Architecture and protection of monuments and sites of historical interest

Series published by the German Commission for UNESCO and the Academy of the Chamber of Architects, North-Rhine/Westphalia, Vol. 12

Prote[ct] [an]d Cultural Animation of Mo[nume]nts, Sites and Historic Town[s in E]urope

The presen[t] [B]elgium, Bulgaria, Canada, the Federal [G]ermany, France, Greece, Hungary, Italy, the Netherl[ands] [th]e United Kingdom, and Yugoslavia

ERRATUM

The author of the United Kingdom section was J Noel White and not N J White as shown.

German Commission for UNESCO

This volume was prepared as a Joint Study on Cultural Policies in Europe, Project No. 12, by twelve European Region members of UNESCO. The contributions were co-ordinated by the Federal Republic of Germany (Professor Gerd Albers, Dr.-Ing., in collaboration with Johannes Cramer, Dipl.-Ing., and Niels Gutschow, Dr.-Ing.).

Edited by Dr. Hans-Dieter Dyroff

© 1980 by German Commission for UNESCO, Bonn
Printed in the Federal Republic of Germany
by Bernecker, Melsungen
ISBN 3 922343 07 4

Foreword by the Co-ordinator

This report is the result of a Joint Study on Cultural Policies in Europe, one of a total of fourteen on different subjects suggested by UNESCO at the Intergovernmental Conference on Cultural Policies in Europe, which took place in Helsinki in 1972. At a meeting of experts held in Bonn in 1975, at which nineteen countries were represented, it was agreed to launch these fourteen projects. Twelve countries have taken part in the study: Belgium, Bulgaria, Canada, France, Greece, Hungary, Italy, the Netherlands, Poland, the United Kingdom, Yugoslavia, and the Federal Republic of Germany as Co-ordinator. This is the largest number of countries to have contributed to any one of the fourteen subjects, a fact which vouches for its topicality and importance. The result can therefore claim to be a representative survey of the different forms of "protection and cultural animation of monuments, sites and historic towns in Europe".

The participating states undertook to inform one another about their respective approaches to the subject and their experience. The aim on the one hand was to present a comprehensive survey of the situation in each country and, on the other hand, to examine in greater detail and evaluate some of the problems on the basis of selected case studies. Experts from the participating countries met three times to co-ordinate the procedure, content and presentation of the study – in Regensburg (October 1975), in Ladenburg (March 1976), and in Rome (July 1977). The draft report was then circulated before appearing in this, its final from.

The aim of this joint study today calls for further explanation. European Cultural Heritage Year 1975 highlighted the importance of an environment that reflects its historical development and therefore retains its own unmistakable identity. In recent decades, however, it has become patently clear that buildings, apart from a few that have a purely museum character, must be put to meaningful use; in other words, they must serve the community without losing their historical features. If this is not the case, even good legal safeguards are of little help. Nonetheless, legislative instruments for preserving historical buildings, the inclusion of this work in the general scope of government, as well as the financial aspects, are of course crucial for any conservation policy.

The obvious starting point, therefore, was a catalogue and description of the legal instruments available in the participating countries as means of protecting and animating historical buildings and sites. They have been presented in such a way as to facilitate comparison.

One of the main problems to which the working group addressed themselves was that of the appropriate use of town centres of the pre-industrial age and also of individual buildings and structures, from the windmill to the country manor, whose functions have disappeared with the passage of time. One particularly important factor in their deliberations was the role of the public, without whose approval and active support the work of the experts will remain piecemeal.

Naturally, however, the study could not be a research project in the true sense as the means and time available did not permit of such an undertaking. So for the most part it was a question of compiling and evaluating documents and data already available in the various countries, supplemented by explanatory sections, some of which are almost surveys in themselves.

On the whole, the study should be of assistance both to experts and the public authorities in their efforts to preserve historical areas and sites as living elements of our towns. The study ends with a summary of possible approaches to the problems – though they should not be understood as remedies, too dissimilar are the individual problems as to nature and scope, and too dissimilar also the other influences which, in addition to the means available to planners, affect the result. All the same, certain types of problems and possible strategies can be discerned and the relevant information used for future work in this field.

The co-ordinator wishes to thank all the experts of the countries concerned who provided material for this report, the German Commission for UNESCO, which was entrusted with the organisational side of the project, and in particular those who have given substantive and financial support, in particular the Federal Ministry for Regional Planning, Building and Urban Development which, by commissioning the study, not only made it possible to present a comprehensive German contribution but also to process the results systematically to provide a basis for international comparison. We further acknowledge the financial support from the Federal Ministry for Foreign Affairs for translation and printing.

In the course of their work, the participants in the joint study expressed the hope that those who use the results will gain information and aspiration from them in resolving the wide variety of problems relating to the preservation and renewal of old towns and thus help make them both inhabitable and more attractive.

Gerd Albers
Munich   November 1980

Contents

Introduction

It is clear from the reports for the Joint Study on Cultural Policies that in most participating countries there has been a change over the past ten years as regards urban development policy. There are some remarkable similarities. In all countries greater importance is now attached to historical areas and drastic redevelopment plans have been revised and in many cases abandoned. The aim now is to conserve as much as possible and carefully to adapt the buildings affected to present-day requirements.

It is hardly possible to draw conclusions from the reports as to the reasons for this change of attitude; they are obviously many and varyous. But the main motive appears to be the feeling that changes in the environment involve a loss of identity, the fear that modern buildings tend to deprive a town of its individual characteristics. This must be seen in the context of the flagging fascination of the idea of "change" – a magical word of the sixties which has now lost much of its appeal because it is realised that not every change has proved to be for the better as had been hoped. But social considerations are also a major factor, resulting partly from the negative experience with urban renewal in the sixties, especially in the United States of America. This has coincided with the realisation that resources are limited and that it is therefore necessary to ensure the proper husbandry of land and buildings. And finally, one observes a change as regards historical significance. The buildings of the late 19th century in many European cities – also those damaged by bombing during the war – still account for a large proportion of the building stock and therefore become increasingly with the passage of time a focal point of historical research. Furthermore, the protection of buildings and sites of historical importance is a widening field of activity, partly because of the more inter-disciplinary approach of the institutions and agencies concerned, which also embraces social history, so that it now covers buildings which previously had not enjoyed a high priority. This applies in particular to the socialist countries which have for some time been protecting vernacular architecture as self-evidence of a culture.

These developments have a twofold effect: they modify the aims of town planning and strengthen the position of those bodies concerned with protection measures on account of the considerable public support. Thus there are two sources of influence on the actual trend: the increased activity and the wider influence of protective measures which have long had an institutional basis and are thus an integral part of government cultural policy, and the more general conservation tendency which takes effect through the instrument of urban planning and is now more akin to the aims of protection policy, though at least in part for different reasons. The widening scope of the protective concept is also partly responsible for the fading distinction between these two areas of activity.

This kind of overlapping, resulting from the related functions of various institutions respresenting the public interest, apparently occurs in most participating countries without its always being specially mentioned. Wherever competence for the protection of historical buildings and sites and urban planning lie with the same authority there is hardly likely to be much cause for argument.

Legal Basis of Urban Conservation

Planning and building regulations

It seems that the aim of preserving existing buildings, especially if they are of historical value, is common to the general planning and building legislation of all participating countries. Although some have special laws pertaining to renewal and preservation, this by no means implies that the others are less active in their efforts to protect old towns but merely that different legal forms are used – usually regulations or comparable legal instruments. This shows the importance attached to general planning and building legislation as a basis for all conservation measures. It derives chiefly from the fact that this legislation, in contrast to all other instruments described below, covers all planning and building measures. On the other hand, there are certain limits to its effect, for instance in preventing the demolition of buildings that are not listed. In Germany it only became possible to prevent such demolition in 1976 when the Federal Building Act was amended. Nonetheless, if the provisions are interpreted in line with the aims of conservation policy and the possibilities exhausted accordingly they represent an important instrument of any urban conservation policy.

In some countries (Federal Republic of Germany, France, Greece, the Netherlands) special laws have been enacted to facilitate urban renewal and preservation measures which contain specific provisions relating to exactly defined fields of activity. For the most part they concern the structure of land ownership, from property dealing to compulsory and other purchase, and financial support for conservation measures. In all countries which have such laws they have proved valuable, but those who do not sometimes complain that there is no sufficient basis for influencing building and the use of property in old parts of towns (e. g. Canada and Greece).

Where renewal areas have been established there arises the problem of differing development inside and outside the area. This is very apparent where conservation is pursued with great care in the renewal areas whilst the buildings in the surrounding parts remain in a poor condition. Preserving isolated parts of urban areas is problematical if it is not part of an overall urban development and conservation scheme.

The legislative requirements with regard to conservation areas are much the same, but in Belgium, France and the Netherlands the authorities can apply far stricter rules with regard to new property than those embodied in the by-laws applicable to "ordinary areas". By-laws relating to design, etc. may be issued on the basis of general building legislation, though in different ways, in Belgium, Bulgaria, the Federal Republic of Germany, Italy and the Netherlands.

Legislation concerning protection of buildings and sites of historical importance

In all participating countries, the definition of such protection, the rights and duties of owners, as well as the responsibilities of the authorities, are laid down by law. The listing of properties worthy of protection has obviously been worthwhile. Although the systems vary, this is the practice in all participating countries. Otherwise the only differences are with regard to the categories of buildings and responsibility for this field of activity. In some countries (e. g.

Bulgaria) listing is deemed to have been completed, in others it has hardly begun (e. g. Greece). And in France and Belgium, for instance, the list has been left open to allow for additions to be made at any time.

Over the past ten years there has been a complete change of attitude in most countries as to what needs to be protected. The authorities and the public are no longer primarily interested in preserving churches, palaces, town halls, etc., but equally private homes, farm-houses and complete groups of buildings. But this process has followed different courses. In the socialist countries the emphasis has been on the documentation and preservation of vernacular architecture. And although in the West, too, buildings in this category have in recent years received increasing attention as property worth preserving, much of what remained has been lost.

The listing of a building usually implies restrictions; this is the case in most participating countries. They relate to structural modifications which destroy or spoil the building's appearance. The owner has to agree to construction work to make the building safe if the authorities deem it necessary.

As regards the method of listing protected buildings, the countries studied fall into two distinct groups. Whereas Belgium, Canada, the Federal Republic of Germany, Greece, the United Kingdom and Italy do not have different categories of property, France has two, Hungary three, and Bulgaria four to mark the degree of importance of the protected buildings, the criterion being their historical and artistic significance. In Bulgaria and Poland, the authorities may also list places of historical or local interest. In France, the requirements as regards the architectural treatment of buildings and financial assistance for conservation measures differ from category to category. The more stringent the protective regulations, the wider the range of possibilities for financial support.

Most countries have made provision for the protection of the immediate environment as well as the actual buildings and have subsequently extended this protection to groups of buildings (ensembles). The various regulations differ considerably in their application to these protected zones. In Hungary and Bulgaria, the requirements pertaining to the conservation of buildings in the lowest category of protection are very similar to those concerning the protection of ensembles. In the Netherlands and France, such zones are listed separately; in France since 1913 with considerable success. Protected zones, which are covered by law in all the countries concerned with the exception of Canada, Greece and Italy, always, as the term suggests, relate to the preservation of groups of buildings, streets, squares, districts, etc.

Organisational Safeguards

Urban planning

In all participating countries, responsibility for building and urban development lies with the local authorities, which set out the aims of and formulate the development plans. All conservation measures start from the fundamental conviction that old parts of the town should retain their historical structures which should be made accessible to modern use. The local authorities can further influence the conservation process by virtue of the fact that they control the financial means. All plans are useless if their aims cannot be put into

practice because the necessary funds have not been approved.

In the West, in contrast to the socialist states where the cultural affairs departments implement conservation measures in accordance with the instructions of the national institutes for the protection of historical buildings and sites, the political decision is usually taken by the local authority. (Only in France can the government prescribe conservation measures.) This is still the case even though in Belgium, the Federal Republic of Germany, France and the Netherlands, development plans have to be submitted to a higher authority for approval.

In the socialist states, town maps and the local plans are prepared exclusively by the local and central government authorities and the plans for the conservation of ensembles are drawn up directly by the national institute for the protection of historical buildings and sites, as in the case of Bulgaria, for instance. In these countries there is no clear distinction between development planning and protection measures.

In Western countries, such plans are drawn up in the same way by local authorities, architects and housing societies. There is a noticeable tendency for larger towns, which account for the greater proportion of the national reports, themselves to prepare and implement the plans. In smaller communities this work is often entrusted to private architects.

Those towns that have organised their departments concerned with these matters in such a way as to meet the special requirements of conservation appear to have been particularly successful. Special conservation offices which co-ordinate activities in accordance with the town map, draw up local plans and handle applications for planning permission, as well as social planning and public relations work, have proved valuable everywhere (for instance, Bruges and Nuremberg). This does not rule out the possibility of individual problems being tackled by private architects (e. g. Rome, Tore di Nona; Faversham, activities of the Faversham Society).

The approach to conservation planning differs considerably from country to country. The common feature of all legislation covering protected zones is that local authorities cannot designate such zones of their own accord. All governments have a say in the matter, obviously because of the financial consequences of such decisions and the scarcity of funds. But whereas in Belgium, the Federal Republic of Germany and the Netherlands there is otherwise no change in planning responsibility, in France it is in some cases transferred from the local authority to an architect appointed by the central government. He supervises all planning activities, assisted by a local architect who also oversees actual building work and has extensive powers of intervention.

Protection of ancient monuments and historical buildings

In all countries the protection of ancient monuments and historical buildings is initially the responsibility of a central authority. The Federal Republic of Germany is an exception to the extent that, not as in the case of legislation relating to development plans, competence lies with the federal states rather than the Federal Government. From the very outset, therefore, as prescribed by the constitution, responsibility is decentralised, whereas the central authorities in the other countries, depending on the constitutional provisions, have regional subdivisions. Some of them (as in Belgium and the Netherlands) are more independent than others (Bulgaria, Greece, United Kingdom, Hungary). Only in Canada are these powers not clearly subdivided.

In France, regional authorities are subordinate to the central government. The obvious advantage of central authority responsibility is that it is possible to establish common criteria and comprehensive plans and ensure an exchange of experience regarding restoration techniques. The quality and efficiency of restoration work in Bulgaria, Poland and France are convincing proof of this. Central decision-making also ensures a degree of uniformity in the assessment of properties and the meaningful distribution of available funds.

Protection measures differ at regional and local level. All countries have regional institutions which support the central authority. This appears to confirm that the links between local conservation office and central authority cannot be dispensed with. At local level protection measures are handled in two different ways. In some countries the government has a local office which ensures that the law is observed and whose staff frequently act in an advisory capacity. In some cases they are also directly involved in the actual construction work. Some governments transfer this responsibility, especially in small towns, to a qualified individual who in many instances serves in an honorary capacity.

Implementation of Conservation Measures: Town Plans in conjunction with Protective Legislation

As mentioned above, the aims and requirements of urban planning and conservation differ on account of their legal and organisational basis and historical development. Urban planning is principally concerned with the overall concept and sees the individual buildings as part of it, whereas the protection approach, both in theory and by tradition, tackles the problem the other way round.

However, it is no longer practicable to maintain this sharp distinction. The fact that most buildings qualifying for protection are at the same time affected by development plans has produced many widely differing forms of cooperation. In the socialist countries, the potential conflict of interests is avoided by transferring planning authority from the town to the national institute for the protection of ancient buildings. These institutes employ not only restorers, art historians and experts on ancient architecture, but also numerous architects and town planners who take charge of urban planning for protected areas. They are in charge of all aspects of planning, from taking stock and assessing the situation to the formulation of new aims.

Western countries do not have such institutions. As described above, planning competence lies with the local authority, at least in principle. Only the *secteur sauvegardé* in France has some similarity with the system in Eastern Europe.

In general, the practice of involving the local office for the protection of historical buildings in the planning of building and conservation measures from an early stage has proved valuable. The office has been consulted on the stocktaking and assessment of buildings and this has been particularly advantageous in Belgium (Bruges), the Netherlands ('s-Her-

togenbosch), the Federal Republic of Germany (Nuremberg and Ladenburg). It is the common conviction that urban development and measures to protect historical buildings, etc. should be coordinated. However, with the exception of the Netherlands, no statutory procedures have been developed for the effective participation of the public department concerned with protection measures throughout the planning process. Elsewhere these departments are no more involved by law than the other authorities concerned.

True, all legislation on urban development pursues admirable aims as regards the protection of historical buildings, but the participation of the conservation departments is usually confined to one or only a few hearings. In no case has any provision been made for joint planning procedures and no such coordination takes place. Many local authorities have meanwhile come to recognise that urban conservation implies more for the planning authorities than was the case in the sixties when the main emphasis was on new buildings. The result has been that those towns and cities that have been making most progress in this field (Bruges, 's-Hertogenbosch, Orvieto) have their own conservation departments made up of members of different professions. In smaller towns the work can also be efficiently coped with by one townscape protection officer (Celle).

The possibilities for advance planning differ from country to country. In the socialist countries five-, sometimes ten-year projections are made; elsewhere, there is hardly any planning on this scale. In France, long-term planning is carried out only with regard to block renewal schemes; in the Netherlands there is a ten-year programme for the renewal of the Hofjes in Leiden, otherwise no long-term planning perceptible to the public exists. This is all the more surprising since wherever this has been the case (such as in Plovdiv, Eger) good results have been achieved.

There are only occasional differences of approach in the actual implementation of modernisation projects and only within officially designated protected areas. In France and Hungary, sometimes in the United Kingdom and Italy, preference is given to block renewal schemes. Consequently, larger contracts can be awarded for construction and repair work, and, possibly, the costs reduced. The disadvantage, however, is that such comprehensive schemes may alter the architectural and social structure of the area and place it in sharp contrast to the environment. It is principally in areas consisting of medieval buildings that renewal projects are tailored to individual structures. This method makes for a gradual and homogeneous restoration process and avoids sharp distinctions between different parts of the town. As most of the national reports only mention the details of actual implementation in passing, it is not possible to make any specific comparison in this respect. In all countries, construction, modification, etc., is subject to control or at least approval by the building authority. The conservation department is only brought in if the building itself is listed or is one of a protected ensemble. Only then does it have extensive powers of intervention which meet their limit only where the financial consequences of its action would be unreasonable.

In Bulgaria, applications for planning permission for protected areas are handled exclusively by the conservation authorities, who are also in charge of development planning. One problem that still exists in several participating countries is that applications for planning permission in respect of buildings which, though not listed, are nevertheless worth preserving often have to be handled by the building authority, which usually does not have staff adequately trained for the purpose. For many aspects that have to be considered before permission is granted (colour scheme, the proposed use of the building, etc.) it lacks the data needed for a proper decision.

The national reports do not always indicate whether adequate consideration is also given to the social interests of the people affected by renewal schemes. But in all cases there is a clear tendency to monitor restoration plans that affect population structures and social interests and to mitigate any likely hardship. In the Federal Republic of Germany and the Netherlands, this is a mandatory element of planning activities.

Treatment of Old Buildings

There are also distinctions in the way old buildings are treated. Some countries are particularly anxious to preserve not only the outward appearance of the building but also its interior (Bulgaria, Italy, Netherlands). They start from the principle that the use of old buildings should depend as far as possible on the existing structure and that therefore extensive alterations should be avoided. In Italy and Bulgaria in particular, studies are carried out at a very early stage so as to determinate the building's future use.

In many countries the authorities have organised construction groups for work on public buildings that pose special problems. These groups are composed of craftsmen with the necessary traditional skills (stone-masons, carpenters, smiths, bricklayers, glassblowers, etc.) directed by restorers and architects. As these groups master modern restoration techniques as well some which are developed in the course of such work, this ensures high technical and artistic standards. Whereas work on old buildings in the socialist countries, especially Bulgaria and Poland, is generally carried out by such groups, in Western countries these activities are mostly entrusted to private firms, with the conservation departments supervising building activity after consultation with the owner.

The colour tones of restored houses are an important field where private owners need advice. Many towns have standard colour schemes which are partly developed by the building authorities in cooperation with the conservation departments. In some cases they represent an attempt to reproduce the authentic colours. In others, new colour schemes are worked out that are not based on historical models.

The design of new buildings in a historical context remains a problem in all participating countries. There are no ready-made solutions and good ones are rare. Most of the successful schemes for the incorporation of new buildings are to be found in Belgium and the Netherlands. The mere use of brick can give an appearance of continuity. In the case of buildings requiring the use of other materials, and this is true of most other countries, the problems are much greater. This applies especially to town centres that are characterised by timber-framed buildings. This problem of modern architecture in old towns has been highlighted in recent years but attitudes still differ. In many countries the authorities have sought to tackle this problem by building new structures in the old style (the "historicising" effect, as to be seen in Hollókö, Hungary, and Ladenburg, Federal Republic of Germany). Often, inconspicious architecture has been chosen to avoid argument and conflict.

Training of Craftsmen and Architects for Conservation Work

One problem in all countries where conservation work is usually done by construction firms is the training of craftsmen. Nearly everywhere, the traditional techniques and the "feeling" for old buildings have been lost. In many countries the first attempts at restoration failed because of the inadequate training of craftsmen and architects. The situation has improved in recent years but craftsmen are still having to acquire the necessary skills through their own initiative. To date, only one school for such specialised training exists – in Venice.

Training for architects also differs. In most countries, with the exception of Bulgaria and Hungary, conservation planning and the modernisation of old buildings are simply part of the general course of study. In France, the authorities expect an architect wishing to supervise restoration work sponsored by the government to have had extensive training in this field.

In recent years, more specialised courses have been instituted for architects but both in socialist and Western countries they are still very limited. In 1978, 28 courses of different duration and serving different purposes were being run at universities and research centres in East and West.

Exchange of Information

Permanent and well organised consultation at all levels of urban planning, building and conservation is obviously essential for successful work in this field. In all participating countries, experts in the different fields have found it useful, especially in the initial planning phase, to be able to call on the experience of others.

This exchange of experience has not developed to the same degree at local level in all countries. In the United Kingdom, for instance, this function is largely performed by the National Trust, which is a private organisation with no direct government participation. Few links exist between the towns themselves but the National Trust is the hub of a well-organised exchange of information. In Italy and the Federal Republic of Germany, permanent contacts among the official bodies concerned with conservation only exist where local authorities have formed working groups or associations, although many meetings and congresses are held. In Italy, the "Associazione Nazionale Centri storico-artistici", which embraces over 200 towns, is involved where it is a matter of passing on tried planning techniques and information on implementation possibilities. A similar function is performed by the "Städteforum" established in Graz and representing local authorities in Austria, the Federal Republic of Germany and Switzerland. In all countries with a central information and documentation centre, this facility has made for better information and the speedy dissemination of established techniques.

As at the communal level, the exchange of information on the protection of buildings, etc. is of special importance and the establishment of a central authority has proved valuable everywhere. The examples of Bulgaria, Belgium and the Netherlands show clearly that centralisation does not necessarily imply that the authority is too remote from the buildings or areas concerned. The unmistakable advantage of centralisation lies in the fact that the success and hazards of previous activities, as well as new techniques, can be quickly assessed and common criteria elaborated without any extensive organisational set-up.

Research Establishments involved in Urban Conservation

The situation with regard to research has not been sufficiently covered in all reports, but it is clear that those countries that have achieved outstanding success with conservation programmes can attribute this to widespread and systematic research work. Only the socialist countries have supplied information on the extent of the research activities of univerities. In these countries universities have separate departments for basic research in this field. In Bulgaria, the Academy of Sciences has its own research institutes for the history of architecture and building. More comprehensive is the information on the means available to the public departments concerned with the protection of historical buildings for improving the quality of their own work through systematic research. In most countries the central authority has various research agencies at its disposal which cover many aspects of conservation. All governments deem it important to list the properties in question and carry out the necessary research.

Several countries maintain laboratories which test and apply restoration techniques. By systematically extending laboratory facilities, the Polish and Bulgarian authorities in particular have achieved high standards of conservation. These laboratories also develop methods of dating and identifying building and other materials.

Financial Aspects

Where the money for urban renewal is not provided directly by the government, as is the case in the socialist countries within the scope of their central planning, various systems of grants and tax relief and other forms of assistance have been develped in all participating countries. This has in every case caused confusion and uncertainty, especially among private owners. In Belgium, for instance, there exists an extensively developed financing system but it cannot be put into practice for lack of funds. The problem generally appears to be that the various possibilities of financial support are not transparent enough for the layman and thus for most private owners. Nearly all the Western countries have made provision for tax relief to a varying degree. Interesting in this connection is the system in France where the amount of deductible expenditure depends on the extent to which the building is made available to the public during the year. In all countries that have legislated on urban conservation, the financial aspect is of special importance.

It is impossible to compare the degree of efficiency of the numerous assistance programmes for buildings inside and outside conservation areas. One common feature is that usually only a small proportion of the actual costs can be covered by such grants. In most cases the money only serves to stimulate private initiative for conservation measures. This also applies to a limited extent to the financial scope for the protection of ancient buildings, etc., there being less money available for urban conservation and renewal. Of course, grants can only be made for buildings of historical or artistic interest and only for the extra costs incurred in meeting the requirements of the conservation department. In Western countries this is handled in very different ways. The size of grants towards repairs and improvements to historical buildings varies between "indefinite" (Federal Republic of Germany, Greece, United Kingdom) and "up to 100 per cent" (France). Most countries meet up to 50 % of the building costs using different systems. In all cases, with the exception of Greece, grants are provided directly by the central government and also by local authorities. In the United Kingdom, in fact, it is the declared aim of the local authorities to preserve those very buildings that are not taken into consideration by the central government.

The Western countries do not have the kind of comprehensive financial planning familiar to the socialist countries. Only the planning for conservation measures under the Urban Renewal and Town Development Act in the Federal Republic of Germany, and the requirement in Italy that 15 % of the amount spent on government-financed housing schemes should go towards urban renewal, point in the same direction.

Recently, modernisation programmes promoted by private companies have assumed greater significance. In all Western countries, but especially in the United Kingdom, the Benelux countries, France and the Federal Republic of Germany, private companies have realised that the buying, modernisation and sale of old buildings can be a lucrative business. However, this usually results in drastic changes in the social structure. The authorities in Canada and the Netherlands have tried to avoid this danger by stipulating that such activities must be supervised by private or semi-official foundations. This makes it easier to influence the population structure.

Participation of the Public

Local amenity groups have been formed in all Western countries, in some cases quite a long time ago. Their aim is to look after the interests of persons affected by urban planning. The United Kingdom has the longest tradition in this respect, going back as far as the 19th century. Interested citizens, sometimes working in an honorary or a full-time capacity, have been involved in urban development and planning for a very long time. The National Trust, which is the umbrella organisation for all local amenity groups, has assumed a major if not the most important role in the field of urban conservation. This organisation can be much more effective than groups acting individually. The political significance of the National Trust is also manifest in the fact that the initiative for legislation on urban conservation comes from it and not, say, the political parties.

Being an organisation which apart from political representation also organises the exchange of information between local authorities, the National Trust has also become indispensable for the implementation of renewal programmes.

Another characteristic of public involvement in the United Kingdom that is likewise the result of a long tradition is the large degree of co-operation between government and local authorities on the one hand and citizens' action groups on the other.

There is no extensive public involvement in the formulation of the aims embodied in development plans. Only in Belgium, the United Kingdom and the Federal Republic of Germany are the views of those affected heard at this level. In all countries, the local amenity groups are chiefly concerned with pressing individual demands. In this connection, groups formed with a view to urban conservation are different in that their demands cover not only individual projects but the wider problems of urban renewal.

On the whole, public involvement with a view to asserting limited demands is most extensive in the United Kingdom, the Netherlands and the Federal Republic of Germany. Only a few initiatives of this kind exist in France and Canada, although some of them are quite effective.

Foundations

The private or semi-official foundations established in the United Kingdom and the Netherlands are other interesting forms of public participation. Again, one has to mention the National Trust, which apart from its function as a political force and information centre also features prominently in the preservation and use of historical buildings. Having the legal structure of a foundation, it purchases buildings, restores them, and puts them to a different use. Although its general aim is to buy only properties that can be put to economic use, the Trust also has an internal financial arrangement (it does not seek to make a profit) to offset losses on individual properties.

In Canada, too, buildings are modernised and given over to appropriate use in much the same way, except that houses are purchased, restored and then sold on a revolving fund basis, i. e. the proceeds are used to finance the next project. There is no attempt to build the fund as an asset in itself. And in the Netherlands old buildings are saved from decay by funds provided by public foundations.

Prospects

Over the past five or ten years all participating countries, though with differing degrees of intensity and with different emphasis, have become increasingly aware of the need for determined efforts to preserve old buildings. On the other side of the coin, there is a growing uneasiness, not only in the United Kingdom, about the tendency to overemphasize and be uncritical of conservation measures and to condemn modern architecture. It is now realised that whilst it is necessary to pursue the aims of conservation they must not stand in the way of sensible urban development. To try and preserve the old part of a town as a kind of museum, more or less arresting its development, is considered to be just as harmful as its total commercialisation or deterioration.

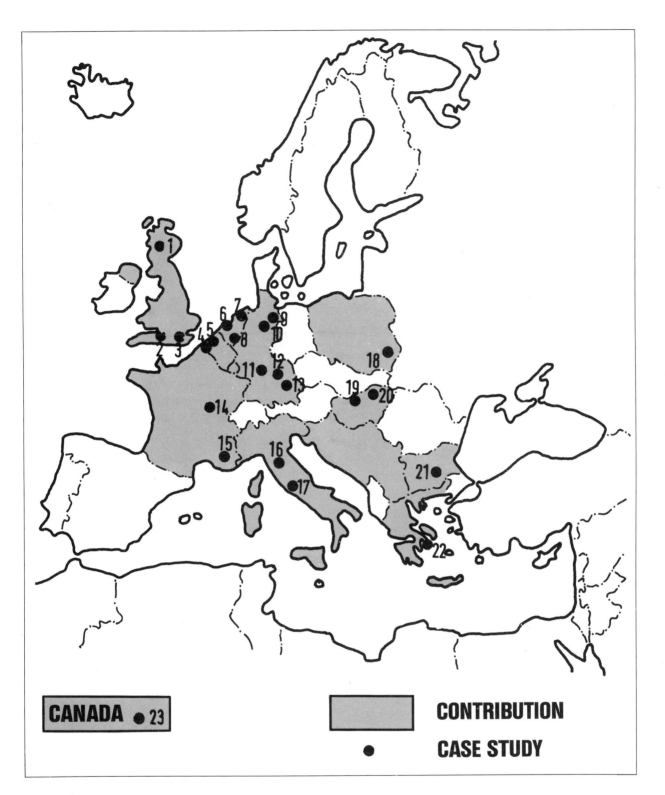

CANADA ● 23

CONTRIBUTION

● CASE STUDY

1 Culzean Castle	13 Regensburg
2 Sissinghurst Castle	14 Arc-et-Senans
3 Faversham	15 Manosque
4 Bruges	16 Orvieto
5 Antwerp	17 Rome
6 Leiden	18 Zamość
7 Dokkum	19 Eger
8 's-Hertogenbosch	20 Holloko
10 Celle	21 Plovdiv
11 Ladenburg	22 Athens
12 Nuremberg	23 Vancouver

BELGIUM

Belgium (Flanders)
LEGISLATION – ORGANISATION – FINANCE

1. Legislation

In 1931, the first complete legislation, aiming at the safeguarding of monuments and sites, came into force, by means of the Preservation of Monuments and Sites Act of August 7. This act deals with real estate (monuments, buildings and sites) as well as with cultural movables.

Although the 1931 act couldn't meet the current requirements for efficient safeguarding, one can't but admit that it was exemplary for its time. The act applies to all monuments, be they religious, civil, public or private buildings, without distinction.

The monuments' immediate surroundings are also taken care of, but this will turn out to be the act's weak element, in due time. A classified monument's or site's legal protection implies judicial regulations, meaning that the owner has duties and rights. Meant here is the right of financial aid from public authorities, enabling to owner to meet the obligations imposed on him, namely the duty of maintaining the building and keeping it in repair. For nearly half a century this act has been the judicial device for the safeguarding of monuments in the country. This device reveals considerable blank spaces due to changed circumstances, a change of mentality, and a new concept of the safeguarding system.

There were contradictions or a lack of precise dispositions regarding the competence of granting demolition or construction licences. Sometimes there is only lack of synchronisation. Due to these imperfections, the definite mutilation of historical centres by new constructions that disturb the city scale couldn't be prevented. Certain applied and other legislative dispositions started competing with the aims of the act on the preservation of monuments and sites. Mainly in the years after world war II, this problem was obvious for premiums for the demolition of dwellings unfit for habitation, the promotion of social housing projects (new constructions) and the green areas.

The sanctions for violation of the applicable law remained the same, for the greater part, but existed only on paper. The first time that an expropriation was carried out, because of insufficient care by the owner, occurred as late as 1975 (European Architectural Heritage Year).

Sometimes, contradictional decisions lead to allowance requests for the discontinuing of demolition or construction activities. The fear of possible complaints had a negative influence on concessions concerning demolition. Implications of such a kind would go too far beyond the very limited budget for the safeguarding of the architectural patrimony.

Those modest budgets, contrasting with the terms of the Subsidies Regulating Act, cause a considerable loss of time for restorations. In some cases this extensive loss of time ran the risk of irreparable damage. However, it was the concept of a monument, as it was recognised in the 1931 act, that gave too much scope for selection, in which exclusively aesthetic, artistic or stylistic criteria could be manipulated. A global vision on the urban scenery was missing: the protecting promulgations only mentioned a very limited and direct environment of monuments; this clause was subjected to various interpretations.

Cultural autonomy, which became a reality in Belgium in 1971, makes us distinguish between a Dutch-speaking cultural community and a French-speaking cultural community (1). From that moment on, the larger part of the cultural policy lies within the competence of the Ministers of Culture.

For that reason, this report is limited to the situation in the Flemish part of the country, which constitutes the Dutch-speaking cultural community.

The growing awareness of the alarming aggression against the environment towards the end of the sixties gave birth to very active ecology groups throughout the country. This movement stimulated the safeguarding scenery considerably.

European Architectural Heritage Year 1975, which was conceived and promoted by the Council of Europe, produced the same result for the safeguarding of monuments.

The enhanced global protection of monuments made coordination between the Ministry of Public Works, the Urban Administration and the Ministry of Dutch Culture much closer, first and foremost regarding the sites and the monuments' surroundings. The circular letter of September 1, 1975, from the Ministry of Public Works to the National and Local Urbanisation Boards proves that this concern exists. The aforementioned circular letter requires the Urbanisation Boards to take the Royal Committee for Monuments and Sites into consultation for the granting of building licences on sites located near classified monuments or sites or other valuable buildings.

From 1971 to 1975, the Cultural Council of the Dutch-speaking cultural community voted on a few enactments that were followed by some Royal Promulgations on the efficiency of procedures regarding the 1931 act, with the aim of creating the required services for an active safeguarding policy:

– Enactment of July 13, 1972, on the modification of the August 7, 1931, Act on the Preservation of Monuments and Sites. These modifications involve the protection procedures.

– Royal Promulgation of June 1, 1972, providing the Ministry of National Education and Dutch Culture with a State Service for the Protection of Monuments and Sites.

  This service will evolve into an institution charged with providing logistic support for the preparation and elaboration of a dynamic architectural heritage protection policy.

– Royal Promulgation of September 24, 1974, implying the modification of the Royal Promulgation of December 13, 1968, on the composition and competence of the Royal Committee for Monuments and Sites, autonomous Dutch-speaking section, with the aim of enabling this Committee to follow the evolution of the preservation of monuments and sites very closely. These structural changes will improve the cooperation with the State Service for the Protection of Monuments and Sites, simultaneously.

Following the advice of the Council of Europe, the Cultural Council of the Dutch-speaking cultural community voted the March 3, 1976, enactment, dealing with the full reform of the legislation and replacing the August 7, 1931, Act, for the greater part. It paves the way towards a preservation policy which is harmonised with the modern and enlarged concepts.

What are the main reforms of this enactment?

1. First of all, the concept of a "monument" was enlarged: "A monument is a real estate, man-made, natural or man-made and natural, being of general interest and having an artistic, scientific, historical, folkloristic, archaeological, industrial or socio-cultural value, movable objects that are part of it and that became real estate, traditionally, included."

2. The introduction of the "urban and rural site" concept, coming near to the architectural patrimony as a whole, in that way.

Article 2 gives the following definition of an urban or rural site:

"The grouping of one or several monuments and/or real estate and environmental elements, such as plantings, walls or fences, waterways, bridges, roads, streets and public places that have a general interest because of their artistic, scientific, historical, folkloristic, archaeological, industrial or socio-cultural value."

3. The main aim of March 3, 1976, enactment is the realisation of a quick and complete protection of the architectural patrimony.

That is why a gradual procedure was applied. The legislation of the past only provided protection by royal promulgation; a provisional protection of nine months covering the lapse of time needed to decide whether the royal promulgation was to be applied or not. The new enactment introduces a three-phase or three-level procedure:

– For each municipality the minister establishes one or several preliminary drafts of a list of monuments, urban and rural sites, that could be protected. These first drafts of the list mention the possible duties to be imposed.

Public administrations and private persons can make a request to the minister to include monuments, urban or rural sites in the preliminary draft of the list. These inclusions will be preceded by a public inquiry, which may lead to observations and complaints. The enactment determines the period of time during which the inquiry must take place and the means of information of the parties involved and the period of time during which the owner must be notified. When establishing preliminary drafts of lists, the minister asks the provincial committee of the Royal Committee for Monuments and Sites and the provincial board of urbanisation for advice.

– The preliminary draft of the list forms the phase that precedes the definite protection by Royal Promulgation.

The Minister of Culture establishes draft lists that are published in the statute book. Judicially, the influence of those drafts starts when they are published in the statute book or when the municipal administration involved is informed about them, and when the owners and the persons given usufruct are notified.

These judicial effects concern the obligation of maintaining and repairing the monument. The entry on the draft list is rightly abrogated when the royal promulgations are not taken up again, at the latest a year after publication of the aforementioned drafts of list in the statute book. This period of time may be extended by means of a motivated decision by the minister, but only once and for a maximum period of six months.

On request of the public authorities and of private persons, the Minister of Culture, after consulting the Royal Committee for Monuments and Sites, can bar monuments, rural or urban sites, from the draft list.

– The King executes the definite classification of the monuments, urban or rural sites, that are entered on the drafts of lists after consulting the Royal Committee for Monuments and Sites. This is published in the statute-book, together with the general prescriptions and, possibly, with the specific prescriptions for conservation and maintenance.

A protecting royal promulgation is proposed to the King by the Minister of Culture; when a settlement plan, approved by the King, or a licence for parcelling out, exists for the region in which the monument or the urban or rural site is situated, the protecting royal promulgation will be given on the joint proposal of the Minister of Culture and the minister who is competent for territorial settlement and urbanisation.

– A register of protected monuments, urban or rural sites, is established for every municipality. The minister determines in which way the register shall be kept. The register must be kept up to date and guarded by the State Board for the Protection of Monuments and Sites, whereas copies remain with the board as well as with the municipal administration, the land registry, and at the recorder of mortgages office, where they can be consulted free of charge.

4. One of the legal garantuees given by enactment is the obligation of the owners or usufructuaries to inform the hirers or tenants about the official publication, by means of a registred letter, also when a monument entered on the register of classified monuments or a real estate situated in a classified urban or rural site is transferred.

5. The procedure leading to definite classification was provided with a synchronisation of the authorities who grant licences, according to the March 29, 1962, Act, regulating the settlement of urbanisation and territory. These authorities must give their advice within a fixed period of time when the building concerned is entered on the draft list.

6. The possibility of urgently intervening when a non-listed monument is in danger of destruction, exists. In that case the enactment accords the power to the Minister of Culture to impose the judicial effects from which classified monuments benefit. The minister makes this statement by means of a motivated decision; the maximum period of time for doing so amounts to 120 days.

7. The concept of a "monument, urban or rural site, having an exceptionally historical or architectural value for the European architectural heritage, placed directly under the protective supervision of the state, who shall cover the costs of conservation, maintenance or restoration", is introduced.

8. The text mentions, explicitly, that private persons have the possibility of taking initiatives leading to the entry of a monument or site on the preliminary draft list of monuments, urban and rural sites, that can be classified.

9. The enactment states the responsibility of the owners and usufructuaries of a classified monument. They must assure its existence, keep it in good shape, and have the necessary works for its conservation or maintenance executed. Mutilation, damaging or demolition are prohibited. Penal provisions exist for the violation of these prescriptions. The minister, the provincial governor, the mayor, the "judicial" police official and officials commis-

sioned by the minister, can invervene in order to stop the works in execution, because they are unauthorised or because they violate the authorisation's conditions.

The aforementioned persons have a right of access for real estate being liable for classification in order to make the necessary determinations; however, in this field they are subjected to certain conditions.

10. The enactment orders a distinguishing classification sign to be given for the classified monuments. Upon the advice of the Royal Committee of Monuments and Sites, the minister decided to adopt, by the ministerial promulgation of April 1, 1977, the sign, determined by the Convention of the Hague, 1954, on the protection of the cultural patrimony in the case of armed conflicts. This treaty was ratified by the Belgian Parliament by means of the August 10, 1960, Act.

11. The dispositions for the extension, organisation and decentralisation of the autonomous Dutch-speaking section of the Royal Committee for Monuments and Sites and of the State Board for the protection of monuments and sites, are treated in this report's second part (Organisation, Administration).

The March 3, 1976, enactment is not the definitive end of the legislation renewal. Three important sectors must be revised: the sites, (landscapes), the movable cultural patrimony and the financing. As was the case for the monuments, the European Nature Conservation Year 1970 stimulated a general awareness and an enlargement of ideas concerning sites ("landschappen"). We can add that Flanders' rural areas were rapidly and extremely urbanised.

When drafting next texts of the enactment about sites, one must reckon with the Urbanisation and Settlement of Territory Act, dating back from March 29, 1962, and with its two modifications, made in 1970 (2). This act's objectives are important for the sites. They are formulated in its first article: "The territorial settlement of the country; the regions and the municipalities will be fixed by means of plans. This organisation was conceived from an economical, social and aesthetic viewpoint, with the preservation of the country's natural beauty in mind."

Meanwhile, the protection of sites will be realised according to the August 7, 1931, Act.

As far as the financing of restorations is concerned, the 2nd article of the 1931 Act remains applicable. In order to achieve an efficient application, the March 3, 1976, enactment orders the Minister of Culture to have the cultural council ratify a royal promulgation.

2. Organisation

2.1 Government level

(1) Both cultural councils are the legislative authorities regarding culture. The Cultural Council of the Dutch-speaking cultural community is competent for the Flemish region (constitutional reform of 1971).

(2) Modified by the Acts of April 22, 1970, and December 2, 1970.

2.1.1 Ministry of Dutch Culture

This ministry has, by enactment, the duty to preserve monuments, urban and rural sites, landscapes and the movable cultural patrimony.

2.1.2 De Koninklijke Commissie voor Monumenten en Landschappen; KCML

(Royal Committee for Monuments and Sites; RCMS)

The foundation of the RCMS is the subject of a royal promulgation, dating back from January 7, 1835. Initially, it was simply called "Royal Committee for Monuments". This somewhat precocious concern for monuments may be amazing, at first sight, as one realises that the young Belgian state hadn't even acquired its definite borders. The motives of the importance attached to this foundation can be explained by the chaotic situation of the cultural patrimony at that time, due to confiscation, requisitions and deportations during the French regime.

The RCMS was charged with giving advice to the Minister of Home Affairs concerning work done to valuable buildings, being valuable either because of their old age, or because of the historical memory they represent, or because of their artistic value. Twenty-five years after its foundation, the Royal Committee for Monuments was extended for the first time; the royal promulgation of May 30, 1860, stated that some corresponding members, working on a provincial level, nominated by the King and meeting every month, had to be added.

The so-called corresponding members assist the Royal Committee for Monuments by giving it information and advice.

By means of the January 23, 1861, Royal Promulgation the Royal Committee for Monuments was charged with establishing inventories of art objects belonging to public property. The establishment of a section for sites (Royal Promulgation of May 19, 1912) started the evolution towards the present character and name: Royal Committee for Monuments and Sites.

The August 7, 1931, act gave Belgium a complete and coherent legislation for the safeguarding of the artistic patrimony. It deals with real estate (monuments, sites) and movables.

The legal protection of a monument or a site (classified) gives it a judicial status with the owner's implied duties and rights: the right of financial aid by public authorities and the duty of maintenance. The RCMS has the right of initiative to present a classification proposal to the government, as the mayor and alderman of the municipality in which the estate concerned is situated can do.

– The RCMS also give advice on the observations handed over by the municipality for the owner before the final decision is made.

– The authorisation or refusal of the work on a classified monument will also be subjected to the advice of the RCMS.

– On request of or after the advice of the RCMS, the King can order the expropriation by the state or by the municipality of a classified monument which is in danger of destruction or deterioration.

– The RCMS shall also be consulted on the classification of a site.

- Prohibited work on a classified site can be authorised by royal promulgation after advice has been given by the RCMS and the mayor and alderman.
- The same advice will be requested when the authorisation for the execution of prohibited work is withdrawn or when the monument or site is declassified.
- The RCMS also gives advice when the municipalities discontinue the public utility character authorised by documents drawn up by living persons or testamentaries.
- RCMS will contribute to the establishment of inventories of objects belonging to the movable cultural patrimony.
- Every person who guards movable objects mentioned in the inventories must inform the RCMS about any loss, destruction or deterioration.
- None of the movable objects mentioned in the inventories can be restored, repaired or alienated without the King's consent given on the advice of the RCMS.

The December 13, 1968, Royal Promulgation on the composition, organisation and activities of the RCMS marks the end of the era of the history of the old committee, dating back to 1835. With the development of cultural autonomy in mind, the RCMS was split up into two autonomous sections: the French and Dutch sections. They are competent for the area, or territory, that depends on their Ministry of Culture. They act together for the area in which both ministries share their competence.

The completely new Ministry of Dutch Culture has the renewal of the safeguarding policy as a main item of its programme.

The same royal promulgation repeats the composition, organisation and activities of the RCMS.

The new Ministry of Dutch Culture immediately took steps with the aim of making the supervision of the architectural patrimony's safeguarding and also the RCMS's efficiency more adequate.

The March 3, 1976, enactment regulating the protection of monuments, urban and rural sites, is a main event in the history of safeguarding in Flanders.

This enactment's provisions largely replace the 1931 Act and pave the way towards a safeguarding policy that is in harmony with the extended and modern concepts.

This enactment's importance was commented upon in the legislation section. What are the renovations of the March 3, 1976, enactment, that concern the RCMS? In the 2nd chapter, article three summarises the RCMS's activities:

". . . advising the Ministry on matters regarding the protection of monuments, rural and urban sites. Moreover, it executes the activities given it by this enactment or being a consequence of it."

In the same article of the enactment it is stated that the Royal Committee consists of a central committee and provincial committees. Upon closer examination the enactment's texts show the following specifications on the central committee's tasks:

- Once the list drafts of monuments, urban and rural sites, that are liable for classification are established, the minister can only eliminate an object from that list when the RCMS has given its advice.
- Before the royal promulgation on the definite classification of a monument, urban or rural site is issued, the advice of the RCMS must be heard.

- The same procedure must be observed when the King decides on modifications or abrogation of a protective promulgation.
- The RCMS advises the minister when he determines the distinguishing sign of classification.

In the second section of the aforementioned article 3 we read:

"The King regulates the competence, the composition and the functioning of the RCMS".

Does this mean that a previous royal promulgation can bring in new competences? Within a lapse of one year after the enactment's promulgation regarding the protection of monuments we find a mandate which was not conceived by the enactment. According to article 2 of the January 28, 1977, enactment, the Minister of Culture must advise the Minister of Home Affairs on armorials and flag-drafts introduced by the new municipalities, originating from the town fusions. Within the RCMS, the Minister of Culture established a special committee consisting of heraldry experts in order to assist him in the accomplishment of this task.

The March 3, 1976, enactment also contains several provisions concerning the RCMS's composition and functioning.

The most important one among those settles the decentralisation towards the provincies. As the volume of safeguarding and protection increases and their activities broaden, a division of tasks between the central committee and the provincial committees became indispensable.

2.1.3 State Board for the Protection of Monuments and Sites

With the efficiency of the protection of monuments and sites in mind, the Ministry of National Education and Dutch Culture was provided with a service called the "State Board for the Protection of Monuments and Sites". This establishment was realised by royal promulgation of June 1, 1972. This royal promulgation fixes this board's task as follows:

1. Establishing and bringing up-to-date the lists of protected monuments and sites;

2. Establishing inventories;

3. Studying and preparing measures with the conservation and preservation of monuments and their artistic patrimony against catestrophes and war danger in mind;

4. Publishing inventories and scientific articles concerning the protection of monuments and sites;

5. Controlling the maintenance and conservation and the restoration of the artistic patrimony of these monuments and also controlling the preservation of sites.

The State Board for Monuments and Sites grants logistic support to the RCMS in exercising its task. The royal promulgation of September 24, 1974, regulating the organisation and the contributions of the autonomous Dutch section of the RCMS gives the following details about it:

- The secretary and the rapporteurs of the RCMS are appointed by the King and chosen from the civil servants belonging to the State Board for the Protection of Monuments and Sites.

- The State Board for the Protection of Monuments and Sites may propose items for the agenda of general meetings and divisional meetings of the RCMS; this board is authorised to propose advice about items on the agenda. The autonomous Dutch section of the RCMS must accept the advice draft introduced by the State Board for the Protection of Monuments and Sites concerning items the aforementioned board had included on the agenda of two consecutive meetings without any definite decision by the committee.

The enactment of March 3, 1976, regulating the protection of monuments and sites, affirms the State Board for Monuments and Sites' mission and enlarges the field of application. In other words: the drafting and execution of the protection, conservation and maintenance and restoration policies for monuments, rural and urban sites, are meant here. The board must assist the RCMS in the execution of its mission. It is also charged with being the RCMS's secretariat. This enactment also contains provisions for the decentralisation of the State Board for Monuments and Sites, giving it a central administration and provincial boards.

2.1.4 Koninklijk instituut voor het Kunstpatrimonium (Royal Institut for the Artistic Patrimony; RIAP)

The RIAP is a scientific institution of the Belgian State. Its conceived mission is the scientific study and the preservation of the national artistic and archaeological patrimony for the benefit of the state museums, the provincial and municipal museums, but also the other public collections, e. g. those of churches and historical monuments. Besides, the institute is charged with establishing the photographic inventory of that patrimony. In some cases this mission has its roots in genuine research. It was found in 1934, when a physical-chemical laboratory, associated with the already existing photographic service, was created in the Royal Art and History Museum.

The Regent's Promulgation of July 24, 1948, established the institute as a scientific institution, called the "Central Laboratory of Belgian Museums" and the "Central Iconographical archives of National Art". A royal promulgation of August 17, 1957, granted it the official name of Royal Institute of the Artistic Patrimony (RIAP – IRPA [French] – KIK [Dutch]).

During the year 1958, the "State Excavation Service" was joined to the Institute, as it was also conceived within the Royal Art and History Museum. From the post-war period the Institute started playing an international part. It was invited to participate in the activities of the Museums and Monuments Division of UNESCO and also those of ICOM (International Council of Museums).

Later it contributed to the control of ICC (International Institute for the Conservation of Art and Historical Objects) and of the Centre of Rome ("International Study Centre for the Conservation and Restoration of the Cultural Patrimony").

The representatives of the natural sciences, mainly physicists and chemists, meet in the three research labs: physical sciences, microchemistry, and historical monuments. Their duty is making use of the rich possibilities at their disposal, thanks to the recent scientific and technical progress, with the aim of identifying compositions and structures deformed by age, evaluating the deep causes of these alterations and, in that way, paving the way for their colleagues, the Restorers of Conservation. They establish ever improving techniques for the preservation of works of art, antiques and monuments. The "Historical Monuments Lab", which was formerly simply a section of the microchemistry lab (stone-like material, mainly materials of old monuments), was detached in order to form a distinctive department. This one is involved in research regarding stonework, treated by Conservation; it also does so for organs outside the institute on which the restoration of the monuments' patrimony depends.

The "Iconographic Archives" department prepares the photographic inventory of the national patrimony. Moreover, it develops new operational techniques in black and white and in colour, with the aid of extremely varied sources of light, also on the field of the invisible. It also in this way gives indispensable assistance concerning preparatory studies for the restorations of masterpieces of great value.

2.1.5 Other Ministries and Secretariats of State having prerogatives involved in the safeguarding of monuments and sites

The Ministry of Public Works and the State Secretariat for Regional Economy, Territorial Settlement and Housing:

In the Urbanisation Administration, there is a section for the renovation of old historical urban centres and sites.

This service treats all problems regarding monuments and sites by applying the Urbanisation and Territorial Settlement Act (March 29, 1962, modified in 1970). In the preliminary drafts and drafts of sectors there is a special clause for housing sectors having an historical or aesthetic value. In those sectors all new construction or transformation must be harmonised with the immediate surroundings of the site in which it is situated.

The preservation of landscapes of an exceptional value is also within the field of application of the Territorial Settlement Act.

The March 6, 1976, enactment regulating the protection of monuments and rural and urban sites pays attention to the coordination between the services and procedures that involve the architectural patrimony:

– for all licences to be given in accordance with the Urbanisation and Territorial Settlement Act (1962/1970), the authorities charged with giving licences and the delegated official for urbanisation must ask the advice of the Minister of Culture or his delegate, when work on protected monuments or protected urban or rural sites, being on the preliminary or draft list of monuments, rural or urban sites to be classified, is involved.

– When a settlement plan approved of by the King or a split-up licence exists for the territory in which the monument, the rural or urban site is situated, the protective royal promulgation is proposed by the Minister of Culture, together with the Minister who is competent for territorial settlement and urbanisation.

– When a classified monument or a real estate situated in a classified rural or urban site is transferred, the executing official must request an urbanisation certificate beforehand and must mention in the transfer document that the monument or real estate concerned is classified.

There is close cooperation between the State Board for the Protection of Monuments and Sites and the Ministry of Public Works (authorisation of new constructions, particular settlement plans, split-ups, classifications).

2.2 Provincial level

2.2.1 The provincial committees of the Royal Committee for Monuments and Sites

In the text about the RCMS, section 1.2, it was already mentioned that the March 3, 1976, enactment includes the decentralisation principle towards the provinces.

The Royal Promulgation of November 16, 1976, issued for the execution of article 3 of the March 3, 1976, enactment, settles the composition, organisation and contributions of the provincial committees. Those committees have some specific tasks:

- advising the minister about the composition of the preliminary first draft lists of monuments, rural and urban sites to be classified;
- introducing protective proposals;
- establishing autonomous advices concerning the immediate surroundings of monuments, urban or rural sites;
- providing autonomous advice concerning work on non-protected buildings, urban and rural sites.

In this royal promulgation we find a few provisions aiming at the coordination and the division of the contributions between the central committee and the provincial committees:

- A central committee delegate can attend the provincial committees meetings.
- The provincial committees send a copy of their recommendations to the minister to the central committee.
- The provincial committees are charged with assisting the central committee in all its activities and with informing it about the following elements, provided they are situated in their provincial territory:

1. the conservation of monuments and of the movable cultural patrimony, their services included;

2. archaeological repairs of monuments and of the movable cultural patrimony;

3. projects concerning religious buildings and other public buildings;

4. projects that can jeopardize the existence or integrity of a site as well as all projects involving the immediate surroundings of a monument; the autonomous recommendations which the provincial committees are entitled to submit are communicated to the central committee on whose behalf they are pronounced.

The provincial committees have their seat in their respective provincial administration. They are presided over by the governor of their province.

2.2.2 Provincial boards of the State Board for the Protection of Monuments and Sites

As prescribed by the March 3, 1976, enactment, the State Board for the Protection of Monuments and Sites is organised in a central board and provincial boards.

2.3 Municipal level

Important towns dispose of a municipal service for the safeguarding of monuments which is often incorporated in the technical municipal services, in the urbanisation services, or in the building services. They are in charge of the municipal architectural patrimony, sometimes independently but mostly in cooperation with the province or the state. Their activities are not limited by technical aspects; they are also in charge of the inventory, publications and information, and promote public awareness of the value of the architectural heritage. A certain number of towns are members of the Association of Belgian Historical Towns. This association was established in 1974 and has already taken some remarkable initiatives in favour of controlling the safeguarding of the architectural patrimony at municipal level.

The Association of Belgian Towns and Villages was founded in 1913 and assists the municipalities concerning all administrative matters in an advisory capacity. The safeguarding of monuments and urban renovation occupy a major place in it.

3. Finance

3.1 General summary

As late as August 7, 1931, in the Preservation of Monuments and Sites Act, the duty of maintaining classified monuments is mentioned for the first time. This is a duty of the owners, accompanied by the means of assistance and pressure; subsidies are the main kind of aid. The facilities and volume of this financial aid will be specified later, e. g., in the Regent's Promulgation of July 2, 1951, regulating the subsidies for classified monuments that are publicly or privately owned.

According to the kind of building and the sort of work, the state intervenes for 30 up to 60 %; the provincial and municipal parts included, grants for private restorations can amount to 90 % of total costs. Taking into account the selectivity provided for in the royal promulgations on classification as applicable until a few years ago, this percentage was about the general rule.

One can consider Belgian legislation as the most generous in Europe. However, as far as the total volume of disposable means is concerned, Belgium doesn't occupy the first place at all. It's not surprising to see the gap between the volume to be subsidised and the disposable means increase.

With the enlargement of the "monument" concept and the activated sensibility since the European Architectural Heritage Year 1975, the process accelerated; the number of royal promulgations on classification was multiplied in comparison with the old days. The disposable means are absolutely insufficient.

Long waiting periods are the result. This negatively affects the monument concerned. When restoration work of a certain volume and importance is involved, the monument is unattractive during a lengthy period of several years and supplementary costs are added because of the successive parts of the activities. On the other hand, it must be said that the preservation of monuments competes, in the field of finance, with other grant systems that sometimes have conflicting interests: demolition premiums against a second-plan ground speculation leads to the applications of the decay procedure, whereas promoting social housing channels a very large volume of financial aid to new constructions, although the intentions may be good. Should a coordination between the authorities and the management that has repercussions for the architectural patrimony, such as urban renovation, public works, etc., be reached, this would be a big step forward. Such a leap forward in the objectives of the different aspects involved in management would be beneficial, directly or indirectly, for the architectural patrimony, implying financial efforts by everyone. Stimulated by this new vision and inspired by several studies and organised colloquiums with the aid of the Council of Europe, UNESCO and ICOMOS on the occasion of European Architectural Heritage Year 1975, the Belgian administration is about to review the whole situation.

By introducing the March 3, 1976, enactment, the Cultural Council of the Dutch-speaking community replaced the August 7, 1931, act for the larger part, at least concerning the Flemish part of the country. The financial dispositions are equally being reviewed; at the moment, a new bill is in preparation.

In conclusion, we can remark that, thanks to an enlarged sensitivity of the public, the number of private initiatives and the contributions of this sector have increased considerably. A certain number of foundations, of which some have very strict objectives and others have broader objectives, have booked considerable results. In this context, for Belgium anyway, the Marcus Foundation of Bruges served as a prototype.

3.2 Contemporary situation

The financial basis was stimulated by the August 7, 1931, act, stating and enumerating the works liable to be subsidised and indicating the financing authorities:

– maintenance, fortifying and supporting, restoration, necessary for the conservation of a classified monument or building, its historical artistic, scientific value (article 2);

– the state, the province and the municipality involved participate in the costs of this work needed to prevent the classified building from being destroyed or from deteriorating.

– The owner may request the expropriation of his building by the state (art. 2).

– The state or the municipalities themselves may decide upon the expropriation for public benefit (art. 4).

– There has been only one case in which this possibility, created by the 1931 act, was applied; it happened in Antwerp in 1975.

– The Governor can have the necessary maintenance works executed at once and can legally obtain the refund of the costs (article 2).

The act also contains a few clauses for classified sites.

– The owners and other persons involved are entitled to a state grant for the prejudice which is the consequence of their restricted rights (article 7).

– The owner, who is charged with the servitude, can demand the acquisition of the real estate from the state, provided he can prove that the minimum value of that estate amounts to more than half of its selling value. The act also states sanctions, in the form of fines, for the destruction or deterioration of a monument or for the execution of unauthorised work (art. 2). Simultaneously, the original form of the building or site must be re-established (art. 23).

The Regent's promulgation of July 2, 1949, determines the genre of work liable for subsidies and also the percentage of the state intervention, provided a public property classified monument is involved (60%). The circular letter No. NC/MS/A/E/1, dating back to July 19, 1951, issued by the Minister of Education, fixes the rules for subsidies for repair, maintenance and fortification of private property classified monuments and buildings.

The state intervention varies from 30 to 60%, depending on these two criteria:

1. The building's nature:

– monument with a rent value

– monument and building without any rent value

– monument turned into a museum, accessible to the public

– mills in operation

– mills no longer in operation

2. The order of work:

– ordinary maintenance or repair work

– archaeological or artistic work.

Next to the state subsidies the province grants a subsidy of 20%, generally; the municipality adds 10%. This contribution is a very considerable burden on municipalities, who inherited a rather rich architectural patrimony.

The division of financing competences, as explained in the second part of this report, makes the subsidy system rather complicated.

3.3 The accents in the revised legislation on the safeguarding of monuments and sites

Both Belgian Ministers of Culture are busy reviewing the legislation on financing the preservation of monuments and sites, totally at the moment.

This project still needs to be discussed in a parliamentary commission before parliament is to vote on it. Nevertheless, we can distinguish a few options that are likely to be incorporated in the new system:

1. Subsidies will be more differentiated than ever in the new act.

2. Local authorities and cultural associations will be able to request state financial assistance, providing certain conditions are fulfilled, for the work and also for the purchase of classified monuments.

3. The state carries the full burden involved in the financing of the work on classified and directly state controlled monuments (Enactment of March 1, 1976, article 11 6 7).

4. Private owners of classified monuments must sign a contract when a restoration subsidy is accorded to them; this contract forces them to repay the total amount or a portion of it when they sell the restored monument. They must also refund part of the interest they receive on the amount granted for restoration.

5. Subsidies for urgent work in connection with preservation are also provided for.

6. The possibility of granting subsidies for other estates on which work need to be executed and which are situated in an urban or rural protected site is also being discussed.

7. Subsidies consisting of loans obtained from recognised credit organisations for that kind of operation are also envisaged; the state guarantees the loan.

8. On certain conditions the owner can obtain financial aid in the form of exemption from taxes, partially or entirely, and also from subscription rights. The establishment of a fund for the safeguarding of the cultural patrimony is under consideration.

This fund would be directed by the Minister of Culture. It would be fed by the state budget, by refunds of certain subsidies, by legacies and by other sources.

1. The Minister: Mrs. R. De Backer-van Ocken, Minister of Dutch Culture and Flemish Affairs. Minister's Cabinet: Jozef II Straat 30, 2nd Floor, 1040 Brussels
Phone: 02–218.12.10

Ministry of Dutch Culture
Central Administration
Kolonienstraat 29–31
B-1000 Brussels
Phone: 02–513.74.61

2. Koninklijke Commissie voor Monumenten en Land-schappen (Royal Committee for Monuments and Sites)
Jozef II Straat 30 (3rd floor)
B-1000 Brussels
Phone: 02–219.04.55/02–217.88.53

3. Rijksdienst voor Monumenten en Landschapszorg (R. M. L. Z. – State Board for the Protection of Monuments and Sites)
Jozef II Straat 30, 3rd floor
B-1040 Brussels
Phone: 02–219.04.55

4. Koninklijk Institut voor het Kunstpatrimonium
(Royal Institute for the Artistic Patrimony)
Jubelpark 1
B-1040 Brussels

5. Minister van Openbare Werken (Minister of Public Works)
Residence Palace, Wetstraat 155 (9th floor)
B-1040 Brussels
Phone: 02–733.96.70 / 02–733.97.60

Hoofdbestuur van Stedebouw en Ruimtelijke Ordening / Diensten van Stedebouw (General Urbanisation and Territorial Settlement Board/Urbanisation Service)
Residence Palace, Wetstraat 155 (8th floor)
B-1040 Brussels

Hoofdbestuur van Stedebouw en Ruimtelijke Ordening / Afdeling Stadskern vernieuwing (General Urbanisation and Territorial Settlement Board/Urban Renewal Section)
Residence Palace Wetstraat 155 (8th floor)
B-1040 Brussels

Staatssecretariat voor Strekeconomie en voor Ruimtelijke Ordening (State Secretariat for Regional Economy and Territorial Settlement)
Anspachlaan 1 (8th floor)
B-1000 Brussels
Phone: 02–219.49.90

6. Provincial boards of the State Board for the Protection of Monuments and Sites:

Province of Antwerp:
Rijksdienst voor Monumenten en Landschapszorg, Provinciale Directie, Koningin Elisabethlei 22–24
B-2000 Antwerp
Phone: 031–37.28.00

Province of Brabant:
Rijksdienst voor Monumenten en Landschapszorg, Provinciale Directie, Blijde Inkomststraat 2
B-3000 Leuven
Phone: 016–22.74.05

Province of Limburg:
Rijksdienst voor Monumenten en Landschapszorg, Provinciale Directie, Minderbroederstraat 6
3800 Sint-Truiden
Phone: 011–67.31.23

Province of East Flanders:
Rijksdienst foor Monumenten en Landschapszorg, Provinciale Directie, Recolettenlei 6
B-9000 Ghent
Phone: 091–23.69.71

Province of West Flanders:
Rijksdienst voor Monumenten en Landschapszorg, Provinciale Directie, Steenstraat
B-8000 Bruges
Phone: 050–33.07.91

7. Vereniging van Historische Steden van Belgie V. Z. W. (Association of Belgian Cities) Stadhuis
B-8000 Bruges
(President: Mr. Andries van den Abeele)

8. Vereniging van Belgische Steden en Gemeenten (Belgian Association of Towns and Villages), Aarlenstraat 53
B-1040 Brussels (President: Mr. Paul Meyers)

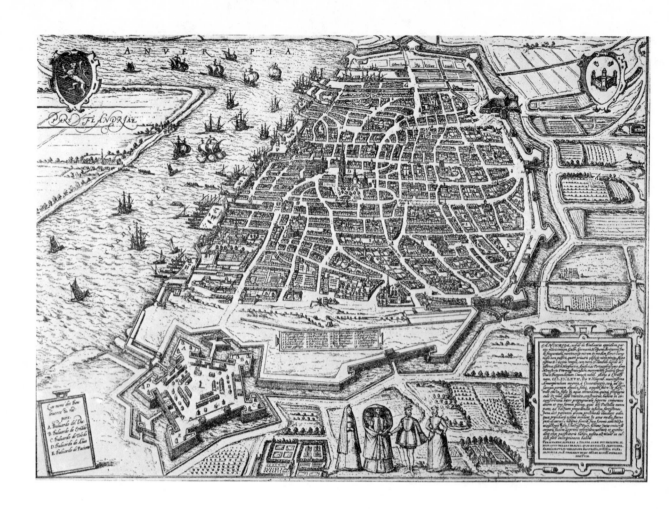

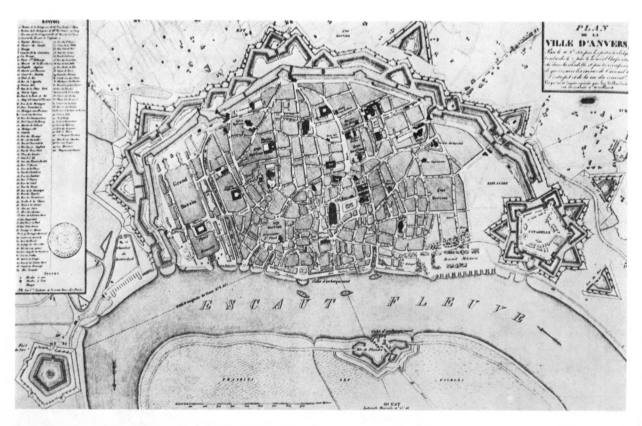

Antwerp: View of the old town of the 18th century (above).
Plan of the old town of the early 19th century with still intact fortifications (below).

Belgium
ANTWERP

1. Situation

1.1 General Introduction

Situated in the North of Belgium, the port town of Antwerp (14,000 hectares – 200,000 inhabitants) polarises a population of 600,000 in the matter of distribution and employment in the agglomeration, the conurbation and the region comprising grosso modo, the Province of Antwerp, and the district of Sint-Niklaas.

In the European context the international vocation bestowed by the port of Antwerp on the Antwerp agglomeration must be underlined.

1.2 History

According to etymology and archaeology the name "Antwerpen" (Antwerp) would derive from the name given to the first settlement "aan de werf" (at the wharf).

The first people who came to establish themselves on the deep bank of the river – presumably very long before our era – found here "a land of fog and mud". Shallows with fords and some slight elevations, undulating between 2 and 14 metres, situated on the river probably with one natural little water-course, branching off from the Scheldt: the ancient roya, a sheltered spot for ships, the first harbour!

It is this situation on the river and on the first natural harbour which have determined the later prosperity and the physiognomy of Antwerp.

Gallo-Roman settlement in the second and third century, premunicipal settlement in the 9th century, Antwerp developed in the 16th century into one of the richest cities, both in the field of architecture and worldtrade.

The first settlements undoubtedly were to be found on the driest (highest) spots: the castle, Hoogstraat, Oude Beurs.

The heights of Kronenburg and the ridge of land situated along today's Lange Nieuwstraat were first built upon in the time of the extensions of the city after the 13th century. The city and the port were already defined long ago.

For the great outlines of the historical expansion, a matter which is of importance from a town-planning point of view, we quote here a paragraph of Floris Prims, the greatest Antwerp historian: "In so far as we know the history, Antwerp appears to have been touched as it were every three hundred years by a magic wand: in the 13th, in the 16th and in the 19th century. Three times a surprising vital strength has come upon this agglomeration, whereby it expanded its ramparts and demolished the old ones, gates and all, whereby it renovated its churches, raised its towers into the sky, demolished its old houses and built new palaces, rebuilt its banks and docks and multiplied new quarters, whereby old streets lost their social rank. It already immediately appears from this simple enumeration that

what is new always has meant the destruction of what is old". We have to place this judgement in the spirit of the time in which it was made (1940). It is a fact that during the successive flourishingtimes, what was old was thoroughly destroyed – as a case in point let us mention the demolition of hundreds of wooden fronts in the second half of the 19th century. The present-day way of thinking does not accept anymore the systematic destruction of an urban environment which can never be re-created.

2. Conditions

We can say that the city as a place where people live and work – and this from of old – has the shortcomings of its qualities. Antwerp has managed – more than any other city – to bring about a symbiosis between an actively living, working city on the other hand, a city with an atmosphere which is reflected in the hundreds of monuments and urban landscapes.

In consequence of this, the city escaped from two great dangers: it has not deteriorated – notwithstanding enormous economic activities in the course of time (viz. in the 19th and 20th century) – into a drab, unimaginative working-city; it has also not become a beautiful, dead city.

3. Goals of Intervention

However, the evolutions which manifested themselves after World War II and especially in the fifties and sixties – let us mention the increasing traffic, the increase in the scale especially of the tertiary sector, the deterioration of the urban environment – have given the bad points another dimension. An acceptable balance between the good points (quality) and the bad points is thereby lost.

Ever since approximately 1970 the town-planning policy has distanced itself from the trends that had been gaining ground since World War II and small-scale solutions were stimulated, public spaces were withdrawn from motorised traffic, and suchlike.

This evolution in the approach to the town-planning problems may best be shown by the following elements:

a. the construction of social dwellings in the neighbourhood of the Butchers' Hall;

b. the drafting of a structural an enlarged Special Urbanisation Plan (SUP) for:

- the inner town: the central part of the city:
  266   hectares
  25,000 inhabitants
  46,800 employments

- the quarter "Antwerp South": linked up with the inner town:
  120   hectares
  14,000 inhabitants

- the quarter "Antwerp Dam":
  64   hectares
  5,372 inhabitants

Antwerp: Historical development of the town
Situation about 1124
first extension 1201–1216
second extension 1249–1250
third extension 1291–1314
fourth extension 1314–1315
fifth extension 1545
situation of the 19th century
actual situation

Antwerp: Historical development of the town

4. Legislation

4.1 Legal techniques
Structural sketch – enlarged SUP for three quarters of the city

The title SUP indicates the double aim which was put first and foremost when it was drawn up.

As regards the "structural sketch" the great options, on the level of the quarter, in the matter of the destination of the territory, the lie of the streets, the planning of mass transportation, the parking problem and suchlike, are laid down.

As regards the "special urbanisation plan", the destination of each plot is laid down, on the level of the building-block, in detailed destinationregulations. Furthermore, building-regulations obtain for new buildings or rebuilding.

All this was only possible with the help of a detailed town-planning inquiry into the physical existing situation and into all aspects of life in the quarter. We mention as the most important ones: the population and the dwellings, employment, recreation, traffic, the inventory of the monuments (embodied in the town-planning study).

The proposed "structural sketch/SUP" therefore mainly contains destinationregulations for each zone which is outlined on the drawing, the purpose being to prevent an increase in the scale and also to avoid mutual hindrance caused by very disparate destinations in one zone or by destinations which would have the opposite effect to the one intended. On the other hand a rigid zoning is avoided by allowing "subsidiary destinations" in addition to "main destinations". Different functions can exist alongside each other. This is also desirable for the preservation of businesses and employment and the animation of the quarter.

In addition to the zoning which is orientated after the purport, the SUP lays down great options and results to a great extent from the existing situation (existing residential zones are mostly laid down in such a way), a demarcation is also proposed which is directed to conventionalism, the visual quality of the surroundings. The idea is: the demarcation of town views and of zones of homogeneous value.

For the first ones the legal protection is proposed according to the provisions of the Decree of 3rd March 1976.

Application of these regulations does not mean "freezing" of the present-day situation. New buildings and rebuilding are often a necessity in these quarters and are always allowed. Only a few guarantees are demanded in the matter of volume, roofing, architectural conception.

An essential point is that the municipality has the disposal of a guide-line and an objective instrument when passing judgement on building applications. In the main this refers to aesthetics, equity and prevention of hindrance.

4.2 Costs and rents of the first series of dwellings of the neigbourhood Butchers' Hall

Total cost price	105,300,000 BF
Share of the land price in the total costs	3,390,748 BF
Total habitable area	4,752 qm
Average cost price per dwelling	1,620,000 BF
Price per qm of habitable superficies	22,160 BF

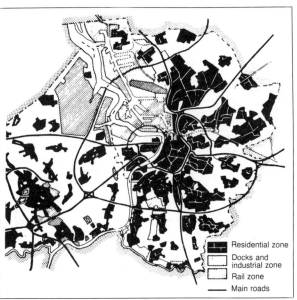

Antwerp: Situation in the region (above)
Ground destination planning for the Antwerp region

Rents (hiring out coefficient of 3.75% on the invested capital:

dwelling with	
1 bedroom (type A)	3,900 BF a month
1 bedrom (type B)	4,650 BF a month
2 bedrooms (type A)	5,000 BF a month
2 bedrooms (type B)	5,700 BF a month
3 bedrooms	6,400 BF a month
4 bedrooms	7,350 BF a month

These amounts will still be increased by 150 francs/month for the extra writing-off on the central-heating installation and on the elevators and by 825 francs a month for compensation of services (cleaning of common parts, telephone, inspection of fire-fighting appliances, electricity, water, inspection and maintenance of elevators, connection cable television).

(Source: statement of account of the Corporation "Onze Woning").

Special Urbanisation Plan for the neighbourhood of the Butchers' Hall

Balance-sheet: costs-assets as seen from the point of view of the municipality (exclusively acquisition and redestination sites – exclusive of newly built houses).

Costs:

Item	area	price	average price/qm
(1) Acquisition sites	9,869 qm	35,757,000	3,623 f./qm
(1 a) sites destined for the grouped construction of social dwellings, appurtenant infrastructure and a common underground garage (including hotel)	(1°)		
(1 b) sites situated outside of the project for social housing (public buildings and laying-out of green zone)	5,384 qm	15,794,000	2,934 f./qm
(1 a) + (1 b)	15,253 qm	51,551,000	3,380 f./qm
(2) demolition costs		2,350,000	
(3) state grant on the demolition		10,742,000	
(4) costs (1) + (2) – (3)		43,159,000	
(5) loss of interest in the period 1955–75 (70 %) of the difference between incomings and outgoings		30,211,000	
(6) total costs (4) + (5)	15,253 qm (1°)	73,370,000	4,810 f./qm
(7) assets from long lease			
(7 a) rentcharge on underground parking-garage	6,088 qm	9,132,000	1,500 f./qm
(7 b) rentcharge on hotel (estimate)	1,239 qm (1°)	8,034,000	6,500 f./qm
(8) land contribution with the municipal Housing Corporation			
(8 a) 60 dwellings	2,800 qm (1°)	2,800,000	1,000 f./qm
(8 b) 100 dwellings	4,849 qm (1°)	4,849,000	1,000 f./qm
(9) implicit municipal land subsidy for social housing 9,869 qm x 4,810 f./qm – (7)–(8)		22,655,000	
(10) resold area (the premises still to be found thereon are subjected to restoration)	312 qm	1,120,000	3,590 f./qm
(11) public garden	1,215 qm	5,844,000	4,810 f./qm (2°)
(12) remaining sites leaves 5,384 qm – 1,215 qm – 312 qm pubic destination viz. education	3,857 qm	18,552,000	4,810 f./qm (2°)
(13) total assets (7) + (8) + (9) + (10) + (11) + (12)		72,986,000	
(14) total area (7 a) not included			14,272 qm (1°)

(1°) The difference in the total area of land (see items 1a, 7b, and (8) amounts to 981 qm resulting from some adjustments to the path of the building-lines; this area has been added to the public road;

(2°) At cost price.

4.3 Participation

Before a structural plan received its final form it was submitted to the population. For the three quarters of the city this happened during public hearings. Every inhabitant received beforehand a compendious explanation and a little plan. During the hearings everybody was able to formulate his remarks.

5. Realisation and Results

Social housing in the neighbourhood of the Butchers' Hall in Antwerp

This project may be regarded in many respects as a pilot operation in the matter of renovation of the city and social housing in particular. The historical record of this project is almost a crystallisation of everything which has lived and was programmed in the matter of conceptions about town-planning and social housing in an existing urban environment since the second world war. The period since 1944 has meanwhile in itself already become sufficiently long to hazard a historical record.

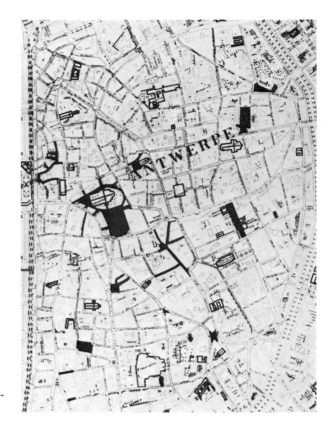

Antwerp: Pedestrian areas in the town.
Realised projects (above).
Pedestrian area around Our Lady's Cathedral and Groen-
plaats.

Antwerp: Neighbourhood of Butchers' Hall. Recent restoration of a 16th century house.

The most essential part of this historical record is rendered here in order to be able to understand what is being built today in the neighbourhood of the Butchers' Hall and especially in order to show how it was ultimately possible to develop an intention of the City of Antwerp into a feasible project.

The first actual datum was the explosion of a flying bomb in 1944 in Oude Beurs/Lange Doornikstraat when a great number of houses were destroyed. Ever since 1945 a number of discussions were started in order to try and draw up a Special Urbanisation Plan. The official order to draw up this SUP was given by the Board of Burgomaster and Aldermen on 19th July 1947. Already at the start a conflict arose between on the one side advocates of a complete renovation of this neighbourhood on the understanding that a contemporary architectural style would be used and on the other hand advocates of a restoration of the traditional situation on the understanding that the existing lie of the streets would be preserved. For that reason, and also because of the time necessary for organising the required public inquiry, a final SUP could only be approved by Royal Decree on 13th May 1953. In drawing up the project the following basic principles had to be observed:

– the preservation of the existing lie of the streets (to be true with widened streets);
– the re-parcelling of the estates covering only a small area;
– the definition of building capacities and town-planning regulations in keeping with the character of the quarter;
– the execution by private architects;
– the construction of public baths for the convenience of the first quarter.

The bathing establishment was built by the municipality. Except for this realisation only one private property was built on the basis of this SUP.

In the mean time the municipality had also conceived (1957) the plan of proceeding to a complete sanitation of the first quarter. The order was given to draw up an urbanisation plan for the entire first quarter and adjoining neighbourhood. The acquisition of properties had to make it possible to build a completely new quarter. In pursuance of the same decision the destinationplan and the reparcelling plan of the original SUP were implicitly suspended. This attitude resulted among other things in the refusal of all building applications for the greater part of the first quarter. The drafting of this "megalomanic" plan was no small order but circumstances were of more than an urgent nature. The Antwerp inner town is an inheritance from the past, largely dating back to pre–1850. It was also at that time that the first quarter was built and modelled, whereby a lot of things even reaching back to the early Middle Ages remained integrated. The most important characteristics are narrow high houses and narrow streets making a densely built-up area, in short the characteristics of every historical city, conceived in such a way that the danger of a siege could be met.

During the very expansive 19th century in Antwerp all open places in the oldest parts, inside and outside the building-blocks, were gradually taken up by destinations which were alien to habitation. The stock of buildings on hand was, certainly in the first quarter, overcrowded and in great need of repair. This led to an accelerated dilapidation of the already old houses. Man oft the 20th century made ever higher demands as far as housing conditions were concerned and also wanted better services and facilities of all sorts. Furthermore, motor traffic after the second world war also pitched its demands high. This was something the old part of the city found difficulty in coping with.

All these problems came up for discussion all at once when it was necessary in Antwerp to proceed in the old city to the rebuilding and the repartition of those parts of the town which had been hit and often completely destroyed by acts of war.

Extensive field work was carried out by, among others, social assistants of the municipality. The problem of the first quarter was not only a technical problem; it was above all a social problem. It appeared from the investigation that 65.7 % of the estates which had been examined were in bad condition. This fact led to a start on work on measures of reconstruction. Making use of the possibilities which in the meantime had been offered by the legislator and the executive power, the municipality systematically proceeded to condemn a number of dwellings. Between 1955 and 1970 477 estates (1,217 dwellings) were acquired in this manner. In order to obtain the state grant the estates had to be demolished.

A first preliminary urbanisation plan saw the light on 13th March 1959, practically providing for the complete demolition and renovation of the first quarter (Fig. 1). Great traffic arteries, great open spaces and detached high-rise buildings were at the root of this project. In as much as the widening of among other things pedestrianised shopping streets appeared to be financially an impossibility on account of the high commercial value and as it apparently did not appeal to the private owners concerned in those streets to become co-partner in this overall renovation plan, this project, after several modifications (the last modi-

Antwerp: The neighbourhood of Butchers' Hall.

fication dates from 8th July 1963), was abandoned. In view of the fact that it was impossible to realise the intended project, the overall plan of the first quarter was then divided into smaller spatial units and the action was mainly brought to bear upon the neighbourhood of the Butchers' Hall.

A proposal for housing development was drawn up by the town-planning department of the Service of Works for this zone. The prevailing idea was to proceed to the grouped construction of social dwellings. The construction was planned of stapled patio-dwellings (on the basis of a system of staple-building, whereby the dwellings are linked together to strings of row houses) with appurtenant infrastructure (shops, spaces for hobbywork, sheds for bicycles and perambulators, playgrounds (Fig. 2). The streets and squares are exclusively intended for pedestrians and service motor traffic. The lie of the streets is completely new. Parking-places were provided for at the edge of this pro-

ject, as well as a great underground parking-garage underneath Willem Ogierplaats (for 264 passenger cars). For town-planning architectural and for socio-economic reasons this project could only be realised as a group building and by an accredited housing corporation. This project departed from the former views as it was conceived on a reduced scale and as it could be integrated into the old inner town.

The project was entrusted by the Board of Burgomaster and Aldermen to the housing corporation "Onze Woning" ("Our House") on 18th December 1967. This corporation accepted the commission to proceed with working out the project of the municipality and to realise it.

In the meantime the municipality drew up between 1970 and 1973 a project of a structural plan for the inner town. It concerned the territory of the first, second, third and fourth quarter. This overall study and the underlying visions are going to play a decisive role in the realisation of the Butchers' Hall project, including the section embodied in this project for grouped construction of social dwellings.

Simultaneously with the build-up of this structural plan intense negotiations were carried on ever since 1972 between the municipality, the central authorities (Direction Urbanisation and Regional Organisation, National Housing Corporation and Royal Committee of Monuments and Landscapes), the Corporation "Onze Woning" and their architects Groothaert and Hagelstein. All this in order to arrive at an acceptable project.

The ultimate project met at long last, after a few adaptations and after a conclusive meeting, with the Town Clerk's approval in principle (letter of 19th April 1974, Fig. 3). The programme included, taking into account all town-planning, architectural and financial desiderata:

1. the construction of a group of about 141 social dwellings,

2. 11 shop-spaces,

3. an underground parking-garage and

4. an hotel.

To be feasible the programme had to be divided into several lots and even among several architects.

The main commission consisting of the construction of the group of social dwellings remained with the corporation "Onze Woning", including the 11 shop-spaces, with the assignment to proceed immediately to the realisation of a first series of 63 dwellings and 2 shop-spaces in the building-block built by Lange Doornikstraat, Oude Beurs and Vleeshouwersstraat.

The construction of the underground parking-garage (450 places) was entrusted to a private firm together with the construction of the hotel at Willem Ogierplaats on top of part of the roof of the parking-garage.

All required sites were given in concession by the municipality (1.8 hectares). It is worth nothing that hereby the use of the underground (on behalf of the parking-garage) was juridically split from the use of the surface of the same site. The realisation of the second series of social dwellings will indeed be executed partly on the roof of the parking-garage which was entrusted to another concessionary as explained above.

From a social point of view it should be remembered here above all that the City of Antwerp has after all granted in this case a landed subsidy, or in all respects has borne this amount of 22,655,000 BF itself so that it would be possible to proceed to the realisation of social housing. The City of Antwerp granted the concession of the site to the Corporation "Onze Woning" on the basis of a price of 1,000 BF/qm. The private concessionary paid on the basis of cost price[1]).

After passing through this very difficult and complicated process, it is now gratifying, however, that the realisation of this project for an important part has already become a fact. The underground parking-garage has been completed and is being used, the main walls of the hotel have also been completed. It will be possible to start work on the

second series of social dwellings in the course of 1978. The first series of 63 social dwellings and the 2 shop-spaces were let out on lease in March 1978 by the Corporation "Onze Woning". This corporation in the meantime has already fixed the cost price and the rent charges on the basis of 3.75 % of the invested capital, so that the rent was kept as low as possible.

The Corporation "Onze Woning" had already received at the end of December 1977 more than 300 applications for renting a house.

The project of the neighbourhood Butchers' Hall is the result of a fight which lasted for years under very thankless circumstances, mainly due to the special nature of the neighbourhood in which the project is situated. It also shows very well how the attitudes changed. At the outset the project was started to repair war damage. Subsequently it became part of the slum clearance and finally it became an important building-stone in the revaluation process of the Antwerp inner town. In the settlement of these problems nearly all town-planning conceptions which prevailed or are still prevailing since the second world war have come into play. Each changing conception finds expression in the historical record of this project. The practical difficulty of acquiring the sites and afterwards again making them available has, however, constantly been present. In order to get round the difficulty the City of Antwerp has had to make an important financial sacrifice. Within the framework of this important project the municipality decided that this contribution would be worth the trouble. It is inconceivable, however, that in the realisation of any other project the local administration would be willing to make such a financial sacrifice. Everybody who today ventures upon operations in connection with renovation of the city must thoroughly take into account the problem of eventually acquiring the sites and making them available again.

This problem presumably will bring in its train in the future even greater difficulties because the pursuance of a housing policy based on building dwellings of inexpensive sites, as in the past decades, threatens to become more and more an illusion. Besides, the housing problem which is still existing to day manifests itself in existing residential quarters and not outside of them. Anyhow, it will be necessary to think of means of eliminating the prohibitive cost price of the sites.

What has now been built in the neighbourhood of the Butchers' Hall on a historic spot in historic surroundings must be the expression of the accepted town-planning standards of the present day. Everyone who bears on this level even a small part of the joint responsibility, either politically or administratively, was concerned more than to a high degree in the realisation of this project.

Still another social aspect must be especially underlined. The City of Antwerp has always maintained that in this formerly working-class quarter dwellings had again to be built which would be accessible to the lower income bracket. This effort has now been realised as much as possible.

To conclude it must be underlined that a hiatus in the municipal structure will soon have disappeared, especially in the structure of the inner town: from March 1978 people will be living again in the neighbourhood of the Butchers' Hall so that this small part of the town will have regained an up to par destination.

---

1) H. B. Cools: "Cost of the Renovation in Belgium", lecture sent in and delivered on 12th–15th May 1975 in Bruges during the international colloquy "The Renovation of the Historical City".

Surroundings of Butchers' Hall

It should also be mentioned that the draft plan Butchers' Hall and surroundings comprises still more than that which has been dealt with in this article. The parts, outside of the zone for grouped construction of social dwellings, are not less important in the optics of the revaluation of this old quarter. The City of Antwerp sold or let out on long lease a number of estates with the obligation of restoration, the project of social housing will be slightly extended in the second phase, a project for building a new Ethnographic Museum is in the course of preparation, it being understood that a number of important historical buildings in the Kaasstraat will be integrated into this project. The reconstruction of the structure above the municipal puppet theatre "De Poesje" next to the Butchers' Hall is in preparation. There are provisions on the local level for schools, a number of houses can still be renovated or reconditioned by private enterprise, and some plots are still available for house-building. Greens have also been provided for and have already partially been planted up. Everything which has been enumerated here is either in preparation or work is in progress. The draft plan Butchers' Hall and surroundings indeed is an extensive frame of reference of everything which can come up when dealing with an urban renewal operation both on the side of the private owner-principal and on the side of the administration as administration or as administration-principal. Within this broader framework of urban renewal in this part of the city the project of social housing certainly has the merit that it has been the great stimulus on the spot for bringing the process of renewal under way.

Bruges: Aerial view of the old town of Bruges (ingenieurbüro Libost, Antwerp)

Belgium
BRUGES

1. Situation

1.1 General Introduction

Bruges is situated in the west of Belgium, 13 km from the North Sea, and is the capital of West Flanders.

There was an amalgamation of Bruges with seven surrounding suburbs in 1971 so that the area of the town increased from 3,546 hectares to 13,100 hectares.

The number of inhabitants stands at 119,000, of which 25,000 people are living in the inner city.

Surfacewise, Bruges is placed sixth on the list of cities in Belgium. Even the old medieval city is rather large: 370 hectares.

1.2 History

The first mention of the name "Bruges" is to be found on money coins of the 9th century. The name is written as "Bruccia" or "Bruggas", which means "landing-stage" or "quay".

The fact that there was an established mint indicates an important habitation in that period.

The region around Bruges was certainly inhabited by Franconian and Germanic tribes before that time. Traces of Roman occupation can be found although archaeological research will have to enlighten us further on this still unknown part of our history. It is generally accepted that a settlement of primary importance was formed around a protected castle during the reign of Charlemagne (9th century).

Our first count was Boudewijn I (862–879). In 1127 a first fortification following the natural course of the "Reie" (canal) was built.

As the population grew and the economy flourished expansion of the town was soon necessary. In 1297 the existing fortification was built. The territory increased in size from 86 to 370 hectares.

The extended fortification of the city was probably necessary to give the inhabitants more protection and simultaneously extend the social control of the different population groups.

During the following centuries Bruges developed into a hub of world economy.

In the middle of the 14th century the number of inhabitants fluctuated between 36,738 and 45,921 and the city was therefore as big as London and Cologne[1]).

The powerful position of the merchants on the local council was brought about by the wealth of the wool trade.

As city councillors they could control the craftsmen, a situation that developed into a more democratic regime after the uprising known as "De Brugse Metten" in 1302.

The affluence of the city appears in its architecture, sculpture and paintings realised in the 14th and 15th century.

Because the rich Dukes of Burgundy were resident in Bruges many important artists of Western Europe were commissioned or attracted to work here; this established the name of the city in history.

Not only the silting up to the Zwin (firth of the North Sea), but also continuing political conflicts at the end of the 15th and the beginning of the 16th century affected the prosperity of Bruges, so that it soon lost its leading position to Antwerp and Amsterdam.

In 1562 the painter Marcus Gerards was commissioned by the city council to paint a complete bird's eye view map of the city. This map had clear commercial aims. The beauty of the city was used as publicity for commercial and harbour promotion. But it failed as a remedy.

In the 17th century further efforts were made to link Bruges to the sea by digging a canal to Ostend but this proved in vain as the "Ostend Company" (to be compared with the East Indian) was in decline.

Important constructions erected in the 18th century at the city harbour prove that this "harbour function" was still deemed important although the main income of Bruges then became agriculture.

The architecture of the 17th and 18th century is of great value. Many of the remaining houses in town date from that period.

In the second half of the 19th century interest in connecting Bruges with the sea was renewed. Under the reign of King Leopold II work on Bruges Seaport (Zeebruges) was started and the port was inaugurated on the 23rd July 1907.

The city of Bruges also experienced a revival. The Gothic architecture remained the big source of inspiration for restoration and new constructions. Complete new neighbourhoods outside the second fortification (1297) were erected around the turn of the century.

We find the famous German Stübben as one of the important planners.

Shortly before and after the second world war the economic situation was unfavourable for Bruges. Fewer jobs were available for the population and the living conditions deteriorated. A change became necessary.

In the fifties, industry in Western Europe underwent an important development which was reflected locally in the numerous industries settling around Bruges, mainly attracted by the possibilities of the harbour of Zeebruges.

2. Conditions

2.1 Problems

The history of Bruges and most old cities is a story of growth and continuous change. The real problem of Bruges is to develop a plan that balances conservation of its essential character and changes necessary for modern living conditions.

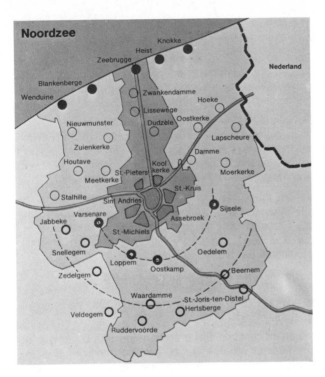

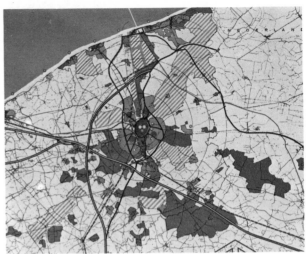

Bruges: Regional setting
Bruges and the suburbs; from: Struktuurplan voor de binnenstad (1976) (above, left).
Struktuurplan voor de binnenstad (1973) (above, right).

Bruges: Historical development
The first fortification of 1127 (left), the second fortification of 1297 (middle) and detail of the first centre (right). Drawings: M. Ryckaert

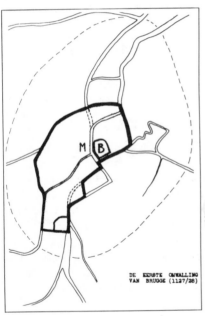

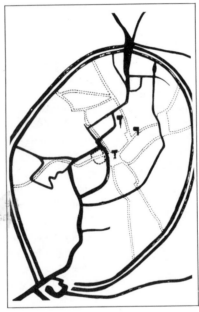

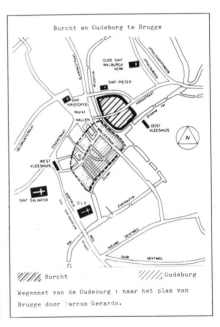

Bruges is a unique mosaic of small buildings grafted to a pattern of winding streets and canals in which the house is the basic element. Bruges was originally built for pedestrians, small building developments, shops and workshops, not for large industrial or commercial schemes.

Today a city like Bruges seems an anachronism. Bruges is remarkably well conserved: this has something to do with the fact that in the 19th century little money was invested in industry. Thus industrial revolution didn't affect the old city: Bruges remained poor and people simply had no money to demolish and to erect new, modern constructions.

The two world wars also passed over Bruges without much damage. On the other hand, these old structures were in growing opposition to traffic needs, evolution of industrial pre-fabrication techniques, pressure of ever expanding functions and the growing welfare. In the battle between conservation and demolition, national policy was unfavourable: up to 1970 there was a real vacuum in the field of urban planning for everything regarding legal, financial and "know-how" instruments for the conservation and rehabilitation of old cities. Worse still, subsidies were granted for the demolition of old dilapidated buildings without considering whether they were valuable or not.

The situation after the second world war was as follows:

– competition between the old city and surrounding sub-urbs,

– a strong loss of functions in the inner city,

– lack of industry and few jobs,

– an impoverished inner city population; well-to-do people moved out to live in new quarters,

– a relatively small city with one in eight vacant old houses,

– more and more slums appeared in the inner city,

– a bad municipal planning policy resulted in a number of catastrophic demolitions of:
major monuments: e. g. romanesque ruins, the 18th century harbour district, the guild chapels of the 14th century, numerous small and large residences, of which some were of great historical and architectural interest.

As a result of all these elements we can conclude that the policy in the period 1945–1970 was not preservation- and restoration-minded.

Bruges was on the way to losing all of its historical character as so many other cities did.

2.2 Initiators of intervention

In 1965 there was a reaction against the attitude and policy of the city council regarding the historical inner city.

A few citizens formed a private foundation which was called the Marcus Gerards Foundation after the 16th century painter. His map had been used as a promotion, so the name was somehow symbolic.

The aims of the foundation were as follows:

– cultural and aesthetic: conservation of an invaluable legacy,

– social: adaptation of the city to present-day norms and living conditions to the advantage of all social classes,

– commercial and economic: a multi-functional city, as amenity centre for the entire agglomeration.

This foundation brought about a change of attitude: they made the population of Bruges as well as the authorities conscious of a number of existing problems and possible solutions.

By buying a small number of dilapidated houses and restoring them they made a symbolic gesture: putting examples of possibilities and stimulating private owners.

They won local authority support for various ideas e. g. conservation, drafting a structure plan, increasing the number of listed classified buildings.

The provincial authorities took the initiative suggested by the foundation to start an inventory of the houses of Bruges (Dr. L. Devliegher: De huizen te Brugge, Tielt, 1968, 2 delen). This work has proved to be of tremendous value.

Another important initiative was taken by the Young Economic Chamber which carried out a survey of traffic patterns. This study was further developed in the structure plan.

In 1971, after the amalgamation of the municipalities, the city council took an important initiative. First of all the creation of the Department of Historical Monuments and Urban Renewal (under the Town Department of Public

Bruges: Historical functions
The "Burg" in Bruges still functioning as the administrative and legal centre of the town.

Bruges: Masterplan for the Old Town.

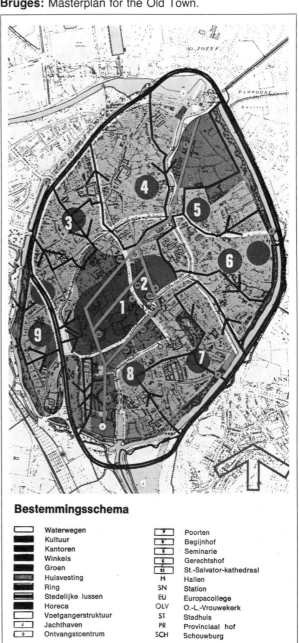

Bestemmingsschema

Waterwegen	P Poorten
Kultuur	B Begijnhof
Kantoren	S Seminarie
Winkels	G Gerechtshof
Groen	SS St.-Salvator-kathedraal
Huisvesting	H Hallen
Ring	SN Station
Stedelijke lussen	EU Europacollege
Horeca	OLV O.-L.-Vrouwekerk
Voetgangerstruktuur	ST Stadhuis
Jachthaven	PR Provinciaal hof
Ontvangstcentrum	SCH Schouwburg

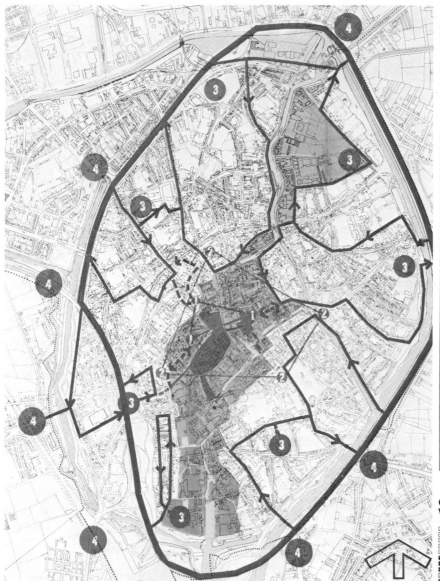

Bruges: Traffic system
Preliminary plan and scheme of
ideal situation (above).
Pedestrian street Breidelstraat
before restoration (1977) and
after (1978).

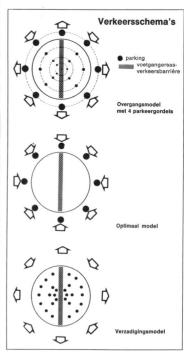

Verkeersschema's

● parking
▧ voetgangersas-
verkeersbarrière

Overgangsmodel
met 4 parkeergordels

Optimaal model

Verzadigingsmodel

**Overgangsmodel -
Verkeer**

▭ Waterwegen
▣ Faze 1 parkings
▣ Faze 2 parkings
▣ Faze 3 parkings
▣ Faze 4 parkings
▬ Stedelijke lussen
▬ Ring
▭ Verkeersvrije zone
▭ Verkeersarme zone
▬ Toegang parkings

Bruges: Visualisation of adverse effects.
Existing situation in neighbourhood 5,4 Ryckepynder: expansion of a brewery (above).
Photo of the situation (centre).
Projected situation – housing in the area becoming available.

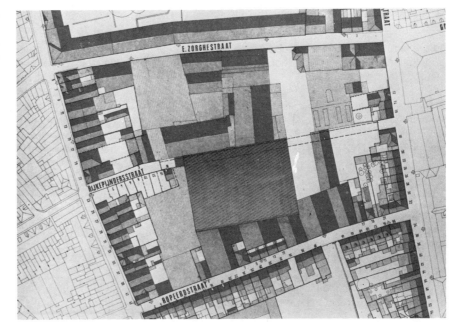

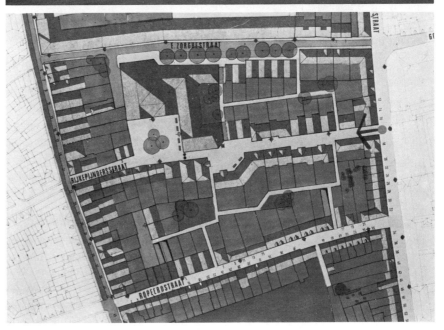

Works) whose task is to advise on all architectural and inner-town planning problems.

Later the municipal authorities also nominated a city councillor for Urban Renewal, thus showing the importance they attached to the matter.

3. Goals of intervention

3.1 Structure plan

The city council, conscious of the complexity of the problems and wishing to give a strong philosophical background and planning vision of urban renewal, started in 1972 with the drafting of a structure plan, which was seen as a "thinking model", an organic planning system, which could evolve and be adapted to the changing problems of urban and economic development.

The methodology of the structure plan is threefold. The first part is the basis of the local town planning policy. The second part contains detailed studies of each city quarter, as well as the planning of activities such as traffic, costs and returns.

The third part will be a feed back from the detailed studies to the first part in order to establish the basic structure.

The threefold division of the method gives room for continuous participation and flexibility. The plan should be achieved in the next 25 years.

This structure plan must be continuously in the hands of a steering team in order that its contents be interpreted and adapted as the need arises.

The aim of the structure plan is diversified as follows:

1. The habitational function of the city must be extended to attract more inhabitants and so guarantee the lively character of the town for all population groups.

   An urban philosophy and rational property policy must replace the disturbing functions and unadapted ground-use by more optimal small town functions.

   The commercial heart of the city should be made even more attractive and lively. It should be able to compete on equal terms with commercial influences from outside. Commercial floor space can be increased in and around three streets in the centre of the city.

   The valorisation and preservation of the best architecture in the historical centre can only occur if this architecture receives economical self-supporting functions. It must be involved in the "life" of the city centre.

2. The character of the inner city can be greatly improved. We have to respond to the existing danger of decay. All elements harmful to the environment (noise, pollution, etc.) must be eliminated.

   In this way the historical centre will become more attractive to life for all kinds of residents and depopulation can be prevented.

   Every new construction and building complex in the historical town must conform in scale, volume, street-pattern, form, rhythm and colour to the highest environmental standards and architectural criteria.

This means that top quality contempory architecture must be encouraged.

3. Traffic solutions were presented, based on the subdivision of environmental areas (coinciding with the city quarters and conservation areas). From this it was assumed that the traffic should be adapted, not the city. The basic elements for the solution of the problems are the barriers (pedestrian diagnonal axis), the inner city ring (primary distributor), the environmental areas and the one-way loops (local distributor roads) linking up the city quarters. Public transport must be primary and private motorists secondary.

4. Strategies and measures

The present council (1976) wishes to continue the plans and projects written down in the structure plan but will stress even more the realisations in the social field.

4.1 Legal, administrative and financial techniques[2])

Law of 1931 and Decree of 1972

The Law of 7 August 1931 on the Protection of Monuments and Sites and the Decree of 13 July 1972 assure the protection of valuable monuments and sites.

Bruges has relatively few houses appearing on the official monument list. Only 96 houses and 2 landscapes are legally protected.

Major monuments such as churches, the town-hall and the Belfry are of course also on the list.

The "protection" assures subsidies in case of restoration (50 % state, 10 or 20 % province, 20 % town).

"Kunstige Herstellingen"

Bruges offers the owners of valuable houses a special system of grants called "subsidie voor Kunstige Herstellingen" (subsidy for historical restoration).

In case of restoration of a historical house not falling under the category of legally protected houses the owner can claim a subsidy. This subsidy amounts to 50 % of the restoration costs for the visible parts (front façade and roof) and 30 % for the unvisible parts (back façade and valuable elements inside the house: beams, chimneys, etc.).

This system which was started in 1877 is unique in Belgium and has stimulated private initiative.

In one hundred years some 400 houses have been restored with this town subsidy.

For the moment 5 to 8 million BF are annually attributed to private owners.

Subvention for the functional improvement of houses

A new subvention system is now under study. It aims to help the inhabitants (owners and tenants) to improve the living conditions in functionally unadapted houses.

A grant of 25 % of the costs (max. BF 60,000) of drying out walls, improvement of the sanitary installations, and so on, is available.

Bruges: Restoration projects.
Restoration of the house Katelijnestraat 96 (before and after restoration) (above).

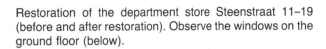

Restoration of the department store Steenstraat 11–19 (before and after restoration). Observe the windows on the ground floor (below).

Bruges: Good examples of contemporary restoration.
Vlamingstraat 70: Modern addition to a 16th century house (above).

Bruges: Gentpoortvest: A new student house within the Old Town.

Bruges: Harmful expansion at Gotje.

This year for the first time credit of 3 million BF is allotted by the city council.

Structure plan and detailed plans

A subdivision of the structure plan offers the municipal authorities another instrument for protecting and controlling the architectural heritage.

The intention is to apply the philosophical and urban outlines of the structure plan to the particular conditions of smaller entities.

Therefore the 9 quarters of the inner city are subdivided into about 50 sections.

One detailed plan consists of a set of 14 different plans (inventorisation, evaluation, projection plans). They are presented together with an extensive dossier which explains all proposals and interferences.

The plans are a study of the architectural, art-historical and structural values of the buildings individually, but at the same time an analysis of the whole town landscape in that particular area.

The options taken in the structure plan are tested against the level of functions and traffic.

The final projection plan, the so-called destination plan, contains all regulations and measures in regard to restoration, rehabilitation, sanitation, conservation and renewal.

Up to now 20 detailed plans have been approved.

Acquisition and restoration of houses

In 1974, in view of Architectural Heritage Year, Bruges was picked out as one of the pilot towns for Belgium.

For that reason it received 133 million BF from the central government. The municipality has used this money to acquire approximately 200 empty dwellings for restoration. Yearly 60 million BF are used for this purpose. After restoration of sanitation the houses remain council property and are rented out.

Houses can also be granted on longlease on condition that they are restored within a limited period. Houses can also be sold under the same conditions to private persons or sub-economical housing organisations (e. g. Brugse Maatschappÿ voor Huisvesting).

4.2 Organisation

For the organisation of urban renewal and restoration projects the municipal authorities are assisted by the Department of Historical Monuments and Urban Renewal.

Its activities are diversified as follows:

1. Processing of building applications
   Every building permit delivered in the inner city is controlled by this departement.

2. Urban planning
   See point 4: structure plan and detailed plans. The department is directly involved in all planning work and in the realisation of the detailed plans.

3. Restorations
   The restorations of private properties as well as council properties are advised upon and followed up by members of the department. For some restorations the plans and research are completely executed by the department.

4. Study, documentation, information and publications. For every activity it is first necessary to compile a comprehensive dossier. It consists of photographic documentation, a collection of slides, a library and iconographic material. In recent years several publications and a film have been made.

Consultative Commission

All important architectural modifications are put before a consultative commission referred to as the "Commissie voor Stedenschoon". Chairman of the commission is the city councillor for urban renewal. The members are "independent" qualified persons interested in the architecture and the culture of Bruges together with civil servants of the department of Public Works.

Steering Committee

The Steering Committee (Stuurgroep) is a group of experts on urban matters which advises monthly on all the urban modifications resulting from the detailed studies. They are also involved directly as advisers during the drawing up process of the detailed plans.

Traffic Commission

This commission proposes resolutions and propositions for the traffic problems.

4.3 Participation and information

Recently some neighbourhood committees are playing an important role in the realisation of urban renewal projects (we mention: the Cultural Circle of Sint-Anna; the committee of Sint-Gillis "'t Zilletje" which stimulates by means of an own gazette, the "taking position" of the inhabitants of the quarter; the Service Centre of the "Ganzestraat" which could realise a "residential plot" (woonerf) in their street; also the "Cactus" organisation which publishes "De Lastige Bruggeling", a magazine sold to an important number of young inhabitants which certainly plays a role).

The local newspapers regularly publish news about the problems and the realisations in the field of urban planning, monument care and town renewal.

We should stress that there has been a serious campaign in Bruges to involve the citizens in the realisations of town renewal. Already at the moment of the drafting of the structure plan, many people interested in the changes are invited to the townhall to discuss their problems.

The results of these discussions are published in the local newspapers, and have been of great importance to the planners. 45,000 copies of the structure plan were distributed to all houses of Bruges to notify the inhabitants.

For the detailed plans, there are three levels of cooperation:

1. Whilst preparing the detailed plans each inhabitant has a say in the projects the city are making. At the moment of house inventorisation, the inhabitants are asked to formulate their wishes and complaints in order to improve the living conditions in their neighbourhood.

2. The authorities contact also what we call the "privileged witnesses" in a neighbourhood. These are the doctor, priest, socialworkers, people who are professionally acquainted with the needs of the families of that particular neighbourhood. These "witnesses" advise the planners.

3. Plans are presented in a comprehensive manner to a large public. Different colours emphasise the situation and the possibilities.

Projects and several alternatives of the detailed plans are on view in the townhall. At this point the municipality invites owners and tenants of these quarters to introduce and explain the schemes.

Cooperation in this field should still be extended.

5. Realisation and results

The city of Bruges tries to realise the options taken in the structure plan.

5.1 The viability of the inner-city has to be preserved and the number of inhabitants increased to 32,000. The first step in achieving this aim is to create good houses.

Good houses can only be obtained

– by restoration and sanitation of the existing ones. This should be executed by the town (their properties) and by the Housing Association of Bruges (Brugse Maatschappij voor Huisvesting).

– by new constructions e. g. this possibility has recently occurred in a particular neighbourhood – Ryckepynder – where a brewery agreed to move out and space became available for nearly 100 houses.

To create a good environment it is also necessary to have enough green areas, play-grounds, and to eliminate pollution (this last point has already partly been achieved with the sanitation of the canals). The authorities note that several hundred inhabitants still move out each year to live in the suburbs. This can only be prevented by creating good houses and a good environment (this year e. g. BF 5 million are set aside for creating play-grounds).

5.2 The inner-city must still present a multifunctional aspect (shops, administration offices, schools, hotels, etc.) but the expansion of these functions must be controlled.

New functions (e. g. socio-medical function Oude Burg) can readily by adapted to historical buildings. These initiatives are very much stimulated.

5.3 The historical continuity of the town has to be assured. This can be controlled at the moment of the delivery of all building permits. Modern architecture, adapted to the town, is promoted and some good results have been achieved (e. g. Youth Library Spanjaard-straat; Student-house Gent-poortvest; office Oude Burg).

Streets and squares can be arranged in a different and more attractive way, yet still corresponding to present-day needs.

5.4 A major objective is the elimination of traffic problems in the inner-city.

Some pedestrian areas have recently been created (e. g. Breidelstraat, Burg, Blinde Ezelstraat, Vismarkt) and more are projected in the near future.

This year an amount of BF 35 millions is reserved for this project.

Traffic barriers are to be created at several places. To eliminate the parking problem many parking-places have to be constructed, all of them underground. One of these parking garages is already in use (Zilverpand ± 420 cars) and one is almost complete (Biekorf ± 200 cars).

It is the planners' biggest wish that the car should adapt to the town and not vice-versa; this of course requires a change of attitude on the part of all drivers.

6. Conclusions

6.1 **The activities of recent years were for Bruges a "step in the right direction"**

Several achievements by the city council can be summarised as follows:

1. restoration work was concentrated on houses as this seemed to fulfil the most pressing need (60 houses have been restored);

2. new dwellings were built (Zilverpand: 120 apartments) or are planned for the near future. They proved to be very important stimulations for private enterprise;

3. the first pedestrian streets are in use and the prohibition of traffic there has not resulted in any extra difficulties. Sufficient parking facilities are projected to support this initiative. Presently a new traffic scheme is being tried out;

4. the sanitation of the canals is almost a reality, a few town quarters still need a sewage-system but all this is under progress or planned.

All these activities also had a repercussion on the national level. They brought about a change in national policy regarding historical towns. The Secretary of State for Public Housing reserves ⅕ of his annual budget (BF 13 million) for urban renewal. Bruges's quota of the national funds has been considerably increased in recent years.

Internationally, Bruges regained some of its splendour and fame. It is no longer only the "Nürnberg" of Flanders. Because it was earmarked as a pilot town for renovation operations in Belgium, lots of foreign visitors interested in this matter are attracted to Bruges. Criticism and admiration by these visitors stimulates the whole process.

6.2 The required mentality change however has not occured fast enough to achieve the aim of realising the goals of the structure plan within the set 25 years. On the administrative, legal and financial level, changes are insufficient and too slow.

The insight of the responsable persons is still a slowly growing process. Too many financial and personal interests are mixed up with the need for a comprehensive, successful and continuous process of urban renewal.

This has certainly to do with the economic crisis which severely curtails the necessary funds.

6.3 The drafting of an action and financial plan for each townquarter could avoid the whole matter of structure and detailed plans remaining beautiful publications: many more books on the shelf doing little or nothing to actually improving the quality of life in the old town and its surroundings.

6.4 Co-operation and participation must be increased: A non-stop co-operative interaction between municipality and private persons (e. g. enterprises) is necessary.

At the level of the inhabitant sociologists are of great use to contact permanently, explain, help and play the intermediary part.

6.5 Looking into the future it has to be realised that many prominent problems will have to be faced. The expansion of Zeebruges will confront the municipality of Bruges with problems of a different kind: such as the decreasing housing possibilities, the deterioration of the landscape and environment and the inevitable increasing economical pressure on the medieval town centre.

Prices of real estate keep on increasing, thus reducing the possibilities of finding good homes or reasonably priced building plots.

A large number of people are therefore excluded from the building process.

The widespread problem of unemployement is particularly felt in Bruges: new jobs have to be created maybe in the direction of specialised craftsmen for restoration and urban renewal works where already a growing lack can be felt.

A choice has to be made: talk alone will not improve the living conditions of human beings but realistic action to prevent a more and mechanised world becoming a worse place to live in.

Bruges must try to set an example[3]).

---

[1]) Prevenier (W): Bevolkingscijfers in professionele strukturen der bevolking van Gent en Brugge in de 14e eeuw, in Album Charles Verlinden, Gent, 1975, p. 284

[2]) BF 100 = 1,7 L, 14.04 FF, 3,06 $

[3]) For this article the publication "Brugge, Strukturplan voor de Binnenstad", Groep Planning-Brugge, 1976, has been used as inspiration.

BULGARIA

Bulgaria
LEGISLATION, ORGANISATION, FINANCE, PARTICIPATION

Introduction

Over the centuries, Bulgaria has experienced several civilizations on her territory. In contemporary times, traces have been found of Thracian tombs dating back to the 6th century B. C. and including the one near Kazanbik with its famous frescoes and thousands of as yet unstudied tumuli.

Roman architecture (3.–4th cent. B. C.) is represented by the remains of a large number of villages such as Philipopolis, Augusta Traiana, Nicopolis and Istrum and Marcianopolis in addition to isolated structures in a more or less satisfactory state of conservation (villas, thermal springs, stadia, tombs and temples).

The testimony to the Byzantine Age (4th to 7th cent.) consists in the walls, fortifications and basilicas to be found at Sofia, Nessebar, Belovo, etc.

Following its foundation in 681, Bulgaria underwent periods of national splendour as well as suffering brutal invasions and foreign domination which destroyed most of the evidence of the country's past culture and prosperity. From that period date the vestiges of the palaces, churches and fortresses to be found in the capitals of medieval Bulgaria – Pliska, Preslav and Tirnovo – and also at Nessebar, Cherven, Zemen, Boiana etd.

The examples of Turkish architecture dating from the period of Ottoman domination (1396–1878) have disappeared almost completely. These were mosques, forts, dwellings, etc.

In fact, only those buildings which have been erected during the last two centuries still remain preserved in full or in part and give the towns and villages their stamp. This is known as the period of the "National Awakening" or "Bulgarian Renaissance".

It is from this epoch that Bulgaria has derived her greatest architectural heritage – a heritage which comprises dwellings (about 8,000), public buildings (inns, administrative authorities, clock towers, churches and monasteries, commercial and workmen's buildings such as windmills, forges, shops, etc.).

0. Strategy

0.1 The Cultural Revitalisation of Historic Centres

As we all know, a site or area of historic interest is the product of its epoch. It represents the outcome of all the factors which created it (social, political or economic), the level of development reached by the nation's culture, its technology, transport system, construction materials sector, aesthetic traditions, etc. Nor are these factors temporary in nature. They exercise a constant influence on historic sites during the whole of their existence. If one or several of the factors undergo a change, this tends to alter the whole face of the site.

As a result, we must endow historic centres with a fresh sense of purpose in order to ensure their survival. By virtue of our giving them a contemporary role, these centres will undergo a process of revitalisation and lead an existence based on satisfying the needs of modern society.

Certain settlements (and above all villages) located in mountainous regions are threatened by total dilapidation, whereas others affected by economic development manage to survive. The following classification may help us to oversee the problem:

A. Historic centres liable to complete neglect.

B. Historic centres bypassed by modern economic development.

C. Historic centres threatened by the frantic pace of modern life.

Although we cannot describe the problem in full at this stage, it may be helpful to say a few words about the above-mentioned categories.

A. Historic centres liable to complete neglect

(The town of Melnik with a population of 400 inhabitants and hillside villages in the district of Gabrovo, Slivene, Bourgas, etc.).

These places could be transformed as follows:

1. Their use as a summer tourist area with privately and publicly purchased houses converted into small hotels and recreation homes.

2. Areas set aside for creative work with houses converted for use during temporary sojourns by members of the central associations of writers, artists, architects, etc.

3. Zones of country homes purchased by private individuals to spend their weekends and holidays there.

B. Historic centres bypassed by modern economic development (Teravna, Chiroka Laka, Koprivchtitza etc.)

An attempt has been made to revitalise these centres by attracting a large number of tourists with the help of:

1. Programmes of music and folk-dancing during holiday periods and on gala days (Koprivchtitza).

2. Annual festivals of songs and folk-dances, congresses of painters, film directors, etc.

3. A revival of traditional crafts (articles made of leather, carved wood, gold and copper).

C. Historic centres threatened by the frantic pace of modern life (Plovdiv, Gabrovo, Smolian, Nessebar, Sozopol, etc.).

These sites, most of them designated as protected zones, are obliged to conserve their monuments and settings, but adapted to the requirements of modern life. The old buildings are now used as administrative or cultural centres or as private dwellings which make use of the available space without spoiling its environmental setting. Thanks to a strict observance of the appropriate proportions, dimensions and building materials, they fit into the given framework without attempting to imitate it.

0.2 The Revitalisation of Monuments

A. Buildings converted into museums

A complete network of museums has been organised throughout Bulgaria and housed in what were formerly private dwellings or public buildings used for religious worship or military training: they are now used for local or regional exhibitions. This solution furnishes visitors with an opportunity of studying not only the exhibited items but also the interiors of various historic buildings.

Unfortunately, a certain number of old edifices have been adapted as museums in which the exhibits clash with the architecture. Painted signs, show-cases, shelves and other elements of interior decoration completely alter the original atmosphere of the interiors. The visitor's attention is directed to exhibits so that he often fails to appreciate the quality of the rooms or the beauty of some of their ornamental detail.

B. Buildings converted into reception centres

A considerable number of old houses have been converted in reception centres where senior administrators and politicians or representatives from the associations of architects, artists, painters, etc. can entertain their guests from home and abroad. These houses are often of a representative character.

C. Buildings converted into centres of recreation and creative work

The associations of painters, writers, artists, architects and film directors have at their disposal a whole series of rest centres for recreational and creative purposes located throughout the country. A considerable number of authors and artists, etc. have purchased old restored houses where they spend a large part of their time working in a peaceful atmosphere, far from the noise of modern life.

D. Buildings used for tourism

Certain buildings have been adapted for use as hotels and restaurants as part of a chain of tourist establishments. As an integral element in the network of hotels scattered across the country, these witnesses in stone to a former style of living are now springing back to life after having undergone certain modifications and improvements in structure and design.

E. Buildings adapted for use by the public authorities

A large number of old houses or public buildings have been converted into schools, kindergartens, boarding schools, shops, art galleries, administrative centres, etc.

More recently, a number of old houses have been adapted as registry offices for marriages and christenings.

1. Legislation

1. History

1.1

The relevant laws on the protection of historic monuments have all been promulgated during the period since the liberation of Bulgaria from Ottoman occupation (1878). The National Assembly enacted its first provisional arrangements for safeguarding the cultural heritage of Bulgaria in 1888 entitled "Temporary Provisions for Scientific and Literary Enterprises" and in 1890 the Law on Historic Research and Assistance for Scientific and Literary Enterprises. At a later stage (1911), the National Assembly passed the Law on Ancient Monuments, an important step to ensure the protection of our heritage from the past. For the first time, the 1936 Decree on the Protection of old Buildings in Towns and Villages extended State safeguards to cover historic and architecturally interesting buildings, districts, streets and squares of architectural, folkloristic or general importance by virtue of their design, type of construction or past history. The same applies to individual houses and monuments having the same significance.

1.2

Since the Revolution of 9.9.44, the Ministerial Council has passed decrees No. 1608/1951 and No. 165/1958, which established the solid and systematic basis for the duties of the State in regard to protecting historic monuments and properties.

The Bulgarian Government's obligation to protect its historic and cultural legacy found full expression in the Law on Historic Monuments and Museums of 1969 and in article 31 of the Constitution. Pursuant to these laws, various provisions were enacted in order to facilitate the detailed application of the Law and the Constitution: these dealt with the problems peculiar to monuments and, by the same token, with those peculiar to buildings. The most important of these provisions have been promulgated whilst ratification of the others is imminent. There is every likelihood that the provisions envisaged by the Law on the Organisation and Duties of the National Institute of Historic Monuments will have been issued by the end of 1978. In accordance with articles 4 and 5 of the Law, the most significant of the national provisions on protected sectors have been approved and published in the Official Gazette.

1.3

As a result, the duty to safeguard historic monuments in Bulgaria has become an independent part of civil, administrative and international law. The penal provisions governing the protection of historic monuments are to be found in the Penal Code (articles 208, 278 and 414). The following are deemed to be crimes: acts which infringe international law on military activities by damaging, demolishing or rendering useless historic monuments or acts which constitute a theft, misappropriation, confiscation or receiving of stolen monuments.

2. Different categories of legal protection for historic monuments

2.1 The legal protection of historic monuments in Bulgaria falls within penal, administrative, civil and international law.

The legal safeguards provided under international law are implemented in Bulgaria by strictly applying the relevant international conventions and agreements on the protection of our national and international cultural heritage.

2.2

The legal measures to protect historic monuments are taken under the above-mentioned Penal Code, which specifies the most serious crimes which may be perpetrated against intact and original monuments. In the case of less serious offences committed against historic monuments, other penal provisions operate with due consideration for the aggravating circumstances.

Pursuant to the principle adopted by the Bulgarian legal authorities when codifyging criminal law within the Penal Code, no penal provisions have been incorporated within the law on historic monuments and museums.

2.3

The administrative measures adopted to safeguard monuments rest on articles 34 and 35 of the Law on Historic Monuments and Museums. Other subordinate legislation on protected sectors lists various dangerous crimes liable to similar penalties. This protection is based on certain clauses in the Law on Town and Country Planning, which govern house-building in Bulgaria and the protection of properties and monuments. This protection is augmented by the special Law on Criminal Offences and Administrative Penalties and by the Law on Administrative Procedure.

2.4

The protection afforded in civil cases rests on the Law on Historic Monuments and Museums and on the relevant provisions of Bulgarian civil law. All the damage inflicted on historic monuments is repaired at the cost of those responsible in addition to the fines and penalties. The provisions of civil law are enforced through administrative channels by penal ordinances (in cases involving only small sums of money).

2.5

This protection under civil law is backed by the relevant clauses in public law on the general requirements of society and the State in regard to safeguarding our cultural heritage. Throughout Bulgaria, there are associations known as the "Friends of Historic Monuments" who unite in this idealistic pursuit and represent the most fervent champions of our rich national legacy. These indefatigable patriots organise an individual or collective defence of the monu-

ments and ensure that the State maintains a continuous control and protection of our cultural patrimony. The aim consists in making sure that no historic monument is left without a custodian whether it be a private individual, an organisation, or a school, etc.

3. Legal provisions for the protection of historic monuments

3.1

Article 31 of the Bulgarian Constitution and the Law on Historic Monuments and Museums govern the protection of old buildings and movable structures and also place this obligation upon all State authorities, public or cooperative organisations and governmental bodies. Moreover, they make it a patriotic duty for every individual citizen in the country.

3.2

In compliance with the rules laid down by the Law on Historic Monuments and Museums, statutes have been enacted with detailed clauses on the protection of historic properties and monuments. These statutes are different for immovables and movables.

Responsibility for publishing the statutes on the protection of "movable monuments" rests with the museums themselves and the competent officials on the committee for cultural affairs. The statutes on buildings are drawn up by the National Institute of Historic Monuments. The general supervision of these activities lies with the subgroup for the "plastic arts and for our cultural and historic inheritance" within the committee for cultural affairs.

Now that this series of legal instruments has almost been completed, they provide total statutory cover free from any inconsistencies – for research, study and documentation in the field of historic monuments (i. e. their identification); the study and elaboration of projects and conservation activities, restoration and adaptation; and other technical measures designed to promote their protection, popularisation and continuous control by special authorities for the protection of monuments.

Let us also add a brief mention of the subordinate legislation to the Law on the Protection of Buildings ("immovable monuments"), the Law on Historic Monuments and Museums; and the Ordinance on the Organisation and Duties of the National Institute for Historic Monuments covered by the present report.

3.3 Ordinance on the research, study, registration and listing of historic buildings

This provides detailed rules for research and study on old buildings and for inventorising them. In the case of monuments, these are classified into isolated items and groups. The Ordinance also sets out the types of research to be pursued, the establishment of a fund to promote our "cultural legacy", the preparation of records on monuments and national archives on documentation. The Ordinance has been approved by the President of the Cultural Committee.

3.4 Ordinance on the utilization and management of historic buildings

This provides detailed rules for the use of old structures: the leasing of such properties, legal provisions, compulsory purchase, etc. as well as for their protection by special authorities. The Ordinance has been approved by the President of the Cultural Committee.

3.5 Ordinance on delimiting historic properties in the countryside

This covers monuments and sites located outside of the towns and villages whose study, listing and protection affect different organisations (Ministry of Forests, Ministry of Agriculture, Committee for the Protection of the Environment, etc.).

3.6 Ordinance on state mortgages on historic monuments rebuilt at government expense

The State bears all expenses involved in the protection of historic monuments in private ownership. With a view to precluding speculation and enrichment at the expense of the State, the Government creates a mortgage on the properties corresponding to their increased value by virtue of the conservation and restoration carried out by the State.

3.7 Ordinance on protection zones, i.e. the surroundings of isolated edifices or groups of buildings and monuments

This comprises the rules drawn up to govern the delimitation of these zones and the inclusion of the latter in town and country planning. It has been approved by the President of the Cultural Committee and the President of the Bulgarian Architects Association.

3.8 Ordinance on the preparation of town planning schemes and architectural plans for the renewal of buildings arranged in groups

In order to conserve the venerable image of these valuable testimonials to the past (whether they be architectural and historic ensembles, old town quarters or protected zones), a series of principles has been enunciated to govern the drawing up of town planning and architectural projects.

3.9 Ordinance on the study and preparation of projects and the execution of conservation, restoration and other activities in respect of historic buildings

This ordinance, which is still in the process of enactment, will offer a complete system for the protection of historic structures.

3.10

In addition, a number of special ordinances have been issued for those protected sectors deemed to be most important. This comprises concrete rules on the study and elaboration of projects and on the organisation, rehabilitation and protection of each protected sector. The ordinances also aim at safeguarding whole quarters as well as single historic monuments.

For example, a number of streets or houses dating back to the first Bulgarian State (7th–11th cent.), those of the second Bulgarian State (12th–14th cent.) have been designated as "listed properties" and no changes may be made there without the prior agreement of the National Institute of Historic Monuments. The planning schemes for these structures were worked out by the Institute itself or in some cases authorised by them.

In recent years, a total of 27 groups of buildings (Plovdiv, Koprivchtitza, Melnik and Nessebar), monasteries (Rila), ruins of ancient Bulgarian capitals (Pliska, Preslav, Tirnov), national parks (Stoletov, Bouzloudia) and other items have been designated as listed properties. Furthermore, 93 places were declared to be "historic sites".

2. Organisation

After World War II, the Governments of the new Socialist Society instituted a policy of safeguarding our national cultural heritage. A series of decisions enacted by the Council of Ministers together with the Law on Monuments and Museums passed by the National Assembly in 1969 have furnished the basis on which to standardise relations between the various bodies entrusted with the preservation of Bulgaria's architectural treasures. The bodies in question are as follows:

The Committee for Cultural Affairs

This is the supreme administrative and policy-making body with overall responsibility for the protection of our cultural legacy.

The National Institute of Historic Monuments

Its functions are to pursue research, work out projects and discharge the tasks attendant upon the conservation and restoration of historic monuments, murals and icons.

Cultural Councils

These administrative and policy-making organs are set up by the regional authorities for the purpose of protecting our cultural patrimony within their particular area.

Councils of this kind have been set up in the five regions of Bulgaria which, in turn, are subdivided into 27 districts.

In addition to these institutions, there also exist governmental or non-governmental institutions which promote the same cause: the Ministry of Architecture; the Archaeological Institute; the Department for the Theory and History of Town Planning and Architecture at the Bulgarian Academy of Science; the section for "architectural heritage" set up by the Bulgarian Architects' Association; and the "Friends of Historic Monuments" association.

The taking of decisions on promotion and restoration and the execution of such activities have been put on an organised footing. In close cooperation with the representatives of the cultural councils in each region, the National Institute of Historic Monuments draws up its plans in line with the sum of money placed at its disposal.

Pursuant to this plan, the same bodies prepare a detailed plan of work at the end of each year in regard to the listing of items, the pursuit of research, the elaboration of projects and their implementation during the coming year. Broadly speaking, the list of monuments to be conserved and restored is completed in accordance with suggestions submitted by the social organisations, private house-owners, tenants, and the representatives of public opinion.

The execution of renewal and rehabilitation measures rests exclusively with the State authorities for the preservation of monuments. In each of the five regions, a public department for construction coordinates all rehabilitation work. These departments have at their disposal specially trained craftsmen for repair and restoration techniques who direct and assume responsibility for the activities of small work groups supported – where necessary – by unskilled workers and constructors. These craftsmen are employed by the "National Institute of Historic Monuments", which employs a total of 1,700 craftsmen in the five regions and a staff of 146 at the main office in Sofia.

The individual districts specialise to a certain extent in specified renewal techniques. Plovdiv, for example, is noted for its large number of wood-carvers and restoration specialists. Tivorno, on the other hand, enjoys a reputation for craftsmen skilled in glass and metal-working. Whenever necessary, exchanges of skilled personnel take place.

The object of reconstruction consists in re-establishing the original condition of a building. As a rule, only recent additions and substructures are removed so as to retain the orginal centuries-old fabric. The restoration is carried out with great circumspection. For example, the frescoes of the monastery of Batchkovo near Plovdiv were restored with tempera so as to give later generations an opportunity to undo the restorative work without any damage to the original condition.

Furthermore, a few small areas of the background are always left in their original condition – particularly in the restoration of murals – in order to document and retain this original.

3. Finance

Pursuant to Bulgarian law, the conservation and restoration of historic monuments are carried out by the State and for the account of the State.

Every year, a total of several hundred private houses forming part of our national cultural legacy are restored to their former condition. Depending on the category of the monument, the restoration charges are borne in full or in part by the national budget. Following this work, the houses are returned to the care of their owners who sign a mortgage for the total sum spent by the State.

Generally speaking, the integral structure of a building does not undergo any modification: this applies in particular to the facades. As for the interior, the process is the same with the exception of certain rooms of less importance whose function is changed into that of a kitchen, W. C., junk-room, etc.

The architect's main concern is to conserve everything of historic, aesthetic or decorative interest – for example doors, ceilings, carved panelling, fireplaces.

The structure itself occasionally undergoes a certain degree of change. If the wooden framework proves to be too old to support the weight, it is replaced in one room after the other. In serious cases it is even possible to replace it by modern materials such as reinforced concrete, steel, etc.

In those cases where the monument stands in a less important category and the interior of the building does not contain anything of historic, scientific or decorative interest, the house-owner himself has to bear the cost of carrying out most of the work. Hence, he is obliged to meet the expense of renewing floors, ceilings, plaster, electrical installations, plumbing, etc.

In this field, the private owners and the administrative authorities sometimes find it fairly difficult to reach agreement. The important thing is to draw up a precise list and to estimate the cost of the work needed to repair the monument and the payment expected by the owner.

As a rule, the dispute is settled by the originator of the project, who makes out separate written accounts – those to be debited to the State and those to the house-owner, who must then remit the sum in question to the municipality.

In 1978, expenditure on construction measures for the protection of monuments amounted to 10 million Lw. This sum will increase to 14 million Lw by 1984.

The allocation of these funds takes place in accordance with the requirements listed by the individual regions and districts. With a view to accelerating the completion of certain projects, a list of priorities is determined. In the year 1978, for example, 2 million Lw were invested in renewing the old quarter of Plovdiv.

4. Participation

As mentioned above, the protection of monuments and historic sites in Bulgaria forms part of the Government's economic policy with the cooperation of Governmental and municipal councils.

The general public is kept informed by the press, radio and television and by meetings convened at local or national level to discuss what is happening in this sphere. In the final analysis, however, it is the National Institute of Historic Monuments which bears the responsibility for the success or failure of conservation and restoration activities.

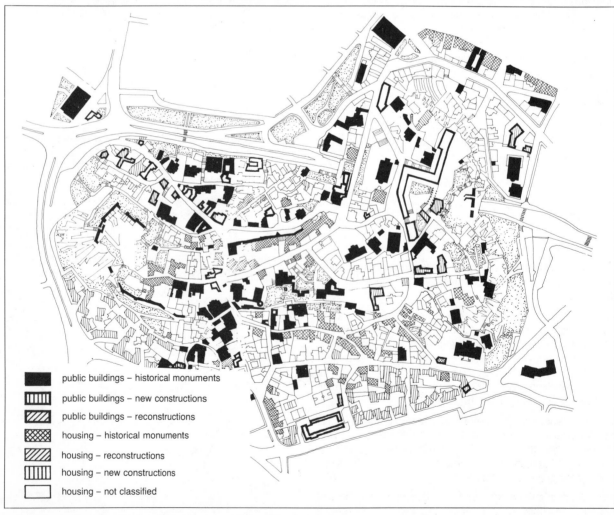

	public buildings – historical monuments
	public buildings – new constructions
	public buildings – reconstructions
	housing – historical monuments
	housing – reconstructions
	housing – new constructions
	housing – not classified

Plovdiv: above: View of the old town about 1930; below: Planning and rehabilitation plan.

Bulgaria
PLOVDIV

1. General Situation

1.1 Historical background

Plovdiv, the second largest city of Bulgaria in terms of population, was built along the slopes and at the foot of six hills. Its location in the fertile valley of Upper Thracia at the crossroads between East and West and astride the river Maritsa destined Plovdiv to become an important commercial and administrative centre from the beginning of its long history.

The first settlement on this site, which originated during the neolithic age, continued to thrive in the bronze and iron ages. During the Thracian age, the town became a fortress in the 4th century B. C. Until the 2nd century B. D., it was called Eumolpia in memory of the mythical hero and Thracian singer, Eumolpe.

In the year 341 B. C., Philip of Macedon conquered the township and enlarged it into an urban centre. To honour its conqueror, the town was renamed Philipopolis and this became Poulpoudeva in the Thracian language.

After a struggle lasting over a century, the Roman legions finally subdued the Thracian people and in the year 46 A. D. Philipopolis became the capital of the Roman province of "Thracia" with the new name of Trimontium.

Today, remains of the town walls and of the monumental structures in the Acropolis of ancient Trimontium can still be found in the heart of the city.

Following the creation of the Eastern Roman Empire in 395 A. D., the town was reorganised and enlarged further still. The Byzantine rulers appreciated the strategic importance of the city and its value as a bulwark against the Turks.

In the course of the 6th century A. D., a large number of Slav tribes invaded Thracia and settled at Plovdiv, changing its name to Paldena.

Under the rule of Krum and Zar Symeon, the town was incorporated within the Bulgarian Empire. Later, Paldena changed hands several times and Bulgarian alternated with Byzantine rule.

The Ottomans seized the town in 1364 and designated it as the seat of the Bey of Roumelia. Its name changed to Philibe.

Towards the end of the 17th century, the Bulgarian people made great economic progress despite their subjugation under foreign rule. Thanks to the accelerated development of craft production for equipping the Turkish army and for exporting goods to the countries of the Near East and Eastern Europe, Plovdiv came to be a focal point of commerce and culture.

All this has exercised a certain influence on the course taken by urban architecture with its characteristic intermingling of oriental detail and baroque forms. Many different kinds of projections, ledges and bow windows impart a highly dynamic character to the street. Light and shadow juxtapose on facades animated by every colour of the rainbow.

In the early 18th century, the typical Plovdiv house became asymmetrical in design and appearance. By the close of the century and at the beginning of the 19th century, the material prosperity of the population grew apace as commercial relations strengthened with Constantinople, Jerusalem, Odessa, Vienna, Venice, Leipzig, Manchester, etc. This exercised a substantial influence on the local style and led to the erection of more representative buildings, whose design became symmetrical. The central line of symmetry in the new town house became the salon around which the other rooms were grouped. The staircase, the ceilings, the door and window frames were made of carved wood, whilst the walls were covered with painted panels. The principal facade was also symmetrical. A four-column porch and a spiral staircase accentuated the symmetrical axis of the building.

After the Russo-Turkish war of liberation of 1877–78, Plovdiv became the capital of Eastern Roumelia and it was here that the incorporation of Eastern Roumelia in the Principality of Bulgaria was proclaimed on 6. 9. 1885.

Economic growth at the end of the 19th and at the beginning of the 20th century gave a fresh impetus to Plovdiv's architecture. The influence of pseudo-Classicism and of the Secession gradually made itself felt. Under the impact of the latter, new residential and commercial quarters sprang up at the foot of the Trimontium. The picturesque features of the winding lanes has been replaced by the straight streets so characteristic of the new departure in town planning. Striking illustrations of this are "Vassil Kolarov" and "Raiko Daskalov".

After the 1920s, the architecture of Plovdiv underwent a period of complete decadence. The functionalism and utilitarianism of the buildings imbued the exteriors with a banal aspect and led to the disappearance of the picturesque traits of the old town.

Fortunately, the uneven terrain and the difficult building conditions (granite rock) have meant that only the historic town-centre is located on the hills of Nebet, Taxime and Djambaz (forming the ancient settlement of "Trimontium") and, even today, this has not been affected very much by the encroachment of modern architecture.

In the course of the last 30 years, Plovdiv has pressed ahead with buildings in the new Socialist style. The new high-rise dwellings help to enliven the somewhat unartistic appearance of the streets.

The rehabilitation of the old quarters was made the subject of an international town-planning competition. That stresses the importance of the genuine opportunities for a modern development of Plovdiv. The various trends now discernible in the building of the new city and embracing the old district have resulted in a need to undertake active measures to safeguard it. All that has led up to the preparation of the current planning and rehabilitation scheme for old Plovdiv.

1.2 Architecture

During the pre-War period, the houses built in Plovdiv were usually one to three storeys in height.

Plovdiv: above: Roman theatre
below: House in Maxim Gorki road
after reconstruction

2. Protection

2.1 Situation

In the centre of the town and located on the three hills of the "Trimontium" (Djambaz, Taxine and Mebet) lies the oldest part of Plovdiv, which has been designated as a protected zone.

In this context, the fine examples of architecture in v. Kolarov and R. Daskalov Street are also the subject of current studies.

2.2 Research

The archaeological research carried out in recent years has shown that the limits of the ancient township exceeded the Trimontium area. At the foot of the hills, significant

As a result of the political, economic and social changes brought about by the War, the number of public buildings and private dwellings erected increased considerably. In the town centre, buildings remained one to three storeys in height whereas in the suburbs multi-storey structures were allowed. Thanks to this fact, the city has retained its famous silhouette with the six hills of Plovdiv rising in the middle.

Plovdiv: The house of Köcümcüoglu after reconstruction; façade and entrance archaeological and historic remains have been discovered beneath the foundations of the "Trimontium" Hotel, v. Kolarov Street and R. Daskalov Street as well as the districts adjacent to the hills in the North East.

In several parts of the town-centre, 18th and 19th century houses were built on top of the ancient structures.

The old part of Plovdiv consists almost entirely of buildings constructed during the period of the Bulgarian national awakening (17th–19th centuries) and these now make up its most distinctive features. The buildings in question were mainly churches, private dwellings and a Turkish mosque.

2.3 Classified monuments

The systematic inventory drawn up in 1964 in the old quarter of Plovdiv comprised 154 "listed" monuments with 12 of them possessing national importance, 42 local importance, and 100 forming part of an architectural whole.

The most significant monuments

Archaeological

The most important archaeological remains are to be found on the "Trimontium" where the line of the walls enveloping the ancient Acropolis is clearly marked. Beneath the South Gate, work has now been completed on uncovering a Roman theatre still in perfect condition. A large part of the foundations, vaults, arches and mosaics of outstanding quality can now be seen.

Diggings have also revealed part of a Roman road and of the Roman arena. Certain evidence points to the existence of a town wall – with "Khissar kapa" in impeccable condition.

On the hill at Nebet, there are important archaeological remains dating back to Thracian times.

Christian monuments

The Holy Virgin Church at 6 M. Gorki Street, better known as the cathedral, was completed in 1844. In design and architecture, it marks a new stage in the development of places of worship during the Bulgarian National Awakening. Its bell was constructed 10 years after the liberation of the country from foreign dominion – in 1888.

St. Mary's (1869) is built completely of timber. Its terrace-type construction imparts an original appearance to the church.

St. Constantin and Helen, located close to the Roman Gate at "Khissar kapia", has a monumental baroque iconostasis and icons dating from the 14th century. It was built in 1830.

St. Dimitar, reconstructed in 1870, is a basilica with two rows of columns subdividing the church into 3 naves. The iconostasis consists of pure marble. On the south-eastern side of the church, the porch is surmounted by a large square bell topped by a cupola.

St. Nicolas (1835) has a single nave with a timber vaulted ceiling and a small balcony above the entrance. Its carved wooden iconostasis is decorated by icons made in 1736.

Plovdiv: The house of Köcümcüoglu, plan of the ground floor (r.) and the first floor (l.)

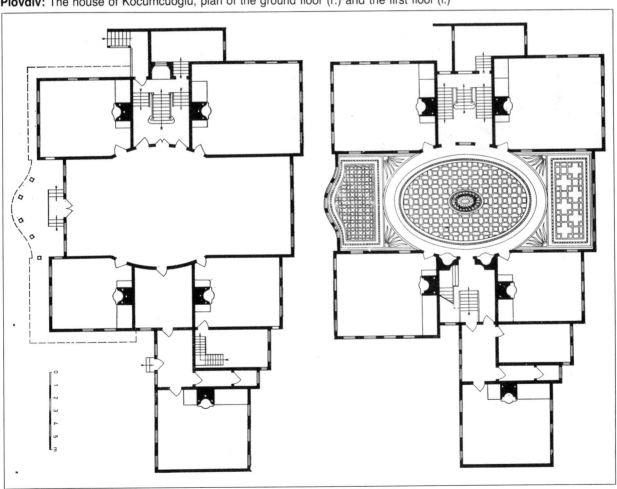

Plovdiv: left: Hissar Kapi, the former gate of the ancient Roman town of Trimontium, on the right-hand side two reconstructed buildings, one of them the house of Köcüm-cüoglu on top of the ancient wall

right, above: The house of Mavridi after reconstruction
right, below: View of the Paldere street
left, below: House in Nektariev street. Detail of the facade with reconstructions of mural painting.

St. Petka, perched on a rocky elevation overlooked by the hill at Djambaz, fits perfectly into this architectural framework. Built in 1835, the church has only one nave: its outstanding feature is simplicity of design.

St. Haralampi (1870) is similar in design to a basilica with three naves. The two rows of columns are made of wood.

St. Nedelia (1832) is not distinguished by any special architecture or decoration, but it does possess a very fine iconostasis made of carved wood.

St. Kevork is an Armenian church in the basilica style with three naves. Historic documents dating back to 1147 bear witness to the long existence of this monument.

Mohammedan places of worship

In the protected zone of old Plovdiv, there is only one Moslem religious monument and that is the Mevlevi Khane,

a square structure with a small balcony over the entrance. During the years 1974–1975, the restored hall was used as a tourist attraction.

Outside the protected zone there are several Moslem places of worship possessing considerable importance such as the Djoumaia Mosque of the 14th–15th and the Imaret of the 15th century.

Public buildings

The major public edifices are located near the protected zone: a Turkish clock (1623) on "Danov halm" hill and two Turkish baths made of stone and topped with domes.

Private dwellings

Nearly all the historic monuments preserved in old Plovdiv are houses built during the Bulgarian National Awakening

Plovdiv: Reconstruction of the "Mevlevi Khane", a former tekke of the "dervich"
above: View of the former prayerhall after reconstruction
below: Interior of the restaurant within the tekke

(18th–19th cent.). Whether large or small, symmetrical or not, these houses impart a picturesque character to this quarter perched on the three hills of the Trimontium.

Despite the overall uniformity of the architecture here, it does nevertheless offer great variety in its range of sizes and facades, doors and windows, gardens and courtyards as well as murals and carved wooden ceilings.

3. The Aim of Renovation

For a number of years now, the old quarter of Plovdiv has been the subject of intensive research. This research was taken into account in the planning and rehabilitation of the town centre and also in the residential quarters along the river Maritsa. Quite recently, V. Kolarov Street and R. Daskalov Street were renovated by restoring the facades of the houses to their original colours.

The introduction of a new pedestrian precinct in the middle of the town created a functional and aesthetic link between the old and the new town.

The necessity of replanning the town centre, the unprepossessing appearance of the old architecture, the presence of numerous archaeological ruins and the large number of monuments from the epoch of the National Awakening, made it imperative to renovate the old quarters of Plovdiv.

4. Strategies

4.1 Renewal of the historic town-centre of Plovdiv – legal provisions

The planning and rehabilitation scheme

This was drawn up by the National Institute of Historic Monuments during the years 1966–68 by a team of experts headed by the architect Mladen Pantchev. Prior to its approval by the Ministry of Architecture, the plan was discussed during two national conferences and at a number of meetings for interested persons, experts, local residents and representatives of Plovdiv municipal council.

Basic plan

The best conserved part of old Plovdiv is located on the three hills of Trimontium with the addition of a few adjacent quarters to the south and west. This area formed the subject of substantial research and analysis by architects, town planners and archaeologists, whose findings were then incorporated within the basic plan. The latter is an integral component of the planning and rehabilitation scheme.

Detailed planning outline

This comprises the following schemes, plans and notes:

a. Zoning plan
b. Zone of new buildings

Plovdiv: above: Interior of the house 55, Maxim Gorki road below: The house of Nicolaidi, south facade towards the courtyard.

a. 1. Zone of archaeological research
This comprises above all the area around the historic town walls as delimited by the diggings carried out in accordance with an appropriate time-table.

a. 2. Restoration zone
Areas with a particularly large number of historic structures (whether isolated monuments or buildings and whole streets of historic interest) earmarked for total or partial restoration.

a. 3. Reconstruction zone
Areas with only the isolated houses of architectural merit still remaining. The street silhouette will be filled out with new buildings erected on the site of the old structures, whose exact dimensions are to be found in the land registry map.

a. 4. Zone of new buildings
This zone consists of the quarters located along the fringes of the protected area – mostly comprising dilapidated buildings. In design and size, the new houses are inspired by the old buildings in the protected zone.

Outside the old town walls, provision has been made for the erection of isolated villas or country houses with two to three storeys on sites obtained by consolidating several smaller plots of land.

As regards the property enclosed within the old walls, the building of new houses will be kept to a minimum.

Certain sites in Paldena Street and Tzeretelev Street, for example, are reserved for the construction of new cafés and pubs to meet the needs of the tourists, whilst others will be set up as studios for painters and sculptors. At the corner of L. Karavelov Street and the 4th January Street, a youth centre will be built whilst the sports centre situated between L. Karavelov and P. R. Slaveikov will have a new sports hall.

4.2 Social, economic and architectural objectives The silhouette of the protected quarter

Certain panoramic photographs taken several decades ago show a streetscape marked by great variety. This diversity has been retained in the planning and rehabilitation scheme, which reverts to the typical outlines of the old streets and underlines the rocky massif of the three hills in old Plovdiv.

Network of communications

The resolution of the problem of communications involves the following two factors for the planning and rehabilitation scheme:

– the re-creation as closely as possible of the character of the streets at the time of the National Awakening;

– the safeguarding of the conditions for providing a modern transport system.

With a view to achieving these goals, the project envisages the restoration of the old lay-out of the streets provided that this does not hamper the movement of modern means of communication. Vehicular traffic must use the outer roads. The remaining streets are reserved for pedestrians, whilst cars are only granted access in extreme cases. Car parks have been set up along the main routes leading to the old historic town-centre.

c. Study of the silhouette of the protected zone
d. Network of streets and roads
e. Tourist itineraries
f. Commercial facilities
g. Scheme for the adaptation of historic monuments for the benefit of the general public
h. Studies on the silhouette of the streets (the "streetscape")
i. The green belt
j. Administration of public services
g. Demographic trends

The details of the above are as follows:

a. Zoning
This was prepared with due consideration for the existing historic monuments within their setting and for the necessity of making full use of archaeological remains. The scheme provides for the following zones:

Tourist itineraries

These itineraries take into account the interest evinced by visitors in the various items of historic interest. These include archaeological monuments located on the three hills as well as numerous streets of architectural merit together with isolated monuments. Near the southern entrance to the tunnel, a lift has been planned to carry visitors up Djambaz Hill.

As regards streets in the central sector, plans have been made to set up restaurants, self-service cafeterias, a post office, a philatelist centre, bazaars for the sale of craftsmen's products, etc.

Accommodation for tourists is assured by the conversion of old houses into hotels as well as by the erection of new buildings.

The adaptation of historic buildings for public use

The planning and rehabilitation scheme envisages the adaptation of a large part of Plovdiv's historic houses as cultural centres, youth clubs, chess clubs, reception rooms for the Municipal Council and Party Committee, rest homes, "creative centres" for members of the associations of painters and artists as well as architects and film directors, a permanent exhibition of local painters' works, etc.

The townscape of Plovdiv

One of the principal tasks in the planning and rehabilitation scheme consists of the restoration (as far as this is feasible) in design and silhouette of the old streets of Plovdiv. In those cases where the documentation needed for the restoration of the town is insufficient, new buildings will be erected in the typical style and size of the historic quarter. Their architecture ought to be inspired by that of the old structures, but at the same time approached in the modern manner involving the use of contemporary materials.

Green belts

The open spaces in the old part of Plovdiv are considered to be sufficient in area, and the planning and rehabilitation scheme does not envisage the laying of new green zones.

The large number of public parks has made it possible to carry out diggings without demolishing buildings. After conservation treatment, the archaeological ruins discovered in the natural parks will be open to visitors in as good a condition as possible.

Moreover, the planning and rehabilitation scheme envisages archaeological diggings at the top of Nebet and Djambaz Hills which will be left as green spaces with a panoramic view of the town after the conservation of the ruins and the renewal measures have been completed.

The rocky massifs around the Trimontium provide the most impressive of its natural treasures and, for this reason, the plan has tried to show them to good effect.

In order to safeguard the intimacy of the old town houses in Plovdiv, the planners decided to retain their inner courtyards enclosed within high walls.

Renewal – municipal services – technical installations

The planning and rehabilitation scheme for the historic centre of Plovdiv also concerns itself with the important problem of renewing the old quarter and ensuring the smooth functioning of all the modern technical installations.

In the ancient town-centre, each of the old houses has a fairly spacious courtyard: however, without the cow-sheds, hen-houses, etc. the restoration of the yards will not pose any serious difficulties. In some cases, however, a building of considerable or less importance (whether very old or not) which does not form part of a historic ensemble is earmarked for demolition. That permits a more unimpeded view of the courtyard and also enables the sun to reach secluded recesses.

The various municipal utilities (such as electricity, water, drainage and telephones) have been considered in the light of the old lay-out of the streets and the requirements of modern traffic. The whole of the electric installations have been laid under the pavements so as not to spoil the view of the streets with pylons and cables. A discreet system of street-lamp lighting and, in certain places, the use of floodlights guarantees a proper artistic setting for a number of the streetscapes.

The studies carried out on the lighting of K. Naktariev Street illustrate the search for an intimate atmosphere in the old district without over-emphasising certain aspects of the whole setting.

The installation of two new transformers has been planned in order to ensure adequate electricity supplies.

The provision of drinking water and sewage facilities is also guaranteed by conventional means for the whole area of the protected zone.

As the restoration of Plovdiv's old houses proceeds apace, each of them is fitted with a complete range of sanitary facilities.

Furthermore, local residents are assured of telephone communication by virtue of the network of subsurface cables throughout the historic town centre.

Unfortunately, it has proved impossible to get rid of the television aerials and these will remain clearly visible on the roof-tops.

Demographic trends

The protected zone in old Plovdiv covers a superficial area of 3,884 hectares and houses a population of 4,954 inhabitants. For town planning purposes, the territory is divided into two parts. The first comprises the site on the Trimontium proper, delimited by its natural frontiers, with a population of 4,378. The second part consists of the area surrounding Gebzarska Street and Stamat Matanov Street – designated a green belt – and also the district at the foot of Djambaz Hill where archaeological diggings are to carried out.

Private accommodation

In order to ensure that the local residents in old Plovdiv enjoy contemporary standards of living and that the size of living space per person is increased from 19 to 25 square metres per person, the planning and rehabilitation scheme provides for a reduction in the population of 1,539 inhabitants. These people will be rehoused in the new part of the town by 1980.

The Municipal Council of Plovdiv has undertaken the construction of the new housing.

Public funds

The adaptation of Plovdiv's historic buildings and monuments for public purposes such as their use as art galleries, creative centres for artists, reception rooms, etc. is intended to help conserve the picturesque features of the protected zone.

Unfortunately, this trend has extended beyond sensible limits and produced a certain exodus of people from the quarter. Houses which formerly accommodated three generations at once are now closed for most of the year.

The new public buildings recently projected will cover a superficial area of 5,697 square metres and thus not exceed that of the existing structures.

Having taken into account the existence of different institutions for young children (nurseries and kindergartens), the planning and rehabilitation scheme has only provided one kindergarten for four groups.

No new schools are scheduled, because a sufficient number already exist in the protected zone.

The commercial sector

Shopping facilities have been concentrated in the quarters adjacent to the protected zone. The requirements of the 3,415 local residents and 4,000 visitors per day will be met, in line with the general plan, by 26 food shops and 20 other types of shops. Studios are to be provided for 34 craftsmen. The total superficial area covered by these shops and studios will amount to 1,200 square metres.

4.3 Finance

The provision of funds for conservation activities and the restoration of the historic quarters (for both planning and execution) is subject to the same system as the rest of the country, i.e. the money is voted in the annual budget of the Bulgarian Minister of Finance.

To begin with, a sum of 200,000 leva was earmarked for this purpose, but this had risen to 1,200,000 leva by 1978.

5. The Realisation of Projects

The execution of projects involving the conservation, restoration and adaptation of historic buildings and monuments in old Plovdiv has been entrusted to a special team of 23 architects, engineers and technicians from the National Institute of Historic Monuments in Sofia.

The author of each project sketches the dimensions and current facade of the building or structure in question. After carrying out appropriate studies on the monument (such as the type of construction, the various layers of paint on the walls, the state of the roof and the foundations, the possible modification of the original plan, etc.), the experts then proceed to prepare a plan of rehabilitation and restoration.

The third phase of the studies comprises the project for adapting the monument in accordance with a programme drawn up or approved by the regional committee for cultural affairs or by the new proprietor (where the house has been expropriated).

In those houses earmarked for residential purposes, an attempt is made to improve living standards by arranging for suitable sanitary facilities, kitchens with running water, electrical installations, etc.

The conserving of archaeological and medieval monuments is carried out in accordance with archaeological studies under the direction of the Institute of Archaeology, a department of the Bulgarian Academy of Science.

The actual conservation, restoration and adaptation work is carried out by workmen directed by Plovdiv's special department – part of the National Institute of Historic Monuments.

During the period 1957–1977, the National Institute of Historic Monuments carried out the conservation and restoration work on a large number of historic monuments. These included the following:

Archaeological monuments

The whole complex of Thracian fortifications on Nebet Hill, the old town wall running below "Mevlevi Khane", the medieval reservoir at Nebet Tepe, the Roman amphitheatre, the ancient site near St. Constantin and Helen, etc.

Monuments dating back to the National Awakening

Most of the houses in the historic town-centre of Plovdiv remain as private accommodation for their proprietors after restoration, but a large amount of conversion is carried out for public requirements.

Below, we have listed some of the largest houses which passed into the ownership of various public institutions following expropriation.

Kouyoumdjioglou is one of the largest houses from the epoch of the Bulgarian National Awakening to be found in Plovdiv. Built in 1847 in the central area of the elevation called Nebet Tepe, it perches on the old town wall near the Southern Gate known as Khissar kapia. This huge building now houses the ethnographic museum.

Mavridi

Completed in 1829, Mavridi is better known by its other name, La Maison de Lamartine, in honour of the great French poet who stayed there in 1833. Because of its very poor state of repair, the house had to undergo considerable reconstruction. Steel girders were used for strengthening purposes without, however, necessitating any change in the position of the ceilings and carved doors. Today, Mavridi serves as a museum.

The House at 15, K. Nektariev Street

This building is now used as a "creative centre" for the association of artists. Erected in the mid-19th century at the end of a little courtyard, it presents a symmetrical facade of monumental design.

Nicolaidi (1868–1870) was restored in 1972–1974 and converted into the Architects' Club.

The house at 55 Maxim Gorki Street has become a reception centre, Pavliti House a rest home for the Committee of Cultural Affairs, the house at 21 M. Gorki a chess club, that at 32 P. R. Slaveikov converted into offices used by the National Institute of Historic Monuments, etc. These buildings all represent felicitous examples of conversion.

A number of houses have been converted into restaurants without this impairing the original interior.

The conversion of a former place of worship, the Mevlevi-Khane, into a restaurant called for substantial rebuilding. New rooms of the new restaurant have been housed in the basement under the main hall. The kitchen and other annexes are also located in the basement.

Furthermore, a new wing with an enclosed courtyard has been added to the storey which includes the old hall.

Reconstruction of buildings

In certain parts of the historic quarter, demolished houses will be replaced in accordance with the provisions of the planning and rehabilitation scheme. The architects in charge of these operations work from old sketches and photographs and endeavour to reproduce the former facades with modern building materials.

This method was adopted to reconstruct "Balabanov", "de Khadji Lampcha", the house at No. 8, Fourth of January Street, and also the house at No. 50 St. Matanov Street, which accommodates the service department of the Directorate for Old Plovdiv.

The Construction of new buildings and architectural complexes

In order to fill out the empty spaces within the protected zone, the planning and rehabilitation scheme has provided for the construction of new houses or even whole complexes, albeit with due consideration for the streetscape of old Plovdiv.

Examples of this are the plot of land at No. 7 Starinna Street where a two-storey villa has been built and the artists' studio at 16 Palden Street or the hotel planned for construction on several pieces of land in Kniaz Tzeretelev Street.

The plastic arts

Both in their exteriors and interiors, the houses of Plovdiv not only present fine works of architecture but also outstanding examples of the decorative arts. For that reason, a large number of historic buildings with fine architecture (houses, churches and mosques) are also classified as monuments of the plastic arts (paintings and wooden sculptures).

The walls of the rooms are decorated in linear style or embellished with imaginary columns or floral garlands. Some of the panels on partition walls have been ornamented with multi-coloured medallions representing exotic landscapes.

The ceilings, gates, door and window-frames and the banisters in the staircases are made of richly decorated carved wood.

The walls of the churches are covered with murals, whilst the altar is separated from the nave by fine iconostases. The decorations on the walls – particularly the exterior walls – are often in a lamentable condition due to the imperfect materials used and the age of the structure.

The projects for the conservation and restoration of works of plastic art are reserved for painter-restorers who belong to the special studio set up at the National Institute of Historic Monuments.

Following detailed studies such as tests on the mural paintings, ornamented wood or multi-coloured decorations on wood, the well-tried methods and techniques of conservation are then applied: thorough cleaning followed by replastering and repair of the damaged surfaces.

The reconstruing of vanished ornamentation (whether paintings or wood carvings) naturally includes the marking of the latter to prevent any confusion with the originals.

Most of the houses and churches quoted above are treated by the painter-restorers simultaneously with the restoration work in an attempt to achieve the multi-coloured effect of former times.

6. Conclusions

Twenty years ago, the old quarter of Plovdiv was threatened by the slow but sure decay of its rich architectural legacy.

Following the encouragement and financial support given by the Government and various local organisations together with the help of the population during the last 20 years, the destruction of the old houses has been brought to a close.

A new policy has appeared – the policy of renewal and restoration. The historic town-centre was declared to be a protected zone, lists were drawn up of the existing monuments and a new planning and rehabilitation scheme introduced.

In order to ensure a better organisation of investment and effort, the Municipal Council created a special local department – the Directorate for Safeguarding Old Plovdiv. In turn, the National Institute of Historic Monuments created a studio of planners and an implementing service.

In spite of the difficulties, the work has made rapid progress. Slowly but surely, the historic quarter is regaining its old appearance. The multi-coloured facades of the restored houses and the surrounding walls with their huge gates will recapture a sparkle of gaiety for this neglected district. In summer, a large number of the courtyards will become exhibition halls to display the works of local painters.

Some of the streets will retain their original surfaces whereas others can look forward to a more modern solution.

In the evening, certain streets are illuminated by discreet lighting. The municipal authorities endeavour to provide adequate lighting in all parts of the town centre and to arrange for aesthetically satisfying street-lamps.

Parallel with the successes achieved by the restorers, however, it must be admitted that the number of houses converted into public buildings (museums, reception centres and rest homes) is somewhat exaggerated since they remain empty most of the time – especially in the evenings. This factor deprives the district of its customary animated atmosphere.

A good solution would be to construct a new tourist centre and also to build new villas on empty plots. In this way, the historic town-centre could become a livelier place, not only for tourists simply passing through but also for the three generations of local inhabitants – the children, the adults and the senior citizens.

Rescued from its seemingly inevitable decay by virtue of restoration and adaptation to meet the needs of contemporary life, old Plovdiv will continue to show future generations something of its eventful history down through the centuries and above all to present them with fine examples of the picturesque architecture built during the Bulgarian National Awakening.

CANADA

Canada
LEGAL – ORGANISATIONAL – FINANCIAL – ASPECTS OF PRESERVATION

1. Legislation

1.1 Legislative competence for protection

1.1.1 General

Canada's fundamental constitutional document, the British North America Act, 1867 (as amended), grants exclusive jurisdiction in certain subjects to either the federal government or the provinces. In certain topics (such as heritage conservation) an overlap is inevitable.

Furthermore, provinces delegate some of their powers to subsidiary levels of government, i. e. municipalities. These levels of government are organized as cities, towns, villages, townships, counties, etc. In addition, a fourth level of government standing between the municipalities and the provincial legislatures has been created in districts where a partial fusion of municipalities has taken place. This level is called a regional community, urban community, etc.

Each level guards its jurisdiction jealously . . . occasionally at the expense of conservation.

There are no easy solutions. There ist, however, a way to alleviate the problem: it is to increase the awareness of heritage on the part of all governmental levels, to translate that awareness into legal and moral obligations, and thereby impose an imperative need for co-operation which does not currently exist.

1.1.2 Federal activity in heritage matters

Legal basis: The legal basis for federal activity is the Historic Sites and Monuments Act of 1952.

Effects: Protection of monuments and sites: Constitutionally, all matters pertaining primarily to "property and civil rights" are of exclusive provincial jurisdiction. Therefore, although the federal government goes through the exercise of naming "national historic sites", it cannot protect the properties so named and such designations have no legal effect.

The federal government can, however, purchase historic sites. Approximately 100 historic sites have been acquired by the government and are being scrupulously restored. The restoration of one site alone has cost over twenty million dollars. The overwhelming majority of such sites are now being used as museums.

Protection of surroundings and districts:

The situation is the same as in the case of individual landmarks.

1.1.3 Procedures

In matters pertaining to historic sites, the Minister of Environment consults and advisory body named the Historic Sites and Monuments Board of Canada. When a structure is brought to the attention of the Commission, it first screens applications which are beyond its terms of reference (e. g. cemeteries) and, after study, makes a recommendation to the Minister. The study period is usually some six months long.

The Commission may recommend that the Minister

a. ignore the structure,

b. designate the structure as a national historic site and erect a plaque,

c. enter into a cost-sharing agreement, or

d. acquire the property.

The Minister is not bound by that recommendation.

Integration into national development policy:

Some forty-five federal departments and agencies affect cultural property directly or indirectly. An interdepartmental committee has been recently established to supervise this effect and to discuss ways of minimizing the damage which public works projects may cause to cultural property. If a site has been declared by a province to be a protected landmark, the federal government (unlike any other party) is under no legal obligation to respect that site if it is carrying out a federal public works project.

Consequently, if a site of heritage significance (designated or not) is threatened by a federal project or is on federal land, the only recourse is to apply for help from the Minister of Indian and Northern Affairs.

1.1.4 The problem of demolition on federally regulated property

Nature of the problem: There is little the federal government can do constitutionally to save threatened buildings. It can buy landmarks: but it cannot buy every significant structure in the country. It can, however, do something to regulate its own demolition of cultural property, and that of federally regulated organizations (such as railways). The creation of governmental committees is a second-best solution.

The federal government's duty with regard to the conservation of our heritage is one of Canada's legal curiosities: namely, the federal government has absolutely no legal duty whatsoever.

The American federal government, by contrast, enacted sweeping legislation such as the National Environmental Policy Act and particularly the Urban Mass Transportation Assistance Act. Australia followed with similar legislation. These statutes insist that any project with federal participation must avoid destruction of historic and architectural heritage unless no viable alternative is possible. Although the new laws did not provoke a deluge of litigation, they led to some important judicial decisions which both saved valuable heritage and instilled a more conscientious attitude in government planners regarding historic and architectural heritage. A subsidiary problem is destruction of heritage on land which, although not federally-owned, is federally controlled. Such land is beyond the reach of provincial statutes, including heritage statutes. The primary example of such land is railway property. Various agencies regulate the use of such properties but have not used their powers for heritage conservation. Consequently, there is little control in practice upon the destruction of heritage on those properties.

Working toward a solution: Heritage Canada is currently conducting legislative research based in part upon the Urban Mass Transportation Assistance Act and related legislation. The unusual feature of these statutes is that the protection of cultural property is no longer contingent upon inventories.

Inventories had always been considered a necessary evil in heritage legislation. They were necessary because a clear delimitation was considered essential between indispensable national heritage and expendable property. They were considered an "evil" for four reasons. The drafting of inventories was subject to lobbying. It placed government in a conflict of interest when the government which was drafting the inventory was also proposing to demolish the structure. It was a never-ending process; for example, the Swedes have not completed their inventory, although they started it in 1666. Finally, it tacitly stygmatized properties which were not, for any reason, on the inventory.

By contrast, the American statutes said that whenever the federal government proposed to destroy an area for a public works project, it would have the responsibility of assessing the impact of its own actions.

Furthermore, the statutes extended to other areas: they prohibited the government from subsidizing any project which wantonly harmed heritage. Since most federally-regulated enterprises (such as railways) receive some kind of subsidies, the statutes also affected their activities.

At the present time, there is no legislation at the Canadian federal level which directly coincides with these precedents. However, the federal government has enacted policy statements which are morally (if not legally) binding, and has established a committee of senior civil servants to promote the government's policies; it is called the Federal Advisory and Co-ordinating Committee on Heritage Conservation.

Tentative projections: Federal procedures regulating governmental demolition and integration of conservation with development policy are becoming increasingly formalized. There is a new Environmental Assessment Review Process, a Federal Advisory Co-ordinating Committee on Heritage Conservation, and an increasing number of public hearings into environmental matters. If this trend continues (and most authorities think it will), then it is likely that a statute will eventually dictate formal procedures for the federal government to follow whenever it threatens a site of potential heritage interest, and that citizens will be able to block the project if the government fails to do so. A bill which resurfaces occasionally before the House of Commons would have precisely that effect; although it is given little chance of passage in the immediate future, many authorities believe that is not only a sign of things to come but will also be an answer to the problems of integration of conservation into national policy.

1.1.5 The provincial governments

Legal basis: Eight of Canada's ten provincial governments are empowered to grant permanent protection to monuments and sites. The only two exceptions are Ontario and Nova Scotia.

The relevant provincial statutes are as follows:

Alberta:	The Alberta Historical Resources Act
British Columbia:	The Heritage Conservation Act
Manitoba:	The Historic Sites & Objects Act
New Brunswick:	The Historic Sites Protection Act
Newfoundland:	The Historic Objects, Sites & Records Act
Prince Edward Island:	The Recreation Development Act & The Archaeological Investigation Act
Quebec:	The Cultural Property Act
Saskatchewan:	The Saskatchewan Heritage Act & The Provincial Parks, Protected Areas, Recreation Sites & Antiquities Act.

Nova Scotia's Historical Objects Protection Act controls only archaeological excavations on government land. The more recent Nova Scotia Historic Properties Designation Act does not control alteration or demolition of properties so "designated".

The only province not mentioned so far is Ontario; it is described under Chapter 1.3.

Surroundings: The only province to protect the surroundings of designated sites is Quebec: the distance is a radius of 500 feet (150m). Any projects within ½ mile (0.8 km) of a designated site in Alberta must, according to regulations passed under the Alberta Planning Act, be submitted for comment to the cultural affairs officials of that province; but their decision is not legally binding.

Groups and districts: Only one provincial statute refers specifically to the provincial protection of districts. The Quebec Cultural Property Act empowers the Minister to declare protected districts.

The New Brunswick Minister of Education can also designate "historic districts", but the designation has no legal effect.

The other provincial statutes do not refer specifically to districts; instead, they usually refer to "sites". A "site" can be as large or as small as the government declares it to be. An entire district can be considered a single site for legal purposes. The Alberta government has recently decided to protect a "site" which includes some sixty buildings, and two British Columbia "sites" (Gastown and Chinatown in Vancouver) each contain even more properties under multiple ownership.

Procedure: The procedure for designation usually comprises a number of steps, not all of which are described in legislation; some are discribed in Regulations, and other are simply carried out in practice without any formal legal requirement. They apply more or less to all provinces except Nova Scotia and Ontario (described later).

Most provinces have historical boards which advise the government regarding structures worthy of protection; but only in Quebec and Alberta is it obligatory for the government to consult with the board.

The owner of a property proposed for protection is frequently notified beforehand of this possibility; this is a legal requirement in both Alberta and Quebec, where such notice must be given sixty days before designation. Such notice must include the reasons for the proposed designation.

Once the property has been designated for protection, it is customary to register this fact at the land titles office. This is a legal requirement in Alberta, Prince Edward Island adds that the designation must be announced in a local newspaper and be posted on a sign on the property.

No provincial statute outlines an elaborate procedure for applications to conduct alterations or demolition on provincially designated sites. There are not very many designated buildings in Canada, and even fewer applications to change them; consequently, this activity is usually treated in an ad hoc manner.

1.1.6 Integration into provincial, regional and local development policy

Many provinces have set up interdepartmental committees to supervise public works which affect cultural property.

The only provinces which will "force" themselves to consider cultural property in their planning process are Ontario and Alberta, which have environmental assessment statutes (Ontario Environmental Assessment Act 1975, Alberta Land Surface Conservation & Reclamation Act, Alberta Historical Resources Act). Even in these cases, however, the integration procedure has been weak: Ontario has exempted most building demolition from its statute, and Alberta has so far concentrated primarily on archaeological resources rather than historic sites in its environmental assessments.

1.2 Selected problems in provincial legislation

1.2.1 Examples of areas of concern

Maintenance: Most provinces do not compel maintenance of designated heritage sites. In Kingston, a former home of our first Prime Minister, Sir John A. Macdonald, was left to fall into such disrepair that the commemorative plaque was removed in disgust.

Building codes: People wishing to renovate structures face the familiar problem of strict compliance with building codes and fire codes. Only Alberta empowers its Minister to waive building code provisions; but this is done only in exceptional circumstances.

The National Building Code, which is the model for such codes throughout the country, specifically permits building inspectors to grant "equivalents", i. e. to approve buildings which do not meet the wording of the Code but are otherwise as safe as the Code buildings. Inspectors, however, are loath to make such decisions: for if there is a fire, the public will tend to blame them instead of the Code. Conservationists hope to overcome the building code problem without sacrificing safety.

Governmental demolition: Provincial governments, like the federal government, have generally not followed the American and Australian example in controlling the destruction wrought by public works projects; nor have they imposed controls upon municipal public works which have similar effects.

1.2.2 Enforcement

General: A statute is worthless unless it is implemented. In Canada, three legal obstacles stand in the way of citizens trying to persuade governments to enforce their own laws:

a. Citizens have no right to governmental information concerning implementation of laws;

b. Citizens have no right to deduct expenses from taxable income when those expenses are incurred to protect the "public interest"; by contrast, all expenses to promote the private interest and profit (including lobbying) are tax deductible;

c. Citizens have no inherent right to legal action even when the public interest is being harmed by blatantly illegal acts.

They are discussed below.

Access to information: In some countries such as the United States, all governmental information is presumed public until declared confidential; if it is declared confidential, there must be a valid reason. Otherwise, the courts may force the government to release the information under the Freedom of Information Act.

Canada presents a different story. Under the Official Secrets Act and the Civil Service Oaths, all information is secret until approved for distribution. Such approval is at the sole discretion of the government. There is no way that citizens can compel the issue of government information related to heritage conservation or any other subject.

Lobbying: It is difficult to quantify the amount of lobbying which speculators and developers have engaged in throughout our provincial capitals. Lobbying on behalf of the public interest is not tax deductible; and if a public interest group is accused of lobbying, it is liable to lose its registration as a tax deductible charity.

Locus standi: "Locus standi" is the name of a peculiar legal doctrine in Canada which blocks access to the courts for most conservationists and other citizens' groups promoting the public interest.

If every member of a community was harmed equally by an illegal act (e. g. a governmental illegality), then no one would have access to the courts except a governmental official (the Attorney General). Needless to say, the instances wherein one governmental official has launched litigation against other governmental officials (often in the same government) have been rare.

It now appears that the only way to guarantee protection for ourselves under the law will be to promote corrective legislation. This task is being vigorously pursued.

1.2.3 Tentative projections

The provincial designation of protected sites is currently possible in most of the country, and many authorities believe that it will soon be possible in every province. It is unclear whether more stringent measures will be taken by provinces to enforce maintenance of heritage property. Provinces currently appear content to leave this question in the hands of municipalities, and there is no indication of significant change in the foreseeable future.

There is no indication of activity to include the surroundings of sites in the protection of the site itself. Only one province

(Quebec) had legislation to that effect, and even Quebec is having second thoughts. No significant legislative action can be expected in that area for the time being.

Building codes are coming under closer scrutiny. Alberta is already working on the development of an alternate building code specifically referring to heritage structures. It is likely that other provinces will eventually follow suit. In the meantime, efforts are currently being made to incorporate instructions in the National Building Code advising building inspectors to treat heritage buildings on a different footing; many authorities believe that this reform is close at hand.

Governmental demolition and environmental assessment are also enjoying increasing attention from all provincial governments. It is generally considered likely that environmental assessment legislation will become more commonplace, and will give citizens more opportunities to block undesirable projects and comple integration of conservation with provincial policy.

Access to information is currently an issue of great public interest. Legislation is currently before legislators at the federal and provincial levels, and major improvements are expected shortly.

No major changes in the current imbalance of lobbying power are expected in the near future.

The future of the "locus standi" doctrine is uncertain. Efforts are being made to obtain corrective legislation but are obtaining little public attention. If the question of access to the courts is left to the courts, significant changes may require decades.

Increasing attention is being paid to the idea of permitting either the province or municipalities to designate buildings for protection. This is already the case in three provinces (British Columbia, New Brunswick and Alberta), and three other provinces share their designation powers with their respective provincial capitals. If this trend continues (and it shows every sign of doing so), then soon most of Canada should enjoy a situation whereby the heritage which is overlooked by one government still has a chance of being designated by another.

If this two-tiered system of designation becomes widespread, and if it is supplemented by an effective environmental assessment procedure for the protection of undesignated heritage property, along with solid financial support (mentioned later), then Canada will probably consider itself on a par with most other countries as far as legislation is concerned, despite the presence of other loopholes. Many authorities trust that Canada can reach this level within five to ten years. In the meantime, there is also optimism that breakthroughs will be scored in some of the other areas where heritage legislation suffers.

1.3 Local authorities

1.3.1 Legal basis

General: There are three kinds of legislation which confer power on Canadian municipalities for heritage purposes.

The first kind is enabling legislation which delegates heritage functions to all municipalities in a given province. The second confers powers on only certain specified municipalities. The third is customary planning legislation which can (with imagination) be adapted for the protection of heritage property.

Heritage legislation of general application:

Five provinces empower all their municipalities to give some protection to cultural sites.

The British Columbia Heritage Conservation Act authorizes municipalities in that province to list properties which will enjoy permanent protection. As mentioned previously, the British Columbia provincial government is also empowered to grant such protection; protection may therefore come from either the province or the municipality.

The New Brunswick Municipal Heritage Preservation Act similarly empowers municipalities in that province to grant permanent protection against alteration and demolition to buildings and areas. Such municipal initiatives must, however, be ratified by the provincial Cabinet. Like British Columbia, this can be called a "two-tiered" system of protection.

Alberta has introduced a similar system; in the latter case, however, no provincial authorization is needed for municipal designations.

In Ontario, on the other hand, the province protects only archaeological ruins. Any other kind of historic site can only be protected by municipalities. Furthermore the protection granted by a municipality to a threatened structure can almost never exceed 270 days; after that delay expires, the building can be demolished whether the municipality likes it or not . . . unless the structure is purchased. The relevant law is the Ontario Heritage Act.

A similar power to postpone demolition (in this case for one year) is vested in Quebec municipalities under the Quebec Cities & Towns Act.

Heritage Legislation of particular application: Some provincial governments have given certain specific municipalities special powers relating to heritage conservation.

Nova Scotia has granted certain narrow powers in the case of Peggy's Cove, and wider powers to Sherbrooke Village. Newfoundland, Prince Edward Island and Manitoba have granted such powers to their respective capital cities, namely St. John's, Charlottetown and Winnipeg.

With the exception of Peggy's Cove, all the above municipalities can give definitive protection to structures against demolition.

None of the above statutes refer to the surroundings of sites.

1.3.2 Protection of districts

Although some cities are specifically empowered to protect heritage districts (e. g. St. John's), the only provincial statutes conferring such powers to municipalities generally are the New Brunswick Heritage Preservation Act, the Alberta Historical Resources Act and the Ontario Heritage Act. In the first two cases, permanent protection is possible; however, as in the case of individual structures, protection under the Ontario law cannot exceed 270 days for a structure located within such a district.

More definitive protection, on the other hand, can be granted under the Ontario Planning Act. That statute permits any municipality to refuse a demolition permit indefinitely on dwellings in a given zone so long as the applicant refuses to guarantee replacement of the structure by another structure within two years.

1.3.3 Local land use legislation

Almost all Canadian municipalities are empowered to control bulk and height of buildings. This power is important for two reasons: infill construction in a heritage area should have a bulk and height which does not detract from the character of the area; furthermore, a low permissible building bulk and height will help discourage demolition and redevelopment within the area.

Use is an equally important subject. Almost all Canadian municipalities can control the use of buildings, which is essential in excluding incompatible uses from heritage areas, and in helping stabilize the area's residential component.

Maintenance is another subject which has been included quite recently in the powers of municipalities. Some provinces confer a curious power: they permit municipalities to clean up dilapidated buildings at the owner's expense. This power can have a similar effect on maintenance provisions, and in the case of heritage areas might even have greater potential.

The location of a building on a lot can significantly affect the appearance of a streetscape, particularly when it breaks the harmony of a row of buildings. The power to regulate location (or "set-back") is clearly spelled out in almost all provinces.

It is obviously desirable to control the design of structures being built or alternations being made in a heritage area. Most provinces specifically empower their municipalities to control design. In such cases, however, the by-law must be sufficiently clear so as to describe exactly what is expected of the owner; in architectural matters, this requirement can cause difficulties in drafting. To meet this problem, some municipalities have requested (and obtained) the exceptional right to establish architectural committees.

Signs can do a great deal to change the appearance of a heritage area. Every province gives its municipalities the power to regulate signs.

Trees and shrubbery also make a big difference in the appearance of a heritage area. Although few provinces have Quebec's provision which permits municipalities to compel proprietors to plant trees, most municipalities (e. g. in Alberta, Manitoba, New Brunswick, Saskatchewan) can at least control the destruction of trees, and occasionally shrubs as well.

Implementation: The sanctions imposed upon offences against municipal by-laws are usually very weak. It is frequently more economical to disregard the by-law and pay the fine than to obey the law. Some municipalities have accordingly turned to the alternative of seeking court injunctions against violators. At first, their capacity to do so was challenged and jurisprudence was divided; but many court decisions now favour the municipality's right to seek injunctions in such cases.

In the case of buildings erected in violation of zoning by-laws, an even more effective recourse usually exists, namely destruction of the building at the owner's expense.

1.3.4 Procedures

Virtually all Canadian jurisdictions insist upon some public notice of changes in land use controls.

In no province are municipalities obliged (as they are under the British Civic Amenity Act) to plan for conservation. In only a few provinces are they obliged to plan at all.

However, once a plan is initiated, some jurisdictions (e. g. Manitoba and New Brunswick) state that it must take heritage conservation into consideration. In some provinces land use by-laws are not the only relevant legal mechanism: in addition, plans have legal consequences. In such provinces a plan is usually not a prerequisite for land use controls of a heritage nature; but if the heritage by-laws contradict the plan they are open to challenge. Some provinces have established provincial review bodies (called "municipal boards") which can invalidate by-laws on the ground of "unreasonableness". This criterion can include almost anything. The experience of the conservation movement with municipal boards has not been extremely happy: some municipal boards have tended to automatically dismiss all municipal attempts to control urban sprawl or highrise construction as "unreasonable" by definition. Once again, conservationists face a considerable challenge in the field of public information and education.

1.3.5 Integration into local development policy

Like other levels of government in Ontario and Alberta, municipal governments will eventually be forced by the Ontario Environmental Assessment Act and the similar Alberta statute to take various environmental considerations into account in planning public works. Where municipal plans specify that heritage conservation is to be a priority in the community, some lawyers argue that the local government would be impeded from undertaking works which damaged heritage. That hypothesis, however, is still untested.

Canadian courts have adopted a relatively restrictive approach to land use controls and the success rate of citizens' groups invoking such controls has been low compared to our American counterparts.

If the reaction of Canadian courts to citizens' groups continues to be so negative, it is unlikely that the integration of conservation into development policy (at the national, regional or local level) will be enforceable.

A recent court case in Victoria, British Columbia, has led to more optimism: the court upheld extraordinary heritage controls because it refused to overrule the city's contention that the threat to heritage constituted a state of "emergency". It is not clear what impact this precedent will have on other Canadian courts.

1.3.6 Tentative projections

The notion that heritage conservation should be an obligatory component of municipal plans is gaining wider acceptance, and it is likely that most provinces will eventually enact legislation to this effect.

As mentioned earlier, it is increasingly likely that more provincial and municipal governments will share responsibility for designating and protecting sites and districts.

If the tendencies in Ontario are symptomatic of a national trend, then it is likely that plans and environmental impact assessments will increasingly limit a municipality's right to damage heritage. Furthermore, as public education increases, the likelihood of such restrictions being misunderstood and overruled by the courts should decrease.

If greater powers concerning heritage are extended to municipalities, it is likely that these powers will coincidentally grant more discretion to municipalities in accepting or rejecting proposals for development. This move in the direction of discretion is already noticeable; provinces have been empowering more and more municipalities to create "development control" districts where such discretion can be exercised. This tendency, however, is viewed with profound suspicion by proprietors.

1.4 Further reading

An analysis of heritage legislation at all levels in Canada is found in Heritage Canada's legislation series, Protecting the Built Environment.

An analysis of environmental legislation generally, along with an overview of methods whereby citizens can invoke this legislation, is found in a book by the Canadian Environmental Law Association: Environmental Management and Public Participation, another overview is in Heritage Fights Back, available from Heritage Canada.

2. Organization

2.1 Government officials

Two federal departments have overlapping roles in the field of cultural protection. The Department of Environment acquires and promotes national parks, including national historic sites.

The Secretary of State Department promotes the incorporeal aspects of culture. It also operates the network of national museums, and thereby has a great influence upon archaeological research.

As mentioned previously, most of the real power in terms of cultural protection and animation is at the provincial level. In virtually all Canadian cities, the administration of heritage sites and areas is administered through the municipal planning department.

2.2 Public and semi-public institutions and advisory boards

The Federal Advisory and Co-ordinating Committee on Heritage Conservation was mentioned earlier.

The federal level: The Historic Sites and Monuments Board advises the Minister of Environment as to designation of "National Historic Sites".

A semi-public institution is beginning to organize at the national level. It is ICOMOS Canada.

A governmental organization has been formed to hold annual meetings of officials responsible for heritage conservation. Those officials are both from the federal and provincial governments. The organization is named the Canadian Conference on Historical Resources.

The provincial level

Five provinces have "foundations" which have an interest in heritage. Those provinces are British Columbia, Alberta, Manitoba, Ontario and Prince Edward Island. They are authorized both to advise governments and acquire properties. A "foundation" usually refers to a non-profit corporation which enjoys some independence from government, thanks to an endowment fund. However, all of these "foundations" are governmentally created and ultimately responsible to their provincial government. Some, however, have endowment funds which supplement the funds received from the provincial budget.

The municipal level: In Ontario, the Ontario Heritage Act specifically empowers municipalities to establish architectural conservation advisory committees. Many communities have done so. Many municipalities elsewhere in Canada have also done so on their own initiative.

2.3 Private associations and non-public resources

2.3.1 Private associations

General: There are several hundred associations which have a direct or indirect interest in the conservation of cultural property. Some, such as the Society for the Study of Architecture and the Canadian Environmental Law Association, are national in scope. The overwhelming majority of such organizations, however, are of a purely local nature.

Structure varies. Legal status depends on whether the association has been incorporated. Once incorporated, it may apply for registration under the Canadian Income Tax Act as a tax deductible charity. This registration means that any person contributing money to such an organization may deduct such contribution from his taxable income. Many associations are registered as a tax deductible charity, the financial structure of most public interest groups however is shaky when they must rely exclusively upon membership fees and donations.

Heritage Canada: The largest non-governmental organization concerned with cultural property in Canada is the Heritage Canada Foundation (Heritage Canada). It is a non-profit corporation founded and incorporated in 1973 under the Canada Corporation Act. It has a Board of Governors which meets periodically, and a full-time staff which currently numbers under twenty.

Its financial base is composed notably of donations, the interest upon a $ 12,000,000 donation which was deposited in trust for Heritage Canada by the federal government in 1973. Aside from the fact that Heritage Canada is legally limited in how it can invest trust moneys, and aside from the presence of two representatives of federal ministries among Heritage Canada's fourteen governors, Heritage Canada has no budgetary or political links with any government.

Heritage Canada does, however, have contractual links with some governments. It has a property-holding agreement with the federal government which permits it to give relatively favourable tax treatment to donors of property. It also has contracts with provincial and municipal governments.

The programs conducted by Heritage Canada have dealt with such things as loans to member groups conducting non-profit renovation projects. It has been concluded, however, that the most can be done with available funds by promoting the protection and renovation of heritage neighbourhoods. This conclusion was reached after considerable study of the internal economic dynamics of such areas and led to a wide-ranging economic and promotional program loosely called the "area conservation program". Heritage Canada's investment in such areas first took the form of feasibility studies for wide-scale renovation. If the studies were affirmative, and if local co-operation (governmental and private) was indicative of a potential catalytic effect for further investment, then Heritage Canada would purchase and renovate properties with the intention of resale and reinvestment in further renovations. Such purchase, sale and reinvestment is sometimes called a "revolving fund" and has been used successfully in the United States. Heritage Canada would also promote the establishment of a permanent local foundation to guarantee the continued administration of renovations in that community.

The publications of Heritage Canada bring the public up-to-date with recent developments in conservation efforts as well as the conclusions of the research. Annexed to the publications component is the media component, which promotes the message of heritage conservation through radio, television and film. Written materials is sometimes printed as specialized publications, but most information is published in the magazine Canadian Heritage.

Research is carried on at headquarters and it is also contracted out. The work conducted at headquarters is almost exclusively on the subjects of economics and renovation technology. Work contracted is almost exclusively on the subjects of education and of urban planning for proposed heritage conservation areas. Virtually no historical research is done except insofar as it is necessary for an urban plan. Instead, a fairly clear-cut division of labour has emerged: the member groups research what to save and why to save it, whereas Heritage Canada researches how to save it; the parties advise each other accordingly.

2.3.2 Philanthropic and non-profit funds

There is no large private philanthropic organization in Canada devoted exclusively to the financing of renovations or restorations.

There are some large foundations, such as the Devonian Foundation in Alberta or the Macdonald-Stewart Foundation in Quebec, which will invest directly in heritage projects. For example, Devonian has budgeted $ 6,000,000 on improving the appearance of small Alberta towns. However, most such organizations will invest directly: they will donate sums to a registered charitable heritage organization to carry out the work. Heritage Canada has published a list of possible funding sources.

2.3.3 Revenue-producing funds

As detailed in Chapter 3.1, a loophole in the Income Tax Act permits those who demolish structures to avoid taxes.

Financial institutions often look upon renovation as a second-best use of the property. This in turn tends to cast doubt upon the business acumen of the loan applicant. This problem can only be solved by the appropriate amendments to the Income Tax Act which conservationists are seeking.

The actual physical cost of renovation is another inhibiting factor. Many Canadian architects are not equipped with the ability to work effectively with older buildings. The choice of architects to handle renovation work can often decide whether a given project will be incredibly profitable or a financial disaster. Unless a lender has some grasp of this phenomenon, he will not be able to assess the risk factor of the loan, and shall refuse it accordingly.

In an attempt to solve this problem, Heritage Canada has published information on renovation projects and in the proper cost management of such projects.

Mortgage loans are automatically refused if it is impossible to obtain a policy insuring the premises for the benefit of the lender. Some conservationists have claimed that insurance companies are refusing to insure some older areas of Canadian cities, thus making it impossible to obtain financing for renovation and thereby accelerating deterioration. The largest single obstacle facing loans for renovation is allegedly that Canadian financial institutions do not know how to appraise older buildings nor do they know how to appraise renovation projects. No single financial institution in Canada has seen enough of these projects to say that it has any understanding of the economic dynamics or the risk involved.

The path toward a solution

The first task toward a solution is to educate the appraisers working for the financial institutions. That work is supplemented by the extensive research conducted by the conservationists to demonstrate the economic desirability of renovation.

Under this proposal, which is currently under study, an institution or agency would guarantee the repayment of mortgage loans to renovation projects when the age of the structure makes conventional financing impossible. Upon default, the institution or agency would repay the loan and acquire title to the property; but since only a small minority of loans would succeed in sponsoring renovation, expenditures would be far in excess of what was spent on the program. This possible program is still in the study phase, and will not proceed to the experimental phase until all the modalities are understood.

The second avenue is to guarantee loans. Customarily, the guaranteeing of loans for socially desirable projects is done by a federal government agency, Canada Mortgage and Housing Corporation.

2.3.4 Tentative projections

No major changes are expected in the allocation of governmental responsibility for conservation.

The establishment of provincial foundation is being encouraged, and it is probable that more provinces will establish them in the foreseeable future.

Conservationists continue to seek a rapprochement with the financial community. Although it is too early to say whether a mortgage guarantee scheme will work, other measures are being taken and financial leaders are increasingly sensitive to the presence of conservationists.

3. Finance

3.1 Purchase

3.1.1 Purchase of property rights

The Canadian federal government, provinces, local authorities and other institutions and associations have, from time to time, allocated funds to purchase sites and to restore them.

The percentage that such expenditures represent of governmental budgets, Gross National Product, and per capita income and expenditures has yet to be determined.

There is an increasing feeling, however, that governmental purchase should be viewed only as a last resort, when no other viable use can be made of a structure. When a viable use exists, the proprietors should put the property to such use and the government's financial responsibility should be limited to any unduly excessive costs which might be imposed by preservation and renovation.

3.1.2 Purchase of lesser interests

It is possible, under both the Civil Law system of Quebec and the Common Law systems of the other provinces, to acquire real interests in property less than full ownership.

Under the Civil Law system of Quebec, a legal mechanism entitled a "personal servitude" can bind an owner (and all his successors) to refrain from doing something on his property, such as altering it or tearing down buildings. This contract can be signed by the owner with any other person or corporation; Heritage Canada has entered into such an agreement with a proprietor who binds himself not to alter or demolish his property without Heritage Canada's consent.

Similar agreements are possible in the Common Law provinces under the name of easements and covenants but the Common Law imposes a condition:

if the contract is to bind future owners, the party with whom the owner contracts must also own land which is directly benefitted by the contract.

Five provinces have enacted corrective legislation (Ontario, Prince Edward Island, Newfoundland, New Brunswick and British Columbia) and more are expected to follow suit.

The fact that the owner's consent is obligatory means that the agreement is attributable either to philanthropy or to remuneration.

In the overwhelming majority of cases, owners will not sign until they are remunerated. Heritage Canada has been researching ways of doing this indirectly through the Income Tax Act; in the meantime, some conservation agencies have been dealing in cash, although they prefer to think of such transactions as grants rather than payments.

3.2 Fiscal aspects

3.2.1 The federal level

Demolition

Due to an anomaly in the definition sections of the Income Tax Act, a person who demolishes a structure has not "disposed" of it.

This oversight is very convenient for speculators. It is upon "disposition" that federal officials can check whether the property has been overdepreciated (and income tax avoided accordingly); but since demolition is not a disposition, there is no way of checking for this tax avoidance.

Another aspect is even more convenient. Although the building has not been "disposed of", it has somehow disappeared. Under the Income Tax Act, the building has become lost, as if it had flown away and nested elsewhere. Since it is "lost", the owner can claim its value as a loss and reduce his taxable income accordingly.

This provision happens to be very costly to the public treasury. For example, the owner of frame structures worth 150,000 on land worth 150,000 who sells the land for 350,000 after eight years can save as much as 75,000 in taxable income by demolishing the buildings before sale. It is probable that tens of millions of dollars of tax revenue are lost annually because of this problem. Heritage Canada has been studying this problem.

Renovation

Renovation in Canada does not receive as favourable a tax treatment as new construction on multiple unit residential buildings because the rules for depreciation are different.

The primary difficulty with renovation, however, is another non-sequitur in the Income Tax Act.

Renovations are usually treated as a "capital expense" which (unlike a "business expense") is not deductible from taxable income. However, the definition of a capital expense is one "made once and for all", i.e. for the expected duration of the structure. When a heritage statute protects a structure the legislative intent is for such structure to last forever. In that perspective, no expense can logically be made on it "once and for all". To treat renovation as a capital expense would be at odds with the legal intent of those statutes.

Consequently, Heritage Canada is researching ways of providing better tax treatment for renovations, particularly on designated heritage structures.

3.2.2 The provincial level

Only one province, Quebec, has formalized a system of tax abatement for classified heritage properties. It states that the evaluation on which municipal taxation is computed can be lowered by as much as 50% on non-commercial premises.

3.2.3 The municipal level

General: In all provinces except Newfoundland, municipal revenue is collected in the following way: all properties are evaluated in the perspective of their market value, and then a certain percentage of that assessment becomes payable in municipal taxes. In Newfoundland the system is highly similar, except that evaluation is directed toward rental value rather than market value. Throughout Canada, this system can cause problems whenever heritage conservation is discussed.

The conflicting interests: If municipal governments are requested to improve services in an area (street lighting, sidewalks, benches, etc.) then they usually expect to see an increase in property values which will be translated into increased municipal revenues to amortize their costs.

Conservationists have been able to reply with figures indicating marked increase in property values for heritage areas which have been the subject of protective and renovative activity. For example, Vancouver's Gastown saw an increase of 81 % in six years.

This does not, however, help the owner of a heritage property in the area. The more he improves and renovates his property, the more he is taxed; indeed, since he is helping the entire area become more picturesque and fashionable (thus increasing the value of his land as well as his building), it is conceivable that his evaluation for tax purposes might increase at an even higher rate than the value of his improvements.

This is no incentive for renovation; but in most non-residential areas (with the exception of some rare cases such as Toronto) these extra costs can be passed on without causing major dislocations.

In residential areas, however, the effect of increased taxes can be disastrous. Increased taxes mean increased rents and housing costs, frequently to those who can least afford them; and many precedents in the United States have indicated that neighbourhood dislocation and social hardship can result.

Conservationists in residential areas must therefore argue that revenues to amortize governmental expenditures can be derived in other ways, aside from increasing municipal taxation on the area. Again, precedents are fortunately on the side of conservationists. Other heritage areas have invariably demonstrated a substantial increase in tourist spending. Thanks to sales tax and economic conditions generally, this increased economic activity sooner or later is reflected in municipal budgets. The City of Quebec is a good example: its heritage character is sufficiently attractive that 35 % of the city's economy is based upon tourism.

This phenomenon, however, also creates pressures for population displacement. People who try to cash in on increased tourism lobby municipal governments to permit more and more restaurants, bars and night clubs to encroach upon residential areas. If the population is not priced out of the area, it can be driven out by noise, fumes and drunks.

Dealing with the problem: If the needs of municipal finance and population stability are both to be met by heritage conservation programs, it will be necessary to keep a number of factors in mind.

It should be possible to find ways of raising revenue through tourism, and thus to avoid (as much as possible) increased taxes upon renovated heritage structures. At the very least, there should be a moratorium upon assessment increases for a specified period. Particular effort should be made to avoid tax increases in residential areas. At the same time, a conscious policy must be adopted to prevent undue encroachment upon residences by other uses.

Heritage Canada has suggested one way of defraying municipal expenditures, at least in part. The current fee for a demolition permit in Canadian municipalities rarely exceeds $ 10.00; some municipalities charge no fee at all. Thought should be given to scaling demolition fees to the assessed value of the structure to be demolished; for example, a municipality may demand 2 % of the assessed value as a fee for the permit. This could become an interesting means of raising revenue.

3.3 Cost-sharing and other financial techniques

3.3.1 The federal level

Introduction: There are two ways that the federal government enters into cost-sharing arrangements. The first is by direct subsidy. The second is by entering into agreements with other levels of government by which the federal government transfers funds but the other governments carry on the administration of the subsidy program.

Subsidies for historic sites follow the first format: they are negotiated directly between the federal government and the beneficiary. However, most renovation programs are simply funded by the federal government (through its agency Canada Mortgage and Housing Corporation) and administered by other levels of government. They are therefore described under the provincial level.

Historic sites: The only direct federal funding program is the one administered by the Department of Environment for sites designated as being of national significance under the federal Historic Sites & Monuments Act. Treasury Board Minute 623840 states:

(1) where title to the historic property is vested in Her Majesty in right of Canada;

(2) where title to the historic property is vested in the name of the other party to the agreement;

(3) where title to the historic property is to become vested in the other party to the agreement.

Regulations

a. when condition (1) prevails, the federal government share should be not in excess of 75 % of the costs of restoration;

b. when condition (2) prevails, the federal government share should be not in excess of 50 % of the costs of restoration;

c. when condition (3) prevails, the federal government share should be not in excess of 50 % of the costs of acquisition and 50 % of the costs of restoration.

CMHC improvement programs: Canada Mortgage & Housing Corporation funds two major relevant programs. The first is the Neighbourhood Improvement Program:

Area characteristics:

1. predominantly residental
2. in need of rehabilitation
3. low to moderate income for residents
4. inadequate social & recreational amenities

CMHC contributions:

A. 50 % of
   1. planning costs & administration
   2. acquisition and development of land for amenities and low income housing
   3. development of maintenance standards
   4. loans for commercial premises
   5. relocation of displaced residents
   The other 50 % to be provided by province and municipality and eligible for low interest loan from CMHC.

B. 25 % of certain municipal services

C. 100 % of 20-year loans for commercial premises up to $ 10,000 at rate of ½–1 % above Government of Canada Bonds.

This program can remain in effect in many Canadian municipalities until 1981; but for the majority of municipalities it has been replaced by the Community Services Grant Program. The latter program will permit subsidies along the same general lines as the former program, but the exact details remain to be negotiated.

The other major program is the Residential Rehabilitation Assistance Program:

Loans up to $ 10,000. Up to 3,750 foregivable and two point lower interest rate for low income earners.

For further information, contact CMHC on Montreal Road in Ottawa.

Other programs

A number of federal programs may indirectly be used for the renovation of heritage structures. They can be used if the building is intended for conversion into a cultural centre, a museum, a hostel, low-rent housing, etc.

Furthermore, on February 23, 1976, the Minister of Indian and Northern Affairs officially announced that the federal cabinet had approved a new "Program for Heritage Conservation". That program would include the establishment of a "Canadian Register of Heritage Properties". This register was proposed by Heritage Canada in 1974 and would comprise a list of buildings designated jointly by the federal and provincial governments. These properties would enjoy, in the Minister's words, "the possibility of financial assistance through matching grants with the provinces". The system is not yet in operation but is expected in the near future.

3.3.2 Provincial and municipal rehabilitation programs

Introduction: Some provincial programs are funded by the federal government; others represent provincial initiatives. Few of the renovation programs deal specifically with "heritage"; they simply intend to renovate structures, to provide adequate housing, regardless of architectural or historic features.

The details of these programs change very quickly; consequently only a broad outline is possible. Several provinces have financial schemes to subsidize renovations to heritage sites which have been designated for protection by the provincial government. Quebec has the most elaborate set of rules to provide financial aid; the systems in Alberta and Saskatchewan are also well-defined. In most of the other provinces, subsidies tend to be determined on a more discretionary and ad hoc basis.

It is extremely rare for government funding for renovations on private property to exceed 50 % of the cost of those renovations, and there is usually an upper limit on the expenditures to be subsidized. Further information on these various programs is available from the authorities responsible for heritage conservation in each province.

In almost every case, financial assistance is contingent upon renovations being conducted; the one major exception to that rule is British Columbia. That province's Heritage Conservation Act forces the province to turn cash over to the owners of designated heritage property if there has been a decrease in the property's value; that obligation is binding, whether the owner undertakes any repairs or not. Furthermore, when a municipality designates a heritage building for protection, the Heritage Conservation Act makes oblique references to "compensation"; although some lawyers feel that the municipality is under no legal obligation to pay the owner of the property, that did not stop school trustees from threatening the City of Vancouver with a multi-million dollar lawsuit if the City designated Vancouver's oldest standing school for protection. The fact that the City backed down from designation proves that this worthy goal of financial assistance to heritage properties has been turned into a deterrent to the protection of the province's heritage.

A similar obligation to pay compensation has been imposed upon Alberta municipalities who wish to designate property for protection under the Alberta Historical Resources Act.

Housing programs are a different story. Many provinces not only participate in CMHC's programs but also add some extra programs of their own to renovate older housing stock. These programs change regularly; however, they can be broken down into several main categories.

Certain provincial programs are aimed at very specific forms of renovation. British Columbia's "Conversion Loans" are available only for the subdivision of large old buildings into smaller units. Another program administered by the Ontario Ministry of the Environment will help an owner kill the termites in his building. Insulation is still a further area in which subsidies are usually available: The Canadian Home Insulation Program (CHIP) provides funding of some description to most of the country for the insulation of dwellings, even though the program has been extensively altered in various provinces to suit local conditions.

The programs mentioned above are directed toward the renovation of residential buildings. Some provincial programs, however, are directed toward commercial areas.

For example, Saskatchewan's Department of Industry and Commerce launched an experimental Main Street Development Pilot Project to renovate the commercial cores of smaller communities. Ontario's Downtown Revitalization Program is far more ambitious, representing a four-year commitment totalling $ 40 million. The difficulty with such programs is that they almost never specify that heritage conservation should be taken into account: more taxpayers' money has been spent "revatilizing" commercial areas by obliterating their heritage aspects than by promoting such characteristics. Nevertheless, conservationists hope that the money in these programs will soon be directed toward revitalization in a manner which best displays the heritage of the community. Some provinces have programs similar to NIP and RRAP; Ontario is an example, with its Ontario Home Renewal Program. Quebec has a similar "Provincial-Municipal Rehabilitation Subsidy"; similar terms are found in New Brunswick's Home Improvement Loans and the Saskatchewan Residential Rehabilitation Program. In some other provinces, however, the program is reserved for "emergency repairs" (as in Nova Scotia's Emergency Home Repair Program and Manitoba's Critical Home Repair Program). In still other provinces, the only people eligible for subsidies or favourable loans under the special provincial initiatives are welfare recipients (as in Newfoundland's system) or senior citizens (as in Alberta's Senior Citizen Home Improvement Program; Saskatchewan also has such a program in addition to its other programs).

Other provincial programs: A wide assortment of cultural programs are available throughout Canadian provinces. They do not necessarily deal specifically with building renovations: they may involve cultural centres, multiculturalism, museums, etc. With some ingenuity, however, they can be adapted for the financing of building renovations.

3.3.3 The municipal level

Some municipal governments (e. g. Montreal) have introduced limited cost-sharing agreements, and some (e. g. Victoria) are currently studying the possibility of doing so. Municipal budgets are restricted, and the concept is so recent in Canada that no generalizations are currently possible.

3.3.4 Other aspects

Compensating social hardship: so far, no concerted program of area conservation has led to massive social displacement. This is perhaps because programs have been few, particularly in residential areas. The threat of displacement is nevertheless a reality, and has been discussed earlier. That threat, however, has been partly reduced by the fact that the existing structural rehabilitation programs are frequently directed to earners of low income, i. e. those who would otherwise be the likely victims of displacement.

Recouping increased values: Some concern has been expressed in other jurisditions regarding the large increase in property values which usually accompany the revitalization of a heritage area. Some have argued that this is sometimes an unearned increment which should be recouped from the owner, particularly when the increase is attributable to public investment.

There is little discussion of this subject in Canada for three reasons. First, there are already enough political problems in establishing heritage areas: to threaten proprietors with tax increases would compound these problems. Second, federal and provincial programs (particularly in the housing field) are not particularly oriented to cost amortization. Third, the municipal system enjoys a built-in form of cost amortization: since municipal taxes are geared to property value, increases in value will usually produce an automatic increase in gross municipal revenues.

Care for surroundings: The care of streets, sidewalks, etc., is a municipal responsibility, although some funding does sometimes come from the federal or provincial government (e. g. the federal N. I. P. program), and even from private foundations (e. g. the Devonian Foundation in Alberta).

The municipality raises revenue through customary municipal taxation. It can also charge certain expenditures through "improvement levies" to the proprietors immediately affected.

3.4 Tentative projections

Various proposals for tax reform are currently under study by the federal Department of Finance. Conservationists hope that the current incentives for demolition will be replaced by incentives for renovation. If such a change does occur in the federal Income Tax Act, much of the pressure for financial incentives at the provincial and municipal levels will be relieved. Furthermore, since it is impossible to place an exact figure on the cost of the tax benefits to the public treasury, this incentive has the added advantage of not appearing in cultural budgets, on which severe limits have traditionally been set.

The balancing of competing economic interests in heritage districts should also become easier as municipal planners obtain information concerning successes and failures of heritage areas elsewhere. That information is becoming increasingly available.

Cost-sharing programs change so frequently that some provincial governments are reluctant to publish any detailed information because it may be out of date by the time it is distributed. The figures in this text are obsolescent, and should be used as a general guide only.

At the time of writing this report, still further changes are expected imminently; these changes would substantially alter several national programs. The only projection which can be made is that the governmental commitment to subsidize housing renovation now appears permanent; the commitment to subsidize other forms of renovation (and planning for renovation) is less certain, and it is unlikely that any clear pattern will emerge for another two years or so. In the meantime, any programs to aid non-residential renovation will, by and large, continue to be "experimental".

3.5 Further reading

See: How To Plan For Renovations, available from Heritage Canada, and Second Canadian Building Congress, available from the National Research Council, Ottawa.

4. Involvement of the Public in Preservation

4.1 Educational institutions and adult education

Elementary and secondary schools: The comprehensive dissemination of heritage-oriented information in our elementary and secondary schools is still at the planning stage.

Some organizations, such as Heritage Canada and the Ontario Institute for Studies in Education, have developed programs to teach the appreciation of heritage structures and communities to students. These programs are still at the experimental stage.

College and university levels: Many colleges and universities offer courses on heritage structures. These courses are usually non-credit, i. e. they do not count for the purposes of obtaining a degree. Diploma programs are offered at:

– Algonquin College, Ottawa, Ontario

– St. Lawrence College, Brockville, Ontario

– Université Laval, Québec, Québec

– University of Calgary, Alberta

The media: Many newspapers have moved from open hostility regarding heritage conservation to vocal support.

Several large newspapers now have regular features appearing at least weekly on the subject. Heritage Canada annually announces "Communications Awards" to writers, journalists and newspapers which have publicized heritage.

The response in radio and television has been neutral: There is no noticeable bias for or against conservation, and no noticeable promotion of it. Unlike the Netherlands, Canada has no regular TV program which mentions heritage; indeed, only a handful of programs have been shown over the past decade.

4.2 Public participation – institutional structure

Legal basis: There are three forms of land use controls affecting heritage conservation in Canada. The first is environmental impact assessment, which is a land use control which regulates governmental projects; the second category includes provincial controls on heritage projects; and the third is general municipal land use legislation (bulk, height, design of buildings, etc.).

The legal basis of the first category is in the environmental assessment statutes mentioned earlier. Public participation is usually in the form of a hearing which citizens can demand if they believe that the environmental assessment procedure is not being used properly. However, the ultimate mechanism available to American conservationists (the lawsuit) is not granted to Canadian counterparts under the Canadian versions of environmental impact legislation.

The second category of controls includes provincial controls on designated heritage property. In those cases, there is no provision for public participation whatsoever, either to coax the government to designate a certain site, or in the supervision of alterations or demolition which are later conducted on the site.

The third category of controls is found in municipal land use planning. Rules respecting public participation at this level are scattered throughout provincial Planning Acts, Municipal Acts, city charters, etc., and vary from place to place. The following, however, are some features which appear in the enabling legislation of most municipalities.

Effects: Since municipal governments have the greatest contact with land use planning, it follows that any proposal to change the status quo must be submitted to the municipal administration. In most municipalities, such proposals are secret. Similarly, there is usually no provision stipulating that reports written on proposed plans for the municipality must be made public, or even that the terms of reference of those reports be published. As seen later on, those terms of reference can be crucial to the conclusions of the report.

Proposals for changes in the status quo are then submitted to the elected municipal council for its consideration. Again, there is usually no stipulation that either presentations to council or council's deliberations be made in public.

However, when the time comes for municipal councillors to vote on a proposed change, such vote must usually be made in public, and citizens must usually be given advance notice of the issue as well as the date of the council meeting. This meeting is the forum at which citizens can make their views known; however, there is seldom any statutory obligation for the municipality to give any details on the expected impact of proposed changes or alternatives thereto.

In one province (Quebec) citizens could force a municipal referendum on changes to municipal land use controls. In some other provinces, the decision of the municipal council can be appealed by the citizens to a provincially appointed board or to the provincial minister of municipal affairs. In the case of appeals to boards, there is usually a statutory obligation to hold a hearing; there is usually no such obligation in the case of an appeal to the minister.

Advisory bodies: Citizens' advisory bodies have been mentioned earlier. Ontario's Local Architectural Conservation Advisory Committees (LACAC's) are expected to play a useful role in promoting conservation in that province. Many other cities across the country have set up similar committees.

Heritage Canada has been promoting the establishment of "Foundations" which, to a certain extent, would institutionalize citizen participation in heritage areas. These foundations would be directed by boards composed of representatives from governments active in renovating an area plus voting representatives of the heritage societies, citizens' groups, merchants' associations and prominent agents in the community. The foundation would not only act as the liaison body for conservation activities but would also receive government funds to carry on its own investments. Such foundations have been established in several cities, the most successful of which is probably St. John's, Newfoundland.

The most elaborate schemes for citizen advisory committees (and those which most closely resemble the Baden formula of "open planning" in Switzerland and West Germany) are probably those of the Le Breton Flats in Ottawa and the complex statutory system in Winnipeg, Manitoba. The latter has come under such vigorous criticism from the politicians that its future is uncertain.

4.3 Public action groups

Citizens' groups: Citizens' groups are the backbone of the Canadian heritage movement. Their incorporation, tax registration and methods of association (e. g. in Heritage Canada regional councils) were described earlier.

Most of these groups become involved in the dissemination of information via meetings and/or newsletters. Demonstrations were once a frequent sight but have declined in popularity.

Merchants' groups: Merchants' groups are organized along lines similar to those of citizens' groups. They have been relatively more influential and have scored some significant victories.

These groups, modelled loosely upon England's "Norwich Plan", have usually received no special institutional framework. An exception to that rule is found in Ontario, where the Municipal Act foresees "Business Improvement Areas". Such areas are created when two thirds of the merchants form an association, which can then oblige the municipality to form a Board of Management for the area. The Board budgets for improvement and promotion of the area; if the budget is approved by the municipality, funds are voted accordingly from municipal taxes raised within the area.

4.4 Some strategies of public action groups

Many Canadian citizens' groups claim to be operating at a disadvantage. Consequently, some have adopted unusual techniques to promote their point of view. Some of the more unusual ones are as follows.

One of Canada's more influential local groups has adopted a systematic policy of wooing lawyers into the organization. Its executive is now composed almost entirely of members of the legal profession. It has capitalized on its legal expertise by invoking the widest assortment of obscure laws to impede unsympathetic development.

Another influential local heritage group decided that co-operation with public officials could best be achieved as follows. Knowing that it enjoyed a good reputation as a respectable historical society, it systematically recruited wives of Cabinet ministers and then set out to convert them into dedicated conservationists. Within short order, governmental decisions were exhibiting a far more sophisticated appreciation of heritage matters.

A different method was legislated in Ontario, which empowered municipal councils to name "local architectural conservation advisory committees" or LACACs. The LACACs were given only an advisory function and some conservationists feared that the LACACs would be used to dupe the public into a false sense of security. However, the LACACs had been given a mandate to study heritage and proceeded to acquire expertise. Furthermore, the nominees tended to be chosen from among the community's more influential members. They did not take kindly to having their recommendations frustrated, and the media have taken due note, thereby sensitizing public opinion.

In short order, and beyond the expectations of many politicians, LACACs have generated a political force to be reckoned with and a powerful argument for more comprehensive legal action.

Another technique is used by conservationists who have decided to make themselves such a regular feature at municipal council meetings that their participation is not only accepted but expected. They claim that this approach not only leads to an unusual degree of intimacy with the council but that (over the long term) it induces the council to equate conservationists with the public (or at least a significant part thereof).

Finally, Canadian citizens' are frequently divided over a persistent dilemma: is it better to maintain a low profile and attempt to make quiet deals with politicians, or should citizens' groups seek a high profile by loudly denouncing unfavorable projects? Conservationists in one major Canadian city believe that they have solved the problem: they have set up two organizations. One is composed of an influential "elite" which has access to decision-makers; the other regularly protests (in relatively radical terms) alleged civic indifference toward conservation. The two groups exchange notes scrupulously.

4.5 Heritage Day

Introduction: For some time, many Canadians (particularly labour leaders) have urged the proclamation of a national holiday in February. It appears that this proclamation is strictly a matter of time.

Conservationists (particularly Heritage Canada) argue that any such holiday should be dedicated to Canada's heritage. Heritage Canada and its member organizations immediately undertook to hold celebrations on that day, even if no holiday has yet been declared.

Almost every promotional technique known to conservationists has been used on "Heritage Day", and consequently a review of Heritage Day activities gives a fairly accurate picture of the movement's techniques. Indeed the promotion of Heritage Day and the development of promotional techniques has even been taken up by groups which are not conservation groups (e. g. Kinsmen Clubs of Canada).

The general direction of promotional efforts: Some provinces, such as Alberta und Quebec, have dedicated different times of year to heritage. That causes certain problems to conservationists both in terms of co-ordination and also for the purchase of common posters, buttons, etc. In those provinces, some conservationists continue to stage events in February on the assumption that an extra day devoted to heritage can do no harm.

On the federal level, Heritage Canada strongly supports any attempt to create a statutory holiday to celebrate the nation's heritage. The Secretary of State has promised a government bill to declare the day a holiday, a measure which enjoys support from all parties.

Political leaders are asked to make a proclamation. Most have done so.

Press releases are issued. Heritage Canada has also prepared a tabloid and an education kit for distribution to member organizations and others interested in the promotion of Heritage Day.

Local conservationists are urged to promote Heritage Day in the same way that Heritage Canada does.

It is suggested that conservationists pick events which are of interest to the community as a whole and try to organize exhibitions and activities which will inform and involve people of the community of their own heritage; encourage other community and service groups to join with them in organizing activities and co-ordinate activities with theirs to ensure a more successful celebration; approach the schools in the community and suggest that they sponsor a debate, an essay contest, a heritage play or short story, and that the students be encouraged to dress in heritage costumes, demonstrate heritage crafts and skills, or participate in some other group activity on Heritage Day; settle on a number of events, appoint a Heritage Day co-ordinator to oversee their organization and start publicizing the Heritage Day celebrations at least two weeks in advance to try to orchestrate the media campaign so that it reaches its peak on Heritage Day.

Heritage Canada provides buttons and posters to each member organization to help promote Heritage Day.

Case study: Renfrew, Ontario: Far and away the most imaginative and active Heritage Day community in the country in 1976 was the little Ontario town of Renfrew (population 8,530). Its activities are a microcosm of all Canada. The following is a partial list of the town's activities.

The Mayor and Council proclaimed the day to be "Heritage Day" (without, however, making it a holiday) and gave assurances that they would assist the local conservation group, Heritage Renfrew, with its celebrations. The Council's proclamation was published in the town paper. Heritage

Day posters (provided by Heritage Canada) were distributed to the town's eight schools, public library, churches, and Main Street buildings. In addition, Heritage Canada bronze pins were given to the schools as prizes for various activities. Lapel buttons were sold at $ 1.00 each to raise money to defray program costs. The day's organizers concentrated much of their attention upon schools. Projects included: a bake sale using old recipes; a walking tour of old neighbourhoods; a display of artifacts of countries from which the area's pioneers had come; a collection of Indian and Eskimo clothing; demonstrations of ice cream, butter and cheese making; a history study of one of the area's early settlers; skating, square dancing and sleigh riding. Snow sculptures (of locomotives, horses and cutters, and wishing wells) were produced. Many teachers and students dressed in nineteenth century costumes. The Renfrew Collegiate Institute prepared a display called "How the Community Looks to Us". Featuring about 50 drawings of early structures, the display was mounted for four days at the Town's Recreation Centre. Another school produced a tabloid on Renfrew history, which was inserted as a special supplement to the local newspaper. Elsewhere, students taped the reminiscences of senior citizens. The tape was broadcast on the evening of Heritage Day. Another school rented a local arena for a history day. Students and teachers dressed in pioneer costumes. The film "Old Renfrew", which had been made by the school's teachers, was screened. Over at still another school, halls and classes were decorated with student-made Heritage Day posters. A Heritage Canada film was shown and students listened to a round of special speakers.

On another front, the Renfrew Heritage Day organizers had great success enlisting the aid of local shops. They persuaded almost every shop owner to resurrect and display the items which might have been sold there long ago.

At the Renfrew Public Library, an open-house was held which featured paintings of heritage buildings. The library also displayed the local conservation group's survey of heritage buildings.

In the evening of the celebration period, 125 townsfolk attended the first annual Heritage Day dinner. Old time music was provided at the reception and a play written by the president of the local conservation society was performed.

The town's Kinsmen's Club joined Heritage Renfrew in promoting celebrations. The Kinsmen also distributed posters, advertised the dinner, and ran radio ads reminding Renfrewites of the day.

Almost all of these activities were promoted and co-ordinated by a volunteer committee of ten local residents.

4.6 Tentative projections

The debate over public participation in land planning appears to have lost some of the intensity it had a decade ago. This is partly because of improvements in legislation, and because attention has sometimes been shifted to environmental impact procedures rather then municipal procedures as such. Many conservationists nevertheless worry that there has been a loss of momentum, and that few major improvements can be expected over the next few years. Indeed, some worry that the current economic slowdown will incite governments to limit participation and environmental procedures in order to expedite projects.

Prospects for improvements to participation procedures are therefore unclear.

The status of citizens' groups may change. Legislation has already been passed to assure that charitable organizations are indeed charitable. Some conservationists hope that the reason for which rules were improving the tax status of charities: several proposals are already before the federal government to improve the terms under which donations are made to organizations.

The current economic situation makes it unlikely that Heritage Day will become a national holiday, for the time being. In the meantime, however, conservationists continue their promotional activities.

4.7 Further reading

The legal powers of citizens' groups are detailed in the Canadian Environmental Law Association's Environmental Management and Public Participation. Another useful text is the Report of the National Advisory Council on Voluntary Action entitled People in Action and published by the Dept. of the Secretary of State. John Hulchansky of the University of Toronto has recently produced a Bibliography on Citizen Participation, No. 1297 of the series published by the Americal Council of Planning Librarians.

HERITAGE LEGISLATION AT THE PROVINCIAL LEVEL (July 1, 1978)

	Recommended by Unesco	Newfoundland	Prince Edward Island	Nova Scotia	New Brunswick	Quebec	Ontario	Manitoba	Saskatchewan	Alberta	British Columbia
Are clear criteria given for the definition of Heritage Property?	Not discussed	No	No	No	No	No	No	No	No	No	No
Must notice be given of impending demoliton of unregistered Heritage Property?	Not discussed	No	No	No	No	No	No	No	Yes	No	Indian archaeological site only
Is Government under any obligation to attempt to protect unregistered Heritage Property?	Yes	Unclear	No	No	No	No	Sometimes	No	Unclear	Archaeological Sites only	No
Can demolition of unclassified building be delayed pending study?	Yes	Yes	No	No	No	Yes	Yes	No	Yes	Yes	Yes
Can definitive protection against demolition be given to a building (short or expropriation)?	Yes	Yes	Yes	No	Yes	Yes	Archaeological Sites Only	Yes	Yes	Yes	Yes
Is radius around monument protected?	Yes	No	No	No	No	Yes	No	No	No	No	No
Can governmental decisions on designation be appealed to higher authority by statute?	Yes	No	No	No	No	No	No	No	No	No	No
Is the definitive preservation of districts specifically foreseen?	Yes	Unclear	Law Protects "Areas"	No	*	Yes	No	*	*	*	*
Can maintenance of Heritage Property be enforced by the Province?	Yes	No	Yes	No	No	Yes	No	No	Unclear	Yes	No
Can Heritage Sites be Inspected?	Yes	Archaeological Sites only	Archaeological Sites Only	No	No	Yes	Yes	During Work Only	Unclear	Yes	Yes
Does government have right of first refusal on sale of Heritage Buildings?	Not Discussed	No	No	No	No	Yes	No	No	"Objects" Only	Yes	No
Can Heritage Properties be exempted from building codes?	Yes	No	No	No	No	No	No	No	No	Yes	No
Can illegally altered Heritage Building be restored at owner's expense?	Yes	No	No	Not applicable	No	Yes	Yes	Subsidized buildings only	Yes	Yes	Yes
What is the maximum penalty for offences?	Not specified	$1000 plus 3 months	$1000	Not applicable	$100 plus 30 days	$25,000	$10,000 plus 1 year	$100	$5000 plus 6 months plus damages	$50,000 plus 1 year plus damages	$2,000 plus 6 months

* The law empowers protection of "sites", which can be as large as a district.

HERITAGE LEGISLATION FOR MUNICIPALITIES (July 1, 1978)

	Newfoundland — St John's	Newfoundland — Elsewhere	Prince Edward Island — Charlottetown	Prince Edward Island — Elsewhere	Nova Scotia — Sherbrooke Village	Nova Scotia — Elsewhere	New Brunswick	Quebec	Ontario	Manitoba — Winnipeg	Manitoba — Elsewhere	Saskatchewan	Alberta	British Columbia
Is heritage conservation an obligatory part of municipal planning?	No	No	No	No	Yes	No¹	Yes	No	No	Yes	Yes	No	No	No
Is municipality obliged to file environmental impact assessment on demolition of heritage?	No	No	No	No	No	No	No	No	No	Not Yet	No	No	Not Yet	No
Can municipality give permanent protection to buildings	Yes	Unclear	Yes	No	Yes	No	Yes	No	No	Yes	No	No	Yes	Yes
Can municipality give temporary protection to buildings	Yes	Unlikely	Yes	No	Yes	No	Yes	Yes	Yes	Yes	No	No	Yes	Yes
Can municipality regulate — Bulk and Height	Yes	Unclear	Yes	Yes	Yes	Yes	Yes	Yes	Yes	Yes	Yes	Yes	Yes	Yes
Can municipality regulate — Design	Yes	Unclear	Yes	Yes	Yes	Yes	Yes	Yes	Yes	Yes	Yes	No	Yes	Yes
Can municipality regulate — Use	Yes	Yes	Yes	Yes	Yes	Yes	Yes	Yes	Yes	Yes	Yes	Yes	Yes	Yes
Can municipality regulate — Set-back	Yes	Yes	Yes	Yes	Yes	Yes	Yes	Yes	Yes	Yes	Yes	Yes	Yes	Yes
Can municipality regulate — Signs	Yes	Yes	Unclear	Yes	Yes	Yes	Yes	Yes	Yes	Yes	Yes	Yes	Yes	Yes
Can municipality accept or reject applications for construction on heritage sites on a discretionary basis	Yes	No	Probably	No	Yes	No¹	Yes	No	Yes	Yes	No	No	Yes	Yes
Can municipality enforce maintenance a) of dwelling interiors	Yes	Yes	Yes	Yes	Yes	Yes	Yes	Yes	Yes	Yes	Yes	Yes	Yes	Yes
b) of dwelling exteriors	Yes	Unclear	Yes	Yes	Yes	Yes	Yes	Yes	Yes	Yes	Yes	Yes	Yes	Yes
c) of non-residential interiors	No	Unclear	Unclear	Yes	Yes	Yes	No	Yes²	Yes	No	No	Unclear	Yes	Yes
d) of non-residential exteriors	No	Unclear	Yes	Yes	Yes	Yes	No	Yes²	Yes	No	No	Unclear	Yes	Yes
Can municipality compel a) protection of trees	Yes	Yes	Unclear	Unclear	Unclear	Unclear	Yes	Yes	Yes	Yes	Yes	Yes	Yes	Yes
b) landscaping	No	No	No	No	No	No	Yes	Yes⁴	No³	No	No	No	No	No
Can illegally altered building be restored at owner's expense?	Yes	Yes	No	No	Unclear	No	Yes	No	Yes	Yes	Yes	Yes	No	Unclear
Usual maximum penalty for offences	$100	$100-$200	$90 + 90 days	$500 + 90 days	$500	$100	$100	Variable	Variable	$1000 + 6 Mths.	$1000 + 6 Mths.	$1000 + 1 Mth.	$500	$2000 + 6 Mths.

¹ Except in Peggy's Cove
² Except in municipalities regulated by the Cities & Towns Act
³ Except under development control schemes
⁴ Except in Montreal, Quebec, and rural municipalities

Appendix:
Bodies involved in Protection

Government officials

A. The federal level

Two federal departments have overlapping roles in the field of heritage conservation.

The Department of Environment acquires and promotes national parks, and co-ordinates the federal government's activities relating to heritage sites.

Parks Canada
Department of Environment
Ottawa, Ontario

The Secretary of State's Department promotes most aspects of culture other than sites of historic and architectural significance. It also operates the network of national museums and thereby has a great influence upon archaeological research.
The Secretary of State
66 Slater Street
Ottawa, Ontario
or
National Museums of Canada
Ottawa, Ontario

B. The provincial level

As mentioned previously, most of the real power in terms of heritage conservation is at the provincial level.

a. Alberta:
The Minister of Government Services and Culture
Legislature Building
Edmonton, Alberta
or
Alberta Culture
8820-112 Street
Edmonton, Alberta

b. British Columbia:
The Minister of Recreation & Conservation
Parliament Buildings
Victoria, British Columbia
or
Deputy Minister of Recreation & Conservation
Parliament Building
Victoria, British Columbia

c. Manitoba:
The Minister of Tourism, Recreation & Cultural Affairs
Legislature Building
Winnipeg, Manitoba
or
Historic Resources Branch
Department of Tourism, Recreation and Cultural Affairs
200 Vaughan Street
Winnipeg, Manitoba

d. New Brunswick:
The Minister of Education
Legislature Building
Fredericton, New Brunswick
or
Historical Resources Administration
P. O. Box 6000
Fredericton, New Brunswick

e. Newfoundland:
The Minister of Tourism
Confederation Building
St. John's, Newfoundland
or
Historic Resources Branch
Newfoundland Museum
Duckworth Street
St. John's, Newfoundland

f. Nova Scotia:
The Minister of Education
Legislative Building
Halifax, Nova Scotia
or
The Director
Nova Scotia Museum
1747 Summer Street
Halifax, Nova Scotia

g. Ontario:
The Minister of Culture & Recreation
Queen's Park
Toronto, Ontario
or
Ministry of Culture & Recreation
Heritage Administration Branch
Queen's Park
Toronto, Ontario

Please note that the actual designation of cultural sites in Ontario is a municipal responsibility, not a provincial one. Furthermore, the functions of the Ministry and the quasi-governmental Ontario Heritage Foundation are often shared.

h. Prince Edward Island:
The Minister of Environment and Tourism
Province House
Charlottetown, P. E. I.
or
P. E. I. Heritage Foundation
2 Kent Street
Charlottetown, Prince Edward Island

i. Quebec:
Le Ministre des affaires culturelles
Assemblée Nationale
Québec, Québec
or
Directeur Général du Patrimoine
Ministère des affairs culturelles
6, rue Université
Québec, Québec

j. Saskatchewan:
The Minister of Tourism and Renewable Resources
Legislature Buildings
Regina, Saskatchewan
or
Supervisor of Historic Resources
Department of Culture & Youth
2002 Victoria, 11th Floor
Regina, Saskatchewan

These are government agencies which should have an interest in this subject matter. However, in five provinces, the ultimate decision to protect a site is made not by the Minister but by the Cabinet (upon the Minister's recommendation). Those provinces are Alberta, British Columbia, Manitoba, Newfoundland and Prince Edward Island. In two provinces, Ontario and Nova Scotia, no provincial official is fully empowered to protect heritage sites.

C. The municipal level

In virtually all Canadian cities, the administration of heritage sites and areas is administered through the municipal planning department.

Public and semi-public institutions and advisory boards

A. The national level

The Historic Sites and Monuments Board advises the Minister of Environment on designation of "National Historic Sites". Contact:

The Secretary
Historic Sites & Monuments Board of Canada
Ottawa, Ontario

Another important federal advisory body is the Federal Advisory & Co-ordinating Committee of Heritage Conservation (FACCH) mentioned earlier. It can be reached, care of the Department of Environment at the same address as above.

A governmental organization has been formed to hold annual meetings of officials responsible for heritage conservation. Those officials are both from the federal and provincial governments. The organization is named the Canadian Conference on Historical Resources and can be reached care of federal or provincial heritage officials.

B. The provincial level

Five provinces have government-sponsored "foundations" which have an interest in "cultural property". Those five provinces are Alberta, Manitoba, Ontario, Prince Edward Island and British Columbia. They are authorized both to advise governments and acquire properties.

The Alberta Historical Resources Foundation's address is 121 8th Ave. S. W., Calgary, Alberta.

The British Columbia Heritage Trust can be reached care of the Department of Recreation & Conservation, The Parliament Buildings in Victoria. Heritage Manitoba can be reached care of the Manitoba Historic Resources Branch, 200 Vaughan Street, Winnipeg, Manitoba.

The Ontario Heritage Foundation can be reached at 77 Bloor Street West, Toronto, Ontario.

The Prince Edward Island Heritage Foundation can be reached at 2 Kent Street, Charlottetown, Prince Edward Island.

In addition, most provinces have advisory boards which assist the Minister in formulating and applying heritage policy.

C. The municipal level

Advisory boards frequently exist at the municipal level. Usually, municipalities do not even need special enabling legislation to create such bodies, as long as their function remains strictly advisory. Some other jurisdictions prefer to bestow upon these advisory bodies the blessing of special legislation, as in the case of Ontario's Local Architectural Conservation Advisory Committees (LACACs).

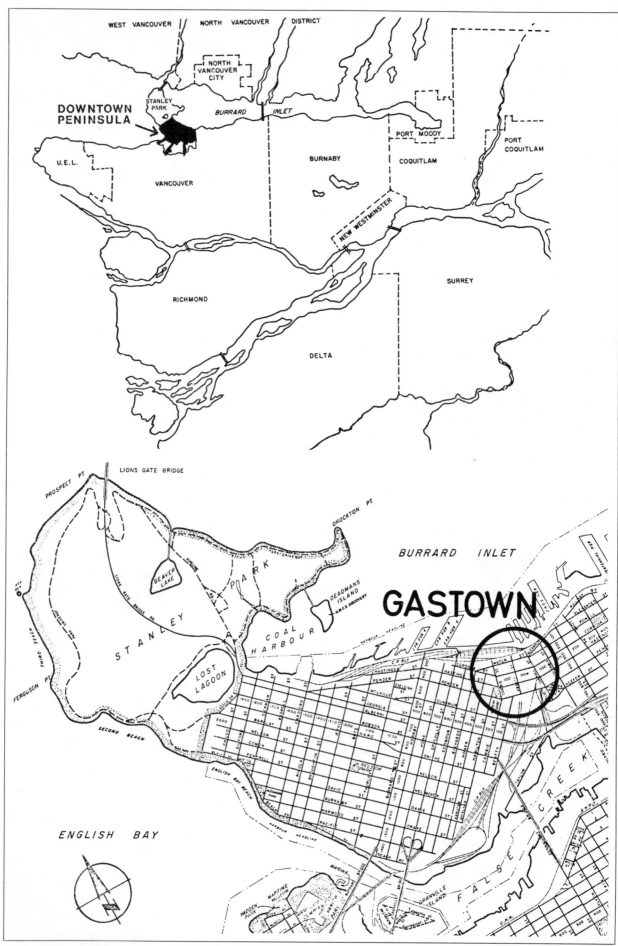

Vancouver/Canada: Location of Downtown and Gastown

Canada
VANCOUVER

1. An Introduction to Gastown, Vancouver[1])

In 1867, a former river pilot named John Deighton landed at Burrard Inlet with two women, a dog and a keg of whiskey.

He succeeded in attracting the enthusiasm of workers at a nearby sawmill, and within twenty-four hours his saloon stood proudly at what is now the corner of Water and Carrall Streets.

The City of Vancouver was born.

Deighton's monologues earned him the title of "Gassy Jack", and the thirsty community that arose around his crossroads became known as Gassy's Town or Gastown.

The rowdy and free-wheeling character of the early community would later "inspire" those who promoted the revitalization of the area.

In April 1886, the town was incorporated as the City of Vancouver. The name honours Captain George Vancouver, who had charted Burrard Inlet in 1792 for the Royal Navy.

On June 13, 1886, clearing fires west of the city were blown out of control by a sudden gale. The town was virtually destroyed within twenty minutes, but it recovered almost as quickly. Buildings sprang up, many of wood construction like those of pre-fire days, but many also of masonry. With the influx of immigrants between 1886 and 1892 the population grew from 5,000 to 15,000.

Vancouver's role as a shipping and distribution centre was reflected in the warehouse and wholesale stores that lined Water Street; its large transient population was served by the area's many hotels. Cordova Street became the principal commercial thoroughfare.

A severe depression struck in 1892, but ended six years later with the rush for gold in the Klondike. Many large commercial blocks and hotels were built with money acquired in the gold rush. The boom continued almost uninterrupted until the First World War; but between 1908 and 1913, when Vancouver underwent its period of greatest early growth, most of the commercial activity had moved into the Eastern Downtown Business District.

Throughout the next half century Gastown steadily declined. Ironically, the lack of economic activity served a useful end; little new construction took place, but at the same time few old buildings were demolished. The area eventually contained little more than warehouses and cheap hotels for the city's poor, frequently called "skid-roaders" after the "skid road" on which logs were dragged to the sawmill and near which cheap rooming houses were built for loggers.

Gastown began to be revitalized in the late 1960s. Old buildings found new owners and have been restored as shops and restaurants. Despite Gastown's new popularity, the age of its buildings holds rent lower than in newer commercial areas.

City planners and Gastown merchants have begun to improve the streets and alleys. In February 1971, the government of British Columbia designated most of Gastown and adjacent Chinatown as historic areas, thereby preventing demolition and controlling restoration and development. Gastown's future as a lively historic quarter appears secure.

Vancouver was launched like a ship: with bottles of booze (though certainly not champagne). This was done in the 1860s, and some people may wonder whether one can label such an area "historic". Gastown certainly does not pretend to be one of the architectural masterpieces of the western world.

On the other hand, Vancouver is one of the few major cities in the western world which can still display the functioning buildings which represented the first twenty-five years of its existence.

The fact remains that Gastown represents the achievement of a society which, in many respects, was still a pioneer society. For that reason alone, it can rightfully be called historic. Its value is also environmental: it provides a needed alternative to the anonymity of the modern city. Its success in this respect is unquestionable and can be measured in the area's continuing popularity among the residents of the city.

Another significant feature of Gastown is the story of its rehabilitation. It is a story not of governmental initiative but rather of citizen initiative.

2. Problem: The Battle of Gastown

2.1 The proposed invasion of Gastown

By 1960, the decades of economic stagnation in Gastown and its seedy population had led many officials to treat Gastown as expendable. When a consortium of major developers proposed a sweeping demolition and redevelopment of the area called Project 200, officials were enthused. Project 200 would destroy almost half of Gastown; almost another half would be destroyed to provide freeway access to Project 200.

2.2 Reviewing the troops

2.2.1 Pro-Gastown forces

– Proprietors:
  They realized that collective action was the key to success, and had organized a clean-up campaign as early as 1958. They were organized in a group called the Townsite Association.

– Merchants:
  Their interests were similar to those of the proprietors. They formed the Gastown Merchants Association.

---

[1]) See Exploring Vancouver, by Hal Kalman; much of the historical information in this section is from that text, reproduced by permission.

Vancouver/Gastown: aerial view of the city.

– Conservationists:
They were represented by the Vancouver Community Arts Council, which promoted a self-help plan (called the Norwich Plan) through films and speeches.

– The Chinese community:
It lived next to Gastown, and its efforts to protect its own neighbourhood simultaneously affected Gastown.

2.2.2 Anti-Gastown forces

– Entrepreneurs:
A consortium of two real estate giants and two department stores (total assets in billions of dollars) proposed Project 200.

– Federal support:
The federal National Harbours Board promoted the freeway construction, and the federal government would be called upon to subsidize it.

– Provincial support:
The provincial government would be called upon to subsidize freeway construction.

– Municipal support:
The city government was the most active promoter of freeway construction, and donated use of its planning staff to Project 200.

– The media:
In its initial stages (and even as late as 1969), Project 200 received very favourable coverage: "Excitingly, Van-

couver was destroying without a qualm the things of its childhood to be better prepared for full stature in a fast-changing world."

2.3 Offensive weapons

– Unsolicited reports: in 1963, unsolicited planning reports suggested massive development and freeway construction. These reports coloured civic planning for the area. By coincidence, some of the people who submitted these reports were later officials in Project 200.

– Secret negotiations: some three years of negotiations took place between Project 200 officials and the city. The public did not learn of these negotiations until 1966.

– Recruitment of planning staff: in July 1966, the city donated the use of its planning staff to help expedite approval of Project 200. It also commissioned supplementary planning studies for the project.

– Secret plans: planning for the project remained secret, and civic meetings to discuss those plans were held behind closed doors.

– Predetermination of planning results: the terms of reference of highway planning studies were drafted in such a way as to predetermine the results of the studies.

– Patchwork strategy: civic proposals for the freeway construction tended to cover only a small part at a time, thereby masking the city's long-term aims.

2.4 Defensive weapons

- Impeding access: Project 200 was unlikely to proceed without freeway access; consequently, impeding access was the foremost feature of Gastown's defense.

- Pre-emptive action: merchants tried to embelish their premises to demonstrate that the area did not deserve obliteration. These expenditures were risky.

- Walking tours: these became the focus of promotional efforts by the Community Arts Council.

- Sunday openings: merchants defied the law by opening on Sundays and developing a clientele which cannot shop anywhere else.

- Recruitment of professional support: a concerted effort was launched to win the support of influential associations of architects, urban planners, and academics. These would eventually pronounce themselves in favour of Gastown and receive good media coverage.

- Petitions: these were launched in favour of endangered buildings, and were interpreted as signs of public support.

- Recruitment of civic support: close links were cultivated with certain key members of civic staff.

- Publications: a newspaper was launched to promote the area.

- Festivals: the first was a small festival held in 1969. Festivals would grow in importance, as seen in Chapter 13.

- Goodwill tokens: the first was a statue of Gassy Jack Deighton donated to the city by local proprietors.

- Public meetings: certain civic actions required public meetings.
  Gastown sympathizers made sure that they attended in force. They used these meetings to present formal briefs to the city.

- Demonstrations: this technique was used only when the situation became desperate, as it did during the freeway controversy.

2.5 The battle in brief

1958: Merchants launch the first small Gastown clean-up campaign.

1959: In order to accomodate development, the City commissions a report which recommends forty-five miles (75 km) of freeways in and around the downtown including a branch through Gastown. The price apparently deters the city, and consequently the public is not informed whether the City has any proposed transportation plan.

1961: Council pays for another study "to review, up-date and recommend action on the 1959 plan and subsequent proposals".
The Mayor then proposes construction of a short length of waterfront freeway, which would make future construction of a Gastown link inevitable to give the waterfront freeway somewhere to go.

1962: The Community Arts Council launches films and a slide show to promote conservation.

1963: Massive commercial development in the area is suggested in several reports to City Council. Only one of

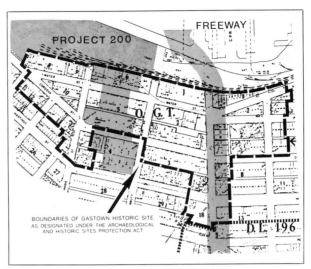

Vancouver/Canada: Boundaries of Gastown/Chinatown Historic Site
(as designated under the Archeological and Historic Sites Protection Act – 1971)

the reports is requested by council; two of them are unsolicited from business interests. Secret talks begin between the developers and City officials.

June 1966: Plans for Project 200 are formally unveiled. This is the first time the public learns of the proposal.

July 1966: City instructs its planners "to submit recommendations to council as to means of expediting approval of the project".

Fall 1966: The City funds more plans for access to the project. To co-ordinate civic and private efforts, the City sets up a committee composed exclusively of government and Project 200 officials.

Spring 1967: Joint planning continues, but all documentation remains closed to the public.
Opposition to Project focusses on the project's weakest point, access. More clean-up and renovation campaigns are launched by merchants.

June 1, 1967: After eight years, the highway plan is finally made public, including the proposed link which would carve through Gastown and neighbouring Chinatown. City Council accepts the proposal.
In public statements, the City emphasizes the freeway will be harmless because shops will be located underneath.

June 10, 1967: A group of planners denounces the freeway.

June 13, 1967: Chinese businessmen denounce "the Great Wall of Chinatown". The Chinese Benevolent Association calls for a public meeting.

June 15, 1967: The City responds by halting further study of the Gastown-Chinatown route pending a public hearing. The project planner is asked whether the freeway could go elsewhere, and answers "that is beyond my terms of reference".

Late summer, 1967: The City agrees that further planning should take place regarding the route of the freeway. Critics are satisfied that other alternatives will avoid the Gastown-Chinatown route.

October 17, 1967: The City gives a final announcement reconfirming the Gastown-Chinatown route; mourning

Vancouver: Gastown, circa 1879 (Vancouver archives)

banners are draped from windows and protesters march through the streets.

October 18, 1967: A university professor announces that the terms of reference of the planners were unjustifiably predicated on a Gastown-Chinatown route. Conservationists call for a public meeting.

October 23, 1967: Mayor Campbell says that the freeway will not be built for another ten to fifteen years anyway. Furthermore, it "will be an improvement rather than take away from Chinatown". He promises consultation, but opposes a public meeting.

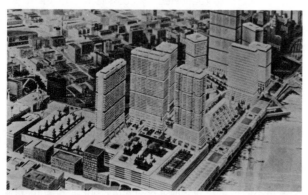

Vancouver: Development of the Gastown waterfront according to plans of "Project 200"

October 30, 1967: The local Member of the Provincial Legislature denounces the planners' terms of reference. The lawyer for the Chinese Benevolent Association accuses the City of pandering to Project 200.

November 8, 1967: Mayor Campbell states that it is too late to reconsider.

November 17, 1967: The City engineer states that the freeway would redevelop an area that "needs rebuilding" anyway.

November 23, 1967: Twenty-seven groups, even including the Vancouver Council of Churches, prepare briefs to be presented at the public meeting.
This in itself is a accomplishment, given the time in which citizens had to operate. The meeting overflows, and is described by the media as "riotous".

December 7, 1967: Mayor Campbell states that the City was never really interested in the freeway anyway; all the City wanted was a viaduct south of Gastown and Chinatown.

Spring, 1968: New plans are quietly undertaken for a freeway along the same route. The distinction is that the new freeway would be depressed, rather than elevated.

July 1968: The Mayor submits a secret transport report to City Council.

August 1968: Before any final word had been received concerning availability of access, the first building (albeit a small one) in Project 200 goes up in Gastown.

September 1968: The developers face internal problems; furthermore, some officials want the developers to pay a bigger share of the costs of a construction bypass made necessary by the project. Instead, developers later announce they will go ahead without a decision or development permit.

September 1968: The Community Arts Council holds the first of a series of popular walking tours of Gastown. The crowd which shows up in the rain even impresses the Mayor, who pledges support for renovation.

Spring 1969: In response to public pressure, the City finally gives formal authorization to its planners to undertake a preliminary plan for the revitalization of Gastown. Merchants open a "Flea Market" in Gastown. It attracts many shoppers, particularly since it is one of the few locations in Vancouver open (illegally) on Sunday.

May 5, 1969: When two Gastown hotels are threatened with demolition, a petition is launched which gathers 550 signatures within a matter of hours. This is interpreted as a sign of public support for Gastown.

June, 1969: A planning firm submits the first report on the conservation potential of Gastown.

July, 1969: The City's Planning Committee recommend beautification of Gastown. Private recycling activity in Gastown intensifies. An antique dealer founds the Gastown Gazette, and uses it to publicize the area.

August, 1969: City Council refuses the development permit for another building in Project 200 until specific conditions can be agreed upon.
Within one week council appoints a three-man negotiating committee between the city and Project 200. Two aldermen recommend that the city grant a permit without a written agreement, on the basis of a promise of later cooperation. In the following week, City Council gives the go-ahead for the project even without a by-pass agreement. It is proposed that taxes pay for three quarters of the cost of roads around Project 200.

November, 1969: A university Professor warns that Project 200 would have "serious economic consequences". Without better planning, the project could:

Vancouver/Gastown: Waterstreet in 1886, shortly before the fire (Vancouver archives)

– slow downtown traffic to a crawl
– cripple the port's efficiency
– displace up to 1,500 people
– attract thousands of residents to an area without adequate schools, parks, etc.

The criticism is dismissed by Project spokesmen, and a Vancouver Sun editorial criticises some members of council for not giving sufficient co-operation to the project.

December, 1969: Part of the Project 200 contract is given the sister company of a company responsible for one of the unsolicited 1963 reports suggesting waterfront development. It is also responsible for the provincially-sponsored 1965 study that recommended a waterfront highway which, by coincidence, would provide access to Project 200. The company's Vice President is the same planning consultant who had repeatedly called for freeway construction in transportation studies commissioned by the City.

January, 1970: As a gesture of good faith, merchants present a statue of Gassy Jack to the City, which is displayed in Gastown despite the Mayor's promise to bring it to the dump.

Spring 1970: Work on another part of Project 200 begins in March 1970; but in April 1970, the City appoints a consortium of consulting firms to conduct studies for a "beautification project" in Gastown.
Meanwhile, the first large restaurant opens in Gastown; it sets an example of structural recycling techniques, and becomes enormously popular.

Summer 1970: It appears increasingly unlikely that an adequate solution would be found for access to Project 200 but prospects for an effective (and popular) revitalization scheme appear better every day, particularly pursuant to the City's new planning studies. Gradually, more and more city officials are convinced that revitalization of Gastown is both more feasible and politically more expedient than flattening it; if Project 200 is to proceed, it can do so outside Gastown's boundaries, or else in a scale and style compatible with the surroundings.
Project 200 developers start considering the possibility of constructing sympathetic buildings in Gastown on empty lots. This work will ultimately lead to the construction of Gaslight Square, which is considered to blend well with its Gastown environment.

November 16, 1970: A major threat faces Gastown business. After several years of open illegality, the City Prosecutor finally threatens to fine Gastown merchants who operate on Sundays. Merchants promise to disregard such action.

November 18, 1970: Upon the advice of conservationists, Mayor Campbell observes that if Gastown were a designated historic site it might be possible to exempt the area from the Sunday closing law.

February 2, 1971: Gastown is designated as an historic site by the province under the British Columbia Archaeological and Historic Sites Protection Act. Henceforth, no police action is taken against merchants who are open on Sunday. It is not immediately clear whether all politicians realize that the measure also assures the protection of Gastown for the future.

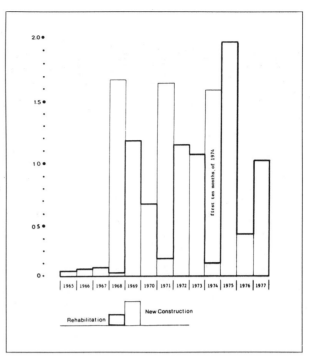

Vancouver/Gastown: Building permit activity in 1,000,000 Dollars.

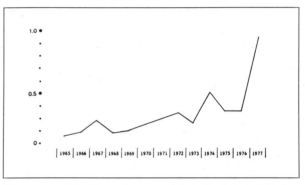

Vancouver/Gastown: Average value of property transactions in 1,000,000 Dollars.

Vancouver/Gastown: Overall assessment; percentage increase 1966–1974.

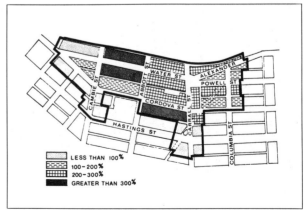

(illustrations: City of Vancouver, Planning Department)

Vancouver/Gastown: Typical restorations of 19th century structures.

3. Results in Brief

Certain problems developed in the offensive on Gastown. Some were internal; for example, the project ran into serious delays because of entrepreneur-city disagreement over the sharing of highway costs. Other problems, however, can be attributed to the efforts of Gastown's defenders.

The first major victory was won when the freeway was stopped, blocking access to Project 200.

The second major victory was the demonstration of Gastown's economic viability. This task was greatly facilitated by the fact that so many businessmen proclaimed Gastown's potential. An important paradox of Canadian municipal politics is that the public interest is seldom paid as much attention as when it is also "good for business".

The third major victory was won when conservationists were able to demonstrate relatively widespread public support.

A fourth factor may also have played an important role: it was the question of Sunday opening. The resulting action of the city in proposing designation of the area may partly be attributed to good luck, but is primarily due to the defiance of the merchants and the ability of the conservationists to make the right suggestion at the right time.

The following is a description of the supervisory framework which resulted from these successes. The policy goals which are now considered important in Gastown emerged gradually, and shall be discussed in the following sections.

4. Strategies and Measures

4.1 Legal protection

4.1.1 Statutory authority

On February 2, 1971, Gastown was declared an historic site under the British Columbia Archaeological and Historic Sites Protection Act (now expanded and renamed the British Columbia Heritage Conservation Act).

4.1.2 Effects

All alterations of demolition in Gastown are subject to provincial approval. The statute places no limits on the discretion which the government can exercise.

4.1.3 Integration into development policy

Since British Columbia has no environmental assessment act, it is under no legal obligation to follow any restrictive procedure when threatening the character of the area. Furthermore, even if the province or its agencies acted illegally, it is unlikely that the province could be brought to court because of the "locus standi" doctrine described earlier. Consequently, there is no immediate legal incentive compelling the province to integrate protection of the heritage area into its development policy.

The City, on the other hand, is bound by the Heritage Conservation Act. To disregard it would undoubtedly be an offence. As with provincial infractions, it is a moot point whether any citizen would have standing to take the City to court; his chances of success, however, might be reasonable. Consequently, it was in the City's interest to integrate protection of the area into its development policy.

4.1.4 Supplementary measures

A series of municipal by-laws were passed subsequent to the designation of the area under the Archaeological and Historic Sites Protection Act. These by-laws regulated details of the heritage area.

The two most important by-laws involved new controls on uses and signs. Incompatible uses were discouraged, compatible uses were promoted in an area which had not previously foreseen them, and highly comprehensive sign guidelines have been promulgated.

4.1.5 Selected problems

Maintenance

The city's power to regulate maintenance is expressed primarily in the "Tidy Lots By-law". There has been no apparent attempt to use this power to compel the maintenance of buildings in Gastown which remain unrepaired.

Radius

Nothing protects Gastown from unsympathetic construction immediately beyond its boundaries. An enormous and totally unsympathetic building, built by the public authorities, is now located to the immediate east of the area.

Building codes

In order to recycle a building there is a legal prerequisite that the building be brought up to building code standards.

Until recently, some proprietors were able to deal with this problem more effectively than others. It took some three and a half years of negotiation before the City would issue a permit to recycle the Mussenden Building, a 5 storey brick building of post and beam construction which had been partially destroyed by fire.

Some entrepreneurs felt the City was being too reluctant to recognize equivalences for building code specifications. This debate, however, has allegedly become academic. Under recent amendments to the building code, recycled structures must now be capable of withstanding an earthquake equivalent to 7.2 on the Richter Scale – although the major seismic threat to Vancouver allegedly comes from tidal waves, not earthquakes.

This new requirement of "seismicproofing" has aroused considerable dissatisfaction among Gastown proprietors and conservationists. They argue that it is a disincentive to recycling and as such will ultimately lead to deterioration rather than strengthening of buildings in the area. One conservationist commented: "Gastown's future is interesting but doomed". Although most interested parties would

Vancouver/Gastown:
Typical restorations of
19th century structures.

Vancouver: Demonstration against the planned freeway October 17, 1967 (Vancouver Sun).

disagree with this bleak appraisal, there is agreement that the building code should pay more attention to the special needs of recycling activity.

Government action

As mentioned earlier, the enforceability of Gastown planning priorities vis-à-vis government agencies is weak.

Federal agencies such as the National Harbours Board appear free to disregard Gastown's objectives. According to some local representatives, it is only recently that arguments for greater co-operation have finally prevailed.

Provincial agencies allegedly fare little better. Although the

area now enjoys good relations with agencies such as B. C. Hydro (which buried its electric cables), merchants claim that co-operation was obtained only after unduly strenuous effort.

Enforcement

Although the governmental advisory bodies in Gastown have pointed to some outright violations of protective legislation, it has occasionally taken years to obtain remedial action. Violations of signage regulations are a case in point. As mentioned earlier, there is little that citizens can do to correct this situation short of legislative reform.

Access to information

Much government information affecting the future of Gastown remains secret.

For example, the National Harbours Board was asked in 1972 what it would do with the waterfront which faced Gastown and which it was busily filling with landfill. N. H. B. Chairman (and ex-mayor) Rathie replied: "I shall have to take the position that there is no need to discuss this further." It is still not clear what the N. H. B. is planning to do with its property, although there is currently more optimism for co-operation than ever before.

4.2   Financial techniques

4.2.1 Investment from the public sector

The extraordinary feature demonstrated by Gastown is the enormous distance which can be covered by a relatively limited public investment.

Vancouver: Promotional activities in Gastown; Gastown Festival.

Vancouver: Launching the bathtub races (Photo: Franco Cirarella).

Gastown has not seen any level of government:

– buy buildings;

– restore buildings themselves, or

– subsidize renovations.

However, since much of the responsibility for Gastown's revival was cast upon the merchants' shoulders, their costs had to be amortized through increased rents. This has had a severe dislocating effect upon the handicrafts which were once identified with Gastown.

There are increasing calls by conservationists for some level of government to buy some commercial space and to make it available to the handicraft producers at a cost comparable to 1970 levels.

Similarly, conservationists are asking why government offices still have a negligible presence in Gastown. Most government offices in Vancouver are leasing downtown office space (at taxpapers' expense) at approximately twice the cost of top-quality recycled space in Gastown. If levels of government were to decide to save taxpayers' money by locating some offices in Gastown, it appears that further revival would be stimulated.

4.2.2 Compensating social hardship

Some 400 low-quality (but low-cost) housing units have been lost in Gastown. The governmental commitment to compensating social hardship has had a low profile in Gastown. In an attempt to offset this trend, the City and other levels of government have either purchased or entered into management agreements with a number of the apartment hotels with the aim of providing low-cost, acceptable housing for the area's residents.

The displacement of handicraft workers was mentioned in the previous section.

4.2.3 Care of surroundings

Almost all public investment took the form of street improvements.

The City invested $ 1,071,000 between 1966 and 1974 in capital improvements in the area by acquiring land, undergrounding utilities, and by improving the appearance of Maple Tree Square, Blood Alley Square and Water Street.

Federal contribution to these projects:	$ 175,000
Provincial contribution to these projects:	$ 544,000
Utilities' contribution to these projects:	$ 459,000
Municipal contribution to these projects:	$ 1,071,000
Proprietors' contribution to these projects:	$ 926,000
	$ 3,175,000

4.3 Administration

4.3.1 Procedure

The Archaeological and Historic Sites Protection Act did not outline either the procedure for protection nor that of applications for changes in the area.

Applications for changes are reviewed by the Gastown Historic Area Planning Committee, described later. As applied to Gastown, the Board functions in the following manner. When a property owner makes an application for construction, signs, alterations, or change of use, the application is forwarded to the Vancouver City Planning Department. The application is then presented to the Historic Area Advisory Board for its consideration. If the Board approves the application, it then proceeds through the regular administrative channels until the permit is issued or refused. When the Board does not approve an application it attempts to reach a compromise with the owner or it requests that the Director of Planning and Civic Development handle the matter on behalf of the Board.

To date, only one demolition has been approved: the building was replaced by a parking garage of "Gastown-compatible" design approved by the Board. The building was applauded by many Canadian architects as the epitome of "harmonious" infill construction.

Several other new buildings of approved "Gastown-compatible" design have been constructed.

4.3.2 Public authorities

The Minister responsible for the administration of the Act when it was applied to Gastown was the Provincial Secretary. It is now the Minister of Recreation and Conservation.

Since the terms of the Act were so vague, an advisory board was established: it is the Historic Sites Advisory Board, under the chairmanship of the Deputy Minister of the relevant department (now Recreation and Conservation). Another primary function of the Board is to act as liaison for the various government departments responsible for heritage conservation.

The provincial government also chose to rely heavily upon advice from the municipal level, to such an extent that provincial and municipal regulations of Gastown have become almost indistinguishable.

Most government officials in Canada guard their prerogatives jealously; in that perspective, the bureaucratic co-ordination shown in Gastown has been exemplary.

Pursuant to the "gentlemen's agreement" which evolved between the province and the city, Vancouver passed a by-law establishing the Historic Area Advisory Board, representing the groups of conservationists, merchants, property owners, academics, professionals and residents.

The Board was expected to recommend guidelines as to the kinds of structures to be protected, altered or demolished, as well as the style of infill construction. The Board would also make recommendations to the City concerning zoning and signage.

The Board was succeeded by the Gastown Historic Area Planning Committee. Of the seven voting members, one represents each of the above groups (except for the property owners, who have two seats on the Committee). The city provides a planner who acts as non-voting secretary of the Committee.

The Committee is now supplemented by the Gastown Historic Area Co-ordinating Committee, composed exclusively of the Gastown groups. It administers the Festivals Committee, special projects (e. g. the musical clock) and general liaison within Gastown.

Changes in Gastown tend to be organized or reviewed by the civic authorities on an ad hoc basis rather than in the perspective of a long-range development policy. This is because the City has no long-range official plan specifying in detail the proposed evolution of Gastown, although the area is mentioned for protection in general terms in the master plan of Vancouver as a whole.

4.4 Renovation activities

The accompanying photographs illustrate some of the renovation efforts conducted in Gastown.

5. Promotion

"A businessman in Gastown shouldn't think like a proprietor; he must think like a promoter."

Larry Killam

"To communicate is the beginning of understanding."

Gastown handbill

5.1 The problem

Legal designation did not guarantee Gastown's future. During the late 1960s, the hippie movement "adopted" Gastown. On the positive site, hundreds of people became involved in the production and sale of handicraft goods on a highly informal basis. It is estimated that only 18% of merchants held the obligatory business licence. This entire phenomenon gave Gastown an unusual air of spontaneity, and encouraged those who worried about the gradual disappearance of Canadian handicrafts.

As usual, however, it was hippiedom's weakest point which was exploited by the press: its propinquity to the drug cult.

5.2 Riot

For reasons which are still unclear, the media chose not to attack drug abuse per se, but rather to blame the entire phenomenon on Gastown itself.

This took the form of almost day-to-day denunciations of this "unsafe" area by an open-line broadcaster and the Mayor.

There were two responses. Merchants rejected a plea to sue the Mayor, and instead urged him to make less sweeping denunciations. Radical hippies, on the other hand, responded to this alleged "provocation" by assembling a "smoke in" in honor of marijuana. The mounted riot squad charged the demonstrators, and the evening degenerated into a riot which a formal inquest later blamed primarily on the police. Radical hippies immediately started to prepare for a larger confrontation.

Merchants and proprietors realized that if Gastown became a battle-ground the reputation of the area would not recover and the area would be doomed. They therefore took pre-emptive measures: they organized a giant "peace party" for the next Saturday evening, at which hippies, policemen, merchants and politicians would be reconciled. It worked.

The "peace party" served another purpose: it was so successful that it inspired many more festivals.

5.3 Promotional efforts

Food was the focus of two promotional efforts. One was a periodic breakfast held in a department store garage in Gastown. As usual, what would appear unusual elsewhere was deemed quite appropriate in Gastown.

The second such effort was the establishment of a farmers' market in Gastown. This attracted great publicity, particularly since it was originally illegal and was the object of meticulously orchestrated civil disobedience.

The wearing of costumes has lost some appeal, and is now restricted to festivals.

The donation to the City of a statue of Gassy Jack had good results. The merchants' next gift was the world's only steam-operated musical clock, installed on Gastown's main thoroughfare.

Special tours of the area are no longer offered, in the absence of government funding.

5.4 Festivals

Gastown's main promotional efforts are concentrated upon six annual festivals:

- The St. Patrick's Day Parade (mid-March);
- The Rain Festival (April), featuring a bathtub race through the streets and a costume ball;
- The Heritage Festival (June), featuring one month of various cultural activities (music, dancing, etc.);
- The Bicycle Races (August), featuring a major race preceded by children's races and a costume race;
- Gastown Days (late September), featuring music and dancing in the streets, as well as a temporary casino;
- The Christmas Festival (December), featuring carolling.

The festivals are organized by the Gastown Festivals Committee, a branch of the Gastown Historic Area Coordinating Committee. As mentioned earlier, this Committee is composed exclusively of Gastown groups, with technical assistance from city planners. The festivals not only attract people to Gastown, they are also profitable. Except for the Christmas and St. Patrick's Day festivals, (where no beer or wine are sold in the streets), profits from beer sales amount to $ 3,000–$ 4,000 per festival.

6. Results

6.1 Social benefits

The Vancouver City Planning Department has summarized some benefits in the following terms:

The most immediate of these was the heightening of awareness on the part of the public and government to the heritage of the City of Vancouver. The Gastown experiment showed that heritage preservation and economic and social progress were at least compatible and probably complementary. As a result of the Gastown experience, the City established a Heritage Advisory Committee to advise Council on the heritage aspects of the city's continued growth and development. On the advice of this Committee, Council has designated two dozen other buildings throughout the city as being worthy of preservation. Vancouver is a young city, and prior to 1967 paid almost no attention to its own past. Gastown has changed that. It is impossible to conceive that Vancouverites will again view their city as one of only future potential with no history worthy of note.

Another area of social benefit which has occurred as a result of the Gastown redevelopment is the reduction in crime within the downtown. While some forms of crime, most notably prostitution, have merely been displaced to other areas of the downtown, some other types have shown an absolute decrease within the city as a whole. These tend to be the types of crimes for which skid road residents are generally the victims, such as strongarmings, petty extortion, and some types of drug and alcohol abuse. Because the skid road has not been displaced but has been merely made more visible, the policing of these types of offences has been made considerably easier. Indications are that Vancouver is a safer city because of this programme.

The city's recent efforts on behalf of skid road residents were mentioned earlier.

6.2 The impact on private investment

The civic improvements obiously made the area more desirable, particularly for retail purposes. Furthermore, the designation under the Archaeological and Historic Sites Protection Act as well as the City's commitment to the area gave property owners and merchants additional confidence in the future of the area, thus freeing some loan capital for renovation efforts. That impact over the period 1965–1974 was documented by the City Planning Department, and partly updated in 1977:

	66–74	66–77
Value of building permits in Gastown	+ 3,300 %	
(value of building permits in Vancouver generally	(+ 59 %)	
Retail space	+ 147 %	
Restaurants and entertainment	+ 107 %	
Office space	+ 60 %	
Warehousing space	− 27 %	
Vacant space	− 50 %	
Total market value	+ 147 %	+ 200 %
Average property sale price	+ 182 %	+ 420 %
Average property sale price (adjusted for inflation)	+ 98 %	
Municipal assessment (for tax purposes)	+ 147 %	+ 147 %[1]
Municipal assessment (adjusted for inflation)	+ 60 %	
(Municipal assessment for Vancouver generally – unadjusted)	(+ 127 %)	
Property tax revenues	+ 132 %	
Property tax revenues (adjusted for inflation)	+ 50,5 %	

Mortgage financing for investment appears available to entrepreneurs with a "proven track record", but there is disagreement over the fairness of interest rates.

6.3 Visitors to Gastown

New "Gastown-compatible" retail/restaurant sales amounted to approximately $ 17.7 million in 1974. Total expenditure by an estimated 1.8–2 million tourists entering Gastown (of the more than 7 million tourists in Greater Vancouver in 1974 spending more than $ 500 million) amounted to approximately $ 9 million. It has been estimated that up to 25,000 people enter the historic area on a warm sunny day in the summer months.

Place of Origin	Time Period 10AM–10PM %
Gastown	2.8
Downtown Vancouver	4.2
City of Vancouver	20.2
Metro Vancouver	17.1
Lower Mainland	3.4
Rest of BC	6.9
Rest of Canada	17.4
United States	22.3
Other Countries	5.6
	100.0

The most frequently mentioned reason for coming to Gastown is "window shopping" and "browsing". This is mentioned by more than 55 % of all responding Gastown visitors.

The most frequently stated aspect of the character of Gastown enjoyed by visitors is the "variety of unique shops". This is mentioned by nearly 32 % of all responding people. The next most enjoyed feature ist the "atmosphere" with nearly 26 %, followed by "the little yards, squares and beautified streets" with more than 16 %. "People" and "walking around" rank together as fourth and fifth with 14 %. Next, "restaurants" and "architecture of buildings" rank nearly together with 10.5 % and 10 %.

When asked what they do not like about Gastown, "traffic problems" and "social problems" (drunks, panhandlers) are the most frequently mentioned dislikes. "Traffic problems" is mentioned by nearly 14 % out of all persons responding and social problems by more than 10 %. "Parking problems" is next with 6.3 %.

73 percent of all Gastown visitors from the Metro Vancouver area come to Downtown Vancouver in the summer months because of Gastown. More than 67 percent of all tourists have at least a general idea of the Gastown area before coming to Vancouver.

More than 31 percent of all Metro Vancouverites visiting, passing through, or on business in Gastown had been in the historic area twenty or more times between August 1974 and July 1975. This would suggest that Gastown is a continuing attraction, enjoying "repeat business".

Although only 30 % visiting Gastown during the summer months come to purchase something, more than 60 percent of the total purchase merchandise or eat in Gastown. This suggests a high proportion of "impulse" buying. In 1975, average money expenditure per person per visit was $ 6.22 during the summer months. The average amount of money

---

[1] "Property assessments have been frozen since 1974 pending provincial review of assessment policies."

Vancouver/Canada:
compatible architecture

Photograph of existing structures on the north side of Cordova Street.
Renovation sketch below indicates the style of ground floor premises as being in sympathy with the architecture.
Note the parking structure. New buildings, where required, should be designed to conform in feeling and scale to the overall area.

spent in restaurants amounted to $ 4.73 for the period between 10 AM and 10 PM, and total average expenditure for all merchandise items was $ 8.72.

6.4 Economic fluctuation

The visitors' survey proved that the majority of visitors come to browse, not to shop. This feature makes Gastown's retail function fundamentally different from that of the typical retail centre; a much higher percentage of purchases are due to impulse in Gastown than in other areas.

A major exception to "impulse" buying in Gastown is the purchase of "specialty" items or "luxury" items (e. g. in art galleries). Furthermore, Gastown's restaurants and bars are a major attraction.

The combination of these four major marketing objects ("impulse", "specialty", "luxury" and "entertainment" items) make Gastown unusually subject to economic fluctuations. During times of economic growth, Gastown can be expected to boom at a considerably higher rate than the economy as a whole, since people have more money to spend on precisely what Gastown provides. Inversely, during times of economic contraction Gastown can be expected to suffer far more than the economy as a whole.

Gastown has almost no residential population. If it did, this would probably have a stabilizing influence upon the fluctuations of retail trade in the area. Above-ground office space already has a significant stabilizing role. It is only by matching retail use of ground-floor space with effective non-retail use of above-ground floor space that the boom-or-bust character of the area can be minimized.

Conservationists hope that proposed amendments to the National Housing Act will make it easier to finance the conversion of warehouses to residential use. A strong demand is detected by the City Planning Department: "The few middle income housing units built in Gastown since 1970 have waiting lists of several years in length. It is too early to say if this trend will develop into a significant one, but indications are hopeful."

7. Some Preliminary Conclusions on Gastown

It was mentioned that the Canadian heritage movement is a coalition. Vancouver is a perfect example. The motivation of the merchants, the historians, the culture fans, and the neighbouring Chinese community was different. But they nevertheless worked successfully together in protecting Gastown and promoting rehabilitation. Gastown also exemplifies the importance of the economic and social rationale for conservation; these arguments were as basic to the citizens' movement as any pure "heritage" considerations.

Conservationists in Canada are faced with a seemingly eternal problem of balancing their comments such that they provoke governmental action without precipitating a breakdown of essential communications.

In Gastown, conservationists chose to act in a highly visible manner. They got away with it for three main reasons;

– they had good credibility (particularly their businessmen);

– they "put their money where their mouth is" by investing in the area; and, most importantly,

– they had well-organized and highly visible popular support, as well as a flair for promotion.

Despite incredible odds, Gastown was saved in such a way that its economic benefits to the community became as obvious as its social and cultural benefits. Gastown's primary lesson is in the usefulness of citizen initiative, economics and promotion in the conservation and rehabilitation of our structural heritage. If these factors could overcome the formidable odds encountered in Gastown, then the future of other heritage areas is indeed bright.

FRANCE

France

LEGISLATION, ORGANISATION, FINANCE, PARTICIPATION

1. Legislation

1.1 The statutory protection of historic monuments

The provisions concerned with the safeguarding of France's architectural legacy rest on the Act of December 31, 1913. Since then it has been amended by the Acts of December 31, 1921, July 23, 1927, August 27, 1941, September 27, 1941, February 25, 1943, and May 24, 1951, together with the ordinance of October 23, 1958, the decrees of January 7, 1959, April 18, 1961, the Acts of July 21 and December 31, 1966, the decrees of February 6, 1969, August 28, 1969 and September 10, 1970, and the Act of December 23, 1970.

Article 1

"Those properties whose conservation engenders public interest due to their artistic or historic appeal shall be classified, either in their entirety or in part, as historic monuments . . .".

Article 2

"Those private properties or parts of properties which, without warranting immediate classification, engender sufficient artistic or historic interest to make preservation desirable shall always be eligible for inclusion on a supplementary list."

Article 4

"Those properties, whether movables in the narrow sense of the term or immovables by virtue of their function, whose conservation engenders public interest due to their historic, artistic, scientific or technical appeal may be classified as historic monuments."

Article 24

(text of the Act dated 23/12/1970) "Those properties, whether movables in the narrow sense of the term or immovables by virtue of their function, which belong to the State, the départements, municipalities, public authorities or cultural associations and which – though not warranting immediate classification – engender sufficient historic, artistic, scientific or technical interest to make preservation desirable shall always be eligible for inclusion on a supplementary list."

The legal status of the proprietor, i. e. whether he be a body corporate or a private individual, does not possess much significance in this context. Only the quality of the property, whether movable or immovable, is retained and handed on from one epoch to the next.

1.1.1 Classification (12,000 classified monuments)

Procedure

As regards the classification procedure, historic monuments and properties are governed by the explicit provisions of the Act of 1913 and its implementing decree of March 18, 1924.

An analysis of the tenor of the Act and the decree reveals six fundamental requirements:

– to consult the First Section of the Commission supérieure des Monuments historiques (article 5 of the decree of March 18, 1924);

– to ascertain the views of the proprietor (articles 3, 4 and 5 of the Act of December 31, 1913);

– to issue an ordinance (arrêté) setting forth the monument's classification (articles 3, 4 and 5 of the Act);

– to inform the proprietor about the ordinance (article 6 of the decree of March 18, 1924);

– to register the ordinance with the bureau des hypothèques ("office of mortgages") pursuant to article 6 of the above-mentioned decree; and

– to publish at periodical intervals in the official Gazette a list of classified properties (article 6 of the same decree).

It is an essential requirement to obtain the opinion of the Commission supérieure des Monuments historiques. This opinion is delivered in an analytical study ("dossier de recensement"), which must comprise all the available information of a historic, artistic and legal nature on the building or site in question. The dossier is drawn up by the locally competent Conservateur régional des Bâtiments de France acting either on his own initiative or in response to a request voiced by the proprietor or a protective association. Before its submission to the Commission supérieure, the dossier goes to the Inspection générale des monuments historiques.

The classification is then announced in an ordinance issued by the Ministry of Culture and the Environment once that the proprietor has given his consent. In the rare event of the proprietor withholding his consent, the Commission supérieure re-examines the dossier. In those circumstances, the classification may be pronounced in an official decree issued by the Prime Minister after consulting the State Council (Conseil d'Etat).

There is also another procedure for dealing with exceptional circumstances know as "l'instance de classement". This is only used in urgent cases such as when the property is threatened by demolition or serious modification or when it has reached a grave state of disrepair. Under this procedure, the ministerial decision is exempt from any adherence to preliminary formalities or undue bureaucracy. After a single consultation with the Inspection générale des monuments historiques in line with suggestions put forward by the Conservateur régional des bâtiments de France, the Ministry of Culture and the Environment may order the prefect to announce the State's intentions to the proprietor, who then has two months within which to communicate his views.

The "instance de classement" is only valid for one year during which time it is deemed to equate with a classification proper. It cannot, however, be extended. The building either falls once more under common law (droit commun) or else the State has to implement the measures laid down for the ordinary classification.

An expropriation may be necessary if the building is needed for public use: such a move must be decided by the ministry or else the prefect or the mayor (ordinance of 23 October 1958). The full implementation of a classification takes place as from the time when the proprietor is informed of the intention to expropriate him, and the classification itself is set forth in a simple ordinance issued by the ministry following the declaration that the building will be put to public use. If that has not taken place within twelve months after the notifying of the proprietor, the new classification then ceases to be valid.

"In pursuance of the provisions of ordinance No. 58997 of 23 October 1959, the Ministry of Cultural Affairs may order in the name of the State the expropriation of a classified property or one proposed for classification by virtue of the interest which it furnishes from the standpoint of history or art". The départements and the local authorities enjoy the same right.

By the same token, this opportunity is also given in respect of those properties whose expropriation is necessary "in order to isolate, restore or emphasize a classified property or one proposed for classification if it impedes the view of such a property".

Article 7 contains a precise provision:

"As from the day on which the administration of cultural affairs has notified the proprietor of a non-classified property of his intention to effect expropriation, the whole statutory effect of the classification applies to the property in question. It ceases to operate if the declaration of public use is not made within twelve months of the notification.

"When the property has been declared to be of public use, it may then receive its classification without any further formality by means of an ordinance signed by the Ministry of Cultural Affairs".

These two articles, 6 and 7, indicate the relationship between classification and expropriation. Where a classification has been given to a property pursuant to a decree issued by the Prime Minister upon the advice of the Council of State but without the consent of the proprietor, the latter has the right to a fixed rate of compensation determined if it has been proved that this change involves a certain financial loss for him.

In order to exercise his right, the proprietor must apply for compensation within six months from the date of having been informed of the classification. In such a case, however, the administration authorities are not bound to pursue the classification project any further: within a period of three months after the judgement, they may cancel the decree on classification or have recourse to expropriation procedure (which may be requested by the proprietor himself).

The effects of classification

– The classified property may not be destroyed, moved or modified, either in its entirety or in part, by means of activities undertaken without the prior approval of the minister (art. 9, first para.).

– Any authorized activities must be carried out under the supervision of the administrators of cultural affairs (art. 9, second para.).

– The property is transferable (i.e. may be bequeathed or sold) provided that the minister has been informed (art. 8).

– It may not form the subject of an investigation on the aims of an expropriation for public use unless the minister has been asked to present his views (art. 11).

– Any legal easements which exist and which could bring about the decay of the monument are not valid for classified properties (art. 13, third para.).

– No legal easements may be enforced by a contractual agreement in respect of a classified property without the authority of the minister in charge of cultural affairs (art. 12, final para.).

– The immediate surroundings of a classified property are also protected (art. 1; art. 6, second para.; art. 11; art. 13 A).

– The work involved in maintaining, repairing and restoring a property may also be supported by the technical assistance of the "service des monuments historiques" (art. 9, second para.).

– This work may also benefit from the financial assistance of the State (art. 9, third para., art. 9, first para.).

– Proprietors who bear the expense peculiar to the conservation of the monument may enjoy preferential tax treatment.

We shall go into the details of these tax advantages and the problems of financing classified properties faced by their owners at a later stage.

1.1.2 Registration on the supplementary list of historic monuments

(18,000 registered monuments)

Procedure

This is virtually the same as for classification. However, the administrative authorities do not need to obtain the proprietor's consent. Subject to this condition, the authorities must:

– consult the "commission supérieure des monuments historiques" or its permanent delegation;

– order an inclusion in the supplementary list by ministerial ordinance.

Effects

Article 2, which defines such registration, stipulates that "inclusion in the supplementary list of historic monuments will be notified to the proprietors, thus imposing upon them the requirement not to carry out any modifications to the property or part of it without first informing the minister of cultural affairs of their intention to do so and indicating the work which they propose to carry out".

It is interesting to note the difference in wording between article 9 (on classified properties) and article 2 (on registered properties). In the former, the ministry must authorize the demolition or modification of a property: in the latter case, the requirement is merely that he must be told of the proprietor's intentions.

"The ministry cannot prevent the aforesaid work from taking place except by applying the classification procedure".

Hence, registration implies more than the sole effect which it had in 1913, i.e. to prohibit all modifications unless the ministry had first been informed. At the present time, it exercises three new effects which brings it close in nature to classification.

- The immediate surroundings of monuments registered on the supplementary list enjoy the same protection in the same conditions and subject to the same limits as classified properties (pursuant to the Act of 25 February 1943).

- The tax advantage under registration match precisely those conferred by classification. The fiscal provisions assimilate registration to classification. Indeed, they speak of "classified or registered properties".

- Finally, any work designed to conserve a registered monument is eligible for financial assistance from the ministry of cultural affairs (pursuant to the Act of 24 May 1951).

The principal differences between classification and registration lie in the following:

The former places buildings under the strict control of the administrative authorities, who may then decide upon the necessary steps to ensure proper conservation. On the other hand, registration does not entitle the authorities to demand of the proprietor that he must carry out the requisite work: they can only encourage him to do so by granting subsidies.

Furthermore, the work carried out on classified monuments must in principle be executed by the architectes des bâtiments de France in regard to maintenance and by the architectes en chef des monuments historiques.

1.1.3 Measures to safeguard "movables"

The Act of 1913 also extended to movable monuments the benefits of the protection provided for buildings (real estate).
As regards procedure, the principles applied are virtually identical.

Procedure

Classification (75,000 classified items of movable property)

If he wishes to classify a movable item of property, the minister must take the following course of action:

- Accept the advice of the commission supérieure des monuments historiques.
  However, he does not turn to the First Section with competence for real estate, but to the Third Section whose composition differs considerably from the former. The appreciation of the problems inherent in movable properties calls for another competence to that needed to judge questions pertaining to buildings. In the latter case, it is necessary to obtain the opinion of architects: as regards movables, the most important people to consult are historians, museum curators, archivists,

- Obtain the permission of the proprietor. Similar to the procedure for buildings, the owner's approval must be obtained prior to the taking of a decision. In the case of movables, this precondition of consulting the proprietor only exists in regard to the classification of movable items of property belonging to private individuals. As regards items belonging to the State, the départements, local authorities and public bodies, approval is sought "after" the decision to classify a monument.

- Similar to the position for buildings, the minister also has to notify the proprietor of the ordinance (or decree) pursuant to article 15.

- On the other hand, movables do not come under the requirement to inform the bureau des hypothèques (mortgage office) so that the legal provisions do not lay down such an obligation for the classification of properties. As a result, the law has replaced registration by the provisions of article 17: "The minister shall arrange for the preparation of a general list of classified movable properties subdivided for each département. An up-to-date copy of this list shall be deposited with the ministry of cultural affairs and the préfecture of each département. Information about entries may be obtained subject to conditions determined by administrative regulations".

The "commission supérieure des monuments historiques" furnishes its advice on the dossier drawn up by the conservateurs des antiquités ou objets d'art and the inspecteurs des monuments historiques and then forwards it in the first instance to the competent departmental commission.

Registration on the supplementary list of historic monuments

Until quite recently, registration was only obligatory for movable items of property (Act of 23/12/1970). The procedure is identical to that for buildings with the important difference, however, that it is not reserved for the minister but for the prefect of each département. The decision to register a property on the supplementary list is announced by the prefect in an ordinance, whilst the consultative body is a local organization, i.e. the commission départementale des objets mobiliers. Nevertheless, this registration has a national character.

A special case: church organs

Pursuant to the Act of 1913, organs were deemed to be movable property and thus eligible for protection in accordance with the arrangements and procedure for protection of that category of items. However, they possess their own characteristic features due to the technical complexity of their construction, so that it is necessary to resort to specialized personnel and different procedures. It is up to the Fifth Section of the commission supérieure des monuments historiques to decide whether an organ is worthy of protection.

The effects of protection of movables

Classification

- A classified property may not be modified, repaired or restored (or even demolished) without the prior consent of the minister (article 23)

- Authorized work may not be executed "outside the supervision of the administrative authorities" (article 22)

- Limited freedom only is granted for the sale or disposal of classified properties belonging to bodies incorporated under public law (article 18)

- The transfer of properties belonging to an individual is free provided that the minister of cultural affairs has been informed within two weeks of the given date (article 19)

- Classified items may not be exported from France (article 21)

- Similar to buildings, they cannot be acquired by prescription (article 18)
- The owners or users of classified items are obliged, subject to a given request, to present them for examination by a duly authorized agent of the minister of cultural affairs (article 23)
- If the owner or user of a classified item is a body incorporated under public law, the latter must observe certain strict requirements concerning the protection and conservation of movable items of property (article 25)
- By way of compensation, these public-law bodies may receive authorization to charge payment fo visitors, the amount in question being determined by the prefect subject to the approval of the minister (article 25)
- The minister may order the provisional removal to a safe place of those classified items whose safety and conservation are deemed to be in jeopardy (article 26)
- Classified items must be catalogued and checked at periodic intervals (article 23).

These requirements take effect as from the notification of the classification decree or, in the case of an "instance de classement", from the notification of the intent to classify a certain item.

These requirements apply to whoever may acquire the properties.

L'instance de classement

The legal effects of this process are identical with those of classification.

Registration (5,000 registered movable items of property)

The legal effects of registration are also very different to those of classification.

Although a fairly close relationship exists between the two measures in respect of the properties, that does not apply to movable items of property.

The effects of the registration of movable items of property are defined in article 24 A.

Registration on the list merely entails "the obligation for the proprietors, managers, occupiers, users, and trustees of classified items not to transfer the latter – except in cases of immediate danger – without having given the administrative authorities one month's prior notification of their intention of doing so".

Hence, registration does not involve very many requirements and in fact it only serves one purpose: to keep the minister informed of the "fate" of the registered property so that he may inform the owner if his envisaged plans are not convenient. That holds particularly true for transfer and modification, repairs or restorations. In the case of a transfer, the obligation resting upon the proprietor to notify the authorities is simply intended to keep the minister informed of the future location of the conserved item. In fact, this recent rule about having to register movable items of property has produced the same result as the registration of buildings, i. e. the acquisition by the minister of a simple right to ensure due protection where necessary by designating the item in question as a classified item.

As such a young institution, the registration of movable items of property has so far only produced constraints and none of the benefits which the statutory listing of buildings

has attained in the course of the years, such as the opportunity to enjoy the support and technical assistance of the "service des monuments historiques" and above all participation by the State in this work.

1.1.4 Legal assistance against measures to protect and conserve historic monuments

The owner of a property (although not a third party) may appeal to the locally competent administrative tribunal that the classification accorded to the former exceeded the powers of the authority in question. Only a defect in law may justify such an appeal. A classification may be terminated by a simple declassification pronounced by the Council of State for building and by a simple ordinance (arrêté) for movables.

1.2 The statutory preservation of sites

The Act promulgated in 1913 on the protection and conservation of historic monuments was supplemented by the Act of 2 May 1930 on historic sites and the Act of 25 February 1943 on the immediate surroundings of a protected monument within a perimeter of 500 metres including both built-up and rural areas. (In exceptional cases, the perimeter may exceed this limit but only on condition that it is fixed by a decree issued by the Council of State after consultations with the "commission supérieure des monuments historiques").

The immediate surroundings (30,000 protected zones)

Under this Act, any work carried out within the "visual range" of a classified or registered building and certain to impair the appearance of the property – irrespective of whether such work has been called for by a private or a public owner – must first be submitted for approval to the minister of culture and of the environment or to his representation (e. g. the prefect) after consulting the "architecte des bâtiments de France".

This Act provides for the classification of a monument not eligible for designation as a historic monument when:
- "its classification is necessary in order to isolate, release or restore a classified property or one proposed for classification"; and when
- the property, "either by itself or when fully constructed, lies within the visual range of a classified property or one proposed for classification".

As in the case of historic monuments, the two most important types of protection are:
- classification and registration.

1.2.1 The classification of sites (6,500 protected sites)

Procedure

This is identical with that for historic monuments. The responsibility for examining protection schemes lies with the conservateur régional des bâtiments de France, who submits each case to the commission supérieure des sites or, in his place, to the commission régionale des opérations immobilières de l'architecte et des espaces protégés.

Similar to the arrangements for historic monuments, a classification can only be given as a matter of principle when the proprietor (whether a private individual or a public body) has given his agreement. In default of this, the Council of State must issue a decree. In such a case, the proprietor may receive compensation.

Effects

These are similar to those emanating from a classification of historic monuments. They invariably hold good for the site and not for the proprietor.

1.2.2 Registration on the supplementary list of sites

Procedure

Again, this is virtually identical with that for historic monuments. However, a close coordination of views may be established with the locally elected representatives during the examination of the case by the "conservateur régional des bâtiments de France" and as a result of the publicity and notification procedure. In effect, the proposal about registering a property is first communicated to the mayors of the local authorities in question by the prefect so as to obtain the advice of the municipal councils. The registration is set forth in a ministerial ordinance issued after consultations with the "commission départementale des sites".

Effects

These are identical with those attendant upon the registration of historic monuments. Two other types of site protection have been envisaged:

- the introduction of "protection zones" envisaged by the Act of 1930 (which we should not confound with the protection afforded to the immediate surroundings of historic monuments. In principle, this covers a wider area than that of classified sites. "All large-scale projects of whatever kind, whether of interest to all or part of the zone, may be submitted for advice" to the minister of culture and the environment.

- The "sensitive zones" (directive issued by the Minister of Construction in October 1960) where building permits remain subject to certain recommendations. Within this framework, it is possible to designate "sensitive perimeters" designed to protect neighbouring zones.

Those sites whose interest consists largely in their fauna and flora may be declared nature reserves, regional parks or even "national parks" whose conditions of protection are deemed to be much more important. Both in order to assist in examining the protection given to the immediate surroundings of historic monuments and to sites, the ministry of culture has set up an atelier de la création architecturale which helps to study the projects. This studio may be consulted by departmental and regional services of the direction de l'architecture.

1.3 Protection of historic quarters

1.3.1 Designation of protected sectors

The Act of 4 August 1962 (known as the Malraux Law) completes this legislation, which extended the concept of a "protected sector" to urban housing possessing architectural value.

Procedure

The creation of a protected sector requires first of all a detailed examination of the project by the local councillors and the representatives of the ministry of culture and the environment as well as by an architect enjoying the confidence of both parties. The cost of carrying out these studies is borne entirely by the ministry of culture and the environment. This study then goes to the municipal authorities for approval and then to the "commission nationale des secteurs sauvegardés" for the same purpose.

If a favorable opinion is pronounced, the perimeter of the sector is definitively fixed by an interministerial Resolution issued by the ministry of culture and the environment and the ministry of equipment. If an unfavourable opinion is pronounced, recourse may be had to a decree issued by the Prime Minister following studies carried out by the Council of State. However, no-one has yet availed himself of this possibility.

Once that the delimitation of the perimeter has been accepted, a permanent plan of protection and development is carefully studied and submitted to the commission nationale des secteurs sauvegardés, in whose deliberations the mayor participates on a consultative basis, and also to the commission nationale des monuments historiques when the sector in question warrants this.

This plan is then promulgated in a decree issued by the Council of State pursuant to a report jointly issued by the minister of culture and the environment, the minister of equipment, and the minister of the interior.

Once published, the plan is submitted to the general population so as to acquaint it with the policy being pursued. The document setting out the protected sector contains the same provisions as a land-development plan (plan d'occupation des sols). It is a relatively complex document drawn up under the supervision of an architect designated by the mayor with the approval of the ministry of culture and the environment and the ministry of equipment.

Effects

The immediate impact of the publication of the interministerial ordinance fixing the limits of the protected sector is to subject to prior authorization "any work likely to modify the state of the property". This control is exercised by the architecte des bâtiments de France, or by the architect entrusted with this function in regard to the protected sector.

In the geographic zone in question, the protection scheme supersedes any detailed town planning scheme or land development plan already in existence and replaces them in regard to future use.

The implementation of safeguarding policies for the protected sector is at present governed by three principal joint methods of restoring decaying properties:

- Les îlots opérationnels, carried out under conditions determined by the decree of 31 December 1958 on urban renewal.

This first method consists in choosing a segment of the protected sector by virtue of its qualities and the urgency of the work and rehabilitation envisaged under the protection plan. The group of houses chosen for restoration (îlot opérationnel) must serve as an example and stimulus for the remaining buildings within the protected sector. A set of records (dossier) is prepared in accordance with an interministerial study conducted jointly with the municipality and then presented to a société d'économie mixte pursuant to the terms of an agreement concluded between the latter and the local government. This company ist then entrusted with the implementation of the work. It obtains its funds from local institutions holding the majority of the shares. These para-administrative companies function in a similar manner to private firms, obtaining their finance from public sources (governmental or municipal subsidies with funds guaranteed by the FNAFU) as well as from private sources such as banks or the proprietors themselves. Examples of these companies are SOREMA for le Marais in Paris, SEMIRELY in Lyons and SEMIRESA in Sarlat. One organization designed to restore our legacy of historic properties possessing national interest, SARPI, was set up by the Caisse Nationale des marchés de l'Etat with the aim of promoting relations between the State and the municipalities within the framework of "sociétés d'économie mixte". Most of these companies stem from SARPI. However, other organizations also take part in the management of restoration schemes, such as the "Société centrale pour l'équipement du Territoire", an offshoot of the Société civile et immobilière de la Caisse des Dépôts et Consignations, or SAREF, which was set up by the Banque de Paris et des Pays-Bas.

AFU

The owners of these properties may also join the Associations Foncières Urbaines (AFU) on terms laid down by the Act of 4 August 1962 as defined in the decree of 26 February 1974 in regard to the conservation, restoration and development of protected sectors.

ARIM

A third possibility flowed from the Act of 12 July 1967 which was designed to inspire the proprietors and tenants of historic properties to subject their properties to norms of health and equipment as defined by decree. This applies to small-scale activities enjoying the support of the Agence Nationale pour l'Amélioration de l'Habitat (ANAH).

Under the aegis of PACT centres (Propagande et Actions contre le Taudis), a number of Associations de Restauration Immobilières (ARIM) may set up at local and regional level and discharge the functions of a société d'économie mixte.

1.3.2 The scheme for the 100 towns

Apart from the protected sectors, it was the exception rather than the rule before 1974 to find the Direction de l'Architecture financing studies on the protection, development and rehabilitation of old towns.

The scheme for the 100 towns, initiated in the autumn of 1974, provided for a steady increase in the scale of budgetary funds earmarked for studies. This new policy marked a genuine move in town planning by the Direction de l'Architecture outside of protected sectors.

In order to give firm substance to the proposals about registration on the list of historic town centres envisaged under the Act of 2 May 1930, a series of studies was set in train, with priority being given to the 100 towns whose architectural legacy seemed to be in jeopardy or where interministerial action was projected or else actually in progress. By February 1977, urban planning studies had been carried out on 46 of the 100 towns with a population of over 20,000 inhabitants which featured on the original list.

The few other projects currently in hand mean that half of the original total has been reached.

As regards the type of urban area studied, the application of the accepted criteria usually results in prime consideration being given to the large and medium-sized towns.

The studies on protection schemes and on the 100 towns undertaken as from October 1974 in the context of effecting an architectural contribution to preparing documents on town planning and a search for means of revitalizing old, declining town-centres have promoted the introduction of operations designed to accompany systematic rehabilitation and formed a third starting-point for the rehabilitation of sectors inspired by the wish to improve housing standards.

The current perspectives for this policy are as follows:

– to pursue and increase agreement with the other administrative bodies and with the "Society for Urban Planning" (Fonds d'aménagement urbain) during the stage when the choice of towns and the contents of studies are being determined;

– to enlist the services of the architects working in the provinces more than hitherto;

– to attempt more systematically the insertion in the P.O.S. (article 11) of the findings of the studies; to encourage a close relationship between the list of tenders for the registered sites and the P.O.S.;

– to render work (such as notes, maps, legends) more amenable to comparison and thus easier to use;

– to increase access by professionals, researchers and students to the funds for urban studies.

1.3.3 The scheme for "villages"

At the present time, one can observe a faster rate of decline in the fundamental and significant features of our rural heritage, i. e. in the villages and hamlets:

– the complete abandonment of houses resulting in the dilapidation of dwellings deemed to be unhealthy and lacking in modern facilities;

– the modernization and development of an old building which, apart from the destruction of interior space, also involves a modification in exterior dimensions, entrances and materials;

– "embellishments" based on an imitation of suburban bungalows;

– new buildings simply erected anywhere without consideration for the surroundings, thus destroying the harmony of the villages and hamlets.

Mindful of these problems, the minister of agriculture and the minister of culture and the environment have endeavoured to find solutions.

The scheme for villages is the objective of a priority programme for upgrading the rural zones.

The aims of the programme do not merely concern the rehabilitation of old buildings within their village setting, but also the development of jointly used areas such as local roads, underground telephone cables, sconts, squares, fountains, wash-houses . . .; the rehabilitation and re-utilization of jointly used buildings (working men's clubs, village institutes, rural societies, old people's homes, etc.).

This operation must go hand in hand with the economic revitalization of the village by means of the study and encouragement of integrated activities in agriculture, small-scale production, tourism and even industry. The essential thing is to prevent villages from simply becoming museums.

The scheme for villages has given rise to three types of complementary assistance by the public authorities:

– the financing of studies on development and also technical and architectural assistance for the preparation of programmes and the execution of work:

– a scheme for providing more information for villagers and arousing their awareness of the quality of their heritage and the need to safeguard it;

– the provision of substantial funds to the municipality for developmental activities and of subsidies to private individuals so as to help them to improve their accommodation.

The scheme began in 21 villages at the end of 1976, and it is expected that about 40 local authorities will benefit from the new scheme in 1977.

Apart from the simple consideration of aesthetic appeal, the restoration and revitalization of our architectural legacy rest on numerous town-planning studies backed by important socio-economic and constructional analyses.

Whether the subject matter is the achievement of a balance in the popular quarters, poor people's ghettos, districts undergoing speculative redevelopment or in the villages, the important consideration remains to find and adopt a global and balanced strategy both at local and regional level.

The means of expressing this overall strategy of balance are furnished by:
the different instruments of regional and local land planning; regional programmes for economic development (P.D.R.E.); overall development and urban planning schemes (SDAU); land-development plans (POS); overall schemes for centres (PRAC) for local planning and for medium-sized towns.

With a view to restraining any undue land and property speculation, the town-planning code permits local authorities to designate zones of differentiated planning, i. e. zones d'aménagement différé (Z.A.D.). These ZADs usually cover larger territories than those of the protected sectors.

A policy of restoration and revitalization could not really be implemented unless all the groups affected are integrated within it and moreover the local population adheres to it. At a later stage, we shall see the importance of the societies set up to defend or promote schemes in this sphere.

2. The Financing of Restoration

2.1 Individual efforts

2.1.1 Classified historic monuments

The responsibility for regional work rests with the architects des bâtiments de France and the architectes en chef des monuments historiques.

Nevertheless it is the private or public proprietor who actually initiates the work which must then be carried out under the supervision of the authorized architects.

The ministry of culture has, however, had the right since 1966 to require a proprietor to execute certain indispensable work if he is a private individual.

The proprietor may appeal to the administrative tribunal against this requirement. If the ordinance containing the latter is quashed by the court, the cost of the work falls entirely on the State.

A proprietor may also call upon the State to expropriate the property. The State's share of the cost of maintenance is at least 50 % of the total expense of the work in question.

Apart from the subsidy given to a proprietor, the latter may deduct in full these 50 % from his income for tax purposes.

If he does not receive a subsidy and moreover keeps his monument open to visitors 50 days per year, he qualifies for a deduction for tax purposes of 93,7 %.

In addition, a proprietor may also obtain assistance from the local and département authorities.

2.1.2 Registered historic monuments

If the proprietor of a registered historic monument is a private person, the State only bears the expense of 10 % of maintenance work and even then this subsidy is only accorded in exceptional cases. If there is a subsidy, the proprietor may deduct the remainder of the cost of the work from his income for tax purposes.

No requirement may be imposed for ordinary registered monuments. The conservation of the property depends solely on the good-will of the proprietor, who may order the work to be done by the architect of his choice even if he receives a subsidy.

Available funds for the restoration of buildings of architectural merit

Normal Designation of the Property	Proprietor	Available Public Assistance
I.		
Historic Monuments and classified items of movable property	Département Municipality Public-law body or private individual	State State-département council State-département council Municipal Council
II.		
Monuments registered on the supplementary list of historic monuments	Département	State
Sites on the supplementary list of sites	Municipality	State-département council
Properties in the immediate surroundings of classified historic monuments or on the supplementary list	Public-law body or private individual	State Département council Municipal council
Properties located in the protected sectors		

2.1.3 Movable items of property

The responsibility for support and assistance devolves upon the inspection générale des objets mobiliers with private owners being at liberty either to carry out the desired work or not. If they do decide in favour, the work must be carried out under the supervision of the inspectors-general for the properties in question or the "conservateurs des antiquités ou objets d'art". Moreover, it must be done at their expense. This financial responsibility also applies to public-law bodies. Nevertheless, the State has the right of compelling the latter to take action if the work in question is absolutely necessary and urgent. But in such a case, the State often bears 50 % of the cost.

2.2 Financial assistance

Alongside the classical types of assistance provided by the State and the local authorities (subsidies, preferential tax treatment, etc.) and in order to enable proprietors of good will to bear the cost of restoration and maintenance, there exist certain kinds of financial help such as supplementary loans by the Caisse Centrale de Crédit hôtelier, industriel et commercial backed by the Caisse nationale des monuments historiques et des sites. These loans, which may account for up to 30 % of the total cost of the work, carry an interest rate of 7 % and must be authorized within 10 years.

Requests for loans must be made to the Conservation régionale des bâtiments de France.

In the protected sectors, the work carried out at the proprietor's initiative benefits in particular from:

– loans from the Crédit Foncier or ANAH in respect of "ordinary" work;

– subsidies from the ministry of culture and the environment for the financing of "aesthetic surcharges";

– subsidies from the ministry of equipment for "town-planning surcharges".

If the work is carried out within the framework of a public scheme, the assistance comes from a subsidy (known as a balancing subsidy) to offset the deficit incurred by virtue of the operation: the société d'économie mixte entrusted with the operation receives loans from the Fonds national d'aménagement foncier et d'urbanisme (FNAFU).

Be that as it may, it should however be pointed out that this financial assistance is usually only granted if the restoration and development work features in a plan régional de développement économique (P.R.D.E.).

2.3 Le Fonds d'Aménagement Urbain (F.A.U.)

This organization for urban planning and development was created pursuant to an ordinance dated 24 August 1976. Its function consists in administering urban development centres. Its members comprise the directors of land development and town planning bodies, of building, architecture, social action, local public-law corporations, the budget, the Secrétariat de la Commission nationale du Logement des immigrés et de l'Agence Nationale pour l'Amélioration de l'Habitat (ANAH).

We should emphasize the essential role to be played by the administrative authorities at département level.

The restitution of unhealthy dwellings and the restoration of buildings are to be promoted whilst, for the time being, urban renewal will only take place on a limited scale. Furthermore, assistance will be provided for rehousing poor families. Credit will be made available for financing the maintenance and restoration of the original architectural quality.

The development activities which the FAU may subsidize are: replastering (with or without reconstruction), the restoring of houses and groups of buildings of architectural merit by private co-proprietors and public or semi-public bodies, the refurbishing of monuments and buildings of outstanding quality with the aim of achieving urban revitalization, and all support of the same kind seen to be the most appropriate for the individual case.

2.4 Other supplementary sources of finance

Apart from the fact that local housing bodies may borrow money from the Caisse des Dépôts et Consignations (deposit bank), several interministerial funds have recently been set up for the purpose of participating at fairly small cost in operations which open up other sources of credit.

– Le Fonds d'intervention pour l'aménagement du territoire (F.I.A.T.), attached to the prime Minister's Office, was established in order to finance "opérations complémentaires d'équipement du territoire". Its contribution is limited to 20 % of the work in question. (The budget for the last two years has amounted to 270 million francs.)

– Le Fonds d'Intervention Culturelle (F.I.C.) created in 1971, whose credits stem from several ministries, falls under the responsibility of the ministry of culture and the environment. It provides funds exclusively for interministerial experimental schemes, which must then subsist without its support. (Since its creation in 1976, it has taken part in 162 experimental measures involving the expenditure of 28 million francs.)

– Le Fonds d'intervention pour l'action sur la nature et l'environnement (F.I.A.N.E.), administered by the Prime Minister's Office, was set up for the "financement complémentaire des investissements intéressant la protection de la nature et de l'environnement". (In 1971, it spent 53 million francs; in 1972, 85 millions)

3. The Promotion and Revitalization of Historic Buildings and Monuments

Just like Italy and Great Britain, France is one of the countries in Europe which still possess an immense architectural heritage representing a large proportion of the buildings which have survived from the past.

In recent years, the problem of utilizing historic monuments has become highly alarming. In effect, many of these buildings still belong to private owners, who encounter more and more difficulties in maintaining them or, if they cannot manage at all, to find people willing to acquire such accommodation.

As regards churches and other religious property, the exodus of people from the countryside and the dwindling number of clergymen present grave problems.

Moreover, public institutions (hospitals, barracks, etc.) tend to concentrate in new, well-functioning centres. Another factor is the impact of the public campaign conducted for the last few years, which has made people more aware of the situation and less willing to accept or comprehend such a utilization of our legacy of historic monuments.

It is also necessary to rehabilitate old houses and old quarters by adopting the requisite measures for meeting the social, economic, cultural and practical needs of our society whether they be everyday or only occasional needs. Hence, the rehabilitation of old quarters and houses must take into account the current standards of comfort in housing and also include the general renewal of the quarter as well as the provision of an appropriate infrastructure and superstructure. The activities carried out in historic buildings must be developed along lines which do not alter their character.

It would be quite wrong simply to restore an edifice for aesthetic reasons. It is indispensable to maintain the original function of the building or to accord it a new one in keeping with its architecture and interior layout and also mindful of the surroundings and character of the town. It is up to the sous-direction de la création architecturale to watch over internal reorganization in order to ensure an adaption of the monument to its new function based on respect for the integrity of our historic legacy.

The same holds true of old town-centres which have to be infused with new life and accompanied by a certain degree of continuity in local traditional trade and industry, whilst care is taken to avoid speculation.

3.1 Education

3.1.1 Adult education at the university

In this context, we shall not draw the reader's attention to the State schools for the fine arts but simply mention the efforts undertaken by certain universities during recent years to organize, parallel to courses in the history of classic art, other courses specially devised for older people.

An interesting experiment in this field has been carried out recently at the University of Nanterre and in a number of other universities in the provinces.

3.1.2 The education of schoolchildren

This poses an enormous problem and one which remains far from a solution in France.

In principle, it is the history teachers who also provide instruction in the history of art and they wish to retain this privilege.

Sometimes in the more senior classes (2ème cycle), drawing teachers also devote part of their lessons to the history of art, although they teach it from a different angle.

Our architectural legacy only occupies a very small part in these syllabuses, and in any case it is a subject which remains poorly represented as a whole.

Nevertheless, one undertaking has been particularly successful within the framework of the new reform of education:

seven hours per week have been set aside for "activités d'éveil" during the preparatory stage of primary school instruction with the intention of arousing children's curiosity in all spheres of culture, including that of France's architectural heritage.

A new system known as "le tiers-temps pédagogique" has been introduced for the junior classes (1er cycle). This differs somewhat from the British approach, for example, in that the idea is not to dedicate the afternoons to cultural instruction and sport but solely to inspire and authorize the teachers to devote a certain number of hours per week to cultural activities of their own free choice. This formula has been welcomed by the ministry of culture and the environment, which sets out to increase the scale of cultural activities provided for young people and to encourage the formation of cultural groups especially for them.

Although the institution of a "tiers-temps pédagogique" was particularly constructive and interesting in theory, it is hardly feasible at the present time for financial reasons. No special credit has yet been set aside by the ministry of education. So far, this experiment has only taken place in those academies to which the local authorities have allotted a financial grant. It is to be hoped that this practice will soon spread.

In addition, schools often organize photography or drawing competitions on local cultural attractions and take part, with the help of the Secretary of State's office for Youth and Sport and the Caisse Nationale des Monuments Historiques et des Sites, in competitions for revitalizing historic monuments and sites. These activities may be held either under the aegis of the individual school or else the academy itself which organizes cooperation between several schools.

In many instances, the Fonds d'intervention culturelle makes a financial contribution to these school activities.

One cultural activity has already been practised throughout the schools in a certain region – the "Roman Year in Poiton – Charentes". Two similar operations are now under consideration: "Burgundy today: the defence of its cultural legacy" (a highly generalized theme) and the "Protection of Lille's architectural Heritage".

In order to prepare teachers for this new type of active cultural instruction, the ministry of education organizes courses with some of them being devoted to outstanding local architecture:

– the evolution of different types of settlement and rural life, the extension of cities and the development of town planning, the permanence and evolution of networks of communication and the mutual links which they forge among the local populations;

– an active search for traces of ancient history: relics and prehistoric objects, historic monuments, old districts in protected zones, and rural architecture.

In 1976, all academies introduced courses in local culture. Under this new approach, art education may also include (as from the 6th class) not only drawing and music but also architectural and town-planning studies. The 5th and 6th classes spend two hours per week on art instruction as do the 1st and 2nd classes. The syllabus has not yet been fixed for the 3rd and 4th classes.

Finally, teachers are able within the general framework of secondary education to devote 10 % of their time at school to any activities of their choice including cultural subjects.

3.2   The dissemination of information via the media

3.2.1 The press

Apart from the revue des monuments historiques edited by the Caisse Nationale des Monuments Historiques et des Sites, which appears every two months as a profusely illustrated magazine for the specialists and general public, there is no periodical in France devoted to historic monuments or the old quarters of towns.

As regards the national or even local dailies or weeklies, there is no regular column on these problems. It must, however, be pointed out that – thanks to direct contacts with the direction de l'architecture, the press and information service of the C.N.M.H.S., the representatives of the associations for defending and promoting France's architectural heritage and also interested individual journalists – articles sometimes appear in the major daily newspapers. The articles cover general aspects of policy in this field or special campaigns or events (the prizewinners of competitions, festivals, interviews with famous personalities, etc.) or the simple dissemination of facts taken from dispatches sent by l'Agence France – Presse.

The local press assigns greater coverage to these problems than the national press, particulary in South France where a high level of cultural activity prevails.

3.2.2 Radio

Here, too, there is still no regular programme on this subject. However, attention should be drawn to France-Culture, which goes to a certain amount of trouble to broadcast interviews. Naturally, important items of information are included in the general news.

3.2.3 Television

There is only one regular weekly feature (on Channel 2) known as "Chefs d'oeuvre en péril". This programme stems from the personal initiative of its author and producer, Pierre de Lagarde, who also launched a parallel programme "le concours des chefs d'œvres en péril" with the aid of radio and television and also the C.N.M.H.S. His programme possesses particular importance because it is currently unique of its kind and in its regular appearance. It exercises a wideranging impact. The series is dedicated to historic monuments in general and castles or private houses in particular, all of them either classified or registered.

Furthermore, Channel 2 provides information programmes on these questions within the framework of its afternoon broadcasts, particulary on the occasion of important manifestations or events.

Channel 2 also has a weekly programme called "La France défigurée" with 2 or 3 hours dedicated to the defence of our architectural heritage.

For about two months now, T.F.I. has broadcast a new monthly magazine on cultural matters entitled "Expressions" on Sundays at 10 p.m.. This series is produced by Maurice Bruzek on the whole range of cultural life with about 10 minutes in each programme devoted to France's architectural legacy.

F.R. 3 also broadcasts special programmes from time to time, usually at regional level but sometimes also on a national basis.

Films are sometimes presented to mark certain events of national significance. An example of this was "Europa Nostra" to mark European Architectural Heritage Year.

But there still remains much to be done in France so as to enlist the services of the press in arousing and informing the general public.

3.3   Inspiring and informing the general public

This task always devolves upon the Caisse Nationale des Monuments Historiques et des Sites.

3.3.1 Information centres and information rooms

The C.N.M.H.S. has set up three centres in France for keeping the population informed:

– in Paris (at its headquarters in Hôtel de Sully);

– at Poitiers (opened in 1974); and

– at Montpellier (due to open in 1978).

At these centres, the C.N.M.H.S. has proposed three types of service:

– gaining the interest of the population and keeping it informed by editing leaflets on Paris and the provinces and by providing colour-slides;

– selling works including several which it edits itself. These books and leaflets are also on sale on the counters of the Caisse at the historic monuments which it manages; and

– providing documentation.

In the case of the most important monuments, the C.N.M.H.S. has set up "salles d'Information" to present temporary exhibitions and tourist information.

In addition, the C.N.M.H.S. participates in a certain number of schemes to promote local attractions such as the editing of leaflets on certain quarters (in Paris, Lille, Lyons).

3.3.2 Audio-visual presentations

These take place on a more limited scale within the framework of visits to historic monuments administered by the C.N.M.H.S..

3.3.3 Specialized guided tours throughout France

These "visites – conférences" form an integral part of the development of historic monuments and old quarters (especially in protected sectors).

The Caisse Nationale des Monuments Historiques et des Sites organizes guides tours of Paris, the Paris region and – within the framework of the activities organized in artistic towns and historic or ancient town-centres – in 70 towns possessing outstanding architecture or a historic heritage of unusual significance. The Caisse also does this for a very large number of historic monuments.

On an average, these guided tours last an hour and a half. They take place under the direction of specialists, very often the holders of degrees in art and history, who are recruited by means of an open competition. The tours afford an opportunity to present both the monuments themselves as well as the historic town quarters, whether in protected zones or not.

In Paris and the Ile de France, these visits are organized every day during the whole year in three forms:

– visits organized for individuals with a widely distributed programme appearing every two months to furnish all the requisite details;

– visits "à la carte" in response to a request by groups;

– walking tours for children with topics adapted to their school syllabuses. This has acquired much greater importance since the institution of the "tiers-temps pédagogique" in French schools. We shall revert to this subject at a later stage.

In 1976, the guided tours attracted more than 600,000 visitors to the art towns alone; with Paris recording 280,000 and the major monuments more than 50,000.

This policy of interesting the general public and carrying out a programme of revitalization has progressed substantially in major campaigns known as "tourisme culturel" promoted by several ministerial departments including those for tourism and the environment and also the C.N.M.H.S., who also expect the local public authorities and private associations to cooperate with them. Every year, they deal with a different theme. In 1973, it was the castles of Burgundy; in 1974, the castles and hills of Auvergne; in 1975, Gothic art in Picardy; and in 1976, Romanesque art in Poitou-Charentes.

3.4 Private associations and foundations

3.4.1 Measures adopted by private associations

The Caisse Nationale des Monuments Historiques et des Sites (C.N.M.H.S.) and the local public associations are not alone in this policy of gaining the interest of the general public and revitalizing our architectural heritage. Gradually, private associations have come into being with the aim of:

– defending France's architectural heritage; and also

– promoting it.

The "associations de défense" were founded spontaneously to conduct a campaign to safeguard a certain quarter or old buildings when the latter are threatened by speculative developers or simple negligence on the part of the proprietor or the public and local authorities or even the two factors together. The hub of large urban areas, for example, has often remained a centre of activities claiming more and more room for facilities – a phenomenon which, in conjunction with the rarity and price of the real estate there, attracts the speculators. The latter then replace the old unprofitable housers by high-rise buildings, thus destroying the unity of the quarter and breaking its architectural and social unity.

Only when the population is confronted day by day with the damage to our architectural heritage caused by massive urban sprawl, the unceasing development of communications, installations, the large scale of urban renovation and the repeated stumbling from one failure to the next in contemporary town planning has a growing part of public opinion become aware of the problem of quality of life and notably, in this sphere, of the whole range of our cultural legacy in the form of architecture and nature. It is this which gives rise to the setting up of "associations de défense" who undertake considerable efforts to achieve their aims (e.g. l'association des amis du vieux Lyon, du vieux Lille, du vieux Annecy, du Paris historique etc.).

They offer the greatest possible resistance to these speculative development schemes for transforming the appearance of old quarters by appealing to the local authorities and public bodies and also by organizing an information campaign based on the issue of leaflets, informational pamphlets or even brochures on restoration techniques (such as that produced by the Friends of Old Strasbourg on restoring old Alsatian houses) and on the organization of restoration competitions.

Promotion campaigns are naturally grafted on to defence campaigns to revitalize a quarter or certain buildings by ensuring the latter's inclusion on established tourist routes, by arranging for good signposting, by cooperating in the establishment of festivals or cultural and trade activities and by writing small books and leaflets.

Whether these associations are geared more to the defence or more to the promotion of old quarters and buildings, they often – though unfortunately not always – work hand in hand with local authorities from whom they may receive subsidies, as well as with public organizations such as the C.N.M.H.S. for revitalization schemes or the direction de l'Architecture for restoration schemes.

3.4.2 Foundations

These are often still very rare in France, at least in the legal sense of the term, because they often blend with associations. The legal phenomenon of a foundation such as it exists in the United States for example hardly receives any encouragement under French tax laws. What we in France call a "foundation" is usually only an association governed by the law of 1901, but whose creation is the work of a single family or a group of persons or an industry with the aim of promoting a good cause. Examples are la Fondation Royaumont (created by a family) to promote music and also to provide a meeting place for other cultural activities, le centre de l'Abbaye de Sénanque (founded by an industry) and le collège d'échanges contemporains de St. Maximim (group of persons and of industries). The only organization with a full right to the title of foundation is la Fondation de France, whose terms of reference are the study of cultural and scientific problems.

3.5 Participation by private individuals in the conservation or improvement of their quality of life

The role played by private citizens in measures designed to ensure the aesthetic protection of our architectural legacy has been a constant factor in French law. However, its application has been extended more and more.

When a site is to be classified or a zone of protection set up, the law stipulates that a public inquiry must be opened so that all those who have something to say may present their observations. The same holds true of the acceptance of safeguarding schemes in protected sectors (Act of 4 August 1962). past experience has taught us that these inquiries, which remained fairly theoretical for a fairly long period of time, now generate a wide measure of interest among the general public who participate in large numbers.

The French law-makers held the view for a long period of time that normal representatives of the public were the elected deputies, who received a mandate for precisely such representation and who were obliged by the statutes and the rules to consult the town councils. The elaboration of the land – development schemes (POS – Plans d'occupation des sols) has been automatically linked with this since the law on the reform of town planning (31 December 1976). This means that the group of those obliged to accept its orders includes not only interested officials and technicians, but also the representatives of the town council. However, this official representation did not seem adequate. The most senior State authorities have insisted that the protection associations must be able to air their views in the committees dealing with the interests which they defend:

Commissions départementales et nationales des Sites, Commission nationale des secteurs sauvegardés. The implementing decree in respect of the law on the protection of nature has clarified the conditions of the authorization to be accorded by the associations. The law-makers' concern has in effect been to avoid giving a blocking vote to associations which cannot fail to be an amalgamation of private interests.

In keeping with the same line of thinking, "associations foncières urbaines" (AFU) may be endowed with privileges derived from the public authorities in order to carry out certain town-planning operations of a limited nature. The same applies to the associations de restauration immobilière (ARIM).

Finally, in their concern to meet the growing interest of the population in the quality of life, the town councils have very often created extra-municipal commissions on the environment. Most of these commissions came into being after the last municipal elections (in March 1977) so that it is still too early to judge their efficiency.

One thing remains clear. It is the general interest produced by all the problems inherent in the quality of life which has led the general public on the one hand to maximum use of all the legal means of providing support and, on the other, to demand access to the files and moreover legal status. The defence campaigns have gained an advantage on one important point: those campaigns which are authorized have the right of audience in court.

3.6 The utilization and revitalization of historic monuments

This may be carried out in various forms and, in particular, in two sectors of contemporary activity: the "tertiary" sector of the economy and cultural life. The activities which these engender are compatible with the character of old buildings which, in turn, usually prove suitable for adaption to their requirements and for satisfaction of the latter.

It is evidently preferable to succeed in establishing permanent activities in historic monuments. This is a difficult exercise by virtue of the scale of capital required both for the establishment of premises (since it is necessary to adapt

the monument to its new function and to adapt the function to the constraints imposed by the monument) as well as for their later role. When the task is impossible, one must try to create interim or semi-permanent activities.

3.6.1 Permanent activities

Economic activities

Sometimes, this utilization comes from private initiatives with the agreement and sometimes with the financial aid of public and local authorities. Illustrations of this are castles or very fine houses converted by their owners into hotels (e.g. Château de Mercuès near Cahors).

Industrial concerns sometimes purchase historic buildings to house their registered offices (e.g. St. Raphael in le Marais at Paris) or to use as a staff centre (e.g. Château de Menars purchased by St. Gobain to set up a permanent educational centre).

In most cases, however, the utilization results from a combination of private, local and public initiative (e.g. the creation of a congress hall in the Papal Palace at Avignon.

Public administrative bodies also use old historic buildings. In Paris, the C.N.M.H.S. occupies l'hôtel de Béthune-Sully: the administrative tribunal is housed in l'hôtel d'Aumont; and numerous ministries and embassies have acted in similar fashion. The provinces furnish many instances of historic buildings being acquired by the préfectures, the mayor's offices, chambers of commerce, research establishments and educational bodies. The accommodation of the European Institute of Ecology in le cloître des Récollets at Meth may be cited as a model example.

Cultural activities

This is a difficult task and one which la Caisse Nationale des Monuments Historiques et des Sites (C.N.M.H.S.) undertakes in addition to its many other activities. As a public establishment under the direction of the ministry of culture and the environment set up by the Act of 10 July 1914, as amended by the ordinance of 7 March 1945, the C.N.M.H.S. pursues two principal courses of action:

– the utilization and revitalization of historic monuments and historic quarters; and

– accommodating, informing and influencing the public.

Clearly, many French museums are housed in historic buildings (such as le Louvre). For a number of years now, assistance has been provided by the C.N.M.H.S. for a more and more frequent conversion of historic monuments into meeting places and centres for cultural exchange. Examples of this are the cultural centre in the chateau de Valprivas, the seat of the Centre internationale de recherche et de création artistique (C.I.R.C.A.) in la Chartreuse at Villeneuve-les-Avignons or the five private centres of art grouped together in the association of the same name (the centres of contemporary art in Lacour and the abbey at Beaulieu-en-Rouergue, the cultural association of la Mayenne housed in the castle of Sainte Suzanne and the art centres at Ratilly and Flains. The function which these five centres have given themselves is to make accessible to a wide-ranging public, particularly in the provinces, the most original and innovative forms of expression in the domain of art.

Activities which are both economic and cultural

Here again the C-N.M.H.S. sets out to promote in the regions a number of centres for meetings and exchanges of views on cultural and economic matters and these centres are housed in historic buildings. Some of these centres have already been set up and grouped in the Association des Centres de recontres et de séjours – created some three years ago on the initiative of the C.N.M.H.S.. Similar examples are the centre at the abbey des Prémontrès at Pont-à-Mousson, the Claude Nicolas Ledoux Foundation for Reflexions on the Future housed in the old salt-work buildings at d'Arc-et-Senans (Doubs), the cultural centre in the abbey at Sénanque and the Cultural Centre of the West soon to be opened in the abbey of Fontevraud and to serve three regions.

3.6.2 Temporary or semi-permanent activities

It is not always possible to establish a permanent activity. That is why the C.N.M.H.S. goes to great efforts and spends substantial sums of money to attract economic, cultural or economic-cultural activities, whether temporary or semi-permanent, to the historic buildings and sites.

This campaign serves a dual purpose: to revitalize and temporarily place the historic monument in the midst of our modern economic life and at the same time to direct the attention and interest of the citizens and their elected representatives to the architectural heritage of France.

The letting of halls

With this in mind, the C.N.M.H.S. administers certain halls and large rooms in its historic buildings and hires them out to individuals or clubs for the holding of meeting, discussions, cocktail parties, balls, dinners, etc. Mention may be made of la salle Saint-Louis de la Conciergerie at Paris, the château de Maisons at Maisons-Laffitte, the château de Chambord, the Alsatian house in le château du Haut Koenigsbourg, the rooms in the palais du Rhin at Strasbourg, the rooms in la Cité de Carassonne, etc.

Festivals

Festivals attract a large audience who discover the setting of the performance in the best conditions.

In Paris, le festival du Marais aroused interest in the old district of Marais, which had been completely neglected and left to decline, and thus played a big part in having it made into a protected sector. The same may be said of the foremost festival of all – that of Aix-en-Provence, the festivals of Avignon and Saintes, etc..

The C.N.M.H.S. makes every effort to inspire and assist these local initiatives. Other administrative sections at the ministry of culture and the environment often join in these efforts: la direction de la musique, sometimes la direction du théâtre, le Fonds d'Intervention Culturelle, etc.

Son et Lumière

These spectacles were an enormous success right from the beginning. The C.N.M.H.S. gives them considerable assistance or even runs them completely (as at Chambord). At the present time it must be admitted that this vogue is declining and they are tending to give way to other types of presentation.

Temporary exhibitions

These important (and mostly touring) exhibitions are set up to illustrate the architectural heritage of France. Examples of some of the most recent ones are: Palladio, les grandes demeures angevines du XIX siècle, les Tardins 1760–1820, les fresques de Saint Savin and Nancy architecture 1900.

Competitions for revitalizing sites and historic monuments

These are currently being organized by la Caisse Nationale des Monuments Historiques et des Sites to arouse the interest of young people in particular in the need to integrate the legacy of the past life of their region.

Les chantiers de jeunes

The C.N.M.H.S. thus embarks upon several schemes for making young people aware of the problems. For example, it organizes every year a competition with prizes for the best results among young teams of voluntary helpers who restore historic monuments in their leisure time. Between 1967 and 1975, the C.N.M.H.S. awarded prizes worth 1,370,000 francs to 200 teams of helpers ("chantiers").

Since 1975, this competition has also appeared in a different form comprising two phases:

– the awarding of scholarship for short courses in technical studies to voluntary associations to encourage them to prepare their scheme of work with great care; and

– the awarding of prizes to recompense the efforts of working teams or those voluntarily taking further technical studies.

These voluntary working teams of young helpers are always followed up by architectes des bâtiments de France ou des sites. They form associations which in turn form federations – the most important one being L'Union Rempart. All these associations and federations depend in a general manner on a liaison body vis-à-vis the public authorities known as "Cotravaux" and meaning "cogestion" (codetermination for the voluntary work of young people). It receives financial assistance in particular from the ministry of culture and the environment (direction de l'Architecture), the Secretary of State's Office for Youth and Sport and the local authorities.

Arc-et-Senans:

Transformation of the saltworks of Chaux into a conference centre

above: congress and meeting hall for 2,000 people. The original timber-structure of the roof was replaced by a concrete structure

Centre: planning of the Royal Saltworks at Chaux and the City of Chaux by Claude-Nicolas Ledoux in 1775–1779

below: restructuring of the original factory

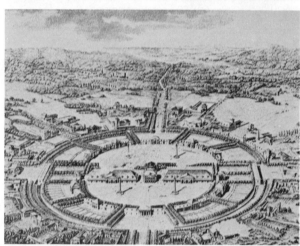

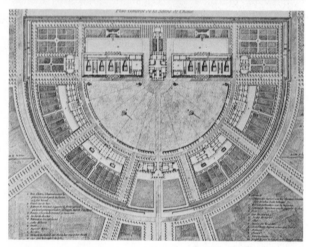

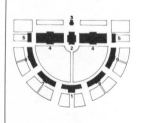

Fra saltfabrik til conferencecenter.
1756: 1, portbygning. 2, direktørbolig. 3, stalde. 4, fa-
briksbygninger. 5, administration. 6–9, værksteder.
1972: 1, reception og portner. 2, administration. 3, depot.
4, teater og bibliotek. 5, bolig for studerende og direktør-
bolig. 6 og 9, boliger for kongresdeltagere. 7, udstillings-
bygning. 8, spisesal og køkken.

■ *Saltworks into conferencecenter.*
1756: 1, gatehouse. 2, director's house. 3, stables. 4,
manufactory buildings. 5, administration. 6–9, workshops.
1972: 1, reception and keeper. 2, administration. 3, stores.
4, theatre and library. 5, rooms for students and director's
house. 6 and 9, rooms for students. 7, exhibitions. 8, dining
room and kitchen.

France
ARC-ET-SENANS
ROYAL SALT-WORKS CHAUX

1. Situation and History

Geographic location

In Franche-Comté, 34 km from Besançon, 100 km from Lausanne, 170 km from Geneva, 390 km from Paris.

- By motorway from Paris to Beaune, then take the route nationale (approx. 4 hours)

- by train via the two main lines Paris–Lausanne and Stras-bourg–Lyons. The nearest station is 6 km away at Mou-chard (at least 4 hours from Paris)

- 25 minutes to Dôle aerodrome and 10 minutes to the small airfield at Artois

- on foot by the GR 59 – chalet at Arc-et-Senans.

History

The salt-works at Chaux rank among the most remarkable European monuments of the 19th century. In 1776, the architect Claude-Nicolas Ledoux was commissioned by his Majesty the King to set up a salt-producing centre. The salt was to be transported from the salt mine by pipes and heated by wood taken from the forest of Chaux.

The factory functioned well until 1830, but then started to decline. By 1880, its operations had virtually ceased alto-gether. In 1927, the proprietor demolished the buildings and started to sell the stones until the Ministry of Fine Arts decided to extend its protection to this historic monument. The département of Doubs then acquired the ruins and reconstructed this famous site. In 1967/68, the Minister of Cultural Affairs André Malraux authorized the provision of credit for the restoration of the building, which had fallen into disuse. In September 1968, someone had the idea of finding a new role for Ledoux's buildings: a centre for studies and exchange visits dedicated to long-term re-search on future developments and innovation.

2. Finance

The period 1927 to 1969 saw the completion of considera-ble restoration work, but we do not know what sum was involved. In 1967/68, André Malraux gave a grant to have the monuments restored (3 millions in terms of modern money). In September 1968, someone had the idea of using the buildings for something quite different: making them into a study centre, where scholars from home and abroad could carry out research into the future and new inventions.

It was against this background that the département of Doubs, the Association for the Revival of the Royal Salt Works, the D.A.T.A.R. and various ministries decided to organize the restoration work on a joint basis. These activities are scheduled to last 10 years and the total cost of restoring the salt works will amount to 7,380 million francs (or 13 millions in constant terms). The interior decoration and appointments will cost 1 million (in constant terms).

The sharing of costs will be as follows:

1/3 by the département of Doubs (5.4 millions; and 2/3 by the State with the following principal participants:

- D.A.T.A.R.   3.5 millions
- Ministry of Culture   2.1 millions
  (Foundation 528,000 + C.N.M.H.S. + Etablissment
  Public Regional)

- Ministry of Education
- Ministry of the Interior
- Ministry of Agriculture   } 2 millions
- Ministry of Industrial &
  Scientific Development

The overall cost of restoring and equipping the building up to the completion of the work will come to between 5 and 8 million francs.

3. The Claude Nicolas Ledoux Foundation

3.1 Establishment

In 1972, the "Fondation Claude-Nicolas Ledoux pour les réflexions sur le Futur" (an association dating back to 1901) was created as a foundation under an agreement conclu-ded with the département of Doubs for a period of 35 years.

This association under the chairmanship of Serge Antoine is financed by founders who undertake to support it for five years. (The fee for 5 years is 60,000 francs for commercial enterprises and 38,000 francs for non-profit organizations). There are 18 founders (i.e. altogether, but sometimes subdivided into groups). They comprise public and private undertakings, research centres and universities, French and foreign foundations and individual researchers.

3.2 Aims and functions

In conjunction with the Association internationale des Luturibles, the Claude-Nicolas Ledoux Foundation promo-tes and arranges meetings on future developments, re-search and innovation in all sectors.

The Foundation has the following accommodation at its disposal:

- 6 assembly halls (with seating for 250 persons and simultaneous translation facilities)

- an auditorium (with seating for 2,000 persons)

- a restaurant for 250 diners

- 30 rooms in the main buildings and 20 at a nearly rural manor within Franche-Comté

- Roche Castle (belonging to the Foundation, but currently undergoing repairs).

Arc-et-Senans:
above: director's house
middle: exhibition hall
below: director's house (middle)
theatre and library buildings
(left and right of the director's house)
(photos: Gutschow 1976)

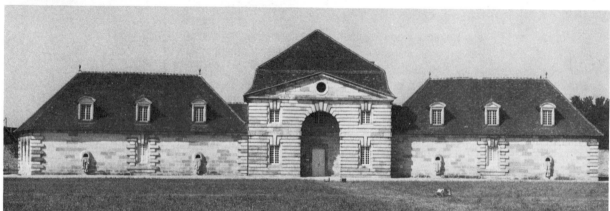

The regular sums earmarked for the running of the centre is 2 million francs, with the founders providing 1 million, the receipts from seminars 600,000 francs and the money from subsidies 400,000 francs. The Foundation arranges about 90 meetings each year: 40 of these deal with long-term future research. These meetings are attended by 4,350 participants annually and 6,000 meals are served. The visitors spend 1,680 overnight stays on the premises and pay 150 to 200 francs for day for participation (including fees of 50 francs for the Foundation).

The Foundation has a staff of 15. The salt-works are visited by 60,000 people each year of whom 35,000 have to pay admission charges. These produce annual receipts of 160,000 francs for the département of Doubs.

The Foundation Claude-Nicolas Ledoux arranges for tuition, the reception of visitors, the provision of audio-visual material, the organization of visits, the holding of permanent exhibitions on Ledoux, visionary architecture or futurology, and also of touring exhibitions (on Gaudi, le Yaouanc, Prassinos, le Corbusier, "free energy"). The Foundation

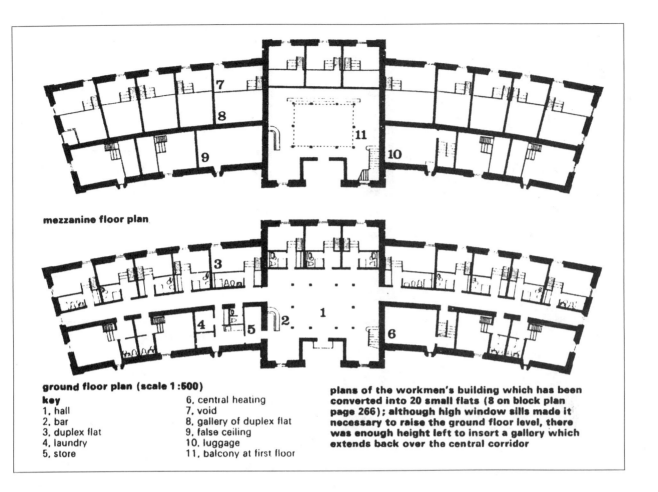

mezzanine floor plan

ground floor plan (scale 1:500)

key
1. hall
2. bar
3. duplex flat
4. laundry
5. store
6. central heating
7. void
8. gallery of duplex flat
9. false ceiling
10. luggage
11. balcony at first floor

plans of the workmen's building which has been converted into 20 small flats (8 on block plan page 266); although high window sills made it necessary to raise the ground floor level, there was enough height left to insert a gallery which extends back over the central corridor

establishes links with the regional associations of culture and organizes meetings between them. It also acts as the seat of the regional centre for the promotion of culture in Franche-Comté.

The cost of its activities amounts to 300,000 francs: a quarter of this is provided in the form of grants to C.N.M.H.S., the Association for the Revival of the Salt Works, Youth and Sport, Quality of Life and the Département and the rest to the Foundation's own special funds.

The present and future role of the Claude-Nicolas Ledoux Foundation is to provide a balanced public service in the field of innovation and future research. It does so by maintaining and increasing the number of founders, organizing a large number of seminars and discussions, studying social innovations, providing regular instruction, etc.

It is a research centre dedicated to promoting international meetings on mankind's future prospects and on innovation.

It was within this framework that the département of Doubs, the Association for the Revival of the Royal Salt Works and the Delegation to the regional authorities decided on joint action for restoring the buildings and equipping them for their new functions. The first international discussion on future developments and research took place here in September 1970 after the initial stage of the restoration work had been completed in record time.

The principal aim of the establishment of the Claude-Nicolas Ledoux Foundation was not in itself the restoration of the historic buildings of the Royal Salt Works or the promotion of the site as a cultural centre. The Foundation was set up in 1972 to promote studies on the long-term future of Europe in general and France in particular in a secluded place far from the bustle of daily life.

Its statutes stipulate that the aims of the Foundation are to study the future trends and innovation in the various sectors of contemporary society, to research the future in general, to encourage interdisciplinary meetings and to promote internal exchange visits in the field of future trends and innovations.

Inspired by these aims, the Foundation arranges and implements at Arc-et-Senans discussions and working meetings, provides accommodation or scholarships for individual researchers and places at their disposal the as yet small library specializing in forecasting the future, Utopian ideals and innovations.

No discipline or problem is a priori barred from potential inclusion. The Centre extends a welcome to all who reflect upon philosophy, the human sciences, technology and, of course, cultural creation. One of the major conferences at Arc-et-Senans attempted a definition of the cultural scene in Europe in the year 2000 A.D.

The priority accorded to reflection and forecasting does not, however, militate against research or initiatives at the Ledoux Foundation designed to increase its cultural and artistic influence. The Foundation considers the Salt Works to be a place of exceptional suitability for meetings and it makes every effort to promote the role of Arc-et-Senans in conjunction with the département of Doubs, the region and the neighbouring départements and the Association for the Revival of the Royal Salt Works. However, its funds are still limited in that they must also suffice for the interior decoration and appointments of the premises.

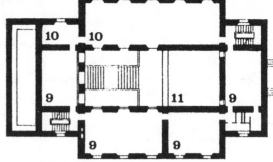

second floor plan

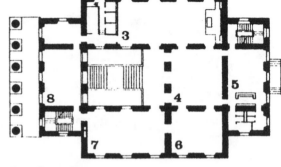

first floor plan

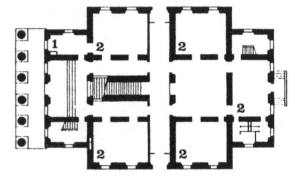

6, the sleeping gallery in one of the flats and, 7, the central hall in the old workmen's building (see plans on left).

director's house: ground floor plan (scale 1:450)

key
1. cloakroom
2. temporary exhibitions
3. conference room
4. hall
5. bar
6. director
7. secretaries
8. lounge
9. workroom
10. reading room
11. void

4. Functions

4.1 Tourism

The salt-works are open for visitors between 9 and 12 a. m. and from 2 to 6 p. m. (and to 7 p. m. in summer). There are 35,000 visitors to this historic site every year:

most of them come from Franche-Comté, the Northern and Eastern regions, Paris, Germany, Switzerland and the Benelux countries.

Guided tours enable visitors to view the reception rooms, recently restored rooms (now suitable for public meetings), the permanent exhibitions on the works of Ledoux, a number of visionary projects of the 18th century and future life in general.

Thanks to the support of the National Fund for Historic Monuments and Sites, the reception facilities for visitors have been improved and the buildings are floodlit every Saturday in summer.

4.2 Seminars

The Centre has the following amenities at the salt-works for organizing conferences and working meetings:

– an amphitheatre with seating for 2,000 persons and a projecting hall for 450;

– a hall with seating for 250 persons;

– a hall with seating for 120 persons (with cubicles for simultaneous interpreters):

– a hall for 45 persons;

– 2 halls seating 30 visitors each;

– 5 committee rooms;

– library and reading room;

– a restaurant for 250 diners;

– 30 rooms within the precincts of the salt-works;

– 20 rooms at the manor of Champagne-sur-Sone, an official guest house of the public authorities of Franche-Comté (5 km by car).

100 comfortable rooms are available for conference participants in local hotels at Arc-et-Senans (6 to 18 km), whilst
Besançon and Dôle are nor far away. The International
Centre for the Future at Arc-et-Senans welcomes all groups
interested in the long-term future and in innovation. It also
welcomes – though still on a limited scale – individual
research workers for periods of several weeks. In some
cases, scholarships are awarded.

Since 1972, the Foundation has held more than 200 conferences and meetings at the International Centre at Arc-et-
Senans (11 in 1975, 64 in 1975 and 85 in 1976).

4.3 Cultural activities

The Ledoux Foundation also provides active instruction for
the 35,000 tourists and 20,000 visitors who come to see the
famous buildings every year. (This total was 8,000 only a
few years ago). Reception rooms have been restored,
audio-visual material prepared, works prepared and guided
tours. Exhibitions have also been organized to illustrate the
work of Ledoux, visionary architecture and futurology.

The Foundation plays host to cultural events each year
(theatrical touring companies, Festival de Besançon) and
also organizes various exhibitions.

Gaudi (1972)
Factory, work and architecture (1974)
Prassinos – Le Corbusier (1975)
Palladio – Le Yaouanc – Messagier (1976)
Life at school – Contemporary French Architecture (1976)

It promotes links with other organizations and arranges
meetings between all the regional associations of culture.
The first meeting took place in 1974.

It is the seat of the Centre Régional de Diffusion Culturelle,
which administers a substantial store of audiovisual material available for use by all cultural bodies in Franche-
Comté.

Manosque: View of the old town from the air

124

France
MANOSQUE

1. Situation

1.1 General introduction

In the course of the last 20 years, the town of Manosque has seen its population triple as the number of inhabitants grew from 7,500 in 1954 to 20,000 in 1975.

This upswing and testimony to the new vitality of the town enables us today after the period of growth and expansion to turn our minds to the historic town-centre and to see what we can do to restore its framework, reaffirm its functions and confirm its role as the heart of the urban area.

The growth in population has been matched by extensive urbanization of the whole of the old Manosque area right up to the surrounding hills.

The new and scattered quarters grouped round the old heart of Manosque have not yet formed an opposing "pole". Instead, they continue to depend on the historic town-centre, which has maintained and even expanded its influence both on the town itself as well as on the region.

2. Conditions

2.1 Problems

The old district has also preserved its architectural unity, which thus enables it to become a homogeneous intermediary between countryside and the town, between sober rural architecture and the more embellished styles of large provençal manors.

Nevertheless, it should be pointed out that, even though the centre has survived and its activities have experienced a boom, private dwellings have been partly neglected and accessibility rendered difficult. As a result, the risk of peripheric poles emerging has become a distinct reality unless the authorities intervene on a massive scale.

Hence, the current problems are those of adapting the old quarter to the requirements of our modern age and of forging links between the two symbiotic entities: the centre and the outer suburbs.

3. Aims of Official Support

– The restoration of houses in the town centre in the light of retaining the resident population, rejuvenating the old district and developing our architectural legacy (scheme No. 1).

– The creation of the collective urban amenities at present lacking which, in addition to social and cultural services, can resuscitate the town centre and restore old buildings of high quality at present in a state of disrepair (scheme No. 2).

– The regaining of public thoroughfares for pedestrians – the squares, lanes and wide boulevards – by means of suitable organization and the creation of additional parking lots in specially designated zones (schemes 3 and 5).

– The opening of green belts and spaces to the public as an essential counterweight to high-density residential areas (schemes 3 and 7).

– Improved accessibility to the old district as the heart of the urban area (schemes 4 and 8).

Furthermore, the future expansion of the centre will have to be prepared now, so as to ensure that new facilities and accommodation may find their place within a coherent whole instead of being scattered at whim.

4. Strategy and Measures

4.1 Residential accommodation

The architectural heritage of the centre of Manosque is a fine example of the historic quarter of a medium sized town not yet touched by the building speculators.

The architectural heritage of the centre of Manosque is a fine example of the historic quarter of a medium sized town not yet touched by the building speculators.

The houses in question are solid in construction but badly maintained due to the lack of funds: these dwellings lack modern amenities and in fact many of them are vacant.

Most of the residents live on modest incomes with 37 % of the households consisting of old people.

On the other hand, the architecture of the town-centre as a homogeneous group of plain but high-quality buildings forms an unbroken fabric reflecting the rural origins of the town in which large and modest houses alike intermingle without any disharmony.

Consideration has already been given to safeguarding the old quarter by designating a "protected zone". The administrative difficulties and the wish to revitalize the centre have led to the definition of a perimeter along the course taken by the boulevard and thus including the whole of old Manosque.

In the face of the given realities, the municipality decided to undertake large-scale action in an attempt on the one hand to enable local residents to remain where they are whilst improving their living conditions despite their modest income and on the other hand to make the fine old houses standing empty a worthwhile proposition for young couples, who would thus rejuvenate the population living in the historic quarter of Manosque.

The hypothesis that all funds and assistance should be concentrated on a single sector of the city has been laid aside. This type of operation is in fact merely a partial response to a problem which, by definition, concerns the whole area.

Manosque situation

Manosque: Strategies for the improvement of the environment of the old town

Density of built-up area

Pedestrian percinct

pedestrianizied
shopping area
amenities
green belt
p parkink lots

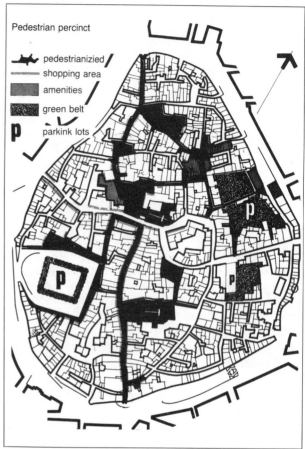

Category I building
(elementary type)

combles-grenier ▶
étage-habitation ▶
r.d.c.-étable ▶
cave →

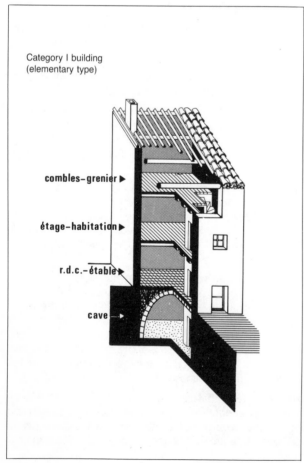

Parking facilities

In consequence, ANAH has adopted as its area the whole of the historic quarter so that it can provide assistance swiftly and efficiently for all the buildings scheduled for refurbishing.

By the same token, an analysis of the rehabilitation measures indicates that only the systematic earmarking of currently available funds will permit the authorities to implement the requisite combination of social objectives and the protection of our architectural heritage which on many occasions appeared to be contradictory.

Analysis and definition of official support. The structure of the built-up area.

The centre of Manosque, circumscribed by the line of the old town wall, covers a superficial area of 13.1 hectares. The utilization of the land is as follows:

- total surface   13.10 hectares
- streets and squares   5.20 hectares
- housing   7.90 hectares
- free space between houses   0.28 hectares
    (3.5 % of the superficial area of the housing)

The first thing to strike us about this list is the high density of housing with the built-up area covering 96.5 % of the superficial area. This high density does not result from the gradual addition of buildings progressively filling up the whole avaible space. It is due to the structure of the plots of land and the distribution of the real estate. Most of the lots only measure 4 by 5 metres, sometimes deeper, and only enjoy any daylight at the front or in narrow inner courtyards – thus forming a dense, albeit dismembered urban fabric.

Even though the shops on the ground floor are not very large, the dwellings (with an average of 1.5 persons per unit) are relatively high. As a rule, they are accessible from steep staircases which thus provide both communication and ventilation.

The rural activities of former times have contributed substantially to shaping the typical Manosque house of today and indeed the original type of architecture may still be found in some of the smaller properties. This consists of cellars often used for storing wine, the ground-floor as cowsheds, the first and second floors often comprising one room each as living quarters, and finally the attics used as a loft or airing room. Certain changes were rung on this first and elementary type of local architecture when the building was meant to fulfil more important functions without, however, undergoing any alteration in its vertical form. Only the appearance of an inner courtyard indicated the difference between this larger town property form the basically logical rural type of house erected from the very beginning.

This reference to the structure of the buildings is necessary to take into account the difficulties of adapting old houses. That holds particularly true for modest properties consisting of small-sized rooms ill adapted to contemporary utilization or the installation of modern equipment and the currently accepted criteria and norms.

Theoretically, it might be possible for a building enterprise to work on several adjoining houses and to join together several vertical dwellings so as to convert them into horizontal units.

Solutions of that kind have occasionally been tried out elsewhere on an empirical basis and the overlapping of properties in different storeys testifies to this experimental approach.

But this idea can only be regarded as an exception within the general framework of restoration activities. On the other hand, it is always necessary to bear in mind the complexity of such changes – changes which are bound to produce extra cost due to technical difficulties.

A definition of official promotion measures

The degree of official promotion accorded depends on an analysis of the state of a building and the comfort of dwellings seen in relation to the tenancy agreement (owner occupier or lessee) since it is the latter which determines the official assistance which tenants and owners may obtain. Consideration is, however, also given to the age of the building with 1948 being taken as the cut-away year.

Assistance is divided into three groups:

a. reconstruction of the building involving, for example, the walls, foundations, electrical installations, woodwork, plaster, etc.

b. sanitary facilities, for example W. C., bathroom, heating

c. restoration of jointly owned parts of the property such as the interior hall. roofs, facades, courtyards, etc.

The number of houses in Manosque in need of assistance was as follows:

	No. of dwellings	Built before 1948	In need of assistance	As a %
Tenants	356	327	271	76.1
Owner-occupiers	305	289	157	51.4
Not determined	25	22	12	48.0
Others	10	–	–	–
Total	696	638	440	64.1

The assistance accorded was subdivided as follows:

	Total	Building + equip. (b + e)	Building b)	Equipment (e)	Jointly used areas (c)
Tenants	271	47	8	102	55
Owner occupiers	157	79	9	183	88
Not determined	12	–	–	–	–
Total	440	126	17	285	143

Cost of assistance

– The cost per unit of the assistance was determined on the basis of estimates for restoring houses and on an analysis of the cost of work already carried out.

The prices used in the overall estimate are average costs. These formed the basis for arriving at the total expense of restoring the 440 dwellings in the town-centre in need of support.

If one establishes an average cost per category of support and per square metre of accommodation in accordance with the tenancy agreement, one arrives at the following results (including added value tax).

Manosque: Strategies for the improvement of the environment of the old town

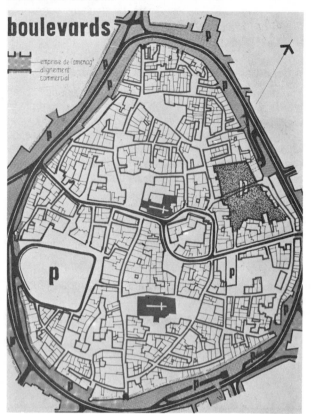

boulevards

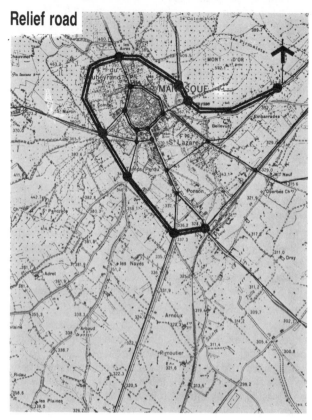

Relief road

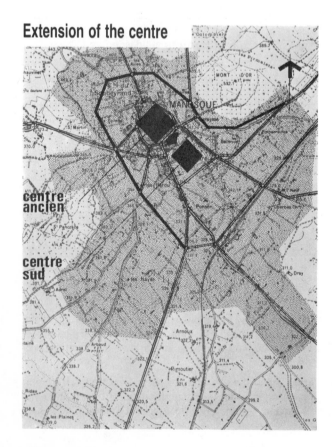

Extension of the centre

centre ancien

centre sud

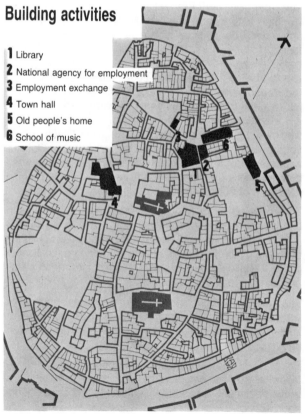

Building activities

1 Library
2 National agency for employment
3 Employment exchange
4 Town hall
5 Old people's home
6 School of music

Nature of assistance

		Cost per m² or unit			
		Tenant		Owner-occupier	
		m² dwelling or unit	cost per m²/dwelling	m² dwelling or unit	cost m²/dwelling
Work on each dwelling per m² Appointments/per unit	Building	50.0	935	66.0	935
	Heating	50.0	125	66.0	125
	WC	1 unit	3,116	1 unit	3,116
	Bathroom	1 unit	6,846		
Work on the house itself per m²	Jointly owned	15.4	323	13.1	208
	Facade	40.0	150	32.0	91
	Roof	26.0	129	26.0	98

Hence, the work per m² or per unit comprises the following:

	Tenants	Owner-occupiers
Building	935 f/m²	935 f/m²
Heating	125 f/m²	125 f/m²
Work on the house	602 f/m²	397 f/m²
Total	1,662 f/m²	1,457 f/m²
Appointments	9,962 f/unit	9,962 f/unit

Pedestrianization

The streets and lanes in the historic quarter of Manosque should be oriented principally towards the use of pedestrians. The current penetration of the car everywhere prevents the smooth functioning of municipal activities and the full enjoyment by local residents of the streets and squares in the historic quarter.

In a densely populated town-centre like Manosque, the available exterior space forms a natural extension of a dwelling. A large part of social life takes place on the streets and squares. The programme for promoting "medium-sized towns" will be able to set in train the systematic restoration of free space to pedestrians and this will be substantially increased in area in addition to the provision of more parking facilities (cf. scheme 4).

The main element in the rehabilitation scheme will consist in establishing a North-South axis destined to form the backbone of the town-centre. A number of lateral extensions have been retained to link up squares or other busy focal points of special interest such as social or cultural centres.

The envisaged treatment is intended to harmonize with the sober architecture to be found in this quarter. By way of exception, the places located in front of public buildings marked by a more ornate architectural style have been treated in more elaborate fashion so as to form special areas.

The programme of action under the present contract constitutes a first phase of the work destined in the end to cover the whole of the historic quarter and to forge complete links with the network of boulevards (cf. scheme 5).

Parking facilities

The Municipality of Manosque has decided to support the rehabilitation of the old historic centre not only by refurbishing dwellings, creating pedestrian areas and providing social and cultural amenities, but also by arranging for the provision of adequate parking space so as to promote commercial and residential development.

The construction of a car-park for 250 vehicles left for either a short or a medium period of time (and supplemented by an annex of about 100 individual reserved parking lots) ought to satisfy the given demand. That in turn should help the flow of traffic in the town centre and on the boulevards where redevelopment will probably take away 207 and 97 parking lots respectively. The creation of an East Square car park will go hand in hand with a better organization of paid parking facilities in the historic town centre and in the adjoining districts so as to adapt the utilization of public space to its final uses.

The full profitability of an investment on that scale cannot usually be achieved until the local population has had to endure for a long period the inconvenience of traffic over-congestion.

On the other hand, such an attitude (which limits the calculation of the profitability entirely to its financial aspects) runs the risk of reducing the attractiveness of the town-centre and even of suffocating it. Indeed, the point is reached where the very reasons which would have initially justified an investment become invalid as a result of "non-investment".

If the parking situation today may be judged "satisfactory" and if one reasons solely pursuant to the criteria of profitability, the justification for the new car parks will not make itself felt until several decades have passed.

By the same token, if parking facilities in the old town centre are not increased in the short term, the competing poles impinging on the old quarter will strangle it to death. With that in mind and also the wish to pursue a more global approach (which is difficult to quantify), the authorities have suggested subsidizing the construction of the car park on a scale which will reduce the duration of the amortization period to 15 years so that either a private or a mixed investment will be able to implement the project. If a decision is taken in favour of a private investment, the authorization will be of limited duration only and will not contain any guarantee on the part of the municipality.

The boulevards

Manosque's boulevards follow the course of the old town wall and in fact circumscribe the historic quarter.

Since the beginning of the 19th century, they have formed the heart of a lively area of commercial activity. At the present time, these generously planned thoroughfares are gradually smothering the town with traffic as the many vehicles in transit and the chaotic parking arrangements impede everyday life and activities.

Faced by the need to coordinate support for the traffic plan and that for the agreement on the medieval town, the municipal authorities have decided to introduce one-way traffic on the boulevards and to reserve certain streets for the use of pedestrians or for commercial and leisure activities. Under this project, there are sufficient short-term parking facilities for business purposes.

Manosque:
Realisation of projects: public library

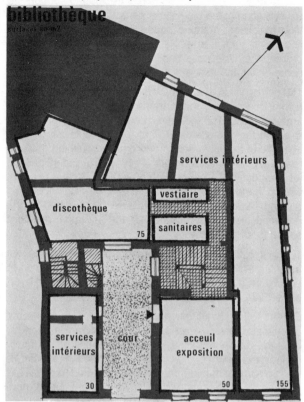

Ground-floor

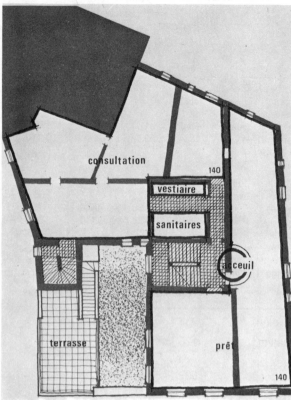

1st floor for adults

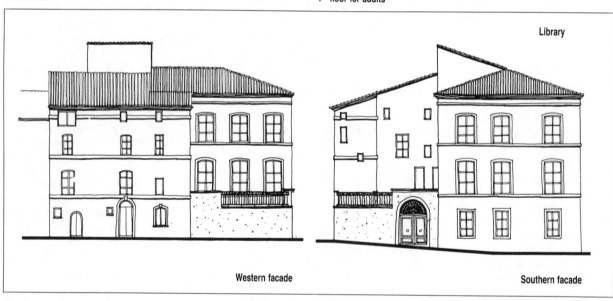

Western facade

Southern facade

Library

It should, however, be added that the planning and utilization of the boulevards will not prove to be completely effective until the most important section of the relief road for the town (scheme No 8) has opened.

When the southern extension of the central area has made sufficient progress during the second phase, the pedestrianization of the boulevard (linking up with the boulevard in the old quarter) my be extended by a footbrigde from la Plaine providing direct access to the public gardens and the "southern zone" (cf. scheme 6). In this way, the boulevards could once more act as a link between the various parts of the town.

The extension of the central area

The history of Manosque does not end in the present age. The population figure predicted by the experts is for 40,000 inhabitants in 25 years' time.

This doubling of the population and augmentation of the various municipal amenities raises the immediate problem of extending the historic centre. Moreover, unless these activities are steered and controlled, there is a risk of them being dissipated with a resulting loss of the town's attractiveness.

A decision has been taken to reserve an area of 4 hectares

bordering the historic town-centre for amenities unable to find a place in the old part of Manosque. Such construction work as the district needs to fulfil its central function will be completed, too.

This zone, to be designated "centre sud", has been extracted from the P.O.S. (Land Utilization Plan) so that a detailed plan can be drawn up on the nature and mode of utilizing land.

It was against this background that the Municipality of Manosque called for a feasibility study to be carried out under the general planning scheme. This study is now being carried out and financed under the funds voted for the programme for promoting medium-sized towns.

The relief road

The building of a relief road for Manosque is a necessity both for transit traffic, which totally congests the boulevards,

and for internal traffic within the town. It also forms an essential element in the development plans for the town.

By reserving for the "dossier d'agglomération" the investments earmarked for the rational organisation of the overall network of roads and the completion of the complementary parts of the relief road, the Municipality of Manosque has opted in favour of including the most "strategic" stretch of the relief road within the present agreement. Even though representing a limited stretch of the relief road, its role will be crucial in the future planning of the town centre in that it will permit completion of the south-western part of the ring road.

Upon completion of the "b" and "c" sections, section "a" will permit a substitute route v–w instead of the route x, y, z, which is now over-congested. Similarly, the boulevards which cannot be planned in any other way will assume their final function of acting as a central urban thoroughfare and active line of communications.

4.2 Finance

Summary of costs

Schemes		Total cost	Other finance subsidies and ordinary programmes	Investments and private loans	Finance for medium-sized towns
1. Housing tender charges		80,000	–	–	80,000
Rehabilitation assistance		6,985,500	1,537,500 (1)	3,352,500	2,095,500
Reinhabitation assistance		5,250,000	850,000 (2)	3,400,000	1,000,000
Social aid		300,000	–	–	300,000
Architectural charges		250,000	250,000 (3)	–	–
Implementation C.I.A.H		540,000	–	–	540,000
Support A.R.I.M		600,000	600,000 (4)	–	–
	Total	14,005,500	3,237,500	6,752,500	4,015,500
2. Homes					
a.n.p.e		725,000	125,000 (7)	–	600,000
Scholarships		180,000	80,000 (7)	–	100,000
Library		2,330,000	1,580,000 (6)	–	750,000
Old people's home		2,280,000	1,302,600 (5)	–	977,400
Town hall		1,020,000	240,000 (7)	–	780,000
Music academy and musical activities		2,560,000	260,000 (8)		2,300,000
	Total	9,095,000	3,587,600	–	5,507,400
3. Pedestrian zone	Total	2,219,000	–	–	2,219,000
4. Parking facilities	Total	6,220,000	720,000 (9)	320,000	2,300,000
5. Boulevards	Total	3,531,000	1,240,000 (10)	–	2,291,000
6. Extension to the town centre	Total	–	–	–	–
7. Drouye park	Total	900,000	900,000 (11)	–	–
8. Relief road	Total	1,990,000	1,990,000 (12)	–	–
Total		37,960,500	11,675,100	9,952,500	16,332,900

The Municipality of Manosque proposes to embark upon experimental measures in creating a "local fund for the improvement of housing" (C.L.A.H.) and to support the implementation of this scheme by providing an exceptional grant pursuant to the policy of promoting historic town centres.

The Functions of the C.L.A.H. (Local Fund for the Improvement of Housing).

Reallocation of the available funds

The main role of the C.L.A.H. will be to rationalize the the granting and utilization of currently disposable monies.

Manosque: Realisation of projects for the improvement of public services: club for elderly people, town hall, school of music

Old people's home

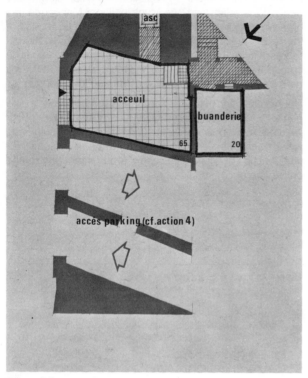

Ground floor

The main concern will thus consist in aggregating the subsidies and loans currently given on an individual basis so that the various beneficiaries (such as recipients of assistance from the C.A.F., i.e. the Family Assistance Fund or the members of certain Pension Funds) may acquaint themselves with the means at their disposal and spend them – and do so via a single interlocutor, namely the C.L.A.H.

By the same token, the C.L.A.H. will have to make the financial arrangements, draw up the financing plans, examine the applications and obtain the best terms for the cases submitted to it.

This scheme, which operates independently of the social and town-planing criteria inherent in C.L.A.H.'s specific asssistance, will be directed towards benefiting the whole housing stock in the historic town-centre.

Assistance for rehabilitation

In order to define the amount and the quotas of C.L.A.H. assistance, account has been taken of the cost of rehabilitation, the reimbursement charges deriving from the work involved (after deducting housing subsidies and grants), household incomes and also the probable number of requests for subsidies during the three-year duration of the scheme for medium-sized towns.

Assistance from the C.L.A.H. for rehabilitation purposes has thus been confined to households with an income equal to or less than that which entitles such families to a P.L.R. classification in the provision of public-assistance dwellings for poorer families. The number of dwellings in this category is 246, i.e. 56 % of those requiring public support.

Town Hall

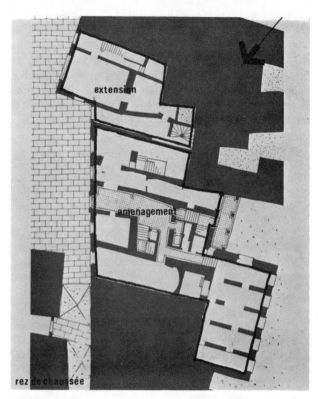

School of music

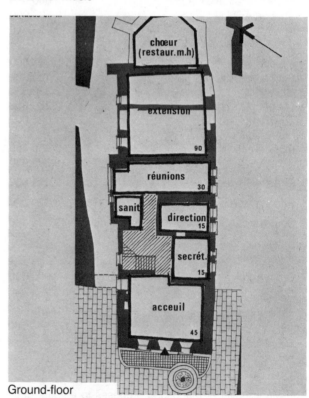

Ground-floor

Assistance in making vacant dwellings re-inhabitable

The large number of vacant dwellings (often of above-average quality) together with the large number of old people living in the town-centre have inspired a scheme to

132

attract the interest of young households by restoring old houses.

The criterion observed by the C.L.A.H. is to grant assistance in the creation of 3 to 4 room flats.

At the present time, an in-depth study on the possibilities of acquiring and restoring 50 dwellings is being conducted by the Municipality of Manosque with the support of the HLM organization (i.e. specializing in low-rent accommodation).

Because of the condition of the vacant premises a flat-rate of 1,000,000 Francs has been earmarked for meeting the expense of rehabilitating these houses.

When private individuals apply to have their dwelling restored, the assistance will be granted in accordance with the criteria defined by the C.L.A.H. (cf. assistance for rehabilition). The aid will be given to HLM construction agencies in those cases where the cost of the work (e.g. on the structure of the building) exceeds the scope of the originally envisaged financing arrangements.

Financing "Social Action"

The sum of 300,000 francs will be set aside by the C.L.A.H. in order to carry out urgently necessary work (such as basic sanitation, safety, sickness-prevention, etc.) in dwellings where the occupants' income does not enable them to carry out any renovation of their homes. This is done by bearing new wiring and removal costs, etc.

Architectural restoration

At the request of the Municipality of Manosque and thanks to a subsidy from the Secretary of State for Culture, the sum of 250,000 Francs is placed at the disposal of the C.L.A.H. for the valid period of the contract. These funds are used for financing the restoration of outstanding architecture.

The conditions for granting such subsidies will be laid down by the Architecte des Bâtiments de France. The allocation of the funds is carried out by a commission comprising representatives of the Municipality, the Direction de l'Equipment, the C.L.A.H. and the Architecte des Bâtiments de France.

The C.L.A.H. is to be set up in the form of a public-law association. Its advisory board will comprise the representatives of the Municipaltity, those of the Direction de l'Equipement and the Architecte des Bâtiments de France, and organizations which participate in financing and assisting restoration work.

Hence, not only conformity in the use of the funds will be ensured but also the systematic employment of the funds will be rendered easier.

In addition, research will be carried out to coordinate C.L.A.H. and ARIM support so as to guarantee perfect harmony in the financial and technical administration of the given operations.

The cost of implementing the activities of the C.L.A.H. during the contractual period of validity has been set forth in the contract at a total sum of 540,000 Francs. This represents the cost ot the permanent staff and the Fund's expenses.

5. Implementation

Public amenities

The wish to provide more amenities for the town has led the Municipality of Manosque to undertake the implementation of six programmes of public works involving either new creations or the development of existing, albeit inadequate facilities.

The choice of locations in the historic town-centre and notably in the nothern part of Manosque (the most decayed area) envisages the revitalization of the old district and more particularly of those quarters where restoration is a priority matter to which an important part of the investment envisaged in the contractual agreement will be devoted.

Hand in hand with this aim of revitalization, the Municipality also wishes to contribute to the architectural restoration of the high-quality buildings left vacant and threatened with decay.

Plans have been drawn up to restore the following:

– The labour exchange which will re-occupy the premises currently reserved for the National Employment Agency (ANPE) so that the latter will have premises completely on its own.

– L'Hotel d'Herbes so as to house the municipal library there.

– The "Mines" building now destined to become an old people's home.

– A property next to the town hall scheduled to house an extension of the municipal offices.

The old monastery "des Observantins" which will house the school of music.

The financial support provided under the programme for promoting medium-sized towns is justified according to the experts by the inadequacy of the ordinary programmes or the high architectural cost caused by the impossibility of financing certain equipment or by the necessity of rapidly undertaking certain working operations at the same time when other efforts are concentrated on the town. Finally, the innovative character of certain programmes or their large scale call for unusual sums of money.

The Library

The municipal library now possesses 15,200 volumes, which are housed in the Hotel de Ville (town hall).

The growth in the population of Manosque and the relative youth of the inhabitants completely justify the creation of a library covering an area of about 1,000 m^2 and designed to fulfil various cultural functions.

The site chosen for the future accommodation of the library is one of the finest old buildings in the town, l'Hotel d'Herbes, which will provide a fine setting for the cultural programme agreed with the Directeur des Bibliothèques.

The substantial structural changes in the building will also lead to a rediscovery of the original architecture as well as permitting convenient arrangements for the reading rooms, the activity rooms and the annexes.

Costs

	Total cost	Other finance	Finance for medium sized towns
Acquistition	330,000	330,000 (1)	
Restoration	2,000,000	1,250,000 (2)	750,000
Total	2,330,000	1,580,000	750,000

1) Munipality of Manosque
2) Including 50 % subsidy from the Direction des Bibliothèques

The implementation of this work will commence in 1976 and last two years. The apportioning of the funds available under the financing of "medium-sized towns" will be as follows:

1976	375,000 Francs (50 %)
1977	375,000 Francs (50 %)

Old People's Home

Quintrand House will accommodate a large number of old people and prepare a new programme (already approved the D.A.S.S.) based on a broad range of the desired services as well as various activities.

This home is designed to meet the needs of old people living not only in the historic town-centre but also throughout the urban area. In 1975, there were 1,900 persons over 65 years of age and 37.1 % of the households in the town centre.

In order to adapt the programme to the needs and wishes of elderly persons, new activities have been introduced at the Home such as callisthenics, a grammophone-record room, studios, etc. It is also agreed that a restaurant ought to be set up to meet the requirements of the people in question.

In addition, exterior changes have been envisaged so that users may find the requisite adjuncts to their comfort and to life at the Home (the constructions of a terrace, a pedestrian precinct between the two Homes, a bowling green, etc.).

Cost of implementation

	Total cost	Other finance	Finance for medium-sized towns
Acquisition Restoration of the building	350,000 1,700,000	350,000 (1) 952,000 (2)	747,000
Exterior work	230,000		230,000
Total	2,280,000	1,302,600	977,400

1) Municipality of Manosque
2) Including a DASS subsidy (40 %)

The work will commence in 1976 and terminate at the end of 1977. The apportioning of the funds available under the financing of "medium-sized towns" will be as follows:

1976	781,920 Francs (80 %)
1977	795,480 Francs (20 %)

Hotel de Ville

Manosque Town Hall furnishes a good example of how to restore an old building.

In order to find the necessary working space for developing the municipal services, the local authorities decided to purchase an adjoining building of outstanding architectural

quality and to undertake its restoration. When these two buildings have been linked together, this will permit simultaneous completion of the current phase of the restoration work on the Hotel de Ville. The implementation of the project will thus permit the completion of the next stage of decorating the property (cf. scheme 3).

Cost of implementation

	Total cost	Other finance	Finance for medium-sized towns
Acquistion	240,000	240,000 (1)	
Restoration	780,000		780,000
Total	1,020,000	240,000	780,000

1) Municipality of Manosque

The extension and restoration activities will commence in 1976. The apportioning of the funds available under the financing of "medium-sized towns" will be as follows:

1976	780,000 Francs (100 %)

School of Music

The Manosque School of Music is housed in the Youth and Culture Centre as a provisional measure, which does not permit it to develop its full range of activities.

The Municipality of Manosque has decided to purchase the old chapel of the Observations Monastery, which was secularized during the Revolution. The state of the building and modifications made in it render it impossible to trace the original architecture (some of it dating back to the 12th century) in all its pristine glory. For this reason it has been decided to accommodate the school of music in the nave and to undertake to rebuild the chancel.

The programme of activities, drawn up in agreement with the musical section of the Secretary of State for Culture, has found a perfect setting for its implementation in the central part of the building, which also furnishes the school with an opportunity for further expansion.

Thanks to the initiative taken by the Fonds d'Intervention, it has been decided to introduce a "music bus" designed to spread a love of good music.

Cost of implementation

	Total cost	Other finance	Finance for medium-sized towns
Acquistion	200,000	200,000 (1)	
Development of the School of Music	2,160,000	–	2,160,000
Restoration of the chancel	p.m.		
Music bus	200,000	60,000 (2)	140,000
Total	2,560,000	260,000	2,300,000

1) Municipality of Manosque   2) F.I.C.

The implementation of this work will take 2 years, whilst the apportioning of the funds available under the financing of medium-sized towns will be as follows:

1976 study
1977 648,000 Francs (30 %)
1978 1,572,000 Francs (70 %)

GERMANY, Federal Republic of

Germany, Federal Republic of
LEGISLATION, ORGANISATION, FINANCE, PARTICIPATION

1. Legislation

1.1 Introduction

The protection of historical buildings and areas and urban conservation are two fields of activity that have developed in different ways. Whereas the protection of buildings and sites of historical importance (Denkmalschutz) has a centuries-long tradition, urban conservation (Stadterhaltung), though preservation was always an integral part of town planning and architecture, is as an aim in itself comparatively young. Only over the past 20 years or so has urban conservation become a separate field and acquired its present-day significance.

As the conservation concept in town planning is primarily concerned with whole districts or areas whilst the protection of ancient buildings and monuments, as the term itself implies, relates to individual objects, the actual tasks and priorities in these two sectors necessarily differ. On the other hand, their subject matter and aims do compare in many respects, as this report will show, so that it is not always possible to make a clear distinction between them. Owing to the substantive links between these two sectors, however, the respective rules and regulations can in some cases be applied to both fields of activity.

This survey will deal first of all with the concept of conservation in terms of building and land law (that is, in this case as regards town planning) and then in terms of legislation relating to the protection of buildings, monuments, etc. It is necessary to point out, however, that a clear distinction has to be made between town planning legislation and regional building regulations. In a nutshell, it can be said that the building regulations, as the term implies, embrace the conditions and the acutal execution of construction work on the land, whilst town planning legislation concerns the legal aspects of the land, especially as regards building and other uses. This distinction indicates at the same time the close connection between protective or conservation legislation and building regulations.

1.2 The conservation concept in town planning legislation

Whereas the Federal Parliament has no statutory powers, except with regard to a few matters of minor importance, in the field of the protection and conservation of buildings, etc. of historical importance and with regard to building regulations (these falling within the jurisdiction of the Länder, the federal states), it does have a legislative competence by virtue of the Basic Law (constitution) for land, and hence of course town planning. The two most important bills enacted so far have been the Federal Building Act (Bundesbaugesetz) and the Urban Renewal and Town Development Act (Städtebauförderungsgesetz). They are the basis for the building plans prepared by local authorities which, since the 1976 amendment of the Federal Building Act,

must take greater account of preservation requirements in town planning programmes. In this way, and through other regulations, the new planning legislation is a further buttress for protective measures but, and this is stated expressis verbis, the legislative powers of the Länder remain untouched.

1.2.1 Federal Building Act

Local planning is based on general aims and specific guidelines which can only be pursued after weighing the pros and cons of all relevant public and private interests. Such interests have included ever since the Federal Building Act was first enacted the cultural needs of the people and the shaping of the townscape. Both relate to urban conservation and building protection measures. The 1976 amendment to the Federal Building Act gives greater prominence and refers directly to the concept of urban conservation. From then on, plans were also required "to take into account areas, buildings, streets and squares of historical, artistic or architectural importance worth preserving". This definition matches the one contained in legislation relating to the protection of ancient monuments, except that it has merely omitted the phrase "public interest in preservation". Thus conservation covers a wider range of property than protection, though it also applies to building in the latter category.

As the criteria pertaining to the protection of buildings and monuments and town planning are much the same, the only real distinction between protection and urban conservation is whether a public interest in conservation exists. Although not specifically mentioned, there is in fact also a public interest in the protection of monuments and buildings within the meaning of section 1 (6) of the Federal Building Act. And although this only means that proposed protective measures have to be considered in relation to other public and private interests, it shows that they form part of the general scheme of urban development.

According to section 2 (5) of the Federal Building Act, the "institutions representing the public interest" – thus including the agencies concerned with the protection of old buildings, etc. – should be brought into the planning process as soon as possible. Those agencies must for their part, according to section 2 (5) of the Act, indicate in their report to the local authority their proposed measures or those already initiated. This ensures mutual information, though not yet any substantive coordination.

And sections 6 (2) and 11 of the Act stipulate that plans must also take other legal provisions into account, for instance those relating to the protection of monuments, etc., since such provisions have to be observed in the approval procedure. As already mentioned, these provisions do not indicate any specific priority rating of building protection or urban conservation in relation to other aspects of town planning; this is decided on an ad hoc basis. Nor does the catalogue of measures (section 9) say that local plans must make specific provision for protective or conservation measures.

When the Act was amended in 1976 its new sections 39 c, e and h created the legal instruments for urban conservation measures. According to section 39 h, the local authority can determine, in the local plan or by means of special by-laws, conservation areas in which permission for demolition, conversion or alteration of structures may be refused if the building is to be preserved because, either alone or together with other buildings, it is an important feature of the town-scape or landscape, or because it is of architectural and in particular historical or artistic significance. If a building in such an area is nevertheless demolished or altered without permission a fine may be imposed. But conservation requirements must have reasonable financial limits and if they are exceeded the owner can apply for the building to be taken over by the local authority (section 39 h (6), Federal Building Act).

Permission for demolition, conversion or alteration may also be refused on the ground that it is necessary to retain the composition of the residential population (§ 3, No. 3) and to ensure that urban restructuring measures make sufficient allowance for the social aspects (§ 4). These additional reasons indicate that urban conservation is a separate concept and mark the distinction from measures to protect ancient buildings and monuments, etc.

The conservation requirment is complemented by a like-wise newly introduced "special right of pre-emptive pur-chase to ensure that urban conservation policies will achieve their aims" (section 24 a). Under this provision, the local authority can purchase buildings worth preserving if it considers that the acquisition of the property by an interested party would militate against the aims of conser-vation as expressed in section 39 h. Section 39 c stipula-tes the use of property. On the strength of this provision, the local authority can oblige the owner to use the building in accordance with local plans. Together with the extensive possibilities for prescribing use contained in the new sec-tion 9, this provision enables the local authority to stipulate in its plan how conservation areas or individual buildings must be used in order to preserve them.

Section 39 e contains provisions relating not only to mo-dernisation (§ II) but to the maintenance of such buildings (§ III). Thus the local authority has the power to oblige owners to carry out the necessary renewal measures. These new provisions have incorporated the architectural elements into local planning.

Within areas built in the same style but without an authorita-tive local plan, new buildings or modifications of existing properties are permissible only if the use, architecture and area to be built up are consistent with the immediate neighbourhood, taking into account the characteristic sett-lement structure. New buildings and alterations in built-up areas are therefore tied more than hitherto to the existing development, which means that buildings of historical importance and other property worth preserving receive greater protection.

1.2.2 Urban Renewal and Town Development Act

The Urban Renewal and Town Development Act offers further instruments for the re-development of renewal areas (Sanierungsgbiete). As regards buildings in a bad state, the Act provides for demolition and rebuilding, but also, and specifically as a measure of equal importance, for moderni-sation and repair. Hence there are additional legal pos-sibilities for urban conservation where this is the primary objective of local authority planning.

Section 10 (1), first sentence, of the Act prescribes that the preservation of buildings, streets, squares or specific areas of historical, artistic or architectural importance has to be taken into consideration within the terms of section 1 (6) of the Federal Building Act. The fact that only this planning

criterion is emphasised is an indication of its special import-ance. The same provision makes clear that regional regula-tions concerning the protection and conservation of build-ings and sites of special scientific interest remain unaf-fected. To that extent the position is the same as under general town and country planning legislation. The local authority may, however, resort to the general instruments now provided by the Federal Building Act for the purpose of conservation planning (especially with regard to modernisa-tion and repair and the establishment of conservation areas).

1.3 Legislation on ancient monuments and buildings and historical sites

Legislative power for this field of conservation lies almost exclusively with the federal states. This is due to the division of responsibilities as provided for in the Basic Law (constitu-tion) of 1949. Consequently, the appropriate legislation is incorporated in the ancient buildings and historical sites protection act of the states and in the regional building regulations.

With the exception of North-Rhine/Westphalia, all of the federal states have meanwhile introduced their own protec-tive legislation, although they differ considerably in content. In addition to this legislation, certain provisions of the general building code have a protective and conservatory nature – North-Rhine/Westphalia relying solely on this source for its protective measures. For the most part, the pertinent regional regulations are identical.

The constitutions of some of the states also contain provi-sions guaranteeing protection for ancient buildings, monu-ments, etc. There are only minor textual differences. In some cases special mention is made of cultural objectives in addition to the artistic and historical monuments. The protection afforded by the state is in most cases com-plemented by corresponding regulations introduced by the local authorities. By and large, the importance of such guarantees lies solely in the fact that they are understood as constitutional mandates to the legislative authorities.

1.3.1 Regional building regulations

All regional building regulations or codes contain provisions relating to conservation and the protection of ancient build-ings, monuments, historical sites, etc. In the majority of cases the provisions are couched in general terms and their common tenor ist that buildings must be faultlessly designed and not deface the environment. They thus mark out the substantive and legal framework for more specific building regulations and determine their parameters. These local regulations may contain (in by-laws and local plans) special requirements tailored to local circumstances.

The fundamental requirements expressed in the general provisions are repeated and sometimes amplified in more specific regulations. Furthermore, the regional building regulations empower the competent authorities to introduce town planning regulations. They are subject to the limits of the powers granted and do not go beyond the substantive town planning principles. The more recent regional regula-tions in particular contain, over and above the classical urban development regulations, a number of other provi-sions dealing specifically with protection and conservation.

And finally, a number of building regulations make the demolition of buildings that are either protected or the preservation of which is in the public interest subject to permission. In the final analysis, this implies with regard to conservation within the framework of town planning and the protection of ancient monuments and historical buildings:

First, the architectural provisions contained in the building regulations – though amounting to no more than the prevention of disfigurement – cover the shape and style of buildings, etc. that are worthy of preservation but not their inner substance. Such property is also protected from changes in the vicinity which would disturb the overall picture. The actual details of such measures may be set out in by-laws.

Second, such architectural provisions cannot obviate total demolition. Nor can they as much as ensure restoration and conservation in keeping with the existing architectural style.

Third, these (as such non-exacting) architectural requirements represent the aesthetic demands of the community and are an expression of the social commitment as reflected in article 14 (1) (2) of the Basic Law; in other words, they cannot lead to claims for compensation.

Fourth, property of historical importance is not usually defined in the building regulations. In some cases the definition is taken over from the appropriate protective legislation; in others it is derived from the interpretation of building regulations. The architectual provisions apply with hardly any distinction to buildings deemed worthy of protection and conservation. Larger areas may only be regarded as the environment of such a building, depending on their effect on its visual appearance.

1.3.2 Legislation on the protection of ancient monuments and historical buildings

All of the federal states have passed laws to protect ancient buildings, etc., mostly in recent years. Although the wording of the definitions varies from state to state, they all concur on the general aim of "preserving buildings, etc. forming part of the cultural heritage". And both aspects of preservation (Denkmalschutz and Denkmalpflege) embrace all the protective elements, including scientific study.

Accordingly, Denkmalschutz covers all provisions aimed at preserving or repairing such cultural property, a policy which can be enforced by legislative means.

Denkmalpflege, on the other hand, implies consultative and financial support for owners and users in the actual preservation or repair of such property. This aspect of protection is only given marginal treatment in the pertinent laws since, as it involves purely administrative matters, it does not need a special statutory basis. Some laws do, however, stipulate that Denkmalpflege also applies to non-listed buildings which, because of that status, do not qualify for the normal administrative protection. Several protective laws name another, longer ranging objective: the inclusion of protective measures in physical planning projects.

The importance of such requirements and of their different extent is reduced in practice because of the fact that the authorities cannot carry out this task themselves but are dependent on the help of the planning agencies. But their obligations as regards planning in general and the protection of buildings in particular stems for the most part from (federal) planning laws, namely the Federal Building Act and the Regional Policy Act, and in some cases state law,

specifically the planning legislation. This legislation, too, draws a framework for the consideration or inclusion of protective measures in regional or local plans. But they require the planning agencies to take other matters into account and to consider them in relation to the protective element, so that the actual weight of the provision prescribing the inclusion of protective measures depends on the actual situation.

As mentioned above, the various protective laws contain different definitions, with the result that their actual areas of application also differ. Only the general definition is more or less consistent. Thus, the object of protection is termed a "Denkmal" or a "Kulturdenkmal". It normally runs as follows: "Kulturdenkmale" are objects, groups and parts of objects, which, for certain reasons, are considered to be worth preserving in the public interest. Total properties and parts of properties are mentioned separately in keeping with the law of property as embodied in the Civil Code, which does not necessarily permit parts of or whole properties to be treated separately or uniformly. But where the general definition is then sub-divided into buildings, sites and movable objects, a clear distinction appears as between the various laws. In the first place, several of the Länder prescribed that a building, etc. can only be an object of protection if it is of cultural interest and belongs to a completed epoch of historical significance. All other Länder have omitted this restriction, so that outstanding examples of modern architecture can be placed under protection.

Other differences lie in the definitions of buildings of historical importance. There must accordingly be historical, aesthetic or similar reasons (see under 3.2.1) in the public interest (see 3.2.2). The category includes "complete structures", "several or groups of buildings", and "conservation zones or areas". These are in particular streets, squares, and townscapes, also parks and green areas. Thus all legislators apparently have in mind the familiar term "ensemble", though it is open to many different interpretations.

With such groups of buildings, too, there must be a public interest in their preservation. The conditions sometimes differ from those pertaining to individual objects, and there are differences from state to state. Moreover, all laws and plans cover the immediate environment of buildings to be protected, which have to be distinguished from complete groups of objects.

1.3.2.1 Historical or other significance of protected buildings

There must be individual or several innate reasons for preserving old buildings. The appropriate legislation contains such phrases as "on account of their . . . value", "their . . . significance", or "for reasons of . . .".

In all federal states the criterion may be "scientific" or "aesthetic", or "historical". Of the various meanings, the "town planning" aspect calls for some explanation on account of the new dimensions it accords to the concept of ancient buildings worthy of protection. The legislation adopted in Hamburg brings out the essence of this criterion. The object is to protect a "milieu" or environment which is a social concern. Protection is afforded to buildings to which local inhabitants and sometimes visitors have an inner, a cultural relationship, which gives them a sense of identity with the local culture and thus encourages social contact and integration. Consequently, buildings or larger units of but little historical or aesthetic importance that add variety to a town or district, giving it a vitality and its own characteristic appearance, qualities which make people feel at home there, also qualify for preservation. Thus the old, dominating concept of protection, mainly the historical connotation, has been considerably extended beyond the classical protection of individual buildings. In some cases the object to be preserved may be listed for protection not because of its individual value but because of its importance within an overall context.

1.3.2.2 Public interest in preservation

The courts have presumed the existence of a public interest where "certain facts establish the building's importance for research, art or local history and culture" and "the community or at least a large body of experts have become aware of its importance". The term "public interest" which appears frequently in legislation on the subject cannot be defined in one generally valid and practical formula. It can merely be said that to interpret regulations designed to safeguard the public interest it is at least necessary to establish the extent of that interest on the basis of the objectives and programmes of the protective legislation and other laws that have some bearing on the matter. Difficulties arise where it is a question of making a sharp division between conflicting public interests, of which the following are typical:

Where a property has the characteristics that make it worthy of legal protection, those characteristics at the same time restrict the owner's freedom to dispose of the property as he sees fit and thus affect the basic principle of protecting property which is also in the public interest. Accordingly, in assessing the public interest in preservation it is also necessary to take into account the interests of the owner – and in many instances the two sets of interests collide. This tends to enhance the importance of the building to be protected. Moreover, the public protection and maintenance of every building to be preserved is a burden on the community, at least in the form of administrative costs, and often in the form of grants. Thus the need to use public funds sparingly must be weighed against the public interest in the object concerned. After all, the conservation of too many old buildings could militate against the productive use of land (Federal Building Act, section 1/VI) in the interest of the economy as a whole.

However, in some areas it is difficult to draw a sharp line between the general public interest deriving from town planning and the specific interests ensuing from protective legislation. This is particularly apparent where a building is considered to be worthy of protection because of its significance in terms of urban development. In such cases it is necessary to take into account the development concept of town planning (where it is expressed in legally binding plans) in determing the extent of the public interest. Considering that conflicting interests can only be harmonised in the course of plan preparation and approval procedure (to the extent that aspects of sector planning are involved), the present basic approach to the application of the concept of protection must be maintained, in other words only the public interest deriving from the concept of protection may be taken into account in giving concrete expression to conservation measures. Thus, in the final analysis, buildings covered by development criteria can only be determined in the town planning process.

If the question of definition has been settled, the appropriate statutory provisions ensuring protection (see below, 3.2.4) can as a rule only be applied after the building has been listed (3.2.3).

1.3.2.3 Listing protected buildings

With the exception of Bavaria, all the Laender have made provision in their legislation for the listing of buildings deemed worthy of protection. If they are not listed the appropriate provisions apply only to a limited extent or not at all. There is a formal listing procedure. The requirements are not always clearly stipulated in the laws but as a general rule buildings must have the characteristics qualifying them for protection under the law.

The Baden-Württemberg protective law, for instance, makes all buildings of cultural importance subject to "general protective provisions". Buildings of "special" importance are listed and receive extra protection (section 12/I). Groups of buildings or units are excluded from this rule and can only be afforded protection on the strength of ordinances issued by the higher authority responsible for protective measures, in consultation with the local authority (section 19).

Berlin, Bremen, Hesse, Hamburg and Lower Saxony also require buildings to be listed to qualify for protection but do not insist that they be of "special" importance.

According to section 8 (I) of the law in force in Rhineland-Palatinate, "zones" are given protective status by means of ordinances. In the other protective laws such a legal form is not necessary.

1.3.2.4 Statutory provisions

All laws concerning protection of ancient buildings of historical importance impose restrictions on owners and users with different contents and conditions. All provisions, though different in scope, require owners and users to keep buildings in a good state of repair or to restore or repair property which has been adversely affected by their own action. Except for the latter case, this obligation is usually subject to reasonable economic limits. In many cases the application of the law depends on the public money available for grants.

Another common feature of protective legislation is the requirement that alterations, etc, to buildings of historical importance are subject to approval by the responsible authority. Such alterations include repairs, restoration, removal from the original site or any change in the environment which would impair the property. The last resort if a property or group of buildings cannot be preserved is compulsory purchase. This is subject to compensation pursuant to article 14 (3) of the Basic Law and happens in exceptional cases only. The laws also contain supplementary provisions requiring owners and users to notify the authorities of any alterations to or sale of the building or to permit access. The building protection laws of Bavaria (article 5), Berlin (section 9/III), Lower Saxony (section 9), Hesse (section 13) and the Saarland (section 11) contain obligations relating to the use of such buildings.

The Lower Saxony building protection law says that "listed properties should be used for a purpose which will ensure their permanent conservation. The Land, the local, urban district and other authorities should assist owners and other users in this respect." Here, too, the provision extends not only to individual but to "groups of buildings".

A survey of the laws and regulations shows that their prime purpose is to protect buildings from intervention by owners, whereas they afford incomplete protection against measures by the public authorities, especially in the planning sector. For instance, there are no detailed provisions on the ways and means of incorporating protective measures in town and regional planning. However, these problems cannot be dealt with by protective legislation since they relate to the legal status of the land covered by planning law and not to the actual building construction and its result.

Nor are there any specific provisions as to how the Land or local authorities should provide assistance to owners and users who have to comply with restrictions. And considering the general tendency to place individual and groups of buildings in one category, there are very few provisions relating specifically to ensembles.

2. Organisation

Under the pertinent legislation, the responsibility for protection usually lies with the Ministry of Cultural Affairs and Education. Thus, because art and culture in general, hence including monuments, buildings, etc., are within the sphere of competence of the Laender, organisation on the national level is decentralised, and on the level of the individual states centralised. From this it follows that organisation depends on the administrative structure and size of the federal state concerned, in other words it is based on the two- in some cases three-tier structure of the federal states, or the organisational structure of the city-states.

In all cases there is a "two-track" system consisting of the consultative specialised bodies on the one hand and the decision-making authorities on the other. The specialised agency is usually a regional office (Denkmalamt), the protective authorities are those of the general (possibly) three-tier structure: Ministry of Cultural Affairs and Education – County President – Lower Administrative Authority (e. g. Landrat or Oberkreisdirektor [chief executive officer]).

Normally, the Denkmalamt has a council for monuments and buildings although in some cases it is attached to the Ministry of Cultural Affairs and Education (as in Bavaria) or the Regierungspräsidium (as in Baden-Württemberg). This council consists of honorary representatives of various social groups and is concerned with fundamental aspects of conservation. In addition, some Laender have a separate organisational structure for castles, palaces, parks, etc. And finally there are various associations and other groupings of a national and international character that have neither the finanical means nor the statutory powers of intervention, so that their influence is for the most part limited to exchanges of views and publicity campaigns, etc.

The Landesdenkmalamt is usually headed by the regional curator (Landeskonservator) whose main function is to ensure consultation and the co-ordination of the activities of all agencies concerned with protective measures as a basis for decisions. The necessary research work is likewise carried out by the Landesdenkmalamt. Only in a few cases have the regional laws on protective measures specified the areas of competence of the Denkmalämter.

As senior authorities, the Landesdenkmalämter are under the direct authority of the Ministry of Cultural Affairs and Education and competent for the entire federal state. In line with the two-track organisational system for protective measures as outlined above, they have no supervisory powers over the higher and lower authorities, which are directly responsible to the Ministry of Cultural Affairs and Education.

Other laws relevant to protection and conservation

The regional laws, plans and programmes contain a variety of provisions relating to the protection of ancient buildings and urban conservation. However, owing to the legal character of regional policy, they can only have a direct effect via town and county planning. They also contain some important parameters for protective and conservation measures. They determine, for instance, the course of major roads, the local authority function in the area, its central role and prospective size. Thus in individual cases decisions can be taken on the long-term fate of buildings deemed worthy of conservation.

The Laender regulations pertaining to local authorities contain provisions on the sale or alteration of property of "scientific, historical or artistic" value owned by the local authorities. They are more binding on local authorities than on private owners.

Protection for Church-owned property is also a special feature. It stems from agreements between the Laender and the Church communities. They usually bind the Churches to see to the preservation of their buildings and not to sell or alter them except in agreement with the public authorities concerned. The regional laws for the protection of ancient monuments and historical buildings issued since 1971 have in general left this provision intact.

Mention is made in conclusion of the Council of Europe Convention of 14 May 1954 for the Protection of Cultural Property in the Event of Armed Conflicts (to which the Federal Republic acceded by law of 11 April 1967 as amended on 10 August 1971) and the draft bill on effective protection for immovable cultural property in Europe.

3. Financial Aspects

3.1 Purchase of buildings by the state

Considering the economic structure of the Federal Republic of Germany, public assistance for conservation measures is not granted with a view to securing public ownership of renovated buildings. The authorities do sometimes buy property, but after renovation it is placed in private hands again, and this is explicitly dictated by the Urban Development and Town Planning Act (section 25). The state normally only retains buildings which cannot be maintained on a private basis.

3.2 Assistance for conservation programmes

There are a great variety of financial assistance measures. The Federal Government, the Laender, district and local authorities, provide non-repayable grants, low-interest loans, and interest subsidies. In addition, there is tax relief.

3.2.1 General sources of assistance

3.2.1.1 Tax relief

In recent years the government has introduced many more possibilities for persons buying and modernising old buildings, especially for conservation purposes, to deduct the costs from taxable income.

3.2.1.2 Government savings schemes

Among the various measures introduced by the government to help secure a wider spread of property ownership, especially housing, saving with building societies is encouraged. As soon as the prospective house owner has saved a specific proportion of the total amount required he receives a low-interest loan from his building society. And for the amounts saved he receives a bonus from the government. All persons up to a certain income limit are entitled to such bonuses. About 10 percent of all money saved with building societies is used for the purchase and modernisation of old buildings.

3.2.1.3 Government-subsidised housebuilding and modernisation schemes

A proportion of the capital borrowed for the building or purchase of new accommodation or for extensions and alterations involving major structural changes can be obtained from the government in the form of low-interest loans, again provided the tenant's or owner's income does not exceed the prescribed limit. As only limited funds are available for such loans, no legal claim exists.

On account of the high cost of land and building, it is often not possible to charge a "cost rent" in the first few years after occupancy; it would in any case be beyond the financial means of many tenants. The same applies to the financial burden incurred in building or purchasing a single- or two-family house. Consequently, loans or grants may be obtained to help cover the tenant's or owner's interest payments during the first twelve to fifteen years after completion of the building, either in place of or in addition to the government building loan. In this case, too, the tenant's or owner's income must not exceed a certain limit.

Single payments or grants for specific periods are available to meet the costs of modernisation and energy-saving alterations. If the alterations are very extensive, low-interest loans can be obtained. Again, tenants and owners have no legal claim. Tax relief may be claimed for modernisation work on certain conditions specified by law, especially if it comprises energy-saving measures.

3.3 Urban Renewal and Town Development Act

The Urban Renewal and Town Development Act starts from the assumption that funds made available for conservation measures are primarily used for local authority schemes to improve urban development and infrastructure and the costs of which are unremunerative. The costs are shared three ways by the Federal Government and the federal state and local authority concerned. These are for the most part the costs of preparation and planning, administration and infrastructure, and a proportion of the costs of modernisation to be borne by the local authority pursuant to section 43 of the Urban Renewal and Town Development Act. Funds earmarked for conservation programmes may only be allocated for the profit-making new building phase in exceptional cases and on special conditions, such as where the purpose of renewal could not otherwise be achieved. Under the federal programme introduced pursuant to the Urban Renewal and Town Development Act, 577 renewal and development projects in 459 towns were being promoted in 1979. The local authorities have together allocated DM 5,155 million.

3.4 Modernisation and Energy Conservation Act

Since 1974, the Federal Government and the Laender have sponsored joint modernisation programmes. The Housing Modernisation Act came into force on 1 January 1977. The object of the new legislation is to provide broad sections of the population with good and reasonably priced accommodation and at the same time to help preserve the housing stock. The law amending the Housing Modernisation Act which entered into force on 1 July 1978 includes buildings improvements designed to save heating energy.

Priority is given to buildings of architectural and in particular historical or artistic importance. The repair work may also qualify for public assistance if the property cannot be modernised by other means. In the case of buildings of the former category, repairs may account for up to 6 percent of the total modernisation costs.

In 1979, the Federal Government and the Laender together made available DM 438 million for modernisation purposes. It is estimated that about 80,000 houses and flats benefited. And another DM 480 million was available for the promotion of energy-saving measures. The most important special government conservation programmes are outlined below.

3.5 Public grants and special programmes

3.5.1 Federal grants

One major element is the programme for future investment "to improve living conditions in towns and cities" adopted by the Federal Government in March 1977. The funds, spread over the years 1977 to 1979, totalled DM 950 million and, as in the case of the special programmes carried out in 1974 and 1975, are used to finance continuous conservation projects under the Urban Renewal and Town Development Act and mainly benefit measures for which assistance is already being granted under the federal programme pursuant to that Act. The different investment categories are "historical town centres", "infrastructure", "transfer of business establishments", and "substitute housing, conversion and extension". In 1977 and 1978, DM 820 million federal funds were allocated to about 2,200 projects. The projects in the "historical town centres" category mainly concerned the modernisation, conversion or extension of buildings or ensembles worth preserving because of their historical, aesthetic or local planning importance.

Another element of the investment programme is village renewal, a problem of preserving the built-up enviroment which has only reappeared again in recently years. Up to 1978, DM 440 million had been allocated for such projects.

In 1978, DM 12 million was made available for the "preservation and reconstruction of large buildings of cultural or historical importance".

The Minister of the Interior may also make available direct grants for the conservation of outstanding monuments. In 1978 he allocated DM 2,500 million for such purposes.

3.5.2 Grants at Land level

All funds used for urban renewal must be administered by the Laender. In many cases they provide funds of their own in addition to the federal grants. The Laender also maintain their own Denkmalamt which may also have its own funds. This money, to the extent that it is not used to meet staff and other costs, is made available as non-repayable grants. It is seen as compensation for additional expenditure resulting from compliance with renewal and conservation regulations. As it has not been possible to increase these funds substantially in recent years, they are at the moment much too scarce.

3.5.3 Grants at district and local authority level

On account of the increasing importance of urban preservation, many districts and local authorities have budgeted for conservation measures, especially with regard to housing. The amounts made available differ from town to town.

3.6 Institutions and corporations

A large proportion of important monuments such as castles, palaces, former monasteries, residences, etc., are owned by the state. Many of them house public authorities, museums, conference rooms, etc. Usually, the expenditure for the upkeep of such buildings falls under the budget heading of ordinary building projects and does not appear as the preservation of monuments and ancient buildings or as a contribution to urban conservation measures. Thus it is not possible to determine the exact expenditure for such projects. This also applies to the Churches, which in the Federal Republic of Germany are self-governing institutions. They receive funds raised by the Church tax but they must meet a large part of Church maintenance costs themselves.

3.7 Private measures

Numerous modernisation projects have been launched in recent years as a result of citizens' action compaigns or through the efforts of private associations. Sometimes, larger amounts are raised by small groups. But the most significant development of recent years has been that private building has tended more and more towards modernisation. This trend has been so pronounced that it is likely to have the most lasting effect in terms of urban renewal and conservation.

4. Involvement of the Public

Public participation in the preservation of historical town centres; legislation, organisation and conservation methods.

Introduction

In recent years the public authorities in the Federal Republic of Germany have been giving increasing attention to the preservation of historical town centres and quarters which up to now has chiefly depended on the propensity to invest of property owners, tradesmen, etc. Where there was no private initiative, old towns fell into decay, and where investment did take place economic interests prevailed. The people living in those areas moved into the suburbs and made way for commercial enterprises; office blocks and department stores took the place of shops and craftsmen's establishments; green areas, open spaces and playgrounds had to give way to roads and car parks. This change in the use of land is also reflected in the townscape, which becomes increasingly dominated by the concrete blocks of modern department stores, multi-storey car parks, banks and insurance company offices.

Local authorities were content to adapt their plans according to owners' requirements and the economic advantages. Often enough they did this not only because they had to owing to the lack of means of control and funds but also because they were convinced that they could not afford to stand in the way of growth and economic progress if they wanted to maintain the viability of their towns and cities.

The consequences of this kind of urban renewal were too obvious: For the most part no consideration was given to the needs and interests of non-owners and the low income groups.

An example: conservation in Hameln (Hamelin)
The Hameln conservation programme was carried out in 1969/70 whilst the Urban Renewal and Town Development Act (Städtebauförderungsgesetz, referred to in Part 1) was in preparation and was regarded by Herrn Lauritzen, then Federal Minister of Housing and Town Planning, as the "No. 1 Model" for urban renewal.

The "Association of the Citizens of Hameln for the Preservation of Their Old Town", however, saw the scheme as the "No. 1 Model for the destruction of our old towns and cities". They accused the town council of setting about doing the very thing which neither the Pied Piper of Hamelin, fire, the Plague, foot and mouth disease, nor foreign armies had failed to achieve: destroying the virility and character of the town:

- Not until after the first local plans had been adopted did the public learn that about one quarter of the houses in the old part of the town were to be pulled down. Only a selected few (representatives of the press and organizations) had, according to the Association, been informed in advance.
- They argued that the decision to place the houses on the demolition list was in many cases wrong and completely incomprehensible. Most of them were to be removed to make room for, of all things, a new department store.
- The concrete masses in the form of four bridge-type multi-storey car parks ("reminiscent of the Bastille") would spoil the integrated character of the old town in the same way as the department store, they said.

Concerned about these plans, this local amenity group asked whether it was really true "that the driving force behind this project, which is unaesthetic and hardly conducive to the advancement of civilisation, are the big building contractors who, now that there is no longer such a grave housing shortage, are anxious they might lose this very profitable source of business? Is it now the intention in this industrial society to degrade houses and flats to the category of consumer goods in order to multiply sales in this branch too?"

The negative trend of urban redevelopment – the decay or commercialisation of old towns and the disregard for the interests and needs of non-owners and low income groups – mobilised both the public authorities and the local population. The following will therefore describe

- what measures were introduced (Part 1: legislation and its application by local authorities),
- what demands are put forward by the local population and how they are asserted (Part 2: the public's insistence on participation).

It will also show how the problems encountered by local authorities in permitting public involvement in policies for the preservation and renewal of historical town centres fit into the wider issue of "participation in the Federal Republic of Germany" (Part 3: general problems of local policies regarding participation).

4.1 Legislation and its application by local authorities

4.1.1 The legal basis for public participation

4.1.1.1 Urban Renewal and Town Development Act

The Urban Renewal and Town Development Act, which came into force on 1 August 1971, on the one hand makes replanning and development schemes subject to public control and thus also opens the door to considerable financial assistance which, though not a substitute for private initiative, can provide a stimulus for such investment and steer it in the right direction. On the other hand, however, it has led to a development which had been quite unusual in the Federal Republic up to then, at least on this scale: wider public responsibility also meant that the people concerned would have a bigger say in these matters.

a. Involvement of the local population as provided for in the Act

Section 1 (4) of the Act lays down that "those affected" should be given an opportunity "to participate in the prepa-

ration and implementation" of urban conservation and development measures. This implies that:

- not everyone may participate, only those affected. Those principally affected are owners, tenants and leaseholders, others with a right of use and the employers of businesses in the renewal area.
- they have a right to participate only in measures involving urban redevelopment and renewal, that is, in their preparation and implementation. Redevelopment measures are only such as serve to considerably improve or re-adapt an area (Section 1 (2).
- the persons affected can merely participate; in other words they do not decide; nor are they the only ones entitled to have a say. Thus the Act leaves untouched the decision-making authority of the institutions stipulated by the constitution and the law (town councils and local authorities), which are merely obliged "to ensure a fair balance between the interests of those concerned . . . and those of the general public" (Section 1 [4]).

b. Provisions of the Act relating to participation

As mentioned above, the relevant provisions of the Act concern the preparation and implementation of conservation and development measures.

(1) Participation in the preparation of conservation measures

In order to ensure that those affected can participate right from the preparation stage, the Act stipulates that

- the local authority should in its preliminary study ascertain the views of owners, tenants, leaseholders and others with rights of use with regard to the proposed conservation scheme and whether they wish to participate, and listen to their proposals (Section 4 [1]).
- The local authority should, as soon as possible during the preparation stage, develop its proposals and discuss with those concerned ways and means of avoiding or mitigating the detrimental effects of renewal plans on those affected (Section 4 [2]).

The local authority is also obliged to publish the date for the preliminary studies (Section 4 [3]); the same applies to the decision on the formal stipulation of the Renewal Area (Section 5 [3]).

(2) Participation in the implementation phase

The Act requires the local authority, during implementation,

- to continue the discussions with those directly affected, taking into account their occupational, employment and family circumstances, age, housing requirements, social influences and local ties (Section [2]).
- and as soon as possible to discuss the proposed redevelopment of the area concerned and the possibilities of their involvement in the implementation phase with owners, tenants, leaseholders and others with a right of use; the authority should also give the employees of businesses in the area a chance to present their views on the redevelopment plans (Section 9 [1]).

4.1.1.2 The Federal Building Act

a. Participation of the public under the Act

The Federal Building Act (Bundesbaugesetz) supplements and widens the scope of the Urban Renewal and Town Development Act in three ways:

- First, it does not limit participation to those concerned but simply provides for "the participation of the local population" (Section 1 [1]). Thus, anyone may participate whether he is affected or not. This does not apply to participation in the sense of Section 13 a., which only concerns the persons affected.

- Second, participation applies not only to comprehensive renewal and development measures but in principal to development planning as a whole, that is, to all procedures relating to the town map and local plan (Section 2 a [1] in conjunction with Section 1 [2]).

- Third, the Federal Building Act applies the provisions of the Urban Renewal and Town Development Act stipulating discussion of the adverse effects of local authority planning and measures to town planning regulations in general (section 13 a).

The Federal Building Act likewise says that participation is not only limited to the local population and that their involvement does not affect the decision-making powers of the local authority departments concerned. The Act does not rule out a modification of the authority's plans after hearing the views of the population (Section 2 a [5]) but it places no obligation whatsoever on the local authority to respond to their objections or suggestions. It is merely required to "study" them and to inform those making the objections or proposals of the result (Section 2 a [6]).

b. Participation in accordance with the Federal Building Act

Under Section 2 a (2) and (6), the local authority must take two steps to enable the local population to have a say in development planning procedures:

- First, it must publicly explain the general objectives and purposes of the plans and give the general public an opportunity to present their views and discuss the matter (hearing). Both must be done in an appropriate manner and in good time; the authority must draw attention to the plan's probable implications and to the main alternatives for the renewal or development of a particular area (to the extent that alternatives come into consideration).

- The authority must then lay out the draft development plans together with the explanatory report or justification for public inspection and receive objections and suggestions. The plan must be available for public inspection for one month and the place and duration must be advertised locally at least a week in advance. As the provisions of Section 13 a of the Federal Building Act largely correspond with those of the Urban Renewal and Town Development Act (Sections 4 and 8, see above), there is no need for them to be explained separately here.

4.1.1.3 Other statutory provisions

Although practically all aspects of "the preservation and renewal of historical town centres" are covered by the provisions of the Urban Renewal and Town Development Act and the Federal Building Act, there are a number of other laws that are relevant to this subject and in some cases contain provisions concerning the involvement of the local community. They are, however, usually less comprehensive than the two acts mentioned. For example:

- The Housing Modernization Act (Wohnungsmodernisierungsgesetz) of 23 August 1976 stipulates that the Federal Government and the Laender should promote modernisation programmes in order to improve the supply of good and relatively cheap accommodation for broader sections of the population and in this way help preserve towns and communities (Section 1). The task of the local authorities is to determine the priorities (Section 11 [1]). Tenants have to accept the publicly financed modernisation measures but must be informed in writing by the landlord about the nature, scope, commencement and probable duration of the modernisation work two months in advance (Section 2 [1] and [2]).

- The legislation of the Laender relating to the protection of ancient monuments and historical buildings defines the monuments and buildings falling within these categories, lays down how they should be preserved and how public money is to be used for the purpose. The Protection of Ancient Monuments and Historical Buildings in Berlin Act of 22 December 1977 provides for the appointment of an advisory committee for monuments and buildings under the authority of the Senator (Minister) for Building. It advises and assists the agencies concerned with protection measures and submits proposals. It consists of three experts (for history, protection of monuments and buildings, and architecture) and three members of the community (Section 4 [1, 2, 3]).

Also important for the preservation and renewal of historical town centres and quarters are a number of regulations providing tax concessions for the purchase or preservation and renewal of old buildings, etc. (cf. Heuer, Schäfer).

4.1.1.4 Summary of the analysis of statutory provisions

Two main factors should be emphasised as the result of the analysis of statutory provisions relating to the involvement of the local community in the preservation and renewal of historical town centres:

(1) The different aspects of preservation and renewal are to a large extent covered by the provisions of the Urban Renewal and Town Development Act and the Federal Building Act which also relate to participation by members of the community.

(2) This legislation does not of course deal with participation comprehensively, only within certain limits:

- For one thing these Acts leave no doubt that whatever the result of participation it has no binding effect on the authorities. Their decision-making powers remain untouched.

- For another, they determine the scope of participation, in other words they say where the community may participate.

Thus it is left to the discretion of the local authorities how the problems not covered by these Acts are to be resolved. They include the following:

- The local authorities can to a large extent themselves determine how they wish to allow people to participate in the decision-making process. Provisions in such terms as "ascertain", "discuss", "study", "consider", "receive" proposals, etc. leave local authorities just as much scope as phrases like "as soon as possible" or "in an appropriate manner". The Federal Building Act makes it clear that the local authority can decide "in what manner, in what area, and within which time limit the local population can participate" (Section 2 a [3]).

– The local authorities can moreover to a large extent themselves determine how far they will take the results of such participation into account. From a purely legal point of view, they can just as easily disregard them altogether as adopt them completely.

The wide scope which the Urban Renewal and Town Development Act and the Federal Building Act accord the local authorities in matters of participation enables them to adapt their policies to local conditions. Although this is without doubt an advantage, the drawback is that there are no standard modalities of participation since the nature and extent of participation largely depend on how individual local authorities view the whole question. The provisions of these two Acts are interpreted and applied very differently.

4.1.2 Organisation and methods of participation under the Urban Renewal and Town Development Act

The following survey is simply an analysis of the way in which the local authorities apply the provisions of the Urban Renewal and Town Development Act relating to the participation of the local population. The amended Federal Building Act has not been in force long enough to permit of any conclusions as to local authority experience with the Act at this stage.

4.1.2.1 Preparation of renewal measures (preliminary study)

The participation process in the preparation of redevelopment schemes usually takes the form of opinion polls. Although the local authorities can in this way in most cases reach the majority of those concerned, polls are of but limited value in ascertaining their future attitudes (e. g. how far they will be prepared to assist in the decision-making process), which is so very important for any redevelopment project, nor are they an instrument "of active or creative participation": the citizen who is consulted "remains the passive partner who may voice an opinion but not play an active part". (Koller, p. 2).

Apart from these general defects of the poll as an instrument, its effectiveness as a medium of participation mainly depends on how it is incorporated in the overall participation process (a) and how far the results it produces are injected into the planning process (b).

a. Participation process and polls

The following two examples are given to show how different local authorities can be in their application of the provisions of the Urban Renewal and Town Development Act.

Redevelopment plans in the old part of Tübingen

The Tübingen public works department had drawn up plans for a redevelopment scheme before the Urban Renewal and Town Development Act was passed by parliament, so that as soon as the Act came into force the town council engaged the Team for Social Planning, an independent group, to prepare a social report. That report was submitted 12 months later and became the first of its kind ever to have been produced in the Federal Republic.

The instruments adopted in Tübingen for conducting the participation process were as follows:

Participation of the local community prior to the social report:

– publication of the proposed town plans in a brochure;
– presentation of the plans at a two-day meeting of the Evangelical Academy in Bad Boll where five open-ended working groups were set up on the proposal of the city council to discuss the draft plans;
– the groups subsequently discussed the plans and drew up a comprehensive catalogue of objections, suggestions and wishes;
– catalogue then presented at a large meeting;
– regular reports in the "Schwäbische Tagblatt".

Participation during the preparation of the social report.

The Team for Social Planning saw its task in "verifying or supplementing the suggestions and wishes by means of scientific surveys, but also in familiarising those sections of the community which up to that point . . . had not been able to participate in the discussion of the redevelopment project, even though they are the ones directly affected by the plans, with the working methods of the local authorities".

The team proceeded as follows:

– An information centre was set up behind the town hall (open daily)
– An exhibition of renewal plans and models was organised (visited by 8,000–10,000 people; discussions with 1,800–2,000)
– Contacts were made with the press, radio and television (including the provision of information for inhabitants of the old part of the town about redevelopment projects carried out in other towns)
– Pamphlets, house-to-house visits
– Seven surveys were carried out (households, businessmen, young people, students, foreigners, people leaving or coming to live in Tübingen; social workers)
– Local authority work was explained to stimulate citizens' action groups.

Redevelopment in Landshut

In its preliminary investigations for Renewal Area III, as provided for in Section 4 of the Urban Renewal and Town Development Act, the Landshut development planning and statistics office carried out a survey among house and land owners, households and local business people. Householders were asked about the type of family (one or more persons), income and mortages, how long they had been living at their present address, the size of the flat or house, its fixtures and facilities, defects, and the amount of rent; they were also asked about their social circumstances and their way to and from work or place of training.

In order to be able to project the "principles for the social plan" pursuant to Section 8 (2) of the Urban Renewal and Town Development Act, "all persons living, working or engaged in business in the renewal area" were asked to make "any changes in their circumstances and any wishes they may have known to the town development planning and statistics office".

If one compares these two examples with preparatory surveys in other towns, Tübingen could be said to be untypical, Landshut typical:

– Since the replanning analysis and opinion surveys normally take place at the same time, the people affected cannot be consulted either on the specific renewal plans resulting from that analysis or on any adverse consequences of renewal for them. Thus people are only asked about alternatives phrased in abstract terms – e. g. new building or modernisation – and not about specific plans as in Tübingen.

– Although most preliminary investigations go beyond mere interviewing, with pamphlets being distributed, the press informed, public meetings organised, etc. all this serves principally to prepare and carry out the survey and not, as in Tübingen, to encourage those concerned to participate and to enable them to articulate their wishes and needs.

b. Taking into account the results of local community participation

In most cases during preliminary studies the results of surveys carried out among those concerned are incorporated in recommendations designed to avoid or mitigate the negative effects on them:

– that they should receive assistance when moving out,

– that their links with the area should be given as much consideration as possible,

– that more assistance should be given to those who are affected more than others (old people, foreigners, large families, those with low incomes, etc.),

– that rents of alternative accommodation must be low enough,

– that flats should be of a higher standard,

– that there should be an improvement in the social structure, etc.

Such proposals, which are usually linked with specific information about the nature and extent of the help necessary for those concerned, show that the principles for the social plan formulated on the basis of the 31 preliminary studies covered are obviously concerned with mitigating rather than avoiding adverse consequences. Thus the wishes and needs of those concerned as established by the preliminary investigations hardly fulfil the aim of "changing the modalities of renewal and redevelopment in the social interest of those concerned" as intended by the Urban Renewal and Town Development Act (Dunckelmann, p. 546).

4.1.2.2 Implementation of renewal projects

Apart from the discussions prescribed by the Act, there are also institutionalised forms of community participation, the main one being the advisory committee on redevelopment:

– The membership of the advisory committee varies between 10 and over 50. The members are normally representatives of pressure groups (tenants, owners, businessmen, etc.), or of organisations (tenants' association, land owners' association, trade unions, chamber of commerce, etc.).
In many cases the municipal authorities and the local press are represented. In some cases, however, as for instance in Kiel-Gaarden, the members of the advisory committee are directly elected and do not have to represent any particular group or organisation.

– The members of the advisory committee are appointed by the municipal authority or the agency in charge of the renewal project, or they are elected directly or indirectly. One would assume that the election rather than appointment of members is better, it being the democratic method, but this is in most cases qualified by the low turnout at such elections: in Kiel-Gaarden, for instance, only 15.2 % of those entitled to vote in the election for the advisory committee on redevelopment did so.

– But although the advisory committees are established in these different ways, they usually have the same areas of competence: they have a right to be informed on certain matters, their decisions merely have the character of recommendations, and their views must be heard on all important aspects of renewal.

4.1.2.3 Renewal and redevelopment without the Urban Renewal and Town Development Act

The Urban Renewal and Town Development Act has saved many historical town centres and other areas but there have also been undesirable consequences:

– All too often, the more comprehensive renewal measures envisaged in the Act have simply taken the form of total redevelopment (Flächensanierung). That is to say, the existing buildings, instead of being renovated, have been pulled down and new ones erected in their place. In Berlin, for instance, the number of old buildings actually renovated in renewal areas up to 1973 accounted for only 0.8 per cent of the buildings demolished (Hämer, Rosemann, p. 4).

– Rents in such rebuilt areas, but also those in old buildings which had been renewed according to the standards applicable to public housing schemes, increased to such an extent as a result of the rising land and building costs that tenants could no longer afford them and had to move elsewhere.

– If word gets about that a particular area is likely to be scheduled for renewal, investment stops and the process of decay is accelerated. "Investment speculators" get to work before the brakes built into the Urban Renewal and Town Development Act can begin to take effect.

– The more comprehensive renewal measures envisaged in the Act generate such a flood of planning, organisational and administrative activity that town councils have no option but to pass the job on to town development enterprises. In such cases they are rarely in a position to exercise effective control (Neuffer, p. 129 seq.).

Under these circumstances it is not surprising that local authorities have begun to seek alternative methods of renewal to those provided for in the Act. One such alternative is the one made possible and qualifying for assistance under the Housing Modernisation Act which is less costly. But as this too is only possible with public assistance and the funds for this purpose are limited, local authorities also try to find alternatives based on the self-help of tenants. If the aim is to induce people to make a financial contribution as well to the preservation of their area, this has serious consequences for their participation in the development process, for in that case they will only play an active part if they can be assured that their wishes and needs will be taken into account.

Berlin-Kreuzberg has since 1977 been the scene of an experiment chiefly designed to mobilise self-help.

"Strategies for Kreuzberg"

The buildings in the area around the former Görlitz railway station in Berlin-Kreuzberg were built at the turn of the century. Once the centre of Berlin but now along the wall on the fringe of West Berlin, the area threatens to become a "slum ghetto for foreigners". Yet it could be included in neither the first nor the second Berlin urban renewal plans. But in order to save what was possible, the Senator (Minister) for Building and Housing, pushed by a priest in Kreuzberg who also had the backing of the local SPD association, launched a competition under the motto "Strategies for Kreuzberg". Participants were invited to develop new plans for reviving the former Kreuzberg SO 36 on the basis of existing local regulations and to adapt available perspectives for a practicable redevelopment programme, the aim being to improve local community life, to enable the inhabitants to identify themselves with this quarter of the city, and to encourage the different population groups to invest in their accommodation. Public involvement was achieved at three levels:

– people could participate in the competition themselves;

– the organisation and methods of public involvement were one of the conditions of the competition,

– two thirds of the jury were local people and members of action groups in the area.

The results of the competition are being tested in model projects and a report will be submitted to the Senate (city government).

4.2   Public demand for participation

It is true that in many cases where the local authorities invite the public to participate the response is not as might be expected, but this does not mean that the local community are indifferent to official decisions. They are to an increasing extent taking action themselves without waiting for decisions by the local authority, or in order to revise decisions taken.

4.2.1   Extent of the demand for participation

4.2.1.1   Potential reserve of active participants in the Federal Republic

The proportion of people who prefer the different ways of directly looking after their interests to representation through the elected bodies is considerable: 59 per cent of the adult population in the Federal Republic of Germany see citizens' action groups as an effective means of achieving specific aims (Emnid Information, p. 6) and as many as 63 per cent consider that important political decisions should be taken on the basis of referendums (Infas Report of 10. 7. 73). Yet this preference for direct involvement does not necessarily imply that people wish to play an active part themselves. Only 34 per cent of the adult population would be prepared to join a citizens' action group and only 3 per cent have actually done so (Infas Report of 23. 7. 73). By comparison: 45 per cent of the population are members of political parties, and 12 per cent are willing to join one (Armbruster, p. 137 seq.).

4.2.1.2   Demand for participation in urban renewal programmes

Urban development, renewal, protection of ancient monuments and historical buildings and measures to preserve the townscape are not issues that tend to arouse the interest of the local community to such an extent that they will play an active part. What they are most likely to get involved in is environmental protection and educational matters; then to a much smaller degree transport, and only then housing and urban development (Infas Report, 23. 7. 73). The Federation of Citizens' Action Groups for the Protection of the Environment (Bundesverband Bürgerinitiativen Umweltschutz) has 931 members (Stuttgarter Zeitung, 12. 5. 77), whereas the "Society for the Protection of Old Bamberg" only had 38 when it attempted to launch initiatives to save old towns (db 1-1974, p. 14). There are two possible explanations for this public inactivity as regards urban renewal:

– One is that those who live in renewal areas do not have the educational, social and economic background which would enable them to participate and are therefore less in a position to articulate their needs (cf. Armbruster, pp. 156 seq.). Hence it is usually the middle class that participate.

– Another is that in view of the long periods of time required for any renewal of a historical town centre or area it is not surprising that the involvement even of those who are willing to participate tends to wane, quite apart from the fact that people show little willingness to play an active part in plans the consequences of which do not emerge clearly until much later.

4.2.2   Citizens' action groups

Citizens' action groups are "in" and quite a number of community self-help organisations, which might in former times have called themselves a "local amenity society", today prefer "citizens' action group" – though many of them do not omit to register themselves as an association with the local court. But whatever the name they have the following characteristic feature: members of the local community form a group spontaneously and without a great deal of organisational investment in order to exert direct pressure on the authorities to meet specific wishes or pursue more complex objectives, or to achieve such objectives through their own efforts.

In contrast there are the traditional citizens' associations which have a long history in Germany but today only play a minor role. Some of them still exist and in many cases have shed their past image as local amenity societies and begun pursuing their activities in much the same way as citizens' action groups, but they cannot compete with the latter as far as their number and importance for urban renewal is concerned; nor do they attract the same public attention.

4.2.2.1   Aims of the citizens' action groups

The 75 citizens' action groups concerned fall into two categories as regards their aims to preserve and renew historical town centres and districts:

– Most of them devote their attention to individual matters; their aim is to preserve specific buildings, parks, streets, etc. Their activities range from

- efforts to save castles, semi-timbered houses and parks, via

- the controversy over cobbled roads (in Dinkelsbühl, for instance, one citizens' action group is fighting to keep the cobbled roads whilst another wants them asphalted to reduce noise), trees and gas-lamps (in Berlin alone there are four action groups trying to save the old gas-lamps), to

- the dispute about local transport plans. Some action groups (there are 21 in all concerned with such questions) say the plans should, like pedestrian precincts, preserve the old townscape whilst others say they are likely to destroy the organically grown structures of old areas.

– The minority of these groups have set themselves more comprehensive objectives; they are concerned with one particular part of the town or all of the old centre. They consider themselves to be "competent" for all problems needing a solution in their area. Their work is long-term; hence they also have more firmly rooted organisational structures (e. g. they are registered associations or they call themselves "area" or "citizens'" forum, etc.).

– Only a minority of citizens' action groups seek to influence the planning and implementation of renewal measures pursuant to the Urban Renewal and Town Development Act.

4.2.2.2 Types of activities undertaken by citizens' action groups

Basically, there is no difference between the activities of groups concerned with urban renewal and those of other groups. Here, too, a "dual strategy" is pursued, i. e. the groups seek to negotiate with the local authority and at the same time mobilise public opinion (by holding meetings, collecting signatures for petitions, calling for donations, articles in the press, demonstrations, etc.).

Example: Erbach/Odenwald Citizens' Action Group

The Erbach/Odenwald Citizens' Action Group has since 1962 been opposed to Local Plan No. 7 c adopted by Erbach town council. The plan provides for the building of a shopping centre, car parks, a communal office building, a high rise hotel and flats in the pleasure garden situated in the middle of the town and dating back to the year 1750. The scheme also covers part of the old town adjacent to the park. The baroque orangerie would be preserved but the complex would be in the immediate vicinity of the palace. The Citizens' Action Group

– prepared comprehensive documentation on the plans

– elicited various expert opinions from art historians, town planners, architects and economists,

– drew those opinions to the attention of the town council together with alternative plans for preserving the palace – pleasure garden – orangerie complex and switching the proposed project to another part of town,

– and initiated a major parliamentary question in the Hessian parliament.

The town council have not yet abandoned the plans but reduced their scope. However, the project has not yet got underway since court proceedings are pending.

4.2.3 Citizens' associations

More in the nature of the traditional private associations are those local amenity societies that aim to make their own contribution to urban renewal – mostly of a financial kind – because they are convinced that appeals to the "competent bodies" are not sufficient to save everything worth preserving. These societies still concern themselves either with just one project, with a specific ensemble, or with the old town en bloc:

– for instance, the "Society for the Reconstruction of the Knochenhauer-Amtshaus e. V." in Hildesheim is asking for donations for the preservation of the butchers guildhouse, which was considered the most beautiful semi-timbered building in the world until it was completely destroyed during the war.

– In the port of Hamburg the "Save the Deichstrasse Society" is trying to preserve a still intact group of old middle-class houses and warehouses built in the 17th and 18th centuries. It helped to have them renovated and newly inhabited.

– The "Society for the Preservation of Monuments and Buildings in the Old City of Augsburg", established in 1959, aims to preserve, restore and clean monuments and buildings of historical interest in the old part of the citiy which, though they survived the war, now threaten fo fall into decay.

Most of these societies co-operate closely with the local authority and associations. For instance, the call for donations by the Save the Deichstrasse Society was signed by four former mayors of the city of Hamburg as well as the presidents of the chamber of commerce, the chamber of handicrafts, the Hamburg chamber of architects, etc; and Augsburg city council has given the Old Augsburg Society financial assistance. The fact that such citizens' action groups do not always seek with such little conflict to achieve what everyone wants in any case is shown by the example of the "Save the Church Square" action group in Bayreuth.

One group campaigned for five years against plans to build new Church offices which they felt would spoil the Church square. The building, which had already been begun, remained a ruin for years until the group, the town planning office and the Church agreed that the front of the building should be moved back 14 metres in order to preserve the square. And the group said that it would not make available the DM 50,000 it had collected unless it was given a say in the design of the building's facade, which was another bone of contention.

Most of these action groups adopt two methods of obtaining donations. They approach potential donors (especially local businessmen) and they appeal to the community as a whole, mostly by means of raffles which apparently offer the best prospects of success, as shown by the accounts of the Old Augsburg Society: of their total income of almost DM 2.5 million, over DM 1.9 million came from raffles, nearly DM 120,000 from members' contributions, over DM 108,000 from interest, and DM 275,000 from donations (Wegele, p. 90).

4.2.4 Prospects of success for citizens' action groups

The fact that citizens wanting to be involved in the decision-making process do not follow the course of the elected respresentative bodies, i. e. they do not usually appeal to the parties, associations or parliament, but rather try to assert their views in a direct dialogue with the local authority must be seen as criticism – though only indirect since it is rarely given expression – of the existing opinion-forming process. One criterion for assessing the measure of success of, for instance, citizens' action groups is their ability to change the opinion-forming process (cf. 2.4.1). Another is the success they achieve in asserting their material aims (cf. 2.4.2).

4.2.4.1 Changing the opinion-forming process

The opinion-forming process can be altered by citizens' action groups on the one hand institutionally and on the other by involving as many people as possible so that democracy really becomes an active process and the for the most part politically abstinent majority no longer submit without resistance to the leadership of the political elite and the experts (Narr, Naschold, p. 157):

– About one third of the citizens' action groups covered by this survey have succeeded in institutionalising their involvement in the decision-making process by gaining admission to local government advisory bodies or establishing the right to be consulted. Two action groups have even intervened directly in the decision-making process by putting up candidates for elections and obtaining seats on the town council:

The "Electoral Association of Independent Citizens" in Berlin-Zehlendorf, which was the product of a citizens' action group which obstructed the building of a street tunnel in order to preserve the old town centre of Zehlendorf, polled 14 per cent of the votes at the elections for the district assembly. This gave them several seats in the assembly and one on the city council.

The "Baden-Baden Citizens' Action Group" which, in order to preserve the townscape, prevented the building of a low-lying road in the bed of the River Oos and instead gained acceptance for plans for a network of tangential roads and bypasses, obtained 5,500 votes in the elections for the town council and thus secured one seat.

– If one takes the number of signatures which an action group obtains in support of its aims as the criterion for its success in mobilising public opinion, it becomes clear that very many can be obtained for this kind of initiative as well (one group in Munich collected 20,000 signatures in opposition to building plans for the Nikolai Platz), but in most cases the action groups have to be content with about 600 signatures.

But such results are no real indication whether the political competence of the people has actually increased to the extent suggested by the large measure of support which the action groups undoubtedly command. The fact that

– people only take an active part when they are directly affected,

– they in many cases take an interest in things like gas-lamps or road services, which may matter to them personally but are relatively unimportant in the context of overall urban development,

– it is the middle class, who are already more competent in political matters, that articulate themselves in citizens' action groups,

is at any rate reason for scepticism. The prevailing political abstinence has not by a long way yielded to a general growth of political involvement.

One confirmation of this theory ist the fact that citizens' action groups are still rare. In matters of conservation and renewal of historical town centres and urban districts, there are initiatives like the "Society for the Protection of Old Bamberg" or the following examples:

– Tenants of Kaussen (purchaser of housing) houses (which are often situated in actual or prospective renewal areas) are trying to form national organisations to defend themselves against the unscrupulous tenancy termination methods of the owner.

– In the Ruhr, 33 action groups have formed a regional association to campaign for the preservation of old miners' houses.

4.2.4.2 Attainment of material objectives

Most of the citizens' action groups covered by this survey have above all been successfull in mobilising the public. With the other groups, complete success and partial success held the balance. Partial success usually takes the form of

– a planning compromise (as in the case of the Erbach/Odenwald action group),

– projects not yet fully completed (as with the "Save the Deichstrasse" action group in Hamburg, who so far have been able to renew only one of the houses),

– or the local authority has delayed its plans to allow time for further deliberations for a survey of the local community (which was the reaction of the Berlin city council to the initiative concerning gas-lamps).

Thus the following applies to citizens' action groups concerned with the preservation and renewal of historical town centres and other districts (as for all other action groups):

– The action groups have achieved considerable success in mobilising the public, which after all is one of the main prerequisites for the effectiveness of their activities.

– But they are to an increasing extent achieving at least partial results in pursuit of their material aims. There are two possible reasons for this:

● The action groups have learnt to define their aims in such a way that they can realistically expect to assert them.

● But the local authorities, too, have learnt to adopt a pragmatic approach; not to reject action groups' demands on principle as they used to but to negotiate with them and, if necessary, to reach compromise solutions.

That the manner in which action groups and the local authorities deal with each other is not always what it should be is shown by the following example:

An action group formed at the time of the "Strategies for Kreuzberg" was set on preserving an old pump and former fire station so that a district centre could be established there. But the district office wanted to pull down both buildings to make room for a sports centre and a combined system settling tank. Members of the action group occupied the fire station and entered the competition "Strategies for Kreuzberg" with their plan to establish a district centre.

The district office at first tolerated the illegal occupation of the building and postponed the demolition of the fire station in order to explain its plan to the jury (which saw itself as representative of the citizens and was accepted as such). Afterwards, it had the occupants of the fire station removed and the building demolished.

The fire station was demolished

- although the district office did not have the unanimous support of the jury for its plans, and

- without waiting for a ruling by the Higher Administrative Court on a complaint; the ruling was to have been given on the day of demolition.

The judge said he was "shocked" by the district office's action and said that it "can no longer be trusted". This comment thereupon prompted the district office to reject the judge on the ground that he was prejudiced in any administrative dispute in which the office was involved. Its application for rejection was dismissed by the Higher Administrative Court (IInd Senate).

4.3 General problems of public involvement

It is clear from the examples given in connection with the preservation and renewal of historical town centres and old districts that several of the central problems concerning public involvement in preservation in the Federal Republic have not by any means been finally resolved. The integration of community participation in the representative decision-making process is still in the initial stage (3.1), and the question as to how the individual is to be made capable of participation also still requires clarification (3.2).

4.3.1 Making community involvement a part of the representative decision-making process

In terms of legal dogma, the question of making public involvement a part of the representative decision-making process no longer poses a problem: such involvement modifies only the process of decision-making but not the distribution of competence as between the citizens and their representatives. But this has not produced a satisfactory solution as far as practical involvement is concerned: both sides, citizens and local authorities, still misconstrue community involvement as a vehicle of direct decision-making by the people.

But after a long phase of research and experiment in the local authorities, solutions are beginning to appear under the caption "open planning". This system makes all aspects of communal responsibilities open to public participation and gives participation a definite and clearly discernible place in the local decision-making process.

Open planning in Munich

The principles of open planning in Munich which, following a motion tabled by the SPD group on 24 April 1973, were submitted by the city development department on 30 November 1976 but have not yet been finally adopted by the city council, read as follows:

1. The decision whether the public is to be involved is taken by the council on the basis of a proposal by the competent authority. The proposal covers the nature and scope of the procedure and the probable costs. The initiative for such decision comes from the council, a district committee, or the department concerned.

2. Responsibility for public participation lies with the district committees. The public department concerned must therefore consult the competent district committee as to its proposals on the nature of the procedure. The opinion of the district committee must be submitted to the council.

3. The representatives of the public interest (cf. Federal Building Act) must also be consulted.

4. Everyone has the right to participate, that is, to state his views at public meetings or submit them in writing.

5. The results of the participation process must be submitted to the city council with a proposal for a decision.

4.3.2 Public interest

4.3.2.1 Reasons for the lack of interest

It is beyond dispute that people's willingness to participate depends on two main factors: the nature of the problem and the socio-economic status of the people who will be involved. This is borne out by the citizens' action campaigns, which are after all the clearest indication of a public desire to be involved:

- Action groups are usually only formed when the excavator is ready for action at the garden gate, in other words when people are directly affected by a problem.

- Most action groups are concerned with fairly straightforward individual problems and less with complex issues; in other words they tend to bother about gas-lamps, the preservation of individual houses, etc. rather than about comprehensive renewal plans or town development as a whole.

- It is nearly always only members of the middle class, that is, people with a better educational background and higher incomes, etc., who get involved in action groups.

It is not so easy to say whether and to what extent the lack of interest is partly due to the lack of decision-making powers of the people. There is no doubt that people's willingness to become involved depends to some extent on how they assess the efficiency of the participation process. The more they feel there is a chance of success, the greater will be their interest. No one can deny that people are less confident about the prospects of the "citizens' action group" as a form of participation than about the traditional forms of participation (especially elections, election rallies, etc. (cf. Radtke, pp. 41 seq.). Thus the argument that the reasons for the lack of interest in participation is due to the little influence they can exercise on the proceedings appears to be justified.

4.3.2.2 Means of increasing public interest in participation

Local authorities can, therefore, if they wish to encourage participation, improve their information policy (a), and make local government a subject of their education programmes (b).

a. Local information

The main object of the local authority's information activities is "to keep the local community informed of decisions in advance so that they can play a worth-while part". (Urschlechter, p. 596 seq.).

Although local public departments have considerably improved their public information activities, they still do not fully comply with this principle:

– Official decision-making tradition is still an obstacle to providing the press with comprehensive information (Peter, p. 19).

– The local information bulletins, still frequently the main medium of information, tend to hide rather than publish information: they have but a small circulation and their method of presentation is mostly inadequate (Höhmann, Kodolitsch, p. 176 seq.).

– And one still finds those brochures, the main purpose of which is to extol the mayor, the local authority, or the achievements of the "governing" party.

– Local authority publications are all to frequently couched in the incomprehensible language of planners.

Local authorities must learn to meet the needs of the local community not only occasionally but continuously, systematically to arouse their interest in information and to foster their ability to articulate themselves.

b. Education and training

Only if the local population have been informed about the substantive issues and decision-making processes, and only if, in addition, as many people as possible have the same knowledge of all these things is optimum participation possible. Neither is the case in the Federal Republic at the present time:

– Unequal educational opportunities benefit some and are a disadvantage to others. Those involved in the decision-making process, whether as a result of proposals by the local authority or of the activities of citizens' action groups, are still primarily from the middle class (cf. above).

– The level of general knowledge about local affairs and decision-making processes, in spite of the widespread interest in local problems, is still low: on account of the usually inadequate training of local journalists (Federal Agency for Civic Education), the information provided by the local press is insufficient; the same applies to the information policy of the local authority, which is concerned solely with individual projects, and to the schools, where in most cases the children are taught about the legislative process at federal level and democracy at the local level is forgotten. Only the Volkshochschulen (evening institutes) run courses, though not sufficient of them, on communal affairs. Unfortunately, the attendance is usually poor, mainly bacause they are not specifically advertised and the "ordinary citizen" is more interested in courses of further vocational training, etc.

The local authorities could correct these deficiencies in many different ways. They could offer local journalists a practical course in administration; they could introduce more evening institute courses concerned with local issues and try to attract in particular those who, on account of their inadequate educational background, are less in a position to come to grips with the problems which they encounter in their own particular situation. And they could induce the regional authorities to give greater consideration to local government aspects in school curricula, etc.

One experiment carried out jointly by the evening institute

and the local authority in Frankfurt was both an attempt to provide better, long-term information on urban development and changes in the decision-making process with regard to a specific planning project.

– The discussion was intensified in courses run by the evening institute in which participants worked out their opinions on the plans.

– These views were then discussed at further large meetings and finally submitted to the City Council.

Participants in the evening institute courses were informed about "other possibilities of discussing and influencing the plans, over and above the work at the institute courses", about the "possibilities of taking action", and their "capabilities for such action" developed as far as possible.

The fact that such programmes do not always have to be offered only from "official quarters is proved by the "working group on school and politics" in Bremen. This working group was formed to collect data for the political opinion-forming process, to strengthen the local authority's democratic awareness and thus to foster democratic action. This group, a private initiative, works in small units but also holds larger meetings for discussion and information purposes. It also holds information evenings at day centres for old people in Bremen.

Evening institute courses on draft structural plans in Frankfurt

In Frankfurt, as a result of "a most successful industrial promotion policy", the local community "completely lost confidence in the continuity and reliability of planning processes". They lost their confidence because office buildings were uncontrollably eating away residential areas; rents were continually rising, tenants were driven out, houses fell into decay because owners wanted to use the land for more profitable purposes. Squatting and street battles were the consequences; conditions were "untenable and scandalous". Draft structural plans were to be introduced to bring this situation in Westend, Nordend I and II, Bornheim, Ostend and Sachsenhausen back under control. They were to be plans for

– the nature and extent of land use,

– infrastructure,

– traffic flows,

– height of buildings.

These plans were supplemented by strategies to gain acceptance for these aims. In order to win the confidence of the local population the plans were to be discussed with them. They had not been coordinated among the local departments and therefore seemed to be still open to modifications. The Frankfurt City Council organised the public discussion in collaboration with the evening institute:

– The plans were introduced and discussed at large meetings and attention was also drawn to the expected areas of conflict.

Celle: above: Historical map of the old town from 1750 (Mattei Seutteri)
below: Map of the town and surroundings. The old town is still the centre of the city

Germany, Federal Republic of
CELLE

1. Introduction

1.1 General situation

Celle lies about 40 km to the north-east of Hanover, capital of Lower Saxony, at the confluence of the Aller, which is navigable up to this point, and the Fuhse entering it from the south. This former residential town of the Dukes of Brunswick and Lüneburg is today the seat of the rural district of the same name, a self-governing city belonging to the county district of Lüneburg.

Since the reform of administrative areas in 1973, the town has a population of approximately 75,000 in an area of 57 sq. miles. About 3,000 people live in the old town and 68,000 in the former central region.

1.2 History

After abandoning the older locality of Altencelle, Duke Otto the Severe founded Celle in 1292 at a ford on the Aller. Until well into the 16th century, the town consisted of a number of circular roads east of the castle . The parish and the town hall lay between castle and town. Around 1530 the town was extended to the south and given a broad moat. Having been raised to the residential town in 1371, it developed within these boundaries until into the 18th century. The moat is the perimeter of the old town as it is known today.

Proposed extensions of the town in the 17th and 18th centuries were only carried out piecemeal; this was because the Dukes of Celle moved their court to Hanover in 1703. At the same time, however, Celle became important as an administrative centre through the establishment there of the higher court of appeal (now the higher regional court). And in the 16th century the Land- und Ritterschaft (rural knights council) of Lüneburg had been moved to Celle, as had the prison and the regional stud.

In the 18th and 19th centuries, Celle had washing, honey, flax and wool markets, showing it to be a processing centre for the surrounding district. The town's function changed yet again in 1845 with the advent of the railway. With industrial expansion it became a catchment area for the rural district, with the result that in 1867, when the suburb towns and villages were incorporated, the old town had a population of 5,500 compared with 11,000 in the suburan areas. After the incorporation of further localities in 1939, the town had a total population of 38,500.

2. Housing

Around 1600, the old town already has as many inhabitants as in 1977, i. e. 28,000. The housing situation is fairly well balanced, notwithstanding the usual deficiencies to be found in old towns. There is no aging of the population. In 1974, 60 per cent of the houses in the old town were occupied by the owners. This no doubt explains the people's constant concern about preserving the townscape. There is a such a great demand for houses in the old town that none have been put up for sale since 1970.

All 390 semi-timbered houses covered by the planning by-law (1977 version) are protected properties. Over the past 20 years, 18 of these have been replaced by new semi-timbered buildings or have at least in part been renovated with the use of historical elements. Those houses not protected were built in areas destroyed by fire. The town was not bombed during the war, the main reason why the typical gable-ended semi-timbered houses have been preserved.

The town centre (old town with the Bahnhofstraße) is the most important central area for a triangular region with a total population of 165,000 in between Hanover, Brunswick and Hamburg. In 1970, the town had 488 businesses with 2600 employees and an area of 74,000 square metres used for business purposes. In addition, there are 69 restaurants and hotels, 59 service enterprises, 23 banks and insurance agencies, as well as 46 manufacturing establishments. It is prinicipally this function as a business centre that maintains the vitality of the old town. Not until recently have the hypermarkets on the periphery of the town begun to offer serious competition. The old town's capacity for development, following a remarkable increase in turnover resulting from the creation of a pedestrian zone between 1970 and 1975, now appears to have reached its limit. Another department store is planned for 1978 but is now in doubt because of the limited business prospects. An increase in the number of business enterprises would seem to depend on the provision of more parking facilities.

3. Aims of Renewal

Developments over the past 30 years do not suggest that the town has pursued a definite preservation policy. On the contrary, it appears that the central area between the cities of Hanover, Brunswick and Hamburg has not been an object of heavy investment. But as the centre of a rural area of influence, the old town has shown itself to have an absorptive capacity without any serious threat to its structure. Up to now the local authority has not developed any strategy for interfering with the market situation. The business area has developed continuously (there are no comparative data available) and will continue to expand in the eastern part of the old town as well, especially as a result of the proposed building of a Horten department store. The old city's function as a supply centre has priority and will continue to be promoted. The residential population has fallen by one half since 1950 and in 1978 seems to have settled at this level.

There is a considerable demand for living space in the old part of the town. In the next few years, traffic noise there is to be reduced even more. As a result, private transport will only be able to use the wall roads. Car parks on the periphery will secure maximum provision of services.

The authorities have since 1958 given priority to buildings with semi-timbered facades and exercise strict control of building materials. But over the years it has become clear that a renewal policy which promotes semi-timbering calls in

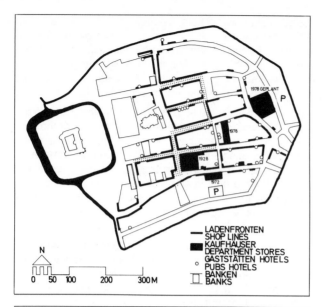

Celle: above: Commercial uses of the old town. Pedestrian area dotted.
middle: Land-use within the old town
below: Commercial use in the ist floor of houses in the old town

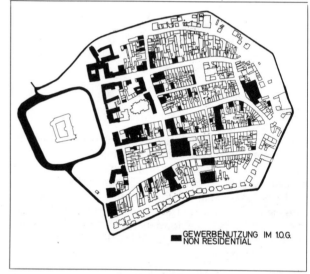

the long run for a massive programme which broad sections of the population desire. Thus, by introducing a drastic redevelopment scheme in 1975 the town council set a good example. The authorities are endeavouring to preserve the townscape.

4. Strategy

4.1 Planning instruments

Building line plans introduced in 1926 provided for wider streets in some parts of the old town but they were never put into practice. A building plan put forward in 1960 envisages three-storey, compactly built houses, and since it is still used as the basis for planning permission there is a danger of old, especially two-storey buildings not being renovated. The "by-law for the preservation of historical buildings and their surroundings and concerning billboards" adopted in 1971 is a decisive instrument for the town's architectural development. A local townscape officer ensures that the aims of the by-law are complied with.

The local authority's policy has been projected by means of a new development by-law (1977) based on the building regulations for Lower Saxony issued in 1975 which provide for public involvement (i.e. plans are open to inspection, the views of the public must be heard).

A development plan introduced in 1976 and the draft town map of 1977 strengthened the function of the old town as a business centre. The local authority has made no provision for binding development plans or the application of the Urban Renewal and Town Development Act. It relies on the "townscape protection officer" who will continue to work on the basis of the development by-law.

4.2 Finance

As the old part of Celle has not been formerly designated a conservation area, federal funds under the Urban Renewal and Town Development Act cannot be allocated. Nor have funds intended for the promotion of economic activity been used in recent years. The remarkable thing is that the town council, rather than complaining about the lack of funds, takes a favourable view of the situation because it is determined that the local propensity to invest should not be made dependent on grants.

Hence the town's special funds amounting to DM 50,000 annually have not been considered inadequate. These funds are used solely to finance measures which go beyond the usual kind of repair work, such as the use of goldleaf, the preservation of sash-bar windows, or the re-use of old semi-timbered parts. The council also provides grants for wrought-iron cantilevers.

Between 1971 and 1977, no more than DM 15,000 was made available from funds earmarked for the protection of old buildings. In general, the town tries to avoid the lengthy processes involved in applying for such funds because it is usually of no help to the person willing to have the necessary construction work done to have the project postponed.

According to statistics issued by the building supervisory office, applications for buildings projects worth about DM 10 million were made between 1967 and 1977 (see map). As actual costs are usually higher (fees are calculated on the basis of the estimate), one can assume that approximately DM 25 million was invested in the old town in a period of ten years.

Most people accept the institution of the townscape protection officer. His advice is indispensable for any building project. No group formulates aims contrary to the project or going beyond the proposal.

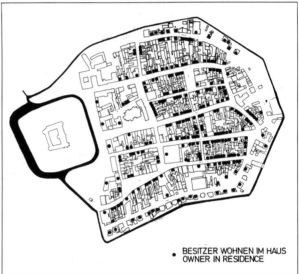

Celle: above: Area with design standards. 390 buildings are listed which will keep in their appearance
below: 276 houses which are inhabited by their owners

5. Planning

The basis for the design of new buildings is the planning by-law of 1971. A new draft has already been prepared on the basis of the new building regulations for Lower Saxony and is an extrapolation of the existing aims. It having become necessary to make a more precise definition of the area covered by the by-law, the side of the old town facing the palace – which used to be the location of the houses of the nobility and is now the site of offices – was omitted. Thus the by-law subjects to control all building projects affecting semi-timbered houses (see map). In this area, 390 (90 per cent) out of 433 houses are protected. The only ones unprotected are those built in gaps caused by fires in the 19th century.

Every application for planning permission in the old part of the town has to be submitted to the townscape protection officer. In critical cases, according to the directives, his report must be formulated in such a precise manner that it can be taken as the basis for refusing planning permission.

In order to explain some of the controversial decisions of recent years as regards the use of semi-timbered facing to give a historical effect, it is necessary to take a closer look at the way the structure of the old part of the town has been changed over the past three generations. In the 19th century there were few schemes for historicising the town. The Post Office and the Museum were built at Schlossplatz (the aim for the latter being to combine all architectural styles to be found in Celle!) Since they were a considerable distance away from the palace, there was no problem of adaptation; the new buildings could justify their own exist-

ence. The Deutsche Bank built in the old part of the town (Kanzleistraße 9–10, see photograph) was characteristic of the proud structures erected at the time of Kaiser Wilhelm. Until recently it had been felt that the buildings representative of that period should be "eliminated", but today they tend to be accepted "breaches of historical standards". A number of coverings of semi-timbered buildings required considerable architectural input but did not involve any serious changes in the basic structure.

Further architectural changes followed with the building of the Kreissparkasse (1905) am Grossen Plan and a department store (1922) abutting the market place, and the enlargement of the Amtsgericht (local court) in 1927, the worst case being that of the department store. The building of the Karstadt department store in 1928 replaced an insignificant hotel building which had been built on the site following a fire in the 19th century. That was the first caesura in the architectural pattern and standards of the old part of

157

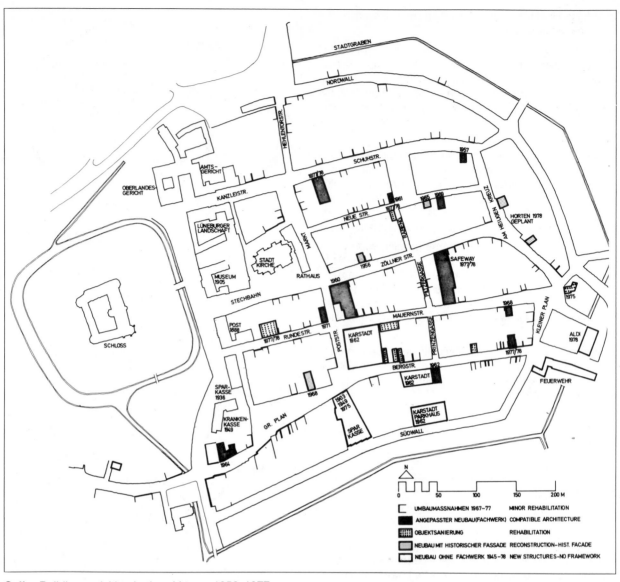

Celle: Building activities in the old town 1956–1977

Legend (map):

UMBAUMASSNAHMEN 1967–77	MINOR REHABILITATION
ANGEPASSTER NEUBAU (FACHWERK)	COMPATIBLE ARCHITECTURE
OBJEKTSANIERUNG	REHABILITATION
NEUBAU MIT HISTORISCHER FASSADE	RECONSTRUCTION–HIST. FACADE
NEUBAU OHNE FACHWERK 1945–78	NEW STRUCTURES–NO FRAMEWORK

the town. A fire at the Schlossplatz in 1930 led to further changes (Sparkasse 1936, health insurance building 1949) in an area which had always led its own life and had not affected the structure of the old town.

The rebuilding of the house at Zöllnerstraße 2 in 1956 and at Schulstraße 37 clearly ushered in a new epoch in the further development of the old part of Celle. For the first time houses were renovated on the historical plots in the traditional style and without any change of use. As a result of the institution of a townscape protection officer, the architecture now intentionally follows the historical pattern. The crucial difference between these two projects was, however, that the house in Zöllnerstraße was "reconstructed" on the basis of the historical plan using most of the old gable, whereas the house in Schulstraße was "designed" in the old semi-timbered style. More living space was created by putting in a second storey and hiding the new building behind a semi-timbered facade. This became the standard practice for about 10 other houses. The rebuilt Kepa house between Zöllnerstraße and Mauernstraße was given three old gables (partly interchanged) with a new gable next to them. A large self-service market was built the depth of an entire block –

the gables intended to restore the historical townscape are degraded and used to cover up buildings for totally new purposes.

The new Karstadt building of 1962 represented the first and to date the last attempt since 1928 to introduce a new style of architecture into the old part of the town (see photograph). It was an obvious attempt to reconcile it with the structure of the old town: the height was reduced by 4 m but it extended the length of the entire block. The vertical sections and the folds made for a strict division but the predominant semi-timbering and brickwork did not entirely harmonise with the small squares introduced into the facade. This was a remarkable piece of architecture which, being a single object, did not establish itself and became a much criticised departure from the gabled semi-timbered houses in the old part of the town.

Later, only new houses in the semi-timbered style were built. Those built by the firm of WARG in der Rundestraße (1971) and in the Westercellertorstraße (1964) considerably enhanced the use of the area and were good examples of this trend. The reconstructed Deutsche Bank (1968, see

Celle: Changes of the townscape 1900–1962
above: Hotel Hannover, built soon after 1800, as it was about 1900
middle: The Karstadt store, built in 1929 on the site of the Hotel Hannover
below: New building of the Karstadt store from 1962

photograph) can also be said to harmonise with the historical picture, though it is not even a semi-timbered building. It has two gables which are reminiscent of a type of building that was destroyed round about 1900. It is apparent that as a result of the building of semi-timbered houses over the past 20 years, the town has been able to preserve its historical structure However, there was a danger that the building of other such houses as substitutes for the old ones might produce a pseudo-historical old town.

But this trend has probably ended with the building of the safeway market between Zöllnerstraße and Mauernstraße (1977/78) and the planned Horten department store (see diagram). This is because the townscape protection officer has asserted his own plans in competition with those of the owners. In the case of the safeway market, for instance, there was no compulusion to erect historical facades. The townscape protection officer would have preferred a semi-steel structure but the semi-timbered facade based on his plans was an attempt to prevent any disfigurement. By carrying out the drastic renovation of the house at Altencellertorstraße 1 in 1975, the town council for the first time showed a genuine alternative which is now being copied.

The same can be said of the Volksbank, which has involved the renovation of two houses in the Rundestraße (1977/78). The floor beams have largely been preserved so that there has been no need to alter the fundamental structure of the buildings.

Where it is a question of renovating facades, all important decisions are taken by the townscape protection officer together with the craftsmen and the owner. This applies above all to the painting. No "colouring plan" was drawn up for the old part of the town, nor does the new draft by-law say anything about paints. The legal adviser in the county president's department felt that the DIN standards should apply, but the townscape protection officer found them of little help as regard medieval tones. There are but a few informal rules which serve as the framework for further decisions: the upright trussing should be painted in a colour which stands out from the filling. In the case of semi-timbered baroque structures, however, both should be painted over in the same way. The colour schemes chosen in the sixties are no longer acceptable. Blue, in particular, is no longer used on the ground that all paints were originally manufactured from plants.

As regards sprocket windows, the compromises reached up to now have been unsatisfactory. A cross in mounted at a distance of 1 centimeter from the window, a kind of dummy facade. Even more problematical is the way the windows open. Typical North German windows open outwards, a matter of considerable importance for the townscape (see photographs). Open windows are visible and extend into the street space, Where houses are renovated, however, there is a tendency to fit windows that open inwards and the townscape protection officer sees no way of intervening.

Celle: Changes of the town-scape.

The market place looking towards the houses Kanzlei-straße 9–10. At the end of the 19th century two timber-framed houses were situated on a site where a bank errected a big new building around 1900. This building was altered in 1968 to make it more similar to the surrounding houses

6. Results

The town has succeeded in preserving and reviving the old parts of the town solely on the basis of the by-law on local development and with the aid of the townscape protection officer. The preservation of hundreds of semi-timbered houses right up to the present day is due to special historical circumstances. The mass of such houses was so dominating that no one seriously considered replacing them. Thus conservation is not necessarily attributable to the town council's consistent policy but to a general concensus. Local shopkeepers and businessmen in particular saw the value of the townscape in good time and encouraged its preservation. They have been able to consolidate their position in the old part of the town, chiefly through the introduction of a pedestrian precinct, without having reached the limit of tolerance. Only the more recent plans for further department stores raised doubts as to the further commercialisation of the old part of the town. But the tradesmen, by utilising most of the ground floor space, have added to the vitality and economic value of the old town. Celle's central position and the old town's function as a service centre are seen as the real reason for revitalising the old town.

7. Conclusion

Celle cannot serve as a model for the conservation of historical old towns. The extensive medieval semi-timbered buildings set the framework for any possible alterations. One could almost speak of a collective compulsion to preserve the old structures and adapt. In this "climate", the townscape protection officer appointed by the town council has been a regulatory but not a determining factor in the redevelopment programmes. It has been seen that architectural by-laws and similar instruments only begin to have effect after intensive consultation with a view to preserving the townscape. It is to the credit of Celle town council that they have gathered experience in this respect over the past 20 years which should be carried forward.

Sources

Otto v. Boehn, Niedersächsischer Städteatlas; II. Abt.: Einzelne Städte, 7. Celle; Celle 1953

Freie Planergruppe Berlin, Information zur Entwicklungsplanung Stadt Celle, 1974–76

ders.: Entwicklungsplanung Stadt Celle – Programme, Konzepte: Mai 1976

Stadt Celle, Statistischer Jahresbericht, 1974

Stadt Celle, Bevölkerung und Erwerbstätigkeit; 970

The authors of this report wish to express their special thanks to Herr Hild, the townscape protection officer of Celle. All photographs are from his archives. We also thank Herr Delius, head of the municipal building department, and Dr. Günther, head of the municipal archives, for their support.

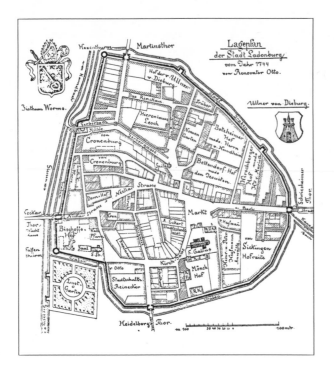

Ladenburg: above: Map of the old town from the year 1744

below: Aerial view of the old town

164

Germany, Federal Republic of
LADENBURG

1. Introduction

1.1 General situation

Ladenburg is situated in the southern part of the Federal Republic of Germany, in an agglomeration embracing the cities of Heidelberg, Mannheim and Ludwigshafen and numerous small towns at a point on the Neckar just before it enters the Rhein. The town was mentioned for the first time in the year 98 B.C., quickly fell into insignificance after the Thirty Years War, and is today a small, central locality between the cities.

1.2 History

Having been settled by the Celts, Ladenburg was newly founded by the Romans in the first century B.C. and developed into an administrative centre. Construction work in the town has uncovered many testimonies to the past (forum, market basilica, theatre, thermas, and various remains of houses). In the year 270 B.C. the town was destroyed by the Alemanni and did not regain prominence until the year 496 as a royal court and later as a bishopric (635 B.C.). After some extension in the 13th century, Ladenburg enjoyed its most prosperous period as a market town and administrative centre up to the Thirty Years War. That period came to a sudden and bitter end and Ladenburg, with its townscape of two and three-storey semi-timbered houses intact, fell once more into oblivion.

2. The Problem

The whole area developed vigorously from the middle of the 19th century. The industrial and administrative towns experienced a powerful economic upswing but Ladenburg benefited little on account of its lack of infrastructure, poor lines of communication, shortage of building land, and not least the poor condition of the houses. All these disadvantages made the town unattractive for both businessmen and house hunters. This meant, however, that there was no pressure for architectural change so that the medieval townscape was maintained largely intact until the sixties.

2.1 Initiators of renewal

Then the initiative for redeveloping the old part of the town came from three quarters at once. The Heimatbund Ladenburg e. V., a local amenity society led by the townscape protection officer, organised various discussion evenings on the question of urban renewal from which emerged the

Planning Group 67. They include keen architects who have since been working on both the strategic plan and the detailed plan of Ladenburg. At the political level, their efforts have been encouraged and supported by the present mayor since 1965.

3. Aims of Renewal

The aims of the renewal scheme derive directly from the problems described above. Although the desire to preserve the historical buildings in the old town and the townscape as a whole is the prevalent consideration, the real purpose of all measures proposed is to modernise the whole town – both as regards the buildings, infrastructure and accessibility. This comprehensive renewal scheme is intended to make Ladenburg attractive again as a residential town and in this way retain its independence between the Heidelberg and Mannheim/Ludwigshafen conurbations. The plans for conserving and improving housing in the old town deserve special mention. The accommodation in the old semi-timbered houses, some of which are in a very poor condition, is to be brought up to modern standards and form the economic basis for the preservation of the old town. Apart from the provision of public facilities for the old town and the new settlements in the south and east, no further locations, say, of the tertiary sector, are planned.

These intentions were set out clearly in 1967 in four main points:

- Preservation of the old town's skyline, therefore no building to have more than five storeys;

- town planning for the central part of the old town to be of a preservative nature;

- retailers in that part of the town to be encouraged, no consumer markets on the fringe of the town;

- the old town to be protected from excessive traffic.

4. Strategies and Measures

4.1 Improvement of the infrastructure

Ladenburg lies astride two very busy secondary roads. As late as the sixties plans existed for the demolition of old buildings so that these two roads, which pass through the town, could be widened. But the plans were abandoned in favour of a road by-passing the old part of the town. At the same time, Ladenburg was directly linked with the new autobahn at Bergstraße, there having hitherto been no link-up with the old autobahn.

The area zoned for economic activity is also to have a direct link with the autobahn. When this project has been completed, long distance traffic will be kept out of the part of the old part of the town.

Educational, cultural and administrative establishments

Through Ladenburg being raised to the level of an "Unter-zentrum" which is the second lowest of the four types of central place, the town council has been able to take advantage of several special programmes and either build or re-equip, in addition to the existing primary school, a new primary school, an intermediate school, a grammar school, and a special school for physically handicapped children. The existing schools have been renovated.

In addition, the Lobdengauhalle has been built in connection with the school centre at the Lustgarten and can be used for a great variety of purposes. The emergency accommodation which had been created in the old Bischofshof was removed and the building converted into the Lobdengaumuseum. The museum also has an open-air section. The offices of the town coucil, which are at present housed in several buildings in various parts of the town, are to be transferred in the near future to a new town-hall situated adjacent to but within the town wall in the west. The adult education centre (Volkshochschule) and a meeting place for old people will then be installed in the old town-hall.

Improvement of the economic structure

Easier accessibility by road in particular has made Ladenburg an attractive locality for industry. As a result, the working population of the town increased from 3,900 in 1970 to 7,000 in 1977.

Release of land for new housing

In order to provide land for the building of single family houses, the Südstadt was released for building purposes in 1966 and the Weihergärten area in 1976. As these areas have not proved worthwhile for retailers, there is a considerable demand for day-to-day and to some extent luxury goods from the old part of the town. As a result of this development, the number ob flats increased by only 1.7 per cent per year on average between 1961 and 1970, but by 6.6 per cent between 1968 and 1972.

4.2 Legal instruments

4.2.1 Planning regulations

The 1967 strategic plan was the first attempt to lay down conservation aims. The plan, for which no provision was

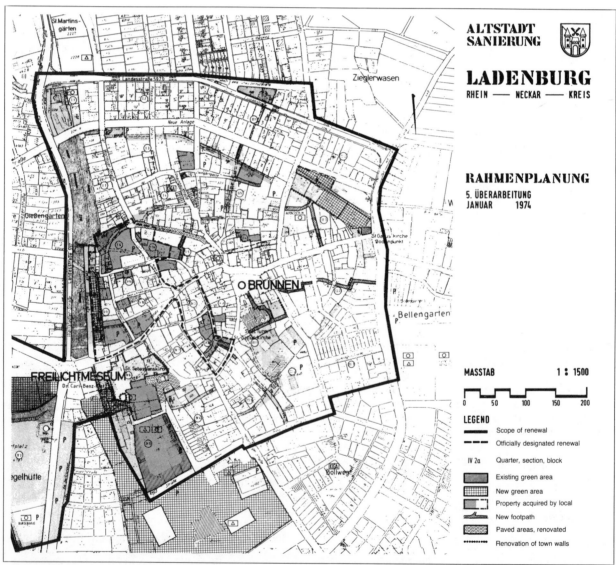

Ladenburg: Planning and town planning.
A green belt was built around the walls of the old town. Passages for pedestrians were created wherever a connection to the new housing areas appeared to be neccessary

Ladenburg: Public amenities are the basis for successful preservation
above: Because of the link with the motorway the town is becoming interesting for people working in the surrounding towns.
It is also feasible for allocation of industrial sites
below: New housing areas take in people leaving the bigger towns of Heidelberg, Mannheim or Ludwigshafen. Schools and other amenities make the town an attractive place to live in

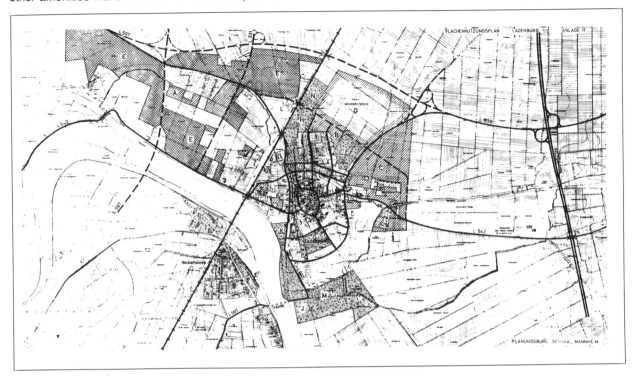

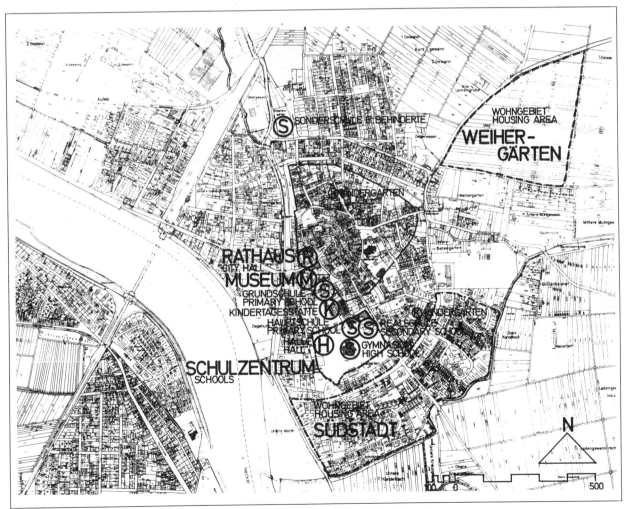

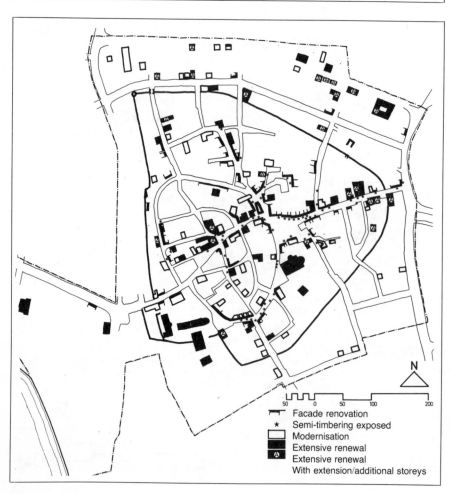

Ladenburg: New constructions and demolition

New buildings since 1967
- Modern
- Historicising
- After demolition

- Demolition before 1967
- Demolition after 1967

Ladenburg: Preservation and conservation

- Facade renovation
★ Semi-timbering exposed
- Modernisation
- Extensive renewal
Ⓐ Extensive renewal
  With extension/additional storeys

Ladenburg: The main street before World War II and today

made in the Federal Building Act, it being binding on the local authority only, constitutes a link between town map and local plan. It prescribes the lowering of traffic noise in the town centre, the concentration of development on the main shopping area, the placing of a green belt round the old town, and above all preserving the townscape. The strategic plan was drawn up mainly for the purpose of making planning aims transparent so that they could be discussed in good time, and in order to be able to coordinate municipal land purchase policy on a long-term basis. In the local plan the provisions of the strategic plan are merely given concrete form with some modifications of detail. In the process of drawing up the plan, all houseowners and tenants affected are fully advised as to the situation. One part of the old town was formally declared a renewal area in 1972. Another area was made a modernisation zone.

4.2.2 Townscape and protection of historical buildings

With a view to preserving the townscape of the old town (an area of about 20 acres), a by-law pertaining to the old town was introduced in 1975. And in 1977, another by-law was adopted to preserve the surrounding area and the skyline of the old town.

On the basis of these two by-laws, the local authority can exercise considerable influence on the design of new buildings, conversions, and the treatment of facades and advertisement signs and boards. In 1977, the list of historical buildings was considerably lengthened, so that now 261 buildings or elements are protected.

4.2.3 Municipal land use policy

In order to further the aims of renewal, the town council also purchases buildings and passes them on to interested buyers without profit. It does so to achieve the aims of municipal replanning and to influence the ownership structure.

4.3 Finance

Between 1965 and 1977, a total of DM 11.5 million was spent on renewal projects. Apart from the funds approved in accordance with the Urban Renewal and Town Development Act, the town council in particular has provided assistance on a remarkable scale, as indicated for instance by the increase in grants to private builders from DM 6,000

Ladenburg: The market place around 1950 and today (photo: Thomé)

in 1968 to DM 180,000 in 1978. By promoting bulding and renovation projects by individual persons the town council ensured a lasting conservation policy.

4.4 Public involvement

As the decision to pursue an active conservation policy was partly due to the initiative of the Heimatbund Ladenburg e.V., the local amenity society, interested members of the public were able from the very outset to put forward their views in the decision-making and planning process, for instance in the group formed to discuss problems relating to the old part of the town. The 1965 election campaign, which was also fought on the town conservation issue, must, in the most direct sense, be seen as public participation in old town renewal projects and the relevant decision-making processes. In addition, a conservation commission has been formed to discuss all planning and legal measures, but also questions of detail. The commission consists of the mayor, representatives of the party groups on the town council, the townscape protection officer, representatives of the Heimatbund Ladenburg e.V., the association of self-employed, the association of property owners, the town building and property department, and the planning group.

Although the commission cannot take any binding decisions, it has proved to be a useful forum of discussion for all concerned. But what seems to be more important than the various institutionalised debating and decision-making groups is the continuous process of discussion among the people themselves and between them and their political representatives, which is possible in a relatively small town. Often problems are discussed not during official visits but during a chance meeting on the street. Larger towns do not permit of this possibility so long as decisions are taken centrally. The argument about listening to public opinion assumes a more direct significance in this way.

Basically, public involvement could be a continuous process. Whereas the aims of the stragic plan, which was the subject of an exhibition and a questionnaire distributed among the local community, gave rise to widespread discussion, it appears that matters concerning the local plan are by and large left to the planners and councillors, who operate from the basis of the strategic plan and general public confidence and have closer contacts merely with the people directly concerned. The Marienbrunnen on the market place was built as a result of the initiative of one single person.

Information on historical facts

Various efforts are made to acquaint the entire community of Ladenburg with results of research on the old part of the town. This is first and foremost the purpose of the Lobdengaumuseum established in the Bischofshof in 1968 and since enlarged. Is has a department of archaeology (local findings verifying the town's Celtic, Roman and medieval history), and a department of town history and folklore. It is run on an honorary basis by members of the Heimatbund.

This museum is linked with an open-air museum which, apart from some of the larger findings, also show parts of Roman and Franconian buildings in the vicinity of the former

170

Ladenburg: The bishop's palace before and after preservation.
The restoration of the mural painting is remarkable. The groundfloor of the building now holds a museum

royal court. Foundations and in some cases parts of the walls have been exposed which give a direct impression of 2000 years of continuous settlement in the area.

The depictions showing the line of the foundations of what was to have been a Roman market basilica serve the same purpose. They are indicated by the different stone surfaces in the area around the St. Galluskirche.

The size of the medieval central area of the town is apparent from the wall, which has been partly exposed and renovated. This is to be thrown into even greater relief by means of a green belt where the town moat used to be. Various discussions and lectures are organised to improve local knowledge of the town's history.

5. Implementation

5.1 Planning strategy

There has been no attempt to make the renewal process follow a predeterminded course. Usually no one is pressurised, let alone forced, to carry out building measures. Up to now there has been no compulsory purchasing and none is planned. The town council merely ensures that the aims of the strategic plan are not obstructed. The information office for building conservation is run by the town planning staff and has been proved very useful in advising citizens free of charge. Here they can discuss their problems and doubts with regard to proposed developments without any fear of confrontation with public departments. Not until the individual and the planner have reached possible solutions with regard to, say, the purchase of land owned by the town is the council brought in as the official negotiating partner.

Private initiative has full play in the planning and implementation of individual building measures. The town makes the necessary planning arrangements, of course, and provides the infrastructure, but so far has appropriated no money for the construction or alteration of private buildings beyond the grants intended for the renovation of facades. Nonetheless, a surprisingly large number of buildings have gone up in the past seven years. One notices above all that apart from the facades that have been renovated quite a number of buildings have been completely restored.

Apart from the encouragemant given to private individuals to carry out building projects, some important decisions are settled by means of competitions. For instance, a public competition was held to find the best design for the school centre at the southern town hall, as well as a competition for experts to determine the layout of the new building area Weihergärten and for the new town hall in the western part of the old town.

In order to prevent bad investment and to ensure that every building project would be consistent with the strategic plan, it was decided that any application for planning permission concerning the old part of the town should be submitted to the planners for their observations. If it does not comply with the town's long-term plans or the townscape it is discussed

171

Ladenburg: The "Neunheller Hof" before the first conservation attempt in the 1930s and after conservation in 1977 (photo: Thomé)

with the applicants with a view to securing the necessary modifications. So far this has always proved successful, so there is no precedent as to how possible conflicts might be resolved. During the discussion the applicant is also counselled on financial aspects and design.

5.2 Achievement of planning objectives

5.2.1 Replanning measures

Replanning is at present concentrated on the extension of the green areas and recreational facilities in the town. The lack of such areas within the old town wall is to be offset by a green belt leading round large parts of it.

5.2.2 Demolition and rebuilding

Several more valuable buildings were demolished up to the late sixties. Afterwards, few changes were made at first and the only major demolitions were carried out outside the western town wall, where the old fortification was made visible again and the green belt enlarged. In the Metzgergasse area several minor buildings were demolished and replaced by new ones to facilitate the provision of services.

The question of the design of new buildings was tackled in two different ways. In the case of major developments, the town council has been disinclined to accept modern architecture. A building on the market place and several new buildings in the Hauptstraße and behind the old town hall have been given a historical stamp so that at first sight they do not appear to be new buildings. Though they are inconspicuous they are in many cases of but mediocre quality. More fitting than this half-hearted planning, which in addition has given too little consideration to the design and

use of ground-floor space, are the pseudo-semi-timbered buildings. Some of them have been brick built and then given a semi-timbered facade. The decision whether a new building should be of historical or modern design is taken by the owner himself. The by-law on the townscape gives no guidance in this respect. More recently, the town has been venturing into modern architectural design, also in prominent areas of town development. One such example is the new town hall at the Godulsmarkt, apart from a number of houses and shops.

5.2.3 Modernization and renovation

Most of the building activity over the past seven years has been intended to improve existing buildings. The emphasis has been on technical improvements such as the installation of new heating systems, baths, toilets, etc., with few structural changes. This work has to a large extent been financed by the owners themselves and in many cases done in several stages. It is only in the past few years that renovation on a more extensive scale has been carried out. The local community are apparently slowly coming to appreciate that such projects are feasible, that they are no longer an incalculable risk.

The town council have also been trying to expose more of the semi-timbering that has been covered over with plasterwork. In recent years 35 such facades have been treated in this way with public assistance and in some cases the simi-timbering has proved to be of considerable historical value. All plaster-coated houses on the market square and many in the Hauptstraße and the Kirchenstraße now have renovated facades.

In order to convince other house owners that it would be worthwhile restoring their facades, thermographic inspec-

Ladenburg: The new town hall within the old town. Design: Auer, Borkowski, Burger, Frotscher, Lackner, Samstag

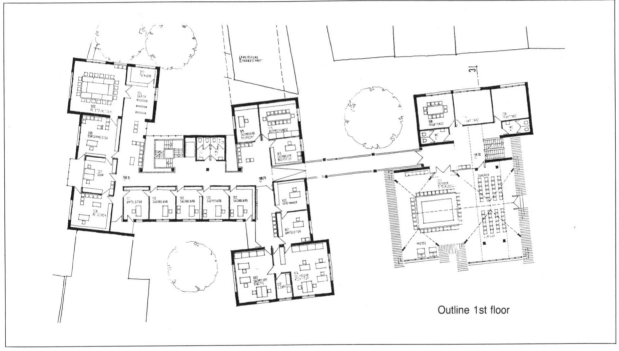

Outline 1st floor

West view, Von der Bleiche

tions have been made of 50 facades as a basis for discussion and negotiations with house owners. Most of the modernisation work ist done by local craftsmen who have gained experience in this specialised field. The planners, and especially the authorities concerned with the protection of monuments and historical buildings, had proposed that craftsmen from several different trades should cooperate in this work and this proved to be a big advantage. The "Ladenburger Bauhütte GmbH" was recently established and embraces several different crafts. It has also been more economical to restore the facades of several houses at the same time. The actual work done by house owners themselves or relatives is a major element of modernisation. There are ramified family ties in Ladenburg, so that by helping one another costs of renovation can be considerably reduced.

5.2.4 Street-level shops, windows

Street-level architecture remains a problem in Ladenburg as elsewhere. It is still difficult, apparently, to persuade

Ladenburg: Open air museum near the former bishop's palace

owners to choose shop windows which correspond to the size and style of the building. Many businessmen still argue that a "proper" shop should have large windows. This is why an architect in charge of the conversion of a building on the market place did not succeed when he proposed that the windowpane should be sub-divided by sash bars. The owner did agree at first but then had a large window put in instead. And recently just the opposite happened: the owner of a shop in the Hauptstraße used blind arcades to sub-divide his large windows.

6. Information and Publicity

In a small town like Ladenburg, there is to a limited extent a constant exchange of information through contacts between planners, local amenity groups, and the town authorities. This continuous process, in which contacts can be made at short notice, is largely responsible for the success of the renewal schemes.

The Heimatbund holds an annual meeting at which successful projects carried out in previous years are discussed and slides shown. This annual survey is very useful because it shows that progress is being made with renovation work and that it benefits all members of the community.

The Ladenburg Altstadtfest, the old town festival held every year on the second weekend in September, also begins with a stock-taking of restoration work. On this occasion the old town is a large festival area which is very popular with local people and visitors from neighbouring villages and towns. The festival is widely appreciated both for its content and semi-timbered setting. Restoration work in the old town has been the subject of numerous newspaper articles and television and radio broadcasts. The 1977 regional press conference on old town renewal was held in Ladenburg and various organisations have chosen the town as their venue for meetings concerned with the preservation of monuments and historical buildings.

In particular, the continuous coverage of successful restoration work in regional and national dailies has given the people of Ladenburg themselves a sense of pride in their own town and increased their interest in preserving old buildings, as have various books on the history of Ladenburg and individual buildings.

7. Conclusions

The renewal schemes and the results achieved have without doubt been successful. The aim of preserving the buildings and social structure of the old town and of improving its economic potential, which was formulated in the mid-sixties, has already been partly achieved and the rest merely a question of time.

It appears that the renewal process has been initiated at all necessary levels and has now developed its own dynamism which makes further success almost compulsory.

The growth of the retail and hotel and restaurant trade is proof of the succes of the renewal programme. With trade in these branches having been stagnant, it is now lively. Many shops have widened and modernised their range of goods and alterations and extensions are frequent.

Many inns and restaurants have been altered and made more appealing; new ones have also been opened. Today, Ladenburg's pubs and restaurants are popular not only with the local community but with people from neighbouring large towns. Indeed, tourism has become an important source of income for Ladenburg.

The quality of Ladenburg as a residential area is clearly indicated by the fact that today it is extremely difficult to buy a house in the old town for modernisation purposes.

Enquiries with the town council and planning architects by far outnumber the houses available for sale. Most people wish to remain in their houses.

One general phenomenon is the tendency of people to migrate back from new housing estates into the old town. After the development of the Südstadt, many young people bought land and built single family houses in the suburban areas. Often their parents followed them and the old buildings were either rented or left empty and hence fell into decay.

Nowadays, the same people are returning to their homes in the old town, the houses having been modernised. But the remarkable feature of renewal programmes in Ladenburg is that apart from the success of the actual measures carried out there has so far been no need to use the various funds available for these purposes. With but few exceptions, decisions have been taken by mutual aggreement so that no compulsory measures, let alone legal proceedings, have been necessary, yet the aims of preservation have been achieved. On the political level, too, there have been no fundamantal differences of opinion as to the aims of conservation.

Bibliography

Gutfleisch, Bruno: Ladenburg und seine nähere Umgebung als Wirtschaftsraum im Wandel der Zeit mit besonderer Berücksichtigung der Landwirtschaft.

Häusser, Rober und Heukemes, Berndmark: Ladenburg – Porträt einer 2000jährigen Stadt, 3. erweiterte Auflage mit deutschem, englischem und französischem Text. 1977

Heukemes, Berndmark: In: Führer zu vor- und frühgeschichtlichen Denkmälern – Mannheim, Odenwald, Lorsch, Ladenburg, 1965 in: Die Römer in Baden-Württemberg. 1976

Die Kunstdenkmäler des Landkreises Mannheim, herausgegeben vom Staatlichen Amt für Denkmalpflege. Karlsruhe. 1967

Mangei, Jutta: Die Wurzel der mittelalterlichen Stadt – die siedlungsgeschichtliche Entwicklung der Stadt Ladenburg. 1976

Schäfer, Günther: Strukturwandel einer Kleinstadt seit 1930 am Beispiel Ladenburg. 1976

Schmitt, Helmut E.: Die Wirkungen des 30jährigen Krieges und der Franzosenkriege auf die Wirtschaft der Stadt Ladenburg. 1959

Schummer, Wilhelm: Die siedlungsgeographische Entwicklung der Stadt Ladenburg nach 1945. 1970

Sievert, A.J.: Lopodunum – Ladenburg 98–1898, Karlsruhe 1900

Nuremberg:
above: Historical view of the town about 1530
below: Aerial view of the old town after the bombings of World War II, 1/4/1945

Germany, Federal Republic of
NUREMBERG

1. Introduction

1.1 General situation

Nuremberg lies in the middle Franconian Rednitz Basin on both sides of the River Pegnitz and is today, with a population of approximately 500,000, the core of an agglomeration. Within a radius of 20 km are Fürth, Erlangen and a number of smaller towns, together accounting for another half a million inhabitants.

1.2 Historical survey

The Castle was built by Henry III about 1050 and beneath it there immediately grew a small market town, "St. Sebald". About 100 years later the "St. Lorenz" settlement developed on the southern bank of the Pegnitz, and the construction of the town wall, which still exists, was begun in 1346. It encloses an area of 402 acres.

There are signs of self-government as from 1219, and by 1313 at the latest the "Free Imperial City" had developed the political and social system which by and large remained intact without any serious internal unrest until 1794. Nuremberg was the home of merchants engaged in overseas trade and of specialised craftsmen whose workshops grew into industrial establishments in the 19th century (pencil and toy making, metal processing, food).

Scholars, painters inventors and artists were active in large numbers here particularly in the 15th and 16th centuries, and poets and musicians until the 18th century.

Up to the second world war, Nuremberg was the best preserved of the large medieval centres in Germany; and an offical map published during the war (1942) shows 2,580 historical buildings, and describes 280 of them as "of special value".

2. The Problem

2.1 Destruction and reconstruction: today's tasks

Up to about 1970, the problems concerning the restoration and revival of the old city ensued mainly from the situation as it is existed in 1945: as a result of bomb attacks, 90 per cent of the buildings inside the walls had been destroyed.

But since the mid-sixties, renewal policies have not differed much from those of other communities of similar size and economic strength. Excessive city expansion with all the negative consequences is a threat to historical buildings in Nuremberg also and to the very existence of the old city.

2.2. Initiators of renewal

In the period of reconstruction, the city authorities initiated and carried out practically all major measures. About 1980 the communal planning system was reorganised. A "Nuremberg Plan Working Group" (AGN) was set up as a co-operative body in the overall city administration with the task of co-ordinating all aims, programmes and measures related to specific plans as well as investment and financial planning.

In recent years public interest in the problems of city preservation and the buildings has increased exceptionally. The "Friends of the Old City of Nuremberg" (established in 1973, cf. section 6) have set a good example in this respect.

3. General Concepts

3.1 The reconstruction phase

In view of the extent of the destruction, the prospect of rebuilding the entire old city was never seriously considered. After assessing the 188 entries for a "competition on the reconstruction of the old city of Nuremberg" (1947/48), the city council adopted in 1950 a Basic Plan which, in contrast to the reconstruction programmes of most other destroyed cities, provided for inter alia:

– the preservation of the most important features of the city outline;

– the exclusion of transit traffic;

– new buildings to be built on the pattern of existing historical buildings, especially as regards roofs (steep);

– reddish and yellow tones for the rendering to harmonise with the colour of local sandstone.

3.2 Nuremberg's present development plan

The "development plan for the old city" prepared by the AGN was adopted in December 1972, the first of its kind. The paramount aim was to develop the old city into a centre of communication for the entire urban area and for this purpose the council promoted economic, administrative and socio-cultural functions. Housing was to be made attractive to specific groups (individualists, students, elderly couples, who play an active part in the life of the city).

4. Strategies

4.1 Legal instruments

The basic plan and its guidelines were referred to in the previous section. As Bavaria did not have any legislation on reconstruction schemes, the plan was for a long time the main instrument of renewal in the old city; to all intents and purposes it was a by-law. Today, measures in this field are

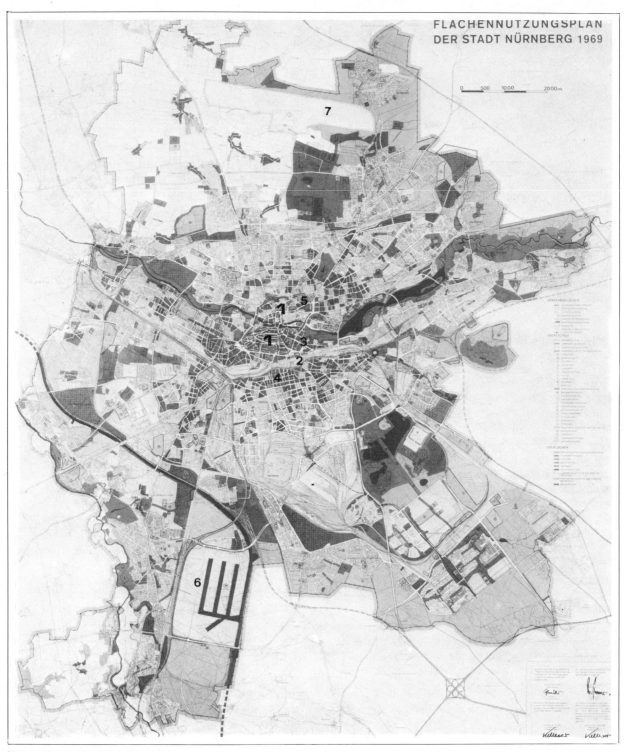

Nuremberg: Masterplan of 1969

1 = Old town, 2 = railway station, 3 = commercial quarter (banks, etc.), 4 = housing areas, 5 = university, 6 = harbour, Rhine-Main-Danube Canal, 7 = airport

based on the relevant sections of the Federal Building Act and the Ordinance on Land Development of 1977, and on the Bavarian Building Regulations as amended in 1974.

Since 1973, efforts to preserve historical buildings have had the backing of the Bavarian Monuments and Historical Buildings Protection Act. The protection list provided for in article 2 of the Act contains at present nearly 2,000 individual and over 50 groups of buildings under the Nuremberg city authority. They are described in detail in the new edition (1977) of the "Short Inventory for Nuremberg".

The 1971 Urban Renewal and Town Development Act does not apply, however, since the only formally designated renewal area is situated in the "Südstadt" outside the city walls.

4.2 Financial aspects

Apart from the funds earmarked for planning in the city budget, other sources for financing old city preservation schemes are:

Nuremberg: The "Hauptmarkt" from the south with St. Sebald (left) and Frauenkirche (right)
above: after destruction of World War II in 1945
middle: Proposal for reconstruction (1st prize in a 1947/48 competition)
below: Same situation in 1977

Nuremberg:
above: "Die Füll", a street formerly mainly inhabited by merchants
below: "Weißgerbergasse", a street formerly mainly inhabited by craftsmen

– the "investment programme for improving living conditions in towns and cities";
– the Housing Modernisation Act (applying mainly in the Weissgerbergasse) and the Second Housing Act (covering the conversion and extension of housing owned by co-operatives);
– city loans for repairs (offered for the first time in 1978, DM 580,000/year.

For the preservation and restoration of monuments and historical buildings the city receives grants from the Bavarian Office for the Protection of Monuments and Historical Buildings in Munich (accounting for five per cent of the total funds available for these purposes), the Compensation Fund of the Free State of Bavaria, from the district authority of Middle Franconia (up to 10 per cent of the costs), and from the budget item "non-urban monuments and buildings requiring protection", these latter funds being administered by the Central Office for Building (townscape and monuments and old buildings department). This office has a vote of DM 680,000 (1977) for the preservation of city buildings. Up to 1977, approximately DM 11,000,000 had been invested in the restoration of the city wall, the biggest object of preservation measures.

4.3 Participation of the local community

Various events are to be held in the squares, courtyards and historical buildings in the old city to strengthen its economic and socio-cultural functions. These include the traditional markets ("Christkindlsmarkt", "Trempelmarkt"), and the "Summer in Nuremberg" programme embracing historical events.

And every year since 1971 a donors' association has organised an Old City Festival under the auspices of the city authorities.

5. Results

5.1 Measures for the protection of monuments and historical buildings

Round about 1960, the work of restoring damaged monuments owned by the city, the state or church were practically completed to the extent that they had the necessary "regenerative capacity" (including the Unschlitthaus, Baumeisterhaus, Dürerhaus, Fembohaus, Kaiserstellung, Heilig-Geist-Spital, city hall and wall with towers and gates, the Castle, St. Lorenz, St. Sebald, the Frauen- and the Egidienkirche). But the situation is less favourable as regards the repair and maintenance of privately owned historical buildings: of 270 private houses which survived the war, nearly 40 have disappeared over the past 20 years and many others have fallen into decay. This situation has prompted the "Friends of the Old City" to take action (see section 6).

5.2 Rebuilding

The rebuilding of completely destroyed parts of the old city has been a long and diversified process. As from the midfifties the basic plan appears to have been applied less strictly: instead of steep, "semi-steep" roofs (i.e. less than 40 per cent inclination) were sometimes introduced, as well as new building materials and types of houses with elements alien to Nuremberg (balconies, loggias fronting the street).

In spite of this, Nuremberg by and large regained its old townscape. The Sebald side also retained its residential

Nuremberg: Activities of the "Altstadtfreunde" (Friends of the Old City)
above: Conservation of the house Untere Krämersgasse 16, owned by the "Altstadtfreunde"
below, left: Buildings Untere Krämersgasse 16 and 18 after restoration
below, right: Buildings in the Obere Krämersgasse with restored timber-framed construction. The restoration was realised with the assistance of the "Altstadtfreunde".

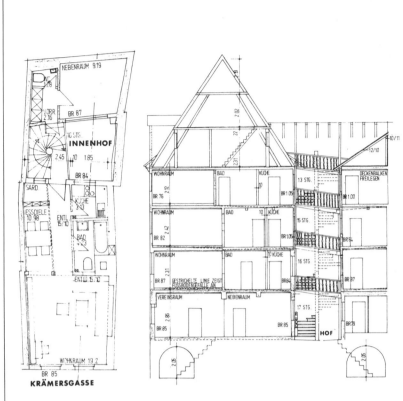

Data of the Nuremberg example

1. Cubic capacity

Front house	688 cbm
Back	266 cbm

Total	954 cbm (without spiral staircase)

2. Area

Ground floor shop	appr. 25 qm
1st floor flat	appr. 54 qm
2nd floor flat	appr. 54 qm
3rd floor flat	appr. 54 qm

Total	187 qm

3. Cost estimate (Dec. 75)

Without spiral staircase	DM 287,00
Spiral staircase	DM 100,00

4. Cost situation (1977)

Costs accounted for and expected	DM 290,000
Without spiral staircase	
expressed as qm/cubic capacity appr.	1,550
expressed as cbm/cubic capacity appr.	303

5. Income

Probable annual rents	DM	15,600
expressed per qm appr.	DM	7

o Restoration of old buildings under such adverse conditions is not an optimum capital investment but if all possible financial sources are exhausted the financial burden is tolerable

o The scheme only works if the owner sees the restoration of historical and cultural buildings as of value to himself and the general public

Nuremberg: Activities of the "Altstadtfreunde"
above: groundfloor of the Weißgerbergasse. The planning was inaugurated by the "Altstadtfreunde"
below: Restorations and towscaping by the "Altstadtfreunde"

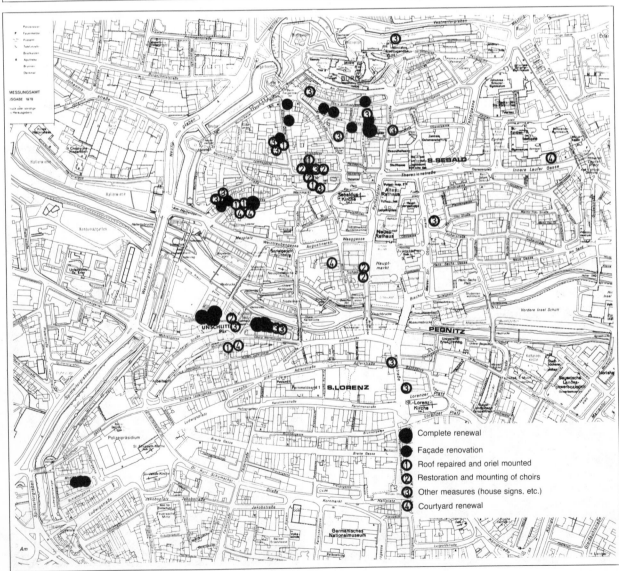

● Complete renewal

● Façade renovation

① Roof repaired and oriel mounted

② Restoration and mounting of choirs

③ Other measures (house signs. etc.)

④ Courtyard renewal

function, whereas the Lorenz side (which is closer to the traffic arteries and topographically more easily accessible) has been subject to the more usual type of change (intrusion of department stores and office blocks).

5.3 Implementation of the "Old City Development Plan"

The AGN made its first assessment of the plan's progress in its "report of the development of the old city" (Dec. 1976). The report says that in particular the proposed modifications of the transport network (enlargement of the pedestrian zones, construction of the underground railway with stations at Lorenzkirche and Weißer Turm, the building of additional multi-storey car parks in the old city) had been completed and the economic and socio-cultural functions strengthened.

Negative effects resulted from the diversion of private transport into the streets of the residential parts of the Sebald half of the city and from the large number of public houses and bars in the "historical quarter".

The conflict situations have been recognised, however, and taken into account in the projection of the Old City Development Plan (Dec. 1977). In future the old city will again provide accommodation for all sections of the population. Today, about 17,000 people still live within the city walls, almost four per cent of the total pupulation and 40 per cent of the populace of 1939. Up to 1975, 8,758 flats had been built or restored, more than the 7,500 planned in 1947; however, 10–15 per cent of the accommodation is in need of renovation, especially on the Lorenz side.

6. Public Involvement

The work of the Friends of the Old City of Nuremberg

Preliminary remark

The activities of this association should be seen not so much in relation to the exceptional efforts being made by the city authorities to preserve and develop the historical city centre but rather in comparison with the action of similar groups in other towns and cities.

An association of Friends of the Old City of Nuremberg had been in existence since 1949/50, but after a few initial moves in protest against, for instance, the modern Kaufhof building next to the Mauthalle, had dwindled to a club of notabilities. What prompted the reorganisation of the association in 1973 was the demolition of one of the 'Sieben Zeilen' (Webersplatz) overnight by the owner.

This was yet another striking example of the generally hopeless situation of private owners and the impotence of the authorities responsible for the protection of old buildings. Ever more of the old houses which had already been decimated during the war threatened to fall into ruin: there were still temporary roofs and semi-ruins yet many remnants of choirs, oriels, and balustrades which had been rescued from the debris were stored in cellars, some of them inadequately and likewise subject to decay.

The association's new committee set themselves ambitious aims: the association's work should not be determined by useless criticism of past mistakes but by alternative action in the form of exemplary restoration work before the eyes of those directly or indirectly concerned, something which everyone could see.

Today, just under five years since the association's rebirth, the Friends of the Old City of Nuremberg now number more than 3,000 – only Nuremberg's sports clubs have more! Of course, the educational and negotiating skills, as well as the technical know-how, of the initiators and most active members of the association were essential for this impressive growth of the membership.

In accordance with the above-mentioned objectives, the association's activities fall into two groups:

1. **Publicity to win more participants, informations, etc.**

a. General 'propaganda': display cases in the subway leading from the station to the old city; 'open door' days, information stands at fairs, markets, festivals; exhibitions in places frequented regularly by the public, with competitions; street activities (first time 1976, sale of brochures, stickers, beer mats, etc.; reports in the press.

b. Specific information for members to fill in their background knowledge of the problems involved:
2–3 circulars a year with topical reports; briefing evenings; 'reports on the old city of Nuremberg'; in 1976, 564 people visited the association's office for information.

c. Illustrating the problems at the actual place or building concerned, especially in the form of 'walks through the old city'; as early as 1974, as many as 1,000 attended each event, and by; 1976 up to 3,000 were joining in the walks. They are held about eight times a year on Saturdays and as many as 30 guides are in action. This work calls for detailed preparation, especially in view of the very different educational background and ages of those taking part.

The association draws attention to complex situations and present deficiencies; the guides explain the history and development of buildings and their characteristic architectural forms and elements.

Direct contacts with action groups pursuing similar aims: In 1974 and 1975, trips were made to Augsburg and Bamberg, and in 1977 to Regensburg (four coaches carrying over 200 participants).

2. **The actual restoration work**

This initiative proved to be the association's biggest success: the membership jumped after the initial projects from 300 (beginning of 1974) to 1150 (beginning of 1975), probably because the city's procedures were visible to all. A street or square regained its former appearance or became more complete; people were able to make a comparison 'before' and 'after'; and the work achieved was made possible by their personal involvement; they were able to identify themselves with the result.

By the end of 1977, 43 projects had been completed:

– 12 facades were restored (exposure or restoration of the sandstone or semi-timbering); cost, depending on the size of the object and the extent of the damage, DM 7,000 – 40,000 each.

– Two roofs repaired, including the oriels, DM 20,000 – 24,000 each;

- Three oriels placed in position, each costing DM 7,000 – 10,000;

- Four courtyards/galleries, rear facades repaired, each costing DM 5,500 – 26,000;

- Five choirs restored/reconstructed, costing DM 6,400 – 50,000, depending on the difficulty involved and whether including assembly;

- One technical monument restored: exposure of the spring water access, DM 8,150;

- Five house signs or house figures were restored and mounted; each costing DM 1,050 – 8,000;

- Two gas lamps installed at DM 1,000 each;

- Six other projects to complete the townscape: installation of fountains (2), baroque garden figures, a historical 'birds' tree', and so on.

But the highlight of the association's activities has been the model restoration of a typical Nuremberg craftsman's house (Untere Krämersgasse 16) which it had purchased (completed in the autumn of 1977), see drawings and cost summary. It contains three flats and the small shop which have been rented.

Another similar major operation was the rescue of the house ruins on the Unschlittplatz for which demolition permission had been granted and the greater proportion of which had already been sold by the city council to a building company for redevelopment; as a result of an intensive protest campaign and petitions, the decisions of the city and district councils were reversed, the Friends of the Old City of Nuremberg managed after hard negotiations to acquire the property. However, the association did not have the funds to finance another model restoration project so the four houses are to be sold to individuals who will pledge themselves to restore them.

The Friends of the Old City participated in the other measures (by meeting incidental expenses, offering advice or supervising building activities), depending on the means and situation of the owners. They tried to draw money from other sources, depending on the nature of the building, for instance ad hoc grants from the monuments and historical buildings fund of the regional office, the district council, the city council, the chamber of handicrafts, or from foundations, industrial firms, retailers, etc. Building firms and craftsmen often gave their services free or charged less than the normal rate.

The association's funds are made up of members' contributions (DM 10 per year minimum, no ceiling), donations and proceeds from raffles (2). In 1974 they had DM 18,656 at their disposal, but this had already risen to DM 146,064 by 1975 (more than the amount made available by the city office for the protection of historical buildings for the preservation of 'non-urban buildings'); in 1976, the association was able to contribute DM 73,332 towards the cost of other measures in addition to the model renewal project at Untere Krämersgasse 16.

All members work on an honorary basis. In the meantime, several groups have been formed to deal with specific sectors which offer a wide field of activity for people of varying abilities, for instance:

- The working group on city and house research: this group draws up inventories of the 231 remaining old houses and prepares documentation. Building photographs are obtained in co-operation with the Academy of Arts. By 1975, they had visited 90 of the houses; of the first 56 on the Sebald side, 21 were in a poor structural condition, 23 could be said to be fair, and 12 good; 21 had semi-timbering which had been plastered over (especially this century), 12 still had emergency roofs, and five had only been partially rebuilt; most of the documentation work was concentrated on the Weissgerbergasse. On the basis of this preliminary work, the city council comissioned the group's co-ordinators, the architects Jurck and Sternecker of the Academy, to prepare a planning report for this the best preserved street consisting of old craftsmen's houses. That report is now used as the basis for all renovation measures.

- The working group Untere Krämersgasse 16 was concerned with the renewal of the association's own house (financing, accounting, renting, etc.);

- The working group concerned with walks through the old city;

- The working group on publicity: the group designed stickers, beer mats, posters, coins and came up with a variety of gimmicks to boost sales. For instance, they went round the city in historical costumes, going into public houses and restaurants, etc; 'walking towers' as an advertisement during raffles, etc.

15 – 20 people came forward to do the necessary typing and office work and a reference library is being built up.

These various activities of the 'Friends of the Old City' can be grouped under the heading 'Action': In contrast to the responsible authorities, which react to requests for planning permission or demolition permits, applications for grants, etc., the association takes the initiative itself, tries to provide stimulus, to offer the owners of the houses concerned alternatives. The emphasis is on measures which everyone can appreciate; they preserve or restore the city's overall picture. A house owner has no direct advantage from the exposure of semi-timbering, but a renovated facade restores the building's significance within the overall context and is an incentive to him; where possible the owner is placed under obligation to restore the interior of the building.

By these methods the Friends of the Old City present a participating, self-organising public, in contrast to the institutionalised citizens' forums, advisory committees and similar bodies which are involved by the local authorities as appropriate.

7. Final Observations

There appear to be two essential conditions for the revitalisation of the old city of Nuremberg: the further preservation of the residential function of the area within the walls and the active interest of the people of Nuremberg in their city. The latter is reflected in the willingness to co-operate shown by the institutions concerned with urban planning and the protection of historical buildings and by the general public. This can at least be partly explained by the history of the Free Imperial City where the constant need to defend its achievements and acquisitions against intruders strengthened the solidarity of the people. To some extent that defensive attitude has been passed down the ages since the 19th century.

Regensburg: above: Historical view of the town (from "Schedels Weltchronik" 1493)
below: Historical view of the town by Hans Georg Bahre 1615

Germany, Federal Republic of
REGENSBURG

1. Introduction

1.1 General situation

Regensburg lies at the northernmost point of the Danube, opposite the Regen und Naab confluences. Here, three geological formations are adjacent to one another which have had some bearing on the settlement and economic structure of the surrounding area: in the west Jurassic limestone, in the east the igneous rock of the Bavarian forest, and in the south fertile loess. In 1977, the city covered an area of 29 sq. miles with a population of 135,520. 14,623 of them live in the old part of the city south of the Danube (45 acres). Today, Regensburg has a University, is the seat of the Oberpfalz county council, and higher order centre of a planning region covering some 1973 sq. miles and an estimated population of 530,000.

1.2 Historical survey and town planning

The Celtic settlements in this area were occupied by the Romans as from the year 15 B. C. In the year 179 A. D. they established the Castra Regina camp on the lower Danube terrace (area 580 × 500 yds.). In the early Middle Ages, "Reganespurc" became the residence of the Bavarian Dukes, the imperial palace of the Carolingians, and at the same time the base from which the migrant bishops Erhard and Emmeram christianised the area around the year 680. Within the boundaries of the former Roman camp were built the Cathedral, the Pfalzkapelle, and numerous chapels and parish churches. Around 920 the town was enlarged to include the St. Emmeram monastery and the tradesmen's and merchants' quarter west of the Castrum. And around 1,300 it was expanded again to include the Westner und Ostnervorstadt. Not until about the middle of the 19th century did Regensburg extend beyond those limits. In the year 1924 it also incorporated Stadtamhof to the north of the Danube.

The period of greatest economic growth between the 11th and the 13th/14th century, also covering the time when Regensburg became an independent Reich city from the year 1245, was also the period of outstanding architectural development. Apart from the churches and chapels already mentioned, the city hall, numerous patrician residences with towers (about 60 of which 20 still exist) and that rare example of engineering and architectural skill, the stone bridge (consisting of 16 arches spanning 350 m), were built.

But in the late medieval era Regensburg was overtaken by Nuremberg, Augsburg and Vienna. Nor could the city's gradual decline be halted by the establishment of the Permanent Reich Diet there (1663–1806); on the contrary, it remained a consumer town with feudalistic structures. It lacked a body of independent craftsmen, which was one of the reasons why the first phase of industrialisation in the 19th century left no impression on the area. And even during the general economic upswing after the second world war, little independent initiative was generated in this peripheral region of the Federal Republic of Germany.

2. The Problem

2.1 Preserving the historical character, developing services

In the case of Regensburg, there are two apparently irreconcilable objectives: to preserve the unique, early medieval city north of the Alps and at the same time to develop the services centre for a planning region embracing 530,000 inhabitants. This means, on the one hand, restoring more than 1,000 historical buildings and monuments, many of which are of incunabula character, and on the other concentrating banks, offices and department stores in the city centre with the concomitant traffic problems: new bridges to create links with the old part of the city, the building of multi-storey car parks and underground garages, and the widening of roads.

2.2 Existing buildings and housing situation

The initial plans for restoration were the result of the sanitary conditions, the high population density, the congestion and condition of the houses in the vicinity of the Danube, and hence the latent dangers of epidemics, fire, and collapse. There are frequent signs of fatigue: the mortar has eroded and the foundations are no longer adequate; changing groundwater levels and currents, the timber construction and piling dating back to early medieval times, are other uncertainty factors for restoration schemes, but so, too, are the repair work, alterations and excavations done later. Consequently, all this calls for thorough and varied preliminary investigations.

A special evaluation of the 1968 census of buildings and housing shows the following data (Source: Social Report, Part 1, 1975):

Housing situation	Renewal area	Stadt-amhof	Alt-stadt	City as a whole
Houses with 3 or more flats as percentage of all dwellings	79.7	67.8	75.2	43.1
Proportion of dwellings built before 1950	91.9	83.8	80.7	20.6
Percentage of flats with bath and WC	24.6	22.0	23.6	65.6
Percentage of flats heated with wood and coal	64.6	64.1	59.0	44.8
Living area per person in sq. m.	24.9	23.6	27.0	24.0
Rent per sq. m. in DM	1.67	1.62	1.75	2.16

Regensburg: above: Map from about 1890
below: Demolitions of World War II and afterwards. Only a few buildings were destroyed during the war, but a great many were torn down in the late 60s and the beginning of the 70s

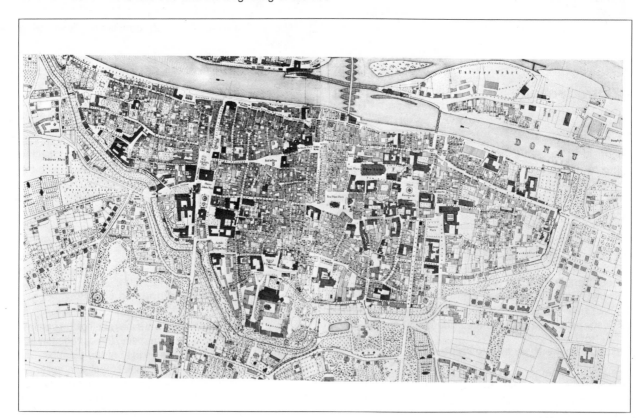

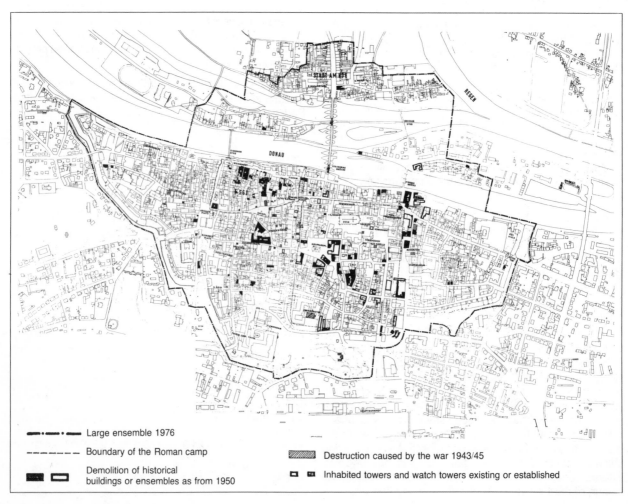

- ━━ ·━ ·━ Large ensemble 1976
- ━ ━ ━ ━ Boundary of the Roman camp
- ▬ ▭ Demolition of historical buildings or ensembles as from 1950
- ▨ Destruction caused by the war 1943/45
- ▫ ▣ Inhabited towers and watch towers existing or established

2.3 Ownership, use, tenancy

In 1976, the ownership structure in the old part of the city was as follows:

39 % private

22 % city council and Stadtbau GmbH

15 % Churches and monasteries

10 % Free State of Bavaria

An analysis of property use carried out between 1974 and 1976 shows the following spread of the gross floor (storey) area:

Living space	49 %
Public administration (excl. churches, etc.)	13 %
Retail trade	20 %
Private services	10 %
Trades and industry	3 %
Other uses	5 %

(Source: Regensburg Plan III–12)

The map shows a concentration of shopping and administrative zones between the city hall and the Maximilianstraße and in the area of the Roman camp (this was mainly the site of public buildings and markets in the Middle Ages), whereas the main residential areas spread into the west of this part of the city. Some 90 per cent of the inhabitants are tenants and subtenants, mostly from the lower social strata.

2.4 Initiators of renewal

In 1955 the city council of Regensburg applied to the supreme planning authority in the Bavarian Ministry of the Interior for financial support for restoration projects. This was the first initiative in this direction. At that time there was no systematic plan for revitalising the entire old city; the council intended initially to save buildings in very bad condition, especially those to the west of the old city hall. An overall study was carried out by an interdisciplinary planning seminar known as the "Stiftung Regensburg" (cf. section 3.1). It had been proposed by the Munich architect Sep Ruf and was financed by the cultural amenities group within the Confederation of German Industry.

3. Concepts and Aims

3.1 Old city as a whole

Restoration concepts for Regensburg followed, though with some delay, the proposals by the city planning authorities for the modernisation and use of town centres. The Lasne Plan of 1919 envisaged the building and widening of roads; it showed consideration only for the city's principal buildings, such as the Cathedral and the city hall. Although it was somewhat utopian for Regensburg, it did have an impact on building development in the city. For instance, it was the basis for building lines determined in the twenties which were still being invoked in the seventies.

Proposals made after the Second World War (report submitted by the German Academy for Urban Development and Regional Planning, Regional Group for Bavaria, 1959; Urban Development Plan prepared by Professor Döllgast, especially for Renewal Area I) envisaged the preservation of medieval ensembles that had been spared the ravages of war, but also their adaptation to modern needs; as a business and administrative centre for the region, the old city must be made correspondingly accessible to motorised traffic.

These aspects were emphasised by the Leibrand Plan of 1961, which proposed direct and large area development, the Road Transport Plan of 1963 based on the Leibrand Plan, and the study carried out in 1972 by Dorsch Consult/ Ingesta, Institute for Area Planning and Urban Development, Cologne, which was commissioned by the city council. A dual carriageway, the B8, is to be constructed in the east and the west leading right up to the edge of the old city, and some buildings are to be pulled down along Hunnen- and St. Georgsplatz in preparation for the north-south connection with the "Bayernwaldbrücke" (see map), which will also be a dual carriageway. These proposals were the upper limit but were only adjusted in 1974 when the Road Traffic Plan was put forward. The Loop system proposed by the "planning seminar" in order to minimise traffic noise in the old city appears to be gaining more acceptance. In 1977, the inter-disciplinary working group on "town development" representing the city departments concerned drew up for the first time (in sections) a "Regensburg Plan" which laid down the following aims for Planning Area III (townscape preservation and development):

1. The prime objective is to preserve the old city as a historical unit, ensure its use on a large and small scale, and conserve valuable buildings, also outside the old city.

2. The old city is again to be made a residential area for all social strata.

3. Conservation programmes should be scheduled so as to minimise any further decay or destruction of valuable buildings. Preference should be given to the restoration of specific objectives.

4. The economic capacity of the old city should be preserved and strengthened where possible.

5. With a view to easing the burden on the historical part of the city, areas close to the old city are to be selected for development which have been the location of facilities which the old buildings could no longer accommodate and for which, for reasons of comprehensive planning, a central location is desirable.

6. Land use in the old city should in principle continue to be based on the historical model.

3.2 Renewal Area I

An area of about 20 acres roughly corresponding to the former "Donauwacht", one of eight medieval city districts, has been the object of preliminary investigations followed, since 1968, by restoration measures to improve the quality of housing. The first plans envisaged the clearing of interiors which, together with the rearward facades, were to be redesigned in accordance with the plan proposed by Professor Döllgast in 1958. The changing approach to planning is evident from the subsequent overall plan or development plan and the measures successively carried out. For exam-

Regensburg: Revitalisation of the old town by implementing central function.
Construction of Horten store. Several historical houses were demolished, only the facade of a neo-classical building was "saved" and used again in the new construction

ple, the new development axis running right through the middle of the renewal area (see diagram) has meanwhile been abandoned and increasing consideration is given to the preservation of historical buildings. Two other plans that are important for planning purposes were submitted relatively late: the "Building Age Plan" drawn up by the Bavarian Regional Office for the Protection of Historical Buildings (1973) and the Social Report (Part 1, 1975) prepared by the Working Group on Old City Renewal at Regensburg University. Both these expert opinions were prepared within the scope of the preliminary studies in accordance with section 4 of the Urban Renewal and Town Development Act.

4. Strategies

4.1 Legal instruments

It is only within the scope of urban development plans and draft strategic plans (Regensburg Plan) of recent years that the possibilities for preservation work envisaged in general planning legislation have been related to the old city as a whole. The 1956 town map was of little assistance as regards built-up areas, where redevelopment was governed by the free play of economic forces. But in order to gain some control of property dealing, the city council, following the enactment of the Federal Building Act on 7 December 1961, decided to draw up a local plan for the whole area of the old city. The first partial plans became legally effective in 1966 and 1971 in Renewal Area I.

When the Urban Renewal and Town Development Act came into effect in 1971, Renewal Area I was divided into two sub-areas of just under six acres each (1 A and IB, see map). The subsequent surveys (Building Age Plan, Social Report), however, apply to the whole renewal area.

Pursuant to article 107 of the Bavarian Buildung Regulations, the city council finally issued an "ordinance on local building regulations for the protection of the old city of Regensburg" on 9 January 1976. It mainly concerns the exterior design of buildings and is effective for ten years.

Before the Bavarian Protection of Monuments and Historical Buildings Act came into force in October 1973, the regional office for protection measures in Munich and the office for the preservation of buildings and the townscape of Regensburg (a section of the city museum) confined their activities to research and counselling. But the regional office is now involved to a much greater extent and a number of restoration measures are administered and financially supported direct from Munich. The (provisional) list of protected properties prepared in co-operation with the city authorities in accordance with article 2 (1) of the Protection of Historical Buildings Act now stands at 1,300. Of these, 1,050 are in the old city (70 per cent of that area's building stock), 126 (74 per cent) in Renewal Area I, and 53 (88 per cent) in its subareas 1A and 1B. It is clear from these figures that it was not until actual work was carried out or the Building Age Plan was drawn up that the valuable buildings were discovered and placed under protection. In accordance with Article I (3) of the Act, the "old city of Regensburg and Stadtamhof" was designated an ensemble in December 1975 on the proposal of the Regional Council for the Protection of Historical Buildings. All structural alterations carried out within this 442-acre area, even if the buildings concerned are not listed, are subject to the provisions of the Protection of Historical Buildings Act.

4.2 Finance

Renewal Area I: The city administration has always tried to obtain special funds for this purpose under public housing schemes but the grant scales are insufficient for preservation purposes, so that in such cases up to 50 per cent of the costs are not covered. This has caused rents to increase to three times the previous price. Up to 1975, a total of DM 23 million came from city, federal and regional (Bavarian) funds. Between 1975 and 1977, DM 9.3 million was provided by the Federal Government and the State Government, which was supplemented by DM three million from the compensation fund, during the same period.

Regensburg: View of buildings in the Roter-Hahnen-Gasse and Gesandtengasse before 1955 (above) and the same situation after the buildings had been replaced by new constructions to take in commercial activities (below)

Regensburg: Conservation area "Donauwacht"
above: Sketch for the area by Prof. Döllgast, 1958
below: Building activities until 1977

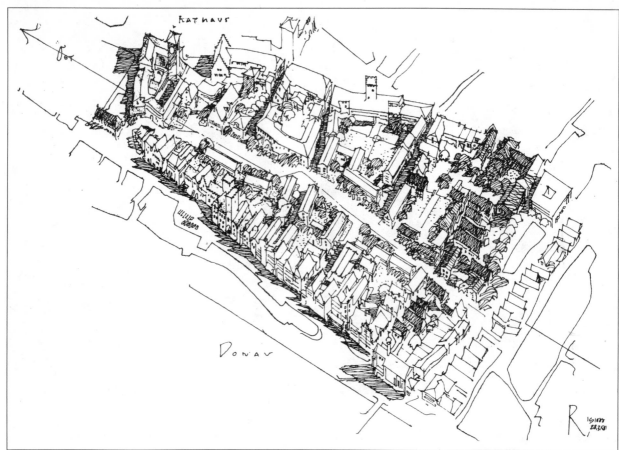

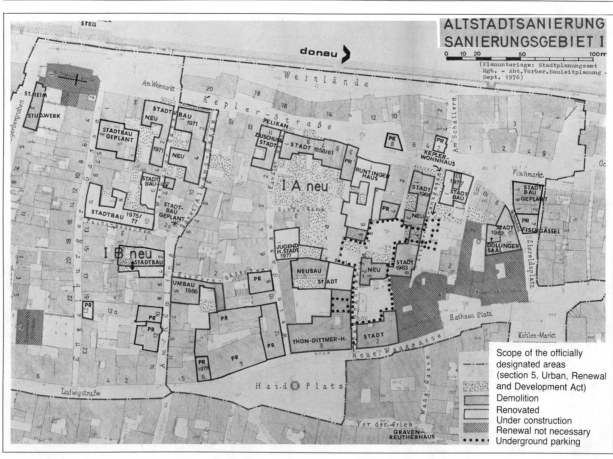

Scope of the officially
designated areas
(section 5, Urban, Renewal
and Development Act)
Demolition
Renovated
Under construction
Renewal not necessary
Underground parking

Publicly owned historical buildings: The costs of projects currently carried out or recently completed by the Churches, the city, and above all by the Free State of Bavaria, can be estimated at approximately DM 50 million (for detailed statistics, see section 5.2).

Privately owned buildings worth conserving: Funds from various public sources have been drawn upon, either for the first time or to a greater extent, for the improvement of privately owned buildings; for instance, those available under the Housing Modernisation Act, the programmes for the promotion of economic activity, and special investment funds, depreciation and tax relief, but especially the compensation fund established under the Protection of Historical Buildings Act in the Free State of Bavaria.

The following two examples illustrate the breakdown of costs:

1. Kepler House, Keplerstraße 2, in Renewal Area I (categorised as a ruin on map indicating the state of buildings), restoration 1½ years (1976/77), 1,462 cbm, area 300 sq. m., flats apart from ground floor:

   – first grant from the compensation fund (approved in 1975) 585,000 DM
   – second grant from the compensation fund/special funds 236,000 DM
   – owners' own contributions (group of heirs) 34,000 DM
   Total 855,000 DM
   (of which net building costs 750,000 DM)

2. Fischgässel 4 in Renewal Area I (previously in a moderate state), restoration 11 months (1976/77), 3,170 cbm, area 713 sq. m., flats apart from ground floor:

   – from funds available under the Urban Renewal and Town Development Act 360,000 DM
   – Grant from the Bavarian Regional Office for the Protection of Historical Buildings 70,000 DM
   – Owner's own contribution 790,000 DM
   Total 1,200,000 DM

4.3 Participation

4.3.1 Offer from city council or agency responsible for renewal

In general, it must be said that up to the seventies the city administration showed little inclination to bring the local community into renewal programmes. At the suggestion of the Friends of the Old City of Regensburg, a renewal centre was set up on 1 December 1975 under the direction of the head of the building department which co-ordinates private, urban and other public initiatives and gives advice on financial aspects and implementation. Those directly affected in Renewal Area I have not received any offers of participation. Up to 1975, the city and the Stadtbau GmbH have confined themselves to "planning for social cases" and for the most part undertaken re-allocation programmes.

4.3.2 Involvement of local amenity groups

The Friends of the Old City of Regensburg formed themselves in 1976 and by 1977 had 165 members (annual subscription DM 20). They have four working groups (townscape/protection of historical buildings; traffic; industry and commerce; "citizens' festival"). Under the guidance of experts, they draw up reports and well-founded alternatives to official plans and make them known to the public. The "Bürgerfest" (an annual public festival held every July since 1973) helps to make the public aware of the old city as an area of urban life.

The "Forum Regensburg e. V." was formed by local citizens and students in 1972 and is mostly concerned with protection of the environment and historical buildings. Today they number about 100 who work in small groups. They draw attention to the various problems of urban development in panel discussions and by means of printed brochures (e. g. "Gries-Stadtamhof" 1975, "Der Bismarckplatz" 1978). They not only criticise but offer constructive alternatives (as for instance for the Regental Autobahn or the Bayernwaldbrück).

5. Implementation

5.1 Revitalising the old city as a whole

The revitalising of the old city of Regensburg by concentrating tertiary sector activities and trade and traffic there involved a large amount of "urban reconstruction" which caused the loss of more historical buildings than the destruction during the war. Wholesale redevelopment, such as the Pustetblock 1955 (seven early and late Gothic houses as well two baroque four-wing structures were pulled down for the building housing the Horten department store and the Sparkasse in 1975 (loss of several Gothic and baroque houses, the sales area being extended from 1,800 to 5,000 sq. m.) altered large sections of the old city considerably. Plans for building a City Centre on an area 90 × 120 m on the site of the Maximilian, a former exclusive hotel, have been thwarted. The building is to be used as a hotel again on the initiative of Dr. Eckert's Technische Lehranstalt (costing about DM six million).

5.2 Implementation of renewal measures in the specified ares (Renewal Area I)

The original programme, starting from a population of 3,000, provided for 490 flats in renovated buildings (i. e. approx. 50 per cent of the units that existed previously) and 600 substitutes in other parts of the city; at present, about 1700 persons in some 800 units live in the specified area. According to the department responsible for renewal measures, the programme has so far been implemented in two periods:

1957–67, measures taken by the city council (building department):

Having built 48 substitute flats in the suburbs, the house "Blauer Hecht" at Keplerstraße 7, was chosen as the first conversion project. In fact only the exterior walls remained standing; the courtyards were cleared, completely new ground plans drawn, and the facades redesigned. Then came the extremely purist restoration projects on the "Runtingerhaus" (cf. 5.3 below) and the new part of the "Dollingersaal" behind the city hall. The council had to meet all the costs since the Protection of Historical Monuments Act had

Regensburg: Conservation of the building Keplerstr. 2 (the former house of Kepler)
above, left: Condition before restoration
above, right: 1st and 2nd floor after restoration
below: View of the house before restoration in 1972 and after restoration with the reconstruction of the mural painting of the 15th century

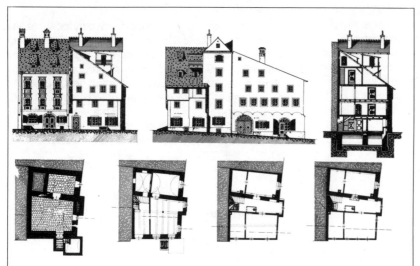

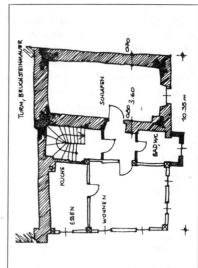

not yet come into force. Two towers (Baumhackergasse 1 and "Am Pelikan", Keplerstraße 11) were designed along historical lines, but larger parts of the buildings at Zieroldsplatz 3 und Silberne Kranzgasse 6, were preserved and renovated.

In this initial period there were obvious planning deficiencies. In particular, the preliminary examinations (research, soundings) concerning the houses themselves and the projection of the work on the basis of the findings were inadequate. Between 1957 and 1966, 81 flats and several street-level shops were provided in Renewal Area I under

the auspices of the city council. Another 21 flats were accommodated in privately renovated buildings; about 270 substitute flats were built in other parts of the city.

Since 1969, measures carried out by Stadtbau GmbH:

After an interruption on financial grounds, the city council transferred restoration work, including the nine houses already acquired, to the Stadtbau GmbH, which recommenced the task with vigour but without any experience in handling old buildings (1969). In the initial period (1969–73),

49 owner-occupied flats, 3 shops, 1 restaurant and 31 parking spaces in two underground garages were made available in the Weinmarkt – Metzgergasse – Keplerstraße – St. Albansgasse area, with the reconstructed high Gothic house tower in the centre. In spite of announcements to the contrary, they are all new buildings, some with historical elements.

Afterwards (1975–77), seven houses in Engelsburger – Metzgergasse, most of them with Romanic and Gothic elements, were partly demolished and renovated. Originally there were 44 units, after renovation 38. Work was carried on at the same time at Fischmarkt 12 and 14, where in the meantime another 12 flats have been occupied. Twenty-three additional flats are to be renovated in subsequent phases (probably ready for occupancy in 1979).

Summary: After initial difficulties, a systematic, more cautious approach has been developed in a working group on "urban renewal" in which all interested parties are represented. After the entry into force of the Historical Buildings Protection Act and the establishment of the compensation fund, the bodies concerned with preservation measures now have a much stronger hand.

5.3 Preservation of specific buildings/publicly owned structures and works of art

The "classical" objects qualifying for preservation in Regensburg are buildings from Roman, medieval and more modern times. A large number of outstanding buildings have been repaired through the co-operative efforts of the government authorities (for instance the regional building office), the Churches and the local authority. One recalls in this connection the permanent institution of the "Dombauhütte" (since 1924, annual cost DM 470,000) which is in charge of masonry renovation. The medieval coloured glass windows are being preserved from further decay by means of protective windows (cost estimate DM seven million). Major Church renovation projects have been carried out in the past ten years, for instance, in the early Gothic Dominican Church, 1967–71 (DM 1,1 million), in the Niedermünster, in St. Ulrich (conservation of paintings made in 1570: DM 850,000), St. Johann, Alte Kapelle and Neupfarrkirche. Apart from the work in St. Ulrich, late Gothic frescoes are being exposed in the Minorite Church. The cleaning of the Obermünster Church ruins (DM 700,000), the only Church in Regensburg destroyed during the war, has involved, among other things, the preservation of the stonework of numerous tombstones. The "Gesandtengräber" (tombs) adjacent to the Protestant Church of the Trinity also had to be reinforced (DM 130,000). Stone replacement was necessary on the clock towers of St. Emmeram on an unusually large scale (DM 1.1 million). Asam frescoes were discovered in the former library of St. Emmeram monastery, which is now the Royal Palace of Thurn and Taxis. In the Reichsaal of the old city hall, the roof had to be repaired and the frescoes carefully cleaned (DM 700,000). In the museum of Cathedral treasures, a section of the Bischofshof, 16th century stucco and paintings had to be restored (DM 400,000). And not least, a part of the Roman wall was conserved in 1973 (DM 70,000).

In recent years the following buildings have been comprehensively renovated and put to a different use: the service buildings of the Obermünster as a diocesan museum; the former St. Mang Chapter (Stadtamhof) as an academy of Church music; Gravenreutherhaus (owned by the University of Regensburg); this four-wing building had become almost uninhabitable. Since 1975 it has been renovated and adopted; the historical substance has for the most part been preserved and the building is now a meeting place of the university, with flats for visiting professors and 25 students (costing DM 5.5 million, grants from the Volkswagen Foundation and the Bavarian Office for the Protection of Historical Buildings); Rüntingerhaus in Renewal Area I – this patrician house was last inhabited by 24 rent-paying families. In an initial "Gothicising" phase 1962–65 (costing DM 1.6 million) the building was "over-purified", with the result that no one was interested in the huge medieval rooms without heating and sanitation. In a second phase the front part of the house has been converted into a branch of the Bavarian Office for the Protection of Historical Buildings and the rear part houses the Regensburg city archives (additional cost: DM 2.4 million).

5.4 Restoration of specific items/privately owned historical buildings

The preservation and revitalisation of private houses of historical importance has never been confined to the Renewal Area. However, there have been more disputes as to the restoration and conversion to other uses of such buildings outside the renewal area than inside, especially in the attractive commercial centres between Neupfarrplatz and the railway station. The following are examples of privately owned buildings renovated at considerable expense: Brixener Hof (originally Bischofshof dating back to the 11th/12th century and of supra-regional importance); Hotel Kaiserhof am Dom (part of the high Gothic patrician house "Heuport" with chapel and rump tower); Scheckenhoferturm – this medieval tower was completely converted into flats, though various parts of the interior and facade have been removed or concealed, such as loam floors, plank staircases, shooting slits, and merlons.

Of late there has been a stronger tendency to retain the original substance and partitioning of the houses. The houses at Keplerstraße 2 and Fischgässel 4 (cf. section 4.2 and photo) are model examples of restoration work, both as regards co-operation between engineer and architect, researcher and those concerned with protection measures, and as to the successful adaptation of the buildings to present-day accommodation requirements.

6. Results

The (partial) results of the conservation work reflect the two rival planning initiatives for the revitalisation of the old part of the city of Regensburg. Thanks to the publicity for conservation work ensuing from European Architectural Heritage Year 1975, the wave of nostalgia and the decline of economic activity, the pendulum appears to have swung more in favour of plans designed to preserve buildings of historical value. Growth-oriented forecasts have not as yet been borne out: the effective increase in the area given over to commercial undertakings amounted to only 25 per cent of the 35–40,000 sq. m. calculated by Dorsch/INGESTA, and the size of the population has remained constant. However, the realisation of projects on the basis of autonomous specialised planning has created a situation which implies the continuation of investment. In Regensburg, this applies in particular to traffic and bridge planning. Projects that have been shelved could well be implemented at the next opportunity, for instance upon a change in the city government or as a result of programmes designed to stimulate economic activity.

Those who advocate the preservation of old buildings still do not have enough comprehensive data at their disposal: the 1977 Regensburg Plan (cf. 3.1), for instance, requires first of all the drawing up of a strategic plan for the development of the old city, analytical studies on townscape and city development, a list of houses and a social plan as part of any renewal programme.

As regards the preservation of buildings of historical value, the scope for action was marked out by the stipulation of the properties in question in December 1975 and the by-law of 1976. Strategies for preserving a townscape on this scale likewise still have to be tried. Too much of the practical work continues to take the form of individual decisions resulting from ad hoc compromises. Plans for determining the age of and other research on old houses should be extended to the ensemble, as should colour studies. The restoration of the house at Keplerstraße 2 and Fischgässel 4 (cf. 4.2) are the first counter-trend to pop colours which clash with the style and to dirty colours which give a wrong picture.

The actual results of renovation programmes in the stipulated area over a period of 20 years are if anything discouraging. It has benn seen that programmes originally drawn up for wholesale redevelopment are hardly suitable for a prescribed historical and social context, although there have been greater efforts to ensure the protection of historical buildings. The grants made by the city council averaging DM one million per year between 1958 and 1975 are rather modest compared with the amounts spent on traffic facilities (DM 10–15 million a year in the same period).

7. Final Observations

Regensburg, similar to Venice, has been described as an extreme case in terms of preservation. Of course, there are analogies as regards the decay of old buildings of historical value, the technical difficulties involved in renovation, and the costs, but also, unfortunately, with regard to the delays in the elaboration and issue of appropriate plans. Regensburg's town map, for instance, dates back to 1956, Venice's to 1962; there are no strategic plans for the "integrated preservation" of the old city as a whole. Since planning falls within the sphere of competence of the city administrations, they must resolve these problems on their own responsibility. Calls for help, however justified they may be, are of little use if the funds coming from outside cannot be employed on the basis of clear concepts and priorities. The task of restoring the old city as a place to live in will involve generations, however. What has been neglected for centuries can only be restored in a continuous process.

Bibliography (selection)

Altstadterneuerung Regensburg. Vorbereitende Untersuchung im Sanierungsgebiet I. Sozialbericht (T.1). Arbeitsgruppe Altstadtsanierung: Walter R. Heinz u. a. Regensburg: Selbstverlag des Geograph.Inst.d. Univ. 1975 = Regensburger Geographische Schriften H. 6

Jahrbuch für Hausforschung (Münster) Bd. 26, 1976: Bericht über die Tagung in Regensburg vom 2.–5. 9. 1975; mit Beiträgen zu Problemen der Stadterhaltung und Bürgerhausforschung von H. E. Hoeller, Cl. Steinbauer, R. Strobel, J. Naumann u. a.

Regensburg – Die Altstadt als Denkmal. Altstadtsanierung – Stadtgestaltung – Denkmalpflege (15 verschiedene Autoren). München: Moos 1978

Regensburg – Zur Erneuerung einer alten Stadt. Städtebauliches Seminar der Stiftung Regensburg des Kulturkreises im Bundesverband der Deutschen Industrie e. V. Düsseldorf, Wien: Econ 1967

Regensburg-Plan 1977. Stadt Regensburg – Stadtentwicklungsplanung. (Loseblatt-Ausgabe im Ordner)

Strobel, Richard: Baualtersplan zur Stadtsanierung Regensburg. München: Bayer. Landesamt f. Denkmalpflege 1973 ff.
I (SG I = Lit.D., Donauwacht) 1973
II (Lit.B., Schererwacht und Lit.C, Wildwercherwacht) 1974
= Baualterspläne zur Stadtsanierung in Bayern 2.3

Strobel, Richard: Das Bürgerhaus in Regensburg. Tübingen: Wasmuth 1976 = Das Deutsche Bürgerhaus XXIII

10 Jahre Vereinigung Freunde der Altstadt Regensburg e. V. 1966–1976. Ein Ausschnitt aus den Jahresberichten (40 S.)

Verordnung über örtliche Bauvorschriften zum Schutze der Altstadt von Regensburg (Altstadtschutzverordnung) vom 9. Januar 1976. in: Jahrbuch für Hausforschung 26, 1976, S. 49–51

GREECE

Greece

LEGISLATION – ADMINISTRATIVE ORGANISATION – FINANCE

Preface

The problem of protection and cultural animation of historic monuments in Greece is at a critical moment now. This is mainly due to a. their number, which increases day by day as the archaeological investigations bring to light new historic structures all over Greece, b. to their great archaeological, historic or artistic and aesthetic value, and, finally, c. to their rather unsatisfactory state of preservation. On the other hand, the industrial development of Greece after World War II has affected both countryside and conservation in a rather great degree, as it causes a serious pressure for redevelopment schemes.

So, it is now well understood that there is a great need for new steps towards legislation, administration and financial resources. On the other part of the public opinion there is now a large number of Amenity Societies that have shown a keen interest in conservation and this naturally is a most promising point for preservation, protection and cultural animation of historical buildings and sites in Greece.

Problems become quite serious when there exists a number of superimposed monuments: under the surface of the ground remains of Pre-historic, Archaic, Classical, Hellenistic, Roman, Early Christian and Byzantine Greece, combined with superimposed buildings dated to the period which followed the fall of Constantinople (1453). And, as far as the former are concerned, the criterion for priority is their archaeological, historic or aesthetic value. But for the latter, the problems are more complicated.

For various historical and social reasons going back to the long Turkish occupation (mid-15th century – early 19th century) and the relevant devastation of the entire country as well as the complete destruction of pre-existed cities and towns there exist but few historic centres in modern Greek towns. Most of them are confined within a narrow area mostly occupied with 19th and 20th century structures. Of course, there is a rather small number of medieval towns like some village in the island of Chios, Monemvasia on the south-west coast of the Peloponnese, Rhodes, the towns of Canea and Rethymno in Crete, Corfu, fortified villages in the islands of Cyclades (Aegean Sea) etc., where one can face problems similar to those faced in other European countries. Finally, there is a large number of approximately 600 villages and towns all over the country dated to the last centuries of the Venetian-Turkish occupation (17th and 18th centuries) including some very fine examples of vernacular architecture as well as many modern towns in southern and central Greece, founded during the reign of King Otto of Wittelsbach after the War of Independence (1821–1827), where one finds some beautiful pieces of Greek Neo-classical Architecture dated to the 19th and early 20th centuries.

1. Legislation

1.1 Laws

1.1.1 Monuments

In accordance with the new constitution of Greece (1975) the protection of the environment and of the cultural heritage is a duty and care of the State. The State ought to take special preventive or repressive steps for their protection, maintenance and preservation. A law shall determine how these powers of the State will be exercised (Art. 24, sections 1 and 6). It is worth noting that it is the first time that such a subject appears in a Greek constitution. This shows an increasing interest on the part of the public in Greece as concerns both environmental problems and the need for new and drastic steps towards conservation. On the other hand, the new constitution provides also some limits as regards ownership but as well as compulsory acquisition (Art. 17).

As concerns legislation things remain unchanged: The two basic laws on whose force the protection and preservation of the archaelogical sites, monuments and historic structures are carried out in Greece go back to the early 1930s and the 1950s, respectively.

a. Law 5351/1932 "on antiquities". This codifies a much older legislation and provides for:

- The protection of all the "ancient" works of Architecture, Sculpture, Painting, Pottery and any art at all, "from the most ancient era until and including that of the medieval Hellenism". In practice, this provision means the protection of all art of works dating before 1453, the year when Constantinople fell to the Turks.

- The protection of churches, monasteries, fortresses, towers and other medieval and post-medieval structures and historic monuments older than 1830.

b. Law 1469/1950 "on the protection of special category buildings and art works posterior to 1830".

This law provides for protection of:

- Buildings and settlement ensembles in places termed as of "special natural beauty".

- Buildings posterior to 1830, if they are termed as "art works needing special state protection".

- Buildings having an historic importance, posterior to 1830, as well as historic sites.

1.1.2 Surrounding areas

Law 5351/1932 (Art. 50) stipulates in principle a protection zone, where it is forbidden to carry out the following activities without a licence:

a. "the quarrying of stones and digging in order to obtain building materials and ancient ruins of cities, settlements, necropolis and at a distance of 500 metres from every visible ancient monument, as well as the construction of lime kilns in a perimeter of 500 metres from antiquities.

b. The carrying out of a project near an antiquity which could directly or indirectly damage it.

c. Any work on buildings and remnants or ruins of antiquities, even if such work will not bring about any damage".

Supplementary Law 1469/1950 stipulates that these provisions apply also on historic sites.

No provision for the protection of the surroundings exists in all other cases of monuments and sites. In practice, however, jurisprudence has accepted the protection of the surroundings, even in cases which do not clearly come under the above provisions, on the grounds that the will of the legislator for the protection of monuments is in this way materialised in a more complete way.

1.1.3 Supplementary legislation

Apart of the two basic Laws (5351/1932 and 1469/1950), the fate of the monuments is also determined by the remaining legislation, such as:

a. The General Building Regulations of 1973 constitute the institutional framework which determines building activity in Greece. They provide for the possibility of an enactment of special conditions and limitations in the erection of buildings or settlement ensembles "of particular historic, folkloric, town-planning, aesthetic or even architectural character", as well as the possibility of imposing additional restrictions regarding the architectural appearance of the buildings".

b. Presidential Decree 941/77 "on the structure of the Ministry of Culture and Sciences" stipulates the competent organs for the protection of the monuments. In accordance with this decree, protection of monuments dating prior to 1830 comes under the jurisdiction of the Directorate General of Antiquities and Restoration, while, for those after 1830, competence lies with the Directorate General of Antiquities and Restoration of Cultural Development, their main consultative organs respectively being the Central Council of more Modern Monuments.

c. Law 360/76 "on arrangement of land and environment" grants the possibility of an intervention in an arrangement of land and on matters of environmental protection, without concretising the way, the level or the object of the intervention. The law provides for the creation of a National Council of Land Arrangement and Environment (Committee of Ministers) with decisive competences on the above issues, as well as an advisory committee consisting of competent administrative agencies. However, Law 360/76 has been applied only once for the taking of steps for the protection of the environment. Recently, moreover, the Council proposed to the Government steps for the traditional settlements.

d. Decree 1003/71 "on active town planning" provides for the development or reshaping of a region with organised building. Implementation of the relevant provisions could solve certain problems of historic centres or traditional settlements, but unfortunately this decree has not so far in the main been implemented.

1.2 Categories of protection

Object: The following categories are protected by the two basic laws 5351/1932 and 1469/1950:

a. All the "antiquities", that is any art work anterior to 1453.

b. Churches and other historic and artistic monuments and buildings older than 1830.

c. Archaeological sites.

d. Places termed as of "special natural beauty", as well as buildings or monuments posterior to 1830 which happen to be located in them.

e. Buildings or monuments posterior to 1830, which have been termed as art works needing special protection.

f. Buildings posterior to 1830 which have an historic importance.

g. Historic sites.

h. Works of painting, sculpture, architecture, of advanced handicraft or noteworthy folk art, posterior to 1830, for which it is deemed necessary to enact special protection.

Except for the items of paragraph "a", which are more or less automatically protected, the rest must be termed by the Minister in charge as worthy of protection to enjoy the special protective provisions. So far, some 4,500 monuments of all categories have been placed under a status of protection. As it is obvious from the categories of protected items or monuments, an ensemble of buildings worthy of protection is protected only indirectly, if it is considered as a site of special natural beauty, which comprises buildings or monuments posterior to 1830. As a result of this, the powers of the Minister of Culture and Sciences, who is competent for the protection, is limited to imposing restrictions only on one specific building each time, without the possibility of expanding also to the right of determining restrictions for more buildings located in the same street, the same block of buildings, or the entire settlement. This deficiency is partly lifted from the 1973 General Building Regulations, which grants competence to another agency – the Minister of Public Works – to impose substantial restrictions on architectural ensembles, by the fixing, for example, of special building conditions.

Historical and social reasons contributed to the fact that greater weight has always been given to the ancient and Byzantine monuments. This discrimination can be seen both in legislation (law 1469/1950 on more modern monuments conveys the legislation provided for the antiquities to its own objects), and in the execution of projects. Restoration schemes are basically carried out on monuments of older times, of historic and cultural importance, many of which do not operate any longer as the purpose for which they were constructed no longer exists.

The easier acceptance by the public of a building, as a monument, when it is of older times, contributes also to this. On the contrary, the acceptance of more modern monuments, especially the "living" ones, as worthy of protection, is meeting reactions especially on the part of the owners, as these do not offer today any return, when another building of much bigger volume can be erected for exploitation in their place. Because of this, there exists a major problem regarding the imposition of the steps which are being taken. Many of the violations are not perceived, or, even when they are noticed, they have already caused irreparable damage and sanctions are not sufficiently strict as to discourage future infringers.

1.2.1 Surrounding areas – protection zones

The immediate surroundings of monuments and historical sites founded prior to 1453 is protected by the law of 1932.

In practice, the degree of protection and the zone within which restrictions are imposed usually depend on the local Inspectorate of Antiquities (when it is not clearly stated in the proclamation decision). The protection of the space surrounding the monument is ignored for the remaining categories of monuments, unless the proclaimed monument happens to be set inside a settlement ensemble which has been termed as "needing special state protection" or located in a "site of special natural beauty". In this case, the protection of the environment is covered of course by Law 1469/1950, but such protection is coincidental.

The lack of a land arrangement plan renders difficult, if not non-existent, a correlation of monument areas with a broader land arrangement programming and the incorporation of their protection in a general development plan, as the laying of certain uses of land according to zones and the organisation of a settlement cannot possibly be covered only by the legislation on the protection of the monuments' inheritance. Various regulatory and land arrangements studies have been drawn up for several regions at various times, but none of them has so far been enacted and due to this, has not been implemented. In this way, the protection of monuments, units or ensembles, is effected individually.

1.3 Procedure

In accordance with the Greek legislation, protected objects are being covered by the relevant protective provisions, if they are judged, termed and registered as worthy of protection by one or more competent agencies. This procedure applies for all the categories of protected items, except for "antiquities" which are protected automatically, without the need of having to be proclaimed preservable. And in practice, despite the fact that Byzantine monuments are included in the previous article, they are often proclaimed as preservable.

In accordance with article 52 of Law 5351/32, churches or other artistic and historic monuments and buildings older than 1830 are termed as "preservable" by action of the competent Minister, which is published in the Government Gazette. And all provisions relating to protection apply both for the monuments which are included in the list of preservable monuments and in annexes made later.

Correspondingly, the protected items of Law 1469/50, i.e. sites of special natural beauty, monuments posterior to 1830, art works and historic sites, are termed as "needing special protection" by act of the competent Minister, which is issued at the proposal of the Central Council on the more modern monuments.

Finally, in accordance with the General Building Regulations of 1973, the possibility exists of "settlements, or sections thereof, qualified as traditional" being termed "preservable buildings" by Presidential Decree at the proposal of the Minister of Public Works and special conditions of building are enacted for them.

Certain problems are created during the implementation of the provisions on protection, due to the different procedure of proclamation, the different agencies and the different advisory organs. The difficulties are intensified by the lack of a register of all monuments and historic structures. The necessity of creating such a register has been recognised since a long time ago, but the limited number of qualified personnel of the official agency constituted always an obstacle for such a long-term effort. There exist, of course,

relevant catalogues, which, however, are not so complete and so valid as a register. The Ministry of Culture and Sciences has already begun relevant work for the registration of monuments in accordance with the proposals of the Council of Europe I.P.C.E. forms (Inventory of Protection of European Cultural Patrimony). This is also provided for by Presidential Decree 941/77 (Directorate of Monuments Registry). During the drawing up of the Registry, an effort will be made to coordinate also the various registration work so far drawn up by various agencies, state and semi-state. More particularly, regarding the traditional settlements, there exists a first registration of same, according to the I.P.C.E. forms, within the framework of the registration of all settlements of the country by the Ministry of the Interior.

The procedure to ensure protection basically is the grant by the Ministry of Culture and Sciences of a relevant approval for any work related with the object under protection.

In the case of repair or conversion of historic monuments and buildings, anterior to 1830, indispensable work is carried out on the basis of an annual programme which is determined by the appropriate service, by this same service itself. As regards demolition, a protected monument can only be demolished after the consent and permission of the Minister of Culture and Sciences.

Protection basically means restriction on ownership – which is the main difficulty encountered by the State in its effort to preserve the monuments. The content of protection in Greece, as it is determined by the two basic laws, is special, that is it faces only individual monuments and not whole ensembles. This arrangement, which is provided for by Law 5351/1932, is due to the fact that the original objective of the legislation was the discovery and preservation of antiquities (mid-19th century). However, its extension to ensembles or sections of settlements, too, resulted in the taking of individual steps for individual cases, which run counter to the constitutional protection of ownership and the principle of the equality of citizens, because decisions are not taken within the framework of more general provisions. Of course, jurisprudence accepts the imposition of considerable restrictions, within the spirit of Article 17 of the 1975 Constitution, but such restrictions should not lead to great reduction of the right of ownership. It is for this reason that when the authorities, in order to protect an object on each occasion, consider indispensable the imposition of stricter limitations, they have recourse to the step of appropriation. In this way, in practice, a competent agency proclaims a building as preservable only when the agency considers that it is absolutely indispensable and has the economic possibility to appropriate it, since that in most cases the new building regulations are so profitable for the owner that the preservation of old buildings is economically unprofitable.

The general protection of settlement ensembles, which is provided for by the 1973 General Building Regulations and is exercised by the Minister of Public Works, has not yet been implemented on a large scale. However, a new draft bill is being studied, which will enact the possibility of general protection of settlement ensembles coming under the jurisdiction of the Ministry of Culture and Science too.

1.4 Agencies

The protection of monuments is exercised by the Government and more particularly by the Minister of Culture and Sciences. The decisions on the kind of work allowed on protected monuments are taken by the Ministry's central service, on the basis of the recommendation of the regional service, without the intervention of other regional or local agencies.

By the 1973 General Building Regulations, the Ministry of Public Works is also appointed as an agency of protection, chiefly for settlement ensembles. Protection by this agency is basically exercised, in cooperation with the Directorate General of Antiquities and Restorations, on new constructions which are built in existing settlements; it also comprises the competence of drawing out regulatory and land arrangement studies, and also reforms and general protection.

The Hellenic Tourist Organisation also takes part in the conservation schemes within the framework of its competence. Until recently, its contribution concerned only the arrangement of spaces around monuments-tourist sites, aiming at their development. However, its new programmes cover entire settlement ensembles, with emphasis on the protection, preservation and limited and controlled development.

Moreover, the Ministry of the Interior, concerned with the study of localising, registering and evaluating the country's settlements and the completion of their registry, on the basis of the I.P.C.E. standard, has laid the basis for a programmed protection of settlement ensembles on a national scale. Even prefects, who administratively come under the Ministry of the Interior, are often responsible for all technical projects which are carried out in the provinces, many of which have a direct relation with the monuments.

Local authorities have no jurisdiction for an intervention in conservation, according to the law, but the position they will take towards the whole issue of their protection often exercises a decisive influence on the behaviour of the inhabitants towards it.

1.5 Indemnities

In accordance with Law 5351/1932, reparation works which are imposed to be carried out on ancient or historic structures, which belong to civilians or other legal persons, are carried out by their owners at their own expense. In case of weakness or refusal of the interested parties to carry out the indicated work, the state carries out the reparation works, paying itself the expenditure involved. But in such a case it can occupy the monuments belonging to monasteries, communities, or other legal persons, or appropriate those belonging to individuals due to public necessity. In practice, an owner who does not want or cannot undertake the repairs and other maintenance work imposed by the administration refuses to carry out the work. But, as in some cases no way of granting to an individual any economic assistance (loans, grants) is provided for, or a reimbursement by the state of the repair cost involved, the protection agency generally undertakes the maintenance when it plans to appropriate the real estate property. Anyway, all the work which is to be carried out on a protected item, which belongs to an individual, is controlled by the competent agent in charge, both in the stage of study and during construction. Work can start only on the prerequisite of the relevant approval by the Minister of Culture and Sciences, which is often given after an opinion of the Ministry's regional services and the competent bodies (Archaeological Council, etc.).

1.6 Protection in relation with the development policy

National programming

The more general policy of Greece, chiefly after World War II, can basically be characterised as a "development policy", the basic objective being a modernisation of the technical infrastructure. This evaluation resulted until recently in the submission of the state's policy on land arrangement and the environment to the priorities of the economic policy, as a consequence of which the space of monuments was isolated and protection was limited, chiefly on monuments which are no longer used and belong to the State (ancient, Byzantine).

It was perceived during the last few years, however, that to face conservation problems one should pass from the archaeological point of view to the area of programming (national or local), land arrangement and town planning. In the legislative sector, this new conception is reflected in the New Building Regulations of 1973, Law 360/76 "on land arrangement and environment" and Decree 1003/71 "on active town planning". However, as the latter two laws have not yet been implemented, General Building Regulations (1973) which constitute the institutional framework for building and the control of the Greek space, remain as the most important, after the two basic laws (5351/1932 and 1469/1950), regulator of the fate of monuments. A serious obstacle to the protection of monuments, particularly for those dated to the post-1830 period, is the big exploitation coefficients which are allowed in Greek cities and settlements, in relation to the small scale of old buildings (usually with one or two floors). Special building conditions can neutralise this difficulty in small villages, towns, and historic cities, but only eight special decrees have so far been issued, against some 600 villages and towns or sections of cities requiring protection; however, a decree is being prepared for 400 Greek villages and towns and its implementation will solve many problems.

Considerable progress has been accomplished during the last few years, particularly in small towns presenting tourist interest, as, in cooperation with the Hellenic Tourism, economic incentives are being given for the maintenance and preservation of old buildings.

Local programming

Due to the concentrated structure of the Greek State, regional and local services do not have much decisive jurisdiction. In the sector of protection, prefects are basically implementing the decisions taken by the Centre, while Municipalities and Communities are dealing with the issue only at the initiative of Mayors; legislatively, they have no jurisdiction at all. Local watching over the work of maintenance of monuments and control, as well as the proposal of steps regarding their protection, is effected by the regional services of the Ministry of Culture and Sciences, which depend directly only from the central service of the same Ministry, but cooperate, of course, with other regional or local agencies too.

2. Organisation

2.1 Legislative jurisdiction

In accordance with the 1975 Constitution, the protection of the monuments is an obligation of the State. More particularly, in accordance with existing legislation, the main competent agency is the Ministry of Culture and Sciences, which has the responsibility for the protection, maintenance and care of monuments. The Minister of Culture and Sciences decides if a monument should be proclaimed as preservable, after taking into consideration the recommendations of the competent bodies. The Minister gives also his approval for consolidation and reparation work on monuments. Other agencies, too, which have been already mentioned in chapter 1.4 take part directly or indirectly, in specific sectors, in this protection.

2.2 Administrative agencies with jurisdiction for the protection

The recommendation study and the implementation of steps concerning the maintenance of monuments and historic buildings is carried out by the Directorate General of Antiquities and Restoration of the Ministry of Culture and Sciences. Recently, by Presidential Decree 941/77, it was decided that the Directorate General of Cultural Development of the same Ministry is competent for monuments and settlement ensembles dating after 1930.

The following work for the protection of monuments is carried out within the framework of the jurisdiction of the Directorate General of Antiquities and Restoration:

a. Studies are been drawn up and supervision work is carried out on the consolidation, maintenance, strengthening, restoration, arrangement of the surrounding area as well as recording of the monuments. In accordance with Law 5351/1932, "movable and immovable antiquities belong to the State and, consequently, care for their discovery and preservation belongs to the State". In view of this, a restoration study is rarely entrusted to civilians in Greece, but, even in such a case, studies are always checked by the Directorate General, which supervises their correct implementation.

b. Excavations or other work carried out in archaeological sites and steps for the protection of the findings are taken.

c. Consolidation, maintenance and restoration work on monuments is carried out and supervision of repair work made by owners of ancient or historic structures (civilians or legal persons) is exercised.

d. Control is exercised on any activity which may be related with monuments, e.g. erection of buildings near an archaeological site, provisional or permanent use of a monument, scientific studies, etc.

e. A registry of monuments and historic structures is being drawn up.

Administrative care for the implementation of the provisions, as well as an on-the-spot examination of all relevant matters, is exercised by regional organs, i.e. 13 Inspectorates for pre-historic, classic and Roman Antiquities and 25 Inspectorates for Byzantine Antiquities, which are spread all over the country. The Inspectorates are exercising a sub-stantial work because, although decisions are taken by the Central Service, this is done after consultation with the Inspectorate in charge. Jurisdiction for more modern monuments (buildings after 1830) lies with the Direction General of Cultural Development and its regional services (seven inspectorates for more modern monuments). In this sector there exists for the time being a mutual coverage of jurisdictions with the Ministry of Public Works. However, this issue will soon be settled by a new law. Contrarily with the ancient and Byzantine monuments, whose protection is well-organised, the sector of more modern monuments has not yet been organised to the degree which is imposed because of the object involved and therefore, cases that studies are been drawn up by the State or that building work is carried out by the State, are rather rare and coincidental. However, under the new structural status of the Ministry of Culture and Sciences (Pres. Decree 941/77) it is hoped that such weaknesses and deficiencies will be lifted.

Already great efforts are also being made on this subject.

2.3 Collective organs

Up to October 1977, the collective organ on all matters related with the protection of monuments was the Archaeological Council, based in Athens. This concentration presented disadvantages, but the following has been stipulated the issue of Presidential Decree 941/77:

1) The Central Archaeological Council with jurisdiction on monuments dated up to 1830, issues its opinion on all important matters concerning the protection of monuments (licences of considerable extent and significance, proclamations of buildings as preservable, excavations, restoration schemes, erection of archaeological museums, acquisition of buildings or land for archaeological purposes, etc.) and important work on antiquities and historic monuments. The Central Archaeological Council consists of 11 members, appointed by the Minister in accordance with the above Presidential Decree.

2) The Central Council for more modern monuments with jurisdictions corresponding to those of the Central Archaeological Council, consisting of nine members, issues its opinion on monuments posterior to 1830.

3) Six local Councils on Monuments are also provided for as regional collective organs. They consist of five members and issue their opinion on matters concerning the region of their jurisdiction.

Participants in these councils comprise senior cadres of the Minister of Culture and Sciences, University Professors (Schools of Architecture and Philosophy), as well as representatives (senior cadres) of other Ministries and State agencies.

Apart from the councils, certain committees are provided for. These conduct and supervise maintenance work on important monuments, such as the Committee for the Maintenance of the Acropolis Monuments, the Committee for the Study of Historical and Archaeological Problems of Rhodes, the Committee for the Maintenance of the Epikourios Apollon Temple (in Figalia) and the Committee for the Study of Archaeological Problems of Thera. The above councils and committees come under the Ministry of Culture and Sciences. Correspondingly, on matters of jurisdiction of the Ministry of Public Works, the role of consultative organ, usually with a decisive competence, is played by local "Committees on Architectural Control", which are formed by cadres of the Ministry of Public Works, a representative of the Technical Chamber and a representative of the Ministry of Culture and Sciences.

2.4 Private organisations

A good number of amenity societies are dealing with the quality of life, protection of the environment and protection of the monuments. However, a systematic work is carried out by the following:

a. The Archaeological Society in Athens. This was founded in 1837 and operates as a Legal Person of Private Law with headquarters in Athens. The Society seeks

1. the discovery, collection, maintenance, safeguard, restoration, repair and scientific research of ancient monuments, including also the Christian, Byzantine and other monuments up to the Greek Independence Revolution, in Greece and Greek countries,

2. the study of the life of the ancients and the exploration of the Byzantine and Middle Ages archaeology and art,

3. to raise interest, in general, in favour of the fine arts and a spreading of the knowledge on the history of ancient and modern art in Greece.

The Archaeological Society consists of 230 members and carries out excavations, organises lectures, issues announcements and publications regarding monuments and acquires property by gift or purchase for excavations or the preservation and maintenance of antiquities. The Society has its own resources from the exploitation of its own privately-owned real estate properties, bequests, contributions and donations of members, but is also subidized by the State. As it has been already stated, the Archaeological Society does not deal with the more modern monuments. In fact, the major part of its activities are focused on field archaeology and antiquities and it has already displayed a very important work on this field throughout Greece.

b. The Hellenic Society was founded in 1972 and aims at contributing to the preservation and improvement of the Greek environment. Since 1977, it operates as an Association based in Athens. The Society seeks "to invigorate the interest and conviction of the Greeks for the value of their cultural heritage (historical, artistic and architectural), . . . to encourage by every means, economic or other, their preservation, . . . to support the architectural, town planning and lawful land interventions which will improve the environment of settlements and the countryside . . .". The Hellenic Society accomplishes work coming under its interests and tries to broaden the participation of the public in the problems of the environment and the maintenance of the cultural heritage. The Hellenic Society sustains itself from private contributions without state assistance, and deals mainly with the protection of the post-Byzantine monuments and traditional settlements.

c. The Scientific Committee on Architectural Heritage which operates within the framework of the Technical Chamber of Greece. The Committee was set up in 1976 to replace certain other committees of the Technical Chamber (Institute of Fortresses and Castles – 1969 – and Ward of Sites and Cities – 1958) and seeks to study "matters concerning traditional settlements and vernacular architecture and problems concerning monuments".

d. Foreign Schools and Institutes (French, German, Italian, English, American, Swedish, Swiss, Belgian, Austrian) carry out excavations in various areas allocated to them by the Greek State, with rights of priority in the study and publication of the findings.

e. A most important contribution to the protection of monuments and settlement ensembles is also the work carried out by professors, the scientific personnel and students of Superior Education Foundations (School of Architects of the Athens Technical University, School of Architects of Thessaloniki University, Philosophical Schools of the Universities of Athens, Thessaloniki, Ioannina and Crete). The efforts made by all of them are often quite important.

3. Finance

3.1 Compulsory acquisition

Due to the existing legal status the Minister of Culture is not entitled to impose strict limitations that would lead to an essential reduction of ownership. In the opposite case, he must have recourse to the compulsory acquisition of land and buildings. In practice, however, appropriation is not desirable, neither by the Administration nor from the owners; therefore, it is applied as an ultimate means, after the previous exhaustion of all other possible solutions. An obstacle to appropriation, apart from the fact that it runs counter to the sentiments of citizens on ownership, is also the high prices of land, especially in urban centres. Despite all this, the existing obligations from compulsory acquisiton amount to about 2,000 million drs., while the sum allocated to this end annually is just one tenth of the required amount. Presently, however, the State is the owner, as a result of donations, bequests and older purchases, of a considerable number of important buildings which have been termed as monuments, as well as archaeological sites. The Church is also of course the owner of monumental buildings, since many of them are churches or monasteries.

3.2 Restorations, excavations

a. Excavations: The entire country is spread with archaeological treasures of various times; the traces of older civilisations are so many that new and extremely important findings are continuously brought to light; yet, there still exists a huge field for research. In accordance with the law, excavations are effected only by the State, Directorate General of Antiquities and Restoration and regional services. In 1975, the agency in charge spent 88,160,000 drs., for excavations and work at archaeological sites. In 1976, the corresponding amount was 153,068,000 drs. and in 1977 it reached 212,503,000 drs.

Despite all this, there exists so many areas which could be excavated that the Greek State has ceded the right of excavation to foreign Archaeological Schools, too. These are carrying out work in designated areas at their own expense under the supervision of the inspectorate in charge. And they have the right of priority for the study, cleaning and publication of the relevant findings.

A most important contribution to the field Archaeology is also that of the Archaeological Society, which finances excavations on a large scale and has already accomplished a very important work.

b. Consolidation – Restoration: In 1975, the Ministry of Culture and Sciences allocated 56,558,000 drs. for the consolidation and restoration of monuments; in 1976, expenditure was 81,524,000 drs. and in 1977 115,875,000 drs. This work was carried out on important buildings, chiefly owned by the State.

The grant of loans to owners for the preservation of monuments was not provided for until 1972. While the institution of granting loans to civilians for the acquisition of a home is sufficiently spread in urban and also in rural regions, the grants of loans still concern in their crushing majority – new houses or extensions, and not maintenance. In 1972, however, the Ministry of the Interior promoted a short-term "Programme of Loan Grants for Tourist Rooms" chiefly in settlements of vernacular architecture. The results of the Programme were very important, apart of their social and economic repercussions and the information and training of the inhabitants.

From 1976 to 1977, important steps have been made towards promoting the private sector for the preservation and maintenance of buildings. This coincided with the activation of the administration for the protection of the post-1830 buildings and settlements, in addition to the ancient ones. It has now become understood that buildings which are termed as preservable monuments are part of the national architectural heritage and, consequently, their protection belongs to the Greek people. The following methods of financing are provided within the framework of this new conception:

a. The Ministry of Culture and Sciences grants economic aid to owners of preservable buildings or buildings lying in conservation areas for the maintenance of their real estate property. Due to the relatively small sum available (7,636,000 drs. in 1976 and 17,390,000 drs. in 1977), such aid usually does not exceed 100,000 drs. for each building.

b. The National Real Estate Bank of Greece is granting long-term loans at a small rate of interest, up to the sum of 500,000 drs., for reparation works on buildings of vernacular architecture or buildings found in conservation areas. This effort is relatively recent (since the second half of 1977), and due to the small credits which are so far available (25,000,000 drs.), the programme is limited to a few villages and towns.

c. Within the framework of the State's economic policy, important credits are allocated for the maintenance of buildings. The objective however is their development for touristic purposes.

– The Hellenic Tourist Organisation (EOT) embarked three years ago on a Programme for conservation areas. EOT acquired the use of buildings found in ten traditional settlements, for a period of 10–15 years, with the obligation to attend to their maintenance at its own expense and turn them into guest-rooms. In view of the fact, however, that the operation of a guest-room cannot be considered independent from other related operations for the organisation of a settlement, work for other uses has also been incorporated in this programme (such as buildings of squares, roads and pavements, etc.).

– EOT, moreover, in cooperation with the National Real Estate Bank and the commercial banks, grants since 1975 long-term loans for the repair and equipment of rented furnished rooms. Priority to the allocation of such a loan is given to the owner of a preservable monument or building of vernacular character. These loans (up to 40,000 drs./room) aim at a double target: on the other, they contribute to the needs for tourist dwellings.

– A subsidisation of up to 35 per cent of the cost of building work involved is provided for the owner of an important historic structure, so that the owner may turn it into a guest house, with a view to preserving important buildings and giving them a new use. Within the framework of the same programme, long-term loans, at a low rate of interest, are granted for up to 85 per cent of the estimated total expenditure for the "repair, consolidation, arrangement and equipment of privately-owned buildings of special architectural character or which have been termed as preservable, for their turning into tourist dwellings (hotels or guest houses).

It should be mentioned at this point that in the selection and final approval for the subsidies and loans granted by EOT, the basic agency in charge of protection (Ministry of Culture and Sciences) is not taking part, and neither are the proclamations of historic buildings or ensembles as preservable taken strictly into consideration (monuments or settlements which have not been proclaimed as preservable are not excluded).

Recently, the National Council of Land Arrangement and Environment proposed to the Government (Minister of Coordination) a series of economic measures, whose objective is not only the protection of monumental units and ensembles but also the economic and social development of the conservation areas. It is worth noting that the proposals provide for the coming under a status of incentives of entire settlements and not only historic structures. The proposals provide for an exemption from transfer taxation of buildings in important conservation areas and the grant of loans under favourable conditions, as well as the organisation in zones and the drawing up of long-term development programmes for those areas. Finally, it is proposed to subsidize interested parties for up to 200,000 drs. for the maintenance and repair of their old houses and the setting up of a National Enterprise on the protection of the vernacular architecture of villages and towns throughout Greece.

As it appears from the above, we are in a critical transitory period during which the question of the protection of monuments in Greece is being faced more broadly and more dynamically. The object is no longer only the antiquities but also the post-Byzantine monuments, historic structures and ensembles. Many agencies are taking part in this effort and it is hoped that the problems which are still appearing will eventually be solved.

Adresses:
Ministry of Culture and Sciences, Aristidou 14, Athens
Public Works Ministry, Direction General of Settlements, 17 Amaliados Street, Athens
Hellenic Tourism Organisation 2, American Street, Athens
Ministry of the Interior, Stadiou and Dragatsaniou 4, Athens
Archaeological Society, 22 Panepistimiou Street, Athens
Hellenic Society, 10 Panepistimiou Street, Athens
Technical Chamber of Greece 4, Karageorgi Servias Street, Athens
Technical University, 42 Patission, Athens
University of Athens, Athens
University of Salonica
Polytechnic School, Salnica
Association of Architects, 3 Ipiti Street, Athens

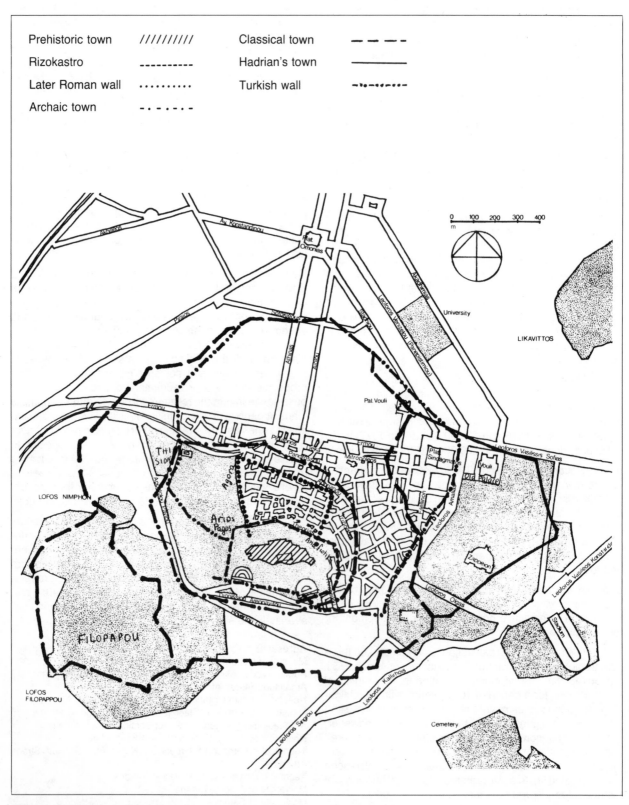

Athens – historical development
(drawing by A. Fostiropoulos)

Greece
ATHENS-PLAKA

1. Situation

1.1 General introduction

There is something unique, at least for Greece, about Plaka, the old town of Athens. The nearly 6,000 people who against all adversities still live there are today united to a man in their determination to save the area.

Conservation for them is not a coffee table discussion or an intellectual or aesthetic pursuit. It involves, as I will explain further, their own life and health and that of their children. Offers to sell their houses to bar and disco owners, compensated by what is for many of them a vast amount of money, are made regularly, coupled with more or less subtle intimidation. But a common answer is, "I love the area and I do not wish to leave". These people surely count among the heroes of European Conservation.

1.2 Physical environment

Plaka is unmistakably identified in the topography of Athens by the nexus of its tile-roofed houses embracing the northern and north-eastern slopes of the Acropolis. It descends gently to the foothills and flatter land around and ends abruptly, facing on one side the archaeological area of the Agora, and on the others the cement barrage of modern Athens.

The hill of the Acropolis which is the landmark for the whole of Athens is even more so for Plaka, part of which literally lives in its shadow.

A large green belt starting at the Agora excavations spreads to the small hills of Thission and Arions Pagos, and over a main road to the hills of Pnyka and Philopappou. There are also two smaller green belts, one between the sheer sides of the Acropolis and the peripheral road around it, and another on the eastern side of the rock above Rangava Square.

The view from the Upper Plaka is extremely pleasant. With one glance one can see first the archaeological area with its monuments, then the hill of Lycabettus, and further along if it is possible to remain oblivious of the shapeless modern town, one can still be carried away by the beauty of the legendary Hymettos and Parnis, two of the mountains that form part of the famous "violet crown" of Athens.

1.3 History

The old town of Athens is probably the only one in Europe that has been continuously inhabited for 5,000 years. The area of the Plaka has been the political, commercial and educational centre of the town of Athens throughout the ages. In different periods of its history the town expanded in different directions, but always retained Plaka as the centre of its life.

The settlement in prehistoric times (3000 BC) developed around the Acropolis and was quite small, no more than 90,000 sq.m.

During the Archaic period (7th century BC) it increased a great deal in all directions, especially to the North and West up to the hills of Thission and Pnyka; it then covered an area of 500,000 sq.m.

The town reached its largest size in antiquity – 15,000,000 sq.m. after the Persian Wars in the 5th century. Classical Athens developed all around the Acropolis which was then turned from a defence bastion into a sacred rock, the centre of religion. Its days of glory continued in Roman times as the Romans felt great admiration for the civilisation Athens had embodied. Under Hadrian the town expanded even further East.

The first major destruction took place in 267 AD, when the Herrulians conquered Athens and set it on fire. The devastation was so great that the Athenians were unable to rebuild and fortify the whole of the old town, and built instead a much smaller wall, the one called Later Roman Wall (see maps). The town included in these walls has been the centre of activity ever since and is roughly the Plaka of today. Athens received further blows in the 5th century (426 and 435), when the Emperor Theodosius II decreed the closure of the philosophical schools, which had continued to flourish.

During the first centuries of the Eastern Roman Empire (Byzantine Empire),Athens lived a withdrawn provincial existence. From the middle of the 9th century to the end of the 12 th century it became once more a thriving town, as is witnessed by the numerous churches which were built during this period, some of which survive and still function in Plaka today.

This prosperity was once more interrupted first by a Saracen invasion (end 12th century), followed by the occupation of the Franks in 1204. For the first time Athens lost its freedom completely. The Frank Dukes (1204–1311), and later the Catalonians (1311–1387), totally disregarded it, and made Thebes their capital. The Florentines Acciajuoli (1387–1456) made Athens their centre, but although some construction and restoration work was carried out, the town withdrew basically inside the late Roman Wall.

The first Ottoman occupation lasted from 1456–1687. Mohamed II visited Athens, and in appreciation of its contribution to civilisation, granted the "mother of philosophy" special privileges, with some degree of local self-government, as well as direct dependence on the Sultan's harem. The Fetihie (Conqueror's) Jami named after him, in the centre of Plaka, was built in 1458 immediately after his visit.

In the 16th century with the arrival of many Christians (mainly Greeks from other places), the town burst out of the bounds of the late Roman enclave, most of which seems to have been destroyed in that period. Only a few remnants remained which can still be seen today. The Acropolis, from that time, was isolated as a fortress for the Turkish garrison, who also built their own houses on it.

The town of Athens was then divided into eight administrative districts, one of which, on the eastern side, as a result of a large slab (Plaka) laid between Adrianou and Tripodou Str., was named Plaka. It is from that neighbourhood that the whole of the old town takes its name today. From this period date a number of churches, and a Turkish bath.

Athens-Plaka:
View from the Acropolis: Plaka is unmistakably identified by the nexus of its tile-roofed houses embracing the northern and north-eastern slopes of the Acropolis

Athens-Plaka: Aggressive entertainment has taken over many streets in Plaka. Neon light signs disfigure the houses

Athens suffered once more one of the most brutal attacks in its history when the Venetians in 1687, led by Morosini, looted the town and bombed the Parthenon, then used by the Turks as a gun store, and which thereafter lay in ruins.

The second period of Turkish occupation (1688–1833) was marked by the oppressive rule of Hatzi Ali Haseki. In the winter of 1778 he literally whipped the Athenians into constructing, in 100 days, a large defensive Turkish Wall (see map). To the North it followed the line of the Classical Wall but its other sides were much shorter.

From that time onwards, the town would be much better documented, thanks to the constant stream of western visitors, who as a result of renewed interest in classicism were keen to rediscover Athenian antiquities. One of the main mosques of the town, Tsisdaraki Mosque, was built in 1759 and is now used as a ceramics museum. The administrative and commercial centre of the town remained again in Plaka.

Athens joined the 1821 Revolution against Turkish rule from the start and soon managed to expel the Turks, but after four years of freedom she suffered another major destruction when the avenging Turkish General Koutahi reconquered it in 1827. The majority of houses in Plaka were destroyed in the war.

In 1833 Athens was chosen to be the capital of the Free State of Greece, and from that time, its development is rapid, as Greeks from all over the world come to settle in it.

Consecutive town plans, urging the demolition of Plaka to create a large archaeological zone around the Acropolis, are put aside under strong local pressure, as the area is once more the centre of the town. Many nice neoclassical houses built then, and still standing, lent the area the basic character it still has today. To grasp the astronomical increase of Athens, one need only be reminded that at the end of the 19th century it had 50,000 inhabitants, while today the Athens region has over 3 million.

The attractive neoclassical town that developed first to the North (the University area) and the East (where the royal palace was built) of Plaka, gradually spread in every direction. Ironically, this neoclassical town, due to a postwar boom, was senselessly destroyed, giving way to a characterless cement city, while Plaka, which was repeatedly decreed for demolition, stubbornly survives as the only witness to the history of Athens.

Above Plaka proper, perched on the steep north-eastern slope of the Acropolis, survives a complex of small intertwined white-washed houses which follows so faithfully the

Athens-Plaka: A beautiful neoclassical house restored by the National Archaeological Service to house one of its departments

contours of the rock that it is barely noticeable from afar. It is called Anafiotika, after the tiny Aegean island from which its inhabitants came in the 19th century to work as builders in the new capital. Built secretly, in the light of the starry Athenian sky, it humbly adds a charming footnote to the history of the old town.

2. Conditions

2.1 Physiognomy of Plaka today

A. Town-planning

Plaka's town-planning has remained unchanged from ancient times to today, dictated all along by the Northern Slope of the Acropolis.

The basic street lay-out also dates back to ancient times, and as is often the case with towns developing around an acropolis, one can distinguish two types of streets; the straight ones descending from the highest point in a beam-like design, and the parallel circular ones (Tripodon Street is one of the oldest) encircling the rock, each at a different height.

B. Architecture

The 1820s War of Independence took a very severe toll, and although a few houses have survived from Ottoman times, the majority of them were built after 1830.

Plaka like the rest of Athens took to neoclassicism with the natural instinct of one returning to his roots. Neoclassical houses and their humbler relatives the "laika neoclassica" ("popular neoclassical houses") lend Plaka its predominant character. Early 20th century efforts to escape into Western fashions were hesitant and produced a mixed 'eclectic' style which still retains neoclassical features.

But neoclassicism and its descendents were often merely a facade, as the Plaka houses even at this stage retained the features of the prototype ancient Athenian house.

This is characterised by the central position of an "AIOP-ION" courtyard, around which are positioned the living and the service quarters. Archaeological evidence has shown that houses like these are found not only in ancient times but in Byzantine and Ottoman ones as well.

Irrespective of their facade (neoclassical, popular neoclassical, or eclectic), most of the houses in Plaka retain the ageold traditional features of a central courtyard surrounded by the living quarters, a lower open gallery and an upper covered gallery "XAΠATI".

This survival of the past in the present is intensified by the constant presence of monuments. Byzantine and post-Byzantine churches still function in dim candlelight and gather crowds not just from Plaka but from all over Athens.

Other monuments (Classical, Hellenistic, Frankish, Ottoman) are not isolated but blend harmoniously with the houses, embraced by the same jasmin or honeysuckle, or shaded by the ever present cypress tree.

2.2 Situation of conflict

Plaka is the apple of discord between three powers, archaeology, commerce, and tourism, waging a fearsome battle over its territory, each with an exclusive claim on it.

A. Archaeology

The archaeological threat, chronologically the first, has been hanging like Damocles' sword over Plaka ever since 1833 when Greece won her independence. With a few exceptions, most of the plans drawn up for the town of Athens by more or less famous architects and planners urged demolition of the whole or a substantial part of Plaka to create a broad archaeological zone all around the Acropolis, which would reveal the ancient city lying right under it.

Due to local protests, but mainly to lack of money, the plans were shelved until in 1930 the American School of Classical Studies provided the funds which resulted in the excavations of the Agora.

The policy of the Greek State's Archaeological Service up to now had been gradually to expropriate areas of Plaka and extend excavations wherever possible, without much publicity. As a result of this the State today owns 20 % of Plaka, and 10 % of its houses.

The archaeologists' argument that it was worth sacrificing Plaka to reveal the ancient town did not at first meet much opposition (apart from locally), as the Greek people believed then that no other period of their history would rival the glory of the Ancient pre-Christian World.

However, the last major plan for the town, drawn up in 1974 under the direction of Professor Zivas, reflects a dramatic change in both Greek and world public opinion. It emphasizes the importance of saving Plaka, and concedes to the archaeologists' spade only a very small area near the Roman Agora and Hadrian's library. It echoes the opinions of R. Lemaire, R. Sneyers and J. Somnier, who in their 1970 UNESCO report on the Acropolis urge the preservation not just of the Plaka but of the Anafiotika as well, if only precisely for the sake of the Parthenon for which the Plaka forms an ideal protective environment.

The archaeological threat which led to many forcible expulsions and demolitions initiated a mood of insecurity which in turn resulted in the vicious circle of abandonment and degradation.

Fortunately today many leading Greek archaeologists recognise the intrinsic value of Plaka itself, and have joined the inhabitants in their recent campaign to save Plaka. A number of houses owned by the Archaeological Service have been restored this last year and it is hoped that they will be used to infuse new life into the area, in harmony with its character.

But as there are still some important archaeologists who are aiming at the ultimate demolition of large parts of Plaka, the mood of insecurity will linger until the State makes a firm commitment to its preservation.

B. The threat of commerce

This threat derives from Plaka's position next to the commercial centre of Athens. As the town of Athens increased to nightmarish proportions, absorbing nearly ⅓ of the total population of Greece, its commercial centre sought outlets and increased its pressures on Plaka. Most susceptible to

Athens-Plaka:
above: typical exterior of a private house before restoration
below: the same house after restoration

these pressures has been the low part of Plaka where many inhabited houses changed function and turned into offices, while others, at some opportune moment, were replaced by apartment houses or office blocks whose scale and style is totally out of place. About ⅓ of present-day Plaka houses do not fit in the area.

Another sign of this pressure is the 2,000 cars (most of them from the commercial centre, as the inhabitants own only roughly 300 cars), which park daily in illegal parking spaces, spoiling the environment of monuments, as well as the views, and creating traffic jams in the narrow streets.

C. The threat of tourism

The vicious circle was completed with the development of an aggressive entertainment industry very different from the genuine traditional tavernas which exploits the best preserved neighbourhood, Upper Plaka, by selling its picturesque character to tourists. These new "folk entertainers", who would send chills down the spines of the Greeks' forefathers, compete across narrow little streets with giant amplifiers propagating their "folk music".

This has resulted during the last ten years in the flight of many inhabitants, while those who remained had to resign themselves to sleepless nights. Plaka turned into a red-light district, with discos, sex bars, drugs and the rest. Means fair and foul were used to convince people to move out of the area. The new entertainers, although a minority even among taverna owners (the majority of tavernas retain their old character), expressed their ambition to control the whole of Plaka by naming it "Dionysopolis" as the tourist world experience has in it a total Greek "let go" trip.

2.3 **Sociological data**

Sociological factors adverse to preservation

As a result of the triple assault on Plaka

– less than 6,000 people live in Plaka today

– only ⅓ of its houses are inhabited (as residences)

– 243 houses are empty (a number of those owned by the State)

- there are 900 shops employing 2,130 people
- 330 handicraft units
- 390 offices employing 2,300 people (the largest employer)
- 193 entertainment units employing 1,600 people, the noisy ones create the greatest disturbance for the residents
- 18 educational centres employing 200 people.

The architecture of Plaka, an interspersed mixture of larger, medium-scale and small houses, traditionally secured a healthy mixture of all social classes. Over recent years, however, the more affluent and influential Athenians who once lived in Plaka moved out and were replaced by people of lower income levels. Now only 27 % of the inhabitants own the property in which they live, a very low percentage for Greece. The lower the social bracket, the less education, the more difficult it becomes to expess legitimate grievances.

Another adverse factor is the drop in the proportion of young inhabitants: only 10 % of the population is under 12 (Athens 18 %), 15 % of the population is over 65 (Athens 9 %).

3. Participation and Realisation

Plaka seemed doomed. But Dionysus, whose ecstasy was anything but commercialised, and who was notorious for his enmity against those who insulted him, took revenge. The last few thousand inhabitants turned out to be more stubborn than expected. They would not budge.

Their anger led them to join hands. Fragmented and isolated groups of people at last came together. A committee coordinating the efforts of 21 local and national organisations campaigning to save Plaka was formed in 1978. It included not only residents associations, but also shopkeepers, and representatives of handicraft firms. It argued

clearly for the view that Plaka should be basically residential, retaining the traditional Greek tavernas but with no loudspeakers and no neon lights. This position is supported by local shopkeepers and a fair number of tavernas too.

The Coordinating Committee has managed to keep the issue alive in the media with news reports or articles about every two weeks over the last year and in this way has succeeded in changing Athenian public opinion. Whereas a year ago the average Athenian would say "It is too late to save Plaka", now he would say, "Plaka should be saved now".

A Europa Nostra statement asking for the prohibition of amplifiers and neon lights has been of great assistance to the campaign. The inhabitants literally bombarded the press with it. Plaka's residents are grateful for this international assistance.

Their next attempt was to get important social groups to support them. One hundred of Greece's most famous artists, writers, and composers, including world renowned figures like Mikis Theodorakis, Michalis Cacoyiannis, Melina Mercouri, etc. signed a letter of support.

At that stage, one of the main counter-arguments they had to face was that Plaka in its present state is good for tourism, i.e. foreign exchange. Everybody, even the inhabitants, believed this. So they were pleasantly surprised when the Federation of Greece's tourist organisations wrote to the press: "Today most tourists are appalled by the noise of the loudspeakers and the general atmosphere of depravity. It is essential the authorities take drastic measures in 1978". Then came a further letter signed by 20 major tourist organisations in the world, among them Thompsons, American Express, TUI, Seatours and many more. It said: "We agree with Lord Duncan Sandys that the foreign visitor is shocked to discover the Acropolis surrounded by neon signs and buried under the noise of loudspeakers. Throughout Europe, our experience has been that tourism is best served by the preservation of traditional areas and by the imposition of restraints on indiscriminate noise and neon lights".

A lot of work has also been done in gaining the support of the political world. Questionnaires were circulated to candi-

Athens-Plaka: A private collector offered the State his very rich art treasures from all periods of Greek art if the State would provide a house in Plaka. So, a new function was found for this attractive neoclassical house which now houses the Kanellopoulos museum

Athens-Plaka:
View (about 1900) from the square of the Aerides (winds) towards the wall of the Acropolis

Athens-Plaka: 1970, same view as above. The cars have now taken over and are parked haphazardly. The first house on the left has given way to a cement structure which for years remained unfinished as the authorities rightly refused the required permission but did not demolish the ugly structure. Now it is being completed in accordance with new plans which harmonise with the environment

dates before the general elections in November 1977 and the replies made public. Parliament has been kept informed as questions on behalf of the residents have repeatedly been asked by friendly MPs. These were in turn fed to the media. A conscious effort was made all along to keep the issue on a non-party basis.

Gradually the inhabitants gained unanimous support in the media, in public opinion, in the political world, and amongst all pressure groups including those concerned with tourism. A proof of this interest is the restoration work which has been undertaken during the last year. Some people are now keen to come and live in Plaka, a few have already come. But this does not help them sleep any better! (So they welcomed an unexpected offer. One of Greece's most dynamic public relations men has offered free his and his firm's advice for a more professional campaign).

During the last few months the Coordinating Committee to save Plaka with its new emblem, a flower plant on a neoclassical balcony, and its new motto "NA ZISI I PLAKA" (Let Plaka Live) has intensified its campaign. As the summer season approached and disco-owners started testing their loudspeakers, the Coordinating Committee sent an open letter to the Ministers of Culture and Public Order, as the two ministers responsible for the area.

The letter, which was given great prominence in the Greek Press, included quotations from the speeches in Parliament of the two ministers themselves when, last December, in reply to a question, they had promised to ensure that the situation would not be repeated this year and more specifically to introduce a new law on Plaka. The letter continues . . . "We ask you therefore, Ministers, what is to happen? Will the State leave us unprotected for yet another summer, exposed to the unbearable cacophony of sounds which have caused some of us even heart trouble? Will you allow the loudspeakers to operate this year? This is a burning issue for us. It is not just a matter of environment aesthetics. It affects our health and that of our children. We ask you therefore to forbid the amplifiers immediately".

Telegrams were also sent to many ministers and members of parliament, to the Mayor of Athens, and other public figures, asking them for their support.

The Minister of Culture responded by asking for the inhabitants' 'lawyers' collaboration in drafting the new legal framework which is being worked out for Plaka. This law would prohibit loudspeakers and neon lights, would create pedestrian zones, would give incentives for conservation. It would also increase the penalties for transgressors and would secure local people a voice in the administration of the area. At the beginning of May he told journalists that he would soon be submitting the new law for Plaka to Parliament. As time passes the Plakiotes keep their fingers crossed.

Finally the Coordinating Committee has for the first time started operating a legal service free of charge for the inhabitants and a newsletter as well.

4. Conclusion

Plaka, which for many years had been condemned to perish, has at last been recognised by Greek and international public opinion as an inseparable part of the Acropolis, enhancing rather than detracting from the beauty and the dignity of the Parthenon. It is the essential stepping stone to the Acropolis.

But the spectre of demolition of a part of Plaka at least still looms on the Athenian horizon and can only be removed by a firm commitment of the State to its existence and preservation. This commitment must primarily encourage resettlement of those of its inhabitants who wish to come back, by offering incentives for residence until a proper balance is reached between the various functions each of which is trying to monopolise it. Ultimately only people who love and care for their houses will be worthy trustees of the cultural inheritance which Plaka embodies.

The new legal framework which has been prepared must leave no loopholes for transgressors and must give every encouragement to residents to restore their houses, by securing procedures that are firm, fair and fast. It sometimes takes years to obtain even permission to restore one's house with one's own money, as a number of conflicting government departments are involved.

Will the summer of 1979 again be long, hot, sleepless, and nerve-wracking for the residents of Plaka? It is probable. What is sure however is that even so they have come a long way since they first coordinated their efforts. As a first step, they have asked the government to forbid the amplifiers which constitute the single most immediate threat to the life of Plaka; the level of noise they propagate makes life in Plaka unlivable.

International support has been not just a moral support but also a leverage for governmental action. The result of the campaign is still uncertain, but the people of Plaka are determined to win.

This simple fact may in the end make all the difference.

Since this article was written there has been some good news. The Under Secretary for housing assisted by a dedicated team of experts is going ahead with the plan to turn most of Plaka into a pedestrian zone. Delivery shops by car will be allowed four hours daily and residents cards (a specific request of inhabitants) will be used for the first time in Greece.

Although pedestrian zones are for Plaka a less urgent need than the abolition of noise pollution by amplifiers, public opinion and the media have greeted the proposal as a courageous step in the right direction.

Bibliography

K. M. Setton: "Athens in the Middle Ages"

Dimitri Gerondas: "History of the Athenians"

D. Kambouroglou: "Rizokastro: Historical Guide of Old Athens"

Professor D. Zivas: "Study of the Old Town of Athens"

Collaborators to Prof. Zivas' "Study of Old Town of Athens"
History: Elizabeth Spathari
Archaeology: J. Travlos, A. Kokkos
Sociology: I. Lambiri-Dimaki
Economics: K. Mandikas

"Plaka Newsletters": issued by the Coordinating Committee for the Preservation of Plaka

HUNGARY

Hungary
LEGISLATION, ORGANISATION, FINANCE AND INVOLVEMENT OF THE PUBLIC

1. Legal Provisions

1.1 Decrees

In Hungary, the protection of historic monuments dates back for more than 100 years during which time several relevant decrees have been enacted. In the present age (i. e. since 1964), the pertinent provisions on safeguarding such monuments have been governed by the Law on Buildings. The problems in this field fall within the purview of the Ministry of Housing and Town Planning, whereas matters of cultural policy come under the Ministry of National Education.

As a result, appropriate agreements exist for statutory direction and practical guidelines for the protection of historic monuments on the one hand as well as the technical and economic functions of related fields (project studies, implementation, urban development, property management, renewal schemes, etc.) on the other.

The set of decrees on the protection of historic monuments together with a relevant commentary and notes were issued in book form in 1973.

1.2 Categories of protection

A Historic Monument (M) is a characteristic and irreplaceable testimony to the past history of our country (such as a building or other structure together with all its appurtenances as well as connected works of fine art or applied art) which serves to illustrate in substantive form the socio-economic and cultural development of the nation and which, moreover, possesses paramount importance from the standpoint of architecture, history, archaeology, art, applied art or ethnography.

A historic monument must always be marked by a plaque bearing the inscription "historic monument" and setting out its main features.

A building or work of art with the character of a historic monument (Mj) is an edifice or other creation which, taken as a whole together with its appurtenances and connected works of fine or applied art, possesses importance from the standpoint of architecture, history, archaeology, fine art, applied art or ethnography.

In both towns and villages alike, any building together with its external appurtenances is deemed to possess importance from the standpoint of urban physiognomy (VK) if it cannot be classified among the historic monuments by virtue of its historic and artistic value but nevertheless plays a significant role in the development of the appearance of a town because of its exterior (site, architecture, facade).

A place possessing the importance of a historic monument (Mjt) is a continuous part of a streetscape which illustrates the formation and historic development of the characteristic structure of the latter (for example the design of buildings making up a square or street) or else a square, street or part of a street where numerous historic buildings possessing the character of historic monuments or edifices of importance from the standpoint of urban physiognomy form a harmonious whole or a typical urban setting.

The setting of a historic monument (Mk) is an architectural and scenic ambience which assures a good presentation and accentuation of a historic monument.

1.3 Procedure

At national level it is the National Inspectorate of Historic Monuments which suggests classifying a structure as a historic monument (M) or as the setting of a historic monument (Mk) or which suggests terminating such classification.

Designation as a historic monument or as the setting of a historic monument or the ending of such classification depends upon a joint decision taken by the Ministry of Building and Town Planning and the Ministry of National Education.

On the basis of an authorization issued by the Minister of Building and Town Planning, the National Inspectorate of Historic Monuments decides upon the designation of an edifice as having the character of a historic monument (Mj) or possessing importance from the standpoint of urban physiognomy (VK) or village physiognomy (Fk) or upon the extinguishing of such classification.

The ownership of the property in question (State-owned, cooperative, ecclesiastic or private) does not play any part in classification.

The right to apply for classification or termination of the latter is enjoyed by all national and social bodies as well as all private citizens. However, the principal role in this field devolves upon the councils, organizations and authorities for the protection of historic monuments.

The decisions about a classification or the ending of a classification are taken by the authority for the protection of historic monuments in the light of the building as well as the implementing committee of the competent council.

The interested parties can keep themselves informed of classified items by means of lists of historic monuments drawn up by the provinces or towns concerned. The verification and possible modification of these lists take place after a number of years have passed.

1.4 The competent organs

The supreme body for the protection of historic monuments is the National Inspectorate of Historic Monuments which, for administrative purposes, comes under the Ministry of Building and Town Planning as the latter's "division for historic monuments".

The activities of the National Inspectorate embrace administrative, scientific and executive functions.

To a large extent, the administrative side involves the procedure for obtaining building permits for construction work on historic monuments or their setting. Although such procedure is governed by a large number of decrees, the granting of support must depend on the merits of each individual case, which is then accepted or rejected in advance. From that point of time, an obligation exists to provide notification of regional and urban rehabilitation plans and investment schemes and to assess them from the standpoint of protecting historic monuments.

In the field of scientific research and technical development, the Inspectorate has the duty to work out the objectives, principles and national provisions for the protection of historic monuments. The inspectors not only engage in research activities but also translate them into reality. On the international scientific scene, the Inspectorate acts as the competent representative body for the protection of historic monuments in Hungary and also plays an active role in cooperation.

As regards its executive tasks, the Inspectorate must discharge all sorts of organizational functions peculiar to the safeguarding of historic monuments and oversee the work of project consultancies and building firms. Furthermore, the Inspectorate operates its own project consultancy, its own building section and a "conservation studio".

With the exception of the capital, the National Inspectorate is responsible for the protection of historic monuments throughout the regions via the services of its regional reporting agencies (departments). Within the framework of departmental guidance, there are also sub-committees for the protection of historic monuments organized at local level and providing a valuable social contribution.

The national project consultancies and council agencies play their role in the studies carried out on the reconstruction of historic monuments (in cases where the examination of a project is not carried out by the National Inspectorate's own consultancy). In the capital city and in those administrative districts with large numbers of "listed" monuments, the project consultancies also carry out special studies on the safeguarding of historic monuments. In many cases, the studies on the reconstruction of groups of historic monuments and historic town centres are carried out on the basis of public competitions.

1.5 Compensation

The fact that an edifice or structure has been placed under the protection of the scheme for historic monuments does not entail any financial loss for the owner.

A considerable proportion of the listed buildings are put to practical use with residential accommodation accounting for a high percentage of the group. The most important properties in this category are State-owned and some of the smaller ones privately run. In the case of such maintenance and renovation of state-owned houses as does not exceed the level of what is deemed normal, funds are available for use in accordance with established rules and regulations. In addition to this financial assistance, "listed" items qualify for a varying supplement depending on the degree of protection furnished to them (M, Mj, Vk) and paid out of central funds. The average sums which may be earmarked for activities connected with buildings listed as M, Mj or Vk or with non-listed buildings are fixed pursuant to norms permitting an estimation of the number of dwellings capable of restoration within a defined period of time at a given place.

The renovation of state-owned public edifices (schools, administrative buildings, libraries, museums, etc.) is carried out in similar manner.

As for privately owned accommodation, the expense of conservation proper for a historic property may be subsidized by the public authorities depending on the merits of the case whereas the cost of other work such as modernization, appointments or extra comfort must be borne by the proprietor.

Where the owner of a private listed property cannot be relied upon to carry out his commitments due to his financial position, the public authorities themselves carry out the renovation or perhaps acquire the house and pay the proprietor compensation.

Popular (rural) historic monuments are given special treatment. If privately owned, they may receive one of the two types of assistance guaranteed by appropriate decrees:

– payment of an "annual flat-rate sum of maintenance" for which such house-owners may apply as undertake to maintain and conserve in systematic fashion their rural buildings pursuant to the provisions laid down by the competent authority.

– payment of "ad hoc aid" if the house-owner could not comply with his obligation to conserve a rural building without financial aid.

A considerable number of the owners of listed buildings which are put to practical use in the tourist trade as hotels, commercial enterprises, etc. feel reluctant to put a listed house to commercial use: they would prefer it to remain simply as a dwelling. At the same time, they do not sufficiently appreciate the value of a building from the commercial standpoint.

Some of the listed buildings – though fortunately their number is dwindling – are put to use for activities which do not permit dignified visual presentation and a peaceful visit to the building (These activities include for example, warehousing, small-scale industry etc.). The curbing of these negative phenomena and the replacement of their current function by one which is more appropriate to the setting has been taking place gradually and step by step.

The cost of restoring non-utilizable historic monuments (ruins, remains of walls, dilapidated churches, etc.) is borne by the State.

The same holds true of items whose use would require prior restoration or even part renewal and which cannot command more than a minimum income from receipts. Castles also fall under this heading and, although they may be converted into tourist hotels, taverns or picture galleries, they cannot guarantee anything like the income needed to defray the expense and work involved. Historic monuments located in museums also fall within this category, as do all the functions maintained and exercised with the help of government subsidies.

Penalties and fines

Where the work to be carried out on a historic monument has not been completed by the person required to do so (or if the quality of the work does not prove to be adequate), the latter may be penalized by means of a fine. However, a more usual course of action is for the authority for the protection of historic monuments to carry out the work at the expense of the responsible person.

It should nevertheless be pointed out that the penalties are not sufficiently strict to guarantee results.

1.6 Relationship between the protection of historic monuments and development policy

In recent years, i. e. since about the beginning of the 1960s, there has appeared the concept of preserving historic monuments and our architectural heritage in the form of a coherent whole.

The first phase of this approach was marked by the establishment in 16 towns and villages of important sites possessing historic significance and of the conditions needed to ensure their protection.

The objective of this move was to guarantee the immediate and assured preservation of the sites so as to obviate the possibility of any irreparable changes.

In our view, it was precisely this "passive" protection which created the possibility of proceeding in our age to "active" measures and of turning our attention to the problems of restoring and revitalizing such places. We deem it to be very important that the old central areas of our historic towns should not be mere museums but living, colourful and animated places which satisfy the needs and functions of modern life. Wherever the historic centre in its ancient setting cannot cope with these requirements, we consider it more appropriate to establish a new centre so as to supplement the other one in an organic manner calculated to enable them to function together.

In conformity with our planning system, every town has its general development scheme setting out in outline its proposed line of progress. In the case of the centres of historic towns, detailed schemes are also worked out and great care is bestowed upon listed buildings and the treatment of their setting and surroundings. When justified by the number of architectural monuments, detailed reconstruction plans have been elaborated with all the instructions needed for the buildings in regard to restoration, modernization, a possible change of function together with consecutive conversion, as well as the solution of communication problems and the creation of green-belt areas.

Competitions are arranged for studies on certain historic centres or on parts of them.

Clearly, the plans in themselves cannot resolve the problems. But they do lay down the general line of development and in fact the outlines of an approved plan are obligatory both for the town (the municipal building department) as well as for the architects of such projects.

It must be admitted that the drafting of successful plans for the protection of historic monuments sometimes encounters difficulties or even substantial resistance. Broadly speaking, towns tend to favour grand schemes (sometimes with concentrated housing in the centre) and they advance economic arguments in support of their case. Another opposing factor is traffic. Those who draw up traffic regulation schemes regard ancient architectural complexes as natural obstacles to the advance of a modern network of streets and roads and they are seldom willing to enter into compromise. Such compromises as do emerge are often inimical to the protection of historic monuments.

Fortunately, there has been a growing number of specialists in recent years who appreciate the need to safeguard such

monuments and who spare neither hard work nor imaginative effort to produce sound solutions.

Another step forward was taken a few years ago when possibilities and means of protecting typical structures and streets (but not listed as historic monuments) were devised in order to safeguard certain settings in our spontaneously developed cities. In this way, we try to save the most important urban places from undue uniformity, maintain continuity in our towns and discover potential future historic monuments.

At the present time, studies have been put in hand to determine which architectural products from the end of the 19th or the beginning of the 20th century are of a quality which justifies future protection.

2. The competent bodies and their organisation

2.1 Terms of reference

The questions of structure and organization have already been discussed in full in chapter 1.

In regard to structural questions, the National Inspectorate of Historic Monuments discharges the functions and enjoys the rights of the Division of Historic Monuments at the Ministry of Building and Town Planning.

Although one cannot speak of private organizations, there do exist social groups with an interest in the protection of historic monuments. These groups possess no official competence nor do they have access to any financial resources, but they make a contribution to the safeguarding of historic monuments with their voluntary work. Among their ranks may be found students of architecture and other young persons still at school who help to register land, to make drawings or to collect facts on historic monuments located in their area.

The regional or local sub-committees for the protection of historic monuments furnish considerable assistance as they are composed of specialists. At present, there are 55 sub-committees or – to be more precise – social committees for the protection of historic monuments. Every year, they meet for an exchange of information and ideas: at the same time, they receive their guidelines from the National Inspectorate.

3. Finance

In accordance with our country's planned economy, the protection of historic monuments also falls under the general plan. As a result, fixed sums of money are earmarked for this field in accordance with an established scale of assistance. The order of priorities and the sequence of work are governed by an overall scheme as well as by the annual plan laid down by the National Inspectorate.

The sums of money provided in the National Inspectorate's budget are earmarked for the policy of protecting historic monuments, mobilizing public opinion and restoring church properties. This budget also includes the sums earmarked for the purchase of properties of special importance when the owner is deemed unlikely to carry out restoration work in conformity with professional requirements.

If the National Inspectorate can find a partner for the restoration or for the utilization of an architectural monument, the accruing costs are then shared.

4. The Importance of Publicity in Protecting Historic Monuments

4.1 National education

The daily newspapers and journals report regularly on the protection of historic monuments on a scale corresponding to their particular field of interest. The national press furnish systematic information on recent finds and the results of excavations as well as publishing photographs of the most significant reconstruction work. Local newspapers provide detailed coverage of the protection of historic monuments carried out in their area and of conferences and similar events (such as the festivals to celebrate the founding of a town and the reconstruction carried out in time for such festivals, the striking of commemorative medals or the awarding of decorations, etc.).

There is also a special periodical dedicated entirely to the protection of historic monuments. It has appeared for the last 21 years. Architectural and town planning journals publish regular features on safeguarding historic monuments.

This theme appears regularly in cultural reviews, scientific periodicals for the layman and literary journals as a favourite item accompanied by rebus, puzzles and competitions. The magazine published for amateur pilots invites readers to take part in flights to view historic monuments and whets their appetite with professional descriptions and photographs.

Concerts and theatrical performances staged against the background of famous architecture enjoy huge popularity. Traditional spectacles are the Magic Flute played and sung in the Roman ruins of Iseum at Szombathely, the floral festival and other spectacles at Gorsium, the open-air plays performed on the main square at the historic centre of Szentendre, the organ concerts in a number of churches, the summer concerts in the courtyard of various castles and palaces, the spectacles in fortresses, the cavalry contests, etc.

The safeguarding of historic monuments and an appropriate presentation of our architectural heritage are regularly featured on radio and T.V. programmes. On television, this field forms the subject of direct transmissions accompanied by discussions and film shows.

Numerous books have appeared on the historic monuments of our country both as de luxe volumes as well as inexpensive popular editions.

The tourist organizations organize regular excursions to famous historic sites.

4.2 Schools and universities

Within the framework of a knowledge of their native country and study trips, school boys and girls go on regular visits to our historical monuments. Those pupils who take a greater interest in historic monuments may consider the subject in depth in a study group. (In such a case, the results obtained naturally depend to a large extent on the personal efforts of the teacher).

The history of architecture is taught as a subject at vocational and grammar schools and universities. At Budapest Technical University, architects and graduate art-historians may pursue postgraduate studies on the protection of historic monuments.

4.3 Social and private organizations

The social committees for the protection of historic monuments are attached to the provincial and urban authorities responsible for social welfare in general. They represent voluntary efforts by specialists who are interested in the protection of historic monuments throughout their region. However, the committees do not receive any official assistance.

The active participation of the general population is backed by the organization of the People's Patriotic Front, the Union of Communist Youth, the Union of Amateur Naturalists and the Movement of Socialist Brigades.

The Hungarian Society for Town Planning also helps to protect historic monuments as do the Associations for the Embellishment of Towns.

House-owners and tenants do not have their own organizations nor do they take part in the drafting of plans. There are no private foundations or similar bodies.

In recognition of their activities on behalf of historic monuments, the Director of the National Inspectorate may award a plaque and diploma "for the protection of historic Hungarian monuments" to persons active in this sphere whether their work be theoretic, scientific or administrative and whether it concern the study or the actual execution of projects.

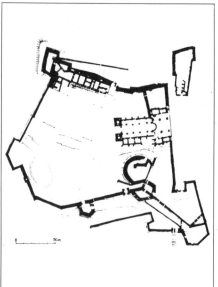

Eger: The town and fortress as shown in 17th century engravings

Hungary
Eger

1. Situation

1.1 General introduction

Eger is one of the oldest and most beautiful cities of Hungary. It has grown up in the picturesque valley of the Eger which flows from the North to the South. To the North stands the mountain of Bükk and to the West its foothills. South of the town stretches the Great Hungarian Plain. The average elevation of Eger is 180 metres above sea level, but the neighbouring hills do not in fact rise above 250 to 260 metres. Eger enjoys an equable climate.

Below the town are located layers of limestone with their famous thermal springs (25 to 30°C) and medicinal baths. The town has a population of 58,000 inhabitants.

1.2 History and traditions

Eger may, with justification, be called the town of the historic monuments. Over 150 of its buildings are listed as having the character of a historic monument. The old district in the centre of Eger also has the status of a place possessing the importance of a historic monument. The fortress of Eger, the relics of the Turkish Occupation, and in particular the Baroque edifices in the Zopf style[1] – veritable jewels of 18th century architecture – the contemporary Teachers' Training College, a masterpiece of neo-Classicism and the cathedral itself, promote the town to artistic distinction and harmonious unity.

The network of medieval roads was fundamentally based on two principal routes. One of them followed the course of the Kossuth Lajos road, starting at the ancient gateway of Hatvan and leading right up to the path which ascended to the fortress. The other one began at the Hatvan, followed the course of the Széchenyi road of Rác. This second route is assumed to have been much wider than the first one. The main square (now called Dobo Square) and Knézich Street have retained their medieval course.

By virtue of Eger's special geographical situation, all the cross-roads lead to the stream which traverses the town – thus demonstrating the likelihood that these streets have existed since the Middle Ages.

The houses constructed at the foot of the fortress (Dobo Street and the Street of 1st of May) are typical of the structures to be found around any fortress.

The city itself embraces three centres: the fortress, the administrative authorities located on Dobó Square and the ecclesiastic centre. These three points are closely linked since Szabadság Square in front of the cathedral is connected with the fortress via Kossuth Lajos Street whilst the civic and ecclesiastic centres are joined by Bajcsy –

Zsilinszky Street. Even though these three units are in fact self-contained, together they form the heart and hub of the town.

The old quarter is thus marked by genuine structured harmony and esteemed as a reliable testimony of old Hungarian town-planning. It is precisely this harmony which makes the medieval district worthy of conservation. the close-knit character of the area, the generous proportion of open space and the felicitous arrangement of the streets – furnishing as they do so many interesting views as the eye is directed towards the church spires soaring to the skies or to the old walls of the town – harbour so many treasures which, whilst the subject of prudent preservation, must also be detached and shown to their best advantage by eliminating all the detrimental elements.

The bulk of Eger's buildings date from the 18th century. No medieval buildings have been discovered in the old district and the Renaissance is not represented either. This is offset by the superabundance of Baroque and Zopf architecture illustrated here by numerous excellent examples. The town experienced its most brilliant period in the 18th century. It was the age which saw the building of the old grammar school (now the teachers' training college), whose architectural pre-eminence in the Zopf style makes it one of the most important monuments in Hungary, the Minorite Church – one of Hungary's finest Baroque churches – the splendid series of vicarages and finally the large number of smaller private houses. This urban configuration of the 18th century manifests itself not so much by Baroque as by Zopf buildings, which may almost be termed a local style since it is virtually a special product of Hungary.

Eger did not experience any urban reconstruction in consequence of the growth of capitalism in the 19th century and indeed none of Hungary's principal railway lines passes through the town. Thanks to the relative difficulty of access to Eger, it has retained most of its historic townscape.

2. Conditions

2.1 Problems

Despite the fact that the difficulty of reaching the town slowed down Eger's development in the immediate postwar years, it has nevertheless undergone an accelerating pace of development since the liberation of Hungary. Its old function as an ecclesiastic, educational and administrative centre has gradually evolved into that of an industrial centre with a virtual doubling of the prewar population.

But even Eger cannot avoid the traffic problems which beset urban areas everywhere today. Some parts of the old principal routes which traverse Eger suffer from congestion and there is a lack of car parks, etc. The long-term plans provide for a solution whereby transit traffic will be diverted along two different ways to avoid the centre and then link up again beyond the town. This scheme will involve the reshaping of large areas at great expense and its implementation will take several years to complete.

---

[1] The late-Baroque style of 18th century architecture in Germany, Austria and Hungary is known under this designation.

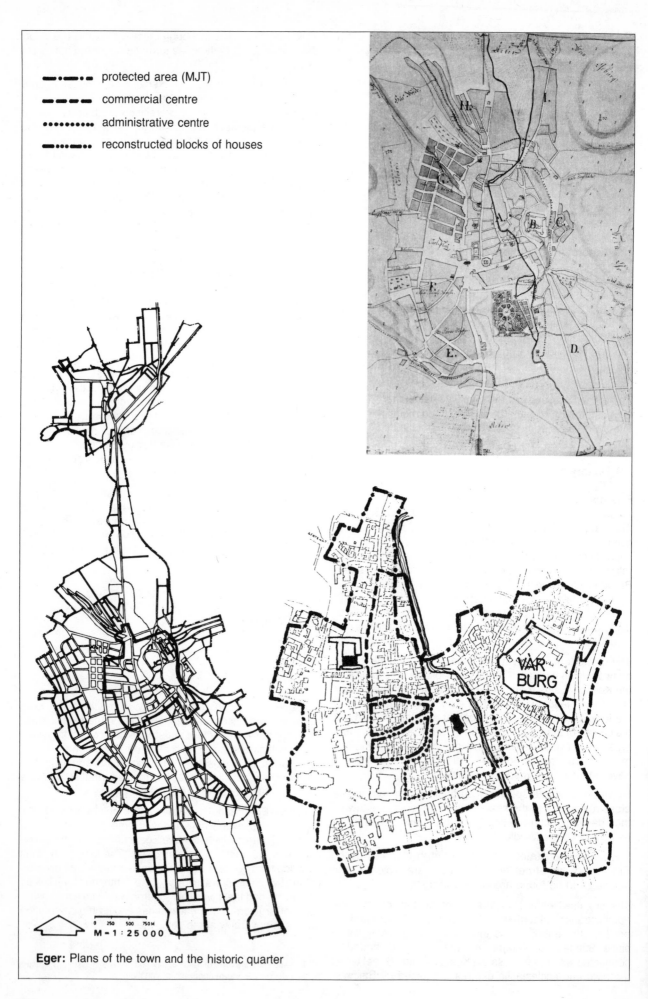

- ▬·▬·▬·▬ protected area (MJT)
- ▬▬ ▬▬ ▬▬ commercial centre
- ●●●●●●●●●● administrative centre
- ▬··▬··▬·· reconstructed blocks of houses

VAR BURG

0 250 500 750 M
M — 1 : 25 000

Eger: Plans of the town and the historic quarter

The long-term plan also envisages the pedestrianization of certain streets. The work of building the by-passes round the centre has already begun.

Another ubiquitous problem concerns the comparatively large number of old people in the historic town-centre. However, the percentage of old persons in Eger has not reached undue proportions because of the numerous public buildings there. (The districts of which a top-heavy age structure is characteristic are to be found to the North of Eger's protected central area).

As for unexpected difficulties, Eger has its fair share of them. Sometimes, for example, an earth tremor causes part of the fortress walls to collapse. The safety measures, the repair work and the rehabilitation have reduced the funds, the construction capacity and the time reserved for other tasks.

Grave concern resulted during reconstruction work from the discovery of cellars and vaults beneath a large segment of the town.

The provision of adequate props and supports has necessitated large-scale exploration and consolidation operations by civil engineers in the dangerous sections. Although the surface reconstruction work has obviously slowed down as a result, the thorough exploration of the underground rooms and passages promises to yield results of considerable scientific usefulness.

3. Aims of Official Support

3.1 Social goals

For a number of social reasons, there is a clear need for a sharper increase in the reliable provision of supplies and services for town populations. However, this is a complex subject embracing a series of facilities and amenities from sewerage to theatrical performances, from nurseries and commercial services to recreational zones. In the midst of this complex is the need to safeguard our architectural patrimony and to present it in a worthy setting.

3.2 Architectural goals

Our architectural approach to this subject consists in fidelity to the past and the reconstruction of properties pursuant to careful researches into the history of architecture and archaeology. Nevertheless, the restoration of a historic group of buildings and the construction of new buildings are conceived in the modern idiom though subject to the restriction that most of these projects must conform to their surroundings. The rules governing new buildings erected within a historic setting concern adherence to the alignment and height of buildings or, in certain specified cases, the character of the roofs (e.g. sloping or flat). In order to satisfy aesthetic considerations, efforts are undertaken to provide architecture of high quality. But it must be admitted in regard to Eger (and certain other towns) that the outcome of these endeavours has not always been felicitous. Among the good-quality reconstructions may be found less convincing examples.

Eger:
View of the old quarter taken in 1930 and 1975. The old part of the town has not altered in appearance. The character of the roofs has not changed

4. Strategy and Action

4.1 Legal provisions

The whole historic area of the town plus the fortress and its surroundings have been designated as a "place possessing the importance of a historic monument". The protection of this quarter is assured by a very strict system of statutory rules prohibiting any construction (or demolition) which would impair the harmonious appearance of the ensemble. Even today, the characteristic feature of Eger is its low-rise buildings – on an average, two storeys in height. Higher

225

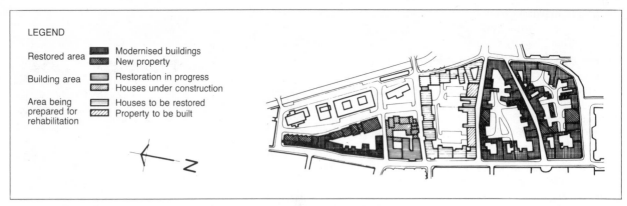

Eger: Centre of Eger. Restoration activities. Aerial photograph of the old district

residential accommodation may only be built outside of the town centre. Hence, no threat to the heritage of Eger's historic quarter emanates from this source.

Nevertheless, a great many economic problems have to be faced in that the rehabilitation of the town's extensive central area requires considerable disbursements.

Since Hungary is a country with a planned economy, the protection of historic monuments as a feature of urban development in general also forms part of the overall plan. As the principal city in the province of Heves, Eger may draw upon the funds provided for the former.

4.2 Investment

Pursuant to the official guidelines laid down by its local authorities, Eger has established the criteria to operate in urban development and to guarantee the availability of sufficient funds for a given period (such as a five-year plan). It has in particular raised the sums required for road construction, communications, public hygiene, teaching etc. as well as the sum available under "new housing" for rehabilitation and reconstruction. This also involves a study of the urban development projects.

4.3 Participation

In their deliberations upon the goals to be pursued in connection with different schemes, the local authorities take into account the views of the whole population. In practice, however, local residents do not voice their opinion on every occasion when they might do so. Despite the regular notification of projects and rehabilitation plans, this seems to evoke little response.

5. Implementation

5.1 Strategy

All towns in Hungary have a general rehabilitation scheme which sets out the general lines of development, the envisaged utilization of land, the density of housing, etc. As regards a protected zone in the town, such schemes also incorporate general rules of supervision to ensure respect for the local ambience of a historic monument.

A detailed rehabilitation scheme is drawn up for the central district of the town – especially if classified as a historic monument – together with a more elaborate reconstruction plan were necessary. This contains suggestions and specific instructions on the buildings to be pulled down, those to be restored or rebuilt, etc.

From the economic standpoint – since the available sums of money never correspond to the required amounts – it has proved essential to stipulate adherence to a sequence of operations in reconstruction work so as to ensure completion as quickly as possible of a certain stage considered as part of the whole. This system of reconstructing one block of houses at a time has been adopted in Eger with considerable success. The method used is described below.

Studies on architectural solutions to the problems of historic towncentres are often made the subject of open competition with the results synthetized in an final scheme. Sometimes, only part of the older quarter forms the subject of an open competition so that the solution of one topical problem only is desired. The competition may be organized as an invitation to participate (project consultancies or groups of project designers) or as a public notification to anyone interested in taking part without divulging his name (but using a pseudonym instead).

In the past, Eger had already competed for submissions to deal with various individual problems, but in 1975 the municipality and the Ministry of Housing and Town Planning invited entries for the reconstruction and architectural design of the historic quarter and administrative centre of the town.

The result of this competition has inter alia demonstrated that, even when preserving the historic fabric and dimension of the old quarter, a careful investigation can indicate how to bring about the necessary increase in capacity whilst simultaneously obviating any detrimental contraction and enhancing the aesthetic pleasure derived from harmonious presentation. Eger has undergone a type of rehabilitation hitherto unknown in Hungary, i. e. the reconstruction of its old-quarter buildings block by block.

The feasibility of applying this procedure rests upon three factors: the clear-cut network of streets; the concomitant large blocks of houses; and the absence of medieval houses so that their rear exteriors (of little value and not affecting the appearance of the street) may be demolished to provide more space. The employment of this architectural potential by the municipality depends upon a third factor, the social dimension: the real estate belongs to the State so that private interests cannot act contrary to the interests of society as a whole.

The method adopted consists in commencing work upon a block of houses circumscribed by few streets as more or less a single operation. The character of the block in question is defined and decided in advance as comprising

Eger: Restoration of the building at No. 1 Zalás Street Condition before and after restoration

commercial enterprises, hotels or even administrative authorities. The essential point is that the basic unit of reconstruction and modernization never consists of a single building but of a whole block. In the course of the work, the properties and dwellings in the block are modernized in concerted fashion, the superfluous and inconvenient backs of buildings removed and the demolished houses, old structures and properties without historic value replaced. The new elements appear in a historic setting; they are not numerous, and as long as they do not predominate such

227

Eger: Restoration of the building at No. 1 Zalás Street

replacements do not seem unattractive. On the contrary, they symbolize that historic evolution never comes to an end; it is still continuing in our own age.

5.2 Building measures

There is another characteristic feature of this kind of overall approach. The reconstruction of an old quarter block by block not only requires solutions to the problems peculiar to town planning and architectural design, but also – and this is often forgotten everywhere – to the problems of technical difficulties. The biggest problem in old edifices is humidity and the lack of insulation in walls. Here, again, Eger has furnished a good example by using modern chemical methods to insulate walls and thus render dwellings healthier and longer-lasting.

5.3 Results

Two blocks of buildings have so far been completed under this scheme of reconstruction. In our opinion, the work carried out has been effective but certainly not impeccable. Among the shortcomings, mention may be made of the lack of preparation and organization as well as certain "compromises" from the aesthetic standpoint with fire-proof walls without any facing, unsatisfactory details, etc.

6. Advertising Campaigns

Closely linked with the efforts to safeguard Eger's historic monuments are the university summer courses which have been held here every year since 1971 for Hungarian und foreign specialists, who welcome the opportunity to review and discuss their current problems.

Since 1971, there has also been a "month of visits to museums and historic monuments" – an event of nation-wide interest organized every year. Eger plays its full role in this scheme by holding exhibitions and other events.

Within the framework of concerts, performances and other cultural events connected with historic monuments, Eger also stages historic plays in the fortress; popular comedies and farces on the main square; organ concerts in the cathedral; and open-air concerts in the courtyard of certain large buildings.

7. Conclusion

By way of conclusion, it may be safely affirmed that the block-by-block reconstruction method practised at Eger has provided a great deal of useful and practical experience. This also includes the problems inherent in the preparing and organizing of the necessary work. Although there are some private interests hindering the implementation of the programmes, it has nevertheless not proved easy to balance and coordinate the participation and contributions by the different organizations concerned. It is difficult to gain the support of tourist enterprises and hotels even though their participation is more justifiable than that of anyone else. They prefer new buildings, show less appreciation of a historic ambience, emphasize both real and imaginary difficulties (such as access for delivery vans, upkeep, compromises in the management of the properties, etc.).

The experience gained in the reconstruction of Eger block by block can certainly be put to use in other towns where similar conditions obtain.

By the same token, it is already possible to make a number of useful generalizations on technical points such as subsequent insulation and wall-drying procedures or on the results of numerous project studies such as decorative facing, the mounting of lanterns and the embellishment of public squares and streets in harmony with their setting, i. e. a successful adaptation to the existing atmosphere of history and tradition.

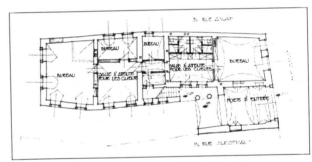

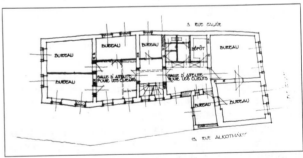

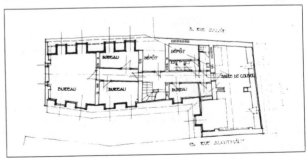

Eger: Restoration of the building at No. 1 Zalás Street
Drawing of the ground floor
1st storey
2nd storey

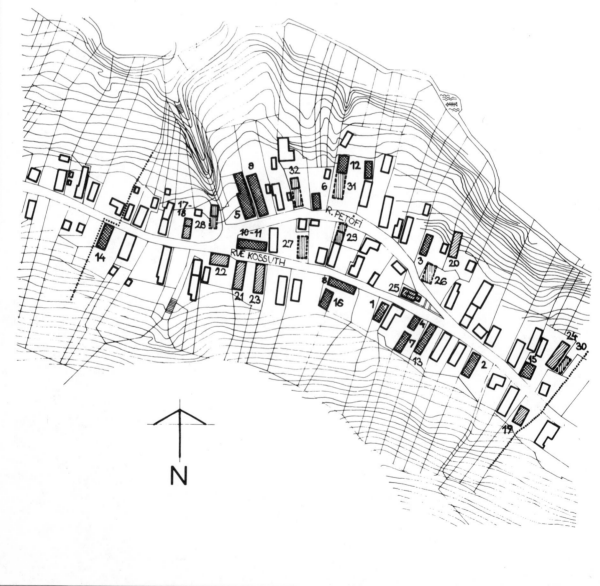

Buildings restored

1 Local museum
2 Hotel
3 Hotel
4 Post Office
5 Ambulance dept.
6 Hotels
7 Works accommodation
8 Services
9 Hotel
10–11 Restaurant
12 Hotel
13 Town-Hall
14 Nursery school
15 Pensioners'club
16 Public services
17–18 Accommodation

Buildings being restored

19 Tourist Office
20 Hotel
21 Craft workshop
22 Library, club
23 Craft workshop
24 Education centre
25 Catholic church

Planned buildings

26 Food shop
27 Local history museum
28 House
29 Souvenir shop
30 Education centre
31 Hotel
32 Hotel

·········· Conservation area

N

Holloko: Plan of the village and situation of the restored buildings

Hungary
HOLLOKO

1. Situation

1.1 General introduction

Holloko presents a fine example of a homogeneous conservation of Palot villages. The ethnic group of the Palots, a branch of the Hungarian people in the North Eastern part of the country, has preserved through the ages its special forms of linguistic expression and popular art which betray a Slovakian influence.

The fortress of Holloko and the village nestling beneath it are located in the mountainous region of Cserhat where the hills vary in elevation from between 500 and 600 metres. This tiny community has a population of only 800 inhabitants.

Palot villages possess a characteristic feature which may also be seen in Holloko, i.e. a hillside settlement built along a country road. This ribbon-building has the appearance of a comb in that rows of houses are built perpendicularly to the road. The distribution of the plots of land is also characteristic of these villages. Following the first settlement in the centre of the village, the houses of large families were constructed on a single plot of jointly owned land covering a large superficial area. The growth of the families brought about a need to subdivide these properties, which had originally been very extensive. The houses built by the head of the first family of settlers overlooked the road, whereas the later dwellings were erected behind them in a row at right angles to the road.

1.2 History

The origin of Holloko dates back to the second half of the 12th century. The relics of that period are now exhibited at the Palot Museum in Balassagyarmat. The oldest documentary evidence of the fortress dates from 1310. The village church (14th century), altered several times in the course of history, constitutes the sole and continuous testimony to the medieval beginnings of the settlement.

As the records show, the Catholic parish was founded in 1342.

After its occupation by the Turks in 1526, the fortress changed hands several times during the next 150 years until the final delivery from the Ottoman yoke in 1683.

Since conditions were unfavourable for the development of agriculture, the village hardly grew at all and the level of population remained stagnant. Moreover, expansion was slowed down by frequent fires.

Only at the end of the last century and at the beginning of the 20th century did the village experience true advancement and economic prosperity. All the old houses were rebuilt following the fire of 1909.

1.3 Historic importance

The 1954 inventory of the historic monuments to be found in the region of Nograd drew the attention of the experts to the significance of the domestic architecture of Holloko. (Because of the natural conditions which rendered the cultivation of land difficult, the village was slow to grow even after Hungary had been liberated. This explains the uniform character of the old village). As a result of the inventory, the first row of houses was placed under the protection of the Department for Historic Monuments. In 1960, there came a simplified planning and rehabilitation scheme and in 1961 a first study by the National Department for Historic Monuments on systematic steps for preserving the village.

2. Conditions

2.1 Problems

There is no threat to the protected part of the village. The new recent additions to Holloko fit in well with the old

Holloko: Typical house and view of a restored house in which a hostel for tourists was established

231

Holloko: Situation of the village and the castle in the landscape

structures. The only regrettable feature of the new buildings is their failure to incorporate any of the Palot traditions, including even their good taste: they represent the new type of 'modern rural home'.

Those of the remaining houses in private ownership which have fallen into a state of disrepair pose a major problem. For a village to remain alive it is necessary to have a sufficient number of inhabitable homes in order to preserve their original function. Generally speaking, the owners are elderly people without sufficient resources to rebuild their home in an appropriate manner. As a subsidy can only be granted on one occasion only (we spoke of this in the introduction) and it does not suffice to cover the cost of reconstruction and modernization, it has become essential to find a suitable way of financing this scheme.

4. Strategy and Measures

In the case of Holloko, the village owes its 'discovery' to the initiative of the National Department for Historic Monuments. It was a felicitous move on the part of the regional authorities of Nograd that they almost immediately followed up this initiative. Better still, they adapted their plans to local conditions in Holloko by declaring part of the surroundings of the fortress and the village to be a protected zone, by setting up a camp and a swimming-pool and by organizing workshops for local industry with a view to protecting rural crafts.

These protective measures really began in 1963 when

steps were announced to nationalize between 17 and 20 houses and to use them for public functions.

In order to ensure a methodical and competent handling of the reconstruction work, the National Department of Historic Monuments prepared a detailed study of the classified monuments of Holloko in 1968 and in particular of the village centre where 58 buildings and a church have been listed as historic monuments. Hand in hand with this has gone the reconstruction of 15 houses and the study of a contemporary plan for the rebuilding or modification of some six or seven houses.

It would seem quite legitimate to modify the function of certain houses with a view to ensuring the provision of the requisite facilities and amenities for tourism and for the development of the village. The principal items hitherto set up or envisaged are: tourist chalets, a post office, a civic centre, shops, a medical consultation centre, municipal baths, a library, a creative workshop of popular crafts, a village museum, a tourist office, a restaurant, a Kindergarten, a citizens' advice bureau, etc.

Holloko:

above: new construction resulting from the Holloko competition
below: a road in the village

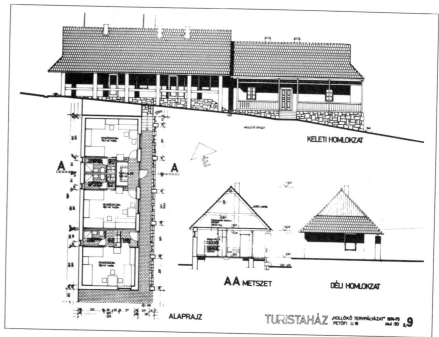

4.1 Institution

The special activities for protecting ancient structures are directed and executed by the National Department for Historic Monuments, whereas the development of the village has been entrusted to the regional authorities.

4.2 Finance

The funding of these operations is carried out as follows. The regional authorities purchase the selected properties and their reconstruction (i.e. the study and the execution of the project) is then realized and financed by the National Department. The furnishing of the houses and the installation of plumbing facilities, electricity, etc. are the responsibility of the regional authorities.

5. Implementation

5.1 Strategy for the implementing of schemes

The regional authorities in Nograd and the National Department of Historic Monuments combined their efforts with the National Office for the Protection of Sites in connection with the 'The Year of Architectural Heritage (1975)' in organizing a competition for the rebuilding of seven dilapidated houses. The problem was to revitalize the village properties which had remained vacant following their dilapidation. The construction projects must be inspired by the principle that buildings constructed as modern architecture will conform in style and character with the classified village zone and with the individual site. The important consideration is to avoid both the archaic and the tawdry in architectural style. The response to the competition has been fruitful, even though it has not resolved all the specific problems inherent in the erection of modern buildings within the framework of a village classified as a historic monument.

5.2 Construction measures

As far as reconstruction work is concerned, we have scrupulously observed the need to preserve the historic authenticity of the materials used and of their processing and shaping. The only exceptions are buildings in which the change in function (post office, tourist chalet, medical consultation centre) or the improvement in the physical fabric (stability, insulation against humidity) call for modern technical installations such as W.C.s, wash-basins and showers. In these cases, we have endeavoured to incorporate within an overall plan a minimum number of changes, a strengthening of the foundations, the provision of an insulation layer, the treatment of wooden structures to render them inflammable or protect them against dry-rot. In all the houses which formerly had clay-brick floors, it is customary today to replace these with plastic floors in a similar colour.

We have also availed ourselves of novel solutions such as the use of artificial roof-trusses in the tourist chalets, for example, whilst making sure that the modern formula is well adapted to the local idiom.

5.3 Results

As for those houses which have remained in good condition and merely require certain repairs, scrupulous attention has been paid to historic authenticity. Most of the domestic architecture in Holloko dates from the 19th century. The houses in question were reconstructed, repaired and – where necessary – slightly modified after the fire of 1909. An examination of the walls provided the basis for these modifications.

It is interesting to note that the Palot architectural tradition persisted until the 50s, particularly in respect of the wooden porches.

6. Publicity

Holloko lies amidst a picturesque site often visited by tourists. The old part of the village classified as a historic monument is tending more and more to become a tourist centre. The 'Palot days' organized every summer provide a programme of interesting events and functions.

7. Conclusions

In Hungary, the only relevant experience which we possess is that acquired in the two villages listed as historic monuments. The other village is situated near Lake Balaton at Tihany, although it differs considerably from Holloko in character and the problems involved. Hence, there is no connecting link between these two sets of experience. Be that as it may, the reconstruction of Holloko has yielded useful results. Despite this fact, we realize that these activities have only been in progress for a few years and that they are far from complete. However, it has already been shown that a place classified as a historic monument is capable of discharging modern functions.

Apart from reconstruction activities proper, it has proved advisable – even in a village setting – to undertake the development of the central area first, to furnish it with the amenities of modern life and to arrange for a harmonious collocation of the old and the new. This poses an interesting problem. In the feverish atmosphere of grand development schemes, the authors of these schemes have got into the habit of turning their minds to large-scale projects whilst failing to clarify the conception and presentation of modest constructions or to evolve an appropriate 'style'.

ITALY

Italy

LEGISLATION, ORGANISATION, FINANCE AND PARTICIPATION

1. Legal Provisions

1.1 Decrees

1.1.1 Legislation on the protection of cultural assets

This consists of two laws, No. 1089 of 1. June 1939 and No. 1497 of 29. June 1939.

Law No. 1089 extends its protection to movables and immovables registered in a list which is recognized in law.

Landed property which has been registered cannot be altered in any way without the authorization of the Ministry of Cultural Assets (the Superintendent). If the ownership of such real estate changes hands, it remains subject to State authorization.

Law No. 1497 deals with the protection of the countryside. It is the instrument with which the Ministry of Cultural Assets may, by virtue of sophisticated procedures, extend its protection to zones of outstanding natural beauty. In these protected zones, every new structure and extension or modification of an existing structure is subject to ministerial authorization.

This provision may apply – though with some complications – to urban areas. As past experience has demonstrated, it may operate for both small or very large superficial areas: from parkland along the slopes of a hill with a famous historic site to coastland covering hundreds of hectares.

We have no information on the overall superficial area of land covered by these safeguarding provisions.

The land in question may form the object of "landscape planning" under which all building activities are totally banned in certain zones. Such plans call for complicated implementation procedure and in fact few of them are in force. The task of drafting such schemes has recently been entrusted to regional governments, who also discharge the functions inherent in town planning.

1.1.2 Legislation on town planning

In reality, most historic town centres can be protected by means of the national law on town-planning (1942), which entered into effect in 1967 and which stipulates certain provisions for historic town centres.

This law prescribes strong limitations "ope legis" on major changes in historic centres not subject to urban development planning. Local authorities have the right and duty to draft and operate their own town-planning schemes. The supervision of the application of this general law is left to regional governments, who have the power to enact laws provided that the latter do not contradict national legislation.

A new law on real estate was recently approved (law No. 10, 1977) with the aim of providing better protection for historic town centres. In effect, it will permit the municipality to establish special funds earmarked for promoting measures in historic town centres, with the sums of money in question being provided under building permits and payable in proportion to the cost of urban development and construction.

The implementation of this law has only been taking effect in recent months and it is still too early to form any judgement on its impact.

This law also lays down that regional governments must amplify and specify its provisions.

1.1.3 Special laws

As regards national legislation, there exist several special laws referring to individual towns of historic interest such as Venice, Urbino, Assisi, Matera and Siena.

Some of these laws were enacted following grave damage caused by earthquakes: they relate to Ancona, Ascoli, Piceno and Tuscania. Others have been redrafted several times: Matera, Venice and Siena.

Originally, these laws envisaged grants-in-aid towards public works and private properties. They then acquired greater sophistication: planning schemes for urban development, administration and implementation were introduced as well as legal instruments for promoting an understanding between public authorities and private properties pursuant to contractual agreements.

Today, these laws can be seen as having introduced useful innovatory instruments.

1.1.4 Regional laws

Regional government have enacted a number of laws to protect historic town centres with the aim of giving practical effect to the object of national laws in regard to the implementation of planning schemes, the definition of criteria governing active support, the financing of surveys (for the catalogue) and the formulation of detailed plans.

1.1.5 Legislation on buildings

In Italy, building legislation is closely linked with appropriate instruments of town planning. The two fundamental texts are Law 167/1962 governing the purchase of sites for inexpensive housing and Law 865/1971 which amplified and modified the above by establishing new criteria for the acquisition and financing both of land as well as the house-building.

To a certain extent, this law permits authorities to intervene on existing sites. The funds earmarked under the law are apportioned among the various regions. These in turn decide which areas qualify for support. In particular, the regions apportion their funds among the financing of new buildings and the conservation of existing ones.

Yet few regions have in fact earmarked funds for conservation purposes and those which have done so only envisage 1 % – a very small amount indeed.

Nevertheless, the application of the provisions of this law to the historic centres is surrounded by controversy. The case of Bologna remains a matter of dispute in this respect as do Tuscania and Apulia.

The experience gained in connection with the law carries a great deal of weight in the current debate on the financing of the house-building law in Parliament and within the Government.

1.1.6 Legislation on rented property

A new law, No. 392 of 1978, was finally promulgated in defence of "fair rents" (equo canone).

The need to reconcile the financial interests of the owner of rented property with the social problems involved in the cost of housing is complex and difficult. The purpose of this law is to protect the less favoured members of the community from indirect exclusion from historic town centres.

2. Organisation

2.1 Legislative responsibilities

The Italian Constitution entrusts the Republic with the task of safeguarding our architectural and cultural heritage.

Legislative competence rests with the National Parliament and the regional assemblies. At the present political juncture, a lot of disagreement prevails on the delimitation of national and regional jurisdiction.

In effect, there exist two laws today dating back to 1939. Some regional administrations have also thought fit to enact their own legislation, which must not, however, clash with national laws.

A discussion has been under way for a number of years on the necessity of revising national legislation. This debate arose after a survey carried out by a parliamentary commission.

So far, however, no new statute has been proposed. Quite recently the Department of Cultural Affairs was separated from the Ministry of Public Education, to which it formerly belonged, following the creation in 1975 of the Ministry for Cultural and Natural Assets.

The protection of our architectural heritage is also effected in Italy by means of legislation on town planning. In this field, there is also complementary national and regional legislation. All these statutes provide important instruments for protecting historic centres.

Another sector which is above all governed by national laws is that of construction where funds have been earmarked for the restoration and rehabilitation of existing buildings. The regional governments are usually asked to apportion their funds both on a geographical basis as well as pursuant to the criteria of use.

2.2 Administrative duties

The responsibility for safeguarding our historic and artistic legacy currently rests with the Ministry for Cultural and Natural Assets. In structure, it consists of five main divisions as well as superintendencies who generally oversee a certain section of regional activities and specialize in: antiquities, architectural treasures and areas of natural beauty, picture galleries and archives.

There are national museums and central institutes (for restoration, cataloguing, etc.) which depend directly on the ministry.

As a matter of principle, no other organization possesses administrative competence in regard to the protection of architectural monuments. In effect, the local authorities have to discharge certain duties – linked to those of the Ministry for Cultural Assets – which devolve upon them by virtue of the valid legislation on town-planning. At all events, the task falls to them of granting the permits for converting buildings in general and thus also historic edifices. When the latter have been "listed" by the Ministry for Cultural Assets, it is also necessary to obtain the latter's authorization.

3. Financial and Fiscal Provisions

As the "listed" buildings possess outstanding public interest, they bestow upon the owner the right to deduct the cost of their upkeep from his tax declaration.

In addition, Law No. 1552 of 1962 provides for the financing of restoration activities (apart from technical installations) up to a maximum amount of 70 % of the overall total. Nevertheless, the funds earmarked each year under the national budget are simply inadequate.

The whole complex of the tax provisions on old buildings is in fact marked by unequal treatment. One new feature is however the privilege of enjoying 25 years of tax exemption, a development which has rendered the restoration of a historic edifice a more attractive proposition. On the other hand, the highly restrictive legislation enacted to protect historic centres has virtually excluded any possibility of rehabilitation in the sense of complete replacement. That has encouraged the continuing decay of old urban districts as well as the concomitant exodus of local residents. That in turn has triggered a greater demand for public services and for new housing.

The years since 1970 have seen the promulgation of a number of legislative measures, which have exercised a considerable impact upon the economics of urban development. The principal factors behind this trend are as follows:

a. The rise in the cost of house-building; and

b. the high cost involved in the urban development of new zones and in the provision of the requisite public services (pursuant to Law No. 10/1977 – see 1.1.2).

This has promoted the idea of providing support for historic town centres. Permission to carry out work in the historic centres may be granted freely to house-owners if this merely implies restoration and maintenance not affecting the original function of the property and if the applicants undertake to charge moderate rents.

Numerous instances of official support for the rehabilitation of historic quarters are at present being implemented or studied in various Italian cities. They involve the establishment of planning zones or development plans for low-cost housing (piani edilizia economia e popolare – PEEP – centro storico) in accordance with the above-mentioned Law No. 167. Under these schemes, the purchasers of property receive grants for the rehabilitation of buildings pursuant to Law No. 865 and the follow-up legislation in Law No. 166 and Law No. 513.

A ten-year urban development plan was recently put into operation under the terms of Law No. 457 of 1978. It contains one section (No. 4) devoted specifically to public support for existing buildings and in particular to historic town centres. Many municipalities are already preparing advance plans or "reimbursement schemes" whereby those house-owners who enter into a contractual agreement with the town council in respect of a certain type of support and the amount of rent to be charged, etc. may obtain interest-free loans for a sum up to 15 million lire repayable in 20 to 25 years.

Finally, mention may be made of certain new factors and fresh financial incentives for individual citizens and public bodies alike to take a greater interest in the rehabilitation of historic centres.

4. The Role of the General Public in Protecting Historic Monuments

4.1 Cultural associations

The attitude adopted by the general public towards conservation problems has been marked by a growing degree of interest and enthusiasm in recent years and great importance is, of course, attached to this in regard to the decision-making processes leading to the provision or withholding of support for our national cultural heritage.

The awakening of the public conscience stems from the great cultural debates which small groups of intellectuals initiated immediately after World War II.

They drew the attention of the Italian people to the negative experience gained from intervention in old towns in the improvement of roads, the demolition of districts or the exodus of people to the suburbs and convinced them of the need to contrast the action now being taken with the realization of similar projects in pre-war years.

These groups of intellectuals, archaeologists, town planners and writers, who began by relying on private initiative, then received the assistance of organized bodies and this influx of supporters gradually expanded their sphere of action until there emerged fully fledged associations capable of making their influence felt throughout the nation.

The following organizations are the few principal private bodies active in this field. They are listed in their order of age since foundation.

Instituto Nazionale di Urbanistica, a pre-war body which was reconstituted with new articles of association after World War II. It has traditionally enjoyed the backing of town-planning, urban development and house-building specialists and experts in administrative law. It played a significant role in promoting the idea of planning controls in the administration of real estate and urban areas. It began to evolve its function following the introduction of town-planning legislation during the war (1942) and later when it set about effecting a firm contribution to the formulation of new legislation for the "code of town-planning" issued in 1960.

Associazione "Italia Nostra", founded in 1956, is a movement expressing the dissatisfaction and opposition of private citizens witnessing the damage caused by the negligence and weakness of the public authorities in protecting our physical and cultural heritage and also the rapid and uncontrolled conversion of property brought about by the profound social and economic transformation of the country. The most significant action taken by this organization consists in the staging of the photographic exhibition "Italia da salvare" (On saving Italy). This exhibition familiarized the general public with a large number of Italian cities by means of documentation showing the state of decay and the destruction of large segments of Italy's cultural legacy, thus evoking a vast protest and keen awareness of the problems among public opinion in Italy. The Association has over 16,000 members.

Associazione Nazionale dei Centri Storico-Artistici (ANCSA), founded in 1960 by town planners and intellectuals, undertook the task of gaining the interest of local authorities for a policy of preserving historic town centres. Its principal programme is set out in the final document codifying the cultural and political principles needed to ensure the revitalization of Italy's historic cities.

Instituto Nazionale di Architettura (INARCH), set up in 1967, has promoted meetings and debates designed to create a climate of opinion among architects and the members of similar professions which favours the conservation of our historic and artistic treasures.

4.2 The role of the press

The enthusiastic efforts and active campaigns of these organizations and their adherents would not, however, have made any significant headway in influencing public opinion in general without the determined support of the responsible press.

The major daily newspapers have never failed to propagate these ideas and the initiatives taken by such bodies and in some cases to back them, thus helping to bring pressure to bear upon the public authorities to take better decisions and to furnish more effective support for preserving our national inheritance. These papers have often printed articles by specialists, art historians, archaeologists and town planners and influenced public opinion throughout the nation by furthering a cultural debate on the criteria to be adopted in conservation policy. As a result, they have played their role in creating a sound knowledge and keen sensitivity about this subject among the general population.

The attention accorded to these activities in the dailies gradually spread to other mass media: first to the weeklies, then to broadcasting and finally to television (which has, however, remained the least enthusiastic about this problem).

4.3 Schools

As an institution, schools are definitely remiss in their duty to teach pupils to protect the beauties of nature and the cultural treasures of the nation. School curricula contain no reference to this problem, even though a vast spontaneous movement is now emerging within schools themselves.

Despite the restrictive character of the laws, decrees and ministerial directives, both the pupils themselves – reflecting the general trend in public opinion – as well as the bulk of the teaching staff endeavour to encourage initiative in this sphere. One powerful impetus towards introducing a study of these problems in schools comes from the creation under a recent law of "institute councils" on which the representatives of the teachers, the pupils and also the parents sit.

At the beginning in particular, the operation of this law produced a striking effect: it helped to curb parochial attitudes and encouraged the establishment of good links with schools' external activities. This has resulted in a growing demand for information and for participation in the management of environmental matters. It has increased the initiatives taken at schools and influenced school timetables and research. Moreover, there is now a greater demand for documentation, facilities and information thanks to the interest shown by pupils, who have today assumed a firm role in fostering a better knowledge of our cultural heritage.

4.4 District committees: decentralization

Parallel to the development of these cultural trends, Italy has also witnessed the growth of a grass-roots movement emanating from urban initiatives.

This movement has proved to be most durable in those areas where it has concerned itself with specific issues, all of them attendant upon the question of our natural environment, either physical or social, i.e. public health, housing, education, municipal parks, transport and other social services.

In places of historic interest, the movement has often sprung from the need to give positive expression to the protests against the neglect and often the expulsion of tenants fostered by the decay, the lack of upkeep of inherited property, and the change of function for the latter as it is gradually taken over by more affluent families or used for "tertiary" or tourist purposes. The demand for services, which has been much keener in recent times, is thus a factor which guarantees the residential role and with it the vitality of historic centres.

Broadly speaking, this grass-roots movement towards active participation has assumed a political dimension and swiftly spread to all quarters in all the large and medium-sized towns to the point of suggesting that administrative and political control in this field should be passed to the regions and local areas themselves. Some of the large municipalities such as Bologna (from 1963) and then Venice, Rome and Naples have encouraged the creation of district committees as consultative bodies and liaison offices.

These first steps have been informal in character and beyond the scope of valid legislation, which did not envisage this type of institutional decentralization.

The movement has been gradually coordinated and clarified by institutions of an essentially local character. The latter provide for advisory organs with membership corresponding to the results of municipal elections in numerous large and small towns (Rome, Milan, Genoa, Bologna, Modena, etc.).

The novel features which have sprung from this movement contributed to the enactment of a national law on decentralization (Law No. 278 of 8. 4. 1976) which envisages the setting up of "area committees" headed by a president in pursuance of special elections held in all municipalities with over 40,000 inhabitants.

At the present time, the town councils have embarked upon the electoral consultations needed before holding elections for these new councils.

So far, little concrete experience has been gained for evaluation purposes since the new institutions have hardly commenced their activities. The small degree of experience gained in recent times in Rome, Milan and Genua points to the conclusion that these new bodies will not replace the spontaneously created "district committees", but simply act as an additional interlocutor and as an agency which is more sensitive to their needs. By contrast, the spontaneous movement of active participation in Rome has expanded and widened in line with the institutionalization of the electoral boundaries. They have assumed greater importance precisely in those situations where decisions on house-building and town-planning have been put forward for general discussion.

In many cases, however, this great vitality is more striking in the suburbs than in the historic town centres. This flows from the general tendency to convert historic centres in Italy which on the one hand have undergone an exodus of population or an increase in the average age of the latter (especially in the less affluent areas) and an economic decline and on the other hand – in the zones marked by intense development – a process of "tertiary development" which has weakened the social cohesion of local residents as well as their spirit of enterprise.

There have also been moves by some of the spontaneously created committees outside of the historic town centres or adjacent to them to undertake non-institutional inter-district coordination and to examine some of the problems in the historic quarters. This has exercised an impact upon overall municipal affairs such as transport, commerce, the protection of monuments, the use of cultural institutions and museums, etc.

Italy

TOWN PLANNING AND REHABILITATION IN 53 ITALIAN CITIES OF HISTORIC INTEREST

1. General

The present account does not concern itself with one place but with a sample group of 53 Italian cities whose local planning policy on their historic old quarters is analyzed and compared. The study was carried out by the Ministry of Public Works and presented at the "National Conference on Historic Centres" organized by the Government in December 1975. The subject matter of this report constitutes a synthesis of the above-mentioned comprehensive study, which has meanwhile been published in Italy and which will be sent to readers upon request. (The comprehensive study in question consists of a full summary and 53 individual reports comprising some 20 pages each.)

1.1 Description of the sample of cities

The 53 urban communities in question were selected from a total number of 8,000 Italian boroughs on the basis of the following four criteria:

1. Boroughs with special legislation which either directly or indirectly affects their historic town centres or where the competent governmental bodies have implemental experimented schemes designed to rehabilitate such centres.

2. Towns which pursue a policy of restoring their own historic centres independently of the motives expressed under fig. 1.

3. Boroughs with historic town centres marked by unusual features such as expanse or location even though no rehabilitation measures have yet been carried out there.

4. The list of towns covered by fig. 1 to 3 was submitted to the competent regional authorities, who then added another list of boroughs pursuing an individual policy for their own historic centres under the aegis of regional programmes.

This is the background to the following list of 53 towns where a total of 12,316,546 people live (according to the census of 1971). The list has been subdivided into separate geographical groups:

a. North Italy, 25 boroughs: 5,933,179 inhabitants Piedmont (Saluzzo, Asti, Alexandria and Turin) Lombardy (Chiari, Como, Bergamo, Brescia and Milan).
Veneto (Treviso, Vicenza, Padua)
Liguria (Lerici, Imperia, Savona and Genoa)
Emilia Romagna (Comacchio, Faenza, Cesena, Rimini, Reggio Emilia, Ferrara, Modena and Parma)

b. Central Italy, 16 boroughs: 3,710,066 inhabitants. Tuscania (Certaldo, San Giovanni, Voldarno, Pistoia and Florence)
Umbria (Orvieto and Gubbio)
Marches (Fossombrone, Urbino, Ascoli Piceno and Pesaro)
Latium (Tuscania, Terracina and Rome)
Abruzzi (Opi, Lanciano and Chieti)

c. South Italy and the Islands, 12 boroughs: 2,673,301 inhabitants
Campania (Ischia, Salerno and Naples)
Apulia (Ostuni, Martina Franca, Molfetta and Bari)
Basilicata (Tricarico)
Sicily (Petralia Sottana, Erica, Syracuse and Palermo)

In order to furnish the reader with a means of comparison, we should point out that the total population of Italy numbers 54,134,843 people living in 8,056 boroughs. The spread of the population is as follows: 46% live in the North; 19% in the central regions; and 35% in the South or on the islands.

As regards a classification in accordance with their demographic structure, 39% of the boroughs (3.3% of the population) covered by our sample study have fewer than 50,000 inhabitants (figures for the whole of Italy being 98.6% and 62.8% respectively) whilst 20.8% of the boroughs and 6.8% of the population in the study are accounted for by cities with between 50,000 and 100,000 people.

1.2 Criteria governing the delimitation of historic areas

Under the municipal planning schemes announced by the local authorities, the historic centres of old towns have been circumscribed in accordance with the provisions made by the Ministry of Public Works, who endeavour to achieve as uniform an application of the law as possible.

The criteria applied when designating an urban area as being of specil historic, artistic and scenic value are as follows:

a. districts where the bulk of the blocks of houses contain buildings erected prior to 1860, even though they lack ancient monuments and individual edifices of outstanding artistic merit;

b. walled towns, either completely or partially conserved and including external items which qualify for inclusion under a.;

c. districts constructed after 1860 but of outstanding architectural merit according to overall documentary evidence.

In most of the boroughs examined, it was found that the historic town centre coincided with the area enclosed by the old walls – whether still extant or meanwhile pulled down. This is the case in Ascoli – Piceno, Como, Florence, Forli, Treviso, Gubbio, Lanciano, Martina Franca, Pesario, Pistoia, San Giovanni, Val D'Arno, Tuscania and Vicenza.

As a result, the selection of an area has often borne in mind one of the typical features of urban renewal, i.e. the inclusion within the historic centre of zones previously used as vegetable gardens and orchards and only completed in recent decades or even districts of recently rehabilitated buildings.

Apart from districts enclosed within walls, other local authorities have designated as historic centres small market towns such as Bergamo and Cesena and districts endowed with special historic or scenic qualities.

Let us consider three examples: Ferrara, Rimini and Certaldo.

Ferrara has divided its historic town centre into three zones, viz

– the ancient walled township, Borgo S. Giorgio, the green strip along the Volano canal and Borgo S. Luca;

– walled districts of recent construction (i. e. built after 1860) and several expansions of the city beyond the walls;

– non-developed areas and green belts adjoining the town walls or of scenic merit.

Rimini is subdivided into the following zones:

– the district encircled by the old town together with S. Andrea, S. Giovanni and S. Giuliano;

– historic quarters or "ghettos" typical of the Romagna region and characterized by outstanding scenery;

– all those buildings which are located in different districts, but classified and indicated in the plan as possessing historic interest or outstanding scenic merit; and

– areas designated by the local planning authorities as "typical" and worthy of rehabilitation.

Certaldo has three zones:

– the old walled town;

– the area adjacent to the walled town with the surrounding villages;

– some of the 19th-century buildings.

Another criterion observed in the delimitation of the historic quarter is the date of construction of the houses and certain characteristic features of town planning and rehabilitation.

Let us now consider the following examples and the agreed definition in these towns of what constitutes the historic centre:

Bari – the urban area which existed prior to G. Murat's plan of 1850 together with the surrounding villages (plan of 1973).

Fossombrone – not simply that part of the town enclosed within the old walls, but the medieval district and the streets dating from the 17th and 18th centuries.

Genoa – the medieval area and the 19th century quarter designated for rehabilitation.

Lerici – five zones including the towns of Solaro and Bologna.

Ostumi – Rione Terra and an adjacent district dating from the 19th century.

Rome – the districts built before 1870 and those built afterwards but possessing considerable interest as an integral example of town-planning and well designed buildings. The historic city centre covers a superficial area of approximately 650 hectares or even 1,000 hectares if one includes the Vatican City and the archaeological sites.

Terracina – the ancient district built upon hills (the upper town) and the flat 18th century zone.

The boroughs of Orvieto and Comacchio cannot be classified among those cited above, since their historic town centres have been defined in terms of certain characteristic features of town design.

2. Organisation

The study prepared by the Minister of Public Works rests on a careful analysis based upon statistics and fluctuations in population during the last hundred years. As a result, the study has taken into account the ups and downs experienced by each city where the conversion phases and the problems manifest themselves in different fashion.

On the basis of the examination, the cities have been classified into three groups. The choice of the sample group was also made in the light of this general analysis.

2.1 Classification and problems

For a first group of boroughs, i.e. those which reached their maximum population level between 1861 and 1921 (3,181 boroughs), the historic centre may in effect correspond to the modern town. Such places are more likely to be marked by decay rather than by property speculation or tertiary-sector development.

A second group of boroughs – numbering approximately 2,327 – may be said to comprise those which reached their maximum population level between 1921 and 1951. Unlike the first group, the old urban fabric has clearly undergone an evolution in its building styles: nevertheless, the relationship between the historic quarter and the new residential streets remains in balance. When one bears in mind that the new districts almost invariably went through irregular periods of growth, these old town centres still remain the characteristic feature of the whole urban area. In view of the full use to which these districts are put, they have not been characterized by any undue speculation or tertiary-sector development.

The third group comprises the boroughs whose largest growth in population was reached by 1961. More than in the two preceding groups, this category incorporates several non-homogeneous elements in that it includes municipalities which have undergone considerable growth not only in the past, but also in recent decades as well as those where the population has gradually fallen in recent years after slow growth in the past.

Table 1 shows that the trend towards urbanization has affected the large urban centres whereas the historic centres of small towns are subject to continuous depopulation.

Table 1
Classification of Towns pursuant to their Growth in Population

Population	No. of Towns	No. of Inhabitants	% of Total
1951			
up to 10,000	6,955	21,180,778	44.94
10,000 to 100,000	764	16,547,770	35.10
over 100,000	25	9,409,687	19.96
Total	7,804	47,138,235	100.00
1971			
up to 10,000	7,181	19,013,803	35.10
10,000 to 100,000	828	19,212,619	35.56
over 100,000	47	15,798,789	29.25
Total	8,056	54,025,211	100.00

The concentration of population in the big cities – a phenomenon which has underscored the varied situations existing in the historic town centres of Italy – acquires a wider measure of significance when one considers that in 1971 the 32 most important metropolitan areas accounted for 43% of the national population distributed over a superficial area representing only 5.8% of the whole country.

Another factor will help to underline the disequilibrium prevailing in the housing sector. According to the 1971 census, 7.6 million rooms equivalent to nearly 12% of the total available number were in fact not used as accommodation. True, some of this large heritage of non-utilized accommodation consists of second homes. However, the problem also stems from the neglect of scattered houses and of the architectural legacy of past ages in small and medium-sized urban centres caused by a steady drop in population due to emigration or by the various difficulties of another kind peculiar to the modernization of old-fashioned homes. Instead, preference is often given to new houses.

The few instances cited above go to show that the historic centres of old Italian cities often reveal totally different and indeed contradictory features in regard to such problems as size, links with the surrounding urban areas, customs, accepted values in conservation and house-building, amenities, the degree of change taking place, economic resources, social structure, etc.

3. The Objectives of the Measures taken and the Procedures adopted in Planning

The aims of the action taken are explained in some detail in the methods, financing schemes and definitions of planning systems used for the various situations which may arise (fig. 2). The result is a typology of historic town centres with this term referring not only to the urban structure but also to the problems inherent in the aims of conservation.

At any rate, it may be safely said in regard to Italy that two principal objectives have been accorded priority:

– the need to maintain the vitality of historic areas in cities whilst safeguarding social, cultural and economic interests; and

– the need to promote a precise plan of continuous action for the conservation of monuments and buildings of architectural merit, thus checking a grave process of general decay.

As regards planning schemes, there are at present four different procedures in use:

1. The town planning schemes are worked out by the Municipal Department of Technical Planning. This is in fact the least frequent method and it usually concerns the modification of urban planning projects of recent origin.

2. The planning schemes are worked out by the Municipal Department of Technical Planning with the collaboration of outside specialists and consultants. This system may be found most of all in large cities with more than 150,000 inhabitants. Its advantage consists in the opportunity it affords municipal authorities of entisting experts from various fields of study and thus enjoying first-class services within their own offices and therefore easier to manage.

3. The planning schemes are worked out entirely by outside consultants with no relationship to the local authorities. This happens most frequently in towns with fewer than 50,000 inhabitants where the municipality's technical servies are inadequate.

4. The planning schemes result from public competition. In such a case, there are two possibilities: either the competition is staged as a preliminary procedure for defining the authors of the project with whom one could entrust the task or else the plan which wins first prize serves directly as the local council's plan of urban development. In regard to the schemes for historic town centres, the Municipal Department of Technical Planning has been assuming growing significance, especially during recent years.

4. Strategy and Implementation

4.1 Scope of action in historic areas

Even though our studies on this subject have revealed a large number of different approaches, we have reduced them to three main types – though conscious that this represents an over-simplicity. We illustrated them with specific examples in our original report and these are now summarized in methodical form.

Situation Type A

The municipality has a planning scheme incorporating a number of general ideas about how to conserve the historic town centre, but decides to postpone all operational details until a subsequent detailed plan for the old quarter is produced. In such a case, the town planning scheme applies to the central district of historic interest the same criteria as hold true for the development zones in that it subjects all measures to the qualification of a later plan.

243

However, the historic town centre is not a free zone where nobody lives and where anything can happen. On the contrary, it is often a densely populated urban area encumbered with a multitude of socio-economic problems and sanitary shortcomings quite apart from the dilapidation of the buildings. This may explain why the urban development plan must necessarily provide for a number of transitional arrangements until such time as detailed plans emerge while allowing for intervention in urgent cases.

Given the complexity of these studies and the financial burdens involved in these initiatives by the public authorities, many detailed plans whose drafting is provided for in the urban development plan have in fact not yet been formulated so that the 'transitional arrangements' become the sole means of taking any action. At least one third of the towns chosen for our sample group are in this situation.

The boroughs in question are either those with a historic town-centre covering only several hectares in size and housing a few hundred people (e.g. Opi with 600 inhabitants) or else above all the big cities with a historic old quarter covering hundreds of hectares with accommodation for thousands of inhabitants such as Florence (506 hectares, 70,000 people, 142,000 rooms), Naples (816 hectares, 280,000 people, 240,000 rooms) or Rome (650 hectares, approximately 95,000 inhabitants according to the census of 1971).

This situation results inter alia from the operational incapacity of some municipal authorities, often brought about by substantial financial difficulties and compounded by the speculative moves of property developers. In some cities, the latter are keen to work in circumstances as free from constraints as possible. Nevertheless, this situation is now evolving along positive lines. Even in the course of this last year, many municipalities in a type A situation have adopted more specific arrangements and thus managed to cope with the uncertainties of 'transitional arrangements' (see situation type C).

Situation Type B

The municipality already operates a planning scheme as in the type A situation, but it has also proceeded to the next stage, i.e. a detailed plan for the historic centre. In essence, the latter consists of two parts closely interlinked in a relationship of cause and effect which vary pursuant to the different urban and social structures and also in terms of the cultural approach to the project.

All the detailed plans have to incorporate a certain number of basic documents stipulated by law. In point of fact, these documents merely represent the lowest common denominator for all plans. In addition, the schemes almost always contain several dozen other graphical representations of the research work being carried out together with various analyses.

We have identified ten topics of regularly recurring research on which all the surveys conducted for the various detailed plans are based.

These ten subjects are as follows:

1. A chronicle of local authority activities and a classification of buildings in relation to the period of construction.

b. The architectural merit of the buildings concerned and their position on a scale of values.

c. The degree of conservation of original architectural structures.

d. An analysis of the various types of building.

e. A survey of residential accommodation.

f. Use of buildings.

g. Survey of property ownership.

h. Statistics on the physical condition and sanitary standards of buildings.

i. Local amenities.

k. Analysis of the physical lay-out of the area.

The detailed plans which we examined were all drawn up in the first half of the 1970s with the exception of Urbino (effected at an earlier date). They refer to historic centres with more or less the same demographic features and all located in the central part of North Italy. The towns in question are as follows (with the 1971 population figures for the historic quarter in brackets):

Tuscania (3,175), Certaldo (1,400), Urbino (3,964), Orvieto (8,635), Lanciano (4,912), Gubbio (5,455), Terracina (8,000), Pesaro (7,753), Coma (18,600), Vicenza (18,300), Bergamo (27,790), Reggio Emilia (14,359)

The feature which makes these detailed plans considerably different from the standpoint of methodology is the varied approach adopted during the analysis and project phase in the examination of architectural design and construction.

In our report, we have delineated in summary form the most notable traits of four specific examples: Urbino, Coma, Bergamo and Tuscania.

Situation Type C

The municipality operates a planning scheme which does not confine itself to indicating a clear-cut 'historic town centre'. Instead, it lists the main features of the area and carries out a series of analyses which attempt to define the problems of the historic centre whilst at the same time offering a solution and drawing attention to detailed plans solely for such zones as necessitate standard treatment and possibly also public financial support (public financial construction plans) and such as are clearly limited to a restricted number of cases.

The type C situation has been introduced during a first phase as a solution to type A and B situations in view of the fact that the detailed plan is often drafted many years after the town planning scheme itself and thus realized within time limits and situations other than those which led to the formulation of the urban development plan. The number of fresh analyses provided under the detailed plan furnish certain results which are contradictory and critical in regard to the forecasts set out in the town planning scheme for the historic area. The type C situation thus emerges as a result of a general modification of such town planning schemes as are already in force. However, a closer look at several concrete examples shows that this situation has also emerged as a separate approach since it permits municipal authorities to provide a concrete answer to the requirements of restoring and restructuring historic centres within short periods of time and without excessive expense. Among the 53 towns in our survey, those named below all fall under the type C group: they are all situated in Central and Northern Italy. The figures in brackets indicate the population of the historic centre in 1971.

Fossombrone (2,627), Chiari (3,652), Comacchio (10,287), San Giovanni Valdarno (2,500), Ascoli Piceno (15,000),

Rimini (9,557), Ferrara (54,468), Modena (16,246) and Brescia (26,055).

4.2 Participation
(see also the general report on Italy 4.4)

In view of the complexity of the problems involved and the need to find the best solution to the exigencies of widely differing interests, encouragement is given to various forms of decentralized participation.

The most relevant decisions are those which essentially fall within the domain of the local authorities.

The outcome of our studies in this field may be summarized as follows (reflecting the situation in spring 1976):

1. Decentralization has been effected above all in those boroughs with over 50,000 inhabitants. Boroughs with a smaller population had examined this problem, but in most cases these efforts did not produce any concrete results.

2. Such decentralization as has taken place is marked by highly differing population figures for the various territorial divisions. Some areas such as the boroughs of Certaldo, Comacchio, Pesaro, Cesena, Coma and Alessandria have a population of only a few thousand people; others such as Salerno, Modena and Parma house 10 to 20,000 persons; there are some (e.g. Naples) with about 50,000 inhabitants or even 200,000 (e.g. Rome).

3. Sometimes, these areas comprise the whole of the historic town centre or a large part of it. In other instances, the historic town centre has been subdivided into two or more districts, albeit all marked by homogeneous territorial features. By contrast, there are examples such as Sienna where an attempt has been made to promote integration between the historic centre and the suburbs by circumscribing areas which are essentially heterogeneous in character.

This was the situation which existed in Italy at the time of our first survey, i.e. prior to the enactment of Law No. 278 of 8th April 1976 on 'Norms for decentralization and participation by the citizens in the administration of the municipality', which took into consideration the whole complex of these activities and which expressed them in more concrete form. Above all, the Law called upon all Italian local authorities to move towards participation and decentralization by drawing up ad hoc provisions and by laying down the election of district committees.

Italy: Situation and number of inhabitants of the 53 towns

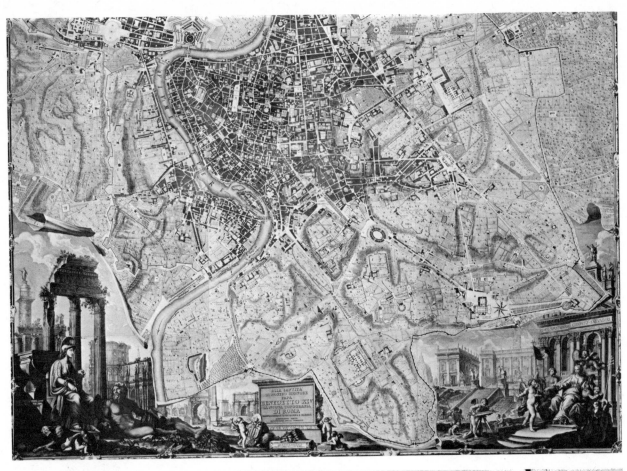

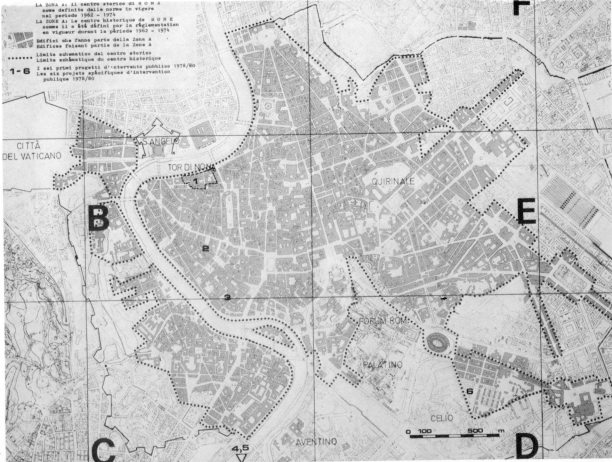

Rome: Shape and size of Rome in the 17th century (above), largely corresponding to the A Zones laid down in the 1964 city development plan (below, a sketch taken from "Roma sbagliata" 1976)

248

Italy
ROME

1. Situation

1.1

Rome is not only the capital of Italy but also the largest municipality in terms of population (2,799,836 inhabitants in 1971) and superficial area (1,508 square kilometres). It is also the administrative centre of the region of Latium which, despite its area (17,203 square kilometres) and number of boroughs (374), only had a population of 4,702,093 in 1971. As may be seen from this, approximately 60% of the inhabitants of Latium live in Rome. However, the latter has only reached its present size in the course of the last 150 years. When it was chosen as the capital of Italy in 1871, Rome had a population of just over 300,000 people. At any rate, the town-planning situation has become very complex in the course of the last 25 years. The growth in population between 1951 and 1971 amounted to 65%.

1.2

The limits of the historic town centre have been defined in different ways. In the fullest sense of the word, the historic centre comprises all of Rome's "rioni" or ancient quarters in contradistinction to the "quartieri" making up the remainder of the capital. For town-planning purposes, the part of the historic central area subject to specific controls (zone A) is more restricted: it covers a superficial area of about 835 hectares. The municipal official currently responsible for the historic centre of Rome has affirmed the need to designate approximately 1,500 hectares as the historic zone of the city.

2. Conditions and Problems

The current population of the historic centre is constantly dwindling in line with the general increase in Rome's population as a whole.

Population of the municipality

1951: 1,695,477
1971: 2,799,836 (plus 1,104,359 = 65%)

Population of the "rioni" (historic quarters)

1951: 424,000
1971: 196,000 (less 228,000 = 53%)

The physical and social changes in the historic centre of Rome have been considerable. The sharp fall in the residential population of the historic quarters corresponds to a growth in demand for new homes in the suburbs. That has aggravated the problem of the housing shortage engendered by the large overall increase in population. The historic central area has also been stamped by physical, social and economic changes. To a certain extent, the relinquished accommodation has been acquired by persons of a different social class (such as professional men or foreigners) enjoying a higher income and making greater demands in respect of standards. This has given rise to substantial plans for typical changes of this kind. Some of the houses in question have been converted into professional, administrative and commercial offices or into hotels. A third segment of this accommodation is in a state of decline and hoping to become earmarked for functional conversion.

According to L'Assessorato, an office established by the city council and placed in charge of the historic city-centre, there were 3,596 unoccupied dwellings in 1961. By the year 1971, this number had risen to 7,250. Simultaneously, the figure for occupied dwellings fell from 59,398 in 1951 to 51,000 in 1971, whilst the number of families declined from 64,520 to 54,000. It should be added that many of the changes effected during the last 20 years are not legitimate as they were not authorized.

Another significant factor has been the rise in the average age of the population in Rome's historic centre where 28% of the residents are over 60 years of age compared with only 17% for the city as a whole.

Finally, major changes have taken place involving the old craftsmen's workshops in the historic quarter in that they have become commercial enterprises, thus engendering a profound modification in the economic and productive structure of Rome's central area.

A separate problem has arisen in connection with monuments, palaces and churches. The large churches naturally have to be maintained by the competent authorities because they continue to exercise their religious function. However, there exist a number of small churches and chapels (a major segment of the famous list of 365 churches in Rome, one for every day of the year) which have become redundant as places of worship due to the drop in population. Today, they are either closed or half abandoned or put to non-legimate use as warehouses, business firms, etc. One factor of considerable importance is the fate of large properties such as monasteries, private hotels, etc. The feeling is that they might and indeed should be put to use as cultural institutions and in this way revitalize the centre of Rome. In point of fact, however, there already exist 94 libraries, 19 academies and 22 cultural institutions.

3. Objectives

The municipal administration elected in 1976 created an "Assessorato", i.e. a special office for the historic centre which formerly did not exist. The historic centre of Rome used to be administered by the same town-planning services as dealt with the whole city.

The short-term aims of the new department consist in initiating and coordinating all the available public and private resources so as to achieve:

– a better utilization of property and financial assets – especially if publicly owned;

– a revision of normative instruments;

– more effective control of unauthorized building;

– an improvement in housing standards and municipal services; and

– promotion of cultural and productive activities (workshops, small-scale commerce and industry).

The first point in the new policy of active support by the municipal authorities concerns the restoration of the bulk of publicly owned housing so as to maintain a fair proportion of residents in the historic centre.

A recent census of the situation of public properties revealed the following situation:

a. Municipally-owned property

dwellings (719)	1,156 rooms
schools	2,582 rooms
offices	1,950 rooms

Rome: City Development Plan of 1964 (cross-section)
In addition to the delimitation of the A zones (the historic city centre), B zones (where the fabric and outward appearance of buildings must remain intact), parks, archaeological and landscape protection zones (V), the plan set out to steer the then indiscriminate urban sprawl in all directions and above all to map out priority areas for the tertiary sector (centri direzionali, 5), for the zones earmarked for restructuring (I), industry (L) and the university (M). In many respects, however, the plan has given subsequent approval to previous haphazard developments and in particular to the multifarious residential districts dotted around the city (recognizable from the dark coloured network of streets)

Rome: Tor di Nona

above and middle: Group of houses in the second section of the rehabilitation scheme in the Tor di Nona seen from Lungotevere (July 1978)

below: Inside the Tor di Nona area: view from the Piazza San Salvatore to the west: to the left, residential housing (some of it restored by private initiative): to the right, the local primary school

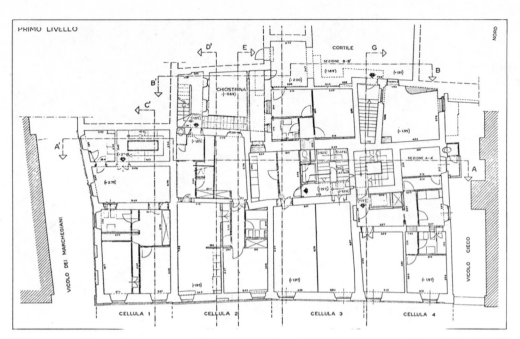

PRIMO LIVELLO

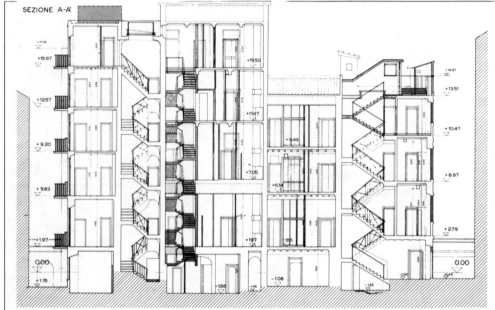

SEZIONE A-A'

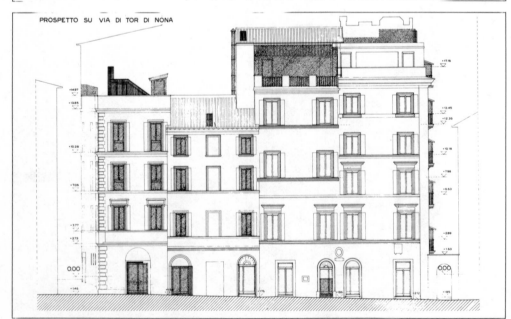

PROSPETTO SU VIA DI TOR DI NONA

Rome:
Tor di Nona
Activities of the public authorities in the Tor di Nona district. The project for the second rehabilitation sector worked out by experts on behalf of the "Istituto autonomo case popolari" (IACP) and commenced in the Autumn of 1978, horizontal projection 1st of storey, profile, view of Lungotevere. New parts to be built:

1 = horizontal structures

Parts to be demolished:

2 = vertical structures
3 = horizontal
4 = vertical

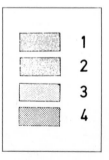

1
2
3
4

b. Property belonging to the "Pio Istituto"

dwellings   1,188 rooms
shops   127 rooms

c. Property belonging to "Opere Pie"

dwellings   1,944 rooms
shops   20,017 square metres

4. Strategy

At the time of writing, six ad hoc projects for the official support of these properties are now being carried out or prepared:

1. Tor di Nona: municipally owned buildings, 300 rooms, 90–100 dwellings;

2. Via dei Cappellari: municipally owned building, 13 dwellings;

3. San paolino alla Regola: abandoned municipal property, no precise figure for number of rooms (100 ?);

4. Ex-abattoir: industrial complex comprising halls, apartments and sheds – to be used for cultural activities, sports, crafts, etc.;

5. Testaccio: land belonging to the I.A.C.P. (public property) – to be used for transit accommodation;

6. Celio: I.A.C.P. land whose future use is at present under consideration.

To these properties must be added the premises belonging to organizations and institutions which are not in a position to utilize them and which place them at the disposal of the local authorities on extremely favourable terms:

a. The old monastery of Via Crispi;

b. The old Roman court of the first instance (a historic monastery);

c. Rivoldi Palace;

d. Property in Via Capo d'Africa.

4.1 Techniques

In order to implement the above-mentioned programme of support, a number of problems have to be solved and efforts are now being undertaken to achieve this.

From the standpoint of procedure, it has proved necessary to put into effect all the administrative and legal decisions needed in order to benefit from the statutory funds earmarked for building purposes and thus implement the agreed projects.

These procedures have been successfully completed in regard to the first project (Tor di Nona). The funds are now available, the projects ready, and the awarding of contracts decided so that the work has in fact already been started.

Let us stress the interest inherent in collaboration between the municipal council and the Istituto Autonomo Case Populari, whose task is to carry out and manage building programmes for low-cost housing. This institute acts as a contract-awarding body and handles the technical side of operations. On the basis of a contractual agreement, it has

also contributed to the preparation of support programmes by furnishing the local government with technical personnel.

The municipal authorities propose to augment this type of collaboration by altering the agreement on the "Tor di Nona" project into a "consortium" designed to include the regional administrative authority, who will probably be the owner of the real estate, and the "Istituto Autonomo Case Populari", who will take charge of the administration and restoration of all public properties falling within the purview of consortium members.

4.2 Finance

The financing of operations will largely rest upon the earmarking of national funds for low-cost housing lent to the municipality of Rome by the regional government. The sums of money in question are:

– 1,100 million lire from past funds, approved but not used; and

– 4,500 million lire earmarked under Finance Laws No. 166 and 513.

The city corporation naturally expects to reinforce its efforts by obtaining funds under the "10-year housing plan", Law No. 457 of 1978. (See also chapter 3 of the general report on Italy).

This scheme provides for a wider framework of action than previously in the rehabilitation sector. In the past, private investment was effected on an intensive scale though without much public supervision. The public prosecutor recently instituted proceedings to curb the support being given to non-authorized conversion activities, i.e. to those which do not conform to the norms and rules laid down in the town planning scheme and in law. The municipal authorities face the difficult situation of reestablishing the force of law by improving the implementation of controls and above all by providing better technical and administrative facilities.

4.3 Participation

4.3.1 The functions of the City Council

In July 1977, the City Council of Rome held a municipal conference to explain its programme to the socially active groups: the association of building industrialists, pressure groups, district committees, professional and trade organizations, and cultural institutions. On this occasion, the competent official at the "Assessorato" presented a report on current initiatives and the funds now available whilst stressing the inadequacy of the latter and the need for more time-consuming research on this subject. The Council gave an account of its short-term (1977–79) and long-term objectives.

4.3.2 Decentralization (see General Report on Italy, 4.4)

4.3.3 District committees

The notification and suppression of abuses in house building carried out in the historic central area of Rome are the outcome of the efforts undertaken in recent years by the cultural institutions to illuminate the gravity of the situation.

Rome: Tor di Nona

above: The district around the Tor di Nona as depicted on the city map made by Giovanni Maggi 1625 (edited by P. Maupin and C. Losi in 1774). The riverside structures were later demolished as part of the scheme to regulate the waters of the Tiber. The embankment is now the "Lungotevere". The Tor di Nona is still located at the same level and thus exposed to the noise and fumes produced by passing cars (see also the photographs).

Detailed plan (1933) for Tor di Nona, some of the existing houses were made subject to a compulsory purchasing order in order to replace them with commercial enterprises and administrative buildings. The war thwarted the implementation of the project, which had failed to give any consideration to the existing structure of the area

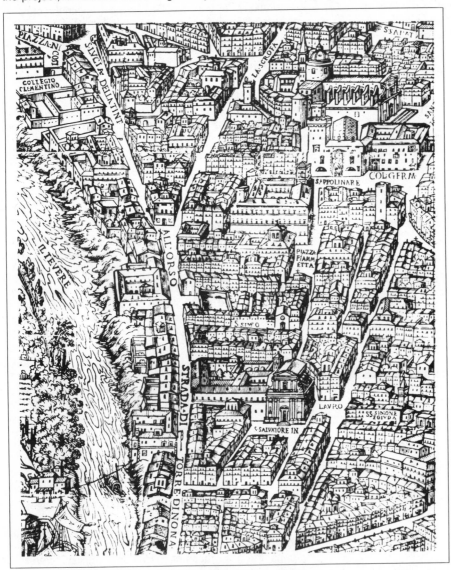

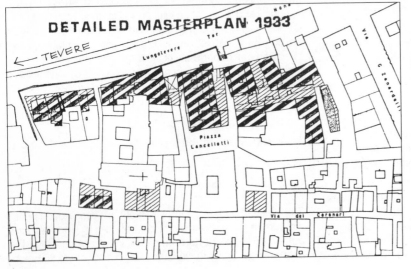

DETAILED MASTERPLAN 1933

 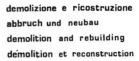
demolizione e ricostruzione
abbruch und neubau
demolition and rebuilding
démolition et reconstruction

parco pubblico
öffentliches grün
public green area
zone verte publique

demolizione
abbruch
demolition
démolition

Rome: Tor di Nona

Cutout from the city development plan (1931). Some of the planned measures in the "quartiere del Rinascimento" were implemented (around the Piazza Navona) whereas others could not be commenced in time before the war (around the Pantheon, Tor di Nona) or else survived as redevelopment ruins (e. g. on Via Giulia). 1 = demolition; 2 = demolition and new high-density housing; 3 = public parks; 4 = private gardens; 5 = (archaelogical) protected zones

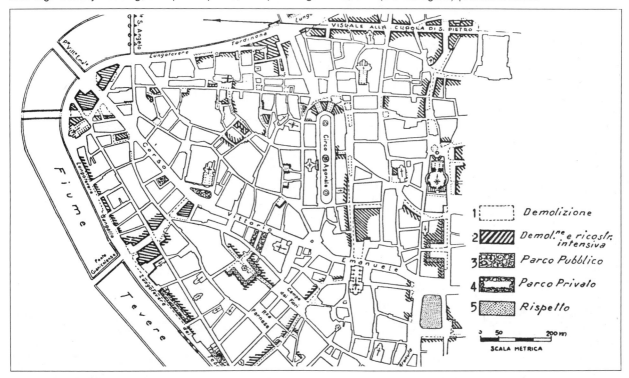

Rome: Tor di Nona

From the preparatory studies for the 1976/77 rehabilitation plan for Tor di Nona and the surrounding area: use/condition of building/ownership of property
I = first part of the rehabilitation scheme; II = second part of the rehabilitation scheme

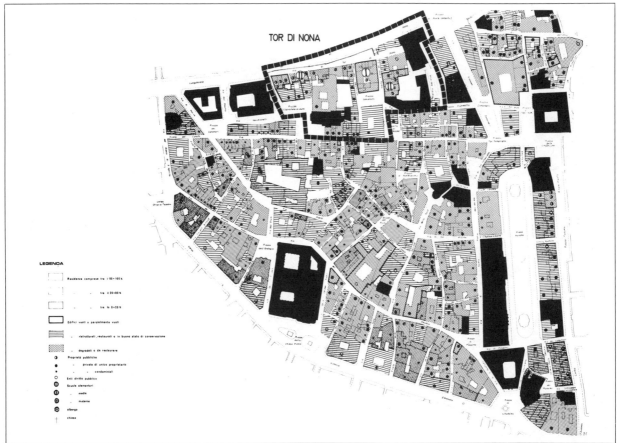

Rome: Tor di Nona
above: Via di Nona to the west
top right: The Lungotevere ring road. To the left are the groups of houses in the first and second sections of the rehabilitation scheme
detail drawing: View from the Lungotevere along Vicolo Cieco

below: First rehabilitation section of Via Tor di Nona/Piazza Lancelotti seen from Lungotevere. Citizens' action groups attract attention to the problems of the district (state as of July 1978)
detail: View from Lungotevere along Vicolo dei Marchegiani (July 1978)

The city council has welcomed these endeavours and the local authorities intend to reapply control procedures to avoid a repetition of this damage and the concomitant need for recourse to the judicial authorities.

5. Tor di Nona: An On-going Project

The first project due for completion is the Tor di Nona. This relates to a block of run-down houses owned by the municipality. At the present time, they are occupied by 37 families. When the project has been completed, a total of 115 dwellings will be available. The scheme is to be completed in three phases. The first one deals with the tendering procedure for the rehabilitation of the apartments where the 37 families live. This phase has just been finished. The second and third phases, to be decided during 1978/79, will provide for the completion of the project and the allocation of the remaining accommodation to families already residing in the historic part of the city, but in houses in need of progressive restoration or in completely run-down dwellings. In order to be eligible as the lessee of a refurbished dwelling, a family must satisfy the preconditions laid down in law for low-cost housing.

The first stage of the project provides for the establishment of a social centre for old people, 14 shops on the ground floor, 97 rooms (46 apartments) with one special 12-room flat for students or elderly persons, 15 one-room flats, 18 two-room flats, 9 three-room and 3 four-room flats. From the technical point of view, the attempt has been made wherever possible to maintain the existing structures. For example, the wooden floors will be partly restored and partly replaced by floors made of iron and hollow tiles. As a result, the estimated cost of rehabilitation will only amount to 45,000 lire per square metre despite the serious state of dilapidation: this sum is 25 % below the price of modern low-cost housing now being erected in the suburbs of Rome.

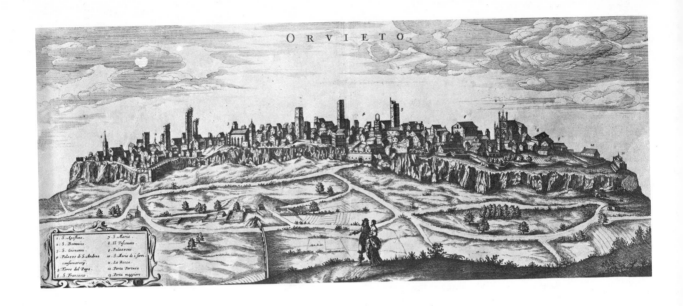

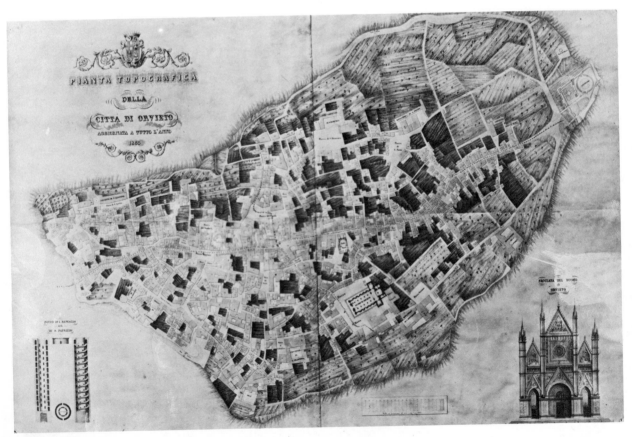

Orvieto:

above: Orvieto from the South West on a copperplate print by Hogenberg (ca. 1575)

below: Land registry plan of the town on the tuff plateau (1865). The dark areas are gardens and vegetable plots whilst the somewhat lighter ones with tree symbols represent orchards and vineyards

Italy
ORVIETO

1. Situation

1.1 General introduction

Orvieto lies amidst the green expanses of Umbria near the Northern limit of Latium and to the East of the Paglia, an Eastern tributary of the Tiber, on a subhorizontal tongue of tuff rock superimposed upon a hill of clay. The waters of underground streams wore away the clay right around the hill and thus isolated it completely. Like most of South-West Umbria, Orvieto is very young in geological terms despite the age of its archaeological treasures.

Broadly speaking, the population trends have been as follows. During the 15 years between 1961 and 1975, Orvieto experienced a slight fall in population. On 31 December 1961, the population totalled 25,100 inhabitants. From then until 1971, there came a steady fall – though varying from year to year – until it reached the minimum level recorded for that period, i.e. 23,252. This trend reversed in 1972 and 1973 when a slight rise took place. In the years 1974 and 1975, the population stabilized at a figure of 23,400.

Broadly speaking, these demographic ups and downs may be explained in the main by population movements. The balance of migration remained negative until 1971 and the exodus even rose quite steeply on occasions. Between 1972 and 1975, the balance became positive or only slightly negative following an increase in immigration or a fall in emigration. Presumably, these fluctuations in population were greatly influenced by major programmes of public works undertaken by the local authorities and neighbouring boroughs during this period such as the dam at Lake Corbara, the Autostrada del Sole or the direct railway link between Florence and Rome.

1.2 History

The early beginnings of the township of Orvieto remain shrouded in deep mystery, much of it susceptible to the most imaginative of hypotheses. According to the traditional view, the Etruscans were the first to inhabit the massif of tufa where they settled after having constructed a road leading into the town – destined to remain the only one of its kind for a long time to come. Despite the abundance of our archaeological treasures, it is difficult to identify the role which Orvieto played among Etruscan towns and their political, religious and military organization. Numerous theories have been submitted by eminent scholars – all of them fascinating and even quite credible. At any rate, one thing remains certain. Given its virtually impregnable position, Orvieto must have been a religious or military centre of prime importance and clearly one of the last Etruscan citadels to surrender to Rome. Orvieto's history becomes enveloped in even deeper mystery and it is not recorded in any chronicle or document. The long period of peace which the inhabitants of the region enjoyed probably brought out a clear decline in the town's fortunes and its rapid decadence. In consequence, some of those people who had sought refuge in times of war and insecurity moved down into the valley in search of work on farms or in the reviving domain of commerce, which was developing above all along the principal routes by land and water. Among the latter was the confluence between the Paglia and the Tiber at the flourishing Roman port of Pagliano, whose existence may still be traced today. Orvieto's eclipse persisted for centuries. Yet when the tottering Roman Empire was invaded by the barbarians, the high plateau of tufaceous rock to which people fled in search of a new life resumed its role of citadel and place of refuge.

The ensuing centuries marked an age of uncertainty caused by the profound social and political changes which convulsed Italy but which then guided it forward into the eventful epoch marking the birth of our modern townships.

That was when Orvieto discovered its true role as Tuscany's military centre. A new future opened up for Orvieto when she took advantage of the political fervour created by internecine struggles between families and factions and their mutually contested aspirations to power by setting up an efficient internal organization backed by free and independent institutions. This political autonomy survived even after the meddling tactics of the neighbouring Papal States augmented to the point of becoming almost intolerable and, as a result, Orvieto never became a member of 'St. Peter's inheritance' – although she did in fact virtually do so at a later stage.

It was in the 13th and 14th centuries that the annals of Orvieto sparkle with splendour and distinction. The town expanded in line with a town planning scheme which has remained virtually unchanged until the present day and which probably adhered to the Etruscan-Roman tradition: it enjoyed the fruits of economic prosperity which permitted it to reach a population of 30,000 inhabitants. The borough of Orvieto grew apace and extended its territories: within the township, public and political life evoked a wide measure of democratic participation. In 1281, for example, a tribune by the name of Neri della Greca ordered the demolition of several houses surrounding his palace to create space for rallies and meetings. The four major religious orders present in Orvieto since the first half of the 13th century played a full role in the cultural, artistic and of course spiritual advancement of the city. It was the adherents of the Abbey of St. Severo and Martirio, the Franciscans, the servants of St. Mary and the Dominicans, who organized a flourishing study of theology under teachers such as Thomas Aquinas. A number of distinguished men either lived at Orvieto or maintained contact with the city, one example being Benedetto Caetani who later became Pope Boniface VIII but who also held very high municipal office for a long period of time.

The churches of Orvieto provided the setting for several important events. St. Francis was the scene of the funeral service for Henry of Germany, killed by Guy de Montfort at Viterbo in 1271, and of the canonization of the French King Louis IX by Pope Boniface VIII in 1297. At St. Andrew's, Simon de Brie was crowned Pope Martin IV in 1281. However, the paramount achievement of the period was undoubtedly the design and building of the magnificent cathedral erected jointly by the ecclesiastic and secular

Orvieto:

above: The old medieval district of "La Cava" between S. Giovanni and S. Giovenale as viewed in the 1930s. In the foreground may be seen the roofs of the Via della Cava and rising up above them the Vicolo del Caccia

middle: A similar view taken in 1978 and showing the numerous extensions, adding of new storeys and "bungalows" in gardens

below: A present-day view from S. Giovenale across the valley to the suburb of Sterracavallo. Many of the residents from the upper city were attracted by the standard of housing and the proximity of road and rail

260

Orvieto:

above: A view of the rocky plateau below S. Giovenale. As a result of erosion, vibration and tree vegetation, the layers of tuff work loose and then scale off

middle: The cathedral and its surroundings from the West. Although this architectural monument has remained incomplete for centuries, its dominating position becomes even more striking when seen from a close distance

below: The town hall (palazzo comunale), commenced by Ippolito Scalza in the 16th century and like many public buildings and noblemen's palaces in Orvieto never finished. To the left is the tower and church of S. Andrea

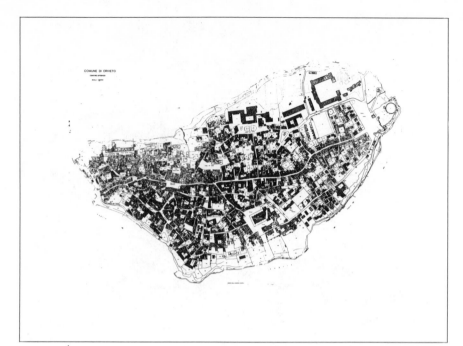

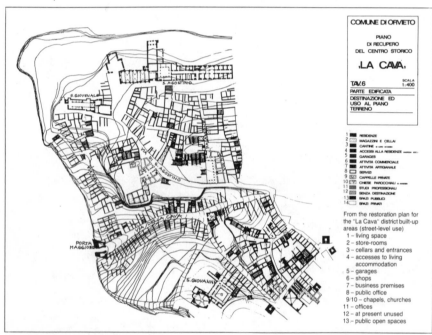

From the restoration plan for the "La Cava" district built-up areas (street-level use)

1 – living space
2 – store-rooms
3 – cellars and entrances
4 – accesses to living accommodation
5 – garages
6 – shops
7 – business premises
8 – public office
9/10 – chapels, churches
11 – offices
12 – at present unused
13 – public open spaces

authorities. Although the Miracle of Bolsena (1263) undoubtedly inspired the construction of the cathedral, it also owes its origin to another reason – the need for a city which had reached the pinnacle of its cultural and political advances to express its glory in a supreme work of art. The history of the cathedral following the laying of the foundation stone by Pope Nicholas IV extended over several centuries and has in fact not yet ended in that the mounting of the bronze doors made by a contemporary sculptor, Emilio Greco, is surrounded by controversy.

In the 15th century, the Papal States finally incorporated Orvieto and its territory. To mark this domination, achieved after so much tenacity, they established a garrison in the fortress of Albornoz and made it into a stronghold charged with the task of controlling the valley of the Paglia which it overlooked as well as the town, which had nevertheless often demonstrated its loyalty to the Guelfs. This ushered in an inexorable process of political decline in Orvieto, a decline from which she proved unable to recover and which

diminished her role from that of a capital city to one of being simply a small provincial town.

Popes and cardinals used to spend long sojourns in Orvieto with their courts because the town's natural and impregnable fortifications permitted them to withdraw there, insulated against the insecurity and vicissitudes of that epoch. The outcome was noblemen and prelates alike built luxurious residences in the contemporary style.

On 5th July 1831, Pope Gregory XVI raised the city to the rank of an apostolic delegation, a tardy recognition of the role which Orvieto had never ceased to play in territories where it had always enjoyed the status of a capital by virtue of its natural destiny and obvious historic and geographic title.

While remaining loyal to the Guelfs and the Popes, Orvieto was clearly inspired by patriotic sentiments. Following a popular uprising, she preceded by ten years the other cities in the 'inheritance of St. Peter', i.e. the Papal States, by becoming part of the Kingdom of Italy in 1860.

Orvieto:
Sheets 8 and 16 of the rehabilitation plan for "La Cava"

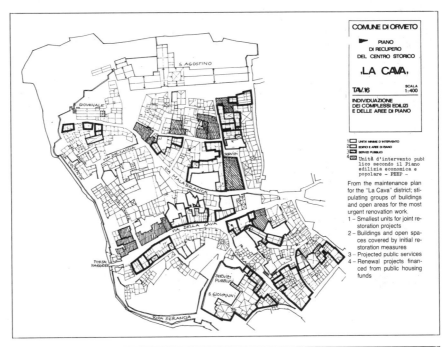

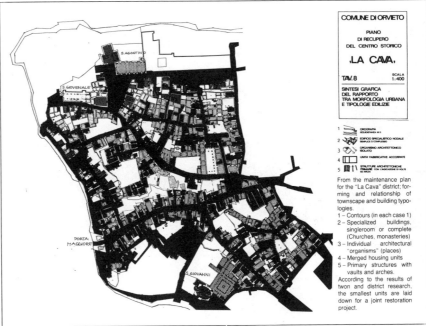

2. Conditions

2.1 Issues: the factors underlying the problems which require Intervention; the dangers to our historic legacy; and geological disturbances

It should be pointed out that the fall in population noticeable throughout the municipality has been particularly serious in the historic central area. The number of residents there dropped from 8,635 to 7,976 between 1971 and 1976, i.e. a loss of 659 persons. By the same token, the number of households fell from 2,960 to 2,728 (i.e. a negative balance of 238 units). It is interesting to note that 568 out of the 659 persons (86.2%) mentioned above and 172 households (74.1%) moved from the old central district to the suburbs. That would seem to indicate that the reasons for this movement do not spring from the pursuit of a higher income but of more satisfactory housing conditions. A parallel phenomenon is the marked tendency to abandon old houses – as may be seen from the reduction in the number of inhabited dwellings – and especially those with a smaller number of rooms. Finally, it should be noted that there is still a real need for more houses even if the number of inhabitants continues to fall and the total figure for dwellings and rooms is theoretically sufficient. The facts described above clearly impinge most seriously of all upon the financially weakest sections of the community (i.e. old-age pensioners, unskilled labourers, etc.).

Hence, it is urgently necessary in political terms to intervene in the historic centre in order to prevent the wastage which has assumed such grave forms in the nation's current crises from occurring in the house-building sector, too.

Indeed, a persistent exodus from the historic centre would produce rises in ground-rents in the suburbs, fresh overall charges for everyone due to increased public services in the development zones and a waste of our legacy of good houses. To that must be added the deterioration in the

Orvieto:

above and middle: Because of the present reduced population of Orvieto, it is particularly difficult to find fresh and adequate functions for the numerous redundant churches. The ex-monastery of S. Agostino served as a barracks; the main part of the church (above) was formerly a garage but it is now empty, whilst the chapel (to the left) recently became a restaurant.

The modified and partially reconstructed convent of S. Chiara (middle) now houses a vocational school whereas the church has became a ruin.

below: Via di Loreto. Until the 1960s, the demolished old buildings and more frequently the gardens and courtyards were replaced by new houses which paid no attention whatsoever to the scale and material of traditional construction methods. Opposite stands a new building in an adapted style.

historic centre due to the loss of the cultural treasures which today constitute one of Orvieto's principal sources of income.

Another danger to the elevated city of Orvieto comes from geological disturbances in the volcanic tuff plateau. The result is earth tremors on the gentler slopes and falls of rock on the steeper ones.

264

2.2 The role of the political and administrative authorities. The preconditions for support and promotion

The efforts undertaken by the municipal authorities to save the historic inner area are illustrated by the role which they have always played in Orvieto's town planning.

Even in the first scheme, drawn up by the architect Beonelli and approved in 1956, the historic centre was segregated from the remaining urban areas and subjected to certain provisions enacted to ensure proper conservation measures. Finally, the architect Piccinato was entrusted in 1963 with the drafting of a new general plan of urban development (plano regolatore generale). This scheme was designed not only to safeguard the historic centre of Orvieto by means of appropriate controls, but also to promote development in the zones around the foot of the hill in the promising economic climate which prevailed in Italy at that time. Nevertheless, the demands of the local population and the cultural aspirations of the period created the need for a more detailed plan and for a scheme better adapted to the historic centre. For this reason, another architect (Coppa) received the commission in 1965 to draw up detailed plans. But the adoption of Piccinato's town planning scheme and the drafting of detailed plans were not sufficient to ensure the revitalization of the old central area which everyone wanted. The causes of this unsatisfactory state of affairs stemmed from the division between the assumptions underlying the town planning scheme and the data emerging from the detailed plans for the historic centre. In point of fact, the vast 'zones of expansion' envisaged in the suburbs represented an immediate alternative for the population living amidst insanitary or congested conditions in the historic centre of Orvieto and unable to satisfy their requirements under the system then in force. Another factor was the heavy expenditure involved in the restoration of old houses, a circumstance which objectively constituted the real reason for the departure of vast numbers of poorer families.

When the economic crises of 1972 presaged the incipient recession and demonstrated the impossibility and danger for the historic town centre of an excessive expansion of house-building as contemplated in the 1960s, the municipality decided to request the Umbrian regional authorities for permission to modify the town planning scheme. The modification scheme was worked out between January and August 1976. The guiding principle in the new approach was that the urban development plan would serve above all to revitalize the historic centre and to make fresh use of the inherited stock of housing.

Among the more important features of the plan, attention should be drawn to the fact that the definition of building areas did not derive from any highly experimental system of uncontrolled 'zoning'. Instead, each item has been decided with such precision as to ensure that the scheme retains its intermediary character between the town planning scheme and the detailed plan. Another element which must be mentioned is the fact that all the old sites within the urban area enjoy the same protection and controls as the major historic centre itself.

3. The Aims of Support Action

This brief account of the problems faced by Orvieto's historic centre enables us to grasp the aims which have been undertaken under the policy of rehabilitation. The principal objective consists in as productive a utilization as possible of the existing resources, both by limiting fresh expansion and the concomitant development costs for the town authorities and by promoting optimum use of old dwellings by those social classes which would otherwise be obliged to move elsewhere. In this way, public expenditure can be cut in relation to the provision of public services and the demand for housing kept to a satisfiable level in the light of the continuing economic crisis. In view of the labour-intensive nature of restoration operations, the measures taken to improve existing edifices will tend to reduce unemployment in the building sector – a trend which sharply increased when the last public works affecting the borough of Orvieto were completed (the barrage across the Tiber, the Autostrada del Sole). Within the context of rehabilitation measures and the need to maintain the level of employment, it is important to help in solving the problem of unemployment among university graduates by enlisting the services of young people in collecting the data required for socio-economic censuses and in directly restoring the relevant buildings.

Finally, we should not underestimate the importance of the fact that only a guaranteed re-utilization of the old buildings will enable us to conserve them for a longer period of time and to maintain this significant testimony to the rich history and civilization of Orvieto. There is ample evidence to show that policies which restrict or only passively conserve our artistic heritage cannot fail to accelerate the process of decline and dereliction.

4. Strategy and Action

4.1 Legal instruments

From the legal viewpoint, rehabilitation is achieved above all on the basis of a detailed plan for the revitalization of the historic town centre. This detailed plan sets out to put into effect the preliminary ideas contained in the town planning scheme.

The municipality draws up the project and must arrange for a correct process of acceptance and authorization. The function of the regional authorities is to implement the scheme on the basis of study conducted by the 'Assessorate Regionale alla Urbanistica'.

Finally, mention should be made of the important role in respect of implementation which may be played by section IV of Law No. 457 (1978), which provided for the instrument of a piano die recupero (rescue plan). See also General Report No. 3 on Italy.

This scheme also permits the coordination of measures between action groups in their support campaign and serves to avoid the lack of unity or the staggering of the necessary steps – factors which are so harmful to the

Orvieto:

left and right: The old district of La Cava, Vic del Caccia: private renewal and restoration work carried out prior to the enactment of the rehabilitation plan. Though relatively uniform in style, the houses do not always conform to local traditions in materials and design.

physical fabric of historic towns both from the standpoint of conserving typical districts as well as that of economic considerations.

In this context, it is important to note that the device of a compulsory purchase order – pursuant to the legislation in force on building (see General Report No. 1.1.5 on Italy) – is often used as a stimulus in order to reach amicable agreements with property owners on rents and on the means of financing restoration activities ('convenzioni'). In most cases, the local authorities are not in a financial position to buy the selected buildings and to guarantee their productive re-utilization. The hope is that the new instrument of the 'piano die recupero' will grant private persons greater scope of action whilst simultaneously furnishing the local authorities with more flexible means of rehabilitation.

4.2 Financial instruments:
public finance – private investment and the activities of private and semi-public organizations

A number of solutions have been proposed in Orvieto to the problem of how to raise the funds needed to carry out the restoration project. In point of fact, the principal concern at the present time is that of extending as much as possible the number of buildings and other items earmarked for restoration. As is well known, the support given to date has rested almost exclusively on public finance. In view of the shortage of such funds, they could only meet a small part of the

money needed to restore all the old buildings. Although the detailed plan again relies on the system of public finance, and the machinery of amicable agreements (re-affirmed in Law No. 457 of 1978), an attempt is nevertheless made to define appropriate methods for encouraging private enterprise. In effect, that constitutes the sole means of widening the revitalizing operation in terms of quantity. The theories hitherto propounded are evidently founded on the problem of amicable agreements: on the granting of permission to carry out renewal measures, particularly in exchange for adherence to controls on prices and rents.

The recent law on landed property (No. 10 of 28 January 1977) also envisages in article 9 a a reduction in, or exemption from, the fees in payment of a restoration permit for such persons as agree to conclude 'convenzioni' with the municipality.

The local community as a whole can also promote the conclusion of amicable agreements with private persons if it succeeds in assuring them of all types of financial or fiscal facility whilst giving preferential treatment to cooperatives or obtaining low-interest loans from local banks.

A 'special law' was promulgated in 1978 on urgent measures for the reinforcement of the plateau of Orvieto following geological research carried out in depth at Orvieto and Todi pursuant to instructions issued by the regional authorities in Umbria. The State has earmarked a sum of 8,000 million lire for the work to be carried out between 1978 and 1981: 6,000 million for Orvieto and 2,000 million for Todi.

4.3 Technical measures

The rehabilitation programme rests on a preliminary classification of the buildings in the historic centre, which in turn is based on a comparison between the property registration surveys carried out between 1819 and 1972 (1843, 1863, 1909 and 1939). The scale used is 1:1,000.

The medieval quarter known as 'La Cava' has been analyzed in greater detail as it contains more buildings of that period than the rest of the old part of the town. A complete survey has been carried out at groundfloor level of this district in order to establish the relationship between the internal structure of the buildings and the use to which they are put. For each group of buildings in the Cava district, the profile has been delineated in each street in addition to the uniform facade of each house and the number of storeys. The survey also includes ownership and distribution so as to be able to draw up priorities of support in regard to the implementation of the plan. Furthermore, building permits issued between 1931 and the present time have been registered so as to have as complete a documentation as possible of the conversions carried out on local houses here during the last 40 year.

4.4 Participation

The modifications of 1976 to the town planning scheme became the subject of a wide-ranging public debate by virtue of:

– meetings, debates and explanatory talks during the period preceding the adoption of the modifications in question;

– an extended exhibition of the documents illustrating the modifications over and beyond the prescribed time-limit following their adoption by the municipal authorities;

– on-the-spot meetings and inspections at all the principal sites within the borough; and

– the advisory services and more detailed information provided by the municipality via an expert of the competent department during the whole period of observation.

On these occasions, an attempt has been made to influence public opinion in favour of the policies set out in the town planning scheme and thus to protect the historic centre of Orvieto and, in more general terms, in favour of an urban development policy designed to reduce the scale of uncontrolled house-building. This awakening of the public conscience has been reinforced not only by applying abstractly aesthetic criteria but above all by emphasizing the decisive influence which these old districts exercise and could excercise on the local economy.

The support for this approach to town planning has been unanimous, as may be seen both from the meetings with the local population and the experience gained during the statutory period.

5. Conclusion

As the rehabilitation plan for the medieval district of 'La Cava' was approved only recently, it is impossible to anticipate the administrative measures which the town

Orvieto: Via della Cava where large-scale changes are envisaged under the rehabilitation plan.

Orvieto: Via del Popolo: other old streets in upper Orvieto are in urgent need of renewal.

council will take in order to guarantee its implementation. At
any rate, it is clear that the renewal schemes are destined to
remain a dead letter if they are not accompanied by a
thorough discussion covering all the subjects in question
and if there is no opportunity for making positive contributions. Hence, there is a need for a phase of public participation. But it must be more extensive and deeper than that
envisaged by the law during the notification period, especially if one wishes to direct initiative and private enterprise
towards higher social goals.

NETHERLANDS

Netherlands

LEGAL – ORGANISATIONAL –
FINANCIAL – ASPECTS
OF PRESERVATION

1. Legislation

1.1 Laws

Monuments and Historic Buildings Act: Monuments and Sites: In the Netherlands, features of special architectural or historic interest in town and country are protected under the provisions of the Monuments and Historic Buildings Act, which came into force in 1961. 'Monuments' are defined by the Act as follows:

1) all buildings or objects not less than fifty years old that are oft benefit to the community as a whole on account of their beauty, scientific importance or ethnological value;

2) sites which are of benefit to the community as a whole because they contain buildings or objects referred to in 1.;

3) all buildings, objects and sites of benefit to the community as a whole because of their historical associations.

These monuments qualify for protection under Section 1 of the Act.

Surroundings: The main emphasis of the Act is on the historic building or object itself and not on the wider context of the monument and its surroundings. In order to preserve large historical sites, the Monuments and Historic Buildings Act contains provisions for the protection of the environment important to monuments. Under the Act, monuments and their surroundings are designated as conservation areas; these consist of parts of towns or villages which still retain a distinct historical character. The Monuments and Historic Buildings Act defines a conservation area as "a group of immovables, i.e. trees, roads, streets and squares, bridges, canals waterways, ditches and other expanses of water which, in conjunction with a monument belonging to the group, make up an area of benefit to the community as a whole on account of its beauty or character."

After designation, the municipal authorities must draw up a local development plan within a period of one year – sometimes extended to two. A conservation area may often be divided of the buildings in it and its structure and different degrees of protection apply in different zones.

Complementary Legislation: The Monuments and Historic Buildings Act is not the only piece of legislation which determines the future of monuments, sites and building or objects of historical interest. The Housing Act and the Town and Country Planning Act are two important additional pieces of legislation which directly or indirectly determine the fate of monuments. Conservation areas in towns and villages are not covered by the permits and penal regulations of the Monuments and Historic Buildings Act but are dealt with by the other two acts. Moreover, as has already been stated, local development plans have to be drawn up for every conservation area and these plans are a direct consequence of the Town and Country Planning Act, which lays down the legal framework for various forms of land use planning: the regional development plan at provincial level and the structure plan and local development plan at local level. Local development plans are used to determine the ways in which given areas of a municipality are to be developed over a certain period; besides laying down the kind of development which is to take place, they establish a set of regulations for the use which may be made of the land and the buildings on it. Local development plans are drawn up by the local councils themselves which means that the practical aspects of protection are in the first instance the responsibility of the local authority.

There are in addition a number of more specific regulations supplementary to the Monuments and Historic Buildings Act, which make it possible for problems arising from the application of the Act to be dealt with more effectively. The decree on financial aid for renovation (1971) is of major importance when all or part of a town centre or a village centre is to be designated as a conservation area.

It provides for government grants towards the restoration of premises situated in a designated conservation area, even though the premises themselves are not protected under the Monuments and Historic Buildings Act. The object of this arrangement is to provide municipalities with conservation areas with more financial assistance for the maintenance of these areas. Municipalities wishing to take advantage of this arrangement must draw up a renovation plan for the area in question, specifying all premises they wish to have restored or improved.

Another piece of legislation of major importance for monuments and groups of historic buildings in town centres is the Urban Renewal Act, which is expected to come into force in about the middle of 1977. Many of the plans for town centres have been made in anticipation of the new law under which local authorities will be able to designate urban renewal areas, that is areas where a more integrated form of urban renewal will take place than one which merely approaches the problem from the point of view of town planning. This means paying considerable attention to economic, social and cultural problems.

An important aspect is the fact that the new Act provides for substantial state aid, which will enable the process of urban renewal to be accelerated. However, it would be wrong not to point out the negative effects on monuments of some of these statutory measures such as the decree on contributions towards reconstruction and urban clearance plans, known as the 80 % scheme, under which the State contributes 80 % towards the purchase of premises designated for demolition in slum clearance areas. This has been responsible for the demolition of numerous premises with historical associations which according to modern thinking could well have been restored.

1.2 Monuments and Historic Buildings Act: categories

Objects: The Monuments and Historic Buildings Act specifies three main categories:

1) a large category of objects and sites which are valuable as monuments,

2) a smaller category of objects and sites that qualify for protection, and

3) the smallest category of monuments which are actually protected.

These distinctions reflect the selection procedure between the initial registration of a large number of objects and sites and the eventual listing of a smaller number of monuments in a statutory register.

The present situation is as follows:

Monuments as per 1 October 1975

Government buildings	625
Fortifications	609
Church buildings	2237
Church buildings listed because of part of the building or an object in it	437
Buildings and dwellings	27994
Buildings and dwellings listed because of a specific feature, e.g. gable, coachhouse, archway	373
Charitable institutions, e.g. orphanages, almshouses	339
Agricultural buildings, e.g. farmhouses	4859
Mills	1038
Roadworks or waterworks, e.g. sluices	289
Catering establishments, e.g. inns	137
Castles	262
Separate objects (not included in the above), e.g. posts, sundials, arches, boulders	813
Total	40012

Source: Central Statistical Office.

The smaller monuments, that is dwellings, form the largest single protected category, but, relatively speaking, the highest number of complete restorations have been carried out on larger monuments of cultural and historical importance. Although theoretically all listed monuments enjoy equal protection, until recently thorough repairs and restoration were carried out mainly on these larger monuments. In the last few years the restoration of dwellings has also received considerable attention. The statutory protection of monuments listed under the Monuments and Historic Buildings Act does not vary according to the nature of the monument as all monuments enjoy equal protection, under Section 14 of the Monuments and Historic Buildings Act.

The great problem with statutory protection is in enforcing it. By far the majority of offences are likely to escape notice; first because some are committed inside the monument and second because the authorities – in this case the Department for the Preservation of Monuments and Historic Buildings – simply do not have the manpower to investigate offences. Even if a person is convicted, the penalty is often insufficiently severe to act as a deterrent to others.

Effective protection of monuments and historic buildings depends in the first place on the attitude adopted by the relevant local authorities. The onus is on the local authorities to see that conservation areas within their territory receive the protection they deserve. The local development plan they draw up should therefore be accompanied by a large number of regulations specifying how the specific character of the area is to be preserved and it is then the responsibility of the local authorities to see that these regulations are observed.

Surroundings/Zones: A monument's immediate surroundings fall in fact outside the law, there being scarcely any reference to them in the Monuments and Historic Buildings Act. How far a monument remains in surroundings more or less in keeping with it depends on the local town planning and building regulations and on development plans, if any. A number of development plans for parts of town centres or for villages contain town planning provisions which could operate both to the advantage and to the detriment of monuments and historic buildings. The surroundings of a monument can only be protected if they are designated as a conservation area by means of a local development plan which the municipality concerned is obliged to draw up. The plan is not approved by the provincial and national authorities until the opinion of the highest advisory body, the Monuments and Historic Buildings Council, has been heard.

Separate mention should be made of those features of a conservation area which are regarded as essential to the whole because they determine the appearance of a particular scene. Such objects are not always monuments according to the law, but are included in renovation plans for conservation areas in a separate category of buildings and objects qualifying for protection. Funds are allotted for their improvement or restoration just as they are for official monuments.

1.3 Procedures

Monuments become protected when they are listed in the monuments register. The Monuments and Historic Buildings Act lays down that such a register shall be kept of monuments protected by the State. It is the duty of the Monuments and Historic Buildings Council set up under the Monuments and Historic Buildings Act – assisted in its preparatory work by the Department for the Preservation of Monuments and Historic Buildings – to draw up a list of the monuments, which in the view of the Council qualify for protection, for every municipality containing monuments. The Monuments and Historic Buildings Council is the leading consultative and advisory body under the Monuments and Historic Buildings Act. In 1903, the first register known as the Provisional List of Dutch Historical and Artistic Monuments was begun. This Provisional List has since been used as an important starting point by local authorities drawing up their lists for the Monuments and Historic Buildings Council. The draft register was completed in 1969. The procedure for drawing up the lists which together form the register is as follows.

In the preparatory stages, the services of the Department for the Preservation of Monuments and Historic Buildings are enlisted. The list drawn up by the Monuments and Historic Buildings Council is sent to the Minister for Cultural Affairs, Recreation and Social Work who then sends it to the Provincial Executive and the municipalities concerned. The draft submitted to the local authorities contains a list of premises within their territory which are considered worthy of protection.

At the same time, the owner and any other persons with rights in respect of the property are sent notice by registered letter that their premises have been provisionally listed. They can make their views known to the Minister for Cultural Affairs, Recreation and Social Work. From that moment the listed premises are temporarily protected for a maximum of two years. After the Provincial Executive , local authorities and owners (or persons with rights in respect of the property) have been given the opportunity to express their views, the Monuments and Historic Buildings Council makes a new recommendation and the Minister then decides on the final list.

An appeal may be made against the Minister's decision to list a building within two months of the date of the letter announcing its listing. An appeal may be lodged by the local authorities and Provincial Executive and by the private owner or persons with rights in respect of the property. On the whole local authorities have reacted favourably to the provisional lists. In 1966, five years after the Monuments and Historic Buildings Act came into force, the response from local authorities indicated that the numbers of listed monuments had fallen by 10% to 15%. Most of the objections raised by the local authorities concentrated on the following points: curtailment of their freedom in cases where they considered certain traffic schemes or clearance plans necessary; the fear that healthy economic growth might be hampered; uneasiness at this new form of state interference in municipal affairs.

A protected monument may only be demolished if a demolition permit is granted by the Minister for Cultural Affairs, Recreation and Social Welfare, who takes his decision within six months (possibly extended to twelve months), after hearing the Provincial Executive, local authorities and Monuments and Historic Buildings Council. The decision is taken under the terms of Section 14 of the Monument Act.

A major problem as far as the lists of monuments are concerned is the age criterion, whereby an object or building must be fifty years old to be classified as a monument. This means that a monuments list is not of a final nature. The present lists cover a period up to about 1850 and include comparatively few objects of later origins although many objects originating from since 1850 already qualify for protection. Countless buildings from this period which could be protected are of an entirely different nature from the buildings and other objects now protected as monuments. A modest start has been made to register them. Yet protection cannot be postponed too long, since many of these buildings are likely to disappear prematurely or become irreparably mutilated as a result of the pace at which society is developing. Moreover, more and more "old" objects are quaifying for protection, partly because of changing ideas as to what is valuable enough to be preserved for the future. Particularly when the harmonious combination of the constituent elements of conservation areas is important, there is an incentive to include simple monuments like small dwellings and workshops on the monument list.

As well as the monuments register there is a special register of conservation areas which is compiled in the following way. The Department for the Preservation of Monuments and Historic Buildings drafts a proposal for the designation of a conservation area, together with the relevant arguments. The proposal is submitted to the Monuments and Historic Buildings Council, which then makes a recommendation to the Minister for Cultural Affairs, Recreation and Social Work. After consultation has taken place between the Minister for Cultural Affairs, Recreation and Social Work and the Minister of Housing and Town and Country Planning (who is involved because a monument not only has to be protected, but a certain area also has to be planned) who both have to agree that protection is desirable, the local authorities in question, the Provincial Executive, the Monuments and Historic Buildings Council, and the Government Planning Board, are then informed of their decision.

1.4 Authorities

The protection of monuments and the care of conservation areas is primarily the concern of local authorities which determine the importance of the historical objects present within their municipal territory. In the first place, municipalities can purchase monuments and then repair or restore them. They can also encourage private owners to restore their own property by providing them with subsidies. In addition, under the terms of the Housing Act (in this case local building regulations) the local authorities can summon private owners to improve historic buildings or monuments in their possession.

The local authorities have an important task as far as conservation areas are concerned in that they are obliged to draw up development plans for them. Here, too, the central government plays a part since the approval required from the Provincial Executive can only be obtained after the opinion of the Monuments and Historic Buildings Council has been heard.

1.5 Compensation

Living and working in premises listed as historic buildings or monuments may have financial drawbacks for the owner. If he wishes to carry out alterations or improvements to the premises, he may only do so provided these are in keeping with the character of the premises as a monument.

There is no financial compensation for adverse effects of listing the premises as a historic building or monument. On the other hand, alterations and adaptations are carried out as far as possible by the owner and the responsible authorities in cooperation with one another. Permits for alterations are required for every alteration, whether to the inside or the outside of the premises, and also for extensions.

Applications should be accompanied by the necessary plans, in duplicate, which are then examined by an architect at the Department for the Preservation of Monuments and Historic Buildings. The Department also asks the provincial and local authorities for their advice and then submits a recommendation to the Minister. The Minister takes a decision and notifies the applicant that he has been granted or refused a permit.

The general rule at the moment is that if alterations are to be made to protected historic buildings or monuments it makes no difference whether or not they are situated in a conservation area. At the same time, designating all or part of a town centre may create considerable economic problems in the future, since it is by no means intended to freeze a historic situation – on the contrary the idea is to ensure that town centres continue to function in keeping with the exigencies of modern times.

1.6 Integration of preservation into development policy

National policy: There are various laws and national regulations that are of importance for the preservation of monuments and historic buildings. The most important of these is the Town and Country Planning Act (1965) which provides the legal framework for future planning and development in municipalities or provinces or parts of them. The Act is important for the development and planning of conservation areas as the municipal authorities are obliged to draw up development plans for such areas in accordance with the Act. The Urban Renewal Act which is in the course of preparation is a further piece of legislation by means of which the government is trying to approach the whole problem of town centres and to carry out urgently necessary urban renewal in a more purposeful manner. In fact it is an extension of the Town and Country Planning Act, which deals more specifically with the central areas of towns. Renewal areas will be designated in these central areas and improvements and/or redistribution plans will have to be drawn up for them. Improvement means that the neighbourhood in question need not really be altered from a planning or architectural point of view. These measures will have an important effect as far as the monuments and historic buildings in town centres are concerned. Through them it will in fact be possible to maintain any kind of building which from the physical point of view and as regards usefulness is considered worth restoring, whether or not it is a monument or historic building, by means of the substantial flow of funds expected under the new Act. This is particularly important for small monuments and distinctive premises not on the monuments list and not part of a conservation area. The bill also creates new ways of protecting urban structures including the surroundings of all restored monuments and historic buildings against all kinds of decay.

A number of the larger municipalities have already started to adopt such an intergrated policy.

There are a number of national regulations that are of significance for urban renewal and for the preservation of monuments and historic buildings.

Besides the decree on financial aid for renovation (1971) another important regulation is the decree on contributions towards reconstruction and urban clearance plans (see above). The scheme has recently been altered so that money is paid out even if the buildings are not demolished.

The national regulations provide the framework within which care for monuments can be given shape and may have a direct or indirect effect on monuments and groups of historic buildings. They may also work to the detriment of monuments, such as when a financial incentive is offered for demolition. In the past many of the regulations have been uncoordinated; they were intended for one particular policy sector and insufficient attention was paid to possible adverse consequences in other sectors. The Urban Renewal Bill ist expected to provide an integrated policy framework to remedy this state of affairs.

Provincial policy: Provincial authorities issue grants for the restoration of monuments and are involved in all procedures concerning municipal monuments lists.

Provincial authorities may also work out development plans for part of their provincial territory, which are then known as regional plans. These plans have no direct effect on the appearance of towns and villages or the situation as regards their monuments. There are, however, numerous indirect consequences. A regional plan is a steering instrument for the content of municipal development plans and may therfore have consequences for the historic character of a town, village or region.

Municipal policy: It is only recently that there has been any question of a particular kind of integration of the preservation of monuments into municipal policy as a whole, for which there are a number of reasons. The main one is

undoubtedly the fact that local authorities have gradually come to realise that demolishing old buildings is not the most suitable way of regenerating a town centre.

It has become more attractive for local authorities to draw up development plans (structure plans or local development plans) for villages or towns in which the restoration and maintenance of monuments and historic buildings or properties plays an important part. Previously, monuments had only been effectively protected if their cultural and historical value was generally recognised. In such cases they were actually taken into account in municipal policy as a whole and funds available for the preservation and restoration of monuments were set aside for them. As a result numerous other less important monuments fell into decay or disappeared from towns or villages. At present two things are of importance in determining to what extent the preservation of monuments and historic buildings becomes an integral part of municipal policy:

1) The extent to which regulations and measures governing restoration and renovation are compatible with the actual situation in towns and villages. The more consistent the government is in its policy, the easier it will be to conduct an effective restoration and renovation policy at local level.

2) The local authorities must be capable of fitting in the preservation of monuments and ancient buildings in their territory with all other social, economic and town planning developments in the municipality, and be willing to do so. They will then have to formulate their plans in the shape of a municipal policy in which the preservation of monuments and historic buildings functions alongside and together with all other policy sectors, as one of the means by which certain democratically conceived social, economic, cultural and historical aims can be achieved . The first signs of this kind of municipal policy are already visible in the Netherlands. An important study on past, present and future municipal policy with regard to monuments and historic buildings was recently made by the European Local Authorities Council.
(Town Centres and Monuments, Maastricht 1976).

2. Organisation

2.1 Legislative competence

Under the Monuments and Historic Buildings Act the main responsibility for the preservation of monuments and historic buildings lies with the central government, and in particular with the Minister for Cultural Affairs, Recreation and Social Work. It is the Minister who, after considering the draft lists submitted by the provincial and local authorities, finally decides which monuments and historic buildings are to be listed. The government also issues prohibition orders. It provides grants for owners who wish to restore monuments and historic buildings and ensures that they are described, photographed and scientifically documented.

Both provincial and local authorities have considerable influence in the monuments and historic buildings policy as a whole, primarily in drawing up the lists of monuments and historic buildings.

2.2 Administrative authorities responsible for protection

The preparation and implementation of measures affecting the preservation of monuments and historic buildings is in the hands of the Ministry of Cultural Affairs, Recreation and Social Work, where the Museums, Monuments and Archives Department has special responsibility for monuments and historic buildings. A large proportion of the practical work in this field is delegated to the Department for the Preservation of Monuments and Historic Buildings. It was set up in 1946 to continue the work of the government department of the same name founded in 1918. The tasks of the Department for the Preservation of Monuments and Historic Buildings are as follows.:

a. To supervise the maintenance and preservation of immovables, i.e. monuments and historic buildings. These duties are carried out by the Monuments Management Department, consisting of architects, town planners, builders, draughtsmen and other staff. The fact that monuments and historic buildings are only the property of the state in exceptional circumstances means that restoration is supervised by private architects chosen by the owners, subject to ministerial approval. The main job of the Department for the Preservation of Monuments and Historic Buildings is to monitor and correct. Its staff advises the owner of a monument or historic building as to the architectural measures which are necessary or desirable and help him choose an architect. They determine the architectural, historical and artistic value of the restoration plans submitted by the architect and advise the Minister accordingly. They discuss the choice of a builder with the owner and his architect. The Department's architect conducts regular supervision of the restoration work. He consults those involved and if he considers a restoration plan should be altered or amended in the light of architectural or historical factors which emerge, he makes a recommendation to this effect. The Department's town planners prepare the designation of conservation areas and deal with town-planning problems around the preservation of monuments and historic buildings.

b. To continue and complete "Geillustreerde Beschrijvingen der Nederlandse Monumenten van Geschiedenis en Kunst" (Illustrated Descriptions of Historic and Artistic Monuments in the Netherlands). The publication was started on the government's initiative in 1903 and so far eighteen volumes have been published on different parts of the Netherlands. The History of Art Division has been commissioned by the Monuments and Historic Buildings Council to draw up an inventory of monuments which qualify for protection under the Monuments and Historic Buildings Act. The History of Art Division is also responsible for the management and upkeep of the library, the archives of photographs and drawings, town planning records, the Architectural Documentation Centre of the Netherlands in Amsterdam (for architecture after 1850), and for photographic and other documentary activities within the Department for the Preservation of Monuments and Historic Buildings.

c. To prepare and carry out measures for the protection of monuments in the event of disasters or war, including the implementation of the Treaty of The Hague on the protection of cultural goods in case of armed conflict (1954) – within the framework of the civil defence organisation.

The Department for the Protection of Monuments and Historic Buildings is organised in such a manner that there are very few separate local offices, except in municipalities where there are a large number of monuments and historic buildings.

2.3 Public institutions

The Monuments and Historic Buildings Act lays down that there shall be a Monuments Council consisting of no less than twenty and no more than forty members appointed by the Minister. The work of the Monuments and Historic Buildings Council is divided into the following five divisions:

Division I	the National Archaeological Field Survey Commission
Division II	the National Historic Monuments Commission
Division III	the National Museums Commission
Division IV	the National Commission for the Description of Monuments
Division V	the National Commission for the Protection of Monuments against Disasters and War Damage.

Divisions II und IV are of particular importance. The fact that they frequently hold joint meetings indicates their close relationship with one another. The National Commission for the Description of Monuments has an important task in advising the Minister of the draft lists of protected monuments. Although the first draft lists were completed in 1969, the Commission still has an important advisory task, not only as regards keeping the lists up-to-date, but mainly in supplying advice on the registration of monuments and historic buildings dating from after 1850 which were deliberately excluded from the 1969 list. Another of the Commission's duties is to coordinate the Geillustreerde Beschrijvingen der Nederlandse Monumenten van Geschiedenis en Kunst. The National Historic Monuments Commission considers that part of its task is to advise and comment on policy with regard to the restoration of monuments and historic buildings. Since the sums set aside for the restoration of monuments and historic buildings are by no means proportionate to the amount required, the Commission constantly emphasises the need to increase the total amount available for restoration grants. The National Historic Monuments Commission also devotes attention to the general importance of the preservation of monuments and historic buildings and is currently using slogans like "home and living environment" to emphasise the social significance of the preservation of monuments. The Commission has a more specific advisory task when important restoration or demolition permits are required for protected monuments and historic buildings. The Commission is responsible for advising the Provincial Executive on local development plans submitted for approval in connection with conservation areas or alterations to them. Finally, the Monuments Council makes official reports for the supreme advisory body in the Netherlands, the Council of State, consisting of recommendations on appeals made to the Crown against the definitive listing of buildings as monuments or the designation of conservation areas.

To give shape to provincial or local policy regarding the preservation of monuments and historic buildings, special monuments committees have been created in some provinces and municipalities. In some cases there is a joint monuments and amenities committee.

2.1 Private associations

There are numerous private organisations in the Netherlands operating in the field of the preservation of monuments and historic buildings, some at national level, others at provincial, regional or local level.

Some of these national organisations will now be discussed in more detail.

The Heemschut League

The Heemschut League was founded in 1911. Its aim is "to protect what is beautiful in the Netherlands" in the broadest possible sense. The League is actively involved in government policy on monuments and historic buildings and acts as an advisory body to all those concerned with the preservation of monuments and historic buildings as well as publishing its own magazine. The League had more than 8,000 members in 1973 and received financial contributions from approximately 600 sources, including official and voluntary prganisations and local authorities. Most of the League's activities take place at local and regional level.

Koninklijke Oudheidkundige Bond (The Royal Netherlands Archaeological Society)

The society was founded in 1899. It studies historic architecture and makes critical evaluations of the suitability of the methods used in restoration. It tries to introduce basic general rules for the restoration of historic buildings and it arranges publicity and makes all kinds of contacts aimed at increasing the knowledge of Dutch historic and artistic monuments.

The Society publishes its own journal, the Bulletin. It has approximately 1,200 members including numerous archaeologists, archivists, art historians and architects.

Vereniging Hendrick de Keyser (Hendrick de Keyser Association)

This association was founded in 1918 with the object of purchasing certain premises that were important from an architectural or historical point of view and preserving them. The association obtains funds for acquisition and restoration from the issue of bonds. The association has 2,000 members.

De Monumentenwacht (The Monuments Guard)

This national association was founded in 1975 with the object of working out preventive measures for the preservation of historic buildings and for combating decay as far as possible. To achieve this, objects are inspected regularly and if necessary minor repairs are carried out on the spot. In undertaking these activities the association aims to shift the emphasis from repressive to preventive preservation. At present the association is active in six of the eleven Dutch provinces.

Vereniging tot Behoud van Monumenten van Bedrijf an Techniek.

This association was set up in June 1976. Its activities consist of taking stock of industrial and technical monuments and preserving them. It intends to purchase monuments and historic buildings in this field and, operating as a trust, to open them as museums to the general public.

Nationale Contactcommissie voor de Monumentenbescherming (National Contact Commission for the Protection of Monuments).

This association was founded in 1972 by the Bond Heemschut, Koninklijke Nederlandse Oudheidkundige Bond, Vereniging Hendrick de Keyser, Stichting Menno van Coehoorn, Vereniging de Hollandsche Molen, Nederlandse Kastelenstichting, Amsterdamse Mij. tot Stadsherstel and ANWB, the Royal Dutch Touring Club.Its objective is to coordinate private initiatives in the field of preservation and to present a united approach to the outside world. In addition, efforts are made by means of scientific study, publications and close contacts with all bodies and organisations involved in protection, to promote the preservation of monuments and historic buildings in the widest sense.

For several years organisations concerned with urban reconstruction have existed in various municipalities. Although not all of them have exactly the same aims, a fairly consistent pattern is perceptible. For example, a primary purpose of these organisations is to carry out the restoration of dwellings thus relieving the burden on the municipal authorities. These organisations have their own basic capital, part of which they obtain from the local authorities (and sometimes from trade and industry or other interests) and part of which they borrow on the capital market. With the help of these funds they purchase premises, which they then restore. They usually rent the premises again afterwards and add the revenue to their basic capital.

Occasionally, housing corporations play an active part in repairing and restoring historical buildings. Recently, organisations which invest on a large scale and large building concerns have shown some interest in restoration projects in town centres.

3. Finance

3.1 Purchase of monuments

The central government, in the form of the Ministry of Cultural Affairs, Recreation and Social Work, only occasionally purchases historical objects for the purpose of restoring them. In such cases these are usually monuments or historic buildings of national interest which no other organisation has been able to purchase and restore. This was the case, for example, with Het Loo, the palace near Apeldoorn. On the other hand, the government itself owns a large number of buildings of which a considerable number are listed as monuments. The provincial authorities hardly ever buy monuments for restoration.

3.2 Restoration of monuments

In 1975 Fls. 76 mill. were allocated for grants and other expenditures for the preservation of monuments and historic buildings. The owner of a monument or historic building who wishes to receive assistance from public funds towards the cost of its maintenance may apply for a government grant if the building needs restoring. The government may give grants for restoration, but there are no automatic rights in this respect. At national level, the grants are allocated by the Ministry of Cultural Affairs, Recreation and Social Work. The provincial and local authorities may also provide owners with grants for the restoration of monuments but these only cover repairs to the actual buildings, for example repairing or replacing foundations, cellars, gables, outside or inside walls, beams and roofs. No financial aid is provided for improvements, adaptations or additions which are not expressly related to the historic character of the building, even if there is no objection to them from a historical point of view. This includes expenditure involved in installing modern facilities such as sanitation or central heating, or adapting a building to economic functions. At national level, the grants are issued by the Minister of Cultural Affairs, Recreation and Social Work, who takes his decision after consulting his official advisers. The size of a grant depends on numerous factors.

It is usual at present for private owners of dwellings or other historic buildings to be given grants amounting to 30 % of the restoration costs which qualify for a subsidy. If the grant is issued jointly by the local and provincial authorities, the former usually pays 30 % and the latter 10 %.

The normal grant paid by the state towards the restoration of churches is 50 % of the cost of restoration. The local and provincial authorities usually pay 30 % and 10 % respectively. Exceptions may be made to these arrangements, particularly when a project is very costly and very time-consuming. In the city of Utrecht, for example, five churches belonging to the Dutch Reformed Church are at present undergoing restoration. In view of the size of the sum required the state provides 66 ½ % (now 61 %), the provincial authorities 7½ % and the local authorities the normal grant of 25 % (now 30 %), so that only 1 % of the cost which qualifies for a grant – and the total cost which does not – has to be borne by the owner, the Dutch Reformed Church. The normal government grant towards the restoration of monuments belonging to public bodies is 40 %. Associations concerned with the restoration and maintenance of monuments can reckon on a government grant of between 40 % and 50 % of the cost of restoration.

Special government grants are given for renovation under the decree on financial support for rehabilitation (1971), which has since been amended. On the basis of renovation plans drawn up by the local authorities, the Ministry of Cultural Affairs, Recreation and Social Work and the Ministry of Housing and Town and Country Planning provide subsidies for the restoration or improvement of dwellings either listed as monuments or considered as essential features of the appearance of a town. The main object of this is to provide more financial scope for local authorities containing conservation areas. The money from the Ministry of Housing and Town and Country Planning is made available to municipalities for the renovation of both municipal and private property. This may amount to up to 35 % of the total cost of renovation. The maximum amount is 35 % of the total cost of renovation. The maximum amount is 35 % of Fls. 150,000 for each dwelling renovated. This is supplemented by contributions from the Department for the Preservation of Monuments and Historic Buildings and the provincial and local authorities, via the improvement regulations for monuments.

The procedure in the various cases is as follows:

a. From the Ministry of Housing and Physical Planning: 35 % of Fls. 150,000 for each dwelling to be renovated (maximum);

b. From the Ministry of Cultural Affairs, Recreation and Social Work; for private property 30 % and for municipal property 40 % of half the total cost of renovation (to an unlimited amount for listed monuments, otherwise to a maximum of Fls. 150,000);

c. From the provincial authorities: usually 10 % of half the cost of renovation;

d. From the local authorities: 30 % of half the cost of renovation, to be paid back from the municipal funds in 25 annual annuities on the grounds of the improvement regulations for monuments.

A number of Dutch municipalities have such renovation plans or are in the process of drawing them up. The amount of restoration so far undertaken on the strength of this decree is still fairly limited, which is not surprising considering the recent nature of the measure.

A regulation was introduced by the government in 1965 to enable grants to be provided without imposing an undue financial burden on the local authorities. The regulation is called the decree on specific rules governing general grants for monuments and contains provisions whereby the local authorities may frequently be reimbursed for a large proportion of the amount they spend on restoration grants, via the municipal fund. This often makes restoration a paying proposition. In various municipalities with large numbers of monuments and historic buildings a regulation has been introduced wherby, roughly, government and local authorities allocate an equal amount annually, mainly for subsidising the restoration of dwellings.

This is known as the dwellings fund.

It is hoped with the help of this regulation to achieve more systematic restoration of dwellings in the municipalities in question and to arrive at a certain continuity. At the moment this fund is somewhat of a problem as the government is unable to release sufficient funds to increase it annually to keep pace with the growing number of applications for grants.

The aim of the regulation is to achieve a more systematic approach to the restoration of monuments and historic buildings in the category of dwellings. Another objective is to enable money to be provided for immediate restoration where necessary and some of the money ist therefore reserved for such purposes. The regulation does not cover the restoration of large monuments and historic buildings, for which government grants are often only made available several years after the work has actually begun and the project been approved for a grant. Within the framework of measures introduced since 1973 to combat unemployment, considerable sums are made available annually for the restoration of monuments. In 1974 the government allocated approximately Fls. 30,816,000 in this way. The work undertaken in this connection was to be completed by 1975. In 1975, 421 objects were included in the scheme to provide extra employment, for which a total additional amount of nearly Fls. 81,000,000 was allocated. These grants, which were financed by the Ministry of Social Affairs, were given on condition the work would be completed within a period of twelve months.

There has been a considerable increase in the number of applications for grants. In 1975, for example, 1947 applications were received, an increase of 17.5 % compared with 1974. At present there are over 2,000 applications waiting to be dealt with. As it is impossible to deal with them in the short term on the basis of the normal budget, restoration is often postponed longer than is justified. Moreover, a large proportion of the budget often has to be used to meet commitments made in previous years, including inevitable price increases. This means that there is not very much money for new projects. As a result, objects that have not yet been restored sometimes deteriorate to such an exent that the cost of restoration increases accordingly. Maintenance is an extremely serious problem at present as far as the restoration of monuments and historic buildings in the Netherlands is concerned. The present Monuments and Historic Buildings Act lays no obligation on the owner of a monument to maintain it in good condition. The Monument Bill did contain a clause to that effect, but it was considered too much of a burden on owners and was therefore deleted. It was also feared that it might be counter-productive, since the owner of a monument might have wilfully neglected it in order to force the government to give him a grant. Moreover, Parliament objected to a provision empowering the Minister to force the owner of a protected monument to carry out the necessary maintenance or repairs. Consequently owners have no statutory obligations in this respect. Grants are given on condition that owners look after their monuments properly, but in fact this stipulation has very little effect; grants are not given for maintenance. This situation is being examined to see how it can be improved.

4. Public Involvement

4.1 Adult education

The press

In general, information in daily newspapers is restricted to straightforward "news" regarding monuments and their care, to such things as the announcement of demolition, renovation or restoration plans affecting well-known monuments or historic buildings, fires and all other disasters, municipal plans that are likely to have a drastic effect on the local situation around monuments or historic buildings, and committees or associations concerned with monuments. The preservation of monuments and historic buildings is not important enough to merit a regular column in the weekly papers whereas urban renewal is. The many developments of a legal, administrative or financial nature in this field, the numerous things actually happening and the activities of action groups often mean that this subject is dealt with by a journalist who is a specialist in the field. Since urban renewal directly affects the preservation of monuments and historic buildings the latter is coming to be increasingly discussed under the former heading.

As things stand at present in the Netherlands, the organisations that enjoy the most publicity in the press and also make considerable publicity for themselves are those which can together be described as action groups. They campaign for clearly defined aims such as the maintenance or restoration of a neighbourhood, they oppose the demolition or alteration of specific monuments and historic buildings, fight against large-scale road construction in historic city centres and maintain critical opposition against the authorities' plans for historic city centres. Groups of this kind regard information in the press as a highly suitable means of exerting political pressure.

Radio and television: Each of the eight broadcasting organisations has a different philosophical or ideological basis, as a comparision of their programmes shows. For example, those broadcasting organisations which, by nature of their principles, are concerned with social problems, broadcast programmes dealing with the social background to the problems around monuments and historic buildings. Often this is as part of a programme on urban renewal; the central theme ist then the human environment at home and at work. The more "neutral" broadcasting organisations emphasize the cultural and historical value of monuments and their special beauty. This enables them to make programmes on subjects such as urban or village renewal, in which the human environment is the main theme and monuments are also mentioned, and on subjects directly concerning monuments and their preservation.

However, these programmes are in no sense a regular feature of broadcasting as they are not made regularly or shown at fixed times. There are however a few exceptions such as a weekly programme on regional topics which always includes reports on monuments and their preservation. During the summer months there are one or two programmes on travel which feature monuments and history. Television programmes for schools include courses indirectly connected with monuments, such as those on town planning or urban renewal.

Adult education centres (Volkshogescholen): The Dutch Volkshogescholen provide a wide range of courses every year on a wide variety of subjects. Although a separate course has not been set up on monuments and their preservation, these issues are dealt with in those courses on urban renewal, participation and the protection of the environment.

Correspondence courses: The Stichting ter Bevordering van de Nederlandse Bouwkunst (Association for the Promotion of Dutch Architecture) and Leidse Onderwijsinstellingen (the Leyden Institute for Correspondence Study) have combined to set up a course on architecture. The object is to arouse an active interest in monuments and historic buildings and to broaden knowledge in this field.

4.2 Schools

History is first taught at primary school level (6–12 age group). The lessons at this stage are of a general nature and the emphasis is on Dutch history. In this connection the children learn something about monuments and historic buildings.

At secondary school level (13–18 age group) more variety is introduced but the way in which history and the history of art are taught depends on the type of school. If the teacher and/or pupils wish to lay greater emphasis on historical architecture or on the preservation of monuments and historic buildings this is certainly possible. Efforts are made to show the past as tangibly as possible by means of slides, excursions and meetings and by the use of materials designed specially for teaching purposes by experts, some of them from the Department for the Preservation of Monuments and Historic Buildings. This aspect of history teaching received special attention during the 1975 European Architectural Heritage Year when numerous activities were organised at national, provincial and local level in which schools could participate.

At the level of higher education, that is higher technical

training and university, things are quite different because it is possible to specialise in history, the history of art or architecture. This can be done either on the technical side at Delft Technical University, where it is possible to take a degree in restoration techniques, or in a more general context by studying history or the history of art.

4.3 Public action groups and private organisations

In the Netherlands there are all kinds of public groups and private organisations and in the last 10 years a large number of action groups has sprung up representative of current trends in society, alongside the more traditional ones. In general these are groups of concerned members of the public who are trying, via some kind of organisation, to draw attention to matters they consider detrimental to a healthy environment in which people work and live. The problems they deal with are often local ones, though sometimes they are regional or national, the latter often in combination with other action groups. There are an estimated 2,000 groups operating at the moment. Many of them only started their work in the last few years.

The following are some of the issues that have been and still are of importance:

1. concern and sometimes indignation of the local population when historic buildings are demolished or are seen to deteriorate more and more rapidly.

2. similar concern caused by drastic events in towns, largely when large office blocks, department stores, hotels, banks, etc. have been concentrated around certain parts of a historic inner city area.

   A similar process takes place on a much smaller scale in village centres. Action groups have often succeeded in changing policy in this field.

3. problems with regard to clearance and demolition areas. People become involved either because their homes or places of work are threatened with immediate demolition without any alternative accommodation being offered in the short term, or because little or nothing is being done by the government to combat the process of deterioration and neglect that has been going on for years.

4. expecially in the larger towns, the local inhabitants of certain neighbourhoods and other interested parties form action groups to improve and preserve their own neighbourhood. People are becoming conscious of the numerous values attached to their own familiar environment in a town centre.

National action groups are the least numerous. They are nearly always well organised and they often have a professional staff and specific aims, in contrast to many of the action groups.

The following national organisations, started by private initiative, have aims that are of importance for the protection of monuments and groups of historic buildings.

1. De Raad voor Milieudefensie (The Environmental Protection Council) is an organisation which coordinates the activities of numerous local action groups dealing with the environment in the widest sense of the word. The Council has its own scientific bureau and receives a government subsidy. Although its primary concern is the conservation of the natural environment, it does also deal with historical matters. Many environmental issues can-

not be dealt with separately from actual planning. When considering whether or not countryside characterised by a particular historical form of land use or form of agriculture should be preserved, the original farms and other buildings (waterworks, mills, bridges, etc.) that form essential elements in it should be taken into consideration.

2. Het Landelijk Ombudsteam (the National Ombudsteam) for urban renewal. This was originally set up by a number of political parties in an attempt to contribute towards a more responsible form of urban renewal throughout the country. It is now to all intents and purposes a professional body. It deals mainly with "inexpensive" forms of restoration and renovation in residential areas in and around the central parts of towns. It frequently supports the activities of local action action groups at their request.

3. Even a traditional organisation like the Bond Heemschut (Heemschut League), founded in 1911 with the object of safeguarding the "beauty of the Netherlands" has in the last few years functioned more and more as a platform for the activities of local action groups interested in monuments. In cases where the character, atmosphere or beauty of a town, village or region are threatened, the Heemschut League has traditionally taken action consisting of submitting expert reports to the authorities ultimately responsible for taking decisions. The League has always tried to involve the public in such matters as far as possible. It also takes part in all kinds of procedures that allow for participation in government town and country planning policy. The League has numerous local correspondents who are often linked to or are members of an action group.

4. Het Nederlands Instituut voor Ruimtelijke Ordening en Volkshuisvesting (The Netherlands Institute for Town and Country Planning and Housing). This private organisation is an association of town and country planners, architects and others professionally involved in this field. It issues a journal entitled Stedebouw and Volkshuisvesting (Urban Development and Housing) which contains articles by experts on topics in the field of town and country planning. Quite often it contains articles on monuments and historic buildings. Because of its reputation in central and local government circles and amongst professional people as well as owing to the quality of its contents, the magazine makes an important contribution towards the formation of opinion on specific problems in the field of town and country planning policy. This applies especially to the preservation of monuments and historic buildings.

5. Werkgroep 2000 (Working Group 2000). This is a national organisation whose objective is the more satisfactory and effective participation by citizens in government planning. In the first place, the Working Group takes a critical view of developments in the field of environmental planning. In addition the Working Group is involved in more specific problems such as planning concerning historical town centres. In 1975 the Working Group was invited by Rotterdam City Council to organise public participation in the city's structure plan. The Working Group is not directly concerned with monuments; the fact that it participates in plans for town centres means that it is indirectly concerned with the fate of monuments and historic buildings.

It is not only at national level that the number of action groups is fairly small; the same really applies at the provincial and regional levels. The groups which exist are usually provincial or regional branches of big national organisations like the Environmental Protection Council. There is a society active in attempting to preserve the characteristic Dutch scenery found between the rivers and dikes and community centres in historic buildings. Efforts are made to find alternative solutions in consultation with the authorities concerned. Another society is active in attempting to restore the quality of life of small rural centres where there are fewer and fewer amenities owing to the declining population and where such buildings as churches are in danger of losing their function. Action is also taken against the fact that numerous people have second homes many of which are historic buildings.

Recently a number of working groups associated with the Delft University of Technology and with the University of Groningen and concerned with the preservation of industrial monuments have come into being. Numerous activities are undertaken at a regional level aimed at the preservation of specific categories of monuments such as mills, castles and fortresses and in such cases there is often cooperation with national organisations.

The greatest number of action groups are to be found at local level, in towns and villages. Many of them came into existence as a result of the discrepancy which arose after the Second World War between municipal policy for villages, urban districts and town centres, town planning, the social and economic consequences of this policy and the feelings of specific groups of the population regarding matters such as a "nice" town centre, an original village centre, the value of their own neighbourhood and the desire to retain those aspects of their immediate environment which remind them of the past. It is impossible to go into the reasons why all the various action groups have come into being. Fairly frequent use is made of methods not entirely acceptable in a democratic system, such as occupying premises, blockades, squatting in empty houses, or disrupting public meetings. However, the main object is to enable citizens to participate where possible in the activities of decision-making bodies. Each of the various representative bodies of every municipal council in the Netherlands is likely to find itself confronted with one or more action group. There is an increasing tendency for councils to endeavour to incorporate action groups into one or other of their institutions. In the city of Utrecht, for example, there ist an advisory council for the inner city which functions as a broad platform for those involved with or wishing to participate in matters concerning the inner city. The Council consists of interest groups and is advised by a group of experts and local officials.

The great advantage of action groups is that they can function as instruments for correcting government policy.

4.4 Participation

Participation, that is the active involvement of citizens in decision-making processes, started hesitantly in the Netherlands in the late sixties. An important part in this was and still is played by the pressure from action groups and interest groups wishing to have a say in plans concerning the future of town and country areas. The highly drastic nature of some of these plans shocked parts of the population into a response. On the other hand, the various official bodies are now becoming more and more open to public participation in drawing up the plans for which they are responsible. This is partly the result of pressure from the action groups and partly the result of the realisation by the authorities themselves that plans should be discussed with representatives from those sections of the population directly involved before being put into effect. Not unconnected with this were certain new forms of government planning which were so drastic that they would have had a direct effect on the essential interests of certain groups of the population. In particular, the renovation of urban areas such as town centres, older residential districts and industrial estates and activities affecting the original village centres in rapidly growing country settlements made it necessary for the government to extend consultation to include representatives of the frequently large groups of the population likely to be directly affected. There ist at present a very strong need for such consultations in connection with the large-scale renovation plans for areas in and around historic inner city areas, where considerable numbers of people live and work. For example, nothing can be done to a densely populated 19th century residential district without those concerned expressing their opinions. There is often little or no organisational structure within the local community so the government itself is faced with the necessity of seeing that a delegation of local residents is formed at short notice.

This projected large-scale renovation of inner urban areas involves large numbers of people living in historic buildings who are often unable to continue living in their homes after restoration because of the increased rent, the high cost of restoration and the high purchase price ot the premises. As a result of public participation these problems now stand out far more prominently than they did before and the situation outlined above has become generally recognised as a "social problem" in inner urban renewal and has developed into a political issue.

Participation occurs most in local planning but there are also certain forms of participation at the regional and national levels. For example, in the preparation of the third government memorandum on town planning, an extensive form of participation was used whereby all government bodies, national organisations, coordinated action groups, and individual citizens (either on their own or collectively) could participate. Participation procedures for all those concerned also exist in respect of important town and country plans at regional level, known as regional plans. The greatest interest in participation is at local level, which is not surprising since many of the regional and national plans are too abstract and the interests they incorporate are often too remote from the average citizen. At local level, however, the knowledge the inhabitants have of factors affecting the welfare of their own community makes problems of government planning much clearer. Above all, the consequences of the plans are far less remote as people are able to relate them directly to their own lives. This often makes participation at local level less exclusive and it is thus possible to involve a larger number of ordinary people. To organise proper participation, the government itself has devised a number of instruments. At the same time, certain methods have become accepted practice as a result of the spontaneous action of individual citizens or actions groups. For example, the local authorities have appointed numerous participation coordinators and community development workers, often working within a special semi-official organisation, the Stichting Samenlevingsopbouw (Community Development Association). These community development workes and participation advisers are often faced with a gigantic task. Large-scale renovation plans for inner urban areas which local authorities wish to carry through at short notive mean that traditional district organisations generally active in the social and recreational spheres have to be turned into discussion partners for local administrators at very short notice. A total lack of training in thinking about municipal affairs or helping to decide about them often remains a big stumbling block. As a result, participation frequently comes after the plans have been drawn up.

The aim of participation is generally to increase the awareness of the general public of all kinds of problems affecting the environment in which people live and work. This awareness then enables them to participate actively in decision-making processes and government plans are democratised. An advantage for the authorities is that this process enables them to make a responsible choice and one which is of better quality. Participation occurs increasingly through special schemes, i.e. discussion on a number of alternatives may take place at any stage of planning, the sequence of participation being that agreement is reached first of all on a number of basic points, which are subseqently explored in ever-increasing detail. What happens in practices is that structured consultations are held on several evenings at which the results of previous participation are expressed in interim draft plans. These can then be used as a basis on which to work towards setting up a more final and detailed plan. For some time now the Municipal Act has provided a statutory basis for greater participation by citizens in resolving administrative problems.

Under Sections 61 to 64 of this Act, it is possible for local authorities to delegate their powers to district councils or committees. The latter may then, under the constant supervision of the local council, take decisions on matters that directly affect the existence and surroundings of the inhabitants of the district or village. If the inhabitants are afraid of taking the responsibility for such decisions they may also choose a district committee whose task is solely advisory. At the moment "exercises" with directly representative bodies of this kind are in progress in a limited number of villages and towns.

4.5 Associations, trusts, private protection

There are a relatively large number of private organisations in the Netherlands concerned with the upkeep of monuments and historic buildings in one way or another. We do not propose to give a list of them here. The emphasis of this account will be placed on objectives and the manner in which the activities are organised. The aims of the numerous private bodies and organisations working on behalf of the preservation of monuments and historic buildings vary; some of them are more or less scientific and involve studying examples of ancient architecture, listing and describing all kinds of monuments (recently including technical and trade monuments, known as industrial monuments), issuing publications, registers and historical atlases and studying restoration methods.

Other organisations have more practical aims; their object is to find ways of preserving monuments and historic buildings threatened by local development.

To this end they endeavour by means of their own magazines, through the press and through involvement in participation and appeal procedures, to mobilise public opinion and to alter the course of the proposed policy. Certain organisations devote their attention entirely to the preservation of specific categories of monuments, such as churches, fortifications, mills and important buildings in towns.

As regards their legal status, most of them are "stichtingen" or "verenigingen" (associations), or N.V.'s (limited companies). The latter operate almost exclusively in the field of urban renewal, often as an extension of municipal inner urban policy, purchasing derelict buildings, restoring and then selling or renting them. The capital required for this is obtained by issuing shares. "Stichtingen" also operate on a basic capital raised by donors or patrons. Unlike N.V.'s (limited companies) they are non-profitmaking organisations. A "stichting" does not have members who can control the policy of its committee. A "vereniging" has both its own capital and a democratic procedure for decision-making, controlled by its members. Up to 26 July 1976 these organisations were governed by statutory rules contained in the Commercial Code (N.V.), the Wet op de Stichtingen and the Wet op Vereniging en Vergadering (Associations Act and Associations and Assembly Act). At present they are all governed by volume two of the new Civil Code.

There are four sources from which the various institutions can octain their funds, namely patrons, membership fees, government grants and investment in the form of shares. An examination of the activities of the various organisations shows that the number of monuments they have repaired or restored is fairly small. Restoration on a somewhat larger scale is not possible owing to the limited funds available nor is it often what is intended. By means of conspicuous restoration projects the institutions aim rather at mobilising public opinion by showing the public and the authorities practical examples of "how things can and should be done". It is usually deliberately left to the voluntary organisations and the government to take the initiative in urban and village renewal by repairing and restoring existing buildings. The picture has however changed considerably recently. Urban reconstruction organisations in particular (with the legal status of limited companies or "stichtingen") have extended their activities on quite a large scale in some towns. They undertake restoration that would be too costly for private individuals, they restore dwellings in places that are not easily accessible and they carry out larger restoration projects in blocks. Local authorities occasionally set up such an organisation to reconstruct an entire inner city area.

There are a few restoration projects in the Netherlands where important results have been achieved because of their original approach. Two good examples are the urban renewal project in Deventer, in the province of Overijssel, undertaken by a limited company and the restoration of the military settlement at Bourtange in the province of Groningen, undertaken by a "stichting". The activities in Deventer have served as an example for other such developments in the Netherlands as they took place at a relatively early stage. N.V. Berkgwartier, Maatschappij tot Stadsherstel (Urban Reconstruction Company), Keizerstraat 13, Deventer, founded in 1968.

The Bergkwartier in Deventer is a part of the town with its own special character. On The Berg, an ancient river dune, stands the medieval church of St. Nicolaas, to which all the streets in this part of the town lead. The buildings have both artistic and historic value: roughly 175 of the 500 or so dwellings and workshops are listed as monuments. They had deteriorated to such an extent that renovation by means of incidental repairs would have been impossible, so a working group was set up, which came to be known as

"Stichting Werkgroep Bergkwartier", to examine the problem.

The group got in touch with the local authorities in Deventer, with the Department for the Preservation of Monuments and Historic Buildings and with the Amsterdamse Maatschappij tot Stadsherstel N.V. (Amsterdam Urban Reconstruction Company Ltd.) and within a year a plan called "Herstelplan Bergkwartier" (Bergkwartier reconstruction plan) had been drawn up.

The Minister of Cultural Affairs, Recreation and Social Work set aside an employment grant of Fls. 1,500,000 for the Bergkwartier. On certain conditions, a few large insurance companies were prepared to participate in forming a limited company on the basis of ideals, to undertake the restoration and exploitation of premises in the Bergkwartier on a commercial basis project. The Stichting Werkgroep Bergkwartier then founded the N.V. Bergkwartier, Maatschappij tot Stadsherstel, and worked out a plan for financing the renovation of the Bergkwartier. Broadly speaking, it involved the employment grant, the local authority contributions, and S shares (nominal S shares, nominal value Fls. 1,000.–) for the ramainder of the selling price.

The above means that the company pays a small proportion of the price for the restored premises it purchases in cash and the rest in S shares. As S shares give only a very limited right to dividends, N.V. Bergkwartier can obtain "cheap" capital with which it can finance unprofitable aspects of further restoration. N.V. Bergkwartier, which has a company capital of Fls. 3,000,000, can then finance the profitable part of the restoration in the normal way by using the remaining share capital and mortgage loans.

Stichting Vesting Bourtange (Mezenhof 22, Ter Apel) (Fort Bourtange Stichting)
Bourtange is an unspoiled farming village in the municipality of Vlagtwedde in Westerwolde in East Groningen. What is striking about it is the unusual shape of the market square and the streets leading into it, a few charming 17th century cottages and the zigzag moat round part of the village. It is obvious that Bourtange was not originally a farming village but was built deliberately at the end of the 16th century as a military settlement with ramparts, moats and gateways.

Nowadays, Bourtange's main significance is as a holiday resort. The municipal council set up a working group to provide adequate recreational facilities and several projects have already been successfully completed.

For example a redoubt (redouté Bakoven) has been reconstructed, street lighting has been improved and street lamps have been installed that fit in with the local atmosphere, a number of sand roads in the village have been paved and the market square and the streets leading into it have been cobbled.

To be able to undertake a project of this magnitude it was necessary to raise funds and the Stichting Vesting Bourtange was set up for this purpose. Its object was to prevent Fort Bourtange from deteriorating any further by reconstructing the fort itself and the fortifications belonging to it both inside and outside the actual fort and the surrounding countryside, or at least restoring the original atmosphere, in a manner compatible with present day standards. Once it has been restored, the entire complex will be preserved as a cultural and historical monuments.

To provide the fort with adequate protection it was found necessary to list it as a conservation area. By law the next step is a regional plan, so a reconstruction plan has been drawn up according to which the fort is to be reconstructed in keeping with its 17th and 18th century origins. The following points of departure have been taken into account:

1. all historic buildings and/or remains still present and capable of being preserved in some way or other are to be retained and if possible restored
2. building will only be permitted on former building sites
3. the walls and moats are to be reconstructed
4. the roads are to be repaired and restored
5. as far as possible only inhabitants of the fort will be allowed to use motor vehicles.

The development of Bourtange does not stop with the reconstruction of the fort. The countryside around the village is equally important, both from a historic and from a recreational point of view and the counryside plan that has been drawn up is intended to give an initial idea of the structure. As will be seen from the foregoing the form of a "stichting" was chosen for development of the entire Bourtange project.

Obviously, the cultivated land will also become the property of the stichting, which will be responsible for its administration and maintenance.

Dokkum: Historical map
below: areal photograph of the historical core from the east, 1977

Netherlands
DOKKUM

1. Situation

1.1 General introduction

Dokkum is a small town situated in the extreme north of the Netherlands. It is in the province of Friesland.

The total number of inhabitants of Dokkum was 11,500 as at 1 January 1976.

1.2 History

Most Dutchmen associate Dokkum with the period of the first christianization of the Netherlands and in particular with a well-known historic event of that time, namely the murder of the Anglo-Saxon missionary Boniface by the heathen Frisians in the year 754. Dokkum was then a settlement built on a "terp" (artificial dwelling mound). The martyr's death suffered by Boniface led to Dokkum becoming a place of pilgrimage and a spiritual centre.

Due to its favourable situation on a deep inlet of the Lauwerzee, the so-called Dokkumerdiep, Dokkum was already a significant port in the early Middle Ages (11th century). The first mention of civic authorities is to be found in a charter dated 1298. Dokkum did not escape armed conflicts. In 1572 the town was plundered, burnt down and part of the population massacred by the Spanish governor, Caspar de Robles. Nevertheless Dokkum managed again and again to recover.

In the 16th and 17th centuries Dokkum flourished as an important port, which in 1597 also became the seat of the Frisian Admiralty. The structure and appearance of the present city centre of Dokkum was mainly determined in this period. Thus in the years 1581–1582 the town was equipped with a defence system of ramparts, bastions and moats. This gave the town its present hexagonal outline. The broad harbour of Dokkum, the Grootdiep, where the sea-going vessels berthed, and the old lock, the Zijl, which shut the harbour off from the inland waterways, were now enclosed within the walls. The importance of the town at that time is still to be seen in the buildings situated along this former artery. About half the total number of monuments in Dokkum is to be found there, including the town hall, with parts built in the 16th, 17th and 18th centuries, the Admiralty building (1618) and some 17th century facades.

Up to 1925, the development of the town took place principally within the ramparts. The municipal boundaries followed the farther bank of the moat, so that the area of the municipality only amounted to 32.5 hectares. One of the consequences of this was that in comparison with other Dutch towns the building density within the city walls was extremely high. Partly due to lack of opportunity for new building in the inner city, the bad residential conditions and the highly intensive use of ground by enterprises, etc., the number of inhabitants of Dokkum steadily decreased: from 4,480 in 1880 to 3,480 in 1920. Under the authority of the neighbouring municipalities, parasitic residential areas and industrial activities grew up adjacent to the inner city. Within the town, council houses and the gas works had of necessity to be built on a bastion.

Not until 1925 was there an alteration of the city boundaries, whereby the municipal territory was increased by 177.5 hectares to a total of 210 hectares. The number of inhabitants thereby rose from 3,500 (1924) to 4,850 (1925) and in 1946 the population amounted to 5,530.

Dokkum was confronted to an increasingly serious extent with the problem of rising unemployment in agriculture and the accompanying drain from the country, especially to the west of the Netherlands. Partly for this reason, Dokkum was in 1959 designated by the government as an industrial core stimulation area. The resultant need for industrial ground and opportunities for housing construction made another alteration of the municipal boundaries necessary (1966), whereby the area of the municipality increased to 760 hectares. The possibilities for structural improvement and filling in of the area round the historic town were hereby greatly enlarged. In about 1950 the first large-scale new residential area outside the town came into being, namely the so-called Westerisselanden. Other large areas followed, such as Hoedemakerspolder (1960), Fonteinslanden (1970) and Fügellän (1975). After 1941 the number of inhabitants in the inner city decreased rapidly. Whereas in 1920 it amounted to 3,480, in 1971 it was only 1,745.

1.3 City structure, characteristics

The inner city has a clear-cut structure, in which the most striking element is the broad waterway running from east to west (Grootdiep – Dokkumer Ee). It forms the main axis, which dominates the fortress from the physical aspect (and, formerly as a seaport, from the socio-economic aspect). The varying width of this waterway is almost exactly followed by the buildings on its banks, which results in a fascinating spatial interplay. Important elements herein are the fairly high buildings round the Zijl, the trees and a few accents such as the town hall with its cupola-type belfry and the mill on the south west bastion. Amongst the principal streets, which are virtually at right angles to the main axis, the Breedstraat occupies a special place. With the weigh house, reconstructed in 1752, as its southern boundary, it is the widest street in the old city centre and has not only a certain physical charm, but also functions as the principal shopping street, where, moreover, the weekly market is held. Another interesting feature is the medieval ring of moats, most of which still exist. It consists of the Westersingel, the Wortelhaven, the Oostersingel (filled in) and the connecting north-west circuit up to and including the Kloostersingel, the latter being a particularly picturesque part of the town with its profusion of trees and characteristic architecture. With the exception of the east-west axis already mentioned, the Breedstraat and the Legeweg, most of the streets are characterised by their narrow profile. The original fairly small scale of building has only been violated in a few places and the architectural pattern is still clearly expressed in the gable-topped and corniced facades.

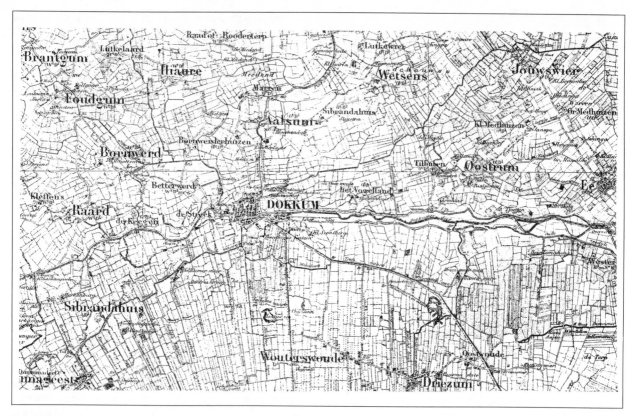

Dokkum:
above: topographical map of 1837–1838
below: topographical map of 1968. The historical core is encirled by expansions started after the Second World War

2. Conditions

2.1 Factors of intervention

Perhaps as a result of the less favourable times through which Dokkum has passed up to the recent past, a good deal of the later building is somewhat squat and sometimes unattractive. A great many one-storey houses with pitched roof are to be found not only in the narrow streets running from east to west, but also in the main streets. Round the Markt, and in particular on the north side, this leads to an unbalanced composition from the spatial point of view. Another defect is the over-intensity of building in the back yards, brought about by the limited space available in the town up to 1925. Thus it appears that of the 140,000 square metres surface area of building blocks more than 85,000 sq. metres has now been built on. With a few exceptions, no developments have taken place since the end of the last century within the ramparts which could harm the human scale of the aspect of the town. Since industrial development did not take place on a larger scale until after the Second World War, and then only in the area outside the ramparts, the town planning structure of the inner city has remained almost intact up to the present day. Only one small breakthrough was made in 1932 and this street was immediately called "Doorbraak" (Breakthrough). To relieve the pressure of traffic in the inner city a partial ring road had already been constructed in 1949 (the plans dated from before the Second World War).

The inner city of Dokkum has from of old functioned as a regional centre for the mainly agrarian area of north-west Friesland. In connection with this function it has a considerable variety of shops and a specific wholesale trade. There is also artisan industrial activity and a fairly extensive service sector. The most important shopping area is located in the centre of the old town. In the Hoogstraat and the Waagstraat the first phase of the pedestrian precinct has been completed. The other functions are spread over the entire inner city area and are not concentrated in a particular zone. The increase in the population after the Second World War was responsible in particular for the expansion of functions in the service sector. The industrial activity takes place almost entirely outside the inner city on the industrial estate. The residential function of the inner city has greatly diminished and now exists principally on the western and southern fringe of the inner city along the ramparts, on the south bank of the Klein Diep (Vleesmarkt) and by the Halvemaanspoort.

Monuments

In proportion to the other buildings and in view of the intactness of the planning pattern, the inner city does not actually possess many monuments. About half the existing monuments are situated along the Groot- and Klein Diep and recall the hey-day of the 16th and 17th century. The rest of the monuments are spread over the inner city. Nevertheless, in a number of cases they still form in conjunction with the other buildings elevations with a differentiated and lively structure.

In the framework of the protected townscapes a supplementary list has been drawn up of buildings which enhance the group effect. In the meantime the neo-gothic Roman Catholic church (Cuypers) has been placed on the list.

2.2 Past policy

In the past the municipal authorities' actions with regard to the inner city area were always governed by a certain degree of emotional consideration for the inner city. This was partly because of a number of factors (see above) which made it unnecessary to interfere directly in building, structure and functioning. An important factor was the "freeze" regulation of 1961, which guaranteed the inner city a continuation of the existing situation, buildings could not be alienated from their original use.

All in all it cannot be said that there was any specific policy directed towards conservation and restoration of the historic elements in the inner city, but rather that there were a number of ad hoc protective measures, more in the personal sphere, as is peculiar to small communities with their special character.

The comparatively few restorations carried out were mainly by private initiative: the Reformed Church, the Admiralty building (in use as a regional museum since its restoration in 1963) and a few dwellings. Apart from the traditional subsidy channels, Dokkum has also had since the fifties a small restoration fund at its disposal, from which small sums were occasionally made available to private persons and which were mainly intended to encourage individual owners to undertake restoration and only for small items, which did not come under the normal subsidy regulation, such as dormer windows, doors, etc. and maintenance work preceding the actual restoration. This fund is included annually in the budget. The total amount spent in the course of the years has not exceeded some ten thousands of guilders.

In the second half of the sixties a change of attitude and action is to be observed with regard to the historic town centre. The cultural and historical elements and the characteristic town planning structure become one of the most important factors upon which to base plans to be developed for the inner city by the municipal authorities.

2.3 Present policy

The boundary changes of 1966 compelled the municipal authorities to give careful consideration to the physical planning of the municipal territory. In the meantime a number of social and economic activities were taking place outside the inner city. In view of these developments it was necessary to adopt a standpoint on the tasks which the inner city could fulfil in the future, especially as the whole inner city was on the nomination list for designation as a protected townscape (conservation area). As a first step a structure plan for the entire municipal territory was developed, which was accepted by the municipal council in 1970. Partly due to the detailed treatment of the inner city in the structure plan, it was possible to start in a short time on the "Inner City Development Plan", which was approved by the municipal council on 15 January 1973. The flexibility with which the plans linked up with one another also accelerated the whole procedure for designation as a protected townscape. On 31 January 1972 the inner city of Dokkum was included on the statutory list. Two points should be mentioned in this connection. In the first place the inner city of Dokkum is one of the first of the larger homogeneous historic areas to be included on the statutory list: previously, the list contained more especially specific streets with their buildings, squares, canals, thus smaller

Dokkum:

above: a restored house at the Baanterbolwerk

below: preservation of a historic watercourse (gracht) and small one-storeyed buildings

3. Goals of Intervention as Articulated in Planning Instruments

The proposals for designation as a protected townscape (conservation area) have from the very beginning been the determining factor for the plans concerning the inner city. In the background there was the idea of allowing the inner city of Dokkum to function as a sort of "model area" as regards the protected townscape, where contemporary functions would go hand in hand with the continuation of the cultural and historic character of the inner city, so that there would be no question of creating the impression of an open air museum. All this can be gathered from the principles upon which the plans for the inner city have been based. Thus the following basic principles are set forth in the structure plan:

1. To conserve the entire fortified town and the scale and structure thereof.

2. To allow the old, but still very much alive city heart to fulfil a variety of typical inner-city functions as the economic and cultural centre of north east Friesland.

In the local development plan for the inner city the same principles apply, except that there more emphasis is laid on strenghtening the typical inner-city functions, and a third point is given, namely the improvement of the traffic flow with the aid of the existing provisions. The foundation both of the development plan and of the structure plan is formed by the striving to maintain the intimate cultural and historic character of the planning area. The old, partly historic decor of the inner city, within which and against which a great variety of functions still take place, is seen as an essential factor in making Dokkum's inner city – also in the future – an attractive meeting place, not only for the municipality itself but also for the whole region.

In the development plan the following objectives for the inner city are mentioned, namely the conservation of:

1. The whole fortress with encircling moat, as well as the old inner canals.

2. The structure and scale of the town planning development.

3. The scale of the accompanying building and the principal form of the elements of which it is composed.

units of a historic whole. Secondly, in Dokkum the statutory term of one year for a development plan to secure designation as a protected townscape was not exceeded. As a result, Dokkum is in the vanguard compared with other Dutch cities with regard to conservation, rehabilitation and the implementation of a protected townscape.

In the meantime, work has started on the protected townscape. Thus part of the fortifications have been restored to their original state. The last bastion is to be restored in the course of 1976.

Dokkum: Local development plan (bestemmingsplan) of 1973

The following guidelines have been laid down for the maintenance and strengthening of the specific inner-city functions:

1. To increase the variety of mutually stimulating functions which are suited to the inner city and which also contribute to a considerable extent to reinforcing the old centre as a meeting place.
2. In determining the surface area required for each of these functions, to take into account the future area which is to be totally occupied and equal to the 125,000 sq. metres surface area now available in the city centre.
3. To fit in as closely as possible with the existing functional strata of the inner city.
4. To preserve the existing town planning structure and scale of building.

Improvement of the traffic flow is to be achieved by the following measures:

1. A strict limitation of through traffic by making some of the streets which attract through traffic – in so far as they are not planned as pedestrian precincts – one way streets.

2. Apart from the short-stay parking facilities in the inner city, which are not to be extended, the construction of several large car parks outside the fortress area at as short a walking distance as possible from the centre.

3. A limitation on the internal circulation by means of a number of projected loop development roads on the periphery of the inner city, whereby incoming short-stay traffic can choose a parking place via one of these loops in the immediate vicinity of this route and can continue on the same loop to leave the centre.

4. Promotion of public transport, which in Dokkum only serves to reach the surrounding municipalities. In order to achieve this it is desirable to keep this traffic in the inner city, as is now the case, and where necessary to accept it as through traffic.

5. Introduction of a pedestrian precinct in the sector where there are now and will also be in the projected pattern of functions mainly retail trade and catering establishments. Delivery of supplies and stocks to the enterprises in this area will have to made between certain times.

Thus it is not a question of pursuing a special monuments policy, but rather that the basis for all conservation of monuments and historic groups is considerably widened on account of the cultural and historic character of the inner city being of decisive significance for almost all action concerning the inner city. The conservation of monuments and historic groups forms an integral part of the plans and therefore of all policy to be pursued concerning the inner city.

Policy: functions

The economic functions within the planning area, in particular the shops and services, "the present-day function", are considered to be of great importance for the profitability of the whole. The residential function will decrease in importance and extent; as far as the residential floor area is concerned, it will be reduced by half in relation to the present situation (by 550 dwellings). Nevertheless, it is hoped that the remaining residential population, whereby the special category of "inner-city lovers" is in mind:

1. will increase the congeniality and vitality of the area,

2. will bring about a sort of social control in the various inner city areas, also outside the crowded periods,

3. will form potential customers in the immediate vicinity of the shops, etc.

Within the variety and multiplicity of inter-related functions concentrated in the relatively small inner city area, each separate building block is viewed as far as possible as a functional unit. The aim is to achieve a certain functional homogeneity within each separate city block in the sense that the dominating function, which now already determines the atmosphere in the block concerned, should in the future be stronger still (if possible for 100 %).

In the provisions accompanying the plan, the notion "cultural and historic character" is defined as follows:

"The character of the inner city (as a reflection of the pattern of civilisation which has developed over the centuries), as it is described in the considerations which have led to the designation c. q. registration of the inner city as a protected townscape, as referred to in the Monuments Act, and which designation c. q. registration is aimed at preserving the character of this unique inner city, namely: the mound upon which Dokkum is built, the 'wet' and 'dry' fortifications of the 16th century, the medieval canals, the east-west waterway, the most important streets, which run at right angles to this waterway, the scale of the street profiles, the street paving techniques and the materials employed, the numerous protected monuments, the scale and dimensions of the buildings, the form of the coping of the individual properties, the pattern of the facades, the use of materials for the facades and roofs."

That this concerns one of the most important, if not the most important definition in the development plan for the inner city of Dokkum is evident from the fact that in the institution of exemptions and specific requirements, which was frequently included in the provisions, it was the cultural and historic character which was repeatedly the determining factor. In this way an attempt has been made to provide a guarantee, whereby the protected townscape does not become an empty phrase but which can help to increase the value of the qualitative level of that protected townscape.

Policy: composition of population

In view of the considerable number of properties standing empty, some for several years, in the inner city, it cannot be said the Dokkum suffers to any serious extent from the problem that restoration work slowly drives the traditional population out of the inner city. In the few cases where this has indeed happened, there were no inexpensive dwellings available for these inhabitants elsewhere in the inner city. It should be borne in mind here that as regards restoration work in the inner city Dokkum acts in general on the principle of sale, with the exception of the one project of the building society. Since the restoration work in the inner city has yet to get really under way, and the interest in the properties of the SSD is not yet unduly great, it is impossible to say at the moment what the consequences of this policy line may be for the future composition of the population of the inner city.

4. Strategies

4.1 Legal techniques

Plans for the inner city

Up to 1970 Dokkum had no legally valid plans for the inner city. On the basis of the old Housing Act some work had been done towards drawing up a plan for the city centre, but this did not reach the actual planning stage. From 1969 onwards a structure plan for the entire municipal territory was developed, whereby the inner city was included in the plan as a separate area and subjected to detailed consideration. In view of the fact that during this period the question of the designation of the whole area within the ramparts as a protected townscape was under discussion, the conservation of the cultural and historic values of this area incorporated in the existing buildings and town planning structure formed an integral part both of this plan and of the associated development plan, a good reason for going into more detail on this aspect in discussing policy with regard to monuments and historic groups. The development plan for the inner city, representing the designation and entry on the statutory list of protected townscapes (31 January 1972), was laid down by the municipal council on 15 January 1973. In 1975 the area covered by the inner city development plan was designated a rehabilitation area, in order to be able to make a start from the financial point of view on dealing with the urban renewal.

Redevelopment areas

Within the historic city ground plan there are five rehabilitation plans to be noted which are going to be or are already being carried out under the existing development plan for the inner city. The plans are for the following districts: Leerlooierspark (continuation of residential function and realisation of a training centre) and the adjacent Parksterbolwerk (demolition of existing council houses). Both these projects are now being carried out. Part of the Westersingel (demolition of houses and development of garages and provision of green space). Buying out the Fortuin candy factory in the Koningsstraat (destined for office buildings) and finally the important redevelopment area Strobossersteeg in the southern part of the town where work is at present in progress – important because a considerable expansion of the shopping area is taking place here. At the same time parking space will be created by pulling down the adjacent residential area between the Wortelhaven and the Molensteeg, a course of action which could impair the intimate nature of this inner canal.

4.2 Financial techniques

Subsidizing of restoration work

The subsidizing of the restoration of dwellings takes place via the normal channels, namely the granting of 30 % of the restoration costs eligible for state subsidy and the reacquisition of the money via the "refinement" regulation of the Financial Relations Act. As a result of the whole of the inner city having been designated a rehabilitation area, money has also become available for the improvement of dwellings and the residential environment by virtue of the order on financial support for rehabilitation work.

Dwellings fund

As has been mentioned earlier, Dokkum has a small restoration fund, part of which is for dwellings. This fund will be considerably increased and the available money will for the most part be given to the SSD. The municipality will make Fl. 25,000 available per annum, which amount will be supplemented by the Department for the Preservation of Monuments and Historic Buildings by another Fl. 25,000. Part of the money will remain for assistance to private persons for specific restoration problems not eligible for subsidy. The fund amounts at the moment to Fl. 100,000; the procedure for the allocation of money has not been laid down in writing.

Acquisition of property

The municipality has been buying up old properties either in the framework of the existing redevelopment plans or in order to make them available to the SSD (at book value) and the building society corporation. The municipal policy is not based on selective principles for the acquisition of properties in the inner city. This would also be contrary to the intention of the development plan now in operation, which is aimed at creating frameworks within which private initiative can develop soundly.

4.3 Participation

Advisory committee

The individual citizen's involvement with the municipal plans has taken a more or less structural form from 1968 onwards. In the first place there was a fairly extensive procedure to allow the citizens a say in the matter concerning the structure plan and the local development plan for the inner city. When this procedure had been rounded off, one of the municipal standing advisory committees, the monuments committee, was reshaped on 27 December 1972 into the advisory committee on the inner city development plan. Apart from a few special tasks, such as aesthetic control of the external appearance of buildings in the protected townscape and the granting of exemptions from the development plan of the inner city, the committee was also assigned a more general task concerning subjects affecting the protected townscape which applies to the whole inner city. As mentioned earlier, the protected townscape has been

worked out in the development plan for the inner city. Part of this general task consists of effecting the continuation of important parts of the participation procedure previously followed, namely the provision of information for the citizens on everything which is happening or which is still to happen concerning the inner city. Hereafter the participation is, albeit in a modest form, institutionalized to a certain extent. The advisory committee is composed as follows: one municipal councillor, the city surveyor, one architect, one town planner, one expert in the field of the preservation of monuments and historic buildings and 3 members of the population. These three citizens must be familiar with the matters with which the committee has to deal, partly because of the supervisory function exercised by the committee with regard to the aesthetic control of the external appearance of buildings. The citizen members are all representatives of group interests, such as the retail trade and the building and contracting trade.

Method

The method of participation (inspraak) chosen to involve the citizens as much as possible in the structure and development plan consisted of three parts: firstly, participation in the programmatic phase (setting of objectives), thereafter in the draft planning phase, and finally in consideration of the plans submitted.

Process

Participation in the programmatic phase was as follows. At the beginning of 1969 two enquiries were held in the inner city by the staff of the "Stichting Stad & Landschap" (City and Landscape Foundation, socio-economic adviser for the plan) and Goudappel and Coffeng's Bureau for Traffic Planning. The enquiries took place amongst the enterprises in the inner city and visitors to the city centre. Two types of information emerged from the questionnaires:

a. quantitative information which was of direct influence on the functional pattern of the inner city;

b. information which could not be quantified and which was in answer to questions of opinion.

Re a. The enquiry amongst the enterprises took place via a questionnaire in which, apart from indicative questions concerning data on the enterprise, such as size and situation of working space, number of employees, turnover, circle of clients, opportunities for delivery and parking, questions were also included on the future number of employees, possible preference for relocating the enterprise, and the desire to expand. The information thus gained – and in particular the last item – has had a decisive influence in drawing up the functional pattern of the inner city.

Re b. Open questions in the questionnaire produced information which either could not, or only with difficulty, be expressed in quantitative results. Although it was naturally more difficult to incorporate this unquantifiable material into the plan than it was the indicative material, the conclusion may nevertheless be drawn that it was of value, since the interest exhibited by the entrepreneurs was a good foundation for further discussion.

Evaluation: the programmatic phase

Participation in the programmatic phase may be characterised as limited. There was no question of direct participation

Dokkum:
above: de Zijl, the central water course
below: the city hall along de Zijl

by all those involved, but rather of the collection of information in the trade and industrial sector and the sounding out of opinions amongst a group of people who were not representative of the citzens of Dokkum but important from the economic point of view, namely those who frequent the inner city.

Method

In the preliminary planning stage the following procedures were used successively:

a. the formation of a participation team;
b. the presentation of the draft plan to the population with the possibility of reactions by means of filling in a questionnaire;
c. the hearing.

Re a. On the initiative of the municipal authorities the Association for Trade and Industry, the Tradesmen's Club and the Cultural Council formed a participation team entirely independent of the municipality. The team consisted of 19 members drawn from the tradesmen (including the multiple stores), the cultural organisations, the road transport and hauliers, the youth movement, education (pupils and teachers), health care, garage proprietors and the catering trade. A member of the scientific staff of the University of Groningen was appointed chairman. The participation team saw as its task the promotion of communication between the population, the municipal government organs and the municipality's external advisers. With this in mind the relevant papers were open for inspection by everyone at the public library and reading room at the town hall.

During the formation of the team there was discussion as to whether alternative models should be used. The time factor in particular led to the choice falling on discussion of the draft plan. The team produced a 60 page report entitled "Uitspraak over Inspraak" (Pronouncement on Participation), which was presented to the municipal authorities. The plan was not essentially affected. The recommendations mainly concerned details which had to be dealt with in the development plan.

Re b. The presentation of the draft plan to the population took place by means of a special newspaper, which came out under the title "Dokkums Toekomstperspectief" (Dokkum's Future Perspective) and was delivered door to door in an edition of some 3,500 copies. A questionnaire with a prepaid answer envelope was enclosed with the paper. The questionnaire contained 12 questions which covered, amongst other things, leaving the structure of the inner city untouched, closing the inner city to through traffic, filling in canals, having public transport through the town, parking zones, pedestrian precincts, The response was surprisingly large. Some 1100 forms were sent in. The results of the questionnaire and the most striking reactions to the questions were brought to the knowledge of the citizens by means of a second information paper delivered door to door.

Re c. In conclusion a public hearing was held at which the Burgomaster and Aldermen were accompanied by the principal advisers. In view of the interest evinced according to the response to the questionaire, a large turnout was expected. However, the numbers were disappointing. About 100 people came to the hearing. The discussions in fact confirmed the opinions expressed in the questionnaire: in general people were in agreement with the basic points of the draft plan. On 27 August 1970 the municipal council approved the structure plan as it stood.

After the approval of the structure plan, work went on immediately on the development plan. The main outlines and underlying principles were already agreed and it was now a matter of the specification of these points in the draft development plan. Thus there was no programmatic phase in the preparation of this plan. When preparations started the (pre-) draft phase at once began.

In this phase the following procedures were used in succession:

a. presentation of the plan to the population, again via a newspaper;

b. organization of an exhibition;

c. information evening and a hearing.

Re a. As was the case with the structure plan, the presentation of the draft development plan to the population took place via a special newspaper delivered door to door. A coloured map of the plan was enclosed with the paper, so that every citizen could in the first instance peruse the draft plan quietly at home.

Re b. An exhibition was arranged which was open to everyone two afternoons and evenings. There were always a number of experts present who could provide further information on request. Considerable use was made of this possibility of going into further details. 317 people visited the exhibition. From a questionnaire handed out to visitors it appeared that 277 of them considered that the exhibition had given them more insight into the plans for the inner city.

Re c. Contrary to what took place in the case of the structure plan, with the draft development plan a distinction was made between people with business interests and others. Two evenings were arranged. The first for the interested parties and the second for the others. All owners and/or users of properties in the inner city recieved a personal invitation. The turnout on the evening for the interested parties was considerable. The session for those not directly concerned was, however, poorly attended.

Evaluation

The municipal authorities did not find the participation method adopted entirely satisfactory. The accent was on information and public relations, whereby actual participation in the sense of having-a-say in the preparation and working out of the plans did not have much chance.

The participation team was not formed until the plans were well under way. As a result the "small" interested parties in the planning areas have had inadequate opportunity to have a say in the matter. This became apparent when the plans were actually being carried out and protests were received from inhabitants whose interests were directly affected by the implementation of a part of the plan. Nevertheless, during the statutory procedure period only two objections were lodged.

Effects of participation

Since the adoption of the structure and development plan some amendments have been made, in particular to the inner city development plan. This was the result both of other views on the part of the municipal authorities and also of initiatives on the part of the inhabitants. Although it is not possible to establish a direct link between them, it may be said that two currents of opinion amongst the population were influential here. A representative of one of the currents was the Bonifatiusplein committee, a small group of citizens resident just outside the inner city, who protested against the demolition of dwellings inhabited by them and the realization of a parking area on the spot. It is true that this car park is outside the inner city, but its purpose is to provide facilities for long parking for visitors to the inner city. The Bonifatiusplein committee's action was clearly plan-conscious in that they presented the municipal authorities with concrete plans for a different authorities with concrete plans for a different solution at that particular point. These things have evidently influenced the vision of the municipal authorities with regard to redevelopment in the form of demolition. The second current of opinion amongst the inhabitants was of a more political nature. Representatives of a political trend of thought have for some time been active with regard to a number of matters concerning the inner city. Thus they objected to the modest residential function of the inner city, to certain traffic priorities, to the demolition of properties and to the sale of rehabilitated or restored dwellings instead of their being let. The representatives of this political trend only began to be active, however, after the plans had been officially approved. Thus it was only possible to exert influence on any possible future alterations. A considerable alteration has been prepared in the meantime. This is mainly concerned, apart from some technical adaptations, with increasing the residential function of the inner city. However, these alterations had all been moot points at a much earlier stage in the authorities' internal discussions. As regards demolition there are in the meantime scarcely any further differences of opinion between the municipal authorities and the inhabitants. The authorities seek alternatives as far as possible, whereby these matters can be forestalled or their effects can be minimized.

Citizens' initiatives

The means by which the inhabitants make themselves felt are mainly of a moderate nature. They consist of letters to the newspapers, the contribution made by sitting on official municipal committees and via the municipal council. An important group as regards the inner city is formed by the Tradesmen's Club (called Club 65). The municipal authorities have monthly discussions with them.

Participation and monuments

With regard to monuments and their restoration there are hardly any differences of opinion. The only point is the system used by the municipality to sell restored properties instead of letting them. This means that the original inhabitants cannot always go on living in their house, or that living in the inner city is only financially possible for a smaller group of the population.

4.4 Involvement of a foundation in the process of urban rehabilitation

The SSD (Stichting Stadsherstel Dokkum) was set up as a foundation in January 1974 mainly on the initiative of the municipal authorities and has as its objective the renovation of old properties, which are of value in the inner city picture, and making them as fit as possible for habitation. Thus the foundation occupies itself with the residential function of the inner city, as envisaged in the development plan. The municipal authorities see the foundation as an important instrument in implementing municipal policy on this point. The foundation's funds are derived on the one hand from the housing fund mentioned earlier, especially in the sense of initial capital, and on the other hand from revenue obtained from the sale of restored properties. At the moment the foundation has some 8 properties in the preliminary stage or in the course of restoration.

Building society and restoration

The building society has in general only a limited, supplementary task in the inner city. It is involved in the redevelopment plan for Leerlooiersperk, where it is a question of three properties for rehabilitation and five new houses. In accordance with its task the building society concentrates in principle on letting these properties.

Purpose and use

As far as the municipality is concerned, there is control over the destination of all ground and properties by virtue of the development plan now in force and the accompanying conditions. Furthermore, the municipality sells properties to the SSD on the express condition that each allocation should be approved by the municipal authorities. The SSD has in its deeds of sale certain specific clauses, which also contain conditions of this nature, such as:

– the property to be sold may not be used as a so-called "second house". Thus it must be in permanent use as a dwelling by the occupier and his family (who are registered as inhabitants of Dokkum).

– the property must be inhabited, used and maintained according to its nature and purpose, in accordance with the purport and provisions of the Monuments Act.

– without written permission from the committee of the SSD the property may not be transferred, either wholly or partially, may not be encumbered with a proprietary right of enjoyment and may not be let. This article is not applicable in the case of sale in accordance with Article 1223 of the Civil Code, i. e. in the case of a mortgage, the conditions of which stipulate that, in the event of default in the payment, the creditor shall be empowered to sell the property by public auction.

– in the event of one or more of these conditions being infringed the offender in question is liable to a fine, immediately payable, for the benefit of the foundation named and amounting to 50 % of the purchase sum, without any notice of default or judicial intervention being required.

Maintenance

The maintenance of the properties restored by the SSD is regulated in accordance with the above-mentioned clause per sale contract. As far as the other monuments are concerned, the normal conditions of maintenance apply which are attached to the provision of subsidies. Neither the SSD nor the municipality of Dokkum is affiliated to the "Monumentenwacht" (Foundation for the inspection of monuments – annual inspection of restored monuments – operates per province).

5. Restoration Projects

The restoration of the properties in the framework of the protected townscape is slowly getting under way. In order to make the approach to and carrying out of this restoration work more systematic, the municipal council, on 26 March 1975, designated the whole inner city of Dokkum as a rehabilitation area, whereby the plans provide for the rehabilitation of ten dwellings per year; a total amount of a million guilders per year for improvement costs must be reckoned with for this work. The first property which was restored in the framework of the protected townscape programme was No. 8 Boterstraat, the oldest house in Dokkum, the completion of which was celebrated at the opening of the Architectural Heritage Year. This property in particular has fulfilled a pilot function for further restoration work in Dokkum, since the municipal authorities had plans for the restoration of this dwelling with adjacent shop as early as 1966 but were not able to carry them out because of subsidy difficulties and the owner's initial plans to pull the property down. Eventually it was possible to finance the restoration with money from the Supplementary Work (combatting unemployment) Fund. This fund has also provided the money with which at the moment the bastions are being restored to their old form, part of the canals are being dredged and the restoration of the Weeshuis (Orphanage) on the Markt and the Jsherberg have been completed. Another important restoration with a pilot function is that of the property on the Baantjebolwerk No. 1, the first restoration to be completed by the "Stichting Stadsherstel Dokkum" (Dokkum Urban Rehabilitation Foundation, SSD).

6. Promotion

The municipality arranges for special events connected with the rehabilitation and development of the inner city to be accompanied by suitable publicity.

To enable the inhabitants to have a say in the matter with regard to the structure plan and the local development plan, a "participation team" was formed; both the structure plan and the local development plan were presented to the population in detail by means of a house-to-house paper with a questionnaire; an exhibition was organised concerning the plans for the inner city and hearings were held. There were and are also regular publications in the local paper "De Nieuwe Dockumer Courant" under the heading "Dokkum Informatief".

The completion of the restoration work on the oldest house in Dokkum, No. 8 Boterstraat, was taken advantage of by the municipal authorities to present the SSD at a festive gathering and at the same time draw attention to Architectural Heritage Year, which had just begun. Other activities were organised to mark Architectural Heritage Year, such as, for example, a photographic contest. When the aquatic "tour of the 11 cities" (the traditional "11 cities tour" is a Frisian skating event) came through Dokkum, this picturesque entourage was used to highlight the completion of work on the first of the properties restored under the auspices of the SSD (on the Baantjebolwerk). The Architectural Heritage Year closed with a so-called "monuments concert" given by the Dokkum Toonkunst Choir and the Frysk Orchestra in the Reformed Church. Through articles in the journals "Plan" and "Stedebouw en Volkshuisvesting" (Town planning and housing) the plans for the inner city of Dokkum have been given national publicity.

7. Future Policy

The future policy concerning the inner city of Dokkum has been laid down via the structure and development plan for a period of 30–50 years. This does not mean that it is impossible to make alterations. Thus, for example, certain principles for adaptation have in the meantime been approved by the municipal authorities. The most important alteration is that the accent has been shifted more towards the residendial function. The instruments to implement the policy will be the same as those at present in use.

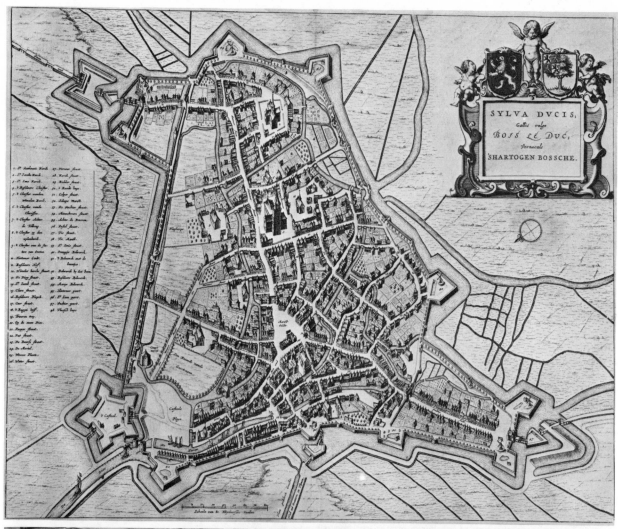

's-Hertogenbosch: Historical map from 1649 (from: Joan Blaeu: Tooneel der steden van de Vereenighde Nederlanden) below: aerial photograph of the historical core with "Markt" from 1977 (photo: KLM Aerocarto)

Netherlands
's-HERTOGENBOSCH

1. Situation

1.1 General introduction

's-Hertogenbosch is a medium sized town situated just South of the big rivers Rhine, Meuse and Waal. It is the capital of the province of Brabant. The total number of inhabitants is 86,000 as per 1970.

1.2 History

In about 1185, the Duke of Brabant granted the place city rights, the oldest municipal rights known in the Netherlands. At that time the town was not much bigger than the present cattle market with its immediate surroundings and the three traditional approach roads, which converge on the market, thus giving this "square" its triangular form. "De Moriaan" also dates from this period, a nobles' dwelling which was built in the first quarter of the 13th century and is thus one of the oldest brick dwellings in the Netherlands. According to estimates the number of inhabitants of the town in about 1300 was some 8,000.

As a result of toll privileges and through its favourable situation at a junction of roads and waterways, Den Bosch developed into a centre for trade and craftsmanship and also for various administrative functions. The economic expansion resulted in a considerable increase in the population. In order to be able to deal with this, the town territory was walled in about 1318. In 1352 the Vughterdijk was added and in 1499 the Hinthamereind. This gave the town its present triangular groundplan. The 17th century city walls, with the medieval ramparts retained in them, are still in existence almost right round the city.

About 1520 the decline of the town started to make itself felt. In this connection it must be remembered that before the Netherlands fell apart into the Southern Netherlands, which remained faithful to the Roman Catholic Church and the Spanish princes, and the independent Calvinist republic, the Duchy of Brabant had formed one of the most prosperous and politically important areas of the Low Countries.

During the eighty years' war between the Republic and Spain, the political, economic and cultural unity between the Northern and Southern parts of the old duchy was destroyed, which meant a mortal blow for the area. This war sealed the city's decline. Trade and industry came to a standstill.

After heavy fights, Den Bosch became a part of the Republic. From that time on, Den Bosch functioned as one of the principal fortresses on the southern flank of the Republic and generally had a large garrison in the town – there were years that there were 10,000 soldiers in the town as against a total population of about 13,000. Thank to this garrison the town still had some income.

On account of the general decline throughout the Netherlands, the town's modest trade also came practically to a standstill. At the beginning of the 19th century the once so flourishing town had become a modest regional centre.

The situation began slowly to improve somewhat. Though the town was no longer considered a frontier fortress, the fortifications were nevertheless maintained.

However, in accordance with the fortress act of 1874 the status of fortress was terminated. The town was then able to expand beyond the ramparts. Work began first on improving the bad state of the watercourses and water supply, which was a result of the inundation system that had been in use. In the period between 1880 and 1890, all the towngates and many of the fortifications were demolished. The ramparts and the Citadel's field of fire could now be used for building. The first expansion of the town took place from 1890 onwards in the area between the Dommel and the site of the railway station. The level of the ground there had to be raised four metres, so low lying was the ground round the former fortress. The connection with the old city centre was effected via the Stationsweg and cut through at the Visstraat. In the seventies and eighties of the nineteenth century the various railway connections came into being, whereby not only did the old north-south connection receive a tremendous stimulus, but it also became possible for the town to participate once more in the international trade between England and Germany.

Further expansion took place and from 1917 onwards various industrial areas were laid out, the first being on land on the Dieze. In the twenties the residential areas Muntel, Hinthamerpoort and the Bossche Veld came into being. The last expansion before the Secound World War added the Vliert district to the town. In the period 1917 – 1940 so much ground was raised that the built-up area of Den Bosch was doubled – it grew from 177 to 366 hectares.

After the hazards of the war years were over there was a rapid expansion of industry and growth of the population (in 1940 still 50,000 inhabitants and by 1967 already 80,000).

The industrial development in particular was now more favourable. The industries were established mainly in the large new industrial areas west of the city, such as the Rietvelden. New residential areas developed on the west, east and south of the city, such as Boschveld, Deuteren, Zuid, Aa-wijk, Orthen-noord, Kruiskamp, Nieuw Deuteren and Noord. In 1971 Empel and Engelen were incorporated to give the municipality of Den Bosch more scope.

1.3 City structure, characteristics

In the report "Towards an integral inner city policy" both the term old town as well as inner city were used for the inner city. As regards the meaning of the notion "old town" no difficulties were experienced. This is the area of the former fortress, as it is enclosed within the moats, which are for a great part still in existence. The Oostwal form part of this demarcation. The Citadel and the strip between the Zuid-Willemsvaart and the northern town moats also belong to the old town. By "inner city" is meant that part of the city area and of the municipality of Den Bosch which the inhabitants and trade and industry experience and use as the "heart" of the city area and the municipality. Thus there is an empirical conception of the notion "inner city". Without this empirical filling in already having taken place, in the plans for the inner city of Den Bosch "inner city" means the area of the old town

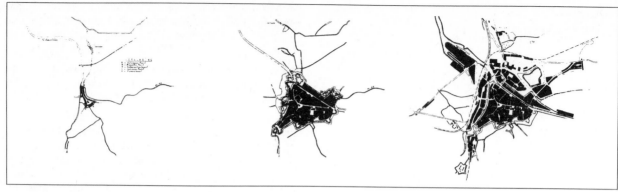

's-Hertogenbosch: Spatial development
left: first settlement 12–13th century, middle: the fortified town, 15th century; right: development until 1945

and of het Zand. The latter is the area between the inner city and the station, which forms the natural boundary as it were on the east side. Certainly from the functional point of view it belongs to the inner city. The "landmarks" (these are the elements by which people form a picture of the notion "inner city" in daily practice) of the inner city area are thus formed on the west by the station and the tunnel under the railway line and the dragon in the station square; to the north by the Dieze bridge with the Citadel, the Aa with the ramparts and the bridge by the watertower; to the east by the park along the ramparts and to the south by the Casino gardens, the town wall Bossche Broek, the Wilhelmina Park and the Provincial Energy Board building.

The core of the historic ground plan is formed by the triangular Market "Square" with the approach roads which have converged on it from the old Vughterstraat, Hinth-

's-Hertogenbosch: The urban fabric of the medieval core, 1973

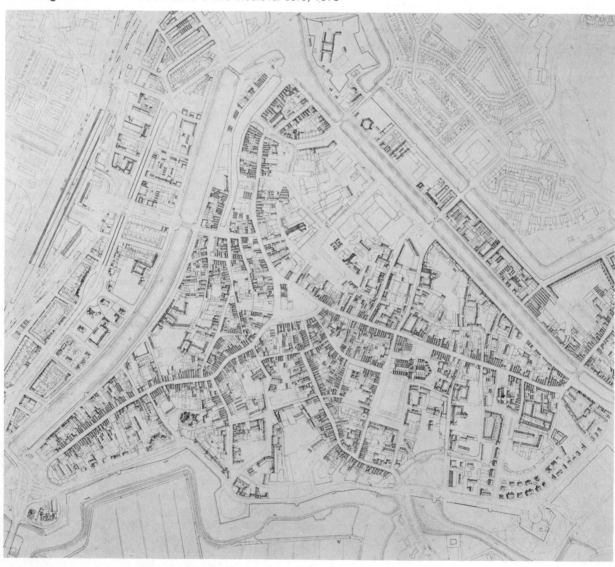

amerstraat & Hoge Steenweg/Orthenstraat. The line of the still partly fortifications from the States period follows the triangular form of the Markt and spans the inner city from these points at which the above-mentioned approach roads enter the city. On the north the Dieze with the Haven forms a fourth opportunity of entering the city. Thus the ground plan the old city of Den Bosch has a peculiar triangular form, which distinguishes it from many other historic towns, which generally have an oval, elongated or square ground plan. The flanks of the triangle, which for long remained unbuilt-on, have in the meantime been fully built up: dwellings, institutions, business premises, etc., of a different and mainly larger scale than the rest of the inner city buildings and thus also of a different character. After 1874 as well as the three traditional approach roads, three other openings to the fortress came into being, situated on the flanks: Kardinaal van Rossumplein-Nieuwstraat-St. Josephstraat, Visstraat-Stationsweg and the Pettelaarseweg.

The Citadel can be considered as the most striking relic of the fortifications to the north, situated on the north side of the historic ground plan. Running almost parallel with the ramparts, the Zuid-Willemswaart here cuts part of the historic town off from the rest. Although at the time the construction of this waterway formed an infringement of the historic city structure, the area in question was of little historical value, since at the time of the canal's construction it was scarcely built on. The course of the Binnendieze counts as an essential part of the historic whole.

Den Bosch differs from many other Dutch towns as far as the role of water in the town is concerned: here it is not a system of canals with quays, but of drainage courses along the backyards of the properties. This provided the opportunity of building above the water as needed, a fact that contributed to the creation of picturesque quarters of the town and specific inner city building (Uilenburgkwartier).

Though the city is based on a medieval structure, its appearance on the other hand is determined to a high degree by the elevation of the streets and squares in the form in which these came into being mainly in the 18th and 19th centuries. Amongst the traditional building structures there are, however, various large scale factory buildings and multiple stores to be found and especially on the flanks there are a number of office buildings, educational institutions, hospitals and semi-religious buildings. The course of the building line and the parcelling up of the land, as well as the structure of the building, are, however, still to a large extent of medieval origin.

Within the historic ground plan no breakthroughs have been made which essentially influenced the character of the inner city. Water and green spaces also make a contribution to the townscape. The water courses, with their numerous branches and apparently rather haphazard distribution, collectively known as the Binnen-Dieze, are structural elements which are of great importance for the townscape as a whole. This is especially the case where the Binnen-Dieze runs parallel to the backyards of the Hinthamerstraat, de Verwerstraat and the Postelstraat. The contribution made by green spaces can be divided into that of the cultivated urban green and that of the uncultivated. As far as the urban green in concerned, the importance of trees in the street profile or of groups of trees at a conspicuous point may be mentioned: for instance, the trees along the Hinthamerstraat near St. Jan's, the trees in St. Jan's churchyard, on the Kerkplein, the trees along the Parade, the park near the Nachtegaalslaantje adjoining the Binnen-Dieze and the

trees along the Muntel wal. At one point the spatial relation between the city and the adjoining countryside is still entirely intact, namely at the Bossche Broek.

Both by the inhabitants and by the municipal authorities the town's indentity is considered to be bound up with the market and the three ancient approach roads, St. Jan's and the Parade, the Uilenburgkwartier, the ramparts with the Citadel and Binnen-Dieze.

2. Conditions

2.1 Factors of intervention

In the report "Integral inner city policy", the developments which have affected the historic character of Den Bosch in the past are summarised as follows: "the construction of the Zuid-Willemsvaart entailed a cut-through which isolated the Hinthamereind and the area between Aa and Zuid-Willems-vaart from the city centre and which has led to partial dilapidation. As a result of its absolutely straight course an elongated space has been created with a breadth of 55 to 70 metres, which forms a sharp contrast to the intimate scale and atmosphere of the inner city, where long vistas do not occur and have been deliberately avoided. The unbuilt-on areas along the flanks of the old town were built up in the course of the 19th and 20th centuries with buildings of a different scale and character. It can, of course, be seen as an advantage that Den Bosch, unlike most historic towns, offers more opportunity for modern buildings to be erected "within the fortress". This does not alter the fact that, especially in the construction of the Groot Ziekengasthuis (hospital) in the redevelopment area of the Tolbrugkwartier, a limit was exceeded both in the scale and also in the height of the building. However, the function of the hospital represents more of an objection than its physical appearance. The hospital on its 3.5 hectares forms a monoculture which contrasts sharply with the diversity of functions and limited area, which are conditions for the bustle and liveliness of an inner city. The concentration of government and provincial offices along the Prins Bernhardstraat, Wolvenhoek and Waterstraat has led to this becoming a rather dull neighbourhood. The cutting through of the Prins Bernhardstraat does not fit into the course of the historic streets. The open area on the west flank was filled up in the second half of the 19th century by the Marienburg (formerly monastery). Although it is hardly possible to object to the monoculture, this will make itself increasingly felt, according to the extent that the city centre develops in this direction. There are also a number of places where much of value had been lost, either because of too drastic and radical clearance, or because preservation of rehabilitation action was taken too late (e.g. round the Louwse Poort).

To these points may be added the following:

– A considerable number of the inner city buildings are of moderate or bad quality. The process of dilapidation was most advanced in the Uilenburgkwartier and round the harbour, which districts are now in the course of being rehabilitated.

– The penetration of large-scale buildings for the service sector in the Tolbrug (former redevelopment area) and the Zuidwal area.

299

's-Hertogenbosch: above: topographical map based on surveys in the period 1837–1838
below: topographical map, 1964

– The continuing drop in the number of inhabitants of the inner city. The following table illustrates this phenomenon:

Survey of number of dwellings and occupants from 1947–1969:

	't Zand		Oude stadt	
	1947	1969	1947	1969
Dwellings	1,120	959	3,900	2,409
Inhabitants	5,110	3,118	20,332	8,904
Resident institutions	83	95	2,410	1,921
Inhabitants less those in institutions	5,027	3,023	17,992	6,983
Average no. of persons per dwelling	4.49	3.15	4.59	2.90

The centre, however, still functions as a residential area for at the most an eight of the town's inhabitants. Of the entire municipal housing stock a twentieth part is still to be found here. Another phenomenon is that there is more and more a so-called typical inner city resident to be found, that is to say over-representation of young adults and elderly.

– In the Baselaars district a residential area has been created which bears the character of a luxurious suburb.

– Since the war three redevelopment operations have been carried out in the inner city, including that in the Tolbrug quarter (1.2 hectares) at the end of the fifties. Here it was less a question of tampering with the ground plan than of impairing the character of function and scale, especially through the high-rise building and divergent scales used for much of the new construction work, including the Groot-Ziekengasthuis, the police station and a complex on the Burgemeester Loeffplein. Moreover, the functions housed in these buildings attract a great deal of traffic. Elsewhere in the inner city two small clearances have been made, namely in the fifties round the Diepstraat for the benefit of providing housing for senior citizens, and in the sixties to provide offices and dwellings. These redevelopment activities have not essentially damaged the historic townscape in its totality. At various points in the inner city gaps arose in the street facades as a result of demolition, such as along the Westwal and by the harbour. Enterprises which had long been established in the inner city begin slowly to move away to the various industrial estates.

Functional pattern

In the heart of the city, the Market and surroundings, and along the three traditional approach roads to the Market, Vughterstraat, Orthenstraat and the Hinthamerstraat, the economic function is predominant (multiple stores, shops, catering establishments, small offices). The more service functions (large offices, education and regligious services, medical and public services, large-scale catering establishments and monasteries) have mainly found a place on the flanks of the old town and in the station area, het Zand. The artisan enterprises, wholesale trade and industry, are concentrated in the area by the harbour and the adjacent Orthenstraat, in the northern part of het Zand and in the space between the Zuid-Willemsvaart and the Aa. Finally, the residential function in fact takes place in a few remaining areas of the inner city, also predominantly on the flanks, namely Uilenburg and environs, Peperstraat and Verwersstraat, Lange Putstraat and environs, Hekellan and environs, Zuidwad and environs, Hofstad and environs, Vughterstraat and environs and the northern and southern part of hed Zand. In the heart of the city and along the traditional approach roads to the Market there are dwellings on the floors above shops and business premises.

The city may now be characterised as a regional and administrative centre of the first order. As regards the inner city, it can be said it will for the most part be able to retain its historic character and historic structure in view of the plans which the municipal authorities have adopted for this area.

Monuments

Most of the monuments are to be found in the Uilenburg-kwartier, along the Hinthamerstraat and in the area of the Market – Verwersstraat – Parade. Den Bosch has a total of 244 protected monuments, of which all but 10 are situated in the old city centre. Many of them, especially the smaller dwellings scheduled as monuments, are of moderate or bad quality as far as their structural condition is concerned. Differentiation according to types of monuments is given in the table. The almost intact 19th century facades on either side of the Stationsweg are not (yet) statutorily protected. There are 45 representative dwellings to be found (12th up to and including 19th century), and the ramparts with bastions which still enclose the old town. These are fortifications which were constructed shortly before and after the capture of the town by Frederik Hendrik in 1627. Important elements of the fortifications are the Citadel (1637), almost fully intact, and the recently restored Kruithuis (powder magazine) (1621).

The municipality owns only 31 monuments.

2.2 Past policy

Planning the inner city

As the first plan after the Second World War for the inner city of Den Bosch, mention may be made of the Reconstruction Plan that was specifically directed towards repairing the fairly considerable war damage in this area. In 1958 a structure plan was drawn up for the municipal territory, but was very soon revised. From 1962 onwards the municipal services were working on the elaboration of a new structure plan for the municipal territory, which on 14 July 1964 was unanimously approved by the municipal council as the guiding line for future policy. This plan, called "Hauen zo, bouwen zo", has in fact never had the statutory status of a structure plan because it was drawn up by the municipal council in the period just before the Physical Planning Act came into force. On the basis of this plan a component plan was made for the inner city. Amongst other things carried out within this framework was redevelopment of the Tolbrugkwartier, after a development plan had been adopted for this area. Traffic measures, such as the reconstruction of the Wilhelminaplein, the introduction of one-way traffic and of pedestrian precincts, as well as major building plans including office complexes and an old people's centre, were carried out in the framework of the inner city component plan, though indeed without a statutory development plan. In this same framework it was possible to prevent the building of the provincial government offices on the southern flank of the inner city (now built near the southern circular trunk road).

In 1969 the insight into, and the views on the inner city had in the meantime altered to such an extent that a group of external experts was engaged to deal with the problems of the inner city and to draw up a policy memorandum on the subject. This group consisted of Prof. Drs. G. J. van den Berg (chairman), Prof. Ir. H. M. Goudappel, Ir. J. A. Kuiper, Dr. A. W. Luyckx, N. A. Nap and P. L. de Vrieze.

In May 1971 they published the report "An integral inner city policy". Making use of elements of previous plans, such as the old structure plan, the structure outline for the urban district and the plans for road structure and parking for the central city area, a memorandum of objectives was produced. On 15 February 1973 the recommendations of the municipal executive concerning this report, containing proposals for an integral inner city policy, concrete ideas on the principal points of the integral inner city policy to be pursued and a filling in of policy concerning a number of inner city areas, were unanimously accepted by the municipal council.

After this an inner city project group was formed, consisting of representatives of the municipal public works department and the town clerk's office under the chairmanship of the relevant alderman. This group worked out in concrete details the objectives for, and basic principals of, an integral inner city policy as formulated in the report "An integral inner city policy" and gave visual clarification in "Zicht op de binnenstad" (view of the inner city). On 21 March 1974 this memorandum was approved by the municipal council. It should be noted that this was not a structure plan for the inner city area in the sense of the Physical Planning Act but was seen as a framework within which the various local development plans for the inner city could be worked out. These are successively: the plan for the Stadskern (city core), Uilenburg, Havenkwartier, Tolburg, Hinthamerdriehoek, Aa-Zuid Willemsvaart, Baselaar, Parade, Zuidwal, Vughterdriehoek and 't Zand. As regards the traffic component, in July 1975 a policy memorandum on road traffic and transport was produced in this framework. In May 1975 the municipal council approved a rehabilitation plan for the inner city so as to be able to proceed with the improvement and restoration of dwellings and of the residential environment, particularly in the light of the protected townscape, more quickly and on a bigger scale. In the

's-Hertogenbosch: Detailed plans for various parts of the inner city. (A – draft, B – draft, second phase, C – legal, D – reconstruction plan for bombed areas)

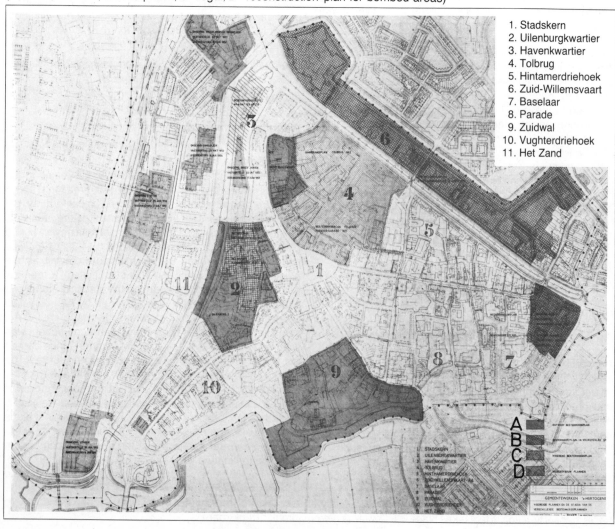

1. Stadskern
2. Uilenburgkwartier
3. Havenkwartier
4. Tolbrug
5. Hintamerdriehoek
6. Zuid-Willemsvaart
7. Baselaar
8. Parade
9. Zuidwal
10. Vughterdriehoek
11. Het Zand

framework of the protected townscape of Den Bosch, which is now operative, work is in progress at the moment on the inner city development plan, which is obligatory in this connection.

Policy concerning monuments

Policy as pursued in the past concerning monuments and historic groups in Den Bosch has not been recorded in the form of specific memoranda on monuments, commentaries, etc. Especially in the first few post-war years there was no action to speak of for the preservation of monuments in all the historically valuable inner city areas. The authorities were confronted with considerable war damage in the urban area, which called for extensive restoration work. A fortunate circumstance was that the historic inner city of Den Bosch had for the most part been spared war damage, so that renewal in this area was not immediately necessary. During this period only a few restorations were carried out, mainly by private persons on the more representative dwellings. The municipality restored amongst others the "Moriaan", one of the oldest brick dwellings in the Netherlands (1966), and the Blaasbalg. The restoration work, which has been in progress since 1860 on St. Jan's cathedral, has also been continued.

The volume of restoration work up to and including May 1970 is shown in the following table:

Subsidies for restoration of properties (excluding churches, institutions and the like)

Year	No. of restorations	Subsidiary costs	Municipal subsidy
1961	2	31,083.80	3,742.–
1962	–	–	–
1963	1	3,573.65	–
1964	1	57,141.–	22,856.–
1965	2	151,928.–	52,560.–
1966	–	–	–
1967	2	71,878.–	21,563.–
1968	–	–	–
1969	4	302,506.–	90,752.–
1970	13	464,628.20	147,303.–
Total	25	1,082,738.65	338,776.–

The funds for this work were made available via the current general subsidy channels; there were no special financial regulations made by the municipality in this field. All in all it may be said that the care for and activities of the municipal authorities with regard to the many historic elements in the inner city have only occupied a modest place in the municipal inner city policy. Thus in the structure plan "Houen zo, bouwen zo" of 1964 there is the following:

"The background to the plan is respect for the beauty that exists. A way has carefully been sought by which new life can function in old spaces and new spaces can be created in order to spare the old form and the old character."

Nevertheless, this plan implied such drastic intervention in the historic town planning structure of the inner city and pattern of inner city building which has grown up within it that it aroused fierce resistance from the very beginning. In this plan the inner city was seen as the heart of the expanding city area. In the forefront in this context were good accessibility with the opening up of the inner city by means of four-lane roads in the southern and eastern parts of the historic ground plan, and the creation of space in the inner city for functions which would promote employment and make the provision of varied facilities possible there. The component plan for the inner city also provided for partial filling in of the Binnendieze, which would have involved such high costs that it did not seem to be justifiable.

As an outcome of this plan redevelopment was carried out in the Tolbrugkwartier – a fairly large area in the inner city, where large-scale buildings were put up, which resulted in a fundamental change in the townscape. Two smaller clearance projects were also carried out. Thus in the daily practice of municipal action great attention to slum clearance redevelopment was to be observed, to which term was attached a significance which is no longer applicable, namely "restoring the inner city to health, where certain conflicts manifested themselves as diseases". This led to small monuments in particular receiving but little attention. The larger, more "luxurious" monuments were fairly generally restored and maintained in a reasonable state.

At the end of the sixties a change occurred in ideas on, and action in, the historic inner city. The proposed filling-in of the Binnendieze, the large-scale road construction provided for in the plan and the effects of the redevelopment already carried out, caused increasing resistance to the plan in this form.

In 1965 the monuments list for Den Bosch was approved. This functioned more or less as a catalyser, since monuments for which there had been demolition plans were now statutorily protected. As a result, the inner city policy formation in the form in which it had been foreseen was seriously hampered and delayed. From 1969 onwards a start was made on an inner city policy in which much more than previously the accent was laid on the value and preservation of historic groups and buildings.

2.3 Present policy

At the end of the sixties a revaluation was evident amongst the municipal authorities of the unique character of the historic inner city and this was accompanied by growing attention to the possibilities for the rehabilitation and restoration of elements in this inner city.

Concept: planning the inner city

This changed concept of the historic features incorporated in the inner city of Den Bosch is also expressed in the "plan thinking" with regard to this inner city. In the report "An integral inner city policy" it is striking how much emphasis there is on the values which are considered to be bound up with the historic character of the city. Thus when speaking of the inner city it is described as "the heritage of the forefathers". This heritage is bound up with the historical and cultural aspects of the old city, a fact which enables this city to continue to exhibit its own special visage and thus also for the future to continue to maintain its own identity.

In the motivation for the preservation of monuments and historic groups the same report says the following:

It has gradually become an internationally accepted conviction that in inner cities, which are important on account of their historic town planning features, the protected townscapes (conservation areas) should form the foundations for a structure plan and an integral inner city policy, if the danger is not to be run that the identity and individuality of a whole town is lost. In Den Bosch this applies particularly to the Markt with the three old approach roads, St. Jan's with the Parade, the Uilenburgquarter, the ramparts with bastions, the Binnen-Dieze. As well as the town planning qualities (environmental areas), the individual properties are of great importance because through the comparative narrowness of the properties they form a small scale (in the sense of: in proportion to human measurements) and thereby also a so-called fine-grained urban area in which, notwithstanding the unity of scale, there is a strong and colourful diversity of outward apperance, functions and historical and cultural significance which lends a great attraction to such historic inner city areas. This power of attraction has always existed as regards the renowned trade function of former days and is still manifest now in the fine historic buildings such as the cathedral and the town hall and the old patrician houses which have been handed down to us, for example, De Moriaan, along the Parade, the Verwersstraat, the Peperstraat, etc.). But it still exists today, not only for business and trade, but also for the residential function. One of the reasons why many people want to go and live (again) in the heart of the old town is that the distance (literally, but especially figuratively) between the far less stimulating residential areas and the old town, which is experienced as an alive and lively meeting place, and as a

centre of attraction, is becoming ever greater. The direct proximity of restaurants and theatres, shops, stores, terraces and cafés gives living in the old town its own charm.

In the municipal executive's recommendations on the proposals for inner city policy as set forth in the above-mentioned report "An integral inner city policy", one of the main points of the integral inner city policy to be pursued is given as the value which is attached to the existence of the inner city and the way in which it is experienced.

"The inner city is the very complex centre of orientation and experience for the population of town and district. It derives this high symbolic value for the most part from its integral functions and specific forms, which should be permanently protected, maintained and adjusted. This should be done by all individuals, enterprises and institutions, who contribute to the life of the inner city. The state also belongs to these contributors."

Restoration policy

When the new plans for the inner city had at last begun to take definite shape, great activity was displayed within the municipal machinery as regards the checking of deteriora-

's-Hertogenbosch: Proposed extension of the conservation area (boundary = 6 Dinise) in 1975 as a precondition for a detailed plan (bestemmingsplan) which covers the whole inner city

tion and the preservation of the historic forms and structures in the inner city. From 1973 onwards, numerous initiatives were taken by the municipal authorities to achieve a systematic approach to the problems. On all sides there was a striving after rehabilitation and restoration of historic elements in the entire inner city area. The idea underlying this was that the character of Den Bosch is determined to a great extent by the totality and, compared with other medium-sized Dutch town, the authenticity – still largely extant – of this totality. The choice of preserving this principal characteristic means that it would then be a mistaken policy to concentrate the urban renewal activities on only a few areas. This would lead not only to other areas, which are certainly as interesting in the totality, being left in an often derelict condition, but furthermore to the acceleration of delapidation since the possible initiators of action in such areas would seek refuge in more active areas on account of the "stepmotherly" treatment of their own area. In practice, however, the authorities were forced to concentrate on those areas where delay could no longer be tolerated. This meant that in the first instance all the plans of the municipal authorities were directed to areas which did not fall within the protected townscape. In some cases the areas were ones which the municipal council had previously decided to demolish, as for example some of the buildings along the harbour and St. Jorisstraat.

As the first phase of the restoration of the historic elements in the inner city, an extensive enquiry into, and inventory of, the structural quality of the buildings was made. Thereafter efforts were made by means of the presentation of detailed plans to acquire the neccessary financial means from the central government. Finally, a rehabilitation-restoration plan for the whole inner city was adopted by the municipal council. Since subsidies from the Ministry of Housing and Physical Planning for the restoration of premises which are of importance to the landscape, but are not protected under articles 8 and 9 of the Monuments Act, are only possible within a protected townscape (or at least in an area where it is the Minister's intention to make it a protected townscape) a proposal was put forward at the same time for extension of the protected townscape to cover the whole inner city area, namely the area bounded by the Dommel, Aa and city ramparts (thus excluding het Zand).

A somewhat conservative view has been adopted with regard to the form in which the restoration of the inner city takes place. This is based not so much on fashionable nostalgia, nor on mistrust of things new, but emanates from the desire to avoid the outward from of the inner city being too much the reflection of a certain period of development. For this reason the preservation of properties, the value of which as monuments is very limited, has been urged and made possible with government subsidies. The authenticity of materials, etc. then takes second place. This does not alter the fact that in 1976 and subsequent years there will be varied contributions to the townscape without there being over-dominant features (filling up gaps, new building for dwellings and offices).

In the near future, provided the municipal council agrees, a building of some 200 sq. metres will be put up at the municipal works depot for the housing and repair of restoration materials. A documentation system is also being built up, whereby cartographic, architectural-historical and town planning-historical data will be easily accessible and safely stored in a sound archives system. It is intended that attention should be paid especially to reporting on restorations and to the revision of drawings.

Technical measures

The municipality of Den Bosch has no city rehabilitation organisation. There has been, and still is, talk of investors and large building organisations wanting to turn their attention to restoration work but not having the general approval of the municipal authorities, since in these cases it was often a question of trying to obtain a monopoly position in dealing with historic buildings. All in all this is at the moment a politically tricky matter.

In connection with the amount of building and restoration work which is in hand, or will shortly be commenced, there is urgent need of a form of city core enquiry. Building remains still present in the ground date from a period for which no maps or archive material exists. They can provide extremely important information on the city's history. Without a specific form of city core enquiry, for which plans are indeed in preparation, this information would be lost.

2.4 Initiators of intervention

Organisation

The tasks in connection with the care of monuments in the municipal machinery lie both with the town clerk's office and also with that of the city surveyor. As regards the preparaton and implementation, however, the emphasis is on the town development department of the city surveyor's office. The inner city department is entrusted both with tasks concerning town planning design (development plans, arrangement of open spaces) and also with tasks concerning restoration work (municipal restorations, guidance for restorations by private persons). A documentation section provides material of architectural and town-planning history for the benefit of these two main tasks. The inner city department has an advisory voice in the aesthetic control over the external appearance of buildings.

Private initiative plays an important part in the municipal restoration policy. Particularly in the housing sector the municipality restores as little as possible itself. The phasing and costing of the properties to be restored in the city rehabilitation plan is to a great extent based on this principle, although the 'planning' of this initiative is a precarious business. The line of policy followed at the moment is that private persons are stimulated where possible to restore their property or eligible properties are 'drawn' to the notice of private persons. In a number of cases the municipality buys properties and then sells them to private persons with the obligation to perform the restoration work. Only in cases where there are no other possibilities does the municipality purchase and restore properties itself. This has occurred, for instance, in St. Jorisstraat. In the Uilenburg quarter, on the other hand, it was mainly private initiative with a few cases of purchase and sale of properties by the municipality with the obligation to carry out the restoration. At the moment the municipality possesses no restored properties which are to let. The properties, which are restored directly by the municipality, are usually sold again. In the restoration policy as it has been pursued up to now, use is made of the existing channels, the state schemes for restoration work.

The importance which the municipality attaches to private initiative in the restoration of properties in the inner city is borne out where possible by the attidute and actions of the municipal services. In the first place there is the intensive guidance given to private persons who are interested in restoring their property. The municipality does not, however, act as an architect for private persons. The aim is to

305

achieve as subtle a process of restoration activities as possible in the inner city by means of the great care which is spent on the documentation and inventorisation of the historic elements and the careful checking of the building plans before they go to the Dept. for the Preservation of Monuments and Historic Buildings. Moreover, the municipality refunds the architect's fees to private persons in cases where the expected state subsidy does not materialize.

3. Goals of Intervention

Objectives as articulated in planning instruments

In November 1970, the municipal council agreed to the designation of part of the inner city as a protected townscape. On 23 March 1973, the townscape in question was officially scheduled. In the explanatory note accompanying the order for designation of the protected townscape the following motivation was used: characteristic elements of the inner city of Den Bosch are the fairly fine mesh pattern of narrow streets and alleys, the fascinating street pattern with its curved building lines, and the presence amongst the "large" monuments of numerous premises with yellow and white plastered corniced facades with stucco ornamentation, mostly 19th century architecture. The usual zone system has been applied to the protected area. On 21 March 1974 the structure concept (plan) 'Views in the inner city' was approved, in which one of the basic principles was the protection of facades, townscape and street patterns, for the entire inner city. The municipal authorities thus laid the emphasis on the characteristic picture of the inner city as a whole, in the way in which it is to a considerable extent determined by the ramparts, the Dommel, the Aa, and the Bossche Broek. From the beginning of 1975 onwards a procedure was set in motion to get the protected townscape extended.

On 15 February 1973, the municipal council, on the basis of the report 'An integral inner city policy', approved these recommendations. The most important points in the council's decision were:

– To maintain and respect the character of the inner city.

– To maintain the monumental course of the Binnen-Dieze and the street elevations.

– To promote and restore the residential function.

– To restore the city ramparts and use them where possible as recreational elements.

In December 1973, 'View of the inner city', a structural concept appeared, in which the objectives, as developed in an earlier planning phase, were specified in more detail:

Broadly speaking, the municipal authorities decided in this plan in favour of maintaining the existing physical structure and of protecting facades and townscapes throughout the inner city, since these physical features are of great importance from the historical, economic, cultural and recreational point of view. This applies in particular to that part of the inner city which is already scheduled as a protected landscape, and also applies to part of the city precincts. For the remaining parts of the inner city and 't Zand the present physical structure, considering the inferior quality of the existing forms, need only incidentally be a determining factor for the future development of the inner city.

As a general rule with respect to the structural and town planning form, the character and the recognition of the inner city, which consists chiefly of the pluriform and the multifunctional, and the way in which the various functions have often adapted to the existing space and forms, should be respected and threats to this identity of form should be guarded against.

Policy: functions

Two aspects of the functions of this inner city enjoy special attention. In the first place the residential function. Housing receives priority in areas outside the heart of the city, in particular in the monuments and the neighbourhoods which have been residential from of old, such as Uilenburg. In an earlier planning phase a number of arguments were put forward in this respect in the report 'An integral inner city policy', namely:

1) The old inner city was originally planned as an area, where dwellings, work, recreation and traffic were an integrated whole.

's-Hertogenbosch: Tolbrug-
straat, results of urban rehabilitation in the sixties

2) Housing is the original function of the majority of the old properties.

3) A residential function promotes the liveliness of the inner city, also after shops and offices have closed and at the weekends.

4) There are groups of people in all strata of the population who prefer living in the inner city, albeit for very varying reasons.

5) The variegated habitation of the inner city is necessary for the functioning of urban democracy.

6) The residential function attracts very little heavy motorized traffic.

A second function which is considered of especial signifi-cance for the inner city is the cultural-recreational. This is determinded in the first instance by the picture of bustle and conviviality of this area whereby for instance some people are attracted to just being there. This picture is supported by the specimens in the economic function, but also by the monumental character of the course of roads and the facades of buildings, by the open space and by buildings, which function of the inner city is therefore so important because the inner city as such is in fact at the service, or will come to be, of culture and recreation in the broadest sense for the whole population. On account of this central function of the inner city, in the widest sense of the word, but also in support of the residential function, the municipal authorities' policy will be aimed at activating the cultural-recreational functions both in and around buildings and also in open spaces to a greater extent.

Policy

In the structural concept the objectives for a number of inner city areas were given concrete form and visual explanation. In so doing a territorial division was made of the inner city area. Thus reference is made to the city core (Markt and immediate vicinity): the part of the inner city where the typical city centre shops and the stores as well as banks and related offices are established, or at least in so far as these together form a linked-up area, with catering establish-ments and parking facilities in between or adjacent. Refer-ence is also made to the 'stadserf' ('city precincts' – round

the city core and along the old main streets), by which is meant that part of the inner city where, under the influence of the 'radiation' from the city core, the use of the inner city is so intense that it calls for specially oriented policy and for an arrangement of that part of the inner city clearly attuned to this use. A strong and striking concentration in the vicinity of various centrally situated functions and the consequent intensification of encounters and contacts between city residents and visitors are characteristic of what takes place in the city precincts. The following functions are intended for these component areas in the future.

a. City core

The principal functions there will continue to be multiple stores, shops, small catering establishments and small services with office premises. Subsidiary functions: (on upper storeys) dwellings and large catering establishments, use for culture, education and religious services, as well as for public services. In this connection an effort will be made to give the most careful guidance in enlargement of the monumental character of the course of the streets and the facades and of the liveliness of the retail trade, where adjustment to a function is necessary, and to promote the residential function where necessary.

b. City precincts

Principal functions same as those of city core, with addition of dwellings, artisan enterprises and wholesale trade. Sub-sidiary functions: same as those of the city core, with the understanding that there can be a greater variety of dwel-lings here. It will also be possible to construct multi-storey garages in this area. This is in keeping with the resolution recently passed on multi-story garages. The greatest atten-tion will also be paid here to historic forms and the multi-functional aspect. Large monumental buildings which become available can be made use of for cultural develop-ment. The maintenance of existing, and the limited develop-ment of new, residential possibilities can take place in this area. This function has a complementary character here. The Binnen Dieze is of great importance for the way in which the cultural and recreational aspects of the inner city are experienced.

307

c. The remaining part of the inner city

plus the part of 't Zand along the Dommel have housing as the principal function and as subidiary functions the principal functions of the core, with the exception of the multiple stores. Other subsidiary functions in this area are the service industries, hospital and nursing homes and multistorey garages. A number of small residential areas already exist here and can be extended. Others can be brought into being. The residential function is primarily here. Attention will be paid to the recreational possibilities of the city ramparts, as well as to the open space (for example, garden of the former Redemptorist monastery), which can support the residential function.

d. 't Zand

The principal functions for this area must be considered as the large offices, the wholesale trade and the service industries, in general the service sector.

As subsidiary functions the functions of the rest of the inner city mentioned under c. above can be developed here.

If this development of functions is to take shape, then there will have to be an attempt at short notice (dependent on the possibilities) to create space to give this development a chance. This naturally leads to the conclusion that in particular industrial activity in the city core, the city precincts and the rest of the inner city will have to be restrained as much as possible and space will have to be created for it elsewhere in the town (De Gruyter (multiple grocery stores), the Bossche Textile Industry 'De drie Mollen', Nederveen Margarine factory and others).

Social implications

The present inhabitants of the premises in the various rehabilitaiton areas will in general be able to go on living there, at any rate as far as the inner city is concerned. This is made possible through the buildding of public sector housing within the old fortress area, for example in the Hofstad quarter. A second possibility could be through 'inexpensive restorations', in fact through catching up on maintenance and repairs for properties of indifferent structural quality, which would be radically restored at a later date. This moderated maintenance could mean that the rents would only have to be slightly raised if the costs could be met from funds for retraining and structural unemployment. Plans for this scheme have still to be worked out. For the rest, a special aspect of the large, combined restoration projects, such as St. Jorisstraat, the harbour, Ortenstraat, Putstraat is that the properties to be restored have not been inhabited for some time.

4. Strategies

4.1 Legal techniques

Control of the intended use of restored properties in the inner city will be possible in the first instance through the various local development plans for this area.

At the moment there is no legally valid plan in existence, apart from the redevelopment and reconstruction plans. A second possibility of control is via the so-called tied con-

tracts, i. e. properties are bought from the municipality either before of after restoration on certain conditions concerning the use to which the premises are to be put. The municipality also has a preferential right should the property be sold within a period of 15 years.

Apart from the obligatory maintenance policy of the municipal building and housing inspectorate, the municipality has no specific methods of controlling the maintenance of monuments. There is no affiliation to the Foundation for the Inspection of Restored Monuments and Historic Buildings, nor is that a condition for the sale of properties to private persons. Now and again, the borough surveyor's department 'raises an alarm' with the municipal authorities concerning the decrepit condition of certain objects. In the future the aim will be to lessen the need for rehabilitation and premature restoration of premises already treated by means of a visiting maintenance team.

At the moment there are six rehabilitaion areas in which an action policy is being pursued, namely Uilenburg, Waaigat, Geertruikerkhof, Putstraat, St. Janskerkhof and St. Jorisstraat.

The protected townscape which is in force in these areas necessitates the drawing up of the obligatory development plans. So far only the Uilenburg plan has been approved by the municipal council. The other plans are at the moment still in the draft and citizen participation stage.

In 1976 it was intended to discuss a supplementary list of monuments in the municipal council. This was not to be in the form of a separate municipal list containing objects of local importance. The aim was rather to include these objects in the existing register of scheduled monuments.

The municipal authorities' actions with regard to all elements and events concerning the inner city are fitted as far as possible into the integral planning design as incorporated in the structure concept for the inner city. This integral inner city policy is described as follows:

'By integral inner city policy is meant a coherent policy which is aimed at one well-defined and deliberately chosen objective; the components and timing and are bundled together in one realistic action programme in which private initiative and state initiative voluntarily cooperate and back one another up'. Thus the nevertheless ambitious way in which monuments and other older buildings are being tackled is not a case of isolated action. There is likewise a concept of the historic whole, embodied in the various policy papers on the inner city. The effects of this specific restoration and rehabilitation policy, in which monuments take an important place, cannot yet be adequately foreseen. 1976 will be the first year in which larger numbers of restored and renovated properties will be delivered.

4.2 Financial techniques

Subsidizing of restoration work

As far as the restoration of dwellings is concerned, up to 1968 it cannot be said that an energetic restoration policy was pursued – the activities were too incidental. Up to 1969 eight restorations had been carried out, subsidizable costs fl. 315,603.–. In 1969 four restorations, subsidizable costs fl. 302,506.–. In 1970 thirteen restorations, subsidizable costs fl. 464,628.–. From 1968 onwards a deliberate restoration policy in dwellings was pursued in close consultation with the Department for the Preservation of Monuments and

Historic Buildings. In that year a so-called "dwellings fund" of fl. 50,000.– became available by the government and was supplemented by the municipality of Den Bosch with an equal amount. Thus a total amount of fl. 100,000.– became available. In 1969 both bodies made a similar amount available (fl. 50,000.– + fl. 50,000.– = fl. 100,000.–), so that for 1968 and 1969 a total of fl. 200,000.– was available. In 1970 the amounts were raised from fl. 50,000.– to fl. 70,000.–, so that year fl. 140,000.– was made available, as well as the total of fl. 200,000.– from the years 1968 – 1969. For 1971 the state and the municipality made amounts of fl. 100,000.– available, so that the assets in the fund up to and including 1971 totalled fl. 540,000.–, of which fl. 270,000.– was made available by the municipality.

Although the municipality was willing to reserve a sum of fl. 300,000.– in the municipal budget for both 1971 and 1972, it was not possible to obtain more than fl. 100,000.– from the state on account of restricted government means. The state subsidy, was to be fl. 250,000.– for 1973, but this amount was eventually raised to fl. 275,000.–. From the total amount available from 1968–1973 seven dwellings and several other monuments were subsidised. For 1974 the municipal executive gave a definite undertaking for subsidies for 13 objects, whilst preparations were made to acquire subsidies for some 25 restoration plans, (the restoration work on St. Jan's cathedral, the ramparts with bastion, the house of refuge, the powder magazine and fort Orthen were not included in this number).

In the structural concept 'View of the inner city' the costs of the restoration work for the most urgent objects from the structural point of view were estimated as follows: including the restoration of the Binnen-Dieze and the ramports (jointly estimated at an amount of some fl. 26,000,000.–) as sum is needed solely for structural provisions amounting to a total of fl. 86,000,000.–.

Specification restoration activities

Plan Uilenburg, phase I, II	fl. 13,500,000.–
Plan St. Geertruikerhof	fl. 6,800,000.–
Plan St. Jorisstraat	fl. 3,000,000.–
Plan harbour	fl. 4,400,000.–
Restoration Binnen-Dieze	fl. 20,500,000.–
Restoration City Ramparts	fl. 6,000,000.–
Inner City, Dwellings	fl. 16,700,000.–
Inner City	
Large-scale restorations (municipal)	fl. 8,200,000.–
Large-scale restorations (private)	fl. 6,900,000.–
Total	fl. 86,000,000.–

Excluding St. Jan's cathedral, but including the catheral tower. A period of approximately 8 years for rehabilitation and restoration has been allocated in view of the structural condition of many of the buildings. In the restoration – rehabilitation plan of May 1975 for the entire inner city, excluding het Zand, 766 of the properties to be rehabilitated were to be used wholly or partially as dwellings. On the grounds of building plans already submitted or anticipated, it is assumed that it will be possible to acquire funds for restoration work in the coming years as follows: in 1976 for 48 properties:

(restoration costs   fl. 9,263,000.–),
in 1977 for 49 properties (fl. 9,852,999.–),
in 1978 for 70 properties (fl. 12,450,000.–),
in 1979 for 68 properties (fl. 12,300,000.–),
in 1980 for 75 properties (fl. 13,350,000.–)
and from 1980 for 456 properties (fl. 88,085,000.–).

According to a very broad estimate fl. 145,000,000.– is needed for this rehabilitation work. This concerns properties, which are to be used wholly and partially as dwellings.

There are also properties with other uses which are eligible for a restoration subsidy: Mention has been made of 14 large properties which according to a rough calculation call for fl. 21,000,000.– and further of small monuments with no residential function for which a sum of over fl. 1,000,000.– will be necessary. The restoration of dwellings often concerns properties which are very important to the landscape. Their restoration could, however, in view of their often deplorable structural condition, better be termed 'new building with restrictions'. The molecular historical genuineness of such restored properties is often minimal, in spite of the careful guidance on the part of the municipal authorities in the real of architectural history. However, in using this method the authenticity of the town planning element has to a great extent been preserved.

DACW fund (Supplementary civil-technical work)

Apart from the general, nationally applicable subsidy regualtions, there is in Den Bosch in the framework of combatting unemployment a considerable inflow of monies from the DACW fund. The following restoration work was carried out thanks to this fund:

Town hall	fl. 660,000.–
City ramparts	fl. 500,000.–
Binnen-Dieze	fl. 3,500,000.–
Housing plan 'Waaigat'	fl. 1,000,000.–
Powder magazine	fl. 650,000.–
'The Twelve Apostles' houses	fl. 900,000.–
St. Jan's cathedral-municipal tower	fl. 2,250,000.–
Total	fl. 9,460,000.–

Since 1970 the following restorations have been carried out:

Restoration of dwellings	Subsidies promises
1968	fl. 110,000.–
1969	fl. 154,000.–
1970	fl. 220,000.–
1971	fl. 220,000.–
1972	fl. 440,000.–
1973	fl. 550,000.–
1974	fl. 1,100,000.–
1975	fl. 2,100,000.–
Total	fl. 4,894,000.–

Finance

The municipality is seeking means of establishing a fund in the future for providing advances for private restoration work or for contributing to the operating deficits on municipal restorations. A possibility may be the profits acquired from earlier restorations carried out by the municipality.

4.3 Partipation – information

As has been mentioned previously, at the end of the sixties there was a change of policy in Den Bosch, whereby the emphasis of the policy for the inner city was again laid more on preservation and rehabilitaiton of the unique historic character. From the very beginning the municipal authorities deliberately set out to make clear what the new intentions for the inner city were. A more of less continuous

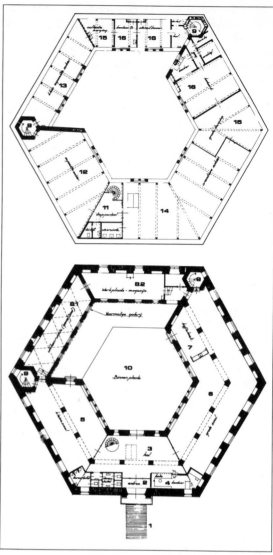

's-Hertogenbosch: Revitalisation of the KRUITHUIS (gunpowder store), built in 1619, reopened as an exhibition centre in 1975; lower right: ground floor. 1. entrance bridge, 2. entrance, 3. hall, 4. 5. little hall, 6. large hall, 7. coffee, 8. former gallery, 9. winding stairs, 10. courtyard; upper right: first floor. 11. staircase, 12. exposition room, 13. small exposition room, 14. 16. office

stream of information was provided. The important structure concept 'View of the Inner City' was published in a large edition and distributed to all interested parties known to the municipality. It was available to the individual citizen for fl. 5.00.

A big exhibition was held in the town hall to illustrate all the plans concerning the inner city; this was done by means of planning maps, scale models, drawings, photos, historical material, etc. It is the intention that similar exhibitions should be organised in the future over all large rehabilitation and restoration plans, as well as filling-in and new building plans.

Participation

There was no participation procedure held for the general inner city plan, set out in the structure concept 'View of the inner city'. The municipal authorities believe that the individual citizen's involvement in the form of joining in the thinking process and possibly in the decision process is more appropriate at the local development plan stage, in which the general concept is worked out in certain concrete components of the inner city. The fact is that the local development plans affect the direct interests of the citizens much sooner. Here it is mostly a question of his own residential environment. There is no hard and fast procedure for participation in the case of the local development plans. What happens is dependent on the existing situation, such as: the most dominating problems in the area, the number of people who still live in the area, or otherwise have interests there, the ownership position, etc. In general the citizens are active in their approach. It even happens that there is often a not unimportant contribution made beforehand by active citizens. They air ideas for the area, offer solutions to problems and give concrete suggestions for the lay-out of the area. The municipality does not ignore these contributions but tries as far as possible to incorporate this representation of interests in the local development plan. As far as the municipality is concerned, the fixed procedure is that the plan is presented to the population in the municipal information centre. If there is sufficient interest a public hearing is held. However, informal contacts with private people involved play the most important part during the planning consultations. All this is connected to no small extent with the character of a grate part of the population of Den Bosch: people are not wont to think so much in urban terms. As a result the influence of the citizens on the main lines of policy is but slight. If one leaves out of account the reactions of the political world and of interest groups directly concerned with the inner city, then the reactions in particular to the structure concept 'Vision of the inner city' were few in number. On the other hand, this need not necessarily be a disquieting phenomenon, since up to now there has been a great deal of appreciation by the population of what is being done in the inner city and there is no question of fundamental criticism after the event now that the implementation of the plans is underway. The intention is that those citizens, and in particular those groups of citizens, who have taken an active part in the last few years concerning the course of affairs in the inner city should be included in a permanent advisory and consultative body for the inner city. The task of this consultative body will be to make recommendations on numerous matters concerning the inner city, such as:

1) Fitting in and function of Hof van Zevenbergen (former Catholic orphanage);

2) Filling in of de Gruyter plot, Orthenstraat;

3) Substitute function for Markt;

4) Filling in of Marienburg (former monastery) plot, Postel-straat;

5) Extension of pedestrian precinct;

6) Lighting plan for the inner city and part to be played therein by advertising (nature and scope);

7) Approach to, and functions for, environs of St. Jan's cathedral;

8) Alternative functions for valuable large-scale buildings in the town (churches, chapels, monasteries);

9) Drastic building and restoration plans (C&A., multistorey car parks, Powder Magazine, Tower of St. Jan's, Brabants Dagblad (daily paper) building, Provincial Energy Board building, Noord-Brabant Museum building, building in Papenhulst area, etc.);

10) Restoration and functioning of the Binnen-Dieze;

11) Draft development plans for the inner city (Uilenburg I und II, Zuidwal, Vughter triangle, Hinthamer triangle, Aa-Zuid-Willemsvaart, De Plein, Het Zang).

In fact an institutionalized form of participation thus comes into being for a number of organisations. These organisations are provisionally: the Association of Dutch Architects, 's-Hertogenbosch Circle, 's-Hertogenbosch Foundation for the Preservation of Historic Building and Monuments, 'De Boschboom' Circle for History and the Preservation of Historic Sites and Unspoilt Countryside (cf. England, 'National Trust'), the Friends of 's-Hertogenbosch Foundation, Business Centre for Wholesale Enterprises, NKOV (Neth. Catholic Entrepreneurs Assn.), Women's Advisory Committee and the SWH (Building Societies Cooperative Den Bosch) Foundation.

Citizen groups

There are a number of citizen groups which have for some time been actively engaged in following the municipal inner city policy with a critical eye. According to the nature of the group this may be concerned with total inner city policy in all its aspects, but it may also apply to specific historic features in the inner city. The principal groups are:

- The local branch of the national Heemschut League (Preservation of Historic Sites and Unspoilt Countryside). This group takes a critical interest in particular in the guarantees which are created for the cultural and historical interests in the various plans. If necessary it makes use of all possible legal means to raise objections to government plans. Amongt other things, the League made a strong protest against the plan for filling in the Binnen-Dieze.

- The 's-Hertogenbosch Foundation for the Preservation of Historic Buildings and Monuments. The Foundation keeps well abreast of what is going on in the realm of the preservation of monuments. It has good contacts within the municipality.

- "De Boschboom" Circle for History and Heemschut (Preservation of Historic Sites and Unspoilt Countryside). This group concentrates in particular on the study of the past history of the special characteristics of the city of Den Bosch. On account of the group's wide knowledge the municipal authorities call upon it in the development of plans.

- The Friends of 's-Hertogenbosch Circle. The circle is concerned with information and education. It produces publications on historical aspects of the town and tries to foster interest in the historical aspects of Den Bosch. Thus, for instance, the circle mapped out a number of historical walks, which were made available in leaflet form for those interested.

Action groups

It may be said that there is an active group amongst the citizens, which has already quickly become institutionalised. To start with this group called itself the "council group for better government management". The reasons for its coming into being in 1966 were general dissatisfaction with municipal inner city policy. In particular the proposed filling in of the Binnen-Dieze was the motive for making this dissatisfaction known on a national scale. The name was later changed to "Den Bosch 2000". By 1970 the group had won 4 seats on the council. At the moment the group has 4 representatives on the municipal council. Analogous to a character in the Carneval of Den Bosch the group now calls itself council group "De Knillis". It has been one of the groups which has greatly influenced inner city policy. Its members were and are emotionally involved in the inner city problems. The relationship between the municipal authorities and the citizen in the realm of monuments and restoration is excellent. Both parties are aware of the favourable climate for these affairs. The citizen knows that the municipality wants to get a great deal done in this field. This finds expression amongst other things in such an enormous wave of applications for restoration and rehabilitation projects that these can only be met in the longer term by the government (central-provincial-municipal).

5. Promotion

The municipality of Den Bosch earned distinction from the national M'75 committee for this respect for its heritage. Further, several leaflets were produced, including "'s-Hertogenbosch Monumentenstad" (Den Boschtown of monuments and historic buildings) and one on the restoration of the Powder Magazine. There was also a folder available with historical cartographic material. A plaque was represented for a restoration work which was completed or in progress. An exhibition in the town hall gave a survey of all aspects of the activities in the inner city.

Apart from these special manifestations, day-to-day information was provided via the information department. In the past a book was published containing all possible information on obtaining government subsidies, building and rebuilding, etc.

6. Future Policy

The future is contained in the present. The future will be characterised by a consistent carrying forward of the memoranda and plans drawn up in the past few years and the substantiation of the council decisions taken. Three aspects may be mentioned here:

1. As regards the municipal services: considerable funds have been promised, but there are sometimes difficulties in assimilating these funds and putting them to effect in time to achieve complete restoration projects via the various plans.

2. The translation of the integral policy concept in the restoration projects realised in the inner city. It is a question of now getting these objects to function in the urban society in accordance with the objectives set.

3. The development of new policy instruments, including those in the realm of advance financing by means of the above-mentioned fund to be established for this purpose, and those concerning the creation of possibilities for the original residents to continue to live in the inner city, by, for instance, specially adapted maintenance of their dwellings, the so-called "inexpensive restorations".

4. In general, present instruments have been found adequate with the additions mentioned above in connection with a city core enquiry and a materials and documentation bank.

's-Hertogenbosch: Appendix cost planning 1975–1978

Plan	Preservation Costs per plan and time		Number of protected objects		Number of objects important for townscape	New Construction Number of aided new flats according to time	
	1975–1978	after 1978	bad	very bad		1975–1978	after 1978
Uilenburg area 2	7,200,000		18 of which 40 flats				34	42
	3,150,000	3,150,000			42 of which 42 flats		
	total costs: 13,500,000						
Havenkwartier area 3	3,000,000				20 of which 20 flats	20	
Waaigat area 3.1	3,000,000	1,368,000	26 of which 26 flats				
Geertruikerkhof area 3,9	2,871,829	4,000,000			23 of which 40 flats	73	
	total costs: 14,239,829						
Zuit-Willemsvaart-Aa							
area 6						173	
St. Jorisstraat area 9,1	1,315,000				10 of which 10 flats		40
	total costs: 1,315,000						
Zuidwal area 9							20
Carolus area 4						100	188
Other areas	4,500,000	9,000,000		90 of which 90 flats			135
	2,400,000	800,000		8 of which 20 flats			
	7,500,000	60,000,000	450 of which 550 flats				
	4,000,000	40,000,000			880 of which 880 flats		
	total costs: 128,200,000						

Total costs in the period 1975–1978:	38,936,829
Total costs in the period after 1978:	118,318,000
Total costs general:	157,254,829

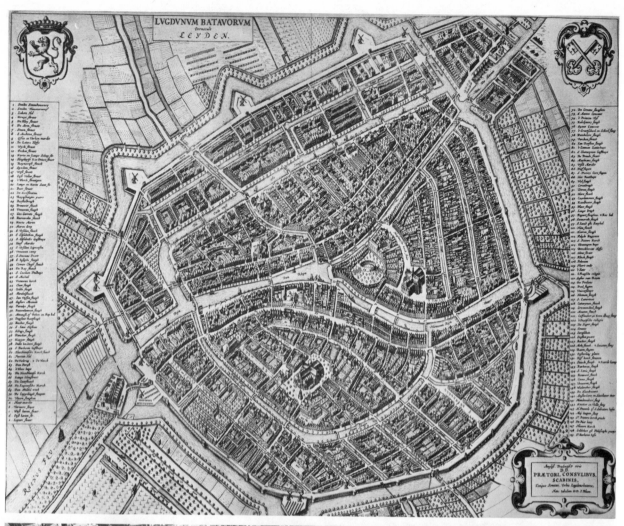

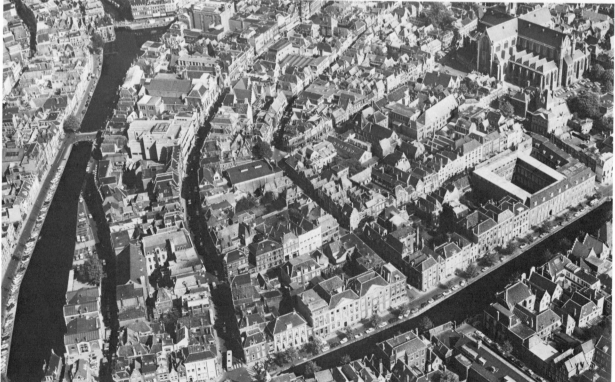

Leiden: above: historical map, 17th century
below: aerial photograph (1976) of the south-western quarter around the Pieterskerk between Rapenburg and Breestraat.
(photo: KLM Aerocarto)

Netherlands
LEIDEN

1. Situation

1.1 General introduction

Leiden is situated in the west of the Netherlands near the North Sea coast. It is in the province of Zuid-Holland. With 177 hectares the inner city is the second largest in the Netherlands with 1,100 statutorily protected historic monuments. The total number of inhabitants is 96,000 as per 1977.

1.2 History

In the second half of the 11th century Leiden must have been a settlement of sufficient importance to the Bishop of Utrecht (who was enfeoffed in 1064 by the Emperor with the present Rijnland) for him to build a fortification against the count of Holland: De Burcht (the castle).

About a century later the settlement, which had developed between the castle and the Count's residential complex (Lockhorst, environs of the Pieterskerk and, later, Gravensteen), had become so large that the Count found it worthwhile to grant city rights.

About 1300 the built-up area had spread out over the Rijnland (Rhine island) which belonged in a civic respect to Leiderdorp.

The last medieval expansion of the town began in 1386 on territory belonging to Zoeterwoude, whose lord of the manor relinquished his rights to the area to be included within the walls. This was the greatest expansion. It provided Leiden with enough building ground to last two centuries.

Medieval Leiden is still clearly distinguishable within the larger 17th–19th century town on account of the width of the circle of fortification canals (still partly in existence).

In the early 16th century a small suburb was already growing up east of the town on either side of the Lage Rijnkijk and Haven; this came within the city walls in 1644. The last expansion of this period took place in the years 1655–1659 with the construction of the outermost 'rind' from the Zuidsingel to the Geregracht, bordered on the outside by the Zijl- and Zoeterwoudsesingel. The area thus gained, Leiden within the 'singels' ('singel' = outer fortification canal for town, hereafter referred to as 'encircling canal'), was again sufficient for some two centuries. About 1640 the number of inhabitants amounted to more than 50,000, which made Leiden the largest town in the Republic after Amsterdam. As a result of the regression in the 18th century and during the French period, municipal expansion was unnecessary.

Not until well into the second half of the 19th century did streets develop outside the encircling canals along the roads to the surrounding villages. Annexations to bring this area under the municipality of Leiden and to create space for expansion took place in 1896, 1919/20 and 1966.

As a result of the industrial revolution, the home industry, which was carried out in the weavers' houses in particular, was superseded at the beginning of the 19th century by work in the factory. In order to house the inflow of employees every empty piece of ground was used to build small dwellings. The few pieces of remaining waste land and even gardens of houses were sacrificed to this building rage. Examples of this are to be found in almost the whole of the old inner city. It was also during this period that a large part of the Levendaal-oost area came into being. The building density of this district amounts to 60 to 70 dwellings per hectare.

Especially after the Second World War, numerous new industries were established in Leiden. Various urban expansion schemes, including the new university city now under construction, bear witness to a new prosperity. The city is the market and services centre for the whole Rijnland region.

2. Conditions

2.1 Past policy

The policy concerning historic buildings and monuments and historic groups in the inner city differed considerably in the period 1945–1970 from that which is now being pursued. Views up to 1970 were not exactly favourable for the preservation and protection of the historic ground plan and the historic buildings. Emphasis was laid on housing and traffic; as a result the monuments (both large and small) were neglected and 'old' structures were treated in a somewhat careless manner. The views expressed in the structure plan of 1958 and the roads plan of 1959 were negative with regard to many aspects of the historic town planning structure and the historic buildings.

A plan for redevelopment and urban renewal followed up, which covered the entire inner city, indicating the consequences of the proposed traffic structure.

As a result of these views the policy pursued during the period was not directed towards the preservation and restoration of the historic buildings. There were no clear views as to the necessity or desirability of restoration work and restorations were only carried out sporadically. The municipality saw to the restoration of the Weighhouse and the Boterhal and circular wall of De Burcht. In this period there was also relatively little initiative taken by private persons. True, some of the large monuments were restored (Pieterskerk, Lodewijkskerk, Gravensteen), but the restoration of dwellings which qualified as monuments remained at a very low ebb (an average of one a year). Up to 1968 the restoration subsidy percentage granted by the municipality for dwellings qualifying as monuments was 10 to 15 %. After the 'refinement' regulation for monuments came into force this was raised to 30 %. The expenditure on the subsidy was covered by the allowance received by the municipality in accordance with the 'refinement' regulation.

The advent of the Monuments Act and the compilation of the monuments list have definitely been of influence. Not everyone reacted equally enthusiastically to this; from various quarters it was feared that the inner city would acquire the character of a museum. In general it may be said that, as a result of the somewhat negative attitude towards the historic town planning structure and the historic buildings, not many instruments were employed at first to preserve the cultural heritage. Thus, for example, no rights of property were acquired so as to be able to protect and restore the properties, no measures were taken towards the maintenance of the historic buildings, no stimulus was given to promote the restoration of private properties. There was no possibility of giving advances for the financing of restoration work, etc. The publicity over the old built-up environment was to a certain extent anti-propaganda, which emphasised the disadvantages and less attractive aspects, whilst the positive aspects were hardly emphasised, if at all.

In 1967 the municipal executive gave instructions for the drawing up before 1970 of an overall plan for the entire inner city, as well as for detailed plans for some of the dilapidated areas therein. Owing to the absence of a complete list of requirements, the Public Works department had to restrict itself to a draft study, which was ready in the spring of 1970. Partly with this in mind the municipal executive proposed to the Council in July 1970 the instigation of an enquiry on the inner city.

Taken by and large, the policy in the period 1945–1970 was not exactly favourable for the preservation and restoration of the historic town planning character and the historic buildings. This has not been without consequences for the inner city. Through insufficient attention and a not very positive view of the cultural heritage, policy in the past has been disastrous for the inner city.

Leiden: Topographical map of 1971 with demarcation of the historical core (17th century)

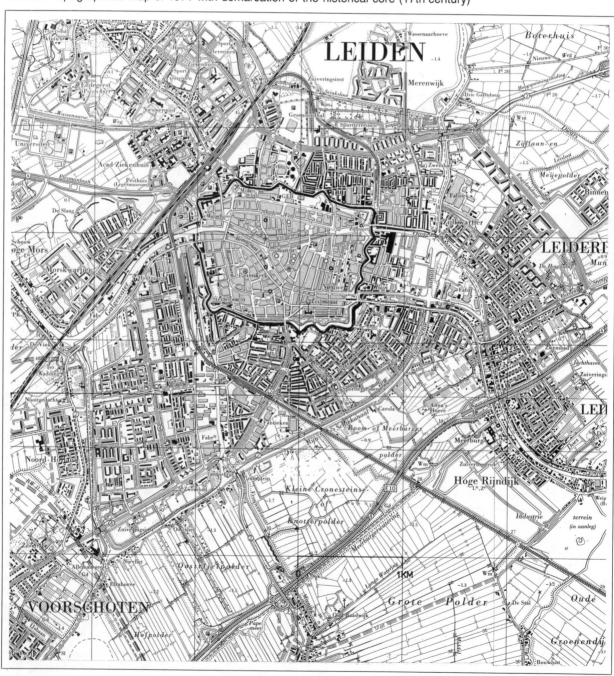

2.2 Present policy

Since about 1970 there has been a change in attitude and policy regarding the historic inner city. Whilst before this time policy bore witness to but little respect for the historic ground plan and historic buildings, after this period there has been much more active interest in the fortunes of the inner city.

The present town council and the present municipal executive are strongly in favour of the rehabilitation of the inner city. As far as structure and scale in the inner city are concerned, policy is 100 % different from that prior to 1970. The aim now is to actually translate these views into active policy and this policy is now in the process of formulation. Staff have now been seconded who deal exclusively with the inner city; the first step is to increase the budget allotments in this field (also for increases in personnel); external advisers have been engaged to draw up an integral inner city policy; the attitude to the protected townscape report is now positive; inventories are being made of all that has to be done in the way of restoration work, a restoration schedule is being developed for the municipal monuments; initiatives are being taken to promote the enthusiasm of private persons for the restoration of their monuments; consultations are being held with the department for the preservation of monuments and historic buildings over the realisation of the plans. All in all these are concrete results in the policy field which bear witness to altered views on the inner city and its historic buildings. The budget allotments have been increased for the first steps.

3. Goals of Intervention

Objectives as articulated in "inner city memoranda"

In 1976 a 'plan of action', based partly on the memoranda of 1971 and 1973, was made public. This plan gives a survey of what has already happened, what is happening now, and what should happen in the future in the inner city. The details are given under three main headings, namely:

– Activities concerned with the rehabilitation of deteriorated buildings;

– Activities concerned with the rehabilitation of deteriorated infrastructure;

– Activities directed towards the rehabilitation of the deteriorated functions of the inner city or change of function in certain areas of the inner city.

In the chapter devoted to the rehabilitation of deteriorated buildings, explicit mention is made of monuments. For the monuments which are municipal property it is proposed that an architectural and structural inventory should be made with a broad estimate of costs for rehabilitation and a restoration programme with an urgency stipulation which should be built into the municipal investment plans and should have its place in the planning for the award of government subsidies. As regards the monuments which are privately owned, the following action points are mentioned:

a. The drawing up of a town-planning inventory of the monuments, this to be done in the framework of the designation of the inner city as a protected townscape.

b. The drawing up of a monuments or restoration report.

c. The drawing up of a policy proposal for the setting up of a monuments committee new style.

d. The drawing up of urban renewal and/or rehabilitation plans for the areas where there are large concentrations of monuments, including the Pieterswijk and Pancraswest, with a view amongst other things to allowing the state subsidy regulations (dwellings with monumental value) to be applied as much as possible.

e. The expansion of service to private persons by means of information and administrative guidance.

Further, it is urged that rehabilitation plans should be made for the various inner city districts and that the rehabilitation and development plans which are in the course of preparation or are being carried out should be proceeded with.

As regards the rehabilitation of deteriorated functions, actions are mentioned which are directed towards the rehabilitation of the residential function in the inner city, the improvement of the accommodation and shopping function, the restoration of lost business and service functions, the improvement of the recreational and tourist function, the centralisation (or not) of the welfare function, closer examination of the educational function in the inner city, and consultations with the university concerning the university's function.

In the meantime the need is increasingly felt for an integral approach to the inner city. In this connection the memorandum 'Verder op weg naar een integraal plan voor de binnenstad' (A step further towards an integral plan for the inner city) appeared in June 1976. This memorandum indicates what should happen to the inner city in its totality. Making use of all that has already been done in the past, the memorandum gives the main objectives for a structure or development plan for the inner city. This plan is at the moment in the participation phase.

4. Strategies

4.1 Legal and financial techniques

Protected townscape

In December 1975 the Department for the Preservation of Monuments and Historic Buildings sent the Leiden municipal council their 'memorandum on the protection of the Leiden townscape' for recommendations. At its meeting on 28 June 1976 the municipal council decided to accept the memorandum. In the memorandum the limits of the townscape to be protected were drawn along the encircling canals. The memorandum gives the reason for this as follows:

'The town planning and historical structural relation of the area within the encircling canals is such a strong one that more confined limits would be very difficult to define.'

The municipal council has, however, decided to make a request to the ministers of Culture, Recreation and Social Welfare and of Housing and Physical Planning for the buildings along the Zoeterwoudsesingel and the Witte Singel also to be included in the protected townscape, since these form an essential part of the territory which has already been indicated in the proposal of the Department for the Preservation of Monuments and Historic Buildings as an area to be protected and whereby the proposed protected townscape of Leiden would be completed. In view of the fact that the value of the component parts of the proposed protected townscape is not uniform, a division has been made into three zones, which can be described as follows:

Zone A: Areas of importance on account of the pattern of the streets and watercourses in relation to the profile and use of the open space and the dimensions and form of the buildings, which include numerous concentrations of monuments.

Zone B: Areas of importance on account of the pattern of the streets and watercourses in relation to the profile and use of the open space and the dimensions of the buildings, which include concentrations of monuments.

Zone C: Areas of importance on account of the pattern of streets and watercourses in relation to the scale of the buildings.

Development plans

For part of the inner city of Leiden there is a development plan in force, though it is under revision. Preparations will start shortly on the development plan for De Camp area, whilst development plans are also in the course of preparation for Levendaal-oost and Marewijk.

Subsidies for restoration work

The subsidy percentage allowed by the municipality for the restoration of dwellings classified as monuments amounts to 30 %. As has already been mentioned, the expenditure on the subsidy is covered by the allowance to be made from the municipal fund in accordance with the 'refinement' regulation for monuments. On account of the municipality's difficult financial situation it is not possible to raise this percentage. Until recently Leiden was an article 12 municipality (municipality with budget deficit receiving financial support from central government) and at the moment it is a municipality with a supplementary allowance. Partly as a result of this same cirumstance there has never been any concrete consideration of advance financing problems for private restoration work.

Acquisition of property rights

Numerous purchases of historic properties are planned. In a few cases the municipality has already actually effected the purchase. However, it cannot yet be said that there is a systematic policy for the acquisition of property rights, although particularly in rehabilitation areas the municipality is beginning to approach the owners according to a certain system. The properties purchased, which are to be restored, are not being sold to private owners at this stage. Some municipal property has, however, been sold to the Diogenes Foundation with the obligation to carry out the restoration work.

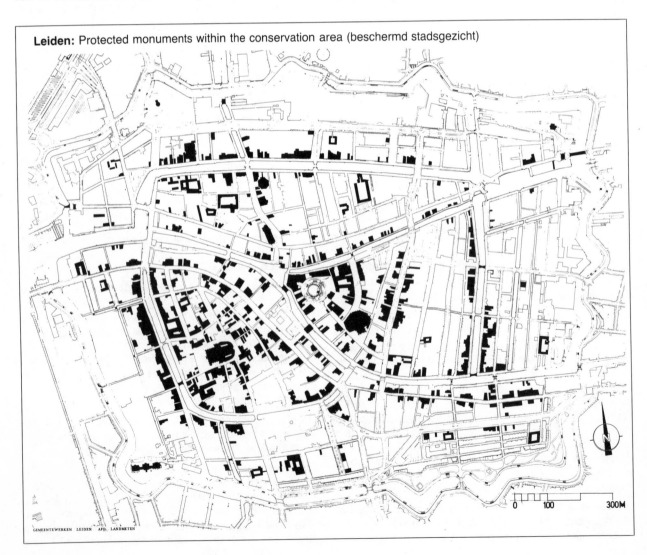

Leiden: Protected monuments within the conservation area (beschermd stadsgezicht)

Maintenance

At the moment an extra sum of f25,000 has been reserved for the maintenance of municipal monuments. There is no specific regulation to guarantee the maintenance of privately owned monuments.

Supplementary list

In the plan of action the importance of the extension of the monuments list has been emphasised. Up to now lack of staff has prevented systematic work on the augmentation of the supplementary list. It has been sporadically supplemented by the Minister of Culture, Recreation and Social Welfare. A report has been sent to the department for the preservation of monuments and historic buildings concerning the possibility of placing 60 examples of 19th and 20th century architecture on the draft monuments list. A request will shortly be made to place a number of properties in the Pancras-oost quarter on the list.

Leasehold

A few years ago the council took the decision only to lease ground in the inner city.

4.2 Organisation

Organisationally speaking, the preservation of monuments and historic buildings comes under the town clerk's office and the public works department. In the town clerk's office the preservation of monuments and historic buildings comes under the traffic and inner city section of the urban development, traffic and land department. 2 members of the staff of this section devote their time to the preservation of monuments. In the public works department there is a technical section dealing with the preservation of monuments which employs three civil servants. A fourth will shortly be added to their number.

4.3 Citizen participation

The municipal authorities have tried in numerous ways to involve the citizens in the various plans for the inner city. The most important action in this field was the setting up in 1972 of an 'inner city advisory council'.

Within the Advisory Council there are five working groups for:

1. structure plan for the inner city,
2. traffic and transport,
3. residing in the inner city,
4. monuments and historic buildings,
5. livability and embellishment of the urban scene.

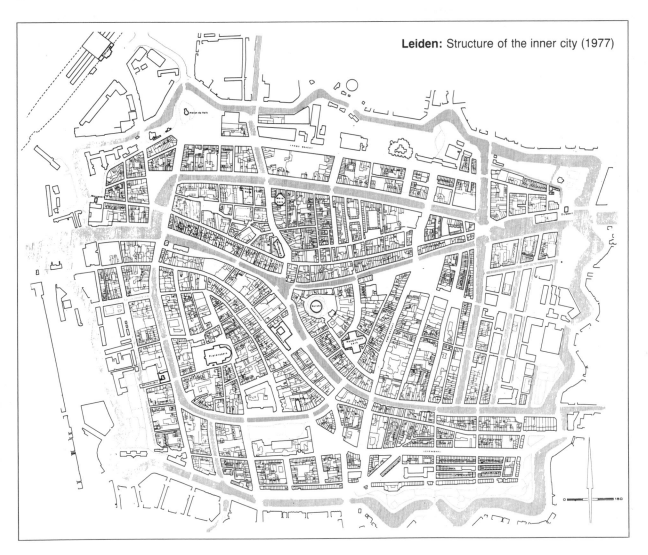

Leiden: Structure of the inner city (1977)

In practice it has been found that the input in the Advisory Council comes predominantly from individual citizens. Representatives of organisations and groups which are involved in the inner city fail to turn up or have withdrawn from the Council. The recommendations made by the Advisory Council are exclusively in the policy preparation sphere. The recommendations to be made are not, however, limited to particular aspects of the inner city.

The Inner City Advisory Council was primarily intended as a broad forum for discussion of the objectives and principles of the first Leiden inner city memorandum (1971). An attempt was made to get the population involved in this plan by means of a house-to-house folder ('Binnenstadt op Zicht' (Inner City on Approval) and by an exhibition in the Weighhouse.

In 1973 the memorandum 'Bouwstenen voor het Binnenstadsbeleid' (Foundations of Inner City Policy) appeared. In this report an attempt was made amongst other things to answer the observations of the Inner City Advisory Council and the main reactions received from the inhabitants. Hereafter the further development of general inner city plans came more or less to a standstill. In 1975 the thread of

Leiden:
above: typical entrance of a "hofje" (almshouse)
below: location of 31 of the 3Є "hofjes" within the historical core (17th century)

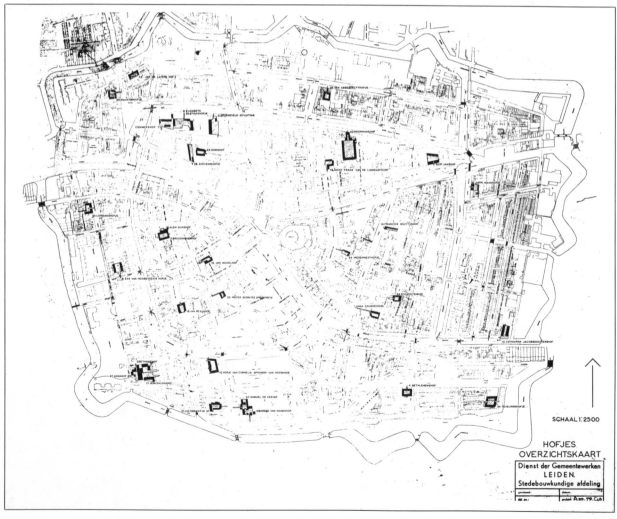

general inner city planning was taken up again via the development of a new integral plan for the inner city made by a group of external experts and civil servants.

The involvement of the population in everything concerning the inner city had, however, not been stagnant in the intervening period. This had become more clearly structurized than previously. Moreover, the participation of the population now concerned more specific, clearly defined subjects. Groups had come into being which may be classified under the common denominator of 'neighbourhood committees'. They stand up for the interests of the residents of a particular neighbourhood or district. The promotion of interests is concerned with maintaining or improving the live ability of the group's own area as much as possible. In general they strive for the restoration and improvement of housing, the presence of good sociocultural facilities, for green spaces in the area, for traffic safety, for matters such as play streets, residential districts with single level roads (yards) for communal recreational use and access traffic only (= woonerf), anti-speed humps, etc.

The neighbourhood committees are not so concerned with the inner city planning in its totality, but rather with component parts which they see as a danger to or a direct infringement of their own neighbourhood interests.

Participation by the economic sector has now been organised via the Leiden Inner City Foundation, in which there are representatives of the Chamber of Commerce, the tradesmen's associations, and other organisations active in that field.

As a result of all this the 'formal' channels of participation offered by the municipality have been put more or less out of action. On account of the continual changes of course in the inner city planning the Inner City Advisory Committee has been unable to make adequate allowance for this; moreover its working methods are not efficient. Its members are mainly individual citizens, whereby there is no real promotion of interests by the various groups in the population. The participation which the municipality had in mind via the information sheets, exhibitions and finally the Advisory Council appear to have met with scarcely any response amongst broad strate of the population.

Among the inhabitants, specific interest groups (especially the neighbourhood committees referred to above) became increasingly vocal when it became evident that certain elements of the planning would have a negative effect for a particular district or neighbourhood. Moreover, these committees exercised ever increasing pressure on the municipal authorities finally to do something for the improvement of the various inner city neighbourhoods, whether or not in the context of an inner city plan. Furthermore, these matters were all more or less politicized to the municipal council.

Now that the inner city plans have 'got going', the conclusion can be drawn that the participation by the citizens has certainly not been negligible. It has, however, taken place via totally different channels than those envisaged by the municipality. Thus the neighbourhood committees had scarcely any contact with the Advisory Council.

The way things happened in the Breetstraat area is illustrative of this. In this part of the inner city an intensification of the shopping and trade function was to be provided for by the introduction of a pedestrian precinct. This would have led amongst other things to increased traffic intensity in the surrounding areas. After objection from the Inner City

Foundation and the neighbourhood committees the content of the plan was altered. For the Pieterswijk a number of technical measures have also been developed, such as protection against short-cut 'sneak' traffic.

In the development of the new structure plan for the inner city it can be said that, compared with events in the past, there is a different strategy. In all stages of the planning development the cards are put on the table as far as possible. The interested citizen, interest groups and such circles, can obtain full information as to the state of affairs at any given moment. Thus it is hoped that conflicts of interest will become known in good time and that the decision-making procedures will be apparent to everyone. This is referred to as open plan procedure.

In the meantime a start has been made on the more permanent form of participation. The principal instrument is formed by an 'inner city shop', where everyone – lessees, owners, shopkeepers, entrepreneurs, neighbourhood committees, action groups and interested citizens can make their wishes or ideas known to the participation coordinator concerning the improvement of the inner city. The latter has a varied assortment of tasks. The coordinator arranges successively for the provision of all kinds of information, the evolving of participation procedures, and the building up of a consultation framework in the component areas, the motivation of groups.

Up to now the principal participation activities have been: the distribution of the memorandum 'Towards an integral plan for the inner city' to all organised groups in the inner city; putting the memorandum on sale to interested citizens; publications on the momorandum and on participation, etc. in the Leiden daily papers; an informative Council meeting with explanation of the memorandum for all those interested; the opening of the 'inner city shop'; giving the inhabitants the opportunity of reacting in writing to the first phase of the planning (in particular the principal objectives). There has been a considerable amount of written reaction. The intention is that these written reactions should be used in some way or other in the next phase of the structure plan. All those who have reacted in writing receive an answer as to the outcome of their contribution. If their idea is not usable they are given the reasons.

In the further course of the participation procedure close contact is kept with all the interested parties. Consultations will be held with neighbourhood and interested groups. All meetings of the project group which is preparing the structure plan will be in public. The participation will eventually be rounded off in the detailed plans for the various component areas of the inner city in cooperation with all those involved. Neighbourhood committees and action groups in particular can then be active in their own field and put forward concrete proposals.

In 1977 work was in progress on various concrete plans for specific areas of the inner city. The development plans concerned are those for Herengracht-Zijlsingel (in preparation), de Camp (in draft stage). The municipal authorities try to involve the population as far as possible before the plans are prepared. The procedure is that an exhibition is organised in illustration of the plan, sometimes in the area concerned, but usually in the town hall; an information letter is sent out and often a well presented information newssheet (as was done recently in the Maredorp area).

As far as the rehabilitation plans are concerned for a number of areas of the inner city (at the moment there are

Leiden:
Schedule for the restoration of the 'Leidse Hofjes' (age-old asylums) from 1976–1982

IIIIIIIII   analysis
/////   planning
▬▬▬   restoration
oooo   already restored

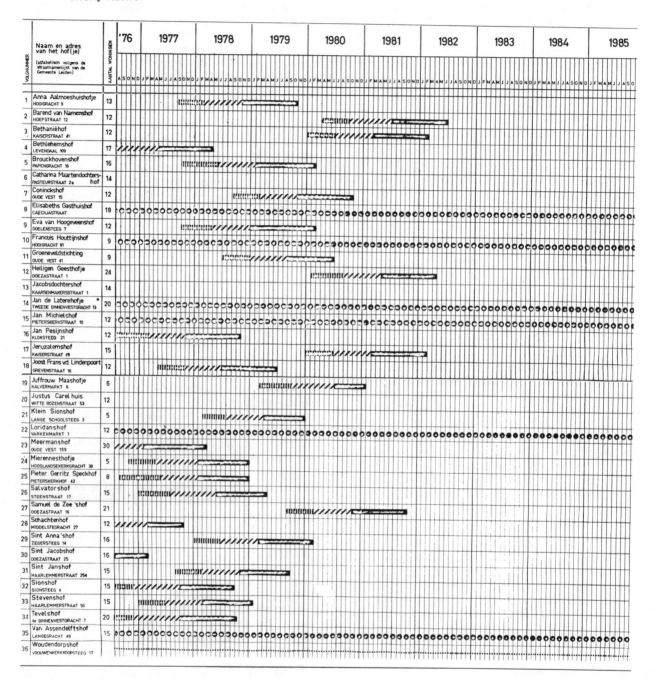

seven ready or nearly ready), the neighbourhood committees play a big part. The contact with the population in these areas functions to a considerable degree via these committees. Monuments and policy on monuments as such scarcely form a problem in Leiden as far as participation is concerned. These are matters which run smoothly both as regards the municipal authorities and the population. The problems are much more in connection with the total framework of the inner city policy, of which the monuments sector form a part.

As well as the neighbourhood committees and the Inner City Advisory Council there are a number of other bodies which present their views depending on the time, place and nature of the problem. These include the Oud-Leiden Association, a group whose interests are principally cultural and historical, the Diogenes Restoration Foundation, and the Leiden Almshouses Foundation, which concerns itself with the preservation and restoration of a number of the many Leiden almshouses.

1

nr.	naam en adres	aantal woningen	komt voor op de lijst van monumenten van:	bestemd voor bewoning door:	situatie van de woningen	indeling van de woningen	bedsteden in gebruik	toilet	water	gas	elektra	stookgelegenheid	kwaliteit van de woning	herstellingen die de kwaliteit en de indeling van de woning kunnen verbeteren
1	Aalmoeshuis, Hooigracht nr. 9.	13	gemeente	vrouwen	goed	goed	neen	in de woning	1 vaste wastafel verder normaal	normaal	normaal	c.v. aanwezig stoken kachel	goed	niet nodig (nieuw)
2	Barend van Namenshofje, Hoefstraat nr. 12.	12	rijk	echtparen	tamelijk goed	goed	in enkele woningen	privaat in de woning	normaal	normaal	normaal	kachel	goed	niet nodig (nieuw)
3	Bethaniënhofje, Kaiserstraat nr. 43.	12	–	vrouwen en echtparen	goed	goed	in enkele woningen	privaat in de woning	normaal	normaal	normaal	kachel	goed	eventueel later herstellen
4	Bethlehemshofje, Levendaal nr. 109.	17	rijk en gemeente	echtparen mannen en vrouwen	goed	matig	neen	binnen w.c. gecombineerd voor twee woningen	normaal	normaal	normaal	kachel	vrij goed	verbeteren
5	Brouckhovenhofje, Papengracht nr. 16.	16	rijk en gemeente	echtparen	goed	matig	neen	in de woning	normaal	normaal	normaal	kachel	vrij goed	verbeteren

2

VERBETERINGS RESTAURATIE plan — subsidies — definitieve bedragen

1 VOLGNUMMER	2 Naam en adres van het hof(je) (alfabetisch volgens de straatnamenlijst van de Gemeente Leiden)	3 AANTAL WONINGEN	4 in voorbereiding bij eigenaar	5 naam en adres architect	6 plan ingediend bij B & W d.d.	7 ministerie van C.R.M. accoord d.d./nr.	8 advies D.G.W. betreffende geld. steun d.d./nr.	9 aantal woningen na verbouwing	10 bestaande huur/mnd	11 begrote kosten (totaal)	12 ministerie van V.R.O.	13 ministerie van C.R.M.	14 college van G.S.	15 college van B & W	16 berekende huur/mnd	17 in uitvoering	18 gereed d.d.	19 kosten volgens eindafrekening	20 ministerie van V.R.O.	21 ministerie van C.R.M.	22 college van G.S.	23 college van B & W	24 vastgestelde huur/mnd
1	Anna Aalmoeshuishofje Hooigracht 9	13																					
2	Barend van Namenshof Hoefstraat 12	12																					
3	Betnaniëhof Kaiserstraat 41	12																					
4	Bethlehemshof Levendaal 109	17	x	ir. M.P. Schutte b.I. Cronesteinkade 18, Leiden.	17-10-75	31-01-75 257.864	03-06-76 2675		f 30,=	f 1.332.150,=	f 532.860,=	f 266.430,=	f 53.296,=	f 192.882,=	f 218,=								
5	Brouckhovenshof Papengracht 16	16																					

3

bestemming — monument[2] — bouwkundige toestand[3]

1 VOLGNUMMER	2 Naam en adres van het hof(je) (alfabetisch volgens de straatnamenlijst van de Gemeente Leiden)	3 AANTAL WONINGEN	4 JAARTAL	5 eigenaar/beheerders[1]	6 OORSPRONKELIJK[1]	7 HUIDIG	8 JA, BESCHERMD	9 NEEN	10 monumentale waarde	11 toilet met voorportaal	12 badgelegenheid	13 centrale verw.	14 brandgevaarlijke indeling	15 trap	16 goed	17 matig	18 slecht	19 naar huidige normen geschikt voor bejaardenhuisvesting	20 opmerking[1]
1	Anna Aalmoeshuishofje Hooigracht 9	13	T 1492	College van Regenten p.a. Rijnsburgerweg 27, Leiden.	maechden ofte vrouwen	bejaarden	●	–	–	ja	neen	ja	neen	goed	–	–	●	ja	Hof in gebruik: 1507; gerestaureerd 1939–1941
2	Barend van Namenshof Hoefstraat 12	12	T 1726	College van Regenten p.a. Plantsoen 51, Leiden.	echtparen	bejaarden	–	●	–	ja	neen	neen	ja	goed	●	–	–	ja	na verbouwing in 1915 oorspronkelijk karakter verloren
3	Bethaniëhof Kaiserstraat 41	12	G 1563	Regenten namens Diaconie Hervormde Gemeente p.a. Oude Rijn 44e, Leiden.	vrouwen en echtparen	bejaarden	–	●	–	neen	neen	neen	ja	goed	–	–	●	ja	in 1907 zijn de huisjes vernieuwd
4	Bethlehemshof Levendaal 109	17	T 1630	College van Regenten p.a. Houtlaan 5, Leiden.	mannen, vrouwen en echtparen	bejaarden	●	–	–	neen	neen	neen	ja	slecht	–	–	●	neen	oorspronkelijk hof aan de Lange Gracht. Sinds 1811 verplaatst naar toermalige hof ,,De Houcksteen''
5	Brouckhovenshof Papengracht 16	16	G 1631	B & W van Leiden Stadhuis, Leiden.	echtparen en weduwen	bejaarden	●	–	–	neen	neen	neen	ja	goed	–	–	●	ja	

4

	Naam en adres van het hof(je)	HUIDIG AANTAL WONINGEN	MONUMENT — JA, BESCHERMD	NEEN	MONUMENTALE WAARDE	INHOUD HOF(JE) IN M³	(GERAAMDE) TOTALE KOSTEN RESTAURANTIE HOF (AFGEROND)	SUBSIDIES — RIJK (MINISTERIE VAN V.R.O. 30 %)	RIJK (MINISTERIE VAN C.R.M. 20 %)	GEMEENTE LEIDEN	PROVINCIE ZUID-HOLLAND	OPMERKING:
30	SINT JACOBSHOF DOEZASTRAAT 25	16	●	–	–	3104	F 1.164.000	F 349.200	F 232.800	F 174.600	F 46.560	
4	BETHLEHEMSHOF LEVENDAAL 109	17	●	–	–	3298	1.240.000	372.000	248.000	186.000	49.600	
16	JAN PESIJNSHOF KLOKSTEEG 21	12	●	–	–	2328	873.000	261.900	174.600	130.950	34.920	
23	MEERMANSHOF OUDE VEST 159	30	●	–	–	5820	2.185.000	655.500	437.000	327.750	87.400	
28	SCHACHTENHOF MIDDELSTEGRACHT 27	12	●	–	–	2326	873.000	261.900	174.600	130.950	34.920	
32	SIONSHOF SIONSTEEG 4	15	●	–	–	2910	1.100.000	330.000	220.000	165.000	44.000	
24	TEVELSHOF 4e BINNENVESTGRACHT 7	20	●	–	–	3880	1.460.000	438.000	292.000	219.000	58.400	
	TOTAAL IN 1977	122				23.668	8.695.000	2.668.500	1.779.000	1.334.250	355.800	

Leiden: Example of a detailed plan for the rehabilitation and preservation of the "Leidse hofjes".
1. analysis of the social, cultural and technical condition
2. programme of architectural and financial planning
3. analysis of technical condition and use
4. detailed financial planning per year

4.4 Restoration activities

A restoration programme has been drawn up covering the municipal properties. A distinction has been drawn between the large and the civil engineering monuments. In the restoration schedule information is given per monument as to the number of cubic metres, the structural condition, the restoration costs per cubic metre, the estimated restoration costs, and the possible destiny of the monument concerned.

In the meantime a few spectacular items are being tackled so as to show clearly what the intention is. These items, mainly large monuments, must be seen as a start which will have a radiation effect on the inhabitants and also on the Council and civil servants. In this way a positive climate is created in which after some time much more restoration work can be done.

As a result of the availability of the so-called 'dwellings fund' from the Ministry of Culture, Recreation and Social Welfare, policy attention has also been directed to the smaller monument, the historic dwelling. This fund was recently raised to f300,000, which is a considerable rise compared to previous years.

Further, through the 'Supplementary Work' regulation a little more opportunity has been created for carrying out restoration work, of which the Diogenes Foundation in particular can take advantage.

Undertakings covering several years have been made by the department for the preservation of monuments and historic buildings for the rehabilitation of dwellings and almshouses situated in two of the urban renewal areas, namely the Haver and Gortbuurt and the Pieterswijk, whereby the planning of housing improvements in these districts is simplified and the realisation of the prognoses for the rehabilitation of dwellings is assured.

4.5 Involvement of foundations in the process of urban rehabilitation

There were 36 almshouses (Hofjes) in Leiden with altogether 491 flats. Two of these were demolished, six were no longer used as flats for the old. These are now administered by the "foundation for student housing" and let out to students after thorough rehabilitation work.

One house is let out to a single couple. The other 27 hofjes are subdivided into the following groups:

- 10 hofjes with 150 flats are considered monuments. Restoration plans are in preparation;

- 1 hofje with 15 flats is not considered a monument. However, restoration plans are already in preparation;

- 6 hofjes with 86 flats are considered monuments – restoration plans are not yet in preparation;

- 4 hofjes with 45 flats are considered integral elements of the townscape. Restoration plans are not yet prepared;

- 6 hofjes with 89 flats are considered neither monuments nor do they form integral elements of the townscape. Restoration plans are not yet prepared.

The Leiden Almshouses Foundation

According to an enquiry carried out in 1961 by the so-called Almshouses Committee at the instigation of the Social Council, 12 of the 32 almshouses within the encircling canals were in such bad condition that it was considered impossible to preserve them: of the remaining 20 almshouses 12 were in good condition, whilst 8 almshouses were eligible for restoration. In the basic plan 14 historically and architecturally important almshouses were to be preserved, whilst the remaining 18, 11 of which are in such a dilapidated state that they were no longer suitable for restoration, would have to disappear in the long run when it would become necessary in the framework of redevelopment.

Contrary to what was stated in the report of 1961 drawn up by the Committee, an enquiry has shown that the 28 remaining properties with 390 flats, which are still used to house elderly people, can be restored. With financial support from the government the 28 almshouses (for location see map) will be able to be made suitable according to present-day requirements for housing the elderly. The rehabilitation work on one of the almshouses is already in an advanced stage; government subsidy has been sought for the restoration and improvement of 4 almshouses. The aim is to have all the almshouses fully restored and modernised before 1982. A detailed schedule for all the 36 almshouses (see figure) states the time for planning and construction and rehabilitation. Complementary lists state the conditions, number of flats and the amount of expected subsidies from the ministries of Culture and Housing as well as the provincial and municipal bodies. From 1977–1981 altogether Fls. 26 mill. are to be spent for restorations. Fls. 6 mill. is to be subsidized by the Ministry of Housing, 4 mill. by the Ministry of Culture, 3 mill. by the municipality and 1 mill. by the province. The Leiden Almshouses Foundation is making great efforts to promote speedy rehabilitation.

Diogenes Foundation

In order to further restoration work the municipality has been actively helpful in the establishment of the Diogenes Leiden Foundation (1974). The foundation buys up properties on the monuments list which are of importance to the townscape. The properties are purchased from the municipality and from private persons; restoration plans are made, subsidies applied for, and the restoration work is carried out. The foundation remains the owner of the properties and lets them out. At the moment the foundation has let 12 housing units, divided over 5 properties. 2 properties are in the course of restoration. It is expected that in the long run the foundation will make a small profit and that they will take on a full-time employee. It is likely that the financing of purchase and restoration work will be easier in the future.

Urban Rehabilitation Foundation

The Foundation for Leiden Urban Rehabilitation has in the meantime submitted a plan for the rehabilitation of the former Bibliothèque Wallone. It is hoped to make a start shortly on the execution of this plan, which provides for the restoration and alteration of the building into seven housing units.

5. **Future Policy**

The appreciation of the historic inner city and the opinion that a municipal policy is needed in this case have grown to such an extent amongst all strata of the population that, judging by the present state of affairs, the views which now exist still also form the basis for policy making in the near future. Although it is considered that it will take a generation to get the inner city into a healthy condition, policy will be aimed at providing the impulses for preserving the old and the beautiful and as soon as possible. In certain respects the inner city of Leiden is still in good condition, whilst in others it is somewhat decrepit. Taken as a whole it is of such significance that it is worth pursuing a policy which is aimed at the conservation of the historic inner city. The policy as it now stands will, however, have to be amplified and elaborated. This will be a question of on the one hand taking measures concerning the inner city as a whole, and on the other hand measures concerning monuments and historic buildings in particular.

POLAND

Poland
LEGISLATION, ORGANISATION, FINANCE

Introduction

Behind all the activities set in train to protect our cultural heritage in Poland stands the fundamental rule that this is not only an obligation for the State but also a duty for every citizen. A look back at the past will help us to understand more easily how it came about that this principle was raised to the level of a veritable institution.

The issues involved in safeguarding our architectural legacy assumed their importance towards the end of the 19th century and at the beginning of the 20th century not only for scientific, artistic or functional reasons but also for patriotic considerations. The Poles, living as they were in a country which had been annexed and divided into three parts – Russian, Prussian and Austrian – wanted to preserve the national character. The forms taken by this protection evolved in the course of the years and the demands based on this sentimental approach finally acquired a systematic character and a legal basis. It should be noted that it was architects and town planners who played a creative role in this process. Thanks to them, the attention paid to individual historic buildings and monuments widened to include blocks of houses or even whole towns with a view to preserving their original character.

The destruction of towns in the First World War became an important incentive for creating the preconditions with which to ensure the protection of these historic structures. It should be borne in mind that the provisional government promulgated the law on this subject as early as October 1918, i.e. on the eve of our independence. This law interpreted historic monuments as comprising buildings, streets, quarters and towns possessing historic importance. The decree issued by the President of the Polish Republic in 1928 and observed until 1962 reaffirmed the preceding law subject to certain modifications.

At the present time, the fundamental legal provisions with a bearing on the protection of cultural assets are to be found in the law on the protection of cultural assets and museums enacted by the Parliament of the People's Republic of Poland on 15 February 1962, (Law Digest No. 10; sect 48). This law replaced the decree of 1928. It defines the concept of cultural assets: determines the aim of the protection of these assets and the ways in which it can be realized; names the categories of protected properties; designates the organizations entrusted with these protective activities; and fixes the limits, procedures and norms for the latter including the orders and prohibitions imposed under administrative penalties and fines.

The law only covers cultural assets. The protection of Nature is dealt with an another legal enactment, the law of 7 April 1949 on the protection of Nature (Law Digest No. 25; sect 180) whose implementation rests with the Minister of Forests and Forest Industries together with the ancillary services controlled by the Ministry.

The term "cultural assets" is deemed to embrace landed property and buildings or monuments irrespective of their age. The importance of the item assigned for cultural development and based upon its historic, scientific and artistic importance is a matter for individual decision. The aim of preservation is not only to keep and preserve cultural assets in good condition, but also to integrate them into contemporary life so that this legacy will constitute a durable feature of our national culture.

In order to guarantee efficient protection, the law stipulates that monuments can only be used in a manner compatible with the principles governing their protection and sensitive to their value and functional capacity.

Because of the large number of monuments destroyed during World War II, the law places on obligation upon all units of our Socialist economy to make maximum and primary use of historic monuments for the purposes of their real function. In this way, the administrative authorities and institutions are directly involved in safeguarding architectural monuments. In keeping with this idea and its broad base of social cooperation are the demands of the protective bodies that numerous historic monuments in Poland should be thrown open to the general public.

In addition to the items to be found in museums and libraries or archives, protection in also extended to cultural assets entered in the registers of monuments and perhaps the non-registered ones, too, if they possess undeniable scientific, historic or artistic merit (Article 4).

The present study confines its attention to analyzing questions involved in the whole field of preserving historic buildings and their settings: it does not concern itself with the cultural assets in museums, libraries and archives or those owned by bodies incorporated under private or public law. A special chapter has been dedicated to the problems of the relations between the conservation of historic monuments and buildings and the planning schemes for them.

1. Legislation

1.1 Legal provisions for safeguarding historic monuments

The law of 15 February 1962 on the protection of cultural assets and on museums subdivide the assets designated for conservation into the following categories:

– buildings and works of architecture and town planning irrespective of their state of preservation, town and village areas, public parks and gardens together with their monuments and surroundings, groups of houses of architectural value, etc.;

– sites of ethnological interest such as typical rural scenes and highly characteristic country buildings;

– places of historic interest such as battle-fields, sites made memorable through the struggles for independence and social justice and extermination camps as well as places, buildings and localities associated with other important events or the activities of distinguished public figures in history;

- archaeological and palaeontological sites, places with traces of primitive man's habitat and way of life, grottos, ancient mines, primitive settlements, charnel-houses, grave-mounds, etc.;

- technical amenities and items of everyday culture such as ancient mines, ironworks, workshops, artefacts, means of transport, etc. which are particularly characteristic of old and modern phenomena in economic life, technology and science.

As may readily be ascertained, Polish law also concerns itself with isolated monuments in addition to groups and areas such as historic town centres and quarters or rural settings characteristic of a region or epoch. Furthermore, protection is also extended to archaeological, palaeontological and ethnological sites.

The legal foundations for the protection of cultural assets rest upon their entry in the register of munuments. The principles and procedure for this entry and the arrangements for keeping the register feature in the provisions issued by the Ministerial Council on 23 April 1965 on the registration of monuments (Law Digest No. 19; sect 181).

The conservation of monuments consists of the following:

- The authorities for the protection of cultural assets have right of access to the latter in order to examine on the spot properties thought to possess historic, artistic or scientific value and thus to verify their status as monuments and their condition of repair or to draw up a documentation on them (Article 18).

- These authorities may affix plaques or inscriptions to historic properties (Article 19.)

- In cooperation with the organs for the control of construction activities, the authorities may promote the conservation of historic urban areas and buildings by introducing building controls for the land in question or by demolishing, reconstructing or rehabilitating certain edifices (Article 20).

- All work and activities relating to historic properties or archaeological excavations require a permit from the regional curator of monuments (Article 21).

- Without the authorization of the regional curator of monuments, it is prohibited to demolish or destroy monuments, to reconstruct them, to conserve, increase the number of storeys, decorate, impair or modify them in any way (Article 27).

- The regional curator of monuments may suspend all activity which does not comply with the above-mentioned provisions or order the responsible individual or organization to restore the monument and its setting to its original state at their own expense (Article 28).

- The proprietors and occupants of historic buildings – whether natural persons or public-law bodies – are obliged to look after these properties and in particular to ensure them against destruction, ruin and devastation (Article 25; para 1, p1). An infringement of this duty by a natural person despite a warning by the curator of monuments may result in the placing of the property under State administration until the time of its conservation (Article 37, para 1) or even in its expropriation (6). By the same token, the preservation of historic properties used by public or social institutions against decay, ruination or devastation rests upon circulars issued by the President of the Ministerial Council.

- The authorities for the conservation of monuments may request the owners and occupants of historic properties to carry out these conservation activities within a certain period of time. If these activities are not carried out, the curator may execute them himself and charge this to the proprietor or to the debit of the mortgage on the property (8). In justifiable cases, the Minister for Culture and the Arts may decide to treat these charges as a non-repayable donation (Article 30–32).

- Offences committed against cultural assets are severely punished. Infringements of formal provisions are liable to administrative penalities involving fines of up to 5,000 zloty (Article 77–78) (15). Similarly, criminal acts such as the destruction or the voluntary devastation of monuments are liable to punishment of up to 5 years imprisonment and a fine of 1 million zloty (Article 73).

2. Organisation

2.1 Authorities for the conservation of monuments

The supreme organ among the authorities for the conservation of monuments is the Minister for Culture and the Arts acting through the agency of the Curator-General of Monuments (currently with the rank of an Under-Secretary of State), who controls the activities of the Department for Museums and the Protection of Monuments.

The subsidiary organs of the authorities for the protection of monuments are the regional curators of monuments who act on behalf of, and subject to, the authority of the voivode (9).

Their competence embraces in particular the right:

- to keep up to date the register of monuments (Article 13, para 1);

- to take the decision of entering a cultural asset in the register of monuments (Article 14, para 1, pl);

- to examine on the spot probable items of historic, scientific or artistic merit so as to establish whether they constitute a cultural asset and also what their state of repair is or to draw up documentation upon them (Article 18);

- to affix plaques or inscriptions to historic properties (Article 19);

- to stipulate in cooperation with the building authorities the preconditions for construction activities within the area of old historic quarters and blocks of houses listed in the register of monuments and to order the demolition, reconstruction or modification of certain properties in the said area (Article 20);

- to issue permits for carrying out work on monuments or on archaeological excavations (Article 21, para 1);

- to issue or withhold permits to carry out such work on monuments as might destory, transform, reconstruct, raise, decorate, complete, displace or modify them in any way (Article 27, paras 1 and 2);

- to discontinue all activites which do not comply with the above-mentioned provisions and to order the restoring of the historic building or its setting to its original state (Article 28, para 1);

- to recommend to the owner or occupant of the historic building conservation activities within a predetermined period (Article 30, para 1);
- to guarantee state debt claims in respect of work carried out on historic properties which the State does not own (Article 32, para 2);
- to ensure the protection of a historic property against destruction, devastation or ruin by setting up a public adminnistration there (Article 37, paras 1 and 2).

In cities and communities with an abundance of historic buildings or monuments of exceptional value, the voivode may – in agreement with the Minister for Culture and the Arts – name a curator of town or commune monuments. The powers of these curators are subject to decisions taken by the voivode (7).

2.2 Consultative organs

The council for the protection of monuments (8) at the Ministry for Culture and the Arts operates in accordance with the decree issued on 6 February 1973 by the Minister for Culture and the Arts (Ministerial Gazette No. 2, sect 17).

The council is the competent body

- to forward upon a request to this effect by the Minister opinions on the annual and five-yearly programmes of ministerial activity in the field of safeguarding monuments;
- to furnish opinions on the annual and five-yearly investment plans drawn up by the Minister;
- to furnish opinions on the advisability of deleting a cultural asset from the register of monuments.

The council consists of the President and members nominated for 4 years by the Minister for Culture and the Arts. These members, whose total must not exceed 25 in number, are recruited from among the representatives of the scientists, experts and activists in the field of safeguarding monuments.

The consultative organ for the voivodes is the council for the protection of cultural assets (Article 10, para 2) (9). The members of these councils are nominated from among the specialists, scientists and practical exponents in the protection and conservation of monuments.

2.3 Documentation centres

With a view to drawing up an inventory of the enormous number of cultural assets and to programme their conservation and development more efficiently, the centre of documentation for monuments was set up by the Minister for Culture and the Arts on 2 December 1961 (Ministerial Gazette 1962, No. 1, sect 6).

The Centre has the following functions:

- to collect, process and make available archives and publications of every kind for interested organizations and individuals;
- to process and present for approval by the Department for Museums and for the Protection of Monuments annual programmes of activities and progress reports;
- to carry out the work envisaged in the Centre's annual programmes on preparing a card-index list of cultural assets in the field of architecture, house-building, town planning and the plastic arts as well as the methodology and technology for preserving monuments.

These activities mostly comprise the following:

- an inventory of cultural assets in architecture and house-building plus a statutory documentation of registered historic properties;
- an inventory of historic towns and buildings, public parks and ornamental gardens;
- an inventory of historic and technical documentation on the architecture and construction of monuments;
- research and studies on history and town planning;
- an inventory of war damage and its indemnification;
- photographic documentation on architecture, house-building and historic town-planning, outstanding specimens of furniture, museum inventories and artistic masterpieces;
- extracts from archives on historic architecture.

The Centre has a large library and also issues its own works, including various series of publications. It publishes a periodical called "Ochrona Zabytkov" (Protection of Monuments).

One essential element in the activities of the regional organization for the protection of monuments consists of the offices for the documentation of monuments to be found in every voivodship by virtue of a decision to this effect by voivodes (even though not envisaged by the law of 15 February 1962). The offices are headed by personel appointed by the voivode pursuant to proposals submitted by the curator of monuments.

The most important duties of these offices include:

- the compilation, analysis and loan of the documentation of cultural assets for the purpose of systematic research;
- the documentation of changes occurring in monuments' state of repair and of the results of the work carried out to preserve these monuments;
- the initiating, directing and controlling of systematic research into the various categories of monuments;
- the preparation of opinions on the documentation of monuments, the supervision of the drawing up of this documentation and the presentation of appropriate propositions to the regional curators of monuments;
- control of completed conservation activities on behalf of the curator of monuments.

2.4 Implementation

By virtue of his decree of 25 August 1950, the Minister for Culture and the Arts set up a special State enterprise known as "workshops for the conservation of monuments" (10), (Polish Gazette No. A – III, sect. 1399) in order to be able to implement preservation work of every kind.

This enterprise pursues the following goals:

- in architecture: preparing technical and scientific documentation, exercising controls in respect of conservation and copyright and the implementing of construction and assembly work for the conservation, restoration and the complete or partial reconstruction of historic properties and their settings;

- in sculpture: preserving historic sculptures and decorative architecture;
- in painting: conserving pictures and murals of artistic merit;
- other conservation activities ordered by the Minister for Culture and the Arts.

The control of the enterprise is exercised by the Minister for Culture and the Arts through the agency of the Curator General of Monuments.

The Workshops for the Conservation of Monuments operate branches in several of the main places in the voivodship in addition to their workshops in other localities.

In 1972, the Polish Government decided to reconstruct the Royal Castle of Warsaw and created a special enterprise to carry out this huge investment.

The branch offices in question may be subdivided into a large number of workshops, which specialize in many different fields. They include 14 project offices with a staff of nearly 400 including 170 university graduates.

The aim of these projects is to restore the balance of buildings by emphasizing their artistic values and adapting them to their role in contemporary life. The workshops for historic documentation carry out research in the field of history, the history of art, town planning and the architecture of history monuments likely to become the object of conservation activities.

In the same way, the workshops for the restoration of sculptures have renovated a large number of stone and stucco statues as well as non-coloured wood.

Even though the workshop for the conservation of monuments have a staff of over 7,000, including several hundred graduates of technical universities, their opportunities for work are not sufficient. This is particularly the case with work on historic buildings and many situations require the help of other State building enterprises or cooperative societies with whom, moreover, the Ministry for Culture and the Arts has concluded an agreement on collaboration (II).

There also exists the inter-ministerial agreement of 30 December 1976 on the principles for sharing construction work whereby enterprises highly specialized in all spheres of work have a duty to carry out work for every investor in need of their help (1.8). Those enterprises, which come under the Ministries of Public Administration, Land Development and Protection of the Environment are inter alia expected to carry out reconstruction work in the historic quarters (III. 3.1)

3. The Protection of Historic Monuments and Town and Country Planning

The prime essential for an effective and efficient safeguarding of historic monuments and their utilization in a contemporary setting consists in effecting an integrated approach to the problems inherent in the preservation of our architectural heritage and in town and country planning.

This principle holds true not only for local planning but also for regional and nation-wide planning, since the latter fulfils a significant function in putting our architectural legacy to appropriate use.

The legislative and administrative arrangements for protecting historic monuments and buildings must be realized in conjunction with existing legislation and in particular with the laws governing land-use planning.

In most cases, a study of the history of urban areas serves as the basis for decisions upon conserving the supreme treasures to be found in historic town centres.

In agreement with the Minister for Culture and the Arts, the Committee for the Problems of Town Planning and Architecture issued a circular in 1956 on historic studies in the context of urban rehabilitation stipulating that such studies "on towns and quarters of a historic character" are obligatory. The provisions in question list in detail the subjects for historical urban studies and for research into the inplementation of town planning schemes.

These studies on ways and means of providing sound protection, conducted for approximately 500 historic town centres, served as a point of departure for working out their general plans. They enable one to avoid wrong decisions when carrying out fresh investment.

The Law of 31 January 1961 on town and country planning (Law Digest of 1975, No. 11, sect. 67 amended by No. 16, sect. 91) does not contain any specific reference to monuments and their settings. But in view of the fact that land-use and all changes in this sphere are subject to the provisions of town and country planning schemes (involving above all local, general and detailed plans), the latter must be coordinated with the services of other government departments and where necessary with those for the protection of historic monuments. This applies in particular to:

- sites where the size of new buildings is limited pursuant to Article 27, § 3 of the Law (so as not to impair the appearance of the monument or one's view of it);
- archaeological sites where the intention is to maintain them on a permanent basis or to cover them over with earth upon completion of the exploratory activities;
- sites where drillings have to be carried out prior to the erection of new buildings.

Under these arrangements, all local plans for historic towns and quarters and for sites with important monuments or buildings must be countersigned by the regional curator of monuments pursuant to the Law of 15 February 1962 before being presented for acceptance by the competent authorities.

The development plans for the historic towns and quarters drawn up by the authorities for the protection of monuments enter info force upon their incorporation within the local town planning schemes.

This is very important since the local plans must form the basis of decisions on land utilization and on the location and implementation of new developments. That also applies to the modification of monuments in historic settings in order to meet modern requirements.

"Protected zones" have been introduced to guarantee the preservation of historic urban structures. These zones are a statutory precondition for the implementation of general area-planning schemes and of conservation directives.

More recently, the Department for Museums and Historic Monuments at the Ministry for Culture and the Arts has worked out such directives on the basis of the substantial experience gathered in this field.

3.1 Object and range of the plans

a. Detailed planning and rehabilitation schemes must be drawn up by all towns and villages which have areas of historic value to be safeguarded, irrespective of their size or economic importance.

b. The detailed planning and rehabilitation schemes must take into account the overall impression of the protected zone or its structural components.

c. The order of priorities for carrying out these schemes is decided by the regional curator of historic monuments in agreement with the local planning and rehabilitation authority.
   The sequence chosen must bear in mind cultural values, the state of the historic substance and potential future development of the area in question.

d. In the case of small areas which have not yet worked out a guiding plan, the latter may be drawn up at the same time as the detailed planning and rehabilitation scheme.

e. In those zones which possess great historic value, development plans are drawn up and implemented under the strict control of the curator of historic monuments and of special teams of experts.
   If the detailed planning and rehabilitation scheme does not yet exist, the development plan must fulfil all the preconditions prescribed for the former.

3.2 Initial ducumentation

The formulation of detailed planning and rehabilitation schemes for an area of historic interest presupposes a complete initial documentation of the type normally envisaged for plans drawn up on this scale. Special attention must be paid to the following documentation:

3.2.1 A detailed inventory of the current state and condition of the area in question
(scale 1:1,000 possibly 1:2,000)

a. Technical state of repair of the buildings;

b. Building materials used, roofing construction style;

c. Size of buildings, number of storeys;

d. Use to which the buildings are put (storey by storey);

e. Analysis of ownership;

f. Density of occupation in each building;

g. Arrangement and laying out of lawns, analysis of the surfacing of streets and squares;

h. Technical infrastructure;

i. Road network.

In special cirumstances, the inventory must contain:

j. Architectural statistics;

k. Results of an analysis of the soil and ground at sites.

3.2.2 Analysis of cultural and historic value of buildings and monuments on the basis of studies
conducted in regard to the requirements of the general planning and rehabilitation scheme but extended to embrace those of the detailed plan.

If no historical or urban examination has been carried out or only partly or if it is already out of date, the analysis of cultural values must also include the problems of the general plan and those of the detailed plan.

The analysis is composed of the following elements:

a. An examination of the principal stages of development of the urban fabric and consideration of its traditional lines of development.

b. Analysis of the current situation and role of the historic centre in the structure of the urban fabric considered on the basis of thorough research on functional and spatial inter-relations with the surrounding zones.

c. Analysis of the structure of the historic town centre and in particular:
   - determination of its homogeneity or of its complexity and also the possible division of the town centre into a number of units;
   - The characteristics of the principal elements making up the urban fabric.

d. Assessment of the methods used in town planning based on an evaluation of the historic value and state of conservation of:
   - historic monuments and buildings;
   - traditional edifices and structures of essential importance for the appearance of an urban area;
   - the historic network of streets and squares;
   - open (green-belt) spaces of historic interest;
   - buildings located next to rivers and lakes.

e. Analysis of the value of a town's visual impact and a definition of:
   - interiors of great aesthetic and picturesque appeal;
   - the alignment of buildings and the architectural style of the streets;
   - the view over and from historic monuments and the various lines of perspective;
   - the dominant architectural accents;
   - buildings which impair the harmony of the whole.

3.2.3 Conclusions concerning measures to be taken to guarantee the protection of buildings and monuments

a. Establishment of protected zones pursuant to the following classification:
   - Zone "A" providing complete protection and embracing areas of exceptional importance in terms of historic structures and architecture or very well conserved. The areas included in this zone must, in principle, form the subject of a special town planning and conservation study. In this zone, the requirements of conservation enjoy top priority.
   - Zone "B" providing partial protection and embracing an area which conforms with the requirements attendant upon implementing some of the major elements of the plan and also upon the historic fabric to be conserved.

The provisions for Zone "B" stipulate the character and the scale of new buildings.

– Zone "E" embracing a safety area for the appropriate settings of historic buildings and monuments, in particular by maintaining non-developed land and limiting the size of new houses.

– Zone "K" designed to protect the scenery and embracing an area which makes up an integral part of the historic building.

– Zone "W" providing archaeological protection and embracing areas affected by, or earmarked for, archaeological exploration and therefore not used for new housing.

The zones must be indicated on the main map for the planning and rehabilitation scheme by means of uniform dots or lines.

It is appreciated that zones may overlap – especially zones E, K and W.

b. Detailed safeguarding measures indicating:

– the historic monuments and buildings to be given meticulous protection;

– single properties and groups of buildings to be conserved because of their environmental value;

– monuments and other historic features of the planning and rehabilitation scheme in particular jeopardy and thus in need of immediate official support;

– groups of buildings or areas of great importance which call for special studies on conservation and town planning;

– zones earmarked for construction activities subject to conditions such as structure, size and subdivision;

– non-developed real estate which ought to be built upon, though subject to certain architectural requirements.

c. Protection requirements on:

– maintaining the alignment of buildings and interiors endowed with aesthetic and picturesque quality;

– solving traffic problems and introducing pedestrian precincts; and

– preventing the construction of buildings which spoil the harmony of the whole.

3.3 Study of the programme for town and country planning

This study rests upon a comprehensive analysis of the town planning and protection scheme undertaken to determine the functional and spatial capacity of historic town centres.

1) Determination of the potential capacity of such centres

– Number of residents and consumers based upon an

a. Analysis of the relationship between cultural values and utilitarian functions with an indication of

– houses and groups of buildings whose current functions deserve to be maintained;

– houses and buildings whose current utilization is inappropriate;

– houses and buildings whose mode of utilization may be diversified;

– the functional capacity of buildings whose construction in a historic town centre has already been envisaged.

b. Analysis of the capacity and access for traffic with an indication of:

– streets and squares where vehicular traffic is strictly prohibited;

– streets designated for possible pedestrianization at a later stage;

– the volume of traffic in streets where it is authorized;

– potential parking facilities.

c. Analysis of the professional, social and family background of the inhabitants.

d. Analysis of sanitation and lighting conditions, density of buildings and population.

e. Analysis of an urban centre's tourist appeal.

2) Qualification of a historic centre's functional capacity in relation to the overall urban development plan.

3.4 Conclusions on the problems of the general plan

1) The function and participation of the historic town centre in the overall urban programme.

2) Possible need (or absence of such need) to organize a new centre of facilities and amenities for the city as a whole.

3) Spatial links with other tracts of land, particularly in neighbouring areas.

4) a. Choice of sites for development and the zoning of such sites.

b. Flow of traffic with particular reference to the main arteries and routes.

3.5 Method of implementing the detailed planning and rehabilitation scheme in areas of historic value

1. The individual nature of zones possessing historic value presupposes the preparation of a three-dimensional project which defines the volume of architecture involved.

2. The complexity of the detailed planning and rehabilitation scheme depends upon the value in historic terms and the peculiar circumstance of the envisaged zone.

3. The plan is drawn up on the basis of

a. an analysis specified in respect of points 2–4 concerning;

– the reported directives for conservation on the principal part of the plan using uniform methods of designation;

– the conservation measures indicated on the synthetic basis of the conclusion arrived at;

b. research and detailed analysis by way of:

– architectural studies;

– study of facade decoration;

– research on the mode of surfacing used for roads and squares;

– study of urban decoration and embellishment;

– research on information and guidance systems.

3.6 Directives on the implementation of work in order to:

1) estimate the various stages needed to complete development and modernization;

2) indicate the aims of investment;

3) indicate the houses and groups of buildings which call for an implementation of the work by teams specialized in the conservation of historic monuments;

4) indicate the number of temporary and permanent dwellings (subdivided into the various stages);

5) indicate the best technologies for fitting new buildings among existing structures, and

6) carry out an economic analysis and draw up a table of fees for each stage of the envisaged work.

In this way, the provisions issued on the realization of town-planning projects lay down the implementation of special studies and take into account the applications submitted by the conservation authorities in the formulation of plans for a zone incorporating historic monuments and buildings. All the architectural projects which affect the houses and groups of buildings in the protected zones must be coordinated with the regional curator for historic monuments. In the event of disagreement, decisions are taken by the Curator-General of Monuments. If new buildings are erected in the zones of outstanding value, it is important to take into consideration decisions of a general nature.

The Law on Building of 24 October 1974 (Law Digest, No. 38, sect. 229) states inter alia "that architectonic forms of buildings must harmonize with their surroundings, bear in mind the qualities of the scenic setting, and help to enhance the aesthetic appearance of the latter (art. 4).

As a result of the enactment of the Law on Building, it was established that no change in the use to which land is put be introduced without the permission of the competent administrative authorities in conformity with the conditions stipulated in special provisions (art. 23, sect. 2).

Mention should also be made of the decree issued by the same Minister on 1st December 1976 respecting the height of multi-family houses (Polish Gazette No. 44, pos. 22). In an annex, this lays down that "in those districts of a town which have a historic character or in those streets of a high aesthetic status, new buildings must be planned and built in harmony with the surroundings" and moreover that the "size and diversity of buildings should be adapted to the style and appearance of the town and take into consideration the outline of adjacent buildings".

In view of the complexity of the subject, the development of historic urban buildings clearly involves problems in excess of the jurisdiction of the Ministry of Culture and the Arts and in some cases that of the local authorities. That is why in 1974, for example, the relevant decisions had to be taken by the Government itself on the development plans for Cracow and Zamosc.

In order to rationalize activities and assure efficient cooperation throughout the country, Resolution No. 101/78 issued by the Council of Ministers on 21 July 1978 created an Inter-Ministerial Commission to handle the development of historic towns and areas. This Commission is presided over by the Under-Secretary of State at the Ministry of Culture and the Arts (Curator-General of Monuments).

Membership of the Commission consists of the following:

– An Under-Secretary of State at the Ministry of Public Administration, Regional Planning and Environmental Protection;
– An Under-Secretary of State at the Ministry of Housing;
– A delegate from the office of the Polish Academy of Science;
– The President of the Union of Housing Cooperatives;
– The President of the Association of Polish Architects;
– The President of the Society of Polish Town Planners,

and other persons invited by the President of the Commission, including the representative of the Department for Museums and Historic Monuments. The Commission may invite the representative of the voivodeships, the town presidents, the town mayors and the representatives of interested communes in addition to specialists and experts.

The Commission fulfils the following functions:

– to draw up the list of historic towns and buildings designated for development; and
– to assess and approve the planning and rehabilitation schemes and the development of historic towns and buildings in all spheres relating to their economic and social development.

The opinions and suggestions voiced by the Commission must be used as the basis and as a directive for the ministers, voivodes and town presidents.

In order to promote a global policy for the protection of historic town centres, the relevant measures have been put on a nation-wide basis. A system of criteria has been evolved for assessing the state of repair of a building and its various elements, its originality and scientific, aesthetic and natural value. In this way, it proved possible to define the relative merits of all the historic buildings and areas in Poland – an essential step if we are to fix a sequence of requirements and a conservation policy on a nation-wide scale. An estimation like that also enables us to gauge the extent of the protection furnished in terms of the relative value of the monument in question.

Clearly, the problem of safeguarding and utilizing historic buildings and monuments requires not only local, but also macro-spatial planning. This aspect of the problem quite rightly constitutes one of the key questions in UNESCO's recommendation on the protection of historic and traditional buildings and monuments and their role in contemporary life (known as the "Warsaw Recommendation").

In Poland, there are town and country planning schemes at voivodeship, macro-regional and national level. As regards the safeguarding of ancient monuments and historic buildings, the most significant role is played by the town and country planning schemes drawn up by the voivodeships.

The problem of pretecting and utilizing structures of historic importance in the regional town and country planning schemes

The town and country planning schemes prepared at voivodeship level play a vital role in the protection and rational use of buildings of supreme importance since it is thanks to them that town planning and socio-economic planning are effectively integrated. The plans prepared at a lower level deal with the chosen locations and areas whenever it is necessary in this field to establish a general policy. The significance of the plans prepared at voivodeship level consists in the formulation of directives to guide planning carried out at a lower level by towns and communes and to submit suggestions for that effected at a higher level, i.e. macro-regional or national.

The cultural merit of historic buildings or monuments must be deemed one of the essential factors in determining the role and function of an area as well as in defining their position in the physical fabric of the voivodeship. On the one hand, it is essential to avoid the decay of precious historic town centres lacking in opportunities for development; on the other hand, it is imperative to curb excessive development in cases where the danger of ruining the historic fabric exists.

The conclusions on these points can only be drawn after a deep analysis of the functional capacity of historic centres and this must give equal weight to the structure of new buildings. The regional plans prepared by the voivodeships must indicate subjects for further analysis and the topics for studies on detailed planning on how to develop and utilize historic town centres.

The regional town and country planning schemes closely linked with the economic plans guarantee access to the necessary funds, the means of production and the selection of required materials. Failure to appreciate this fact could put the realization of the most important propositions at risk.

The formulation of that part of the regional plan relating to the safeguarding of our cultural heritage must rest upon an analysis of the latter within the voivodeship. This analysis is completed with the help of the regional curator of historic monuments, the regional curator for natural assets and for public guidance on this subject and the regional committee of physical education and tourism. Their role consists in drawing up programmes designed to incorporate historic monuments and buildings in the social and economic development plans at voivodeship level.

The Ministry of Culture and the Arts assumes the role of coordinator.

The activities undertaken to safeguard historic town centres may be geared more to development or more to rehabilitation. The expression "development" is applied to buildings whose architectural substance has remained intact or deteriorated to a small extent only and which require the assistance of teams of specialists at the project and execution stage. The term "rehabilitation" relates to buildings and areas for which the plans and their implementation may be handled without external help and simply in pursuance of detailed directives issued by the curators. The criteria for distinguishing between these two terms must not proceed from the value of a building as a historic monument but from the character of the structure in question and its architectural substance, both of which call for a process of adaptation during the period envisaged by the plan.

The applications on protecting the historic features of old towns are submitted to the Department of Museums and Historic Monuments at the Ministry of Culture and the Arts, who then express their considered opinion. After that, the applications have to be approved by the Interministerial Commission for the Development of Historic Towns and Buildings.

The regional planning and rehabilitation schemes must take into consideration the problems of historic villages as well as the adaptation (conversion) of such monuments as are either not utilized at all or put to inappropriate use. The authorities recognize the need to invest monuments with the functions envisaged in the socio-economic programmes by effecting fresh investment.

The directives on drawing up regional planning and rehabilitation schemes take the following requirements into account:

I. Analysis of the cultural heritage of the voivodeship

Any examination of cultural assets must embrace the principal features set out below:

1) Protected areas and buildings of historic interest and their value as monuments at national, regional and local level.

2) Historic areas and buildings which require protection in the form of

   a. development plans for complete protection zones and

   b. rehabilitation for partial protection zones.

3) Places and sites of great value from the standpoint of town and country planning with an indication of those subject to restrictions on fresh investment.

4) Villages whose historic fabric has been preserved with particular attention to those able to adjust to tourist and recreational requirements.

5) Places of importance as historic monuments threatened by dereliction for want of development potential.

6) Historic monuments and buildings of particular appeal and conducive to the vitalization of the cultural scene.

7) Historic monuments and buildings devoted to social purposes but utilized in inappropriate fashion.

8) Sites and monuments of topographical and natural merit.

9) Tourist itineraries and regions (either existing or planned) with suitable historic monuments and sites of natural beauty.

10) It is strongly recommended in respect of voivodeships containing areas of outstanding scenic beauty that the exact number and size of historic structures there should be determined together with the site of the buildings and monuments as well as points of natural beauty.

II. The designation of activities indispensable for the conservation and utilization of cultural assets in the voivodeship's socio-economic development plans

1) Listing of priorities and operational stages for the renewal of historic town centres in respect of their
   a. development
   b. rehabilitation.

2) A list of indispensable funds, productive capacity (building and conservation facilities), availability of materials and accommodation pursuant to the various stages in the realization of the project.

3) Guidelines and principles for the cultural revitalization of small towns and villages of great historic importance threatened by decline and decay.

4) Formulation of a programme for a diversified use of historic monuments and buildings earmarked for social purposes in general and tourism, leisure and recreation in particular.

5) Indication of new itineraries and regions for tourists in the light of a rational utilization of historic monuments and buildings.

6) Specification of indispensable studies and their objectives in regard to the means of safeguarding our cultural heritage and putting it to modern use.

7) Directives on the range of plans drawn up at a lower level.

8) Proposals on higher-level planning.

Notes

1) This law also benefits the curators in respect of those properties which are not listed in the register of monuments if the preconditions exist for registration. In this case, a decision taken by the curator loses its statutory force if registration has not taken place within a period of five months. This period may not be extended (Article 29).

2) The compulsory acquisition of a historic building may take place by virtue of the provisions of the law of 12 March 1959 governing the principles and conditions for the expropriation of properties (Law Digest 1974, No. 10, sect. 64).

3) Circular No. 83 issued by the President of the Ministerial Council on 31 July 1971 on preventing the destruction, ruin or decay of historic buildings by making full use of public and social organization stipulates, inter alia, that the ministers and voivodes in question must take the following action in order to protect historic buildings and monuments against dilapidation and to guard them against destruction or devastation:

 – Issue orders to their subordinate authorities who benefit from historic properties to undertake regular investments in and restoration of these buildings pursuant to Article 70 of the Law on Buildings and Art. 2b, sect. 1, of the Law on the Protection of Monuments and on Museums.

 – Introduce funds for major restorations in the budgets for the occupants of historic properties and ensure the proper use of these sums in compliance with their earmarked purpose.

 – Recommend the organizations in question to apply disciplinary sanctions against those guilty of not having carried out the necessary restorations within the prescribed period.

 Circular No. 57 of 28 July 1972 on greater protection for historic properties recommends voivodes to make the necessary arrangements for ensuring efficient control over the implementation of the Law of 15 February 1962 and the other provisions enacted on the strength of that law and in particular for ensuring the execution of the major restorations of historic buildings and the effective employment of funds earmarked for this purpose.

 At the same time, the organs of public administration at all levels are empowered to transfer part of the budgetary surpluses from regional bodies so as to cover the cost of conservation activities and the restoring of historic buildings. Such work may also be financed out of the economies achieved during the execution of the investment schemes drawn up by the voivodeships, the municipalities and the communes.

4) The guarantees furnished for State bonds operate in accordance with the principles and provisions of the Law of 22 April 1959 governing the restoration and reconstruction of buildings and their height and the conclusion of building work (Law Digest 1968, No. 36, sect. 249).

5) Pursuant to Art. 43 of the law of 25 January 1958 on the people's councils (Law Digest 1957, No. 26, sect. 139), the supreme administrative body within the voivodeship is the voivode. By virtue of Articel 61 of the said law, the voivode may authorize his deputies to discharge certain tasks and to take decisions in his name.
In practice, the curators of monuments in all the voivodeships have been authorized to take decisions in this field and to sign such provisions on behalf of the voivode.

6) This stipulation also applies to work which could impair the setting of a historic building or the view of the latter (Article 27, para. 3).

7) Such curators have been named for such historic towns as Torún, Lublin, Zamosc, Kazimierz Dolny, etc.

8) In regard to the protection of historic monuments, this council assumed the functions of the Council for Culture and the Arts envisaged by Art. 10 para 1 of the law of 15 February 1962.

9) Decree issued by the Minister for Culture and the Arts on the structure and competence of the councils for the protection of cultural assets (Polish Gazette No. 56, sect. 281).

10) Abbreviation in Polish: P. K. Z.

11) Agreement between the Ministry for Culture and the Arts and the Central Union of Housing Cooperatives signed on 14 February 1976.

12) This resolution replaces and broadens the former resolutions adopted by the Ministeral Council No. 102 of 21 March 1957 on the location of investments in historic properties (Polish Gazette, 1961, No. 1, sect. 6).

4. Finance

As we have already noted, all the owners and occupants of historic properties – whether public-law corporations or natural persons – have a duty to keep these structures in good repair and to prevent their decay. Nonetheless, many buildings and their surroundings were in a state of ruin or devastation after the war or as a result of prolonged neglect. It would not be feasible to place their current owners under the obligation of defraying the cost of restoring them to their original condition, of developing such properties or adapting them for up-to-date use. The bulk of these expenses thus falls upon the State within the framework of its investment plans and funds earmarked in the main budged of the Ministry for Culture and the Arts for the conservation and development of historic buildings or that of the Ministry for Public Administration, Land-Use Planning and Protection of the Environement for the rehabilitation and restoration of housing or, finally, the budgets of the voivodships in the municipalities and communes.

By virtue of Resolution No. 179 issued by the Ministerial Council on 8 December 1978 on the utilization of historic properties for the benefit of society (Polish Gazette No. 37, sect 142 – annex III) (12), it is possible to meet part of the cost from the budgetary funds of the Ministry for Culture and the Arts in cases where the investor decides to adapt for his own use a historic building which is either not used or improperly used. If the building possesses a high cultural value, the customary grant of 23% of costs may be exceeded subject to the approval of the Minister for Culture and the Arts (Article II, paras 2 and 3). This credit is available to both public institutions and natural persons.

In order to encourage the widest scale of fresh investment in buildings of historic interest, Resolution No. 179 stipulates in each case that an analysis must be carried out to see if the investment in question could not be effected in an edifice which is either not used or used for an inappropriate purpose. A refusal to invest in the latter must rest solely on significant considerations of a financial or technical nature.

If a historic property belonging to the State is threatened with destruction, ruin or devastation and the public or nationalized bodies cannot or do not wish to undertake its conservation, the local organ of public administration may assign the building to a natural person on a purchase basis, as a heriditary leasehold or pursuant to a lease provided that he accepts the obligation to convert the property into usable condition and to maintain it as such (Article 6, paras 2 and 3).

All these institutions and private individuals enjoy priority in the purchase of rationed materials needed for the reconstruction and conservation of historic buildings used for accommodation (Article 13 and the relief provided for under the financial provisions – Article 12).

5. The Social Protection of Monuments

The principle expressed in Article 1 of 15 February 1962 that "the protection of cultural assets . . . is an obligation for the State and a duty for its citizens" has been widely promoted in Poland by the organization of a network of "social custodians of public monuments" (Polish Gazette 1963, No. 17, sect 97).

The social custodians fulfil their functions on an honorary basis, but they are entitled to have their expenses refunded. Their duties consist of the following:

– to ensure that the monument and its surroundings are kept in a good state of repair;

– to help in the active development of the monument;

– to popularize the idea of the historic and cultural importance of monuments for education and teaching.

The custodians may be appointed for single monuments, for groups of them or for all monuments within a certain locality.

The year 1974 saw the rebirth of the Society for the Protection of Monuments, founded in 1906 and closed down in 1939. The object of the Society is to familiarize the widest possible sections of the community with the requirements and the importance of the social trusteeship of monuments as the legacy of our national culture and to carry out as many activities as possible for its preservation and conservation.

The aim of the Society is:

– to stimulate social initiatives for the safeguarding of monuments;

– to take care directly via its members of various monuments and their surroundings and also to organize as much as possible conservation activities under the control of the State authorities for the conservation of cultural assets;

– to inform the community about the state of repair of monuments and their surroundings and about the efforts undertaken to protect them;

– to cooperate with the public administration authorities and in particular with the Curator-General of Monuments at the Ministry for Culture and the Arts and the regional curators of monuments;

– to collaborate in the safeguarding of monuments with the regional associations and bodies, political and trade-union organizations, tourist and sports bodies, scientific institutions, museums, archives and libraries;

– to edit a periodical and other publications; and

– to cooperate with associated, foreign and international institutions and organizations.

In addition, there are sections for the protection of cultural assets at organizations such as the Association of Polish Architects, whose main function is to ensure a systematic flow of information about this subject.

Independently of these permanent organizations, civic action committees are sometimes set up: examples of this are the Civic Committee for the Restoration of the Royal Castle of Warsaw (1971) or the Social Committee for the Renovation of Cracow's Monuments (1978).

These committees pursue the primary aim of initiating the community into the role and the importance of these monuments for national culture and of encouraging public generosity.

On many occasions, large nationalized enterprises and trade unions pay for the restoration of historic monuments or their surroundings in order to adapt them for their own social or cultural needs.

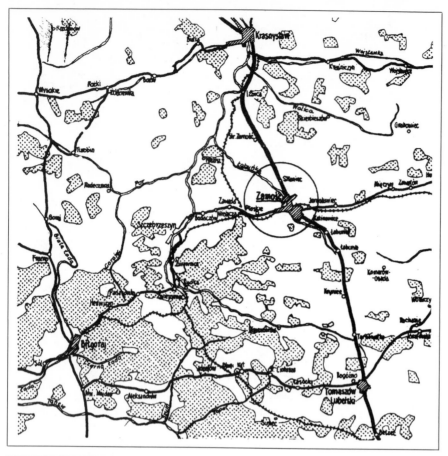

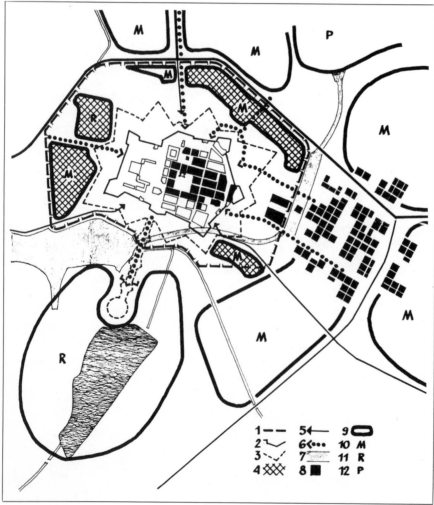

Zamość:

above: Map showing Zamość's location

below: Relationship between the historic town centre and the surrounding area.

1. Limits of the zone covered by the plan
2. Urban area during the Renaissance
3. Limits of the old 19th century citadel excluding the forefield
4. Erection on the forefield of structures which destroyed the harmony of the historic quarter
5. The guiding principle of siting communications outside the town
6. Direction of the principal pedestrianized streets
7. Railway line to be closed down
8. Concentration of social amenities in the town centre
9. Creation of the modern town
10. Housing
11. Recreation
12. Industry

Poland
ZAMOŚĆ

1. Situation

1.1 General introduction

With a population of 30,000 inhabitants and its position as the principal town of a voivodship, Zamosc provides a historic setting of exceptional quality and one of the outstanding examples in Europe of a Renaissance city. The entire urban area is still in a relatively good state of conservation in regard to the physical fabric of the streets and the architectural composition. This historic township within a protected zone can only be described as a precious jewel.

1.2 History

Zamosc was founded in 1580 by the Great Hetman (i.e. Commander-in-Chief) and Royal Chancellor Tan Zamoyski. Its founder, one of the most illustrious statesmen and humanists in Europe, gave Zamosc a charter as an independent town. It was built completely in the Renaissance style in accordance with the construction plans of the Italian architect Bernardo Morando. The execution of the first plans took place very rapidly, lasting only nine years (1580–1589). However, the perfecting, extending and embellishing of the buildings lasted until the mid-17th century. The following years marked the period of new additions which had not been envisaged in the original plan. The completion of Zamosc's urban layout took place in the 18th century. Zamosc is a Renaissance town in the real sense of the word. Its use of space consisted in linking an urban development with the seat of a nobleman in a single unit and provided with a system of common defence. This concept represented a new departure in town planning at the time. Surrounded as it was by bastions in conformity with the rules of the new Italian School, the fortress possessed all the elements essential for the defence systems of that epoch. Henceforth, Zamosc served as a model for other and older towns, which were remodelled along similar lines during the following years. The layout of the town betrays the influence of Renaissance design: the main square in the centre, the central lines of crossing streets, the town hall aligned with the houses bordering the main square, the two connected market squares and the homogeneous architecture of the whole. Nevertheless, a spirit of independence pervaded the creation of this ensemble – an ensemble adapted to the real conditions of the area where it was founded in territorial, functional and traditional respect.

Following the loss of independence at the end of the 18th century, Zamosc fell into the hands of the Austrians: later, after the Congress of Vienna (1815), it became part of the Kingdom of Poland. Its military features attracted attention.

It was in fact a fortress and the Czarist authorities recognized it as a military zone. Under the direction of a military engineer, General Mallet-Malletski, the creator of Vauban-type defences during the Napoleonic wars, the original bastions were enlarged and modernized. The town was remodelled, the houses along the main square modified, several churches laid waste and Hamoyski Palace deformed and spoiled.

In 1865, the fortress of Zamosc was deemed to be out of date and destroyed. Parts of it were blown up whilst others simply decayed in the course of time. local residents used the walls as building material.

Nevertheless, it should be recognized that the existence of the fortifications halted the march of time and rendered possible the historical development of this fortified town and its environs. Today, the Renaissance centre surrounded by a green belt stands somewhat apart from modern Zamosc.

2. Conditions

2.1 Problems

The Object of the Plan. Historic town centres constitute a component part of the larger urban fabric of our times. As a subject for conservation, they cannot be regarded in isolation and left out of our study of contemporary city life. They cannot and must not be considered as a separate group of buildings or as an open-air museum of urban architecture.

Clearly, certain contradictions and even discrepancies exist between the goal of safeguarding our legacy and the pressure of contemporary life with its advanced technology, vicissitudes and different approaches to the concept of modernism. Be that as it may, past experience has taught us that these differences largely stem from misleading appearances and a misunderstanding of the objectives and ideas under discussion. The object of the plan consists in a search for compromises and the elimination of excessively radical opinions, intrusions and overhasty or casual decisions.

2.2 Because of the rapid growth of towns expected for the future, a competition was introduced in 1969 on the theme 'The Development of a New Centre'. The project, designed by a group of architects under the direction of T. Tedynak, won first prize and was nominated for implementation. It envisages the creation of a new central area linked pursuant to the blueprint with the historic quarter, but located to the east. The aim of the new centre is to free the historic quarter of the functions with which it has been overburdened. At the same time, work has been put in hand on the development of a number of blocks of houses.

The approach of the 400th anniversary of the foundation of Zamosc (1980) has accelerated the pace of restoration and rehabilitation in line with the governmental resolution of 1974.

Zamość:
a. Panoramic view from the East side: reproduction of the complete architect's plan
b. Vista of the town towards the East

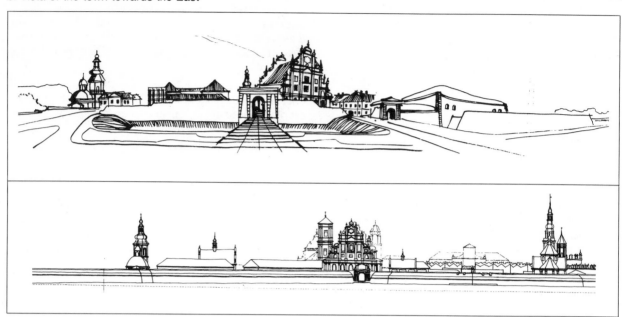

3. Aims of Official Support

The objectives of the plan may be described as follows. The main aim is to establish and coordinate the decisions and activities relating to the provision of complete protection for defined cultural values by means of an appropriate utilization and integration of the historic areas and buildings in the present-day life of the town.

The analysis of the architectural evolution of Zamosc illuminates the essential elements of its use of space, i.e. the Renaissance complex, its subsequent modifications, the fortified town of the 19th century and the changes then taking place in its design and planning over the years up to the present time.

The remodelling of the Renaissance bastions and their transformation into a modern defensive system in the 19th century created a new set of values both from the standpoint of conservation policy and that of town planning. Since then, these two points have received due respect and emphasis. The authorities decided to establish a protected zone covering the entire site.

The growth of the town was the reason for the change in functions of the land surrounding the fortified town. The former role of this land, i.e. to ease the surveying of the surrounding terrain from the town and later from the fortress, now changed and it became a vantage point from which to obtain a pleasant view of Zamosc from outside. The whole set of historic monuments became a protected zone providing a fine overall view of the urban scene.

Functional and architectural studies have demonstrated the need for new solutions to the problem of combining a historic quarter with the fabric of a contemporary urban area, particularly in regard to the flow of traffic. The planning and current utilization of the historic area no longer correspond either to the traditions or the goals envisaged under the planning and rehabilitation scheme. The complex solu-

tions adopted stem in fact from the research work and analysis carried out during the actual implementation of the original plan. The plan also takes into consideration the groups of buildings where redevelopment is still in progress or even completed.

The Renaissance part of Zamosc where the edifices contrasted with the background of the historic area, the remains of the 19th century defences and the forefield created the diversity of problems which had to be taken into consideration during the implementation of the project.

4. Strategies and Measures

4.1 Legislation

The principles adopted in drawing up the plan based on a more comprehensive system and still in force in Poland involve a methodical approach which rests upon the statutory provisions governing town and country planning schemes.

This system is based on the Law on Town and Country Planning (1961) as well as other enactments connected with it and providing the whole country with a uniform network of planning services and supervisory offices for town planning and architecture.

The broadly conceived protection of monuments based upon the Law on the Protection of Cultural Assets and of Museums (1962) introduced a uniform legal system throughout Poland.

The town planning scheme and development of the historic complex of Zamosc furnishes a good example of integrated cooperation and coordination between the two legal systems forming the statutory basis of the plan.

This system of town and country planning determines the implementation of the plan, the principles underlying the 'code' for the registration of such a plan and the statutory provisions to which it will be subject. The system for safeguarding cultural assets determines the means of research and the order of priorities and in particular subordinates all aspects of the plan to the overriding need for safeguarding cultural values.

4.2. Planning

The plan is drawn up in three stages and five phases. This subdivision is typical of all rehabilitation schemes prepared within the framework of town and country planning.

First stage

This ist the preparatory stage and simultaneously phase '0'. It embraces the collection and processing of the initial documents for the plan and in particular the survey maps of the foundations on the scale 1:5000, 1:2000, 1:1000, 1:1500, 1:2500 plus the various directives governing the execution of the plan, the data and the technical preconditions for the infrastructure, the former physiographical documentation, searches in the archives and former rehabilitation projects.

The identification of the site constitutes the basis of the plan. It is carried out by the group of architects who drew up the

Zamość: Current position according to the findings of the architects of the 1976 plan / use of the conventional signs

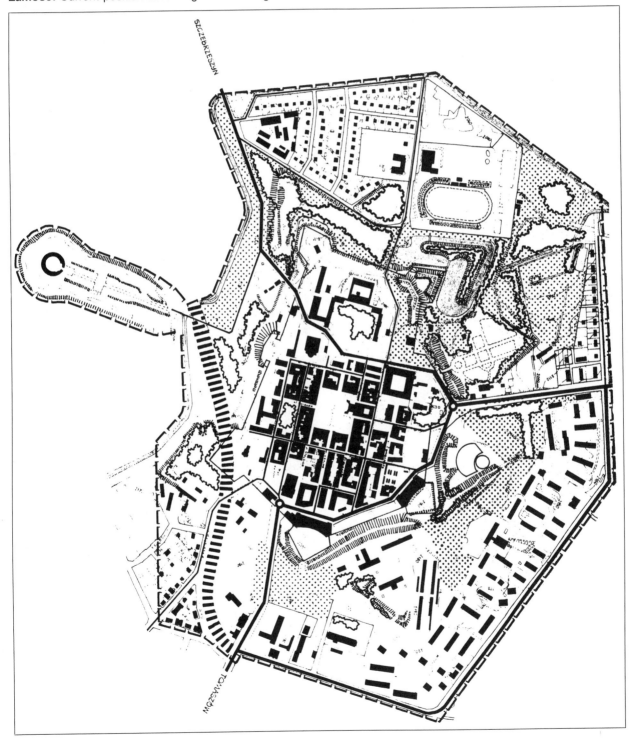

project on the scale (1:1000, 1:5000 and 1:2500) and comprises two aspects: that of town planning with its synthesis of functional and spatial realities and that of architecture illustrating as it does in detail the current state of the urban fabric and including cross-sections of the buildings on the scale 1:250. The identification thus comprises a three-dimensional approach: silhouette drawings of the town (scale 1:500), alignments of the houses along the streets (1:250) and a highly detailed photographic inventory.

It also portrays the current state of the townscape: sketches and nature studies, series of photographs and related descriptions.

An identification carried out in this way illuminates the prevailing situation in the town and also enables the

Zamość: Compositional structure
1. Limits to the study – protection zone "A"
2. Existing buildings adapted to new functions
3. Renewal or reconstruction of buildings, groups of buildings and facades
4. Project for new buildings
5. Surface of streets and squares which require a thorough analysis from the standpoint of their aesthetic appearance
6. Revitalization of botanical gardens
7. Reconstruction of walls in accordance with the original design of old fortifications
8. Relief map of the defensive works
9. Adaption and relief map of the principal line of the ramparts

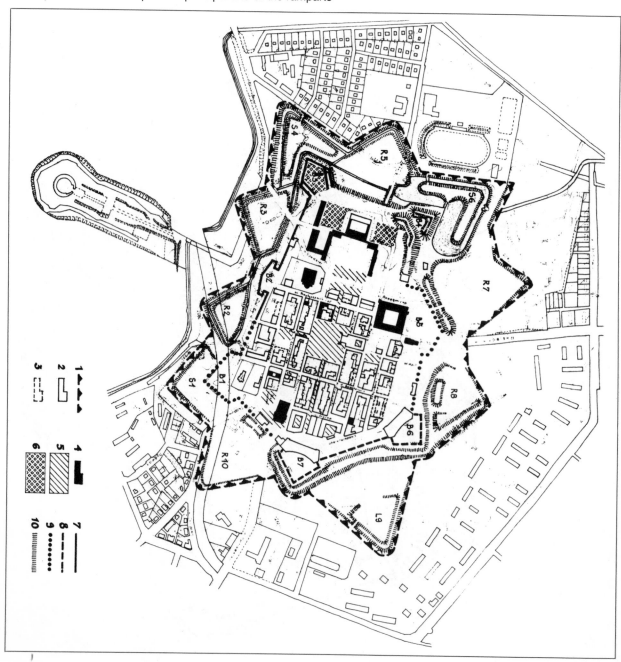

originators of the project to obtain thorough and detailed information about the subject of their study. One of the primary considerations underlying the formulation of plans is that they should help us in the fullest sense of the expression to 'learn our city by heart' down to the most infinitestimal details. Phase '0' and the first stage also include the collecting of documents needed for historic research. Two situations may occur. On the one hand, the town may never have formed the subject of a study and analysis or else the studies carried out did not inspire full confidence because of the passage of time in the meantime or because of the excessive generalizations or the exagger-

Zamość: Functional structure
1. Limits to the study
2. Concentration of social amenities in the centre of the town
3. Concentration of housing and basic services
4. Other urban services throughout the town
5. Recreational and walking areas in protection zone "A"
6. Recreational and walking areas within the limits of the present study
7. Vehicular traffic and car parks
8. Principal pedestrian paths outside the historic town centre
9. Aquatic amenities

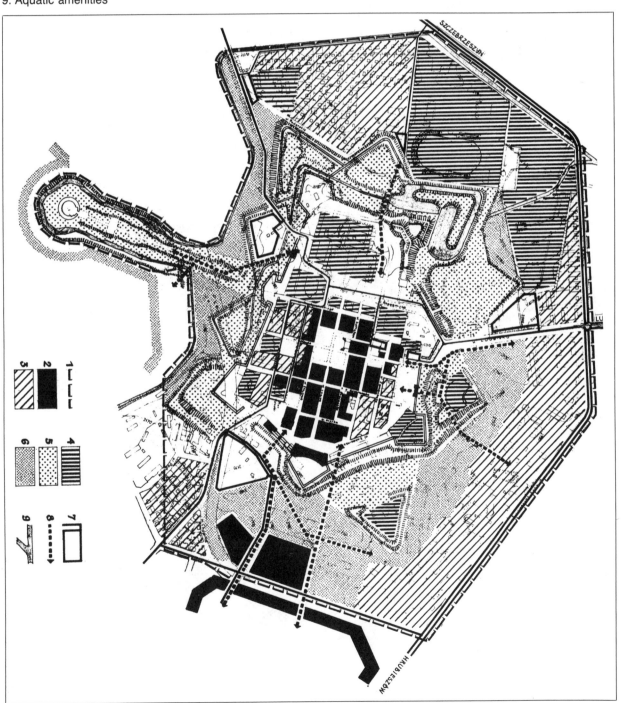

ated partisanship shown. In these circumstances, a fresh historic study and town planning becomes necessary. During phase '0', one must collect the cartographic and iconographic materials, the source documents and bibliographical lists needed before embarking upon any study of a town's past history.

The other situation which may occur is the existence of an up-to-date and adequate study of the subject so as to test the processing of the plan in regard to the safeguarding of monuments. Only the possession of the complete material in this study will satisfy the requirements of the envisaged plan.

In the case of Zamosc, the first stage of the work progressed under the conditions described above – though with an intermediary stage emerging during the apportionment of the historic material. A large part of the study of this unique place in the history of Polish town planning had first to be put together and then amplified with basic documentation.

Zamość: Conservation arrangements

1. Limits of the study
2. Planning and rehabilitation design for the Renaissance quarter – conserved
3. Planning and rehabilitation design for the Renaissance quarter – obsolete
4. Employment of fresh investments outside the Renaissance quarter
5. New investment, still to be settled
6. Non-developed land outside the Renaissance quarter earmarked for permanent use
7. Historic routes outside the city
8. Building of historic importance within the Renaissance quarter
9. Other buildings in the Renaissance quarter put to new use
10. Zone A (complete protection)
11. Zone B (indirect protection of the layout of the town and its environs)

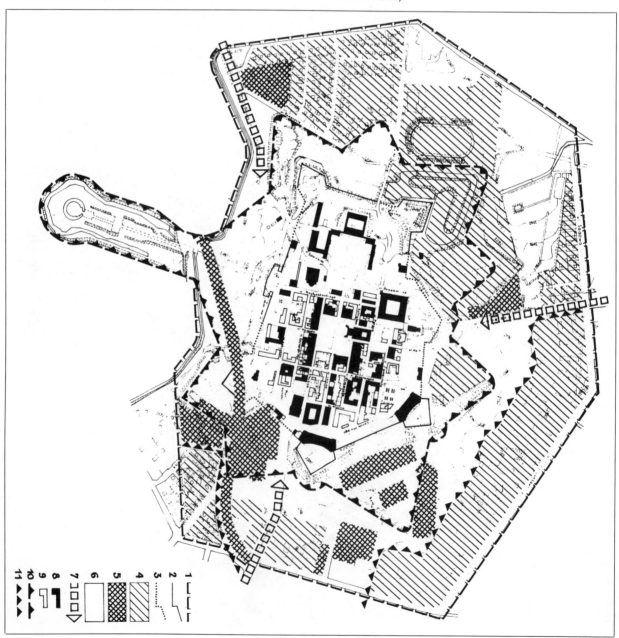

Finally, a new history of the town and its architecture was completed and this standardized and augmented the results of preceding research.

Second stage

Studies and analyses on the plan.
This stage comprises two consecutive phases
– first phase: analyses and applications
– second phase: study of the projects.

Zamość: traffic – changes

1. Limits to protection zone "A"
2. Limits to the extent of the Renaissance quarter
3. Streets with normal and free moving traffic/perspectives
4. Classification of streets
5. Street with free moving traffic / stretch (of road)

The first phase consists of a set of special analyses in the three fields listed below. Conservation: a study on the history of town planning, a study on the current town-planning situation and the conservation directives for the envisaged plan.

The Programme of Town Planning: a study on the land between the historic centre and the new town and the links between the two, on communications, the utilization of buildings and undeveloped land together with ancillary

6. Squares and streets earmarked solely for pedestrianization
7. Streets destined for pedestrians with access to the countryside
9. Railway line due for closure
10. Urban bus-lines (perspective)
11. Urban bus-lines (section)
12. Bus stations

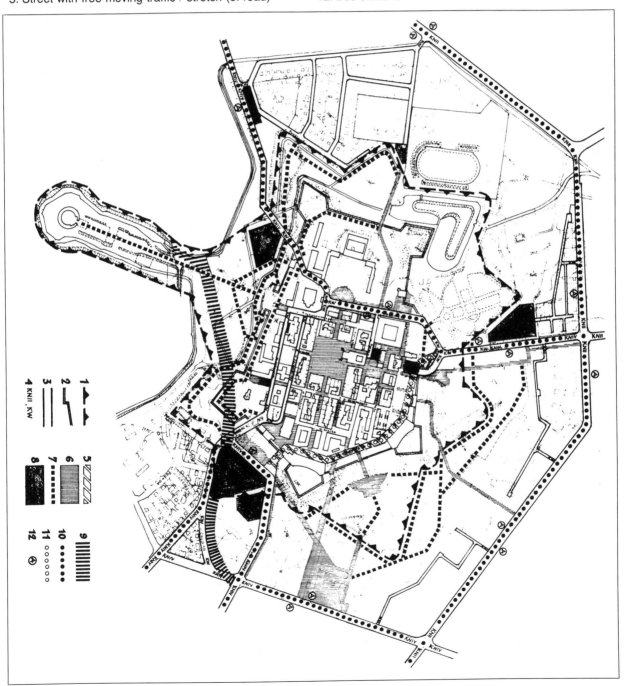

Zamość: Directives on the arrangement of buildings, cross-section of the ground-floor 1:250. Black-and-white copy in the original colour on the dotted frames pursuant to the symbols.
Guide to the buildings, front view 1:250

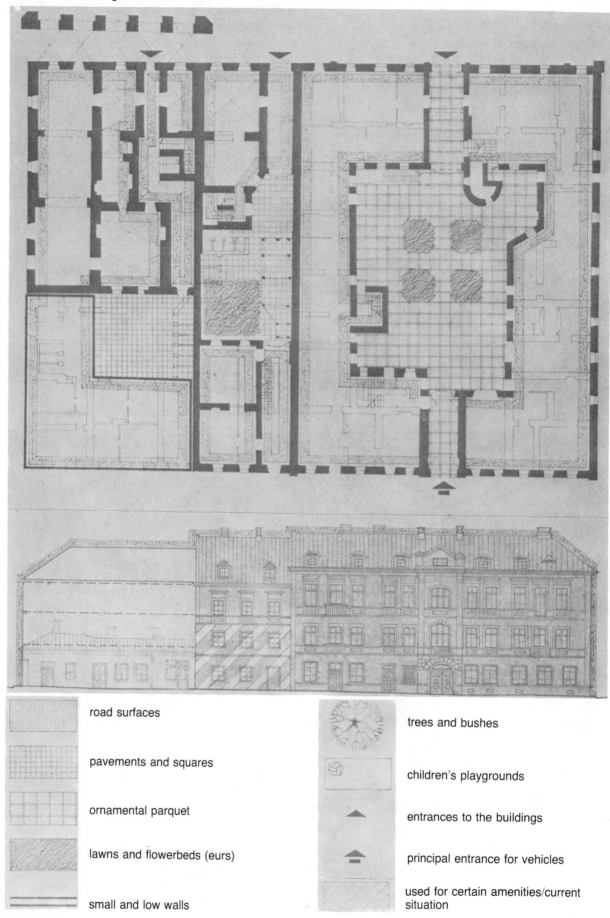

road surfaces	trees and bushes
pavements and squares	children's playgrounds
ornamental parquet	entrances to the buildings
lawns and flowerbeds (eurs)	principal entrance for vehicles
small and low walls	used for certain amenities/current situation

applications, a study on the composition of the landscape and its development. Technical Studies: an analysis of the physical condition of buildings and the infrastructure of the land in regard to current requirements.

During the first phase, the specialists' analyses and decisions are effected and adopted independently of each other. The originators have the right to tackle the problems in personal fashion and to voice radical opinions.

The second phase is marked by a process of integration of the conclusions and assessments essential for the execution of the plan. Furthermore, the objectives of the plan are compared with the genuine possibilities for their realization. During the same phase, widely diverging assessments and conclusions and differences of opinion are coordinated and the attempt is made to achieve reasonable compromises. Upon the conclusion of the study, a functional programme is presented while a technical investigation of the infrastructure of the terrain indicates the possibilities of carrying out the scheme.

The synthesis of these two phases of the first stage of the plan permit the formulation of the fundamental provisions of the plan representing a substitute for the main plan in which all aspects have been classified and most of the compromises adopted.

The fundamental provisions of the plan are submitted for acceptance to the authorities, who later approve the results of the studies, i.e. the processed plan.

Third stage

This comprises two consecutive phases:

third phase: the draft plan

fourth phase: (final) confirmation of the plan.

The third phase incorporates the conversion of the fundamental arrangements for the plan and the study concepts in a processed plan in its definitive form.

In the next chapter, we shall take a look at the substance of the plan. At the present juncture, however, we need only mention that the execution of the plan in its third phase is subjected to multilateral coordination and to the assessment of the experts and of society. The plan is then presented in outline to the general public. All the observations, applications and restrictions are taken into consideration and analyzed both by the originators of the project and by the interested organs and institutions, who resolve the differences and pronounce the final decisions. Having been verified and approved, the draft plan is presented for acceptance by the competent authorities.

The fourth phase comprising the procedure for the confirmation of the draft together with its implementation usually takes place independently of the office which originally drew it up. The draft ist submitted to the confirmation procedure which consists essentially of a dual authorization:

a. On behalf of the conservation authorities, i.e. the regional curator of historic monuments, and in a case of disagreement by the contral authority in this sphere the Curator-General of Historic Monuments. The latter deals with the most important or the most difficult solutions such as the plan for Zamosc.

b. On behalf of the public administration authorities – the town president (mayor) in the case of the detailed plans. In certain circumstances, the plan may be approved by

the municipal council on the basis of a decision adopted in the course of a council session.

These two authorizations constitute the final element in the process of drawing up a plan. The draft plan acquires legal force and from then onwards acts as a law in this sphere. At the same time, it represents the integrated solution to the town planning problem as well as the duly prepared legal document. A plan of this kind cannot be set aside or ignored in the course of official measures to promote the protected historic zone. No change is admissible unless the plan is completely or partially amended and this means that it must go through the same procedure as before.

5. Information

The main consideration and activity in regard to the Renaissance part of the town is conservation. The programmes adopted took into account the general function of this quarter as well as its role as a component of the modern city with its two urban centres. This function has been enriched by other elements linked with the tourist attractions of the site. We can thus set out the following guidelines:

– a reduction in the number of residents to an approximate limit of 2,000 persons with the aim of guaranteeing the historic quarter its natural and traditional level of activity;

– the new functions must be compatible with the tradition and character of the site;

– the grants-in-aid must only be given on condition that the historic building in question may be adapted for the assigned functions and that its most precious rooms are thrown open to the general public; and

– the functions in question must be located along the most attractive routes (Ormiáanska, Lenina, Staszica, the area round the main square and the Salt Market).

The conservation and accentuation of the historic substance of the town exercise an influence on the implementation of the optimal programme for the utilization of our heritage and its integration into contemporary life.

The site embraces the remnants of the 19th century fortifications: the forefield of the latter is mostly a non-planned zone. A number of different roles have been assigned to this site such as that of a public park, a promenade, car-park or recreational grounds next to the housing area. However, the main function of the envisaged site will be to set off the historic town centre.

As Zamosc lies in flat countryside and its silhouette traces a delicate contour seldom broken by vertical lines, the town really has to be viewed from a certain distance. The aim of planning and development consists in attaining such a perspective without any high-rise buildings, but with large numbers of well arranged trees and plants.

The bounds of the Renaissance town and the fortified walls of the 19th century will be traceable thanks to the preserved remnants of the old defence lines and above all Renaissance fortifications set off by the line of ramparts. In certain cases and for educational purposes, partial reconstruction is admissible.

The arrangement of communications based on the three historic approaches to the town constitutes the second element connecting the two sites. As in the past, access to the town is via the roads from Hrubieszov, Lublin and Szczebrzeszyn with a lot of the traffic – especially tourists – stopping at the foot of the town at one of the three car parks. Within the town itself, vehicular traffic has been limited within the framework of the historic streets. The pedestrian precincts have been arranged along those thoroughfares which are the most attractive from the standpoint of social amenities and urban scenery.

The routing of out-of-town traffic takes place via a ring road to the North of Zamosz outside of the historic quarter and this enables the latter to be easily linked with the recreational and aquatic facilities to the South, thus according with the general situation of the town.

All the preparatory activities, the studies and the analyses and the development plans aimed at the goal of realizing a programme based on this thesis:

– the conservation of a historic town centre cannot be effected unless it is integrated as a vital part of contemporary and growing Zamosc. This integration permits the historic quarter to achieve the conditions needed for safeguarding its qualities.

6. Conclusions

It is quite impossible to describe – even succinctly – the whole process for the town and country planning scheme and its translation into reality. Nevertheless, it is essential to make a number of observations on the situation which has resulted from the drafting of the plan for Zamosc and of similar town plans (Taroslav, Rzeszov, Krosno, Przemysl).

1. Studies of this kind take a great deal of time and money and that excludes their application in the planning schemes adopted for a large number of towns.

2. Independently of the study, the conditions governing the realization of the plan illustrate the need for a more flexible approach in the solutions. If the town is developed at a rapid pace, one can argue in favour of precision in detail. If development takes place extensively, such detail is harmful and the need for flexibility in the solutions found becomes a problem of the first rank.

3. A whole series of questions raised by the drafting of plans has not yet been resolved from the theoretical and methodological standpoints. The programming of certain matters affecting the whole quarter such as the smooth flow of vehicular traffic, provision of car parking facilities, adequate greenery, etc. must be brought to perfection by means of scientific analysis and a more profound method of logical approach.

4. Even the most carefully drafted of plans must be viewed as an "open plan", i.e. one which can be perfected even more than before during its implementation. The widening and improvement of the scientific base and fresh combinations in research represent factors which must directly influence the interpretation of decisions. Hence, we must envisage a constant process of improving on the solutions already applied.

UNITED KINGDOM

United Kingdom
LEGISLATION, ORGANISATION, FINANCE, PARTICIPATION

---

1. Foreword

1.1 General

(European Architectural Heritage Year in 1975 prompted an assessment of the policies and programmes for conservation in Britain. The Civic Trust particularly organised the Heritage Year Awards and published a book under that title which admirably reviewed the state of Britain's architectural heritage. The next 13 paragraphs are extracts from that book).

The architectural heritage of Europe, in all its rich diversity, represents one of the crowning achievements of western civilization. Unlike the other products of man's creative skill, great monuments and little houses, market squares and village skylines, cannot be put into glass cases. They remain vulnerable not only to the elements – and nowadays, often, to gross atmospheric pollution – but to the selfishness, thoughtlessness and short-term objectives of preceeding generations. Not only public opinion but official action in Britain have moved strongly in recent years towards increased protection for historic buildings and areas. But how much should we seek to preserve? By what criteria? And at what cost? France has listed some 28,000 buildings and sites (of which 12,000 are given statutory protection), while Britain has listed som 240,000 (all of which receive a modest measure of protection). France concentrates her efforts on 50 or so "secteurs sauvegardes" while Britain has designated some 3,400 Conservation Areas. (1977: 30,000 buildings and 6,500 hectares of sites protected by statute, and 60 secteurs sauvegardes).

Is it preferable to concentrate upon the impeccable retention of important "museum pieces" or to spread available resources upon up-grading the urban environment generally? Social and economic implications are here mixed inextricably with the historical and the aesthetic. Differing philosophies of preservation and conservation can and do exist together.

There are differences of opinion, too, in relation to the action that is appropriate to specific buildings, specific areas. A distinction is made to mean to retain intact, as far as possible, the total integrity of a structure, with its original finishes, decorative features, its landscape setting and so on. To conserve has come to have a wider meaning, which can embrace the rational use, re-use, adaption, extension and enhancement of scarce assets. It is thus possible to preserve a building or group of buildings (though equally possible to use them for new uses); towns and villages, on the other hand, except in a small number of quite exceptional cases, can only be the subject of conservation.

Within such generalities, however, it must remain a matter of value judgement as to the relative gains and losses occasioned by a particular course of action. A great country house is impoverished when it ceases to be in private ownership and is turned into office accommodation – but who would wish its total loss as the most likely alternative? There are small chapels in Scotland which are now used to house electricity sub-stations: can a new use be so totally at variance with the original purpose of a building that this outweighs the value of its retention?

1.2 Economic and social needs

It must be apparent that conservation must be part of the overal plan for land use and not divorced from other aspects of environment planning: housing, transport, the provision of shopping and leisure facilities, the siting of industry, the desirable social mix, and so on. To take a simple example. It is of no avail to inject public money into the upkeep of handsome houses if these have been rendered uninhabitable by the volume of heavy traffic using the street in which they stand; the money should be put into the provision of a by-pass so that they become desirable properties once more (see case study of Faversham).

In cases of straightforward restoration, it is clear that the problems of abbeys and cathedrals, great houses and national monuments are different in kind, as well as in degree, from those of small vernacular buildings. At some point essential maintenance shades into something more positive. Factors to be borne in mind include the following: the degree of creativity demanded by a particular solution; the degree of scholarship, technical expertise and craft skill called for in a particular case; the quality of design and execution expended upon interiors; the external contribution made to immediate surroundings and townscape; the apparent social and economic viability of the scheme within the foreseebale future; the likely effect of a scheme in encouraging the cause of conservation.

In conservation work in Britain there is clearly an extraordinary sense of group effort, in which many different sectors of society are playing a part (see case study of Faversham). Central to that effort is the contribution made by the Government, through the Department of the Environment and the Property Services Agency. But there are also the efforts of local authorities over a wide field; the endeavours of ecclesiastical authorities with very limited means at their disposal; the estate policies of banks and insurance companies, property and development companies, industrial and commercial companies; civic societies and local trusts; down to the army of individual owners who, often with their own hands, have restored and adapted buildings for their own use.

There is a danger of over-enthusiasm. Not all old buildings are good, not all new buildings are bad. We are still, often, insufficiently rigorous over what we demolish and what we keep. Clearly, in an architectural composition which was conceived as a unit – a square, a crescent, an area of uniform terraces – any accidental break should be rebuilt to restore the overall unity. On the other hand, in areas which have grown organically through the years, there will be occasions when it will be more appropriate to seek a good modern design, capable of making its own contribution to the street scene, than to prolong the life of the indifferent building which is already there. In the rehabilitation of individual buildings for domestic or commercial or office use, a suspect note too often becomes apparent. Victorian buildings are transmogrified into Georgian, complete with carriage lamps on either side of the new pillared door; shops which had good, straightforward shop windows suddenly begin to sport bow fronts in areas where these are neither traditional nor appropriate; old barns are converted for use as weekend homes, totally changed in character by new fenestration and car-ports and set between suburban rockeries and sweeping gravel drives. Such things may be cosy and reassuring, they are also effete and have as little to do with creative design as they have with the protection of architectural heritage.

1.3 Legislation and finance

Conservation must, in the nature of things, sometimes embrace short term, finite objectives. More importantly, however, conservation is an attitude, a continuing process, a strategy which is inextricably used with all the other elements of land-use planning. Britain has very comprehensive planning legislation; much of it remains premissive however, and our planning machinery must be used more purposefully and sensitively.

In the last 10 years a remarkable change of attitude has taken place and much has happened in recent years that is encouraging. Conservation Areas have been established and, potentially, some degree of protection is available to all buildings within them. Government grant-aid for preservation and conservation has increased steadily (it must be remembered that 25 years ago no such assistance from central funds was available at all) and some 60 "Town Schemes" are now in operation. Gardens have recently been brought within the scope of aid from central funds. Assistance towards the upkeep and repair of churches, long made impossible by the "ecclesiastical exemption", is now foreseen.

The National Trust for Scotland's "Little Houses" scheme is by now well known – indeed it was one of the Council of Europe's 50 Pilot Projects for Heritage Year – but it remains a shining example of what can be achieved through the concentrated efforts of a self-motivated body.

1.4 New uses

A building without a use is almost a contradiction in terms. There are follies of different sorts which may be considered luxury objects in their own right – beautiful, decorative features in the street scene ceased to fulfil their original function but which now meet a new need as cultural and educational documents, enriching the understanding of the past for tourists and visitors. But the number of such buildings which a society is able to maintain as museum pieces will always be small. In general, a building without a use is a building doomed.

In the conservation of historic quarters the recycling of old buildings, their adaption to modern needs, presents a problem of paramount importance. The more grand the building, the more difficult, often, to find for it an appropriate use. Smaller vernacular strucutres can usually be adapted for domestic use – but what of the big town house with salons and reception rooms of such splendour that their subdivision would destroy the very thing that makes them precious? What of the ever increasing number of redundant churches, so often major landmarks within their town or villages, and the pivot of their community's sense of identity? . . .

An obvious use for many historic structures – in all parts of Europe – is to house museums. There is no less a limit to the number of museums we can support than to the number of show-piece buildings . . .

Allied to these are two visitor reception centres in Scotland – a leader in the field of interpretation – at Culzean Country Park (see case study) and, very imaginatively, in the Old Waterworks, Perth . . . Amongst other recycling operations . . . are two gaols, in Bath and Dornoch; railway workshops and two stations; mills of various kinds; barns and farm buildings in some numbers. All these changes have been handled with imagination and affection . . . In schemes like these may be seen the process of organic adaptive change by which most of our towns and cities were shaped through the centuries.

2. Legislation and Organisation

Department ot the Environment

The first Ancient Monuments Act, passed in 1882, entrusted to the Commissioners of Works, whose responsibilities are now vested in the Secretary of State for the Environment, the preservation of ancient monuments in Great Britain. Since than, the scope of the Department's activities has been progressively widened by successive Acts of Parliament and the Acts that are the foundation of its work today are the Ancient Monuments Acts of 1913 and 1931, the Historic Buildings and Ancient Monuments Act of 1953 and the Field Monuments Act 1972. Under the Transfer of Functions (Scottish Royal Parks and Ancient Monuments) Order 1969 and the Transfer of Functions (Wales) Order 1969 responsibility for ancient monuments in Scotland and Wales was transferred to the respective Secretaries of State but, in order to make full use of their expert services, responsibility for the detailed executive work remains with the Department on whose Votes the expenditure is carried.

The Department's responsibility for ancient monuments

The Ancient Monuments Acts define the term "ancient monument" so widely as potentially to include almost every building or structure of historic interest of any kind made or occupied by man from ancient to modern times. The term, however, expressly excludes ecclesiastical buildings in ecclesiastical use, with the result that cathedrals, churches and some other buildings used for church purposes fall outside the scope of the Ancient Monuments Acts. Further, the powers conferred by the Acts, for most purposes, apply only to uninhabited buildings and buildings used as dwellings (unless by a caretaker and his family) are in general excepted from their operation.

Acquisition and grants

The Secretary of State may accept a gift of, or may purchase, with the consent of the Treasury, any ancient monument. He may also offer grants for the repair of ancient monuments in private ownership (other than an occupied dwelling house).

Guardianship

The Secretary of State may become the guardian of a monument by means of a deed executed by the owner. Under guardianship the Secretary of State accepts in perpetuity the duty of preserving, maintaining and managing a monument but the legal ownership remains unaffected. He may not, however, become guardian of an inhabited building (premises used by a caretaker or his family are excepted). Certain local authorities are also enabled to become guardians of monuments but in practice they have rarely used their powers.

Scheduling

Another principal provision in the Act designed to protect ancient monuments is knows as "scheduling", a duty carried out solely by the Secretary of State. This consists of the compilation and publication of lists of monuments, the preservation of which is considered to be a matter of national importance: but, again, this provision does not apply to ecclesiastical buildings in use as such nor to inhabited buildings.

Normally, monuments suitable for scheduling are recommended to the Secretary of State by an advisory body, the Ancient Monuments Boards for England. In Scotland and Wales similar Boards make recommendations to the respective Secretaries of State. Meetings of the Boards are attended by the Chief Inspector of Ancient Monuments and, as appropriate, the Principal Inspector for the country concerned.

Compulsory protection

If a monument is in danger of destruction, removal or damage from neglect or injudicious treatment, the Secretary of State may serve on the owner and occupier an Interim Preservation Notice placing the monument under his protection. The Notice lapses after 21 months but during that period the Secretary of State may make a Preservation Order placing the monument under his more lasting protection. During the currency of either of these any work affecting the monument requires the written consent of the Secretary of State. If, while an Interim Preservation Notice or Preservation Order is in force, the monument is liable to fall into decay by neglect the Secretary of State may, with the consent of the Treasury, make a Guardianship Order under which he takes responsibility for preserving, maintaining and managing the monument. In all such cases ownership is unaffected and compensation is payable. Whenever possilbe the Department seeks to persuade owners to treat their monument with due care thus avoiding the need to consider the use of compulsory powers.

Organisation: architects' branch

The preservation and maintenance of monuments in the Department's charge (about 800 in number) is the essential function of this branch. This is carried out by a Section under a Superintendent Architect dealing with monuments in England which is divided into Areas each under the control of an Architect based in London.

The branch uses its own directly employed labour staff numbering approximately 1,000 in the three countries. To keep local control and to supervise the work each Architect has an Area Superintendant based in the area who in turn has Superintendents of Works resident in sub-divisions of the area. The industrial staff includes masons, carpenters and joiners, etc. who are highly specialised in their crafts and many of whom have spent their working lifetime in the Department's service. These craftsmen, with labourers, and working under a Foreman, carry out the work on the monuments and their sympathetic and careful treatment of the structures are necessarily of the highest standard. The work is varied and ranges from the removal of vegetation to complicated systems of structural consolidation at all times retaining archaeological evidence disclosed on close examination. Reconstruction is rarely undertaken but if for structural reasons a particular portion of a monument has to be dismantled, a precise record both by survey and photography is made, stones or timbers are numbered and the work rebuilt to correspond exactly with its previous appearance. Excavations, called for by the Inspectorate, are also arranged by contract or, in the case of the Department's monuments, by its own labour force, all under archaeological supervision.

The branch is responsible for producing technical reports on buildings in the Department's charge and for recommending, with estimates, treatment considered necessary. Architects and their staff are also called upon to give advice on monuments not in the Department's care. In certain cases actual work for private owners of monuments by its direct labour staff is undertaken, the costs being recovered from the owner. The Architects are involved in research into the weathering of and other decay to traditional building material.

Role of Ancient Monuments Laboratory

The Ancient Monuments Laboratory of DAMHB, whilst providing considerable scientific support to the national programme of archaeological excavations, also provides certain advisory services in the "protecton of monuments". Examples include assistance through its geophysical teams which undertake about 50 surveys annually on potentially important archaeological sites in advance of land development and possible archaeological excavatiion. Buried remains and features thus mapped may be taken into account in subsequent decisions to preserve, destroy or excavate threatened areas. Sites may vary from a fraction of an acre to as much as 50–100 acres. Principal instruments employed are the fluxgate gradiometer, which detects variations in the concentration of magnetic iron oxides in the soil, and the resistivity meter whose use depends on variations in moisture content; both reflect man's past activity in digging ditches, building walls, etc. Results are computer processed within the Laboratory.

The Ancient Monuments Laboratory also provides services such as "mortar analysis" of ancient specimens; sampling and evaluation of painted surfaces in the interiors of historic buildings, and has also developed techniques to remove intact (as a last resort) very weak small surviving structures such as metalworking furnaces and pottery kilns, which may weigh up to 30 tons.

Listing

The Secretary of State is required by the planning Acts to compile lists of buildings of special architectural or historic interest. Lists are compiled on the advice of the Department's investigators, who are trained architectural historians. The standards adopted for listing are recommended by the Historic Buildings Council, an advisory body of outside experts. The fact that a building is listed does not mean that it must be preserved intact in all circumstances, but anyone who wants to demolish a listed building or to alter one in any way that affects its character must obtain listed building consent from the local planning authority. The authority cannot grant consent without first notifying the Secretary of State and giving him an opportunity to intervene. If an application is refused there is a right of appeal to the Secretary of State. It is an offence to demolish or alter a listed building without listed building consent and the penalty can be an unlimited fine or imprisonment for a maximum period of 12 months, or both. Listed building consent is also required for the demolition of unlisted buildings in conservation areas, i.e., areas of special architectural or historic interest designatied by the local planning authorities. Most, if not all, of our historic towns are conservation areas. Many other less important places are protected in this way and there are now over 3,200 conservation areas in Britain.

3. Finance

Grants

Discretionary grants are available from central and local government funds for the repair of buildings and for the enhancement of historic areas. The Secretary of State has power to make grants towards the cost of repairs to buildings of outstanding architectural or historic interest. Only a few listed buildings are in this category. This year £ 1¼ m. is available for these grants. The Secretary of State may also make grants for the repair of buildings of lesser quality in outstanding conservation areas and for general works of enhancement in these areas, e. g. paving schemes, tree-planting, etc. This year £ 1¼ m. is available for this work. The Government and the local authority may combine to make joint grants for the repair of good groups of historic buildings in what are known as town schemes. In these cases the owner usually pays 50 % of the cost, and the Government and local authority each pay 25 %. The funds for these grants form part of the £ 2¼ m. mentioned above. Local authorities' scope is wider as they may make grants for any building of architectural or historic interest, and are not restricted to outstanding buildings or even to listed buildings. The grants are discretionary, however, and only about £ 300,000 is given annually by all authorities.

Urgent works to unoccupied buildings

Where the preservation of a listed building, or an unlisted building which is important to the character or appearance of a conservation area, is at risk a local authority may carry out emergency repairs to make the building weatherproof and may recover the cost from the owner.

Compulsory acquisition

Local authorities have powers to compulsorily acquire listed buildings for their preservation.

(Throughout this note the term "Secretary of State" should be interpreted, as regards monuments in Scotland and Wales, as appropriate.)

This report consists of extracts from the following published documents for which grateful acknowledgement is made to the authors and publishers:

Foreword: 'Heritage Year Awards – Civic Trust 1975. Public Sector: 'Report of Ancient Monuments Board of England 1974. Report of Historic Buildings Council for England 1972–73. Letter Ditchfield to Harris 3.X.75 and memo. Preservation and Protection of Ancient Monuments.

4. Involvement of private Associations in Preservation

4.1 The Amenity Movement in Britain: The National Organisation's History and Legal Status

Like so many modern institutions in Britain the first of the national voluntary organisations concerned with amenity were born during the last century as a consequence of the industrial revolution. The destruction of common lands, antiquities, medieval architecture, and a countryside shaped by long use, produced outcries first from individuals and then from organisations established specifically to defend them from an expanding population and industrialisation.

Some of the leaders of the first national conservation organisations were in the forefront of the movement for social improvement. Overcrowded living conditions in industrial cities were also the result of the industrial revolution and so the battle for improved housing and public health provision inevitably linked with the battles to protect existing amenities. The distinction between positive improvement and defensive resistance to unwelcome change seems to have been as unimportant in the minds of the pioneers as it often is today.

This connection between social improvement and conservation can be seen in the very first national amenity society – the COMMONS PRESERVATION SOCIETY (now the COMMONS, OPEN SPACES AND FOOTPATHS PRESERVATION SOCIETY) formed in 1865. By the 1860s the outward spread of London threatened such commons on its border as Hampstead Heath and Epping Forest. In medieval times a common was land belonging to the Lord of the Manor over which certain other persons had rights, such as the right of pasture, and the system had persisted. With the growth of the population the commons acquired a new value as open space for the enjoyment of the population generally, and at the same time a financial value as building land. The Commons Preservation Society was determined that the London commons should not be built on and encouraged commoners with existing rights to fight proposed enclosures in the Courts.

The SOCIETY FOR THE PROTECTION OF ANCIENT BUILDINGS was founded next in 1877 by Willian Morris largely as a reaction to the ruthless and wholesale restoration of churches and cathedrals which was then proceeding. The society's manifesto written by Morris recognised the new interest that had arisen within the previous fifty years in ancient monuments of art, but then saw as "fatal" the idea of restoration that involved stripping from a building the appearance of antiquity so that a feeble and lifeless forgery resulted. Rather than drastic "restoration" Morris advocated "protection" and called on those who dealt with ancient buildings "to stave off decay by daily care". The Society therefore stood, and stands not just for ensuring the continued existence of "anything which can be looked on as artistic, picturesque, historical, antique, or substantial: any work, in short, over which educated, artistic people would think it worth while to argue at all", but also for a philosophy of continuous care and respect for the organic evolution of buildings.

Both the Commons Preservation Society and the Society for the Protection of Ancient Buildings were lobbying and campaigning organisations – they could not own lands or buildings. A suggestion was therefore made in 1884 by the then Secretary of the Commons Preservation Society, Robert Hunter, that a new body be formed and incorporated under the Companies Acts, to buy and hold land and buildings for the benefit of the nation. Hunter together with Octavia Hill and Canon Rawnsley (who had been introduced, when working as a priest among the poor, to Octavia Hill by John Ruskin) acted together to gain support for THE NATIONAL TRUST FOR PLACES OF HISTORIC INTEREST AND NATURAL BEAUTY, which was eventually registered in 1895. The Trust immediately began to acquire property by gift and purchase but it did not hesitate to make representations about controversial issues unrelated to its property, such as the condition of Stonehenge or the proposed Snowdon railway. Only later, as its ownership extended and other bodies were active as propagandists, did it confine itself exclusively to the care of its several hundred historic properties and hundreds of thousands of acres. Membership now (1975) exceeds half a million – an astonishing contrast to the first thirty years in the Trust's life during which it never exceeded 1,000.

There seems to have been something of a pause between the turn of the century and the end of the first world war. The next two bodies to come into existence were the ANCIENT MONUMENTS SOCIETY concerned with the protection of buildings of all periods, formed in 1924 and the COUNCIL FOR THE PRESERVATION (now PROTECTION) OF RURAL ENGLAND (CPRE), formed in 1926. The inter-war years saw a continuing urban sprawl, ribbon development and the growth of motoring which encouraged roadside advertisements. No one body covered these and various other threats to the countryside although many were concerned with aspects of the countryside, and the CPRE was formed to bring these bodies together. The CPRE encouraged the formation of country branches where equivalent county-wide bodies were not already in existence and also sought affiliation from smaller rural societies. A formal link was thus created between local and national bodies.

Though primarily concerned with the promotion and co-ordination of field archaeology, the COUNCIL FOR BRITISH ARCHAEOLOGY formed in 1944 has been in the forefront of national organisations seeking to protect the fabric of historic towns. But no national body existed to promote such societies or to concern itself with amenity in ordinary towns falling outside the field of the CPRE.

This gap was filled in 1939 by the CENTRAL COUNCIL OF CIVIC SOCIETIES which existed until 1962 and whose work was largely superseded by that of the Civic Trust, formed in 1957. The Civic Trust neither owns property nor is it a society with members, but it maintains a register of local societies and supplies them with a newsletter. Its interests have ranged from industrial dereliction to the problem of heavy lorries but perhas its principal contribution has been to encourage people to make the best of what they have and to take their eyes away from individual buildings and to look at their surroundings as a whole. New buildings must fit in with old ones, but the best use should be made of the old. This idea found its fullest expression in the concept of the conservation area created by the Civic Amenities Act 1967. The Act, which was promoted by the Trust, laid a duty on local authorities to designate areas of character as conservation areas. From then on it was possible for local societies to argue that a particular area had a character which should be conserved and enhanced and that immediately gave societies a creative role. Once an area was designated as a

conservation area there was an immediate change in emphasis.

No longer was the developer with a proposed new building automatically making a "positive" contribution – with any objector seen as "negative". Instead the advocate of enhancement of what exists in a conservation area is seen as "positive" and someone proposing a radical change must show that it is an improvement.

4.2 Local Organisation

4.2.1 Local amenity societies

These societies are, on the whole, the specialists on conservation and amenity among the wide range and number of all local, voluntary groups which have some interest in these matters. They are also fairly numerous nowadays with 1250 of them registered in early 1976 with the Civic Trust in London (not including local federations) and possibly several hundred more which are, in practical terms, very similar in their work and interests but which are not currently on this register.

Thus local amenity societies are, taken together, a notable element of the entire "citizen participation" movement in Britain (covering not only environmental and planning matters but also tenants, residents, ratepayers, coloured minority community groups, social benefits claimants, school parents, medical patients and yet others). They are a major part of the "participation" movement as it arises in environmental and planning matters although it is essential not to overlook the tenants', residents' and other local community groups who are also involved and who would not call themselves "amenity societies" or, indeed, ever use the word. The Civic Trust has a moral constitution to guide local societies.

4.2.2 Societies and their members

The movement is a young one. Of the responding societies only five were formed last century and only 44 before 1941. From 1941 to 1957 (the date on which the Civic Trust was founded) there was a slow but steady growth after which date the numbers climbed dramatically.

Like all cliches, the joke about the British forming a committee to achieve almost any purpose is quite true. Local and national voluntary bodies are usually run by an elected committee and based on a constitution. Local amenity societies who wish to enjoy charitable (that is, tax-exempt) status and to be registered by the Civic Trust in London (or the several regional Trusts) must have a suitable constitution. Most societies (68 %) either do all their work through one committee or regard their executive committee as the centre or focus of their work.

A common pattern for a society which is of average size and breadth of interest is to have a general or executive committee which deals directly with particular items, including finance, and receives reports on its more long-term or specialist interests from one or more sub-committees or working parties. These may come and go with events and issues.

Although basic rules and procedures are never to be despised by a voluntary body (which could lose key officers who "know the ropes" at any time without warning) it remains true that the individuals concerned will have more influence for growth and success than any particular structure or formal procedures. The Civic Trust's model constitution is probably a notable benefit to local societies, at least as a guide.

4.2.3 Societies and local planning authorities

One of the interesting findings of the Civic Trust's 1974 "census" of its registered societies was that, during 1972–74, societies more often appeared at a ministerial local public enquiry to give evidence in support of the local authority's position than to oppose it.

4.2.4 The amenity society in the community

All local bodies, particularly voluntary groups with little money, rely heavily on their local newspapers to publicise their views and activities free of charge as part of their news and comment about local affairs. Amenity societies have a special need for coverage because their interests are much broader and less definite and familiar than those of the voluntary groups devoted to their own leisure pursuits or service to some defined group, such as elderly or disabled people.

It is worth noting how serious is the position of the voluntary body fighting against some local government decision or policy and not being reported in the local press by deliberate editorial choice. If the editor agrees with the council's policy – or feels that the amenity group is unrepresentative or in some way wrong in its views – the group has little chance of reaching local public opinion. It may need to adopt some direct action tactic which will be reported as "news".

The characteristics of a really successful amenity society are:

- "it always tries to speak up publicly for good planning principles even if this causes some unpopularity in some local neighbourhoods which are adversely affected"
- "it must be selective on preservation and planning cases even if this causes some local unpopularity"
- "it tries to keep a cordial relationship with the local authority even if this causes some loss of its popularity among local residents in some cases"
- "it ensures that it has a large paid-up membership to show its representative character"
- "it is careful to have a cordial relationship with the local press".

4.2.5 Economics

Local amenity societies are voluntary groups and their financial resources are minimal. For an example see Faversham case study.

4.3 The National Trust

It is only within comparatively recent times that either the need or the duty to preserve what was best of England's legacy of wilder beauty and of historic buildings revealed itself as in any degree urgent. In the mid-nineteenth century there was a widespread belief that commercial expansion, peace, general well-being and prosperity would go forward hand in hand. But there were other forces at work by which the National Trust was ultimately to be brought into being.

. . . Cases arose in which land or an old building could be "saved" if it could be put into safe hands for the future and three remarkable people determined to found a permanent Trust for that purpose. They were Octavia Hill, whose housing work had led her to a vivid appreciation of the value of such places as Parliament Hill fields to the urban working classes, Sir Robert Hunter who, as a solicitor, had been closely concerned with the Commons Preservation Society since 1868, and Canon Rawnsley, then Vicar of Wray in Westmorland, who had in 1883 shown great vigour and pertinacity in opposing a threatened railway from Battermere to Braithwaite. The three founders made an admirable combination.

4.3.1 Legal status

In January 1895 the Trust was incorporated as a public company not trading for profit . . . In 1907 a new status was acquired by the incorporation of the Trust under a special Act of Parliament. Part of the Trust's achievement has been the arousing of interest which has led the State and local authorities to take an even larger part in the protection or preservation of the beauty and historic interest of our land. The founders of the Trust obviously envisaged their object mainly as a defensive fight against despoiling by "development". In fact, preservation cannot be achieved by any single act. Even the lands and buildings protected in the past ten years by covenant will require constant watchfulness. Nature is herself a despoiler. In this country the "natural aspect" is always conditioned to a considerable extent by man's operations. And preservation does not, and cannot, mean the stasis of a specimen preserved in spirit in a pathological museum; it means a highly specialised type of management and control aiming at preserving such an aspect as will be felt to be beautiful. (see Culzean case study).

4.3.2 Organisation

The Trust has therefore a varied task. It must find a way of being a national body with a national policy, and yet remain in close touch with tenants and their needs. Endowment lands must be well managed to produce revenue. Agriculture – and especially grazing – must be continued on many lands frequented by the public if their beauty is to be retained. Other wilder lands must be artificially kept from changing to the type of primative scrub, to which they naturally revert. All this work – hardly envisaged by the founders – involves the development of a quite specialized and new technique of estate management.

Behind the work of the staff is the generous help of a body of expert honorary advisers on all sorts of special problems connected with the properties. There must be brought to their work the eye for landscape of the artist as well as professional efficiency. However the State's control and protection of land uses may grow, there will always remain an important field for an independent body like the Trust with long special experience in the management and upkeep of a unique type of property – land and buildings held primarily for their beauty or interest, to which the public have as great a measure of access as possible.

4.3.3 Financial and human values

Properties come to the National Trust in various ways, often by gift or by bequest, and often by purchase, financed either by some single benefactor or by public subscription. The Trust has to make it a rule not to accept a property unless it is self-supporting. Some properties can pay for their own maintenance, not a few by agricultural rents or by the letting value of a house or by gate money raised from the visiting public. But if a property has no such intrinsic annual value, the Trust must ask for an endowment in money for its maintenance. This rule is absolutely necessary for financial solvency, but its application often causes disappointment both to the would-be donor and to the Trust. An owner who wishes to keep the rent and the proprietorship of an area of land, but is ready to part with its development value either by gift or by sale, can enter into a covenant with the Trust whereby the Trust will for all time to come have the right of veto or control of building or any other possible developments on the land in question.

In the management of its properties the Trust endeavours to avoid the evils of bureaucracy and over centralisation. It has a flexible system, not uniform in all the various properties scattered over the country. Some are managed by local committees, of course in close touch with the Trust's agents. But some local committees are advisory only. And for yet another class of property, usually a small one, there is no local committee and the management rests entirely with the officers of the Trust. The Trust also wishes to avoid turning its properties into "beauty spots" or "museum pieces". Its object is that natural beauty should remain "natural" and that agriculture should continue to flourish as agriculture. But the need to preserve natural beauty by the National Trust and otherwise is not merely a question of preserving holiday ground for masses of people from the town. It is also a matter of preserving a main source of spiritual well-being and inspiration on which our ancestors throve and which we are in danger of losing for ever. For the value of the holiday ground as such depends not merely on supplying air and exercise to the city worker, but on offering him the spiritual delight and sustenance that he cannot get in the modern city, so completely divorced from nature. . . . Unless we can refresh ourselves at least by intermittent contact with nature we grow awry.

1975 marked the 80th birthday of the National Trust. Membership reached and exceeded half a million. But 1975 also posed financial problems of extreme gravity; they were due almost exclusively to inflation. In 1965 expenditure was under £ 2 million; in 1975 it was £ 7 million (see Appendix 1 for financial statements for 1975). The special function of the National Trust is . . . the ownership and care of the properties committed to its charge in England, Wales and Northern Ireland. There is a similar but quite separate Scottish National Trust.

4.4   The National Trust for Scotland

The National Trust for Scotland was founded in 1931 as an independent voluntary organisation for the purpose of promoting the "permanent preservation for the benefit of the nation" of lands, buildings, and articles or objects of historic or national interest. In 1935 a special Act of Parliament gave the Trust the status of a charity and specific privileges and powers, in particular the power to hold lands and buildings and their contents inalienably (ie in perpetuity) "for the benefit of the nation". It continued, as at present, to rely for support on membership dues, donations and legacies; the current membership is approximately 80,000.

This report consists of extracts from the following published documents: for which grateful acknowledgement is made to the authors and publishers:

Private Sector: "Local Amenity Movement" – Civic Trust 1975.

National Trust: "The National Trust" Batsford 1945 Introduction by G. M. Trevelyan and Appendix by D. M. Matheson. Annual Report 1975 – National Trust.

National Trust for Scotland: Year Book 1976

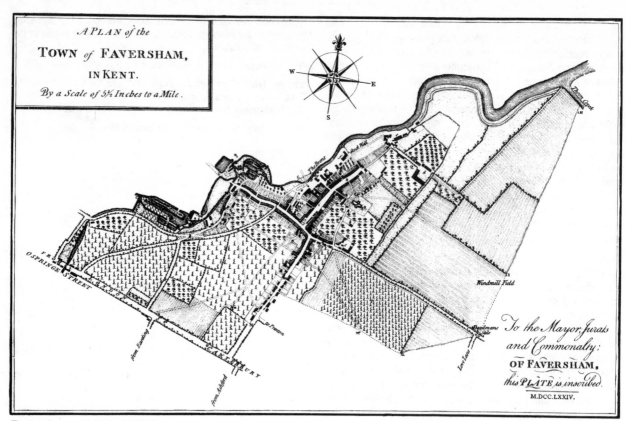

Faversham: historical 1774

United Kingdom
FAVERSHAM

1. History of the Faversham Society

1.1 Summary of a local society's first ten years

Though 160 people attended the inaugural meeting in the Guildhall, the decision to launch the Society was taken without great enthusiasm, and this appeared to be an inauspicious start. In fact, it very soon became apparent to those who might have been critical on these grounds that the new organisation was soundly based and that perhaps it was time to take a little more care of what we had inherited. Faversham, like many other pleasant old towns, faced numerous threats that could not be beaten off by half-hearted condemnation from the sidelines. Since the Society was formed much that might have been thoughtlessly destroyed has been saved. This has come about mainly because there has been active co-operation from the Borough Council and because a sense of civic pride has been engendered among townspeople.

The town clerk realised that an active local amenity society was essential if the town's unique character was not to be slowly eroded. Useful guidance was also received from the Civic Trust, which was – and remains – the 'godparent' of local amenity societies. The Society for the Protection of Ancient Buildings played a key role in persuading the Borough Council not to bring into effect their original plans for the redevelopment of Abbey Street as council housing.

By the time the Society was founded in October, 1962, Faversham had in one important respect already turned the conservation corner. Five years previously Arden's House, home of Faversham's famous murdered mayor and the

Faversham: aerial photograph; scale appr. 1:8000, about 1977

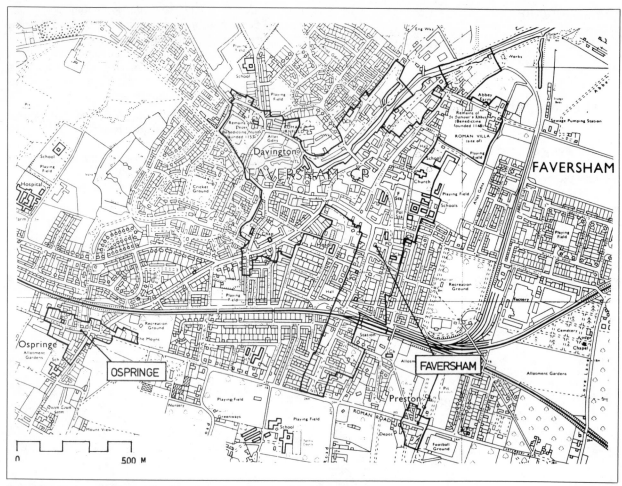

Faversham: boundaries of the three conservation areas

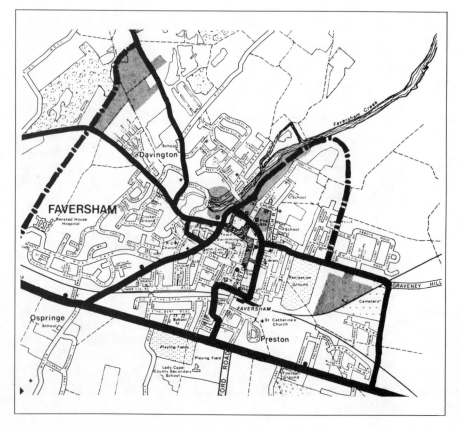

Faversham: Situation of industrial areas (grey), pedestrian areas in Preston Road, and proposal for traffic system by Kent County Council (black) and Faversham Society (dotted). In the latter heavy traffic does not affect the inner town seriously

Faversham: Preston Street before and after restoration

Preston Street, Faversham.

finest half-timbered house in decaying sixteenth-century Abbey Street, went on the market at £ 900. The buyer brought in the Society for the Protection of Ancient buildings, and their consultant architect urged Faversham council, instead of demolishing the street, to restore it.

A new town clerk, Mr. F. G. Bishop, persuaded the council to buy houses in danger and sell them at minimal profit to buyers who would undertake to restore them. Later central and local government combined to offer grants in one of the first town schemes, matching the owner's spending on approved repairs; and Abbey Street became one of the first instances of narrowing the roadway instead of widening it as a response to a problem of lorry traffic.

The Society came into being partly because the town clerk, and one or two people like Mr. Percival, thought the new policies needed encouragement from a pressure group; partly because the one piece of 1950's redevelopment, a supermarket and shops, failed dismally to fit in with the

townscape about it or visually replace the two good buildings demolished. If that was redevelopment, Mrs. Percival and his friends were determined it should not recur.

The Faversham Society, with more than 600 members, is recognised as one of the leading civic societies in the country, working for one of the most attractive towns in the country.

Reasons for the way in which the Society took root and developed were all quite simple. The first, that Faversham is a particularly attractive town that suffered less than most from clumsy redevelopment during the inter-war period; the second, that Faversham people, natives and 'foreigners' alike, are mostly proud of their town and possessed of a potent community spirit; and the third, that by good fortune the Society started off with a great deal of goodwill and an excellent team of voluntary workers (many of them are still working hard for it, and in fact harder than ever!). The 'contingent factor' was the redevelopment of the Barber/

363

Dolphin site in Preston Street. Between them these two buildings somehow typified Faversham, and their memory was sustained by Jack Salmon in one of the first Christmas Cards he drew for the Society. Barber's was a cheeky, creaky and picturesque Tudor building of immense charm, while the 'Dolphin', built much later in dark brick, was a dignified, large and well-proportioned building which stood sentinel-like near the neck of Preston Street. Both were eminently worth preserving, but made uneconomic use uf precious town-centre land, and so were demolished. There was very little fuss at the time, but slowly local people began to wonder if the right thing had been done. The adjacent shops, however up to date they were, didn't quite fit in. All this took place shortly before the formation of the Society, and probably it was very much at the back of many people's minds at the first meeting. The new Society felt that the new shops, though they could have looked a great deal worse, might also have been a bit more in scale with their surroundings. Ten years later, the Society is larger and more active than ever before – but still there is no shortage of tasks. There will always be jobs to do, and however large resources, they will never be big enough to tackle everything at once.

1.2 The first year's activities

In 1962 there were representations on a proposal to widen South Road, Tanners Street and Lower West Street (see map) to improve lorry access to the Oare industrial estate; the Borough Council were supported in their plan to preserve some of the fine trees on the St. Ann's Estate; the proposed caravan site at Hollow Shore was opposed – and refused; attention was called to the scale and design of new brewery buildings, with satisfactory results; steps were taken to remove the threat of demolition frome some Abbey Street cottages; efforts were made to save Davington Court and the ancient Davington Court Barn (both of which, unfortunately, were later demolished); and the first moves were made to secure the preservation of the Chart Gunpowder Mills.

In the first year, too, a group of volunteers cleared a mountain of rubbish from Stonebridge Pond, a move which seems almost to have halted the practice of using this pleasant stretch of water as a dump; tree planting schemes around the town were devised; and the first items in a Faversham Museum Collection were put on display in a room in the Maison Dien, at Ospringe.

Groups of volunteers also found time to clear lorry loads of rubbish dumped in some of the woods around the town, a worthwhile task in which they received kindly co-operation from Swale Rural District Council. The Society's first 200 members were busy on other projects in that first year, too. They were examining the unwarranted obstruction of footpaths; calling for the provision of a town brochure; preparing a photographic survey of the town; recording the memories of older townsfolk; campaigning for proper clinics; and collecting the views of townspeople on the future of Faversham.

1.3 First important task

Many of these matters have been pursued in the years that followed, but perhaps the Society's most important task was to oppose the Kent County Council's road proposals contained in the Draft Town Map, which was published in 1964.

The plan put forward was a very bad plan because it made provision for what was later termed a 'lorry route' through the streets of a town described by the same planners as a 'medieval gem', which would have involved the demolition of many residential properties, of the Queen's Hall, of the medieval hall house at 10, 11 and 11a Court Street, and the widening of Partridge Lane.

The Faversham Society objected to the proposals and there were numerous individual objections, too. A public inquiry into the road plan was held by the Minister of Housing and Local Government in September 1967.

Members of the Faversham Society opened their case by distributing copies of their own volume containing complete alternative road proposals. Some 80 members of the Society had worked on the alternative proposals over a long period and there is no doubt that the KCC plan was doomed from that moment.

In fact, the Inspector's recommendations, published some two years later and accepted by the Minister, represented acceptance of the Society's alternative scheme.

1.4 Conservation legislation

Had the Faversham Society performed only this service to the town its existence would have been justified. But its members have done a great deal more, much of which has since been incorporated in conservation legislation.

The designation of conservation areas provided for by the Civic Amenities Act of 1967, also owed something to the Society, and the restriction of lorry juggernaut weights to 32 tons instead of 44 tons, for which a powerful Commons lobby was organised, was the result of direct action by members of the Society. This particular restriction is being challenged now that Britain is joining the Common Market and the Society is among those backing up the Minister for Transport Industries in his efforts to see that this country with its rich heritage of ancient towns and villages is not battered to destruction as the result of blind 'harmonisation' of lorry weight limits.

Members have also concerned themselves with the conservation of the Swale; views on local government reorganisation have been formulated for both the Maud Commission and the Boundaries Commission; common land has been registered (including the west bank of the Creek from the bridge along Front Brents); and the the Sheppey Group and the Kent Federation of Amenity Societies were nurtured from within the Society.

Ever since it was formed, the Society has sought to ensure that the East Swale and its hinterland remains quiet and secluded – a place where recreation is un-organised and un-commercialised, where the public can simply walk in peace along footpaths undisturbed by noise and other trappings of modern urban life. Of course there can be no commercial profit from the use of the area in this kind of way,. and so the pressure for exploitation is continuous. Such exploitation can benefit the developer and some specialist private interest – but it is against the interest of the community as a whole. The last two or three years have seen a marked increase in general public concern about the dangers of creeping subtopianisation in unspoilt areas such as the East Swale, and it is fortunate that the Society's view on the East Swale are broadly shared by the Kent County Council and the Department of the Environment.

One major landmark in the campaign to protect the East Swale came in 1969 when the Kent Trust for Nature Conservation acquired about 1,500 acres of mud flats and saltings on the south bank as a Nature Reserve. This area has since been designated as a Statutory Local Nature Reserve by the Kent Country Council, which is proposing to make bye-laws to regulate its use. The object of these is not (as some people have maintained) to keep people out of the area, but simply to see that people who do visit the area treat it properly.

2. Activities of the Society

2.1 Preservation

2.1.1 New Look in West Street

The West Street 'New Look' scheme was set up in 1969 as a direct successor to the scheme for giving a new look to the Market Place area in 1964, which was itself doubtless inspired by the success of the Abbey Street restoration scheme started by the Borough Council in 1961 – one year before the Society came into being – in conjunction with the Historic Buildings Council.

The 'New Look' schemes are run jointly by the Borough Council, Chamber of Trade and ourselves and aim to take one street, small area or group of buildings and, with plans, advice and help from the Borough's consultant architect, encourage the owners of each building to redecorate them and restore, if necessary, in such a way that the individuality of the building is preserved while blending harmoniously with its neighbours so that they present an attractive, interesting group.

The economic advantages of redecorating a number of properties at once, using the same contractor, are obvious, and the property owners take an interest in their surroundings as a whole instead of concentrating merely on their own small part.

Faversham: Traffic problems caused by heavy lorries in the narrow streets (above), pedestrian area (below, left) and view of the river Swale (below, right)

That the habit of consultation before restoration and redecoration will continue in this town, much to its advantage, must be a cause for satisfaction to the Joint Committee and everyone else concerned. The Chamber of Trade has taken the initiative in suggesting a further extension of the scheme.

2.1.2 Chart Gunpowder Mills

The faithful band of volunteers continued work at "the Mills". An extra £ 220 had to be found for the purchase of part of the site from Messrs. Parham's, and this has unfortunately hampered the progress of restoration. A start has been made on the job of reassembling the mill machinery itself, parts specially made being used to replace those which were missing. This has involved the reconstruction of oak drive brackets; the fixing in the stone edge runners, and lining up, of huge elm naves hewn from blocks 5'6" long and 1'4" square; and the insertion in these of an iron shaft 4" in diameter, nearly 9'0" long, and weighing over 3½ cwt. The drenching gear has also been assembled and will be in working order when the trigger mechanism has been restored.

The brick walls of the Mills were built on timber rafts and are having to be underpinned where the timber has rotted – this is tedious and laborious work. The roof and protective grille still have to be reconstructed over the water wheel before the sluice gear and replacement vanes can be fitted.

It is difficult to say when all this work will be completed because the Society has been unable to trace anyone who has ever actually commissioned a gunpowder mill of this type and who knows what difficulties still have to be overcome, but it is hoped that after more than 60 years' rest the wheels will turn again in the not-too-distant future.

Even in their present incomplete state the Chart Mills continue to attract a large number of visitors who show great interest in the restoration. The Department of the Environment are considering scheduling the building and site as an Ancient Monument, and this is a great tribute to the skill and authenticity with which restoration has been carried out.

The Society therefore hopes that with replenished funds and continuing volunteer efforts the project will be brought to a successful conclusion and reflect credit on the whole town of Faversham.

2.2 Archaeological Research Group

Rescue archaeology is a term that has thrust itself into the national headlines over the past year. In Kent the need was seen and action taken as long ago as 1965.

1972 has seen the formation of the CIB Archaeological Rescue Corps. A small local group cannot hope to cope with the work of recording previously unknown sites that major developments bring to light. The pattern for the future must be one of mobile teams of well-trained field archaeologists drawn from local groups, led by full-time directors and supervisors, and capable of tackling what amount to civil engineering projects.

There is a place for our local group as organised at present, concentrating on observation and recording of new sites, helping at Chart Mills and the Fleur-de-Lis. But if our work is to keep pace with the rate of development taking place locally a team, trained in rescue archaeology, must be formed around the nucleus of the members we have at the moment. If we are to succeed in recording the 70 % of our history that still lies in the ground, we need the co-operation and goodwill of landowners, local authorities, and contractors. Mention archaeology to most contractors and visions arise of developments held up, with archaeologists clamouring for everything to be preserved. This is not the case: the policy is to preserve the best where possible, and record everything. The Kent team proved that it is possible to achieve these two aims where, with the co-operation of landowners, local authorities and contractors, consultation had taken place before work starts. In many cases the archaeological work has been planned to ensure that the progress of the development goes ahead unhindered.

2.3 Planning and traffic

Planning and traffic are the main preoccupations of any local amenity society, and the Faversham Society is no exception. The Society has taken action on both the local and the national front.

Lying off the A 2, Faversham has no real through traffic problem in the usual sense of the word. However, as almost everyone living in or near the Borough knows to their cost, the town's residential roads and some of the shopping streets form the last leg of their journey for heavy lorries travelling to or from the various distribution depots, warehouses, coldstores, breweries and factories around the northern fringe of the town. In its evidence at the Town Map Inquiry the Society argued that the only effective way of solving the town's traffic problems and meeting the needs of lorry operators was to provide a road or roads linking the industrial areas direct to the A 2 and thereby to the M 2. The Minister accepted this argument and asked the Kent County Council to undertake the necessary studies.

In the meantime both the Borough Council and the Society have attempted to assess the needs of the main lorry operators in the town by distributing questionnaires, but rather surprisingly neither attempt to secure the co-operation of these firms was more than partially successful.

In 1964 the Society suggested to the Borough Council at a Town Forum that it should consider restricting use of the town centre shopping streets to delivery (and collection) vehicles and that West Street (between the Market Place and North Lane) should be the subject of a first-stage experiment.

Many reasons were advanced why such an experiment was unlikely to succeed, many reasons were advanced why it should not even be tried. Meantime many other towns were carrying out such experiments, were finding them successful, and were making them permanent. After 8 years of consideration and much pressure forme the Society the Borough Council has finally adopted a scheme.

Routine and mostly unobtrusive though it may be, the work of scrutinising planning applications is probably the most important job done by any local amenity society. Particularly in an attrative area like the Faversham one, it is essential that new development should be of the best possible qualitiy, that good schemes should be encouraged, indifferent ones improved, and the inappropriate ones rejected. The task of development control falls to the local authorities, but voluntary organisations such as the Faverham Society can often assist them in their work by offering pertinent comments and (if need be) backing them up at public

Faversham: Restored buildings in the Court Rd (1974 – above) view of a street before and after restoration (middle and below)

inquiries when they make wise decisions which are contested by developers.

Though development control is often a negative process – a process of protecting a particular environment which is threatened or of rejecting particular proposals because they are out of keeping – this is not always the case. Some of the applications inspected are a joy to behold, and in these cases the Society is pleased to be able to offer its support.

What is more, perhaps because of the high level of public interest in planning in the town, the standard of applications is improving all the time.

2.4 Museum

Work on the Fleur-de-Lis falls into two categories – actually converting the building for use as a Museum and Meeting Place, and raising the necessary funds.

The Fleur is a larger building than it looks from Preston Street and when the Society took possession it found that a lot of space was wasted by unnecessary and rather insubstantial partitions. It also found that before any really constructive work could begin, many minor repairs were needed. The small team of volunteers who have been working on the building therefore had to spend a lot of time on dirty and rather unrewarding preparation work before they could begin to tackle pleasanter tasks like painting and decorating. Two upstairs meeting rooms have now been rehabilitated, a third is nearing completion, and much preparatory work has now been done on the main Museum room downstairs. In the "service quarters" two kitchens have been completely modernised and equipped and a Museum Curator's office created out of a former scullery. The two cellars needed least attention and one of them has already been turned into a gallery of agricultural implements and other machinery. Further display cases have been begged or bought at knock down prices, and the Hon. Curator (Mrs. G. Cruickshank) has been particularly adroit in spotting likely sources of supply and carrying out the necessary negotiations.

The Society can now be said to be operating two museums, though one is small and contained in one room (at the Maison Dieu, Ospringe) and the other (at the Fleur-de-Lis) is far from complete. The Hon. Curator has arranged several displays in both places. The titles give some idea of the richness of the Museum collections:

Spring Cleaning – as our Foremothers knew it, Easter Parade, Christian Aid Week, Shopping in Faversham in Yesteryears, Victorian Faversham, Upstairs and Downstairs, M'Lady's Boudoir, Domestics, Our Sporting Forefathers.

Displays illustrating the Society's range of "About Faversham Abbey, Inns and Taverns of Faversham, Faversham Gunpowder Industry, 1000 Years of Faversham History, Parish and Town of Faversham, Arden of Faversham, Walks around Faversham, Education in Faversham.

Since 1963 when the Society decided to form a Museum of Local History more than 2,000 items have been presented, or lent, to the Collection.

Apart from being properly accessioned and entered in a double entry card index, material for the Collection has to be labelled, repaired where necessary, and cleaned. Another small team of members is involved here, and some quite remarkable feats of restoration have been carried out on items such as tools, clocks, domestic machinery and clothing.

Finance for the Museum

In its issue of 8 December 1977 Country Life reported that the brewery sold the Fleur de Lis to the Faversham Society for £ 6,500. The Society raised a loan to buy it guaranteed by the Borough of Faversham. The Society also obtained £ 20,000 from the Department of the Environment in conservation grants, and £ 10,000 from the Arts Council for displays and smaller grants from the Kent County Council, Swale District Council, the Pilgrim Trust and Carnegie Trust and others. Manned by volunteers, the completed project opened in spring 1977.

The total needed for purchase, restoration and interpretation was £ 50,000.

3. Promotion and Information

3.1 Visits

The Society's first-ever organised outing took place on 18 May 1968 with visits to Davingtown Priory and the Municipal Offices, where a special display of finds from Faversham Abbey was on view. Since that date, a varied programme of coach outings during the summer months have become an extremely popular feature of the Society's calendar. Since its formation in 1962 the Society has actively encouraged visits from individuals and groups who might enjoy Faversham's charm and historic associations. It continues to play an active part in the work of publicising the town's attractions in this way, and the number of "innings" countinues to increase. Although no charge is made for the services provided by the Hon. Organiser of Visits and his team of voluntary guides, most groups are more than pleased to make generous contributions to one or other of the Society's funds as a token of their appreciation for the time and trouble taken to ensure that their visits are interesting and enjoyable, and both the Chart Mills Fund and the Fleur-de-Lis fund have benefitted in this way.

3.2 Publications

When the Faversham Society was formed it reckoned that one of its most important functions was to promote interest in the past, present and future of the area by publishing booklets and other material of local interest. It calculated on the basis of the experience of similar organisations elsewhere that such activities would probably have to be subsidised out of numbers' subscription, but felt that the intangible dividends would be worth the outlay. It came as a pleasant surprise to find that money could be made out of publications and so the Society now has a wider range of these than probably any other similar organisation.

Faversham Papers have been produced and published on such subjects as the town's ancient Mayoralty, the murder of Mayor Arden, the local gunpowder industry, and the Inns of Faversham. Faversham Magazines, with very valuable contributions on the town and the district scene, have appeared from time to time; postcards and Christmas Cards have found a ready sale; and even old town posters have been reproduced.

3.3 Library

Since the formation of the Faversham Society, the need for a library and a place to house books and papers easily available to members has been kept in mind. Yet, it is doubtful if anyone then could have foreseen that in only ten years not only would there be a home for a library but it would form part of a Museum and Art Centre complex.

This report consists of extracts from the following published documents, for which grateful acknowledgement is made to the authors and publishers:

Faversham town and port – walk around map, The Faversham Society. Article in The Times 7. 8. 75. Article in Kent Life July 1973 (photograph of Fleur de Lis). Faversham Society – Publications List. Faversham Society – 10th Annual Report.

Culzean Castle: Drawing of Culzean Castle (above), view of the castle today (below)

United Kingdom
CULZEAN CASTLE AND COUNTRY PARK, SCOTLAND

1. Foreword: Culzean Castle and the National Trust for Scotland

A new chapter in Culzean's history began in 1945 when the 5th Marquess of Ailsa and the Kennedy family gave the property of Culzean Castle and its surrounding 531 acre estate to the National Trust for Scotland. The Trust inherited land and buildings whose character and present day appearance had already been determined by the strong influences of the Kennedy family over centuries.

Note on the Kennedy family

Old records tell us little directly of Culzean before the 18th century, but the original castle must have been very similar to the tower houses of Dunure and Greenan situated to the north and now in ruins. Such structures were primarily defensive and command fine views of the Firth of Clyde and the Ayrshire countryside.

The Kennedys, who are known to have been associated with Culzean for more than 500 years, had, like many clans, a turbulent earlier history. In the later 16th and early 17th centuries the fierce feuds between the Kennedys of Barghany and those of Cassillis and Culzean resulted in more bloodshed. It was not until the 6th Earl, who succeeded in 1615, became head of the family that local peace was established.

In the second half of the 18th century Thomas, 9th Earl, and David, 10th Earl of Cassillis, were, like their contemporaries, fascinated by land improvement. They did much to promote improved methods of agriculture and horticulture on their own and neighbouring estates. We know from The New Statistical Account of Scotland, published in 1845, that the Kennedy lands were among the most extensive in a steadily more productive county. Undoubtedly, such valuable assets enabled their owners to beautify their houses, woodlands and gardens, and to employ eminent architects like Robert Adam.

Estate duty, payable on the death of the owner, was introduced in 1893. This often proved crippling particularly when heirs inherited in quick succesion (a situation aggravated by war). An inevitable result of the 1914–18 war was the break-up of many great estates; agricultural depression and unemployment went from bad to worse and the land, which had been brought into such good heart by the intelligence and toil of successive generations, sickened. A few far-sighted individuals realised that a new form of landowner must be invented to ensure that part of this

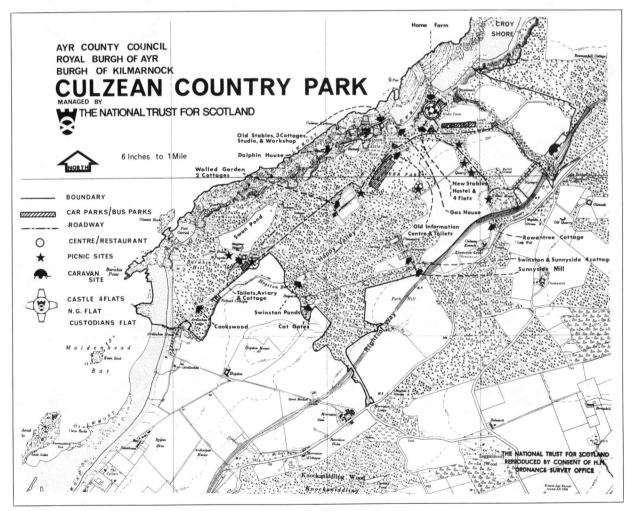

Culzean Castle: Plan of the Culzean Country Park

heritage survived. In 1931, the National Trust for Scotland was created. The Trust always strives to be able to accept properties which are of outstanding interest.

Meanwhile at Culzean the 3rd Marquess and 14th Earl did not die untile 1938 in his 91st year. Each of his three sons succeeded him in turn. In 1945 the 5th Marquess of Ailsa offered Culzean Castle and 531 acres of the estate to the Trust. He continued to live there. The 7th Marquess of Ailsa,

however, has returned with his family to Cassillis which had been their seat until 1759.

The Castle and its policies were of such outstanding national (and indeed international) importance that they were enthusiastically accepted even though there could be no endowment for maintenance. So the whole cost of this fell upon the Trust and its supporters. The Trust has been able to increase the estate by the purchase of the Nursery,

Culzean Castle: Various parts of the Culzean Country Park

372

and Glenside Railway Station as a camping and caravan site.

Culzean was one of the first great houses to be opened by the Trust. Two national appeals have been made over the last 28 years to help meet expenses, aggravated by inflation. During this period over £ 800,000 has been expended on restoration, conservation, maintenance and, of course, on local employment. Thousands of visitors have enjoyed the gardens and policies.

2. Legal Status: Establishment of a Consortium

The Countryside (Scotland) Act 1967 was passed by Parliament for the double purpose of conserving landscape and providing for public recreation in the countryside. The Countryside Commission for Scotland was constituted in 1968 to advise the Secretary of State, Scotland's chief Minister, on many matters, including the making of grants for specific projects. Local Planning Authorities, which derived a broad range of powers from the Town and Country (Scotland) Act 1947 and subsequent legislation, became the principal instruments in direct application of the new measure.

There were three Planning Authorities in Ayrshire concerned with Culzean-Ayrshire County Council and the Town Councils of Ayr and Kilmarnock. All knew from previous experience that it is a basic principle of Trust policy to work with central and local government agencies in any form of activity consonant with the Trust's aims and objects – and with the Trust's independence (see Appendix V. for finance).

An agreement between these authorities and the National Trust for Scotland for the establishment of the Culzean Country Park was concluded in 1969, following consultations with the Countryside Commission for Scotland, and received the approval of the Secretary of State for Scotland. A joint committee representative of the three authorities was formed. For this body the Trust undertook to provide the secrerariat and operate as management agency of the park, at the express wish of the three Authorities and it is reimbursed for providing the expertise and administration. The stipulation by the Authorities was specific that in order to ensure the closest liaison with the Trust they asked that the Trust's Chief Executive should be the Secretary to the Joint Committee.

At the reorganisation of local government in Scotland in 1975 the Country Park agreement was renewed with five authorities in place of the original three – Kyle and Carrick District Council, Strathclyde Regional Council and the District Councils of Kilmarnock and Loudoun, Cunningham, and Comnock and Doon Valley.

The Trust continued, and continues, in ownership of all of the Culzean estate: it is an inalienable property. A management plan for the Country Park was formulated in concert with the Countryside Commission for Scotland and the Scottish Development Department, the executive 'arm' by which the Secretary of State fulfils his function under the Countryside (Scotland) Act, and is applied by the National Trust for Scotland as the management agency.

The Culzean Country Park is of singular interest in that it was one of the first to be established in the United Kingdom and has been operated since the date of its creation by a consortium of local government authorities and the National Trust for Scotland, a non-governmental organisation.

3. Organisation

3.1 Culzean Country Park

The Park is situated on the Ayrshire coast 12 miles south of Ayr. It is approximately 546 acres in extent, and consists of the 'policies' (landscaped parkland), woodlands and gardens attached to Culzean Castle. The Castle, a magnificent mansion on a cliff-top, was built in 1777–1792 by Robert Adam to be the principal seat of the Kennedy family. It is excluded from the Country Park agreement, but is open to view and the Adjacent Home Farm, also designed by Adam and completed in 1777, has been restored, adapted and equipped as the Park Centre, the focal point.

Nothing could be more felicitous, for the Culzean complex was the invention of one 'improving' laird, a leader of the Agrarian Revolution in Scotland.

The Object is not merely to give pleasure to an optimum number of visitors, but by means of interpretative services to lead them to genuine understanding and appreciation of the countryside and the multifarious activities within it. Part of the land remains in agricultural use. Woodlands are managed with economic as well as aesthetic considerations in mind, and they, together with gardens, parkland, cliffs and seashore, are the habitats of vigorous animal, bird and plant communities. The whole provides in a small compass a variety of open air interests, including the swan pond, the walled garden and the fountain court.

The gift of the Castle and Estate to the Trust created widespread interest. It enabled the Trust to make available for public enjoyment a 'country house' property many times larger und infinitely more diverse than any which it held at that date.

Interest was intensified almost immediately by the creation of 'Scotland's National Guest House', a self-contained residence on the top floor of the castle, and the offer of the tenancy for his lifetime to General Dwight D. Eisenhower, Supreme Commander of Allied Forces in Europe in the Second World War. General Eisenhower accepted, and his visits attracted the attention of the international media, notably during his Presidency. It is now regularly used by distinguished guests from the United States.

3.2 The Park Centre

Implementation of the plan went forward in step with the Trust's increasing expertise in the operation of ranger services and interpretative services. At Culzean a significant step was taken towards the enlistment and tuition of professional personnel for duty in the countryside, when the MacRobert Trusts made to the Trust a grant of funds with which to organise and run training courses for rangers until the Countryside Commission could take on the obligation. This the Commission did in 1974.

The essential ranger and interpretative service in the Culzean Country Park was supplied in 1973 when the Home Farm buildings, designed by Rober Adam in 1977, were brought into use (see map).

The fashioning of the buildings of the Home Farm to their new purpose was an enterprise which taxed workers in many disciplines, not omitting that of stonemason. Much of the fabric had suffered erosion, especially the archways at the four corners of a central courtyard. Restoration and reconstruction having been completed, current techniques were applied in the formation and equipment of a multi-purpose auditorium and a suite of teaching rooms. A series of exhibitions deal with all manner of subjects from geology to the economic and social history of Culzean and the Ayrshire countryside, explaining what the land has meant to the people over the centuries.

All was designed to enliven and inform the minds of a constituency in the age range from seven to seventy, and to do so without solemnity or overpersuasion. (It has to be demonstrated that multiple and harmonious use of land, a

Culzean Castle: Park Centre after restoration (above), restoration of the interiors (left) and the famous oval staircase in a former open courtyard (right)

necessity at this date and in the future, can continue to afford room for recreation so long as the individual and the community accept a number of restraints on visitor behaviour). There is an on-going programme for classes from a large number of schools in the region, involving 15,000 children per annum. The facilities at the Centre include a restaurant and a shop.

4. Economics

4.1 Capital cost

Of the total capital cost of the Centre, £ 250,841, 75 % was met by Government grant. The remainder was subscribed in equal part by Ayrshire County Council and the Town Councils of Ayr and Kilmarnock. The running cost is now about £ 55,000 per annum for the whole Country Park.

4.2 Access and attendance

The five authorities on the Country Park Committee put together, in addition to the Centre, a considerable list of physical assets. They brought other buildings into use, contrived viewpoints and picnic places, and established a system of pathways and trails (one of the trails follows the line of a disused railway outside the Park and still the property of the Kennedy family, the Marquess of Ailsa kindly granting permission for this use). They also modified the road system and made appropriate extensions to parking areas at stragegic points.

The ultimate object within the Park, nevertheless, is to curtail unnecessary use of vehicles and to reduce their speed in the interest of the person on foot. It is no coincidence that the scale of admission charges is in effect a tax on wheels. There are parking charges for motor cars and coaches entering the Park, a matter of equity in the first instance but the visitor on foot goes in free.

The record of attendance climbed from 166,325 in 1971 to 248,834 in 1973, and 292,128 in 1975. At the Park Centre approximately one third of this number are received and the ranger service gives personal attention on guided walks, lectures etc. to up to 5,000 per annum, in addition to the school children.

Conclusion

Conservation of Culzean's natural and man-made features is central to the Country Park agreement, and this heritage property, which has no counterpart in Scotland, is capable of assimilating large numbers without harm to its character. Numbers of visitors are monitored with the utmost care, in reference to specific areas of the Park over the year besides total daily attendances at the peak of the season in July and August.

The Culzean Country Park is a spectacular example of the 'combined operations' in which the National Trust for Scotland acts with governmental agencies. It has been examined by many other authorities at home and abroad considering similar enterprises. There are many others in which a Trust initiative has encouraged public authorities to extend their operations into areas in which expenditure of public money could produce measurable returns for the public good.

This report consists of extracts from the following published documents, for which grateful acknowledgement is made to the authors and publishers:

Case Studies: Culzean Castle by Schomberg Scott for National Trust for Scotland 1975. Memo Bryant to Wyeth 30. 9. 76. Culzean Country Park by Douglas Bremner for National Trust for Scotland 1973. Culzean Ranger Events 1976 with map.

Sissinghurst Castle.
View of the castle in 1931 and after restoration of the buildings.

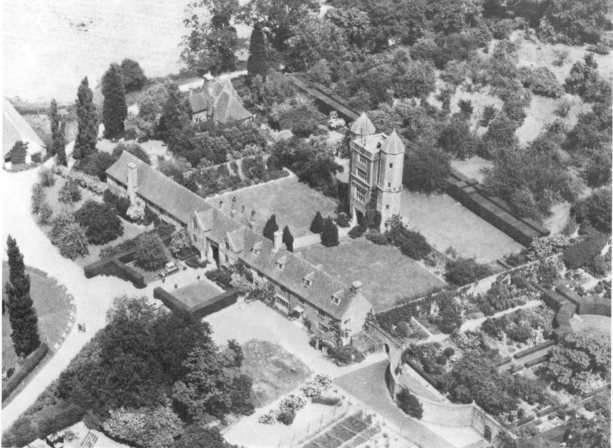

Sissinghurst Castle:
View of the castle in 1931 and after restoration of the buildings and the park in 1968

United Kingdom
SISSINGHURST CASTLE AND GARDEN, KENT

1. Foreword
Sissinghurst Castle and Garden

Sissinghurst garden was made by two people, the late Sir Harold Nicholdson and his wife Vita Sackville-West. He was the designer and she the plantsman and they worked in perfect harmony. He liked rational, classical things and she liked the poetic and romantic but fortunately their conception of an ideal garden was a fusion of the two.

In 1930 V. Sackville-West, poet, novelist, biographer and gardener, was searching the Weald of Kent for a place where she could make a new garden, when her own house, Long Barn near Sevenoaks, was threatened by commuters' development. She first saw Sissinghurst on April 4th 1930, following a chance suggestion from an estate agent and immediately realised its possibilities. The place had been on the market for several years since the death of the last owner, a farmer who naturally had not regarded the surroundings of the castle as a garden, but merely as a convenient dump for his rusty iron, or as allotments for his labourers, or as runs for their chickens.

2. The Situation

Sissinghurst is a true country garden. The view from the top of the tower is wholly rural, with the patchwork fields of the Kentish weald stretching as far as the eye can see. There is a dark fringe of woods to the south and single ancient oak trees, which look dumpy from this height, are dotted about the landscape. Two towers of village churches pierce the horizon on a clear day, that of Frittenden to the north and Biddenden to the east. The approach to the castle is by a winding country lane and the buildings of Sissinghurst Castle farm cluster round the castle entrance. Just outside the gatehouse is the farmhouse itself, a robust Victorian building with handsome chimneys, a group of oasthouses, an Elizabethan barn and white weatherboarded granaries.

The site is a rectangle, but one bounded on two sides by a moat, and inside the rectangle the castle buildings are all askew. The tower is not parallel with the entrance buildings, so that the first courtyard is not a true rectangle, the space between the Moat Walk and the nuttery is an odd coffin shape, and as V. Sackville-West herself wrote, there are many "minor crookednesses" (see map) at Sissinghurst.

Since both Nicholsons were indefatigable diarists and recorders of plans, dates, anecdotes and impressions, the history of the garden is well documented, but there is one quality which no writer can describe or analyse. The visitor must sense its magic for himself. Read the extract form V.S.W's. poem 'Sissinghurst'.

The castle and the pasture and the rose
Beauty and use, and beauty once again
Link up my scattered heart and shape a scheme
Commensurate with a frustrating dream.

Here, tall and damask as a summer flower
Rise the brick gable and the springing tower
Invading Nature crawls
With ivied fingers over rosy walls
Searching the crevices.

Clasping the mullion, riveting the crack
Binding the fabric crumbling to attack
And questing feelers of the wandering fronds
Grope for interstices,
Holding this myth together underseas
Anachronistic vagabonds.

3. Organisation

V.S.-W wrote of the plan in the R.H.S. Journal of November 1953 "Yet the place, when I first saw it on a spring day in 1930, caught instantly at my heart and my imagination. I fell in love; love at first sight. I saw what might be made of it. It was Sleeping Beauty's Garden: but a castle running away into sordidness and squalor; a garden crying out for rescue. It was easy to foresee, even then, what a struggle we should have to redeem it. We did, however, agree entirely on what was to be the main principle of the garden: a combination of long axial walks, running north and south, east and west, usually with terminal points such as a statue or an archway or a pair of sentinal poplars, and the more intimate surprise of small geometric gardens opening off them, rather as the rooms of an enormous house would open off the arterial corridors.

The garden with all its separate rooms and sub-sections must be a garden of seasonal features throughout the year. Harold (Nicholson) believed that our superb climate conditions our style – the English lawn is the basis of our garden design. The garden designer must recognise that the foundations of any good English garden are water, trees, hedges and lawn.

The master plan was as follows: There was to be an avenue of trees leading up to the castle entrance, then entry through the archway to the front range of Tudor buildings into a courtyard dominated by the tower. One would then pass through the tower into the garden proper in which there were to be two main axial vistas and a number of minor vistas (see Appendix VII for plan).

The first vista runs (approximately) from west to east, from the steps of the tower, across the Tower Lawn, through a gap in the yew hedges, and across the orchard, and ends at a statue of Dionysus placed at the far side of the moat.

The second vista runs across this at right angles. Starting at the north end, it runs from an archway on the boundary between the garden and the open country, through what is now the White Garden, under an arch called Bishops' Gate, across the Tower Lawn, through the Rondel in the centre of the Rose Garden, and ends at a statue of a Bacchante at the west end of the Lime Walk. Three important subsidiary vistas are the Lime Walk itself: the Yew Walk which runs parallel with the second vista: and the Moat Walk.

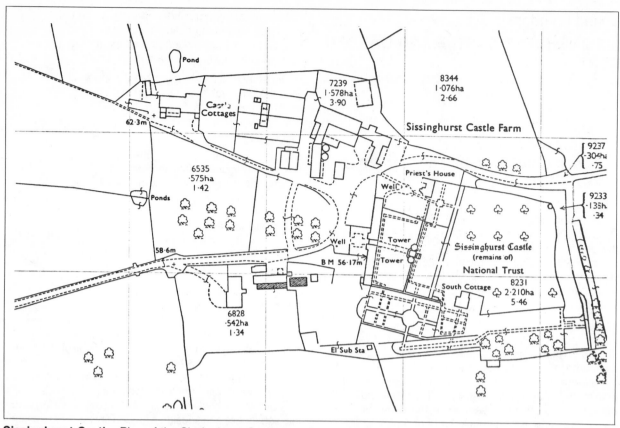

Sissinghurst Castle: Plan of the Sissinghurst Castle and Country Park

Sissinghurst Castle: Details of the garden after restoration

One of Sissinghurst's greatest assets was beautiful walls, and in addition to the old walls, Harold (H.N.) built high new walls to complete the enclosures. All these were to be the background and shelter for hundreds of climbers". (see poem 'Sissinghurst').

In the fifty years of her married life she had but two gardens of her own – Long Barn, near Sevenoaks, from 1915–1930, and Sissinghurst Castle, from 1930–1962. The first was the laboratory for the second. She made her mistakes at Long Barn; fewer at Sissinghurst. She never stopped experimenting, but gradually she came to form three or four principles of gardening.

The first principle was ruthlessness. You must never retain for a second year what displeased you in the first. It must be eradicated. Secondly, she was the opponent of too much tidiness. But thirdly, there must be a plan – an architectural plan and a colour plan and a seasonal plan.

As the designing of the garden neared completion and the planting became the main task in hand, Vita's (V.S-W) role became gadually more important than Harold's (H.N.) She was a supreme plantsman with a style of her own. There are Sissinghurst plants and Sissinghurst ways of combining plants and Sissinghurst colours and Sissinghurst conceits and fancies. The Sissinghurst style was clear for all to see by 1939 and after the war the planting was resumed, restored, improved, enriched every year until Vita's (V.S-W) death in 1962, and after that the tradition was faithfully followed by the gardeners and the family, and subsequently by the National Trust.

4. Economics (The National Trust)

The castle and garden had been made between 1930 and 1962 into a unique work of art, a treasure which must on no account be lost, and the obvious solution was to arrange

379

their transfer to the National Trust. Vita (V.S-W) had been sounded on this idea eight years earlier, in 1954, and had rejected it violently.

It was possessiveness alone that made her so averse to the proposal; not hostility to the Trust which she and Harold (H.N.) had always strongly supported.

It was clear to Nigel (her son) that the property could not be kept up without some such support.

Nigel Nicholson therefore asked the Treasury if they would accept Sissinghurst in part satisfaction of estate duties and the Treasury agreed, provided the National Trust would take it over, which they were delighted to do, gaining a glorious new jewel for their crown. The negotiations were completed in 1967. Nigel Nicholson helped the finances by giving an endowment for improvements and upkeep and the Historic Buildings Council gave an annual grant for several years until the enterprise could be got on to an even keel. Today (1974), with income from visitors, rents, the sale of plants and extras such as teas, Sissinghurst is balancing its budget.

The two head gardeners, Pamela Schwerdt and Sibylle Kreutzberger, . . . were highly experienced when the time came for them to direct the garden. They now (1974) head a team of six gardeners. The gardeners have been outstandingly successful. . . . the standard of cultivation and of plant health is extremly high. When the National Trust took over, the planting of the garden was in excellent shape, but there was much to be done in the way of construction and repair.

Some of the architectural parts of the garden were literally giving way, owing in part to the ravages of time, in part to the rapidly increasing numbers of visitors. In 1961, 13,200 people visited Sissinghurst. In 1967 the number had risen to 47,100.

In 1973, it was up to 91,584 (in 1975, it was 93,000). Therefore grass paths were beginning to wear down to basic mud; stone paths, laid before without foundations for the use of the family and their friends, were breaking apart, some flights of steps were proving inadequate. Nature contributed her blows. Some venerable almond trees in the White Garden died under pressure from the enormous climbing roses they were expected to support. The moat had no proper overflow so there were drainage problems in the Herb Garden and Orchard.

A substantial programme of architectural repairs had to be undertaken, and it was planned and carried out by a small informal committee consisting of Nigel Nicolson, the head gardener, Graham Thomas and other representatives of the Trust.

In 1971 Nigel Nicolson gave the lake and its adjacent field to the Trust – they had not been included in the original transfer – and work began on the drainage and restoration of the lake and there was some new tree planting in the field.

machine-made pot can never equal, so were the imperfections of Sissinghurst utterly delightful. They were part of its intensely personal character.

But the flaws were unsuited to the new conditions and tactful changes were inevitable . . . Two or three people can pick their way across a broken piece of crazy paving, but when there is a stream of visitors, somebody is sure ro twist an ankle. Sissinghurst hat to be restored if the public was to continue to enjoy its beauty.

The important thing is that the restorations have been excellently done . . . the basic plan of the garden is exactly as Harold (H.N.) designed it except for the removal of one or more minor hedges . . . The planting is a different matter. A design can be permanent, but planting has to change. . . . Every gardener knows, and Vita (V.S-W) and Harold (H.N.) knew, that a static planting scheme is both undesirable and impossible. Every part of a garden must be looked at afresh every season.

The philosophy at Sissinghurst has been to preserve Vita's (V.S-W) actual plants for as long as possible, to follow her style of planting faithfully, to keep Sissinghurst colours, the Sissinghurst profusion, the Sissinghurst richness of interplanting schemes when necessary.

For fourteen years, from 1947 to 1961, she wrote weekly gardening articles for the Observer which did more to change the face of English gardening than any other writing since Robinson's 'The English Flower Garden'. Concise and informative, but tinged with poetry, they were models of journalism and their influence on other gardeners was incalculable. Once she had begun to write about gardening, Vita's (V.S-W) influence on other gardens became profound and nurserymen knew that a loving reference to a particular plant in a V. Sackville-West article would create an instant demand. The Sissinghurst disciples were mostly of an upper social class, for gardening has its social strata like everything else.

Of the grand gardens of England, only the great landscapes and the formal Italianate gardens remained unaffected by the Sissinghurst influence.

This report consists of extracts from the following published documents, for which grateful acknowledgement is made to the authors and publishers:

Sissinghurst Castle – illustrated guide – National Trust 1975. National Trust Report 1975 (p. 29) see above. Sissinghurst by Anne Scott-James (Michael Joseph 1975). V. Sackvill-West's Garden Book (Michael Joseph 1968) p. 11.

5. Conclusions

Has all this restoring and tidying spoiled the garden? It has certainly changed it, for the garden has lost some of its mystery. Sissinghurst was full of flaws, but just as the flaws of a hand-thrown pot have a charm which a smooth,

YUGOSLAVIA

Situation

The wish and effort to preserve sites and "monuments" of historic interest in Yugoslavia involve many of the same problems encountered everywhere in Europe. At the same time, however, some of these problems stem specifically from the peculiar circumstances of this region's present or past epochs.

To begin with, the process of listing and evaluating our cultural assets in general and our architectural heritage in particular has not yet been completed. This situation results not only from the growth of a system of values to assess the legacy of the past more accurately then hitherto, but also from the delays suffered in the development of the protection services. The organizing of a modern service for safeguarding historic monuments with its activities based on statutory provisions was not created until the New Yugoslavia emerged after World War II. Needless to say, this observation is not intended to pass over in silence or to minimize the endeavours undertaken by numerous specialists in the past to protect our cultural property. We merely wish to attract attention to the impact of this delay on the course of events with the result that the protection service is not yet able to resolve the problems of growing complexity with which it is confronted – despite the number of specialized teams at work in this field and the institutional structure of the organization.

The first law on the safeguarding of "cultural monuments" was promulgated before the end of the War. It authorized not only the establishment of a specialized service, but also the provision of administrative powers to prohibit the demolition and impairment of cultural assets. This law underscored the primacy of general and social interests over individual interests. Irrespective of the wishes of the owner, certain buildings or other monuments were declared to be of general interest by virtue of their historic, commemorative and artistic merit. This fundamental law (which was renewed and amended on several occasions in the legislation enacted during each Republic) clearly did a lot for the conservation of cultural assets in Yugoslavia. Nevertheless, its limits became more and more evident with the passage of time. As the name of the law implies, its aim was to protect "monuments" and this term traditionally conveys an association of ideas surrounding something special and exceptional. In practice, numerous difficulties emerged when the provisions of the statute had to be applied to entire towns or to streets or groups of buildings. This was particularly the case when the value of the surrounding setting or framework came to be appreciated and it was realized that the latter might well comprise structures devoid of any resemblance to "monuments of historic merit".

Be that as it may, the weak point in the law was the disproportion between the full powers which it gave the protection service and the funds available for implementing its specific functions. Because of this discrepancy, a large number of cultural assets – and particularly those comprising our architectural heritage – were covered by what can justifiably be described as "passive" protection. It

was precisely in conjunction with this architectural legacy of ours that numerous problems emerged in regard to property – problems which supplementary articles in the law endeavoured to resolve by encouraging the owners or tenants of the buildings in question to carry out the necessary conservation measures (by granting tax relief, giving loans etc.). However, the passage of time brought to light the divergence between "abstract" values of interest to the whole community and the real values inherent in these buildings or sites and of interest to certain individuals only.

All in all, the whole legal sphere of safeguarding cultural assets and the fundamental questions involved in their conservation and restoration falls within the competence of the educational and cultural authorities. Clearly, it is cultural motivation which is opposed to the ruthless destruction of historic treasures which took place in the 19th and which has taken place in our century, too. The safeguarding of our historic legacy in towns furnishes a cultural conscience rising to counter the domination of economic motivation. But when cultural forces oppose economic growth in regard to the historic assets of a large number of towns and cities, this trend has fostered the progressive isolation of the champions of culture. In many instances, the demands voiced by the conservationists seem to lack any economic basis and they militate against the initiative displayed by private persons and various organizations concerned with these matters. Although the demands for protection are not without their professional supporters, they rarely offer any alternative and even less encouragement for the official support which they recommand and which would accord with the principles of protection.

During recent decades, the new dimensions of economic and social life have emerged with great clarity throughout Yugoslavia and more especially along the Adriatic coast. As the maintenance of buildings becomes more and more expensive, this naturally clashes with historic structures so that the problem of relations between "ancient" and "modern" becomes aggravated to an unusual degree.

This attitude towards places of historic interest and individual buildings and indeed towards the "past" in general has basically determined our system of social values with its emphasis on reconstruction, development, progress and modernization. During the decades after World War II when a spate of new methods of production enabled mankind to abandon outmoded and largely inferior forms of social and economic life, it has proved fairly difficult to defend the protection of old monuments, which rested on estimates incapable of either precise quantification or economic expression. This is an epoch in which the growth of communications from the modern super highway to radio and television has transcended the narrow confines of local, micro-regional or regional life; in which the standard of living has steadily increased and given people an ever greater choice of consumer goods; in which the orientation towards the various types of "modern life" has created by itself a hostile disposition towards the "antiquated". The introduction of new standards of housing inevitably led to the abandonment of old historic buildings. The crisis experienced by the owners of old houses and their changed standing in the community began to form a vicious circle: the investments in housing by-passed the old quarters more and more with the result that the conditions there deteriorated. Furthermore, the steady growth in car ownership was naturally inimical to the system of narrow streets and small squares. The trend towards a fresh set of values went hand in hand with an indifference towards old buildings. Indeed, this change in attitude induced the handing down of heartless sentences on old buildings in some cases. Only gradually did technical considerations begin to offset the concepts of growth and development. The opposition between private interests and general interests became evident, first of all in the continuous menace to the environment and then in the continuous loss of communal assets formerly deemed sacrosanct (fresh air, clear water, an unimpaired landscape). At the same time, people became more and more aware that the bulk of the new buildings, having been erected in the wide spaces surrounding the old town-centres without adding any new dimension to the quality of urban life or to historic sites in general, now provide fresh opportunities for official intervention based on the wish to maintain and reconstruct the legacy of the past instead of destroying it.

Today, it has become clear that the safeguarding of historic sites is not only a matter for the special environmental authorities. It also forms an essential element in the overall town planning schemes. Clearly, there still exist numerous discrepancies between the given agreements and everyday practice. It is no rare occurrence to witness litigation between different specialists, who in turn have been motivated by other quarrels frequently based on economic interests. Nevertheless, the situation in a large number of towns and along a major stretch of the Adriatic coast has clearly reached the point where the concept of saving the environment and historic places has become the prime ecological issue.

Maintenance, renovation and revitalization

Central to the complex problems of maintaining and renewing historic sites is the concept of "cultural animation". It was thanks to this "cultural animation" that the most significant official support has been accorded to Yugoslavia's historic buildings and streets. The first major initiative related to two large groups of medieval structures located within the walls of Diocletian's palace, an edifice built in the later period of the Roman Empire at Split, which first started to thrive in the 7th and 8th centuries A. D. The first group, a number of Roman and Gothic houses, is similar in design to the peristyle type of architecture. Prior to the granting of official support, it consisted of a number of dilapidated buildings – virtually ruins, in fact. After a long study intended, inter alia, to rediscover the original forms, the requisite preconditions for support and a new function for the buildings were created. Today, the buildings house the "Workers' University" with its classrooms, library and lecture halls.

The same type of cultural function, though on a somewhat wider scale, also inspired the second set of official measures to restore the medieval structures located near the access to the imperial palace from the North, the famous golden gates. These two cases involved dilapidated structures belonging to the old urban fabric and finally evacuated by the poorest members of the community who had sought refuge there. Hence, this official intervention was not only practical in character, but also theoretical and predetermined in regard to methodology. It provided the answers to a number of questions beginning with the methods employed in research on historic structures and the techniques of documentation up to and including the technology of reconstruction and restoration. To a certain extent, the most significant response was the actual execution of the project because it revealed that those historic edifices which

seemed definitely lost may, by dint of assiduous efforts, regain their former qualities and become a useful part of modern life.

The accommodating of various cultural institutions in historic houses and buildings has enabled the authorities to provide official support for numerous sites and thus ensure a longer life for them. Admittedly, this is not the only way of assuring the conservation of these localities. A large and lively city such as Split can set up large cultural facilities in its oldest quarter in a manner which many smaller historic towns cannot hope to emulate.

The fundamental question which arises in this context is to determine the vital relationship between the population and its individual way of life. This question is sometimes neglected in the major intervention schemes, financed from outside sources. After all, apart from those persons who are actually forced to give up their accommodation to make way for cultural institutions, the decisions and official support in respect of such changes always result in the exodus of sections of the population to the suburbs. Housing is replaced by public organizations.

The oldness of historic places obviously constitutes one of the factors which invariably result in their evacuation. An opinion poll carried out in many of the old towns revealed a large percentage of inhabitants in favour of leaving their homes and moving elsewhere. In certain places, it can be demonstrated in precise terms that the money spent by people to build new houses outside the historic town-centres amounts to much more than would have been necessary to restore the old quarters and render them fit for human habitation. There are many factors in the scale of values which determine the behaviour of a large part of the population in the historic quarters and which militate against their living there. Only the implementation of appropriate policies which stimulates individual efforts to reconstruct old places and a wide measure of support to improve communal standards may help to achieve the conditions needed to revitalize many of our towns and cities.

The problem of safeguarding historic structures also arises, to a particular degree, and on a wide scale, for Zagreb. The historic centre of this large conurbation with its 800,000 inhabitants has remained more or less intact – a centre which developed in three stages during the period from the 11th to the 19th centuries. The case of Zagreb has, quite rightly, presented for the first time the problem of conserving a large part of the central area of a city, which was constructed during the last century and at the beginning of this century. The preservation of this "new part" of the town provoked a certain degree of potential resistance in professional circles as well as among many other involved groups – ranging from the interests of those who wished to increase the value of landed property by erecting high-rise buildings to the wishes of those champions of freely moving traffic who were, and still are, inhibited by the rectilinear network of unduly narrow streets. In that sphere, too, the conservationists can but make the first step by ensuring the "passive" safeguarding of these large areas until a later time when the huge sums needed for preservation may become available. Although certain parts of the town such as Gornji grad and Kaptol possess neither the functions nor the establishments to sustain the economic basis for their rehabilitation, a large area in the centre of the town consists of buildings which mostly house commercial enterprises, public organizations, banks and cultural institutions from all over the local area. Despite this, it is impossible to obtain the funds needed to restore numerous buildings, which nevertheless fit in well with their surroundings. Zagreb is faced by the difficulty of finding the economic basis of work for conserving historic sites with greater intensity than any other town. It is a social problem which involves the difficulty of apportioning the funds which a historic quarter can raise in specified conditions. And whereas the problem of conserving the historic fabric of certain old towns may be justifiably considered as the problem of centralized support i. e. the provision of finance by various higher-level authorities, the case of Zagreb brings home to us the complexity of the problems of ground rents, the letting of property, the utilization of buildings, amortization and all the other economic factors which tend to encourage the concentration of investment on something new at the expense of the old. It appears here that the struggle between ancient and modern has, to a certain extent, not yet been overcome in practice despite all the declarations to suggest that this discord clearly has its social and political dimensions.

For this reason, the preparation of new laws on the conserving of cultural assets currently in progress in Yugoslavia in line with profound changes in the whole of the country's political structure (i. e. the continuous and systematic achievement of self-administration at all levels) is quite rightly oriented towards the solving of these economic and social issues.

UNESCO

Recommendation concerning the safeguarding and contemporary role of historic areas

UNESCO, Nairobi, 26 November 1976

The General Conference of the United Nations Educational, Scientific and Cultural Organization meeting in Nairobi at its nineteenth session from 26 October to 30 November 1976,

Considering that historic areas are part of the daily environment of human beings everywhere, that they represent the living presence of the past which formed them, that they provide the variety in life's background needed to match the diversity of society, and that by so doing they gain in value and acquire human dimension,

Considering that historic areas afford down the ages the most tangible evidence of the wealth and diversity of cultural, religious and social activities and that their safeguarding and their integration into the life of contemporary society is a basic factor in town-planning and land development,

Considering that in face of the dangers of stereotyping and depersonalization, this living evidence of days gone by is of vital importance for humanity and for nations who find in it both the expression of their way of life and one of the cornerstones of their identity,

Noting that throughout the world, under the pretext of expansion or modernization, demolition ignorant of what it is demolishing and irrational and inappropriate reconstruction work is causing serious damage to this historic heritage,

Considering that historic areas are an immovable heritage whose destruction may often lead to social disturbance, even where it does not lead to economic loss,

Considering that this situation entails responsibilities for every citizen and lays on public authorities obligations which they alone are capable of fulfilling,

Considering that in order to save these irreplaceable assets from the dangers of deterioration or even total destruction to which they are thus exposed, it is for each State to adopt, as a matter of urgency, comprehensive and energetic policies for the protection and revitalization of historic areas and their surroundings as part of national, regional or local planning,

Noting the absence in many cases of a legislation effective and flexible enough concerning the architectural heritage and its interconnexion with town-planning, territorial, regional or local planning,

Noting that the General Conference has already adopted international instruments for the protection of the cultural and natural heritage such as the Recommendation on International Principles Applicable to Archaelogical Excavations (1956), the Recommendation Concerning the Safeguarding of the Beauty and Character of Landscapes and Sites (1962), the Recommendation Concerning the Preservation of Cultural Property Endangered by Public or Private Works (1968), and the Recommendation Concerning the Protection, at National Level, of the Cultural and Natural Heritage (1972),

Desiring to supplement and extend the application of the standards and principles laid down in these international instruments,

Having before it proposals concerning the safeguarding and contemporary rôle of historic areas, which question appears on the agenda of the session as item 27,

Having decided at its eighteenth session that this question should take the form of a Recommendation to Member States,

Adopts, this twenty-sixth day of November 1976, the present Recommendation.

The General Conference recommends that Member States apply the above provisions by adopting, as a national law or in some other form, measures with a view to giving effect to the principles and norms set out in this Recommendation in the territories under their jurisdiction.

The General Conference recommends that Member States bring this Recommendation to the attention of the national, regional and local authorities and of institutions, services or bodies and associations concerned with the safeguarding of historic areas and their environment.

The General Conference recommends that Member States report to it, at the dates and in the form determined by it, on action taken by them on this Recommendation.

I. Definitions

1. For the purposes of the present Recommendation:

a. "Historic and architectural (including vernacular) areas" shall be taken to mean any groups of buildings, structures and open spaces including archaeological and palaeontological sites, constituting human settlements in an urban or rural environment, the cohesion and value of which, from the archaelogical, architectural, prehistoric, historic, aesthetic or socio-cultural point of view are recognized.

Among these "areas", which are very varied in nature, it is possible to distinguish the following in particular: prehistoric sites, historic towns, old urban quarters, villages and hamlets as well as homogeneous monumental groups, it being understood that the latter should as a rule be carefully preserved unchanged.

b. The "environment" shall be taken to mean the natural or man-made setting which influences the static or dynamic way these areas are perceived or which is directly linked to them in space or by social, economic or cultural ties.

c. "Safeguarding" shall be taken to mean the identification, protection, conservation, restoration, renovation, maintenance and revitalization of historic or traditional areas and their environment.

II. General principles

2. Historic areas and their surroundings should be regarded as forming an irreplaceable universal heritage. The governments and the citizens of the States in whose territory they are situated should deem it their duty to safeguard this heritage and integrate it into the social life of our times. The national, regional or local authorities should be answerable for their performance of this duty in the interests of all citizens and of the international community, in accordance with the conditions of each Member State as regards the allocation of powers.

3. Every historic area and its surroundings should be considered in their totality as a coherent whole whose balance and specific nature depend on the fusion of the parts of which it is composed and which include human activities as much as the buildings, the spatial organization and the surroundings. All valid elements, including human activities, however modest, thus have a significance in relation to the whole which must not be disregarded.

4. Historic areas and their surroundings should be actively protected against damage of all kinds, particularly that resulting from unsuitable use, unnecessary additions and misguided or insensitive changes such as will impair their authenticity, and from damage due to any form of pollution. Any restoration work undertaken should be based on scientific principles. Similarly, great attention should be paid to the harmony and aesthetic feeling produced by the linking or the contrasting of the various parts which make up the groups of buildings and which give to each group its particular character.

5. In the conditions of modern urbanization, which leads to a considerable increase in the scale and density of buildings, apart from the danger of direct destruction of historic areas, there is a real danger that newly developed areas can ruin the environment and character of adjoining historic areas. Architects and town-planners should be careful to ensure that views from and to monuments and historic areas are not spoilt and that historic areas are integrated harmoniously into contemporary life.

6. At a time when there is a danger that a growing universality of building techniques and architectural forms may create a uniform environment throughout the world, the preservation of historic areas can make an outstanding contribution to maintaining and developing the cultural and social values of each nation. This can contribute to the architectural enrichment of the cultural heritage of the world.

III. National, regional and local policy

7. In each Member State a national, regional and local policy should be drawn up, in conformity with the conditions of each State as regards the allocation of powers, so that legal, technical, economic and social measures may be taken by the national, regional or local authorities with a view to safeguarding historic areas and their surroundings and adapting them to the requirements of modern life. The policy thus laid down should influence planning at national, regional or local level and provide guidelines for town-planning and regional and rural development planning at all levels, the activities stemming from it forming an essential component in the formulation of aims and programmes, the assignment of responsibilities and the conduct of operations. The co-operation of individuals and private associations should be sought in implementing the safeguarding policy.

IV. Safeguarding measures

8. Historic areas and their surroundings should be safeguarded in conformity with the principles stated above and with the methods set out below, the specific measures being determined according to the legislative and constitutional competence and the organizational and economic structure of each State.

Legal and administrative measures

9. The application of on overall policy for safeguarding historic areas and their surroundings should be based on principles which are valid for the whole of each country. Member States should adapt the existing provisions, or, where necessary, enact new laws and regulations, so as to secure the protection of historic areas and their surroundings taking into account the provisions contained in this chapter and in the following chapters. They should encourage the adaption of regional or local measures to ensure such protection. Laws concerning town and regional planning and housing policy should also be reviewed so as to co-ordinate and bring them into line with the laws concerning the safeguarding of the architectural heritage.

10. The provisions establishing a system for safeguarding historic areas should set out the general principles relating to the establishment of the necessary plans and documents and, in particular:

– the general conditions and restrictions applicable to the protected areas and their surroundings;

– a statement as to the programmes and operations to be planned for the purpose of conservation and provision of public services;

– maintenance to be carried out and the designation of those to be responsible for it;

– the fields to which town-planning, redevelopment and rural land management are applicable;

– the designation of the body responsible for authorizing any restoration, modification, new construction or demolition within the protected perimeter;

– the means by which the safeguarding programmes are to be financed and carried out.

11. Safeguarding plans and documents should define:

– the areas and items to be protected;

– the specific conditions and restrictions applicable to them;

– the standards to be observed in the work of maintenance, restoration and improvements;

– the general conditions governing the establishment of the supply systems and services needed in urban or rural life;

– the conditions governing new constructions.

12. These laws should also in principale include provisions designed to prevent any infringement of the preservation laws, as well as any speculative rise in property values within the protected areas which could compromise protection and restoration planned in the interests of the community as a whole. These provisions could involve town-planning measures affording a means of influencing the price of building land, such as the establishment of neigbourhood or smaller development plans, granting the right of pre-emption to a public body, compulsory purchase in the interests of safeguarding or rehabilitation or automatic intervention in the case of failure to act on the part of the owners and could provide for effective penalties such as the suspension of operations, compulsory restoration and/or a suitable fine.

13. Public authorities as well as individuals must be obliged to comply with the measures for safeguarding. However, machinery for appeal against arbitrary or unjust decisions should be provided.

14. The provisions concerning the setting up of public and private bodies and concerning public and private work

projects should be adapted to the regulations governing the safeguarding of historic areas and their surroundings.

15. In particular, provisions concerning slum property and blocks and the construction of subsidized housing should be planned or amended both to fit in with the safeguarding policy and to contribute to it. The schedule of any subsidies paid should be drawn up and adjusted accordingly, in particular in order to facilitate the development of subsidized housing and public construction by rehabilitating old buildings. All demolition should in any case only concern buildings with no historic or architectural value and the subsidies involved should be carefully controlled. Further, a proportion of the funds earmarked for the construction of subsidized housing should be allocated to the rehabilitation of old buildings.

16. The legal consequences of the protection measures as far as buildings and land are concerned should be made public and should be recorded by a competent official body.

17. Making due allowance for the conditions specific to each country and the allocation of responsibilities within the various national, regional and local authorities, the following principles should underlie the operation of the safeguarding machinery:

a. there should be an authority responsible for ensuring the permanent co-ordination of all those concerned, e. g. national, regional and local public services or groups of individuals;

b. safeguarding plans and documents should be drawn up, once all the necessary advance scientific studies have been carried out, by multidisciplinary teams composed, in particular, of:
specialists in conservation and restoration, including art historians;
architects and town-planners;
sociologists and economists:
ecologists and landscape architects:
specialists in public health and social welfare;
and, more generally, all specialists in disciplines involved in the protection and enhancement of historic areas;

c. the authorities should take the lead in sounding the opinions and organizing the participation of the public concerned;

d. the safeguarding plans and documents should be approved by the body designated by law;

e. the public authorities responsible for giving effect to the safeguarding provisions and regulations at all levels, national and local, should be provided with the necessary staff and given adequate technical, administrative and financial resources.

Technical, economic and social measures

18. A list of historic areas and their surroundings to be protected should be drawn up at national, regional or local level. It should indicate priorities so that the limited resources available for protection may be allocated judiciously. Any protection measures, of whatever nature, that need to be taken as a matter of urgency should be taken without waiting for the safeguarding plans and documents to be prepared.

19. A survey of the area as a whole, including an analysis of its spatial evolution, should be made. It should cover archaeological, historical, architectural, technical and economic data. An analytical document should be drawn up so as to determine which buildings or groups of buildings are to be protected with great care, conserved under certain conditions, or, in quite exceptional and thoroughly documented circumstances, destroyed. This would enable the authorities to call a halt to any work incompatible with this Recommendation. Additionally, an inventory of public and private open spaces and their vegetation should be drawn up for the same purposes.

20. In addition to this architectural survey, thorough surveys of social, economic, cultural and technical data and structures and of the wider urban or regional context are necessary. Studies should include, if possible, demographic data and an analysis of economic, social and cultural activities, ways of life and social relationships, land-tenure problems, the urban infrastructure, the state of the road system, communication networks and the reciprocal links between protected areas and surrounding zones. The authorities concerned should attach the greatest importance to these studies and should bear in mind that valid safeguarding plans cannot be prepared without them.

21. After the survey described above has been completed and before the safeguarding plans and specifications are drawn up, there should in principle be a programming operation in which due account is taken both of town-planning, architectural, economic and social considerations and of the ability of the urban and rural fabric to assimilate functions that are compatible with its specific character. The programming operation should aim at bringing the density of settlement to the desired level and should provide for the work to be carried out in stages as well as for the temporary accommodation needed while it is proceeding, and premises for the permanent rehousing of those inhabitants who cannot return to their previous dwellings. This programming operation should be undertaken with the closest possible participation of the communities and groups of people concerned. Because the social, economic and physical context of historic areas and their surroundings may be expected to change over time, survey and analysis should be a continuing process. It is accordingly essential that the preparation of safeguarding plans and their execution be undertaken on the basis of studies available, rather than being postponed while the planning process is refined.

22. Once the safeguarding plans and specifications have been drawn up and approved by the competent public authority, it would be desirable for them to be executed either by their authors or under their authority.

23. In historic areas containing features from several different periods, preservation should be carried out taking into account the manifestations of all such periods.

24. Where safeguarding plans exist urban development or slum clearance programmes consisting of the demolition of buildings of no architectural or historic interest and which are structurally too unsound to be kept, the removal of extensions and additional storeys of no value, and sometimes even the demolition of recent buildings which break the unity of the area, may only be authorized in conformity with the plan.

25. Urban development or slum clearance programmes for areas not covered by safeguarding plans should respect buildings and other elements of architectural or historic value as well as accompanying buildings. If such elements are likely to be adversely affected by the programme, safeguarding plans as indicated above should be drawn up in advance of demolition.

26. Constant supervision is necessary to ensure that these operations are not conducive to excessive profits nor serve other purposes contrary to the objectives of the plan.

27. The usual security standards applicable to fire and natural catastrophes should be observed in any urban development or slum clearance programme affecting a historic area, provided that this be compatible with the criteria applicable to the preservation of the cultural heritage. If conflict does occur, special solutions should be sought, with the collaboration of all the services concerned, so as to provide the maximum security, while not impairing the cultural heritage.

28. Particular care should be devoted to regulations for and control over new buildings so as to ensure that their architecture adapts harmoniously to the spatial organization and setting of the groups of historic buildings. To this end, an analysis of the urban context should precede any new construction not only so as to define the general character of the group of buildings but also to analyse its dominant features, e. g. the harmony of heights, colours, materials and forms, constants in the way the façades and roofs are built, the relationship between the volume of buildings and the spatial volume, as well as their average proportions and their position. Particular attention should be given to the size of the lots since there is a danger that any reorganization of the lots may cause a change of mass which could be deleterious to the harmony of the whole.

29. The isolation of a monument through the demolition of its surroundings should not generally be authorized, neither should a monument be moved unless in exceptional circumstances and for unavoidable reasons.

30. Historic areas and their surroundings should be protected from the disfigurement caused by the erection of poles, pylons and electricity or telephone cables and the placing of television aerials and large-scale advertising signs. Where these already exist appropriate measures should be taken for their removal. Bill-posting, neon signs and other kinds of advertisement, commercial signs, street pavements and furniture, should be planned with the greatest care and controlled so that they fit harmoniously into the whole. Special efforts should be made to prevent all forms of vandalism.

31. Member States and groups concerned should protect historic areas and their surroundings against the increasingly serious environmental damage caused by certain technological developments – in particular the various forms of pollution – by banning harmful industries in the proximity of these areas and by taking preventive measures to counter the destructive effects of noise, shocks and vibrations caused by machines and vehicles. Provision should further be made for measures to counter the harm resulting from over-exploitation by tourism.

32. Member States should encourage and assist local authorities to seek solutions to the conflict existing in most historic groupings between motor traffic on the one hand and the scale of the buildings and their architectural qualities on the other. To solve the conflict and to encourage pedestrian traffic, careful attention should be paid to the placing of, and access to, peripheral and even central car parks and routing systems established which will facilitate pedestrian traffic, service access and public transport alike. Many rehabilitation operations such as putting electricity and other cables underground, too expensive if carried out singly, could then be co-ordinated easily and economically with the development of the road system.

33. Protection and restoration should be accompanied by revitalization activities. It would thus be essential to maintain appropriate existing functions, in particular trades and crafts, and establish new ones, which, if they are to be viable, in the long term, should be compatible with the economic and social context of the town, region or county where they are introduced. The cost of safeguarding operations should be evaluated not only in terms of the cultural value of the buildings but also in relation to the value they acquire through the use made of them. The social problems of safeguarding cannot be seen correctly unless reference is made to both these value scales. These functions should answer the social, cultural and economic needs of the inhabitants without harming the specific nature of the area concerned. A cultural revitalization policy should make historic areas centres of cultural activities and give them a central rôle to play in the cultural development of the communities around them.

34. In rural areas all works which cause disturbances and all changes of economic and social structure should be carefully controlled so as to preserve the integrity of historic rural communities within their natural setting.

35. Safeguarding activities should couple the public authorities' contribution with the contribution made by the individual or collective owners and the inhabitants and users, separately or together, who should be encouraged to put forward suggestions and generally play an active part. Constant co-operation between the community and the individual should thus be established at all levels particularly through methods such as: Information adapted to the types of persons concerned; surveys adapted to the persons questioned; establishment of advisory groups attached to planning teams; representation of owners, inhabitants and users in an advisory function on bodies responsible for decision-making, management and the organization of operations connected with plans for safeguarding, or the creation of public corporations to play a part in the plan's implementation.

36. The formation of voluntary conservation groups and non-profit-making associations and the establishment of honorary or financial rewards should be encouraged so that specially meritorious work in all aspects of safeguarding may be recognized.

37. Availability of the necessary funds for the level of public investment provided for in the plans for the safeguarding of historic areas and their surroundings should be ensured by including adequate appropriations in the budgets of the central, regional and local authorities. All these funds should be centrally managed by public, private or semi-public bodies entrusted with the co-ordination of all forms of financial aid at national, regional or local level and with the channelling ot them according to an overall plan of action.

38. Public assistance in the forms described below should be based on the principle that, wherever this is appropriate and necessary, the measures taken by the authorities concerned should take into account the "extra cost" of restoration, i. e. the additional cost imposed on the owner as compared with the new market or rental value of the building.

39. In general, such public funds should be used primarily to conserve existing buildings including especially buildings for low rental housing and should not be allocated to the construction of new buildings unless the latter do not prejudice the use and functions of existing buildings.

40. Grants, subsidies, loans at favourable rates, or tax concessions should be made available to private owners and to users carrying out work provided for by the safeguarding plans and in conformity with the standards laid down in those plans. These tax concessions, grants and loans could be made first and foremost to groups of owners or users of living accommodation and commercial property, since joint operations are more economical than individual action. The financial concessions granted to private owners and users should, where appropriate, be dependent on covenants requiring the observance of certain conditions laid down in the public interest, and ensuring the integrity of the buildings such as allowing the buildings to be visited and allowing access to parks, gardens or sites, the taking of photographs, etc.

41. Special funds should be set aside in the budgets of public and private bodies for the protection of groups of historic buildings endangered by large-scale public works and pollution. Public authorities should also set aside special funds for the repair of damage caused by natural disasters.

42. In addition, all government departments and agencies active in the field of public works should arrange their programmes and budgets so as to contribute to the rehabilitation of groups of historic buildings by financing work which is both in conformity with their own aims and the aims of the safeguarding plan.

43. To increase the financial resources available to them, Member States should encourage the setting up of public and/or private financing agencies for the safeguarding of historic areas and their surroundings. These agencies should have corporate status and be empowered to receive gifts from individuals, foundations and industrial and commercial concerns. Special tax concessions may be granted to donors.

44. The financing of work of any description carried out for the safeguarding of historic areas and their surroundings by setting up a loans corporation could be facilitated by public institutions and private credit establishments which would be responsible for making loans to owners at reduced rates of interest with repayment spread out over a long period.

45. Member States and other levels of government concerned could facilitate the creation of non-profit-making associations responsible for buying and, where appropriate after restoration, selling buildings by using revolving funds established for the special purpose of enabling owners of historic buildings who wish to safeguard them and preserve their character to continue to reside there.

46. It is most important that safeguarding measures should not lead to a break in the social fabric. To avoid hardship to the poorest inhabitants consequent on their having to move from buildings or groups of buildings due for renovation, compensation for rises in rent could enable them to keep their homes, commercial premises and workshops and their traditional living patterns and occupations, especially rural crafts, small-scale agriculture, fishing, etc. This compensation, which would be income-related, would help those concerned to pay the increased rentals resulting from the work carried out.

V. Research, education and information

47. In order to raise the standards of work of the skilled workers and craftsmen required and to encourage the whole population to realize the need for safeguarding and to take part in it, the following measures should be taken by Member States, in accordance with their legal and constitutional competence.

48. Member States and groups concerned should encourage the systematic study of, and research on:

– town-planning aspects of historic areas and their environment;

– the interconnexions between safeguarding and planning at all levels;

– methods of conservation applicable to historic areas;

– the alteration of materials;

– the alteration of modern techniques to conservation work;

– the crafts techniques indispensable for safeguarding.

49. Specific education concerning the above questions and including practical training periods should be introduced and developed. In addition, it is essential to encourage the training of skilled workers and craftsmen specializing in the safeguarding of historic areas, including any open spaces surrounding them. Furthermore, it is necessary to encourage the crafts themselves, which are jeopardized by the processes of industrialization. It is desirable that the institutions concerned co-operate in this matter with specialized international agencies such as the Centre for the Study of the Preservation and Restoration of Cultural Property, in Rome, the International Council of Monuments and Sites (ICOMOS) and the International Council of Museums (ICOM).

50. The education of administrative staff for the needs of local development in the field of safeguarding of historic areas should be financed where applicable and needed and directed by the appropriate authorities according to a long-term programme.

51. Awareness of the need for safeguarding work should be encouraged by education in school, out of school and at university and by using information media such as books, the press, television, radio, cinema and travelling exhibitions. Clear, comprehensive information should be provided as to the advantages – not only aesthetic, but also social and economic – to be reaped from a well-conducted policy for the safeguarding of historic areas and their surroundings. Such information should be widely circulated among specialized private and government bodies and the general public so that they may know why and how their surroundings can be improved in this way.

52. The study of historic areas should be included in education at all levels, especially in history teaching, so as to inculcate in young minds an understanding of and respect for the works of the past and to demonstrate the rôle of this heritage in modern life. Education of this kind should make wider use of audio-visual media and of visits to groups of historic buildings.

53. Refresher courses for teachers and guides and the training of instructors should be facilitated so as to aid groups of young people and adults wishing to learn about historic areas.

VI. International co-operation

54. Member States should co-operate with regard to the safeguarding of historic areas and their surroundings, seek-

ing aid, if it seems desirable, from international organizations, both intergovernmental and non-governmental, in particular that of the Unesco-ICOM-ICOMOS Documentation Centre. Such multilateral or bilateral co-operation should be carefully coordinated and should take the form of measures such as the following:

a. exchange of information in all forms and of scientific and technical publications;

b. organization of seminars and working parties on particular subjects;

c. provision of study and travel fellowships, and the dispatch of scientific, technical and administrative staff, and equipment;

d. joint action to combat pollution of all kinds;

e. implementation of large-scale conservation, restoration and rehabilitation projects for historic areas and publication of the experience aquired. In frontier areas where the task of developing and safeguarding historic areas and their surroundings gives rise to problems jointly affecting Member States on either side of the frontier, they should co-ordinate their policies and activities to ensure that the cultural heritage is used and protected in the best possible way;

f. mutual assistance between neighbouring countries for the preservation of areas of common interest characteristic of the historic and cultural development of the region.

55. In conformity with the spirit and the principles of this Recommendation, a Member State should not take any action to demolish or change the character of the historic quarters, towns and sites, situated in territories occupied by that State.